D1214022

The Charities of London
1480–1660

The Charities of London
1480–1660

THE ASPIRATIONS AND THE ACHIEVEMENTS
OF THE URBAN SOCIETY

BY

W. K. JORDAN

Archon Books
1974

Library of Congress Cataloging in Publication Data

Jordan, Wilbur Kitchener, 1902-
    The charities of London, 1480-1660.

    Reprint of the 1960 ed. published by Russell Sage Foundation, New York.
    Includes bibliographical references.
    1. London—Charities—History. 2. London—Social conditions. I. Title.
HV250.L9J6 1974   361'.9421   74-8700
ISBN 0-208-01410-1

In memory of the eight sons of
T. J. *and* M. K. J.

PREFACE

The first volume of this work, published in 1959, under the title *Philanthropy in England, 1480–1660*, was an essay commenting on evidence drawn from ten English counties which together comprised something like a third of the land mass of the realm, about a third of the population of the nation in 1600, and perhaps half of the wealth of England in the age with which we are concerned. An effort was made to assess the social problems of the sixteenth and seventeenth centuries and to describe the nature of the problem of poverty in this era and the heroic measures which men took to deal with its control, if not its cure. Though remedial legislation was adopted, it was our conclusion that men of the age reposed their principal confidence in private charity, gathered by the instrumentality of the charitable trust into large and disciplined aggregates of wealth with which formidably effective social institutions could be founded and endowed, as they undertook to relieve widespread and degrading poverty and to secure its prevention by a vast enlargement of the ambit of social and economic opportunity.

We have seen that the philanthropic impulse was derived from many sources during our period and that it evoked a steadily and rapidly mounting charitable response which reached a great climax of giving in the first generation of the seventeenth century when, it is not too much to say, the basic institutions of the modern society were securely established. Men's aspirations underwent a notable metamorphosis in the century following the English Reformation, an almost complete absorption with secular needs and a stalwart concern for the visible needs of the society marking this transformation. All regions and all classes yielded, rapidly or reluctantly as the case might be, to these powerful forces of change and to the resolution to build a better, a more comfortable, and a more civilized society for mankind.

England remained throughout the course of our long period a predominantly rural society in which there were not more than a score of large market towns, three or possibly four provincial cities which exhibited truly urban characteristics, and one great city, London, which in terms of its size, its wealth, and its corporate confidence was an urban colossus fixed in what can only be described as a rural setting on a national scale. It is with the urban mind, the urban social conscience, and with the precocity and power of urban aspirations that we are concerned in this volume. And this really means London. Elsewhere, we shall deal with the contributions of Bristol, the second city in the realm, and we shall in the course of our study of ten of the English counties examine the charities and the social aspirations of all the other principal urban communities in the realm, but it remains true that London stood quite alone in England as a great urban monadnock. We shall seek to comment on the great charitable contributions which London made, to describe at some length the aspirations and the social philosophy of the merchant aristocracy which controlled its affairs, and to measure the immense social dominance gained by London in this era as the flood of its charitable generosity poured out across the face of the whole realm.

In the next, and third, volume of this study we shall deal with the contribution of a selected group of rural counties and shall observe a quite different pattern of aspirations, a slower yielding to the secular metmorphosis which marks our period, and a surviving parochialism which is most dissimilar to the almost evangelical concern of London with the whole of the society. There will remain, in addition to our treatment of Bristol, several other studies of rural counties which will in due time appear in appropriate form.

It is perhaps appropriate here to refer the reader to the first volume of this study, where, in an extended section entitled 'The Method', several important cautionary notes involving the whole work are discussed, where several underlying assumptions are set forward, and where we have explained why it seems desirable not to attempt to adjust our statistical data to the rising curve of prices over the course of our period.

We have endeavoured to examine all the printed as well as the principal manuscript sources in our study of London, with the result that the bibliographical apparatus is very large. Since it is not possible to present a formal bibliography, an effort has been made in the instance of a first citation to give the full bibliographical particulars, a short title form being employed thereafter. The documentation is also heavy; so certain conventions have been adopted in the interests of brevity. When more than one reference is made in the text to an individual donor, on the occasion of the first reference the full bibliographical citation covering all particulars for that and later references is given in the footnote. No biographical particulars have been included when the subject is treated in a *Dictionary of National Biography* memoir unless it seems desirable to suggest corrections or to add new facts to that treatment. Similarly, in our biographical notes on merchant donors, particulars have not always been included of the canonical progress from alderman to sheriff to lord mayor, if these facts are available in A. B. Beaven's invaluable *The Aldermen of the City of London* (London, 1908, 1913. 2 vols.). Finally, we have wherever possible employed convenient abbreviations for manuscript materials and for frequently cited printed sources, as the following table of abbreviations will suggest.

W. K. J.

Strafford, Vermont
July, 1959

ABBREVIATIONS

Alumni cantab.	Venn, John, ed., *Alumni canta-brigienses* (Cambridge, 1922–1954, 10 vols.)
Alumni oxon.	Foster, Joseph, ed., *Alumni oxonienses* (Oxford, 1891–1892, 4 vols.)
Arch. cant.	*Archaeologia cantiana,* Vol. I (1858)—(London)
Bib. top. brit.	Nichols, John, ed., *Bibliotheca topographica britannica* (L., 1780–1790, 8 vols.)
B. & G. Arch. Soc.	Bristol and Gloucestershire Archaeological Society, *Transactions,* Vol. I (1876)—(Gloucester)
BM	British Museum.
BM, Add. Charters	British Museum, Additional Charters
BM, MSS.	British Museum, Manuscripts
DNB	*Dictionary of National Biography*
Fry, *Inq. p. m., London, I*	Fry, G. S., ed. *Abstracts of inquisitiones post mortem . . . London . . .* 1485–1561 (L., 1896)
Fry, *Inq. p. m., London, III*	Fry, E. A., ed., *Abstracts of inquisitiones post mortem . . . London . . .* 1577–1603 (L., 1908) Part II of the series, for 1561–1577, ed. by S. J. Madge
Hist. Soc. L. & C.	Historic Society of Lancashire and Cheshire, *Transactions,* Vol. I (1849)—(Liverpool)
Husting	Sharpe, R. R., ed., *Calendar of wills proved . . . in the Court of Husting, London* (L., 1889–1890, 2 vols.)

Lansdowne MSS.	Manuscripts in the Lansdowne Collection, British Museum
L. & P. *Hen.* VIII	Letters and Papers, Henry VIII.
LCC *Survey*	London County Council, *Survey of London*
L. & M. *Arch. Soc.*	London and Middlesex Archaeological Society, *Transactions*, Vol. I (1860)—(London)
London Top. Rec.	London Topographical Society, *Annual Record*, Vol. I (1900)—(London)
Misc. Gen. et Her.	*Miscellanea Genealogica et Heraldica*, Vol. I (1866)—(London)
N. E. Hist. & Gen.	*The New-England Historical and Genealogical Register*, Vol. I (1847)—(Boston, Massachusetts)
PCC	Prerogative Court of Canterbury
PCY	Prerogative Court of York
PP	*Parliamentary Papers* (Great Britain, *Reports of the Commissioners for inquiring concerning charities*)
S. P. *Dom.*	*State Papers, Domestic*
Surrey Arch. Coll.	*Surrey Archaeological Collections*, Vol. I (1858)—(London)
Surrey Rec. Soc.	*Surrey Record Society, Publications*, Vol. I (1914)—(London)
Va. Mag.	*The Virginia Magazine of History and Biography*, Vol. I (1894)—(Richmond, Virginia)
VCH	*Victoria County History*

CONTENTS

The City and its People

Inevitably, if inexactly, we shall tend to speak of London and Middlesex quite interchangeably during the course of our discussion. Our data are drawn from the whole of the county, though the fact is that London parishes together with those of Westminster account for all save a relatively modest proportion (13·25 per cent) of the whole of the charitable benefactions of the geographical entity which was the county of Middlesex. It is difficult to remember that even in the closing decades of our period much of the county was rural, with pleasant farms and stretching woodlands in regions long since consumed by the sprawling urban complex which is metropolitan London. The county was, save for Rutland, the smallest in the realm, with an area of not much more than 280 square miles. It was principally agricultural during the whole of our era, with a heavy concentration on market gardening and with a rural economy benefiting greatly from the nearness of the metropolis. There were, as well, small industrial centres, normally linked with London's requirements or facilities, of which tanning was the principal, with an adequate supply of hides assured from the numerous London slaughter-houses. Throughout our period, however, the irresistible pressure of population was expanding the urban arc beyond the ancient boundaries, with suburban fingers reaching out in the first process of urban absorption. The forerunners were the rich and the fashionable who as early as 1600 were purchasing manors and building their great houses in still rural Middlesex in order to escape the congestion, the noise, and the pestilences with which the city was chronically afflicted. The first exodus was led by the nobility and upper gentry whose great town houses had graced sixteenth-century London but of which only a few remained at the close of our period.[1] More important, though a little later, was the movement of the great merchant families to the suburbs or to the more distant rural parishes, particularly by men who had at least begun to contemplate the bucolic joys of retirement.

Through the whole course of our period London was growing very rapidly in population as well as in economic importance. Most authorities regard as reasonably accurate the estimate made in 1199 by Peter of Blois, then Archdeacon of London, who informed the Pope that the city comprised 120 parish churches and contained a population of about 40,000 people. The city grew very slowly, if at all, during the next three centuries, the population probably ranging between 40,000 and 50,000 during this long interval.[2] But there began in the reign of Henry VIII a steady and a rapid growth in the city, quite bewildering to men of our period, and most alarming to the government, which in an interval of not more than 130 years was to result in a prodigious increase of population of between 700 and 800 per cent. The population of the city just prior to the expropriation of its monasteries was probably of the order of 60,000. At the accession of Queen Elizabeth the number of London's inhabitants seems to have been slightly fewer than 90,000, while shortly after her death Creighton advances a carefully considered estimate of 224,275 as the population of what had by that date (1605) become a true metropolis. Despite the earnest efforts of the Stuarts to discourage or at least control further growth, the population of the city may well have numbered 275,000 by the time of James I's death and certainly had reached the huge total of 350,000 before the outbreak of the Civil War.[3] There is persuasive evidence that the city continued to grow rapidly during the two decades of political and economic disturbance, though John Graunt's estimate of 460,000 for the year following the Restoration may well be too high.

The remarkable growth of the urban complex which metropolitan London had become by 1600 cannot easily be explained. It was spectacular, indeed, even when assessed in relation to the steady growth of the realm at large during the course of our period. Accepting Gregory King's estimate for the population of England as reasonably reliable, it would seem probable that London in 1500 did not number more than about 1·5 per cent of the whole population. But by 1600 the city very probably included slightly more than 5 per cent of the inhabitants of the kingdom and, most pertinently, controlled nearly 80 per cent of its foreign trade. This immense gain was in part accomplished because the city secured growing room from the extensive areas which had heretofore been jealously held by monastic owners and which were in the main opened to speculative and very lucrative building of densely populated tenement areas by their secular owners some years after the Expropriation. Quite as importantly, space was gained for ever-increasing numbers when the city literally burst through its medieval bounds, pushing out urban fingers, usually heavily populated, in every direction; absorbing the borough of Southwark in the reign of Edward VI; and spilling out into a corner of Kent before the death of Elizabeth.

The London of 1600 was, then, a great urban complex. It was a metropolis in every sense of the word, with an immense wealth and a size which comparatively made cities of the next rank seem no more than large provincial towns. Its trade, its restless capital wealth, and its commercial skills had by 1600 made it the economic centre of gravity for the whole of the realm. Its traders had by that year, for example, stripped even the aggressive Bristol clothiers of their trade to within ten miles of the bounds of that western city; well might these harassed clothiers complain to James I that London merchants conducted themselves 'as if God had no sons to whom He gave the benefit of the earth but in London'.[4] The wealth and greatness of London in our period depended on trade, reflecting most sensitively the commercial revolution which had brought increasing prosperity to the whole of the realm in a commerce which came to be funnelled principally through the port of London. We shall have occasion to point out in detail that through the course of our period London was led and dominated by a merchant aristocracy of most remarkable ability whose interests and speculative energies ranged over the whole kingdom and who made of their city a national centre for risk capital as well as for more conservatively disposed commercial wealth. These were men who quickly mastered the intricate arts of large-scale commerce, of assembling and ordering huge capital aggregates, and who lifted London in a precocious development to a position which in 1600 left it unrivalled amongst the great cities of Christendom.

The prodigious growth of London was ill understood in the late sixteenth century and was truly frightening to the responsible authorities. So immense was the energy and so attractive were the opportunities afforded by the city that it drew men to fill all classes of its society by an irresistible magnetism from all parts of the realm. There were constant complaints by the lord mayors and aldermen of the city that most of the swarms of vagrants and unemployed were not London born at all, these respectable burghers quite forgetting the fact that the merchant class to which they themselves belonged was likewise principally filled from the provinces. The bills of mortality and parochial records in general suggest all too certainly that during most of our period there was little if any natural increase in the population of the city, even in the merchant class, so severe and so chronic were the pestilences rooted in filth, over-crowding, and poor medical care. But hordes of men poured in to the metropolis to fill its ranks and more as the population continued to rise at a rate which suggests that London can best be described as a 'boom town', enjoying a continuous and an almost prodigal prosperity for rather more than a century.

By 1580 the extensive open areas gained from the monastic confiscations had been absorbed and the great town houses with their spacious gardens, many of which had likewise once been monastic precincts, were being converted into tenement warrens or being razed in order to provide still more room in an already dangerously over-crowded city. At about this date congested and most flimsy building was likewise beginning in the whole suburban arc about the city, which the Queen sought to halt by a proclamation prohibiting the erection of additional houses within three miles of the city gates, on the grounds that dangers from plague, fire, and fuel shortage were being gravely increased.[5] Some years later (1593) Parliament sought by statute to enforce the prohibitions of the Queen's proclamation.[6] But both Queen and Parliament were really powerless to halt a process of growth rooted in the immense vitality and prosperity of the city. This was recognized when a few years later, in 1598, the Privy Council sharply enjoined the municipal authorities to see to it that the laws against further building should be enforced. The city government was in point of fact fully in accord with the Crown in its own apprehensions, particularly since the economic dislocation occasioned by the Spanish wars had caused real suffering in the city, which was also filled with wounded or discharged soldiers and sailors who refused to move on to the parishes of their birth. A survey conducted in this period suggested that there were 4132 persons in the city requiring relief,[7] though it should be pointed out that such a number of unemployed, or unemployable, constituted rather less than 2 per cent of the then population of London. A sterner proclamation was issued in 1602, once more prohibiting all building and sub-dividing within three miles of the city boundaries and with the further provision that unfinished houses and stables were to be pulled down.[8]

Far more persistent efforts were made by the congenitally apprehensive James I to halt the tidal wave of growth, and with some cause, since a particularly vicious epidemic of the plague had destroyed possibly as many as 30,000 of London's inhabitants at about the time of the King's accession. James issued, in all, nine proclamations attempting to prohibit or to restrain further building, particularly in the suburbs, while the civic authorities sought to control further growth by laying heavy fines against illegal contractors, insisting on the use of stone and brick in construction, and on occasion throwing persistent offenders into gaol for short terms. These restraints did serve to slow down building, especially in the suburbs, but they could not deter the steady and very rapid growth of the city during these years, and they seem on balance to have encouraged even worse over-crowding in an already seriously congested urban area. By the close of the reign of James I the whole structure of the metropolis had been changed in a fashion which would have seemed incomprehensible to men a century earlier.

London is blessed in having had as its historian a man of rare gifts who loved its sprawling mass and who over a long lifetime had watched it grow into the metropolis which he described in 1598. Any historian who has had occasion to depend heavily on the *Survey* of John Stow must pay warm and humble tribute to the greatness of that work. London as it was at the close of the Elizabethan period simply comes alive in his

THE CITY AND ITS PEOPLE 19

pages and the reader stands in awe at the immense range of the author's knowledge and his skill and accuracy of reporting. Stow was at once saddened by the disappearance of the medieval city which he had known and filled with pride at the creation which the very vitality that was London had wrought by the closing years of his life. The whole of the work is warmed by affection and illumined by a moral sense which lashed out against selfish men who profaned London's beauty or greatness while it extolled those sober virtues of charity which were transforming an inchoate urban mass into a great city.

Stow correctly sensed the greatness of London and of the merchant class which had made her famous. He understood, as well, that this was at bottom a moral greatness, formed as men of the age wrestled mightily with the forces of social evil and strove to create a good and a civilized community of men. In so doing the men of London were to call into being soundly based social and cultural institutions for their own city and then to reach out as they exercised a cultural and institutional dominance over the realm at large, quite matching the economic dominance which London had attained over the whole of England.*

*Stow's *A Survey of London* was first published in 1598. We have ordinarily cited the definitive edition by C. L. Kingsford, 2 vols., Oxford, 1908. The edition prepared by John Strype (2 vols., L., 1720) contains much additional material for the last two generations of our period and is accordingly frequently cited, with an indication when this later edition is employed.

II

General Comments on the Data

Benefactors of the city of London in the course of our period were to provide an almost incomprehensibly large total of charitable wealth as they sought manfully to deal with the social problems of their age. Raising up new institutions which would guard men against want or create areas of opportunity in which they might gain new strength and resources, they hoped in time to cure both poverty and ignorance. In all, these burghers of London were to give the truly immense total of £1,889,211 12s of charitable benefactions designed to better the lot of men in their age and to establish institutions which would ensure a fairer future for men of their city and country.[1] This great sum was the gift of a relatively small number of 7391 individual donors, resulting in a remarkably high average of £255 12s 2d for each contributor, an average quite unmatched in all England.[2]

The immensity of London's charitable wealth is suggested when we reflect that somewhat more than 60 per cent (60·89 per cent) of the whole of the great accumulations we have examined in detail for ten counties of the realm was provided by this one almost prodigally generous city. Even more impressively, at least rough samplings of the charitable wealth given in all the counties of England and Wales would lead us to believe that of the total of philanthropic funds disposed during this long era by the whole of the kingdom, slightly more than 34 per cent (34·20 per cent) was supplied by London's donors. When we reflect that at no time during the decades under study did London's population amount to much more than 5 per cent of that of the realm, the dominant role of the city in founding the necessary insitutions of a new age becomes most abundantly clear. In other words, the greatness of London's cultural and historical achievement can be assessed only against that of the realm as a whole: it can be compared sensibly with that of no county, while it was vastly greater than that of all the remaining urban centres of the realm combined. London stood *solus* in England and, for that matter, in the western world.

Taking in view the general structure of London's charitable wealth, one is impressed by the very large total that was provided for the various uses connected with the care of the poor. In all, the enormous sum of

£664,608 14s was vested for one or another form of poor relief, this amounting to rather more than a third (35·18 per cent) of the whole of the charitable funds of the city. An immense outlay of £331,502 4s, most of which was capital, was given for the direct relief of poor men in their own households, to which may be added £92,530 19s given for generally defined charitable purposes but normally employed for this use. The vast sum of £237,636 11s was designated for almshouse foundations in London or elsewhere in the realm, while the relatively very modest capital sum of £2939 was established with restrictions limiting the use of the income to the relief of aged men and women.*

The bold and imaginative quality of London wealth is amply suggested by the sums provided by merchants of the city for a great variety of experimental efforts for the social rehabilitation of the poor. The most substantial total of £251,728 13s was given for such purposes by men of our period, this amounting to 13·32 per cent of the whole of the charitable wealth of the city, a far greater proportion being devoted to this salutary purpose than in any other county in the realm.[3] The scale of London's giving for charitable uses of this most interesting and hopeful kind is suggested when we say that it amounted to nearly four times (3·71) the total provided for such purposes in the remaining nine counties included in this study and, beyond doubt, to considerably more than the whole for this purpose given in all the remainder of the kingdom.

The merchants and tradesmen of London were relatively very conservative in their giving for the various uses which we have included under the general heading of municipal betterments. In all, only £93,593 16s was designated for these purposes, or not more than 4·95 per cent of the whole of London's charities. It should likewise be pointed out that a heavy proportion of even this modest total was given in the form of endowments for the various city companies, the income to be employed for the public benefit in a great variety of ways. London merchants were evidently loath to give for such purposes as the repair of streets, the building of conduits, and the care or erection of public buildings, one would suppose because the more efficient and proper instrument of taxation had long since been employed by a sophisticated city government for securing desirable municipal improvements.

The huge total of £510,890 17s was given by London donors during the course of our period for the foundation or the improvement of educational facilities in the city and throughout the realm, representing 27·04 per cent of all the charitable wealth provided by the city. Roughly half of the total amount was designated for grammar-school foundations in London or elsewhere, the immensity of this contribution being sug-

* *Vide* Table 1 (Appendix) for the details from which a brief summary is drawn for purposes of this discussion.

gested when it is recalled that £1000 of capital was sufficient to found a reasonably well endowed school and that Londoners gave for this specific purpose the sum of £259,263 2s. The devotion of the urban aristocracy to the advancement of education is further suggested by the total of £154,591 5s given for the endowment or general support of the universities, while £92,465 8s was provided for the foundation of scholarships and fellowships either in schools or in the universities.

When the pronounced and almost precocious secularism of the burgher aristocracy is considered, we find it rather surprising that the relatively large total of £368,389 12s was given by London donors for the various religious needs of the age. This amounts in all to 19·50 per cent of the charitable funds of the metropolis, though it should be remarked that almost half the total sum is represented by the £164,004 1s given for church building in London or in other parts of the realm, which so frequently attests rather a kind of civic pride than any particularly dedicated concern with the ends and offices of religion.

The profoundly important and swift metamorphosis in the structure of burgher aspirations may be documented by a brief and preliminary comment on their habits of giving in the successive intervals with which we are concerned. It will be remembered in this regard that London had been a large and a rich city for many generations before our study begins and, what is more important, had been governed and dominated by a wealthy and articulate merchant aristocracy during these earlier generations. Hence, even in the decades prior to the Reformation (1480–1540), we find that the relatively large total of £250,077 6s was given for the charitable needs of the city, this amounting to slightly more than 13 per cent of the whole of the charitable funds given over the course of our period. Even at this early date the remarkably slender proportion of 44·78 per cent of all benefactions was designated for religious uses, with chantry endowments accounting for well over half the total of £111,997 1s given for religious needs. The concern of the burgher aristocracy with the educational needs of the realm was already mature, the £76,581 9s given for that use amounting to nearly a third (30·63 per cent) of the total of all charities. In all, £37,378 7s was given in these early years for the relief of the poor of the city, this amounting to not quite 15 per cent of all charitable wealth accumulated during this interval. It is especially interesting to note that well over half of all benefactions for poor relief were concentrated in the remarkably large total of £18,576 7s provided as endowment for the founding of numerous almshouses in London and elsewhere by men and women who were courageously attacking the problems created by hopeless indigence. At the same time, the relatively modest total of £8429 15s, representing only 3·37 per cent of the whole, was designated for various experiments in social rehabilitation, while almost double this amount, £15,690 14s, was provided for various municipal needs. The whole feel and structure of London benefactions during these early decades suggest that London had passed from the Middle Ages into modernity a full generation before the advent of the Reformation and that the fabric of its life and culture was beginning to display a pervading secularism.

We observe a notable and a very rapid quickening of charitable giving during the short interval of the Reformation (1541–1560), when £152,841 10s was given for all charitable purposes, this amounting to 8·09 per cent of all such funds provided during our entire period. One is struck particularly by the amazing increase of interest in the various instrumentalities for social rehabilitation, to which £66,183 14s was given, representing 43·30 per cent of all benefactions during these two decades.[4] There was as well a sharply heightened interest in the care of the poor, for whose needs the considerable total of £31,481 13s was provided, this being more than a fifth (20·60 per cent) of the whole. An even larger sum, £32,586 5s, was disposed for the further strengthening of the educational resources of the community and of the nation at large, this amount being about evenly divided between the needs of the grammar schools and those of the universities. At the same time, the total given for religious purposes during this tumultuous interval fell abruptly to £15,580 15s, or no more than 10·19 per cent of all charities for the period, as contrasted with the 44·78 per cent given for such pious uses in the preceding interval. The age of secularism had come with dramatic quickness and, as time was to show, with finality in London, and London may well be regarded as a particularly sensitive social and cultural barometer for England at large during the whole of our period.

The Elizabethan era was one of rather cautious giving by the burgher aristocracy of London. It is in fact remarkable that the £260,344 10s provided for charitable purposes in these decades (1561–1600) amounted to not more than 13·78 per cent of the whole of charitable funds accumulated in the city during our entire period and represents a "per decade" rate considerably less than that observed in the preceding interval of the Reformation. At the same time, it is interesting that the flow of funds into charitable uses proceeded in this prosperous and settled age at a remarkably even rate, the total of gifts in each of the four decades ranging between £60,315 14s and £68,961 2s. It is especially noteworthy that benefactions for religious uses fell away sharply to £17,330 13s during this long generation, this amounting to no more than 6·66 per cent of all benefactions for the period and being rather less than the amount provided for various municipal improvements. The proportion of charitable funds deployed for the attack on poverty rose markedly as compared with the earlier decades, the substantial total of £86,891 3s provided for this purpose representing a third

(33·38 per cent) of all charities in the period. A significantly large proportion of this sum was designated for household relief in the various
parishes of the city, while a smaller sum, £23,754 1s, was disposed for
almshouse foundations. The attack on ignorance, so clearly and so
correctly associated in the Elizabethan mind with the assault on poverty,
commanded very nearly as large a proportion (32·00 per cent) of the
charitable resources of the age. The large total of £83,319 12s, of
which almost the whole was capital, was marshalled for the strengthening of the educational resources of the realm, with £32,530 being given
for grammar-school endowments and an almost equal sum (32,503 13s)
being distributed by London benefactors to the expanding universities.
But in some ways the most remarkable aspect of the structure of
charitable interests in this era was the bold experimental concern with
the various schemes for securing the social rehabilitation of the worthy
poor. In all, £53,077 4s was devoted to this general purpose, this being
more than a fifth (20·39 per cent) of the whole and being spread over a
great variety of interesting and often sophisticated uses. Upwards of
£20,000 was vested in the now famous hospitals of the city, while the
£18,795 13s designated for loan funds exceeded considerably the total
given for the whole nexus of religious uses during this amazingly
secular age.

The full tide of London's prodigal generosity was to flow during the
early Stuart period (1601–1640), when the enormous total of £959,032 19s
was given by its citizens for charitable causes. This huge sum amounted
to almost exactly half (50·76 per cent) of the total of London's benefactions during our entire period. Some measure of the limitless generosity
of London in these years is suggested when we note that in each of three
successive decades, 1611–1640, London alone provided more for
charitable uses than the total accumulation of any other single county
in England during our entire period. This immense generosity was
brought to bear, and that most intelligently, principally on the needs of
the poor, to which in all £388,272 9s was dedicated, this representing
40·49 per cent of the whole of the city's charitable accumulations
during the interval. The huge sum of £172,587 9s was vested to secure
the household relief of the poor. Not much less (£143,473 17s) was given
to found still more almshouses and further to strengthen older establishments, while nearly £70,000 was left for general charitable purposes
which held the needs of the poor principally in mind. Somewhat more
than a fourth (25·70 per cent) of the great total of London's charitable
wealth in this generation is represented in the £246,492 3s given for the
extension and betterment of the educational facilities of the city and the
kingdom as a whole. The principal concern was with the founding of
schools, for which the immense total of £148,263 17s was provided, an
amount, be it noted, exceeded in these years only by the sums left for

the outright care of the poor. At the same time, £51,885 was settled for scholarship and fellowship foundations, and the universities were greatly strengthened by the £43,537 6s which flowed to them from London merchants, very few of whom had ever entered their precincts as students or as visitors. Not quite 10 per cent of the total of charitable wealth was devoted to further experimentation in the processes of social rehabilitation, the principal concern being with the betterment of hospitals, the relief of prisoners, and the strengthening of loan funds of a most bewildering variety. There was, a least relatively, only a modest interest in municipal betterments, the £41,680 14s given for this general purpose amounting to no more than 4·35 per cent of the whole. Finally, there was in this period a marked increase in giving for religious uses, the very substantial sum of £194,765 5s having been designated for these purposes, or about a fifth (20·31 per cent) of the whole for the interval. It is noteworthy, however, that of this total, well over half (£111,571 6s) was provided for church building in London and other parts of the realm and that substantially more than half (53 per cent) of the entire sum given for religious uses during these four decades was centred in the Laudian decade (1631–1640), when London was under especially heavy pressure to assist in the restoration of the ecclesiastical fabric of the nation, which had suffered from an almost contemptuous neglect during the two preceding generations.

London was, of course, most seriously affected by the great dislocations of the Civil War and the decade and more of political experimentation which followed. The city bore a heavy burden of taxation during the whole of our final interval, its trade was seriously disturbed, and substantial men, whatever their political and religious convictions, must have viewed the future with considerable apprehension. The flow of London's generosity was accordingly quite sharply diminished. But it was by no means halted, the rate of giving during these two unsettled decades being roughly half that obtaining during the preceding and almost extravagantly generous era. In all, the substantial total of £266,915 7s was provided for charitable purposes during this short interval, this amounting to 14·13 per cent of London's charitable wealth during the whole course of our long period. These benefactions were heavily concentrated on the betterment of the lot of the poor, to which in all £120,585 2s was given, this being slightly more than 45 per cent of the whole. A proportionately very large sum was also given for further experimentation in the agencies of social rehabilitation, the £36,215 12s given for this purpose constituting 13·57 per cent of the whole, with an especially concentrated interest in apprenticeship foundations, for which £11,467 of capital was disposed. The £71,911 8s provided for educational needs represented more than a fourth (26·94 per cent) of all charities funded in these two decades, of which the

greater portion (£48,635 8s) was added to the grammar-school resources
of the nation. There was a very sharp decline in giving for religious
needs, the £28,715 18s disposed for these uses representing not much
more than a tenth of the whole, and of this total, it should be observed,
almost half was devoted to foundations with an expressly Puritan bias.

The moulding, the shaping, impact of charitable gifts is of course
quite as much determined by the quality and care with which they are
framed as by their mass. London's influence in establishing the social
institutions of the whole nation was consequently quite as much
determined by the prudence and legal safeguards with which its great
benefactors were accustomed to arrange their gifts as by the huge, the
almost overwhelming, mass of these gifts. One is impressed particularly
by the fact that so heavy a preponderance of all London charities was
vested in the form of endowments designed to further in perpetuity the
aspirations which had moved the donor in his foundation. Gifts for
immediate use so evidently leave only a momentary impact; they have
only a scant historical effect in the shaping of the institutions with which
a society is at once supported and ordered. Further, the occasional, the
eccentric, alms so typical of medieval charity quite clearly tended to
worsen the social conditions they were designed to assuage, however
pious and noble the intentions of the donors.

It is, then, important to observe that of the massive total of London's
charitable gifts the huge sum of £1,560,422 16s was vested in capital
aggregates, in endowments of one sort or another. This sum represented
82·60 per cent of all charitable benefactions and was, with very few
exceptions, most carefully and thoughtfully ordered by terms of the
deeds of gift. The care taken by London benefactors in the framing of
their charities exhibits the burgher prudence so typical of our period,
the proportion vested as capital being unmatched in any other county
examined save for Bristol.[5] It is also evident, and the matter deserves
further and most careful study, that the investment of so large a capital
aggregate of trusteed funds, heavily concentrated in the period from 1581
to 1640, must have exercised an extremely important effect on the
commercial revolution then under way as it certainly did on the value of
the desirable tracts of urban and rural land which were in such steady
demand from charitable trustees.

Very nearly all the charitable purposes which were capable of being
institutionalized were founded or supported by endowed funds. Thus
the benefactions for such uses as almshouses, general charity, apprenticeship foundations, loan funds, workhouses, schools, the universities,
lectureships, and scholarships were vested in capital amounts exceeding
97 per cent of all the gifts made for these diverse purposes. Similarly,
a very high proportion of funds devoted to the support of libraries, the
hospitals, and the aged were in the form of endowments. It is particu-

larly noteworthy that even of the great total of £331,502 4s devoted to
the outright relief of the poor, the very high proportion of 83·81 per
cent was carefully vested in trustees in order to provide income in
perpetuity for the care of poor men and women in a prescribed area and
usually under thoughtfully prescribed conditions. It is also significant
that more than half of the £53,666 10s left in the form of immediate
alms or doles for the poor had been given prior to 1580, by which date
funeral doles particularly had come to be viewed with general suspicion
by the burgher society which was London. It was only for such purposes
as the repair of streets and roads, church repairs, and, necessarily,
church building that prudent London donors gave as much as half their
benefactions as gifts for immediate use.

It may likewise be noted that a very large proportion of London's
total charitable wealth was established by bequest. The mercantile
aristocracy tended to hold its wealth intact until the time of approaching
death, though in case after case the will itself reveals that the charitable
bequest so carefully framed had been under long and earnest consideration with friends in the donor's company or with his future trustees.
In all, 70·37 per cent of London's benefactions were made by bequest,
a proportion exceeded in only two other counties of the realm.[6] We
must add that this percentage is necessarily inexact, despite the care and
effort taken to note the benefactions made by donors during their life-
times in this and other counties. We may be reasonably certain that
almost all the testamentary benefactions have been found, but we have
no such comfortable assurance regarding living gifts. It is true that
probably all the larger capital foundations made by living men assumed
a legal form which ensured a record, but the small outright gift to help
a scholar in a grammar school, to apprentice a poor boy, or to relieve
conscience by casual alms must in a great many cases have escaped the
net of our method. These spontaneous gifts are neither historically nor
statistically important, but they none the less possessed a great social
and moral value from the very fact of their spontaneity.

The Aspirations of Women Donors

London was a vigorous and a forward-looking city not only in the immensity and the boldness of its charitable dispositions but likewise in the organization of the social system which created and disposed this wealth. It was accordingly a community in which the status of women was particularly advanced and in which their property rights enjoyed substantial respect. The merchant class tended to contract its marriages within a quite strictly defined fraternity of commerce, and the widow of a merchant, on whom the pressures for remarriage were very heavy indeed, normally married within the circle of her late husband's livery. In point of fact, in hundreds of wills of the period husbands all but prescribed the remarriage of their widows by careful property dispositions which made it at once difficult and unrewarding if the widow married outside the company of the late spouse. Within this tightly knit community, which respected property quite as much as sentiment, the position of the wife who had brought a marriage settlement to her husband's business or the widow who had been left with working control of a substantial trading firm was very secure indeed. In an age of heavy mortality among men in their early prime, substantial wealth found its way into the hands of women, much of which was disposable and most of which seems to have been managed with a prudence and success suggesting how fully women bred and married in this remarkable class had absorbed its *mores* and values. We shall likewise have occasion to comment on a considerable number of charities, often very large ones, which were evidently the creation of merchant couples, the survivor completing or augmenting the sometimes most elaborate design begun by the spouse who happened to die first. We are, then, dealing with a period in which the legal rights of women were improving slowly indeed, but in which the status of women and their actual rights were undergoing substantial amelioration in all urban communities, and particularly in London.[1]

There were 1100 women donors in London, these numbering not quite 15 per cent (14·88 per cent) of all benefactors of the city. This proportion exceeds somewhat that noted in any other county, save, significantly, for Bristol. It should also be mentioned that the proportion of women donors in the successive decades of our whole period was relatively high in the last two decades of the fifteenth century and then remained quite stable until 1620, when a remarkably rapid gain set in which reached its climax in the period of the Civil Wars. In the years 1641–1650, somewhat more than 20 per cent of all charitable benefactors were women, reflecting in London, as in all other counties, the interesting tendency of women to make great social and economic gains during periods of profound political unsettlement.* During these years men were away at war, were seeking to protect their estates by the prudent device of vesting at least part of their property in their wives, or were yielding to the new and radical social views regarding the status of women evoked by the reforming thought of a revolutionary era.

The women benefactors of London gave in all £172,635 5s to the various charitable causes, or an average of slightly more than £156 18s for each donor. The whole of their contribution to the charitable needs of their community represents 9·14 per cent of the vast total of London's charitable wealth, a proportion considerably less than that observed in the rural counties of Buckinghamshire and Yorkshire.

We have been able to gain reasonably full particulars regarding the estates of sixty-nine of these women donors who were members of the merchant class of the city, which would suggest that the wives and, of course, more particularly, the widows of the great merchants were in many cases very rich in their own right.[2] Of this group, forty-two were widows and the remainder wives dying earlier than their spouses, the former group being in average terms slightly more than twice as rich as the latter. In all, these sixty-nine women left estates with a total worth of £85,611 2s, charities being included, which they disposed of their own right, or the very substantial average sum of £1240 15s for each member of the group. These estates ranged in total worth from the £50 12s of a goldsmith's widow in 1568 to £11,205 left in 1618 by a merchant's widow, certain lands of an unknown value not being included in this last huge estate. It is likewise interesting to note that eighteen of these women bequeathed lands held in their own names and subject to their own testamentary control, ranging from those who left London houses or small parcels of property, usually in Middlesex or Surrey, to six women testators who possessed at least one manor and including

* The proportion of women donors in the several decades is as follows:

Per cent	Per cent	Per cent
1480–1490—15·13	1541–1550—10·68	1601–1610—14·53
1491–1500—15·34	1551–1560—12·46	1611–1620—13·59
1501–1510—11·54	1561–1570—14·75	1621–1630—15·70
1511–1520—11·04	1571–1580—12·62	1631–1640—16·72
1521–1530—10·64	1581–1590—14·07	1641–1650—20·29
1531–1540—12·50	1591–1600—15·00	1651–1660—17·90

two who disposed real property worth upwards of £400 p.a. These women as a group left £8598 16s to various charitable uses, this amounting to 10·04 per cent of the whole of their disposable estates, which, though a generous proportion, suggests feminine prudence when compared with the extraordinary generosity of the merchant class as a whole, whether in London or elsewhere.

Taking in view the entire group of 1100 women donors, it should at once be remarked that the structure of their charitable interests differed rather sharply from that of the generality of benefactors of the city. They were particularly concerned with the plight of the poor, towards whose relief they disposed more than 41 per cent of all their gifts, as compared with just over 35 per cent for the city at large. Quite surprisingly, they were also relatively more interested in the various schemes for social rehabilitation than were their husbands, these uses commanding 14·81 per cent of all their benefactions as compared with somewhat more than 13 per cent for all donors. Their interest in the several forms of municipal improvement was scant (3·05 per cent), though not markedly less than that of the city as a whole. They were also less concerned with the improvement of the educational resources of the nation than were men, just under a fourth (24·78 per cent) of all their benefactions being devoted to this great need, while the proportion for the city at large came to 27·04 per cent. It may also be noted that their support of education was largely concentrated on the universities, to which women donors gave in all the substantial total of £25,053, this being 14·51 per cent of the whole, of which, however, the immense sum of £18,000 was the gift of one woman donor, the incomparable Margaret Beaufort. And, finally, London's women donors were more secular in their aspirations than were its benefactors as a whole, they having designated slightly less than 16 per cent for religious uses as compared with 19·50 per cent for the city at large. Moreover, it must be observed that nearly half the scanty total afforded by women donors for the various religious uses was represented in the large sum of £12,694 3s which with a quite persistent zeal formidably Puritan ladies vested in lectureships from 1583 onwards.

We might well comment on the difficulties involved in certainly determining the social status to which women donors of our period belonged, often even when they possessed considerable wealth. The decorous title of 'widow' with which they so frequently clothed themselves in social anonymity is on occasion quite impossible to resolve unless there is additional and more informative evidence in the will, the inventory, or some other legal document. In London, rather surprisingly, we have had more difficulty in providing a social census of women donors than in the rural counties. Of the women in our donor group, a large total of 467, these being 42·45 per cent of the whole, simply cannot be positively identified as members of a particular social class, though incomplete evidence would suggest that at least twenty of this number were merchants' wives or widows and that well over half were of the shopkeeper or tradesman class, while the remainder (206) defy even the processes of conjecture. The largest single group of definitely identified women donors were merchants' wives, widows, or daughters, who numbered 260 in all, or slightly less than a fourth (23·64 per cent) of the whole. There were ninety-seven women certainly of the tradesman class, while forty-eight were of the somewhat amorphous group we have had to describe as 'additional burghers', and twenty-seven were the wives or widows of professional men. There were twenty women donors drawn from the nobility, while there were nineteen who were widows of clergymen and four who described themselves as of yeoman status. Most surprisingly, there were in all eighty-nine women donors in London who were clearly of the upper gentry and sixty-one who were drawn from the lesser gentry, it evidently having been common for widows of men of these normally rural classes to take houses in London after the death of their husbands, one would suppose because of the greater comfort and security to be gained in the city.

The women of the merchant class constituted by far the largest, though, somewhat surprisingly, by no means the dominant, group of charitable donors of their sex. These 260 women gave in all £68,303 12s to various charitable uses, this amounting to slightly less than 40 per cent (39·60 per cent) of the whole given by women donors. Most of these benefactions were of course relatively modest, though there were thirteen of these women who were considerable donors with charitable gifts amounting to £1000 or more, all of whose benefactions will be treated in some detail in later pages. Widows and wives of the upper gentry, of whom there were eighty-nine, gave the impressively large total of £31,518 1s for charitable needs, five of these bequests amounting to £2000 or more, though it might well be noted that two of the largest charitable gifts made by members of this class disposed wealth only one generation removed from the trading halls and wharves of London. There were as well twenty members of the nobility who as a group gave the considerable total of £28,330 for various charitable uses, a large proportion of which was accounted for by the great benefactions of Margaret Beaufort, who left a charitable fortune quite large enough to excite the greed of her royal grandson. We have certainly identified ninety-seven of the women benefactors who were members of the tradesman class, their combined charities amounting to £11,065 3s. The large group of women of uncertain social class, numbering 467 in all, gave a total of £23,873, the average of their benefactions as well as more persuasive evidence making it probable that a considerable number of them were the widows of tradesmen. All the remaining social classes gave in total £9545 9s for charitable uses, women of the professional classes and of the lower gentry together accounting for well over half of the whole amount. But from whatever class they may have been drawn, the women donors of London were at once numerous and generous and shared with the urban society of which they were an increasingly significant part a mature understanding of the shape and direction of a new England just coming into being.

The Web of Parishes

A. LONDON

London was throughout our period a city in process of rapid growth and, as we have indicated, was an urban complex already burgeoning out of its ancient limits as it encroached deeper and deeper into the county in which it was geographically situated. It was likewise a city extraordinarily fluid in its social structure, without permanently fashionable precincts, in which the very rich lived side by side with, or more often above, the very poor. We have sought at least to chart the tangled and complex parochial structure of the city in order to determine the sources of charitable giving and to set out the residences of men of the various classes who made contribution to the social needs of the city and nation. We have counted in all 117 London parishes in the course of our period, or about the same number as reported by Peter of Blois in 1199[1] and by John Stow in 1598.[2] If the Abbey Church may be counted as one, there were likewise six Westminster parishes, all of which were essentially suburban by the middle of the seventeenth century. And there were as well seventy additional parishes from which benefactions have been noted in the remainder of Middlesex, the social and occupational complexion of which by 1660 would suggest that at least half were in the early stages of urban absorption.

It would not be meaningful, even were it possible, to analyse the charities of each of the parishes of the city. Most of the larger donors held in view the whole needs of the city when they framed their bequests, others spread the benefit of their benefactions over many parishes, and still others were employing London wealth for the benefit of distant towns and counties. Indeed, the most impressive fact about London donors of our period is that they were in no sense parochial-minded, save perhaps for small and almost customary bequests for the poor or for church repairs in particular parishes in wills which embraced the whole city or the whole nation with the bulk of the charitable funds being disposed.

Our effort has rather been to estimate the total of charitable wealth flowing from each parish in the city in order to determine at least roughly the wealth of each area and to arrive at some view of its social composition at various intervals in our long period. A donor has been assigned to a particular parish, therefore, when his will or some other document names it as his place of residence or, that failing, when he expressed a wish to be buried from a particular parish church. Somewhat surprisingly, it has been possible to determine the place of residence of nearly 84 per cent (83·96 per cent) of all known donors by this method, of which number (6206) it is interesting to observe that 76 per cent were residents of the city, approximately 6 per cent lived in Westminster, and the remainder (18 per cent) in the county parishes, with a heavy concentration in the suburban reaches which ringed the city round.

These residents of known parishes gave in all the huge total of £1,494,292 1s of charitable benefactions, or about 79 per cent of the whole of the benefactions for the entire community, reigning sovereigns as well as persons of uncertain place of residence having 'een excluded. Of this very large total, £1,186,550 1s, or 79·41 per cent, was provided by residents of the city parishes; £109,676 16s, or 7·34 per cent, by Westminster; and £198,065 4s, or 13·25 per cent, by the remainder of Middlesex County. This would seem to suggest a rather more even distribution of wealth over this whole considerable area than might be supposed, the gradual movement of the great merchants and the 'urban gentry' to the suburban areas and to still genuinely rural parishes clearly being the explanation.

The great bulk of London's immense charitable wealth was provided by less than a third of its parishes. Thus £889,429 2s of the total given by donors resident in known city parishes, and this was about 75 per cent of the entire sum, was amassed in thirty-seven parishes. These were parishes which, as we shall see, were scattered in a patchwork fashion over the entire urban area, in which merchants and tradesmen tended to live and to have, in most cases, their business connections. Each of these parishes was to contribute the relatively substantial sum of £10,000 or more for charitable uses, the median parish (St Sepulchre) having had 191 donors who gave in all £18,501 2s. These, very evidently, were the highly favoured parishes from which there flowed in the course of our period not only much of the charitable wealth of London and of England but from which there sprang as well the dominant secular aspirations which were to frame a new social and cultural order. It might be well to examine in some detail the structure of giving in at least a few of these rich and incredibly generous parishes.

Quite set apart amongst the very rich parishes is a group of five which together were to contribute the enormous total of £331,528 4s, or well over a fourth of the whole of the charitable resources of London, and far more than that provided for charitable uses in any single county in the realm. By far the largest total from this parochial group was that disposed by the parish of St Bartholomew the Great, which grew rapidly after the dissolution of the great priory from which it took its name and was the place of residence of such sixteenth-century stalwarts as Richard, Lord Rich, and Sir Walter Mildmay. In all, we have noted charitable contributions amounting to £140,067 12s from residents of this parish, this being 11·8 per cent of the whole charitable wealth of London, though it should at once be added that the amount is greatly swollen by the perhaps debatable addition of Thomas Sutton's immense bequest to the *corpus* of its charities.[3] But there were many other notable benefactors who claimed this parish as their residence, of whom five were great merchants, fourteen merchants, and twelve members of the several professional classes, the latter group having been strongly represented in the period from 1541 to 1610. We must regard as exceptional, too, the huge charitable contribution made by the parish of St Olave Silver Street, much of the £64,375 10s credited to this parish being accounted for by the great charities of Henry Smith, who died resident in the parish and who was, strangely, the only merchant we have noted as living in this otherwise quite humble parish during the entire course of our period.[4]

The three remaining parishes in this most favoured group were more typical in the sense that their very large charitable contributions were not dominated by one immense gift but represent the accumulated charities of a substantial number of rich and generous men. The parish of St Olave Jewry, with thirty-eight known donors, provided charitable funds in the amount of £45,199 2s, a large proportion of which was given after 1600 when the parish became a favourite seat for merchants, and especially for ironmongers. There were eleven donors of this parish who may be reckoned as great merchants, while another fifteen were members of the several livery companies.[5] Ranking close behind it was the parish of St Mary Aldermary, the immense generosity of whose merchants excited the civic pride of Stow. This parish, consistently generous throughout our era, gave in all £41,357 6s for charitable purposes in a particularly impressive pattern of generosity, there having been no one donor whose benefactions amounted to as much as £2000. There was a remarkable concentration of eighteen great merchants who are numbered as donors from this parish, drawn principally from the Merchant Taylors, while there were also thirty-three lesser merchants who were members of the great livery companies.* Equally famous as the home of great merchants, and nearly as generous, was the parish of St Helen Bishopsgate, in which there were in all sixty charitable donors who were to provide £40,528 14s in benefactions, or 3·42 per cent of the charitable funds of the city. This parish gained slowly in wealth and prestige as our period wore on, with the great concentration of

* See footnote on following page.

merchant donors appearing just at the close of Queen Elizabeth's reign.†

The second grouping of rich and extremely generous parishes numbered six, with charitable benefactions from known residents ranging in total amount within the quite narrow limits of from £25,121 13s to £30,622 5s. These parishes were spotted in a haphazard fashion over the whole urban area from St Andrew Undershaft to the east to St Dunstan in the West, these being situated outside the city walls. The most munificent of these parishes was St Andrew Undershaft, whose charitable benefactions amounted to £30,622 5s, or 2·58 per cent of the whole for the city, with a notably heavy concentration of gifts in the early Stuart period. Stow, who described the virtues of this parish with loving pride, would suggest that this was a bustling and highly prosperous urban region, taking great pride in its church, in which a large stock of books was kept for the edification of the neighbourhood, and possessing a tone set by the substantial and civic-minded burghers who peopled it for so long. We have counted fifteen

* The pattern of donors by social classes was as follows:

Class	1480–1540	1541–1560	1561–1600	1601–1640	1641–1660	Total
Great merchants	5	1	2	6	4	18
Merchants	5	3	12	9	4	33
Tradesmen	1	—	—	—	1	2
Burghers	—	—	—	3	2	5
Artisans	—	1	—	3	—	4
Uncertain	—	—	1	1	—	2
						64

The amounts given by intervals were:

	£	s	d
1480–1540	6,057	9	0
1541–1560	2,049	9	0
1561–1600	14,275	3	0
1601–1640	8,088	5	0
1641–1660	10,887	0	0
Total	41,357	6	0

† The pattern of donors by social classes was as follows:

Class	1480–1540	1541–1560	1561–1600	1601–1640	1641–1660	Total
Upper gentry	1	—	—	—	—	1
Lower gentry	1	1	—	—	—	2
Lower clergy	1	—	1	2	—	4
Great merchants	1	2	3	5	3	14
Merchants	1	2	2	5	7	17
Tradesmen	1	1	—	6	2	10
Burghers	1	1	1	1	4	8
Uncertain	—	1	1	1	1	4
						60

great merchants, including several lord mayors, who were residents of the parish, not to mention twenty-five substantial but lesser merchants who were members of the several livery companies.* The social and economic complexion of St Dunstan in the West, which provided the large sum of £28,038 6s, or 2·36 per cent of London's total, was very different indeed. Its donors were an interesting mixture of gentry employed on crown affairs, chancery clerks and officers, professional men generally, and a large number of substantial merchants and shopkeepers, including, however, no great merchants. The great period of prosperity and growth for the parish was concentrated in the early Stuart era, when £24,618 15s of its total contributions were made.† There followed the parish of St Bartholomew the Less, next the great hospital of the same name, whose charitable benefactions totalled £27,580 6s, this large sum being provided by a quite evenly distributed group of merchants, tradesmen, and burghers, including, however, only two great merchants, both of whom died in the first of our intervals. The parish of St Christopher by the Stocks, whose church was substantially improved in 1621, was throughout our period a favourite place of residence and business for merchants, particularly for mercers, merchant tailors, and men engaged in the Flemish and Spanish trades. Most of its benefactors were great merchants, including five lord mayors, while an additional twenty-six were lesser members of the great livery

* The pattern of donors by social classes in this parish was as follows:

Class	1480–1540	1541–1560	1561–1600	1601–1640	1641–1660	Total
Lower clergy	1	—	—	—	2	3
Professional	—	—	—	1	—	1
Great merchants	1	—	2	8	4	15
Merchants	3	1	6	12	3	25
Tradesmen	—	—	5	—	—	5
Burghers	—	—	2	4	3	9
Artisans	—	—	—	—	1	1
Uncertain	1	—	1	2	—	4
						63

† The pattern of donors by social classes in St Dunstan's was as follows:

Class	1480–1540	1541–1560	1561–1600	1601–1640	1641–1660	Total
Upper gentry	—	—	—	—	1	1
Lower gentry	—	1	1	3	—	5
Lower clergy	—	—	—	2	—	2
Professional	—	1	2	10	2	15
Merchants	1	4	11	14	—	30
Tradesmen	1	1	4	8	3	17
Burghers	—	—	4	10	2	16
Artisans	1	1	4	9	1	16
Uncertain	1	—	1	2	—	4
						106

companies. In all, its eighty-seven donors were to give £26,874 1s, or 2·26 per cent of the whole for the city, to various charitable causes. Just to the north of the then Customs House lay the parish of St Olave Hart Street, whose church was to escape the Great Fire. This small but evidently very rich parish was to contribute £26,222 8s to the charitable funds of the city. Its benefactors included six great merchants, of whom four were grocers, as well as two noblemen, the first and the second Viscounts Sudbury, who were respectively son and grandson of a grocer, as well as thirteen lesser merchants, of whose number five were members of the Grocers' Company. And, finally, there was the parish of St Botolph Bishopsgate, whose church lay just to the north of the wall, which was through the whole of our period a popular place of residence and business for merchants and tradesmen of the middling sort. It might be mentioned that we have recorded no benefactions in this parish of any donor not a member of the various commercial classes, one seaman aside, and that of the whole number exactly two-thirds were either lesser merchants or tradesmen. In all, the benefactors of this parish gave £25,121 13s for various charitable uses, with an unusually high proportion for poor relief.

The third grouping of parishes making substantial contribution to the charitable needs of London and the nation included eleven which together were to provide the massive sum of £208,794 7s, a total considerably larger than that accumulated during our whole period in as rich and influential a county as Norfolk. All these parishes save for St Sepulchre, which lay just outside the walls at Newgate, were old and substantial communities within the precincts of the ancient city. Their charitable wealth ranged rather narrowly from the £15,407 4s given by the tiny parish of St Faith under St Paul's, this being 1·30 per cent of the city's benefactions, to the £22,672 17s given by the mercers and other merchants of St Michael Bassishaw. All these parishes were evidently dominated by the mercantile aristocracy, which accounted for nearly 80 per cent of all their charitable resources, with the rather interesting exception of St Sepulchre. This last was throughout our period a populous parish given over to trade and industry, but was at no time the seat of any really rich merchant or any particularly notable donors. None the less, it was a parish with a consistent and a well-developed sense of charitable responsibility, with the largest number of benefactors, 191 in all, whose place of residence can be certainly determined. Over the course of the years charitable funds totalling £18,501 2s were accumulated within the parish, with the result that it ranked eighteenth amongst the parishes of the city in terms of its generosity. We have noted only one great merchant resident in St Sepulchre during our period, while its thirty-seven lesser merchants were on the whole drawn from the poorer livery companies. Its many tradesmen were concentrated most heavily in the brewing and cooperage trades, while a fair number of innkeepers have also been noted as modest contributors to the needs of this interesting urban community.

We have dealt in some detail with a relatively small group of twenty-two parishes in which not only the wealth but the civic leadership of London was most heavily concentrated. In decided contrast, there were approximately the same number of parishes, twenty-six in all, comprising about a fifth of the whole number in the city, which were either areas of great poverty or which for various reasons made only a slight contribution to the prodigal outpouring of charitable wealth from the London of our era. These parishes are most dramatically set apart from all the rest, none having accumulated charitable endowments of as much as £2000 during the whole course of our period. Their contributions ranged from the £10 recorded for the parish of St James Duke Place (not established until 1622) to the £1797 19s of benefactions in St Matthew's parish, the median parish in the group being St Benedict with a total charitable contribution of £846 1s. The poverty of these parishes can perhaps be better documented when it is noted that even the five of this group with the most considerable benefactions contributed within the range of 0·13 per cent to 0·15 per cent each of the whole charitable wealth of the city. Further, when taken as a group, the total of their charities scarcely equalled the contribution of St Botolph Bishopsgate, which in turn ranked no higher than eleventh amongst the parishes of the city in the generosity of its donors.

With two exceptions all these parishes lay within the walls of the city, most of them being small communities that were densely populated and already partially derelict well before our period was out. Many of them were clearly urban slums, without merchant leadership and without much indigenous tradition of social or economic responsibility. These parishes must on the whole be regarded as areas of economic blight, so wanting in resources that their situation would have been desperate indeed had it not been for the immense and the encompassing charity of the city as a whole. We are now, of course, doing no more than seeking to plot the parochial origins of the charitable wealth of the city, wealth which happily for these areas was rarely vested specifically or exclusively for the parish of the donor. These were simply the 'debit parishes' which because of extreme poverty or smallness failed to carry their social weight within the complex urban structure which was London. We should now examine in some detail the social structure and charitable traditions of at least a few of these poorer parishes.

Passing over the recently created parish of St James Duke Place and the quite specially constituted parish of St Peter in the Tower (ad Vincula), the parish making the smallest contribution to charities was St Andrew Hubbard, in Billingsgate Ward and but a short distance inshore from Billingsgate Dock. There were only ten charitable donors resident in this parish, three being merchants and all the rest artisans and shopkeepers, whose total of benefactions was no more than £427 15s. The parish was evidently derelict long before the Great Fire ravaged it. The church was not rebuilt after the Fire, the area being united to St Mary at Hill and the church grounds being converted to public uses. Farther up the river, near Paul's Wharf, was another decayed parish, St Peter Parva, of which Strype sadly records, 'nor any gifts or legacies to church or poor'. This was not quite the case, a total of £488 17s of benefactions having been noted, of which, significantly, £223 17s had been made prior to the advent of the Reformation. Very close to St Andrew Hubbard was the small parish of St Margaret Pattens, which, though in Stow's time on a street 'with many fair houses for merchants', none the less seems to have been in process of rapid decline. We have recorded only sixteen donors of this parish during the whole of our period, seven being lesser merchants, and the total of contributions being no more than £555 10s, or 0·05 per cent of the charitable funds for the whole of the city. The parish of St Mary Staining, in Aldersgate Ward and in a too heavily 'churched' corner of the old city precincts, suffered at once from being small in area and over-populated with poor workmen. The total of its charitable contributions was £597 18s, there having been nothing provided after 1640. The parish was the residence of an occasional merchant until about 1620, but was wisely united with the larger and certainly more prosperous parish of St Michael Wood Street after the Great Fire razed the church. Just in from the river at the Queen Hithe was the small and always struggling parish of the Holy Trinity, the church being so far decayed for some years prior to 1606 that it 'leaned upon props, or stilts' until it was rebuilt largely by donations from other parishes of the city and by gifts from the Vintners and Merchant Taylors. Though still the preferred residence of a number of substantial and old-fashioned vintners, including one great merchant, the parish did not give in charity more than £648 10s during the whole course of our period. This church was rebuilt as a Lutheran chapel after the Great Fire, the parish having been united with St Michael Queenhithe.

The particulars which we have supplied for at least a few of the lesser and poorer parishes will perhaps suffice in suggesting that the processes of decay as well as of growth were at work within the precincts of the city.* We may have erred in concentrating only on those parishes which were either exceptionally rich and generous or which were quite untypically poor, to the neglect of the scores of parishes within and without the walls which were not only providing for their own poor and their own social needs but were on balance contributing significantly to the

* See footnote on following page.

requirements of the whole of the city, and, for that matter, of the realm. But this omission we shall seek to remedy as we comment on certain of the benefactions of residents of these healthy, stalwart, and 'average' parishes.

As we have suggested, a not inconsiderable proportion of the whole of the charitable benefactions of the metropolis must be credited to areas which lay outside the always expanding limits of the city. Thus more than 6 per cent of all benefactors with known places of residence were inhabitants of the several parishes of Westminster, this group of 401 donors contributing in all £109,676 16s of charitable funds, or 7·34 per cent of the whole of Middlesex benefactions given by donors whose places of residence can be determined. By far the largest total was provided by the then huge parish of St Martin-in-the-Fields, during the last two generations of our period a favourite place of residence for the gentry, public officials, and those merchants who wished to escape the congestion of the city. There were in all 158 benefactors in this parish who were to provide charitable funds reaching the substantial total of £43,742 14s, most of which was given in the early Stuart period when the parish was particularly fashionable and rich. We have likewise regarded Westminster Abbey as a parish for present purposes. Excluding all gifts and bequests by outside persons to the abbey or the school, we find that the generous total of £34,998 7s was given for charitable purposes, in the main those connected with the needs of the abbey or school, by the abbots, the clergy, the crown, certain crown officials, and residents of the school. Next in rank among the Westminster parishes was St Margaret's, whose most variegated population gave in all £16,945 11s for charitable uses in the course of our period, with, it should be noted, consistent philanthropic strength being evident in each of our time intervals. The parish of St Mary-le-Strand, which we have treated as of Westminster, contributed the substantial sum of

---

* We may, however, list a few of this group of relatively impoverished parishes, indicating as well the total of their charitable contributions and the proportion this bears to the whole of the charitable funds of the city.

	£	s	d	Per cent
St George Botolph Lane	671	19	0	0·06
Allhallows Honey Lane	727	8	0	0·06
Holy Trinity Minories	814	8	0	0·07
St Benedict	846	1	0	0·07
St Michael Queenhithe	914	9	0	0·08
St Mary Mounthaunt	1,005	0	0	0·08
St Leonard Foster	1,125	5	0	0·09
St Margaret Fish Street	1,230	10	0	0·10
St Mary Somerset	1,269	1	0	0·11
St Benet Gracechurch	1,425	14	0	0·12
St Nicholas Olave	1,492	12	0	0·13
St John the Evangelist	1,556	5	0	0·13

£9466 11s to various charitable uses, with a persistent interest in the needs of the poor, most of its donors being either of the gentry or of the tradesman groups. The nearby parish of St Clement Danes gave in all £4463 13s to charitable needs, twenty of its donors having been members of the lower gentry, eighteen lesser merchants, and sixteen of tradesman status. All these parishes, most evidently, were part of the structure of London life and shared completely in the immense energy and enthusiasm with which the merchant leaders of the metropolis were shaping a new social order.

B. MIDDLESEX

There were as well seventy parishes in Middlesex County, lying beyond the area which we have defined as London and Westminster, which made significant contributions to the charitable needs of the age. We have identified 1088 donors as residents of these parishes, or about 18 per cent of all donors with certainly known places of residence. These benefactors gave the large total of £198,065 4s for charitable causes in the course of our period, or 13·25 per cent of the huge accumulation which may be credited with certainty to individual parishes. This sum, substantially larger than the charitable wealth deployed in the rich county of Norfolk, of course at once suggests that we may have drawn the line of definition much too tightly around the urban complex which was London. The city had in fact spilled out, or, more precisely, many of the men who possessed and could dispose its wealth had spread out in a great and ever-moving wave of urbanization which had by 1660 profoundly altered, when it had not engulfed, rather more than half the area of a once largely rural county. As we assess these parochial contributions, we shall move out of the city through several strata of population and economic organization, which may be described as urban, suburban, semi-rural, and in one surviving area of the county, rural.

Well before the close of our period much of the area to the north and west of the city, included in the hundred of Ossulstone, had become urban, such parishes as St Giles in the Fields and St Pancras being already favourite dwelling places of merchants and gentry who had fled the teeming mass of London. Thus the charitable contributions of St Pancras parish totalled £12,637, respectable even by London standards and given almost wholly by merchants and gentry living there in the period after 1615. The parish of St Giles in the Fields, including as it did much of the present Bloomsbury district and Lincoln's Inn Fields, gained rapidly in population during the last sixty years of our period, the old and small church having been replaced in 1623–5 by a large and more appropriate structure. The charitable contributions of the parish amounted to £2986, of which nearly the whole was given after 1601. The social aspirations of the donors, who were especially concerned with poor relief, reflect most vividly the urbanization which had by 1660 almost wholly transformed the area. Other parishes in this region, including the area now roughly defined as Holborn, St Pancras, St Marylebone, Paddington, and Hampstead, were by no means so completely urban, Paddington, for example, having contributed no more than £1020 for charitable purposes and Hampstead only £212, while the structure of benefactions in both parishes makes it clear that these were regions only beginning to yield to an inevitable urbanization. The total contribution of this area to the charitable needs of the age came to the substantial sum of £24,265 12s, the support of education commanding £11,785, the relief of the poor £9692 6s, experiments in social rehabilitation £1610 4s, and with relatively modest sums for the support of religion and for municipal betterments. There were in all 143 charitable donors who resided in the region, with a particularly heavy representation of gentry and merchants who had built pleasant houses in a still uncrowded but increasingly urban setting.

The hundred of Finsbury, to the east and north of the area just described, was in part heavily urbanized by the close of our period, in part was suburban, though in its more distant parishes, such as Friern Barnet, close against the Hertfordshire border, it remained essentially rural in character. Yet it is significant that in every parish in the hundred we find merchant donors who had established seats outside the city, including two great merchants in Friern Barnet itself. The parish of St Luke, Finsbury, heavily populated by merchant and tradesman donors, gave in all £11,500 for charitable uses, the growth in population of this area being suggested by the fact that all save £900 of this sum was provided after 1561. The far more heavily populated parish of St James, Clerkenwell, contributed £7633 15s for various charitable causes, with a particularly heavy concentration on endowments for almshouses and poor relief, while the parish of St Sepulchre, Finsbury, vested charitable funds totalling £6442 10s. The still largely rural parish of Islington gave the substantial total of £7130 12s for charitable causes, much of the sum having been provided by two generous merchants and one member of the upper gentry who had seats in the parish. The twenty donors of Hornsey, of whom seven were London merchants and tradesmen and nine lower gentry, gave the considerable sum of £4154 6s, while the contribution of Finchley amounted to £3235, and that of Stoke Newington to £2105 13s. In total, the charitable endowments of the hundred, largely designated for extra-parochial uses, amounted to £43,608 3s, the bulk of which was the gift of the many merchants and fashionable gentry whose country seats were spread across the whole area.

The now densely populated reaches from the ancient boundary of the city eastward to the Essex border were also in process of rapid urbanization before our period was out, some areas of which, such as Hackney, Shoreditch, and Stepney, it is difficult to remember were regarded by rich merchants and tradesmen as particularly convenient and pleasant suburban communities in which to establish their families. The largest contribution made by the numerous parishes of this region, St Botolph without Aldgate having been counted as a London parish, was that of St Leonard Shoreditch, whose sixty-eight donors gave £9957 13s for charitable causes. The parish of Stepney followed, with endowments of £7393 12s, given by eighty-nine donors, the variegated social structure of the parish being suggested by the fact that sixteen were rich merchants and twenty-eight were seamen. Hackney ranks next, with £5789 14s, then All Saints Poplar with a total of £2402; St Katherine's by the Tower gave slightly more, and St Leonard Bromley provided £1786 18s for the social needs of the age. All the remaining parishes of the region were evidently poor and probably still thinly populated, their contributions ranging from the £569 10s given by Stratford Bow (Poplar) to the £100 provided in Norton Folgate (Shoreditch-Stepney). The total contribution made by this entire region was £42,156 7s, with a notably heavy concentration of interest in poor relief and experiments in social rehabilitation, betraying the great number of merchants who favoured this pleasant and still uncrowded countryside.★

Still another rapidly changing area lay well to the west of London, stretching along the Thames from Chelsea to Ealing and as far to the north as Willesden. This spacious and lovely countryside, almost completely rural during the whole of the sixteenth century, was rapidly being taken over by the gentry and by older London merchants who were planning their retirement or whose affairs permitted them to live at such a considerable distance from their city connections. It is

★ The charitable wealth contributed by the region was designated for the following broadly defined uses:

	£	s	d
Poor	28,266	7	0
Social rehabilitation	6,316	10	0
Municipal betterments	350	0	0
Education	2,810	11	0
Religion	4,412	19	0
Total	42,156	7	0

The interesting social structure of the area as it then was is suggested by the following listing of its charitable donors:

Nobility	1	Husbandmen	2	Public officials	3	Burghers	9
Upper gentry	7	Upper clergy	2	Great merchants	14	Artisans	44
Lower gentry	40	Lower clergy	7	Merchants	36	Sailors	41
Yeomen	20	Professional	13	Tradesmen	50	Uncertain	36
					Total	325	

especially significant that of the substantial contribution made to charity by this western area, rather more than 90 per cent was provided after 1600 and almost 75 per cent after 1625. The largest charitable total was given by Chelsea, the £17,219 13s it vested for various uses comparing favourably with the benefactions of most city parishes, Chelsea of course being the earliest of these communities to take on definitely suburban character. Almost as much was given by the twenty-one donors of Hammersmith, about half its total of £16,570 18s having been designated as endowments for direct poor relief or for almshouses. Several rich merchant donors also lived in Acton, where the quite surprising total of £12,843 13s was given, with a particularly heavy emphasis on social rehabilitation, for which £4400 was disposed. The parish of Chiswick gave in all £4779 15s, while Willesden and Fulham followed in order with £2132 6s and £1385 6s respectively. The remaining villages, as they then were, ranged downwards from the £754 given by the donors of Ealing to the surprisingly small total of £318 4s provided by the twelve contributors of Kensington, only one of whom was a merchant. In all, the parishes of this generally suburban area gave £56,003 15s for charitable uses, with an especially heavy emphasis on the needs of education and religion.

Finally, there was a band of semi-rural and truly rural regions in the most distant stretches of the county, into which the fingers of urbanization had only begun to reach by the close of our period. Northward and to the northeast, the hundred of Edmonton was still almost wholly rural, the large parish of Enfield having had only two donors whose occupations bespoke London connection, while the nearer parish of Tottenham High Cross already exhibited evidences of urban infiltration. In all, the five parishes of the hundred gave £8213 14s to charitable causes in amounts ranging from £532 4s which we have noted in South Mimms to the substantial total of £3360 3s given by Enfield.* Similarly, the

---

* The dispositions made by donors in this hundred were more typically rural than in most other parts of Middlesex:

	£	s	d
Poor	3,917	7	0
Social rehabilitation	703	10	0
Municipal betterments	12	0	0
Education	1,765	0	0
Religion	1,815	17	0
Total	8,213	14	0

The social composition of the donors in the hundred follows:

Nobility	1	Lower clergy	2	Tradesmen	7
Upper gentry	5	Public officials	2	Artisans	2
Lower gentry	17	Great merchants	1	Uncertain	15
Yeomen	21	Merchants	11		
				Total	84

hundred of Gore, to the north and northeast of the city, stretching along the Hertfordshire border, appears to have been principally rural and as yet untouched, though from about 1600 there were heavy purchases of land in the region by London merchants seeking investments rather than residences. Six of its parishes contributed in all £7035 13s for charitable uses, ranging from the tiny total of £4 7s given by two yeoman donors of Kingsbury to the £3551 17s provided by fifteen donors in Stanmore, including, it may be mentioned, one great and three lesser merchants. So too may we regard the parishes comprising the hundred of Spelthorne, stretching along and to the north of the Thames towards the southwestern reaches of the county, as still predominantly rural in character and in social aspirations. We have noted benefactions in nine parishes in this part of the county, with amounts of less than £100 in Feltham, Hanworth, Laleham, Shepperton, and Teddington, but ranging upwards to the £710 1s given in Hampton and the substantial benefactions of £2479 8s recorded for Stanwell. In all, the parishes of the hundred contributed £4184 4s for various charitable uses, there having been only a few urban occupations listed for the donors of the region. Quite substantial benefactions were made for charitable uses by the still rural villages of Ickenham and Twickenham, also on the western borders.

But certainly the most completely rural region remaining in the county was the hundred of Elthorne, with its parishes disposed along the Buckinghamshire borders and the western reaches of Middlesex generally. Benefactions have been noted from thirteen of these parishes, mostly in quite modest amounts such as the £32 given for the poor of Cranford or the £16 2s provided at Harmondsworth for the poor, the church, and a tiny bequest of three shillings for municipal uses. Such larger and more populous parishes as Harefield and Hillingdon disposed charitable funds of more than £1000, while Hayes contributed the substantial total of £5625, most of which was designated for the relief of the poor. In all, the parishes of this hundred gave for charitable uses £9648 11s, of which over 80 per cent was for the succour of the poor. The rural character of this region is attested by the fact that of the eighty donors noted no more than four seem to have had present or past connection with the sprawling urban complex which was London. But it will have been observed that the rural regions, retaining their indigenous agricultural character and institutions, were by 1660 few and remote in the county. We may say with fair accuracy that by that date London was Middlesex. Almost as truly may we say that London had attained, because of its immense vigour and its almost overwhelming generosity, a dominant role in the life and aspirations of the nation.

The Structure of Class Aspirations

A. THE DOMINANCE OF THE MERCHANT ELITE

1. *Observations on the class*

We have spoken at some length of the immense and ever-spreading growth of London during the period under study. That growth was in a true sense a function of the great gains in wealth and power of the merchant aristocracy of the city, a class small in numbers but possessing a remarkable cohesion of purpose, aspiration, and vigour. We shall consequently be especially concerned with this remarkable and powerful group of men, who played such an important role in framing and founding those institutions and those attitudes upon which the modern society may be said to depend. Yet, at the same time, substantial contributions were being made to the rapid development of the life and institutions of the city by other classes of men whose charitable concerns must be noted and assessed against the background of the dominant social achievement of the merchant leaders of this great urban complex. We shall therefore seek to examine the structure and nature of the aspirations of the several classes of men which together constituted this society.

As noted earlier, there were in all 7391 known individual donors in London who together gave the huge total of £1,889,211 12s for the several charitable uses, or an average of £255 12s 2d for each of these benefactors. It has been possible to establish clear social identification of 6524 of these persons, or the relatively very high proportion of 88·27 per cent of the whole number.[1] All the remaining donors were residents of London when their gifts or bequests were made, a large proportion being women. The amount and nature of these gifts by unidentified donors, as well as certain other evidence, would suggest that probably a third were of the lesser merchant community, something more than a third were almost certainly shopkeepers or their widows, while the remainder were probably well scattered through the other urban classes.

The most immediately evident and certainly the most important fact with respect to the structure of class contributions in relation to the charitable needs and resources of London is the enormous power and generosity of the merchant aristocracy. Numerically a very small class, even in London, these men none the less comprised well over a third (36·22 per cent) of all the donors of the city, while their huge contribution of £1,067,883 6s accounted for 56·53 per cent of the whole of the great charitable wealth given by the city.* This almost prodigal generosity was in part accounted for by the great wealth enjoyed by the class during most of our period. It is also most evident that even at the close of the Middle Ages the tradition, the habit, of leadership, and the ability to translate aspirations into institutions were already well-established traits of the merchant aristocracy: that the dominant role assumed by members of the group during the Tudor and Stuart eras represents but an enlargement, a fulfilment, of capacities for leadership already well matured. This class, too, was doubly empowered because its wealth was so largely liquid, so easily and completely disposable, and because it had been gained by men who throughout their trading careers had been obliged habitually to take heavy risks for possibly enormous gains. These men, or at least the greatest of them, were in point of fact speculators to their very core, and surely the disposition to found and endow institutions which reflect one's aspirations for the future of a society is in itself the most speculative of all human undertakings. It is likewise true, and this is important in explaining the great generosity of the class, that these were rising men whose status within their own society was still ill defined, or at the very best in no sense commensurate with the power and wealth which they disposed. They were

* *Analysis of the social structure of charitable benefactions in London:*

No. donors in the class	Social status	Per cent of all county gifts	Per cent of all county persons	Total for the class £	s
9	Crown	6·29	0·12	118,766	19
78	Nobility	3·79	1·06	71,566	16
141	Upper gentry	1·28	1·91	24,136	7
388	Lower gentry	1·14	5·25	21,447	13
159	Yeomen	0·27	2·15	5,192	14
9	Husbandmen	—	0·12	6	19
34	Upper clergy	3·73	0·46	70,467	11
146	Lower clergy	3·59	1·98	67,757	5
2,677	Merchants	56·53	36·22	1,067,883	6
[438]	[Great merchants]	[48·04]	[5·93]	[907,623	3]
[2,239]	[Lesser merchants]	[8·49]	[30·29]	[160,260	3]
1,087	Tradesmen	5·20	14·71	98,212	6
788	Burghers	2·64	10·66	49,809	15
518	Artisans	0·16	7·01	3,030	13
[466]	[Artisans]	[0·13]	[6·30]	[2,376	3]
[52]	[Seamen]	[0·03]	[0·71]	[654	10]
490	Professional	6·59	6·63	124,524	7
867	Unknown status	8·81	11·73	166,409	1

evidently seeking to lay the foundations of a new England and of a new kind of society, a society animated by values which were all but unknown to medieval men and which were neither wholly accepted nor understood by men of their own age. They were, in fact, fashioning the foundations of the liberal society of which they were in so many significant senses the first exemplars. They, their aspirations, and their immensely important contributions deserve our close and full attention.

Men of this class were knit together by numerous and lasting ties which bound them as a remarkably homogeneous society with common modes of conduct, aspirations, symbols, and what may be described as a common way of looking at life and events. It was for one thing, even in London, a relatively small society of not more than six hundred liveried merchants at the beginning of our period, perhaps eight hundred to nine hundred towards its middle, and not many more than a thousand at its close. While men who described themselves as merchants were almost invariably members of one or another of the twelve great livery companies, it by no means followed that their commercial and speculative activities were wholly or even principally confined to the area of trade with which the company was presumably concerned. The class, tightly organized though it was, is exceedingly difficult accurately to define, and it has been our practice in counting a man as of the class to take the testimony of his own will or that of his executor, for men were more prudent in their language and in their claims on such august occasions in this period. But at least we may say that the merchants comprised the commercial aristocracy of London. They were men principally concerned with wholesale trade, though there was a considerable number of them whose affairs were so great and diverse that they may more properly be regarded as speculators and entrepreneurs. Miss Thrupp's happy phrase, when she described them as men of 'mixed enterprises', comes very close to the mark, and, we may add, they were men of large enterprises.[2] Well before the beginning of our period this class had gained an all but complete control of the city government of London, the selection of aldermen, sheriffs, and the lord mayors being almost invariably confined to members of the great merchant companies. As we shall observe, by no means all merchants were rich men, nor does it appear that the possession of a great commercial fortune lent any automatic prestige within the class, partly no doubt because there was a kind of fragility to these fortunes which were so easily and so quickly won and lost. But it may be said with equal truth that membership in this remarkable fraternity was the only possible way in which a great trading fortune could be made in the course of our period.

It is also important to observe that a distinction can and should be drawn within the merchant fraternity between groups which may quite accurately be called the 'great merchants' and the 'lesser merchants', all, of course, being members of the great livery companies. This distinction was well and clearly made by men of the age and drew its criteria principally from wealth. The great merchants were men who had enjoyed steady trading success and exhibited those personal qualities which led to selection for high civic office or to the mastership of a livery company. In fact, it is notable that very few lord mayors of London had not at some time been chosen to head their companies. These were high but they were also burdensome honours, which many men sought to escape, though that was not easy in an age when designations of prestige and responsibility were buttressed with a kind of inexorable weight. We have regarded 438 members of the class as great merchants, this group comprising about a sixth (16·36 per cent) of the whole number of merchant donors in our period.* We have, perhaps somewhat arbitrarily, listed a benefactor as a great merchant if he attained high civic dignity as a lord mayor or sheriff, if he had ever been designated master of his company, or if his wealth at the time of death exceeded the very large worth of £4000. Though no more than 438 merchant donors of the age meet these most rigorous criteria, it is notable that this small and certainly immensely generous mercantile

* This proportion varied considerably from decade to decade. The following table may be of interest in exhibiting the numerical relation between the great and the lesser merchants and also in charting somewhat inexactly the slow but steady increase in the number of merchants. It should be remarked that women relatives are not included.

	Great merchants	Lesser merchants	Total
1480–1490	10	29	39
1491–1500	11	30	41
1501–1510	18	72	90
1511–1520	12	47	59
1521–1530	10	60	70
1531–1540	19	72	91
1541–1550	15	98	113
1551–1560	16	106	122
1561–1570	13	128	141
1571–1580	18	121	139
1581–1590	24	103	127
1591–1600	20	166	186
1601–1610	30	153	183
1611–1620	37	225	262
1621–1630	36	199	235
1631–1640	45	200	245
1641–1650	31	110	141
1651–1660	38	171	209
	403	2,090	2,493
Full number, women relatives included	438	2,239	2,677

elite contributed the enormous total of £907,623 3s for charitable uses, or nearly half (48·04 per cent) of the whole for the entire city. These men were a commercial aristocracy indeed.

The merchant class of London was closely integrated, had been trained in the same efficient discipline of apprenticeship, and had sprung from broadly comparable social origins. The young man completing his apprenticeship and gaining the freedom of his company normally found it possible, often in partnership with another young man, to begin trading with a capital of something like £100, which the Mercers tried to set as a minimum capital in 1503. This substantial sum the young merchant gained from his family, from one of the numerous loan funds now available, by slowly accumulating savings in continuing on with his master for some years, or, and it happened frequently, by a suitable marriage within the trading fraternity. As we have already indicated, marriages were usually contracted within the class, it being almost predictable that a widow would, if she chose to remarry at all, contract a union within the merchant group and most commonly within her late husband's company. Yet tightly organized as was the class, it possessed an extraordinary fluidity throughout the course of our period. One can think of only four or five merchant fortunes of the age which were increased by sons of the same calling and of no merchant dynasty persisting through the third generation. The class renewed its vitality constantly with fresh and principally provincial blood, for fortunes went to the well-trained, the aggressive, and the bold, these being characteristics not inheritable at a father's wish. Then, too, there was a growing tendency on the part of rich merchants to invest a large proportion of their wealth in land in their late years and if they did not thereupon effect the translation into the ranks of the gentry, to arrange that their sons should do so. Further, we have commented on the fragility of mercantile fortunes in the period, for when such wealth was in process of accumulation it lay subject to very great hazards indeed. Fortunes could be lost quite as easily as they had been made, as is attested by the fact that late reverses not infrequently invalidated the testamentary intentions of men of this class. And, finally, it seems certain that this class remained so remarkably fluid in its composition because of the very high mortality rate prevailing throughout our period in the city where merchants had to live and work during the mature years when their fortunes were being gained. It has been reckoned that a very substantial proportion of merchants in a slightly earlier period died leaving no male heirs, while still another substantial proportion left children so young as to be subject to the hideous infant mortality rate prevailing in London throughout our period.[3] There is, in fact, impressive evidence suggesting that the merchant class failed to reproduce itself in any one generation in the period of almost two centuries with which we are concerned.

The active merchant was gregarious, tending to live and keep his goods and the whole apparatus of his trade in quarters convenient for his calling and for contacts with other men of at least roughly comparable social and commercial interests. We have already seen that the charitable contributions of particular parishes depended in large degree upon the number and quality of merchants residing in them. These merchant clusters were by no means fixed for long periods of time, but none the less the concentration was particularly heavy in certain favoured parishes. We have been able to discover the place of residence at death of 2325, or about 87 per cent of the whole number of London merchant donors in our period, of whom 2173 lived in the city proper, 37 in Westminster, and 115, who were normally older and richer men, had been able to establish their residences in outer suburbs or in more distant rural parts of the county. The concentration of these men was particularly heavy in twenty-two city parishes, quite interestingly spread across the face of the city, in which a total of 874 merchants were to be found, this constituting the commercial heart of the metropolis.*

2. *The wealth of the great urban classes*

In describing and defining the status of the merchants in the early seventeenth century, Breton spoke of the decorum of their lives and

* Number of merchant donors in these twenty-two parishes:

Parish	1480–1540	1541–1560	1561–1600	1601–1640	1641–1660	Total
Allhallows Barking	8	3	10	19	3	43
Allhallows Bread Street	10	2	6	12	3	33
St Andrew Undershaft	4	1	8	20	7	40
St Augustine	4	5	9	11	3	32
St Bartholomew by the Exchange	1	2	8	34	1	46
St Christopher by the Stocks	5	2	12	13	5	37
St Dunstan in the East	11	4	15	22	7	59
St Dunstan in the West	1	4	11	14	—	30
St Helen Bishopsgate	2	4	5	10	10	31
St Lawrence Jewry	10	12	17	10	5	54
St Magnus	13	10	17	16	3	59
St Martin Ludgate	9	3	8	11	1	32
St Mary Aldermary	10	4	14	15	8	51
St Mary-le-Bow	7	1	9	14	5	36
St Mary at Hill	10	3	9	9	3	34
St Mary Magdalen	10	—	5	18	3	36
St Michael Bassishaw	3	4	6	12	6	31
St Michael Cornhill	13	3	15	13	2	46
St Sepulchre	8	4	6	13	7	38
St Stephen Coleman	6	4	12	7	7	36
St Stephen Walbrook	12	3	12	6	3	36
St Vedast	7	5	7	9	6	34

874

went on to enquire: 'and how manie poore do they relieue at home? what colledges? what hospitals? what alms-houses haue they builded and in effect, what cities haue they enlarged, and what countries haue they enriched?'[4] The immense generosity of the London merchant class, which all men came grudgingly to admit, was to flow from the great wealth which they disposed during much of our period and which we should now examine in detail.[5]

We may take first the group we have described as the great merchants. We have reasonably full and reliable data regarding the worth of the estates of 181 of their number, or about 41 per cent of the whole group. The total worth of the estates left by this considerable body of men, charities included, but the value of real property holdings being fully determinable in less than half the cases, reached the enormous sum of £2,462,641 6s, or an average worth of £13,605 12s 3d for the group, spread, of course, over a very long period. These men, again in average terms, without much doubt disposed more wealth, and it was likewise largely fluid and hence more effective wealth, than did the upper gentry even of southern England and substantially more than did the upper gentry of the northern and most Midland counties. These fortunes ranged widely from the £12 13s which seems to have been the fragment of wealth left in 1487 by a grocer who had served as lord mayor to the fortune of Sir John Spencer, who on his death in 1610 was without much doubt the richest private citizen of England. The median estate was that left in 1621 by Richard Hale, a grocer and also a former lord mayor, whose fortune, including two manors in Hertfordshire, can be fairly accurately set at £6760. It is also important to note that 152 of the total number in this group, or nearly 84 per cent, held real property of some value, while 138 owned lands outside Middlesex of very considerable worth. In fact, of this group of rich men, eighty-seven, or almost half, held at least two manors for investment or for other purposes, while as many as forty-one might be described as really large landholders on a scale unusual even amongst the upper gentry.

The wealth of the great merchants increased markedly from generation to generation during the course of our period, as did the proportion of their number holding lands of considerable value. In the years prior to the Reformation there were in all forty-one great merchants the average worth of whose estates was of the order of £2292 6s 1d, while the median estate was that of a salter who died in 1491 leaving property which may be quite exactly valued at £1794 13s. The average worth of the estates of twenty-one members of the group who died during the period of the Reformation exhibits a very sharp rise indeed, having been £4496 7s. The interest of these men in acquiring monastic as well as other real property is well demonstrated by the fact that seventeen of the twenty-one held such lands outside London, while thirteen of their number were landholders whose property included two or more manors. We have counted thirty-two great merchants in the Elizabethan age, with estates ranging widely in value from £86 8s left by a former lord mayor, who had suffered severe reverses, to one great fortune of £53,097. The average worth of the group during this interval had risen to £5316, while the more meaningful median estate was valued at £3345 7s.

The great period of merchant wealth was of course during the early Stuart age when, despite occasional years of sharp depression, the whole trading economy in London waxed rich while becoming increasingly restless in its political and religious sentiments. The sixty-seven great merchants of this interval left wealth totalling £1,902,204 9s, or an extremely high average figure of upwards of £28,000 (£28,391 2s 2d), which was, however, quite seriously distorted by three immense fortunes of the period. But even the median estate, that of a grocer who died in 1620, was valued at £10,166 13s, excluding, it must be said, lands in Middlesex, Essex, and Staffordshire of whose worth no estimate is possible. In other words, the median estate in this period was almost exactly three times as great as that of the Elizabethan age. Of the great merchants of the early Stuart period, fifty-four held lands or other real property, while forty were substantial landed proprietors with two or more manors included in the extensive inventories of their estates. There was a sharp but by no means a catastrophic decline in the wealth of members of the class during the revolutionary era. We have counted in all twenty great merchants during these years with fortunes ranging in amount from £2408 to £43,451 2s 7d, the average estate being valued at £9645 17s 1d, and the median fortune totalling £7060.

It must also be emphasized that these great merchants were quite as generous as they were rich. In all, this relatively small group of 181 men gave the enormous total of £446,579 10s for various charitable uses, or something like twice the amount provided by all classes of men in the next most generous county of the realm. Taking our whole period into account, these men designated for charitable causes 18·13 per cent of the whole value of their estates, an extremely high proportion for men of any class in any age. In the pre-Reformation years, it is interesting to note, the tradition of charitable responsibility was already thoroughly engrained in the class, which disposed the amazing proportion of 29·42 per cent of all its wealth for philanthropic purposes. In the next and unsettled period (1541–1560), this proportion fell to 19·74 per cent, only to increase very sharply to about 25 per cent (25·21 per cent) during the Elizabethan age. Despite the fact that the great outpouring of charitable wealth, reaching the immense sum of £326,270 10s, occurred during the early Stuart period, the proportion of estates left to charity declined to 17·15 per cent of the vast merchant wealth left by donors in these years. During the revolutionary generation, there was a further, though slight, decline in the generosity of the great merchants, who disposed not quite 15 per cent (14·79 per cent) of all their wealth for the social uses of their city and nation.[6]

Ranking far below the merchants in wealth, prestige, and civic pride were the tradesmen of the city. This somewhat amorphous class we have defined as including shopkeepers and retailers not of merchant rank, members of the lesser companies, and a number of miscellaneous occupations, such as founders, innkeepers, and chandlers, who are not so easily classified but who were evidently solid members of the urban middle class. Somewhat surprisingly, we possess reasonably reliable data regarding the value of the estates of only ninety-one of the 1087 donors who have been identified as members of this social group. These men left in all estates with a total worth, charities being included, of £133,138 10s, or a relatively very high average of £1463 1s 1d for the class. The range of wealth was wide indeed, thirteen of these men leaving estates valued at £100 or less, while seven of them were very rich men, even by merchant standards, whose estates were valued at £5000 or more. The median estate, left by a girdler who died in 1621, possessed a worth of £858. About a third (thirty) of these men held land outside London, eight of their number being substantial landowners whose property comprised one or more manors. The class was relatively extremely generous in its sense of responsibility towards the social needs of the age, 14·13 per cent of all its wealth having been left for charitable uses.

It is evident that the tradesmen were gaining rapidly in wealth as our period progressed. We have particulars regarding the estates of thirty-one of these men who died in the interval 1480–1600, the median worth being no more than £255 19s, though there were a few rich tradesmen even in this earlier period. The margin of disposable wealth was apparently inconsiderable during these years, since no more than 5·84 per cent of the whole value of the estates of the group was left for charitable purposes. But a marked increase in prosperity among the tradesmen is to be observed in the last two generations (1601–1660) of our study. The average worth of the estates of sixty tradesmen donors who died in this interval was £1717 8s, while, more significantly, the median estate was valued at £1007, or nearly four times the wealth of the class in the preceding century. Moreover, the participation of the class in building the charitable endowments of the city was increasing rapidly, since 16·55 per cent of the whole worth of tradesmen's estates during this interval was designated for charitable uses.

There are insufficient data regarding any other urban class to permit significant comment on their wealth and their relative generosity, save perhaps for two of the professional classes. We have quite full information regarding the worth of the estates of ten London lawyer donors who died during our period and who left in all estates valued at £44,884 2s. The range of wealth for the class was very great, extending from an estate valued at £314 to a large fortune of £15,620 6s, while the average estate was £4488 8s 2d and the median fortune was almost exactly the same, possessing a value of £4471. Somewhat surprisingly, these representatives of their class were almost niggardly in their support of the charitable needs of their community, only 4·27 per cent of their wealth having been dedicated for such uses. We likewise possess information regarding the economic status of nine London physician donors in our period, who as a group left estates with a total worth of £23,244. The average worth of members of the class was £2582 13s 4d, while the median estate was valued at £1505. These men were as a class, then, much less rich than their lawyer contemporaries, but they were none the less incomparably more generous in undertaking the responsibilities required by the age. These nine physicians gave in all £7376 to various charitable uses, this representing the amazing proportion of almost a third (31·73 per cent) of the whole of their disposable wealth.

We may now turn to an analysis of the charitable interests and contributions of the various classes of men to the social institutions which were being so rapidly and so generously created by London wealth. Our attention will be directed particularly to the changing pattern of aspirations within the several social classes and to the ever-increasing secularism which marked London's giving.

B. THE CROWN

The Crown was relatively most generous in assisting London in meeting its basic social needs, in part no doubt because even sovereigns residing in or near London could scarcely help seeing the pressing realities with their own eyes and still more importantly because the powerful and articulate city authorities were at once vigorous and pertinacious in presenting London's case at court. We have credited as royal benefactions only those which seem on balance to have been laid against a sovereign's own purse and only those which were specifically designated for charitable uses within the county of Middlesex.

Nine sovereigns, or their spouses, made charitable contributions to London's needs during our period, their benefactions having totalled £118,766 19s, or 6·29 per cent of the whole *corpus* of London's charitable resources. This substantial sum was rather more than that provided during our period by the tradesmen of the city and slightly less than that given by the professional classes of the capital. A considerable proportion (45·39 per cent) of the whole amount is represented by the £53,906 given by the Crown for the establishment or endowment of hospitals within the city, while slightly less than a fourth (23·84 per cent) of the total was provided for various religious uses. Sovereigns of our period gave in all £18,733 15s, or 15·77 per cent, for the endowment of prayers and were likewise generous in affording £9133 15s for church building in London and in Westminster. The Crown's support of the poor of the city was relatively very modest, only 15·47 per cent of the whole of royal benefactions having been disposed for poor relief, though it should be remarked that as much as £11,321 16s was given by these sovereigns for the founding or strengthening of almshouses within the limits of the metropolis. A slightly smaller proportion (15·28 per cent) of the whole was designated for the strengthening of the educational facilities of the city and for the support of the universities. In all, Henry VII and Henry VIII gave about £12,600 towards the needs of the expanding universities, while later sovereigns contributed £3411 towards the establishment of schools within the county and £2140 for scholarship and fellowship endowments. These were, then, large and generous benefactions which in any other county or region in the realm would have been dominant in the framing of the social institutions of such areas; they are relatively insignificant in London only because of the vastness of the scale of charitable giving by the merchant aristocracy of the city.

C. THE NOBILITY

We have very possibly included too many of the nobility in the ranks of London donors, though the fact is that many of the class were seated within the city or county and that an even larger number contrived to die in London. There were in all seventy-eight members of the class who may best be counted as London donors, who together left £71,566 16s for various charitable purposes in the course of our long period, or a relatively high average benefaction of £917 10s 6d. The nobility comprised 1·06 per cent of all donors for Middlesex, while their benefactions accounted for 3·79 per cent of all London's charitable funds, the class having possessed a 'charitable weight' roughly comparable to that of the lower clergy or of the upper clergy.

Taking our whole period in view, the nobility were to display a marked concern for the needs of the poor of the city and nation. In all, their gifts for one or another form of poor relief amounted to nearly 48 per cent of their benefactions as contrasted with the 35·18 per cent given for this purpose by the city at large. They were especially enlightened in their persistent support of almshouses, to which they gave the large total of £28,220, or 39·43 per cent of all their contributions, an amount considerably larger than that provided for any other charitable head. The nobility were likewise most generous in the support which they lent to education, this interest accounting for over a third (34·79 per cent) of the whole of the charitable funds provided by the group. It should, however, be remarked that this interest was narrowly concentrated on the needs of the universities, to which members of the class gave in total £23,100, while providing no more than £1170 for schools and £557 for scholarships and fellowships. These donors were likewise consistently secular in their aspirations, no more than 14·13 per cent of all their gifts having been made for religious uses, as compared with 19·50 per cent for the city as a whole. In no interval did their support of the church absorb much more than a third (36·90 per cent) of their benefactions, and in the Elizabethan era the proportion fell to the very low figure of 5·30 per cent of the whole. Their principal religious concern was with church building, to which they gave in all £5648, or 7·89 per cent of the total of their charities, with also a considerable interest in chantry foundations, which commanded £2639 17s (3·69 per cent) of their funds. As we might expect, their concern with the various schemes of social rehabilitation was most limited, amounting in all to only 2·85 per cent of their gifts, such amounts as £620 for hospitals, £405 for prisoners, £490 for loan funds, and £400 for apprenticeship plans representing the larger of their contributions for this spectrum of interest. But even so, their concern with undertakings designed to secure the social rehabilitation of the poor was substantial indeed when compared with the meagre support which they lent to various plans for municipal improvements, contributions totalling £180 for roads and streets and £110 for general municipal uses representing the whole of their support for this broad charitable head.

D. THE UPPER GENTRY

We may also deal briefly with the support lent to the charitable institutions of the city by the considerable number of upper gentry who may be regarded as resident in London or in the county of Middlesex. There were 141 of these men and women who gave a total of £24,136 7s in charitable funds, or an average of £171 3s 7d for the class. While members of this group comprised 1·91 per cent of all the donors of the county, it is significant that their benefactions amounted to not more than 1·28 per cent of the total charitable wealth of London.

The upper gentry were chiefly concerned with the plight of the poor, to which they contributed well over a third (37·59 per cent) of their total gifts for charitable uses. This concern was heavily concentrated prior to 1560 on outright distributions of alms and funeral doles and thereafter with creating endowments for the direct care of the poor in their own homes, these charities together comprising 28·60 per cent of all the gifts of the class. The great gentry gave only the relatively insignificant total of £1260 to almshouse foundations, benefactions for this purpose having attracted the support of only four members of the class during our entire period. The needs of education commanded well over a quarter (28·31 per cent) of the charitable resources of the class, £3690 (15·29 per cent) having been given to the universities, £2542 (10·53 per cent) for the support of schools, and £600 (2·49 per cent) for the endowment of scholarships and fellowships. It should be remarked that the upper gentry were by far the most persistently devoted to the needs of the church of all the social classes of London, they having disposed almost 24 per cent (23·60 per cent) of all their benefactions for such uses. Their interest was especially concentrated on prayers, for which they vested £1810 2s (7·50 per cent), and church repairs, for which they designated £1182 (4·90 per cent), though relatively modest sums were also provided by the class for all the needs included under the broad head of religion. The interest of the class in plans for social rehabilitation was, at least when compared with that of the nobility, relatively great. In all, not quite 9 per cent (8·84 per cent) of their contributions were for this broad purpose, though their giving was heavily concentrated on the support of the hospitals of the city, to which they gave £1006 13s (4·17 per cent), and on the founding of apprenticeship schemes, for which they provided £890 (3·69 per cent). The concern of the class with municipal betterments was most limited, only 1·67 per cent of the whole of their charities having been designated for this general purpose.

E. THE LOWER GENTRY

The 388 members of the lower gentry who made charitable contributions from London or from the county comprise a considerable group of donors, though at least a third of them disposed landed fortunes which had been mercantile in the preceding generation. These donors gave in all the surprisingly meagre total of £21,447 13s to the charitable resources of London, or an average of not more than £55 5s 7d for the class. While they accounted for 5·25 per cent of all donors, the whole of their charitable benefactions amounted to little more than 1 per cent (1·14 per cent) of the immense charitable wealth accumulated in the city during our era.

The lesser gentry were throughout our period most seriously concerned with the needs of the poor, to which they gave the amazing proportion of 58·61 per cent of all their gifts.* Their interest was even

* The proportion given for this purpose in the various intervals will suggest the persistent quality of their interest:

Per cent

1480–1540—28·45
1541–1560—30·17
1561–1600—52·13
1601–1640—75·28
1641–1660—48·84

more heavily concentrated on outright relief than was that of the upper
gentry, over 42 per cent (42·51 per cent) of all their contributions having
been made for this one purpose. At the same time, they gave relatively
substantial amounts, particularly in the early Stuart interval, for almshouse foundations, the £2994 1s given for this purpose accounting for
13·96 per cent of all their benefactions. It seems evident in scores of
wills that the gentry were distressed by what they saw of poverty in the
streets of London and that these bequests for outright relief, whether
as doles or as endowments for permanent relief, represent the admirable
and sympathetic concern of men who perhaps possessed no mature
grasp of the problem or the means for its solution. The lesser gentry
did, however, lend at least moderate support to the many and fertile
schemes for the social rehabilitation of the poor, these undertakings
commanding in all 8·76 per cent of their charitable wealth. But these
gifts were not substantial, scaling downwards from the £916 13s given
for the care of the sick to the £84 7s provided for marriage subsidies.
The support lent by men and women of the class to the educational
needs of the city and realm was likewise relatively modest, such uses
absorbing no more than 17·12 per cent of all their benefactions. In all,
members of the group provided £1919 10s for the strengthening or
founding of schools and £1741 for the universities, gifts for the other
educational uses being no more than nominal. At the same time, the
gentry were among the most secular of all London's social groups, the
several needs of the church having commanded no more than 14·16 per
cent of all their benefactions. The gentry were until 1560 as much devoted to religious purposes as their provincial *confrères*, but from 1561
onwards their giving betrays a severe and an almost unmitigated
secularism.* Their principal religious interest, taking the whole period
in view, was with the founding of chantries and prayers generally, to
which they gave £1477 9s in the early decades of our period, or nearly
half their total contribution for all religious purposes during the whole
of the age under study.

F. THE YEOMANRY

There was also a fairly large group of yeomen in the county whose
benefactions are particularly interesting because of the evident influence
the city and its aspirations exercised on the thinking of such men. There

* The proportion given by this class for religious uses in the several intervals
is revealing:

Per cent

1480–1540—55·01
1541–1560—32·26
1561–1600— 2·01
1601–1640— 4·49
1641–1660— 8·59

were 159 members of this social class who gave in all £5192 14s for various charitable uses. They were most evidently prosperous men, for the average contribution of members of the class was £32 13s, which, it may be observed, was not strikingly less than that noted for the lower gentry. These men comprised 2·15 per cent of the whole number of London donors, while their charitable contributions amounted to only 0·27 per cent of the whole of London's charitable capital. Modest as their contributions may seem, it is noteworthy that their gifts exceeded substantially the charitable giving of the whole and enormous mass of the urban poor of the metropolis.

The charitable concern of the yeomanry went out especially to the poor, for whose succour they left slightly more than half (50·68 per cent) of all their benefactions, of this nearly the whole being for outright relief. Their interest in education was likewise very great indeed, for well over a third (35·85 per cent) of all their charitable funds were vested for the endowment of schools or scholarships. In all, members of the class gave £1342 for school foundations, including, it may be said here, the founding of Harrow, while £520 was provided as capital for scholarship funds. It is also interesting to note that men of this class, the professional groups aside, were the most completely secular of all social classes in the county, the whole of their contributions for religious uses amounting to less than 10 per cent (9·51 per cent) of their total benefactions, while even this modest contribution was considerably more than half represented by the £280 given towards the founding of lectureships. As we should expect, the share borne by the class in the support of plans for social rehabilitation was very slight (2·30 per cent), while the proportion (1·65 per cent) provided for various schemes of municipal betterment was almost negligible.

G. THE CLERGY

There were thirty-four of the upper clergy who contributed to the social needs of the county. These men, the bishops and the abbots, gave in all the considerable total of £70,467 11s, which represented 3·73 per cent of the whole of the charitable resources accumulated during our period. It is significant that though well over half the whole amount was provided by the great clergy prior to 1560, the structure of the giving of the class, taking our whole period into account, has a distinctly secular cast. The central preoccupation of these men was with the educational resources of the city and nation, towards which considerably more than two-thirds (68·28 per cent) of all their gifts were dedicated. Thus they provided the large sum of £17,680 10s for the support of the universities, this being 25·09 per cent of their whole contribution, as well as £25,532 for the founding of schools and £4890 7s for the endowment of scholarships and fellowships. These great clerics gave slightly less than a fifth of all their benefactions for the maintenance of the church, church building attracting their principal interest, as we would suppose, with £6010 (8·53 per cent) of gifts, and the general uses of the church ranking next with £4617 7s of supporting benefactions. It is especially interesting that the great clergy left only very modest sums, totalling £2022 and representing but 2·87 per cent of all their benefactions, for the endowment of prayers. The combined contributions to education and to the church absorbing as they did upwards of 88 per cent of all their charitable gifts, the great clergy were to lend but slight support to all other forms of charitable activity. The needs of the poor were evidently only formally understood by the upper clergy, a meagre 7·36 per cent of all their substantial total of benefactions having been given for this great and, for most classes of men, central area of need. So too only modest sums were given by members of the class for the various uses we have grouped under the heading of social rehabilitation, while the opportunities for municipal betterment commanded less than 1 per cent of all their gifts.

The many hundreds of lower clergy who served their cures in London and in the county during the long sweep of our period are represented by the surprisingly small number of 146 charitable donors. These men, who accounted for 1·98 per cent of all the donors of the county, gave 3·59 per cent of its charitable wealth, the average clerical benefaction having been at the extraordinarily high level of £464 1s 9d. It should, however, be pointed out that the substantial total of £67,757 5s given by the lower clergy for charitable causes is explained by the fact that rather more than £16,000 of this sum was the gift of clergy who were in fact the sons and heirs of great merchants and who gave in a pattern which their fathers would certainly have approved. But, even so, the median gift for this group of donors is £174 7s, suggesting that the parish clergy of London were throughout our era much more comfortably situated than were their rural brethren.

The interests and aspirations of the lower clergy form a most interesting pattern of giving as compared with that of the prelates. These men, too, were deeply interested in educational needs, to which they devoted 52·84 per cent of all their benefactions, such gifts falling below 48 per cent of their total benefactions in only one of our time intervals.*

---

* The proportion of total gifts devoted to educational purposes in the various intervals was as follows:

Per cent

1480–1540	80·71
1541–1560	25·18
1561–1600	76·96
1601–1640	48·03
1641–1660	66·70

Taking the whole of our period in view, the clergy gave £11,001, or 16·24 per cent of all their benefactions, for grammar-school foundations, £14,025 19s (20·70 per cent) for various university needs, £8210 17s (12·12 per cent) for scholarship and fellowship endowments, and the substantial sum of £2559 (3·78 per cent) towards the support of non-university libraries. The concern of the lower clergy with the needs of the church was only slightly greater than that of their great brethren, just over 21 per cent (21·17 per cent) of all their benefactions having been vested for this purpose. Their principal religious concern was with church building, to which they gave in all £7742, this being 11·43 per cent of the whole of the benefactions of the class. Interestingly, the total of £2560 given by three Puritan divines in the early Stuart period for the founding of lectureships accounts for 3·78 per cent of the charitable resources given by the class. All other benefactions for church uses were relatively small in total, it being notable that the £1231 7s given by members of the group for prayers represented no more than 1·82 per cent of the whole of their benefactions.

It was only gradually that the lower clergy became aware of their personal responsibility for the relief of the poor, though, taking our whole period into account, they disposed slightly more (21·70 per cent) for this purpose than for the needs of the church. Moreover, it should be said that there was an impressive quality of strength in their outlays for the poor, their contributions of £12,865 10s for the founding of almshouses representing almost 19 per cent of all their charitable capital and being in point of fact the largest amount vested by the clergy for any one charitable purpose, save for the support of the universities. The lower clergy disposed 3·33 per cent of their benefactions for municipal uses, of which almost the whole was represented in the £2204 8s given for the repair of roads and streets and other public works. The experiments under way in social rehabilitation enjoyed but scant favour from the class, less than 1 per cent being given for all the uses comprehended under this general head.

H. THE GREAT MERCHANTS

We shall speak first briefly of the immense contribution of the merchant fraternity of London as a whole before treating in detail the quite different structure of aspirations to be observed among the great merchants when compared with their lesser brethren. It has been suggested that the body of merchants in London was at all times relatively small in number but that it was disciplined in its responsibilities, articulate with respect to its aspirations, and aggressive in the pursuit of its goals. We shall also have later occasion to point out in detail that the merchant group of London held in view the needs of the whole nation; that they were the least parochial of all classes of men in their age, in part because they were recruited from all over the realm and in part because the very nature of their calling had taught them to think in capacious terms. The charitable contributions, the institutional direction, supplied by these men was accordingly to be decisive not only because they gave so largely, but because they gave so broadly and so well.

The whole number of merchant donors in London was 2677, some scores of wives and widows being included, or rather more than 36 per cent of all the benefactors of the city. This relatively small group of men and women gave in all the prodigious total of £1,067,883 6s, or 56·53 per cent of the immense charitable funds to be supplied by London during the course of our period. This capital is so vast as to be all but incomprehensible. Norfolk aside, the sum given by these few donors exceeded the total provided by all the other counties included in this study, numbering as they did some of the largest and richest in the realm. It seems probable, in fact, that the merchant donors of London alone provided nearly one fifth (19·40 per cent) of all charitable benefactions made during our period in the whole of England and almost 30 per cent (29·40 per cent) of the whole charitable accumulation of the nation, London being excluded. This incredibly generous vesting of charitable wealth was, however, even more powerfully effective than its sheer size would suggest. This wealth, as we have noted in county after county, was not casually disposed, but was vested in large amounts for the foundation and sustenance of institutions which could and did shape the society. This wealth was employed for the creation of new and better social institutions for a whole nation; it possessed, in other words, a qualitative virtue far exceeding its certainly impressive quantitative strength.

But upon closer examination it becomes clear indeed that the generosity and the social leadership of the merchant class were principally seated in the relatively very small group of men whom we have already defined as the great merchants. In this tiny body of men, in point of fact, the leadership of a movement of social reformation and of cultural enlightenment with truly revolutionary implications for the whole realm was vested. There were in the course of our period only 438 of these benefactors, who gave, however, the immense total of £907,623 3s for the establishment and endowment of the social institutions of London and the realm at large. This group of donors, in other words, while constituting no more than 6 per cent (5·93 per cent) of London's benefactors gave very nearly half (48·04 per cent) of all the charitable wealth disposed by the metropolis. These men were the mercantile elite of the city. Roughly 40 per cent of their number were former lord mayors of London;[7] another 43 per cent had been masters of their livery companies or had served as sheriffs; while all the remainder were traders of great wealth and of high standing in a closely knit, highly articulate, and now confident society. The tremendous strength and impact of the charitable dispositions of this small body of mercantile elite is suggested when we consider that they comprised only slightly more than 1 per cent (1·25 per cent) of all the donors in the ten counties we have intensively examined, yet their benefactions account for very nearly 30 per cent (29·25 per cent) of the whole of the charitable wealth disposed in these great and spacious regions. Even more impressively, this single, but infinitely generous, group of donors gave something like a sixth (16·50 per cent) of the total of the charitable resources accumulated in the whole of the nation during our entire period, and, if London be excluded, their great generosity accounts for a fourth of the entire *corpus* of the nation's charitable resources.

But significant as this statistical recital may be, it greatly underestimates the historical importance of the benefactions of these men, for their gifts possessed a qualitative weight far exceeding their immense bulk. These endowments averaged upwards of £2000 (£2072 3s 11d) each, and this, it will be remembered, was an amount quite sufficient to found a richly endowed school, to establish a great almshouse, to endow a lectureship which would in a generation re-mould the social and religious thinking of an entire community, or to care for the normal needs of the poor in an average parish.[8] The great endowments vested by these men were most prudently arranged, their trusts were shrewdly invested by knowledgeable and responsible feoffees, and they were strategically disposed in such wise as to accomplish the purposes on which the donors had long reflected. Further, as we shall see, they were scattered over the whole of the realm in a pattern which suggests a conscious design on the part of these men to alter and to organize the social resources of the nation according to the cultural aspirations so clearly and tenaciously held by the class. The fact is that this beneficent scattering of these immense resources was the consequence of genetic accident—of the incredible geographical fluidity of this class—but the effect could not have been more compelling or more decisive had it flowed from an articulated design. Both qualitatively and quantitatively, then, the benefactions of these men were to wield a dominant influence on the social and cultural growth of modern England. These men possessed and exercised a power far stronger and more decisive than they or their age comprehended. They built well, they built securely, and the edifice which they were rearing was the liberal society whose institutions and whose aspirations were to be accepted as axiomatic by mankind for very nearly three centuries.

If we take in view the whole of our long period, the principal concern of the merchant aristocracy of London was with the betterment of the lot of the poor. In all, nearly 40 per cent of their huge charitable contributions were disposed for one or another form of poor relief and, it is most significant to note, almost the whole (93·71 per cent) of their benefactions for these purposes were in the settled and enduring form of endowments. The large total of £137,822 19s, this amounting to 15·18 per cent of the whole contribution of the group, was designated for the outright relief of the poor in their own homes, and in this instance a large proportion of the whole was vested for the benefit of London parishes. Almost as large a sum, £134,271, an amount larger than the whole of the charitable resources of as rich a county as Somerset, was disposed for the founding and endowment of almshouses, principally, it should be observed, in counties other than Middlesex. Nearly 10 per cent of the benefactions of the great merchants is represented in the £83,333 15s left for general charitable uses, usually in large and carefully ordered trusts, which were principally administered during our period to better the lot of the nation's poor.

A very substantial fraction of the charitable gifts of these men was experimentally made in an effort directly to attack the sources of poverty by providing mechanisms for social rehabilitation, by refusing to admit that poverty and misfortune needs must blight humanity irremediably. In all, nearly 14 per cent of the immense resources left by the mercantile elite was disposed for one or another of these most interesting undertakings. By far the largest commitment is represented in the sum of £51,989 13s provided as endowment for hospitals, principally in London, and the institutional care of the sick. The really great sum of £28,818 15s was given in the form of loan capital for aspiring merchants and tradesmen, this amounting to 3·18 per cent of the whole of the charitable funds supplied by the group. Quite surprisingly, the great merchants displayed only a relatively mild interest in the founding of apprenticeship endowments, to which they gave no more than the modest total of £12,326 15s of capital. They were, in fact, much more generous in providing the substantial sum of £19,246 4s for the relief of prisoners and the general betterment of prison conditions in greater London, with an especial concern for the plight of prisoners for debt, betraying no doubt the haunting fears which in this age did not exempt even the great and successful speculators. And, finally, we may mention the relatively modest contributions of £6643 18s made to marriage subsidies and the capital of £6266 15s supplied by great merchants for the founding of workhouse schemes, particularly in the provincial towns.

The interest of the great merchants in outlays for various forms of municipal betterment was modest, their gifts for this purpose accounting for somewhat less than 6 per cent of their whole contribution, as compared, for example, to the very nearly 11 per cent disposed for such purposes by their lesser brethren. By far the largest amount given under this general head was the considerable sum of £29,314 14s left to city companies for general charitable uses, this accounting for 3·23 per cent of the tôtal. The respectable sum of £18,153 1s was expended on streets, roads, water supplies, wharves, walls, and other forms of public works in London and elsewhere, but this amounted to no more than 2 per cent of the *corpus* of the gifts of these men. Finally, the great merchants were even more circumspect in outlays for general municipal purposes, for which they provided only the modest total of £5941.

It was on the extension and betterment of the educational resources of the realm that the aspirations and attention of the great merchants were pertinaciously and most generously focused. In all, 27·55 per cent of their immense total of charitable wealth was disposed for educational uses: for the enlargement of educational opportunity and for the cure of ignorance throughout the nation. Though they were to endow new colleges in the universities, their concern with higher education was none the less relatively slight, the £23,110 1s which they disposed for the strengthening of university endowments amounting to only 2·55 per cent of all their benefactions and being, in point of fact, far less than the £53,073 2s given to universities by the professional class of the city, which concentrated almost 43 per cent of its charitable wealth on this one use. The disciplined bent of the merchants as they addressed themselves to this great task is suggested by the huge total of £48,190 13s which they alone provided for the founding of scholarship and fellowship endowments for the youth of the entire nation. This great capital sum represented 5·31 per cent of their whole charitable giving and was substantially more than half the total provided for the purpose by all of London's donors. The incalculable benefits of these endowments were spread over the entire realm, often in conjunction with school foundations. It is also important to observe that interest in this form of educational advancement was widespread among the merchant aristocracy, this large total having been given by seventy-eight of its members, only four of whom gave £2000 or more for the purpose. This great educational contribution was, then, the fruit of the concern and dedication of a whole class to one of the greatest of the social needs of the age.

But the almost obsessive, and certainly the persistent, concern of these men was with the founding of grammar schools across the whole face of the realm. As we shall later observe in detail, the great merchants of London were in a true sense the founders of the endowed schools of England. The immense total of £178,132 13s was dedicated by this small band of men to school endowments, this sum representing nearly 20 per cent (19·63 per cent) of all their vast charitable total and being far larger than the amount provided by them for any other single charitable use. The contribution made by this social group amounted to 70 per cent of the huge total given by all London donors for grammar-school foundations and accounts for the incredibly high proportion of almost 40 per cent (39·68 per cent) given for this purpose by all donors in the ten counties with which we are concerned in this study. In all, nearly a fourth of these men made substantial contributions of £100 or more for the founding of new schools or the augmentation of existing endowments, while eighty-seven of their number may be regarded as the founders of new and, with few exceptions, adequately endowed and carefully administered schools in all parts of the realm. Surely no class of men of comparable size and wealth has ever employed its funds as wisely or as fruitfully in the whole history of the western society. These men, in a very true sense, were to dispel the pall of illiteracy and ignorance in England and were to make freely and widely available new channels for ability and ambition across the whole terrain of the society.

The concern of the great merchants with the needs of religion was, taking our whole period into consideration, at once limited and perverse. The whole of their gifts for the many uses of the church amounted to no more than 13·52 per cent of all the great charitable wealth which they disposed, as compared with slightly less than 20 per cent (19·50 per cent) for the city at large. No social class in the city was more secular, the tradesmen and the professional groups excepted, and certainly none was as nearly dominant in the visibly and aggressively secular pattern of giving established by these men. Moreover, it is important to observe, by far the largest of all their religious benefactions was represented in the massive total of £37,296 which they gave for the endowment of Puritan lectureships, a form of benefaction suspect, even when it was tolerated, by the ecclesiastical authorities during most of our period. Further, the next largest amount, £30,457, was provided by these men for church building, a sizeable proportion of which was in turn devoted to the construction of chapels in various parts of the realm in conjunction with a resolute intention to spread the gospel as it was most purely construed in Geneva. A total of £19,665, or 2·17 per cent of the whole, was given for the augmentation of clerical stipends, while £11,339 3s was provided for church repairs in London and elsewhere. Significantly, the relatively tiny total of £6687 5s was given by these men for the general, and certainly the multifarious, uses of the church, while no more than £17,112 14s, or 1·89 per cent, had been vested by members of this group during the first two generations in various forms of endowments to secure prayers for the repose of souls which in their mortal frame had been aggressive, earnest, and not infrequently edged with ruthlessness.

The social dominance of the great merchants was well established even in the earliest of our intervals, and the sense of social responsibility which was the hall-mark of the class was already well developed. In the years prior to the Reformation, their benefactions reached the impressive total of £60,634, or almost 7 per cent of the whole given by them during our entire period. The principal aspirations of this group were in this period, of course, still chiefly centred on the uses of religion, though even at this early date not more than 44·82 per cent of all their charities were for religious purposes, a proportion smaller than that to be observed for any other social group in the city save, ironically enough, for the lower and the upper clergy. The concern of these men with the plight of the poor was already substantial, 18·73 per cent of all their benefactions in this era having been devoted to one or another form of poor relief, with the especially heavy concentration of £6317 7s being designated for outright household relief or for funeral doles. The surprisingly high proportion of 13·42 per cent of their charitable funds was devoted to municipal betterments in this interval, while the sophistication of their aspirations even at so early a date is suggested by the fact that rather more than a tenth (10·20 per cent) of their bene-factions were made for the several heads which we have grouped under the rubric of social rehabilitation. The concern of the class with the educational needs of the realm was only just developing, though the 12·82 per cent of their gifts devoted to this purpose suggests an already lively interest in this great area of need and opportunity. Thus various great merchants were to give in total £5800 for school founda-tions, £1193 13s to scholarship resources, £670 14s to the universities, and £104 7s to public library facilities even during these early years.

The uncertainties engendered during the tumultuous years of re-formation were most dramatically reflected in the scale of giving by the great merchants in this interval. Whereas for the city at large 8·09 per cent of all benefactions date from this short generation, only 3·26 per cent of the gifts of the merchant aristocracy were made at this time, the total of the contribution being £29,558 9s. But the period is none the less extremely interesting in that it reveals a most pronounced shift in the structure of aspirations among these men and the development of a stalwart secularism which was from this time forward to characterize their benefactions. Thus, proportionately, their gifts to the various religious uses were only one-sixth as large as they had been in the preceding period, the 7·32 per cent which they gave for such purposes actually being smaller than that given even for municipal uses (8·41 per cent). At the same time, the concern of the great merchants with the needs of the poor rose markedly to 40·12 per cent of the whole, while their gifts for experiments in social rehabilitation were likewise sub-stantially increased to command upwards of 15 per cent of the whole of their charities. There was also a very steep increase in the proportion of charitable wealth disposed for educational uses, the several purposes comprehended under this head commanding nearly 29 per cent of all the benefactions of the group. Already the absorbing concern of these men with grammar-school foundations was mature, the relatively very large total of £8182 having been given for this single purpose and representing by far the largest proportion (27·65 per cent) of their charitable wealth devoted to any one use.

The merchant aristocracy of London was relatively modest in its charitable contributions during the long and certainly prosperous Elizabethan era, the £123,932 2s given during these years accounting for no more than 13·65 per cent of the total charitable wealth to be given by the class.[9] The age was marked by an intense secularism which among these men was to leave the church with no more than token support. Only 3·40 per cent of their charitable wealth in the period was designated for religious uses, the total being less than that given by the class for the support of a number of relatively minor charitable uses such as, for example, companies (5·38 per cent) and hospitals (9·76 per cent), and not much more than was given for the relief of prisoners (2·67 per cent). The largest single religious use receiving support was the foundation of Puritan lectureships, for which £1953 was provided, while £894 2s was given for the augmentation of clerical incomes, £700 for church building, and, incredible as it may seem, only £9 14s for the general uses of the scores of parishes in the city. Not only the great bequests but the smaller gifts as well were now flowing almost entirely to the secular requirements of the age. Slightly more than a quarter (25·55 per cent) of the benefactions of the great merchants were made for the assistance of the poor, with a particularly heavy concentration (17·55 per cent) represented in the £21,745 vested as endowments for the maintenance of the poor in their own households. This was also the era in which experimentation with the various agencies of social rehabilitation reached a climax, the amazingly high proportion of 26·71 per cent of all charitable gifts having been made for this general purpose. Thus £12,693 7s was added to loan funds, £12,095 3s was provided for the augmentation of hospital endowments, and £3309 6s was given for the relief or release of prisoners, to mention only those undertakings which enjoyed the greatest favour among the mercantile elite during these years. Gifts for various municipal betterments commanded 8·45 per cent of all benefactions made during these years, a considerable number being designated for the benefit of communities in other parts of the realm. There was also a marked increase in the funds being disposed for educational purposes, the staggering proportion of 35·89 per cent of all gifts having been concentrated on this one use. The large total of £21,160 was given for grammar-school foundations alone, this representing a proportion (17·07 per cent) of charitable wealth only slightly less than that given during this generation for the outright relief of the poor (17·55 per cent). The universities were supported with gifts totalling £14,810, while scholarship and fellowship endowments were strengthened with capital in the substantial amount of £8515 13s.

It is difficult to explain how or why the incredibly high proportion of 59·04 per cent of all the contributions of the great merchants should have been concentrated in the one relatively brief interval which we have defined as the early Stuart period. Taking London as a whole, the very high proportion of half (50·76 per cent) of all benefactions were made in this generation, but no single class of men quite approached the great merchants—the unimportant contribution of the artisans aside—in the proportion of charitable wealth vested in these years. Further, this outpouring was heavily concentrated in the brief period 1611–1630, when well over two-thirds of the total for the early Stuart period was given and approximately 40 per cent of the immense total given by this small group during the whole long range of our period.[10] Most of the great charitable fortunes left during these years had of course been won by speculative skill a decade or so earlier, but it remains true that in London as elsewhere much of the period of great prosperity which we tend to call Elizabethan was in fact Jacobean, just as much of the building of the great country houses somewhat inexactly, albeit happily, honours the name of the great queen.

During this period the total given for charitable purposes by the great merchants—there were 158 of them, forty-five of whom had been lord mayors—reached the prodigious sum of £535,902 7s. The enormous contribution made by this small band of men in this interval of a long generation is suggested when we reflect that their giving exceeded the total of charitable wealth accumulated during the whole of our period in the large and rich counties of Kent and Yorkshire combined. The principal preoccupation of these donors was with the effective relief of poverty, to which they conveyed more than 43 per cent of this great wealth. The large sum of £91,096 13s was literally poured into almshouse foundations across the whole length and breadth of the realm, this one interest alone absorbing 17 per cent of the great *corpus* of charitable wealth provided. Very nearly 14 per cent was in the £72,824 17s designated for endowments planned to relieve poor families in their own homes, while another large amount (£66,896 15s) was assigned to particularly interesting and well-devised endowments for general charitable purposes. Another prodigal outpouring went into the various educational uses, which commanded about 30 per cent (29·32 per cent) of the whole. The great merchants concentrated during these years with what can almost be described as ferocity of interest on grammar-school foundations, to which they gave the enormous total of £122,719, this being 22·90 per cent of the vast whole for the interval and somewhat over two-thirds of their total benefactions for this worthy purpose during our entire period. In these same years the substantial sum of £28,885 was provided by the great merchants for scholarship foundations, while £5346 7s was given to augment the endowments of the universities.

The concentration of the merchant aristocracy on improving the lot of the poor and bettering the educational resources of the realm was so great as to command nearly three-quarters (72·57 per cent) of the great stream of wealth with which they were establishing or consolidating the charitable institutions of the entire realm. None the less, almost 10 per cent of their gifts were for various projects of social rehabilitation, for example, prison betterments, loan funds, and hospitals, each receiving more than £10,000; the relatively modest proportion of 5·09 per cent of their gifts was designated for various forms of municipal improvement. There was also, it is agreeable to note, a rather marked increase in the proportion of charitable wealth flowing to the now desperate needs of the church, though the 12·88 per cent devoted to this purpose is significant only when placed against the Elizabethan background of an almost complete, an epical indifference. Nor were the choices made by these shrewd and usually Puritan donors those which appealed to either the civil or the ecclesiastical authorities of the age. The largest sum, £23,160, was designated for the founding of lectureships, while of the almost equal sum (£23,107) provided for church building a substantial proportion was for the building of chapels in remote parts of the realm in which the first incumbent tended to be a very fervent preacher of God's word. At the same time, useful, if relatively modest, support was given for the augmentation of clerical stipends (£12,892 4s), the repair of decaying church fabric in London and elsewhere (£5090 10s), and for the general uses of the church and its services (£4750).[11]

The benefactions of the great merchants declined less markedly than one would suppose during the revolutionary period considering the economic and political dislocations to which London was subjected. The £157,568 5s contributed in these two decades represented 17·36 per cent of the whole of the charitable wealth vested by the great merchants and, it may be noted, was a substantially larger total than had been provided during the long Elizabethan age. There were in all seventy-seven donors in these years, eleven being former lord mayors; so the average benefaction was very close indeed to that which we have noted for the group through the whole course of our study.

The great merchants of the revolutionary period were sensitively concerned with the needs of the poor, to whose relief about 44 per cent of all their gifts were dedicated. Thus the substantial total of £30,939 12s was provided for outright or household relief, this representing 19·64 per cent of the whole of the gifts of the merchant elite during these years, while nearly as much (£28,358) was vested in still more almshouse foundations, and rather more than £10,000 for general charitable uses in all parts of the nation. Clearly connected with their great contributions for poor relief were of course the outlays of risk capital made for furthering various schemes of social rehabilitation, to which the great merchants of the Cromwellian era devoted the very high proportion of 19·50 per cent of all their philanthropic funds. The large total of £10,406 13s (6·60 per cent) was provided for the needs of hospitals, and almost as much (£9620) was designated for apprenticeship foundations in all parts of England. The needs of prisons and of prisoners commanded a total of £3968; loan funds were increased with capital amounting to £3490; and workhouses, especially favoured during this period, were established or augmented with gifts reaching the considerable total of £3150.

There are indications in many wills proved during these years that a number of great London merchants, and they were by far the most sophisticated donors in the entire society, believed that the task of enlarging the range of educational opportunity had been well advanced by preceding generations; that, as it were, the law of diminishing returns was beginning to apply to further large foundations even of grammar schools. This persuasion may well explain the rather sharp decline in the proportion of charitable funds devoted to education by this class through these years, the 20·35 per cent vested for such uses being substantially lower than in any interval since the Reformation.[12] None the less, the considerable total of £20,271 13s was given for school endowments in many parts of England, and £9390 was provided for still more fellowship and scholarship endowments. As we might expect during this interval, the universities were ill favoured, receiving no more than £2100 in new gifts, while £300 was given for the support of public libraries.

The proportion given by the great merchants for religious uses during the revolutionary years remained roughly steady at 12·70 per cent of the whole, though it should be remarked that of these funds a large amount, £12,183, was designated for Puritan lectureships of a variety of kinds. The strengthening of clerical stipends absorbed 2·77 per cent of all merchant giving through these years, and church repairs were supported with 1·66 per cent of the whole, this being, incidentally, the highest proportion given by the great merchants for this purpose since the years prior to the Reformation. The remaining church needs received but scant attention, the £400 given for general church uses, for example, representing no more than 0·25 per cent of the whole of the funds provided by this group during this, the last of our intervals.

1. THE LESSER MERCHANTS

These great merchants possessed a wealth as well as a capacity for assuming great burdens of social and civic responsibility which, as we have seen, simply placed them upon a different plane when one compares them with their lesser brethren of the great livery companies. Yet it must be remarked that the ordinary London merchant seems unimportant or ungenerous only when he is compared with the great and hugely successful men of his company, men with whom he had served his apprenticeship, carried on many of his dealings, and whom he knew intimately through a whole lifetime. We must remark, too, that even the lesser merchants of London as an economic group possessed wealth roughly comparable with that of the lower gentry of the counties, and wealth which would have made the London lesser merchant a very great burgher indeed in Bristol, York, or Coventry. Moreover, the tradition of charitable responsibility was fully understood and respected by these lesser men of the livery companies, almost all of whom established by will or gift a charitable fund which would have loomed as a kind of charitable monadnock in a rural parish but which seemed most modest when compared with the vast generosity of the mercantile elite. There are, however, striking and not easily explicable differences in the structure of interests and aspirations of these lesser men as we compare them with the giants of their companies. In part, certainly, they were simply unable to provide the endowments required for the founding of great charitable institutions with their own resources and hence were more likely to spread their charities over a broad spectrum of worthy interests. It is also true that the lesser merchants were not so frequently disposed to vest substantial endowments in distant counties, even when, as was usually the case, they were not London born; one would suppose principally because they were not so likely to invest in great landholdings, because they often lacked the intimate knowledge of distant needs, and also, and importantly, because they were evidently simply better and more devoted Londoners. Then, too, it seems clear that they lay under real and doubtless complex inhibitions as they viewed the almost epical generosity of their richer brothers who were disposed to change the whole structure of a community by the great and most effective institutions which their wealth called into being. The lesser merchants were less bold, less prescient, and far more modest in their aspirations as they arranged their affairs in their last days; but, then, so had they been during their whole lifetime.

Rather more than four-fifths (83·63 per cent) of all the merchant donors of our period may with some certainty be regarded as lesser merchants, as the moderately successful members of the great livery companies. There were 2239 charitable donors drawn from this group, or 30·29 per cent of all the benefactors of the city. The charitable wealth contributed by these men reached the substantial total of £160,260 3s, or not much less than the whole of the charities of the rich county of Norfolk. The great merchants aside, this was the largest contribution made by any single class in the city, though it amounted to no more than the modest proportion of 8·49 per cent of the charitable funds of London and yields an average of only £71 11s 7d for each benefactor, an average amount, it should be remarked, considerably less than that left by the tradesmen.

The structure of aspirations displayed by this large body of men in their charitable giving differs most interestingly from that of the great merchant donors.* Taking our whole period into account, the lesser merchants exhibited an absorbing concern with the needs of the poor, to whose relief they contributed the heavy proportion of 42·57 per cent of all their benefactions, as compared with slightly more than 39 per cent by their richer colleagues. Moreover, the lesser merchants were especially interested in building up resources within their own or other London parishes for the care of the poor in their own households, to which they gave in all the most substantial total of £58,453 10s, or 36·47 per cent of the whole of their charitable funds, this being, it may be observed, almost exactly four times as much as was disposed by them for the next largest charitable use. The £7891 4s provided by this group for alms-houses amounted to not quite 5 per cent of the whole of their benefactions, as contrasted with the nearly 15 per cent given by the great merchants for these foundations. And, finally, the lesser merchants gave the modest total of £1885 10s (or 1·18 per cent) for general charitable needs, most of this sum being in the form of gifts for immediate use.

In one very important respect these smaller merchants were notably more bold and aggressive than were the elite of their companies, in large part because their interests were so heavily concentrated on London and its institutions. They gave almost 22 per cent of all their considerable benefactions for the several experiments in social rehabilitation, a proportion far greater than was risked in these most interesting and forward-looking ventures by any other class in London, and far exceeding the 13·81 per cent provided by the great merchants for this

* We shall not treat the structure of aspirations of this group in as great detail as we have those of the mercantile elite. The changing pattern of their giving will, however, be suggested by the following table which lists the proportion of total charitable wealth designated for the great charitable heads in each of the intervals into which we have divided our period.

	Poor	Social Rehabilitation	Municipal Betterments	Education	Religion
	Per cent	Per cent	Per cent	Per cent	Per cent
1480–1540	18·05	4·18	14·26	2·12	61·23
1541–1560	40·42	28·58	17·97	4·38	8·65
1561–1600	40·00	34·41	10·61	11·74	3·24
1601–1640	52·41	22·22	9·27	6·27	9·81
1641–1660	52·03	19·17	5·57	13·18	10·04
1480–1660	42·57	21·96	10·57	7·70	17·20

purpose. Thus they designated the substantial total of £13,658 17s (8·52 per cent) for the support of hospitals and the care of the sick, as well as adding £10,964 (6·84 per cent) to the huge capital available as loan funds which the various burgher groups were so rapidly accumulating during our period. They were generous too in the £5685 14s which they gave for the relief of prisoners, and especially debtors, while they provided a total of £2158 10s (1·35 per cent) for the endowment or augmentation of a number of apprenticeship schemes. Lesser, but still useful, amounts were vested for marriage subsidies and for the support of workhouses by these men who evidently possessed a more lively sense of the great and curing virtues of such undertakings than did the very rich merchants.

The lesser merchants also exhibited far more interest in municipal betterments, particularly in London, than did their great brethren. They gave in all 10·57 per cent of their charitable funds for such purposes, in contrast to the 5·88 per cent provided by the great merchants. They were likewise, relatively speaking, better and more loyal 'company men' than were their richer colleagues, having left £11,988 17s, or 7·48 per cent of the whole, to their companies for general charitable uses. Clearly the company loomed very large indeed in the lives of these men, whereas the great entrepreneurs and speculators ranged far outside their company in their ambitious and often financially hazardous pursuits. The considerable total of £2873 was provided for a variety of public works by the lesser merchants, who also gave £2030 19s to the municipal government of London for an extensive range of civic uses.

But it is in the support of education that these lesser men exhibit the most pronounced differences from the aspirations and concerns of their very rich brethren. It is true that there were numerous founders of grammar schools among them, but the class as a whole displayed only the most modest interest in lending help in the enlargement of educational opportunity, an interest which, as we have seen, the great merchants pursued with an almost obsessive zeal. One is struck particularly by the fact that only 128 of the lesser merchants (5·70 per cent) made any contribution to an educational use over the whole course of our period. It seems probable that the great merchants, by their profuse generosity, set a pattern of merchant giving for this purpose which the lesser merchants, as much as they would have liked to do so, simply could not follow. This is suggested, indeed, by the fact that when a lesser merchant gave at all for an educational purpose, he gave on a scale far above the normal charitable benefaction of his social group, the average of these particular gifts having reached the quite high total of £96 5s 11d for the class. The great merchants, then, had apparently established in London the not particularly wholesome tradition that when one gave at all to education he needs must establish a college at Oxford, a grammar school in

the provinces, or a richly and completely endowed scholarship foundation. In all, the lesser merchants gave only 7·70 per cent of their
charitable benefactions for educational uses, as contrasted with 27·55
per cent given by the great merchants and 11·82 per cent by the less
inhibited tradesmen of the city. Their greatest support in this particular was lent to scholarship needs, to which they gave in all £6372 19s
(3·98 per cent), while the foundation or augmentation of grammar
schools commanded £5124 12s (3·21 per cent) of their charities. As
we should suppose, their interest in the needs of the universities was
most modest, only £678 7s (0·42 per cent) having been given by the
group for the purpose. Further, members of this interesting and important, though somewhat restrained, social group gave £150 (0·09 per
cent) for the needs of public libraries in London, where in all respects
their interests were so heavily concentrated.

Finally, it may be observed that the lesser merchants devoted a
somewhat larger proportion (17·20 per cent) of their charitable wealth
to the advancement of the cause of faith than did the mercantile elite
(13·52 per cent). The group lent their heaviest support to the endowment of prayers, the £12,327 15s given for this use being slightly more,
for example, than the whole sum employed by these men for the maintenance of education. They gave as well almost 3 per cent of their
charities for the repair of church fabric; not quite so much (2·55 per
cent) for the betterment of the lot of the parochial and regular clergy.
The lesser merchants gave in total £2439 9s for the general uses of their
churches and somewhat more, £2599 10s, for the founding of Puritan
lectureships, while their contributions to church building were limited
to £1375 7s, this being no more than 0·86 per cent of all their charitable
benefactions.

We should, in concluding our discussion of the structure of aspirations of this interesting class, point out that these lesser merchants grew
steadily more secular as our period wore on. In the years prior to the
Reformation they were as a class deeply devoted to the needs of the
church, the various religious uses absorbing somewhat more than 61
per cent (61·23 per cent) of all their considerable philanthropies. But
this devotion simply withered during the Reformation decades, when
no more than 8·65 per cent of their charitable wealth was given for
religious needs, and all but disappeared during the amazing Elizabethan
age, when only slightly more than 3 per cent of their gifts were made for
such uses. The early Stuart years were for the lesser, as for the greater,
merchants the period of high prosperity and generosity, nearly 38 per
cent of the charities of the group having been vested during this generation. But the increase of concern with the needs of the church was much
less pronounced than was the case with the great merchants, only about
a tithe (9·81 per cent) of all their benefactions having been devoted to

such uses in this era and almost exactly as much (10·04 per cent) in the troubled course of the revolutionary years.

J. THE TRADESMEN

Somewhat inexplicably, the pattern of aspirations displayed by London tradesmen was much closer to that of the great merchants than to that of the more modest members of the great livery companies. These shopkeepers and men of a middling sort[13] were of course far more numerous than the merchant body of the city, though most evidently they were not animated by such tight and almost universal traditions of civic and social responsibility. We have counted in all 1087 charitable donors among these men, the group constituting 14·71 per cent of all the donors of the city. These shopkeepers gave in total the considerable sum of £98,212 6s, or a relatively high average of £90 7s, to the charitable wealth of London, their contribution accounting for 5·20 per cent of the whole of the city's charities. By no means all these men were of modest wealth, not a few disposing resources which rivalled even those of the merchant aristocracy. Thus there were fifty-four of these donors who left very substantial charitable endowments of £500 or more, while there were sixteen in all who established philanthropies with a capital worth of £1000 or more. At the same time, many of them disposed very modest estates indeed, there having been 116 whose charitable bequests ranged under £20 in total value. The tradesmen were, then, an extraordinarily diverse, an energetic, and withal a prosperous community—the true urban middle class—who were to make valued contributions to the building of the expanding commercial society of which they were an important part.

The tradesmen were deeply concerned with the plight of London's poor throughout our period. In all, they were to designate somewhat more than 48 per cent of their considerable benefactions for the several forms of poor relief, as compared with rather less than 40 per cent for the whole body of merchants. It is likewise noteworthy that the tradesmen were pertinacious in their devotion to this compelling charitable need, having even in the years prior to the Reformation given about a third of all their philanthropies for this purpose.[14] The interest of the class was especially concentrated on outright gifts to the poor and on endowments for household relief, towards which the substantial total of £34,189 3s was provided, this amounting to more than a third (34·81 per cent) of all the benefactions of the group. The foundation of almshouses was aided by gifts totalling £10,695 1s, this being 10·89 per cent of their whole giving, while £2673 was provided for endowments for general charitable purposes.

The tradesmen were bold and aggressive in their support of experiments in social rehabilitation, to which they devoted about a sixth (16·40 per cent) of all their gifts, as compared with 15·03 per cent for the merchant fraternity. This support was well spread over the whole spectrum of these experimental undertakings, with, however, particularly notable interest in the care of the sick, to which they gave in all £6674 9s, and the augmentation of loan funds, for which they provided a total of £4818 6s. They were as a class somewhat more generously disposed towards the several uses which we have grouped under the head of municipal betterments than any other social class in the city, nearly 11 per cent of all their gifts having been disposed for this purpose.

The interest of the tradesmen in the extension and strengthening of educational opportunity was relatively most modest. In all they gave 11·82 per cent of their funds for educational uses, or substantially less than they provided for the purposes of social rehabilitation and only slightly more than they devoted to various schemes of municipal improvement. Their greatest educational concern was with the augmentation of scholarship endowments, to which they contributed a total of £6348 8s, or 6·46 per cent of the whole, while they were to give £4722 10s (4·81 per cent) for school foundations in London and elsewhere in the realm. The support lent by the group to the universities was inconsequential, being exceeded in fact by the £290 which they disposed for the support of public-library foundations.

The tradesmen were likewise the most intensely secular social class in the city, with the one exception of the various professional groups. During the whole course of our period, they disposed no more than 12·46 per cent of all their charitable funds for religious uses. The largest amount given was £4034 5s for prayers, all of course prior to 1560. The tradesmen also gave £3822, or 3·89 per cent of all their benefactions, for the founding of lectureships and about half as much (£1991 11s) as endowment for the augmentation of clerical stipends in parishes in various parts of the realm. Church repairs commanded £1616 6s of their benefactions, while members of the class gave in all £765 5s, or 0·78 per cent of the whole, for the general needs of the church and its services.

We know that an almost savage anti-clericalism was centred in this class for decades prior to the Reformation. The secularism of the group appears to be well documented by the structure of their giving, for even in the years before the Reformation the total of their religious benefactions amounted to only 45·82 per cent of all their charities, a remarkably low proportion for this early interval. But in the years of the Reformation this proportion fell abruptly to 9·76 per cent of the whole and was then halved again during the Elizabethan era, when only 4·82 per cent of all benefactions of the group were designated for religious needs, only about half as much, for example, as these men left to the lesser companies of which they were members. The proportion of benefactions made by the shopkeepers for religious purposes rose to a modest 11·11 per cent of the whole in the early Stuart interval, but fell back to just over 5 per cent of all their charities in the decades of political revolution with which our period closes.

K. THE 'ADDITIONAL BURGHERS'

We have also recorded benefactions from 788 donors, comprising the considerable proportion of 10·66 per cent of the whole number for the city, whose social status can be no more accurately assessed than by the somewhat ambiguous term, 'additional burghers'. These were men, or very frequently their widows, who had held minor municipal offices or who were enrolled as freemen of the city, but whose precise occupation or company affiliation, if any, has not been ascertained. This group gave in all the quite substantial sum of £49,809 15s to the charitable wealth of London, or 2·64 per cent of the whole of the great amount vested by the benefactors of the metropolis. These donors were evidently substantial citizens, their average benefaction having been £63 4s 3d. Both the size and structure of their charities would suggest that most of them were tradesmen with, almost certainly, a fair number of unidentified lesser merchants or their widows in the group.[15]

At the same time, it should be said that the structure of the benefactions of the burghers differed markedly in one important particular from that of the tradesman class. Very nearly 60 per cent (59·66 per cent) of all burgher gifts were disposed for one or another form of poor relief, if the whole of our period may be taken in view. It will be observed that this far exceeded even the 48·42 per cent so provided by the tradesmen of the city and suggests an intensity of concern with the needs of the poor rivalled only by that displayed by the artisans. The burghers were especially inclined to leave their funds for endowments to secure household care of poor families in the various parishes of the city, almost 48 per cent (47·65 per cent) of all their gifts having been concentrated on this one use.

L. THE ARTISANS

We have seen that the merchant class in London was numerically a very small group indeed. The tradesmen class, including those whom we have been obliged to list as burghers, was, of course, much larger, but it too represented a relatively thin stratum of the population. By the most generous reckoning, and with the addition of all apprentices and other dependents, it seems doubtful that the merchant aristocracy and the much more broadly based tradesmen and shopkeeper class could have numbered more than 10 per cent of the total population of London in the earlier decades of our period and probably considerably less in the last two generations when the population of the great city was rising so very rapidly.[16] This conclusion and, more importantly, the steady and often frightened contemporary comments suggest that a very large proportion of London's population in our period was composed of artisans, servants, industrial workers, the casually employed, and a drifting mass of unemployed. There was evidently a considerable and on the whole an increasing labour surplus in the city throughout our period, fed constantly from the provinces and restrained only by the hideous epidemics which so continually ravaged the poor of this now teeming metropolis.

Though we have employed particularly careful and thorough methods in recording the charitable benefactions of the London poor, whom we have grouped under the heading of 'artisans and the urban poor', it remains all too evident that the working mass of the city was at once too rootless and too poor to leave wills, much less to provide even nominal charitable bequests. By contrast, in all the rural counties we have examined, a considerable proportion of all testators were husbandmen, were of the rural poor. These too were poor men, but they possessed sufficient property and a sufficient status to leave wills, and a quite surprising number of them also left at least modest contributions to the institutional needs of their communities. But not so in London, where the poor lived and died as a socially insignificant class of men who then sank into oblivion with only rare historical traces.

Thus we have been able to identify only 518 donors who were drawn from this large and steadily increasing population stratum. Moreover, of this number a considerable proportion (60·10 per cent) were clearly of the working-class elite, being artisans, craftsmen in the skilled trades, or seamen. In all, therefore, the urban poor comprise only 7·01 per cent of all London's charitable donors, while their total of charitable benefactions was no more than £3030 13s, or 0·16 per cent of the immense charitable wealth provided by the various classes of men.

Small as was the contribution of the artisans to the social and institutional needs of the city, the structure of their charities is markedly and significantly different from that of any other social group. They were themselves poor men, most of whom had doubtless lived and worked with the terror of unemployment or illness ever around them and their families. This brutal reality must account for the fact that more than two-thirds (66·84 per cent) of all their contributions were for poor relief and that almost all of this amount was given in the form of outright doles for the poor of their own parishes. Not quite 8 per cent (7·87 per cent) of their gifts were for purposes of social rehabilitation, with a particular concern for the relief of prisoners and the care of the sick, and a slightly smaller proportion (7·56 per cent) of their meagre charitable dispositions were made for various municipal uses. In the whole course of our period the artisans gave but £8 13s for all educational uses, this being only 0·29 per cent of their slight charitable total, suggesting a complete indifference to the educational opportunities which the burgher aristocracy was so feverishly intent on creating for the sons of the poor in London and elsewhere. Moreover, the class displayed but slight interest in the religious needs of the age, only 17·49 per cent of all the charities of these men having been disposed for the benefit of the many uses of the church. Their principal concern, in this respect, was with the general needs of their parish churches, to which they contributed in all £234 12s (7·74 per cent), while £141 4s (4·66 per cent) was given for church repairs and about as much (4·04 per cent) for the augmentation of clerical stipends. These were all too evidently rootless, frightened, and socially submerged men, about whom one wishes more could be learned.

M. THE PROFESSIONS

We have noted charitable benefactions, as well, from 490 members of the rapidly increasing and the relatively very prosperous professional classes which, drawn from all over the country, found occupations and fortunes in the great city. These men comprised as a social group 6·63 per cent of all the donors of London, while their impressive contribution of £124,524 7s amounted to 6·59 per cent of the charitable wealth of the city. The professional groups were to give approximately as much as the nobility, the upper gentry, and the lower gentry combined and substantially more than did the much larger tradesman class of the city.

Though the professional class was comprised of numerous elements, the structure of its interests was amazingly uniform and displayed from interval to interval a comparable metamorphosis.* The concern of the

* The professional groupings and the totals of their charitable contributions follow:

Class	Number of donors	Total of charitable benefactions		
		£	s	d
Lawyers	223	53,904	15	0
Notaries	8	202	13	0
Parish clerks	3	167	0	0
Scriveners	32	5,936	15	0
Doctors	89	16,689	12	0
Apothecaries	18	1,023	13	0
Teachers and professors	17	9,786	15	0
Artists, musicians, scholars	7	9,160	10	0
Administrators	9	632	11	0
Public officials	84	27,020	3	0
	490	124,524	7	0

class with the needs of the poor was relatively limited throughout our entire period, only 31·57 per cent of all the benefactions of these men having been disposed for the various forms of poor relief. Their gifts for this purpose were quite heavily concentrated on almshouse endowments, for which £19,586 8s, or 15·73 per cent of the whole, was provided, while a slightly lesser sum of £18,648 17s (14·98 per cent) was given, almost wholly in the form of endowments, for parochial relief in one or another form. These always prudent men displayed only slight interest in experiments in social rehabilitation, this whole spectrum of need commanding no more than 3·83 per cent of all their benefactions and with totals of more than £1000 having been designated only for the relief of prisoners and to aid the work of the hospitals of the city. Nor was there much more enthusiasm for municipal betterments, which together absorbed only 4·41 per cent of the whole of the generous benefactions of the class.

The dominant interest of the professional classes was in the strengthening of educational opportunities, particularly in the universities, which, of course, most of them had attended. In all, they vested more than half (52·11 per cent) of their charities in educational endowments, a proportion exceeded only by the gifts of the clergy of the city. The great generosity of the class was heavily concentrated in the enormous total of £53,073 2s (42·62 per cent) which they gave to the universities, the other and possibly more pressing educational needs of the age having been supported by the relatively modest totals of £6997 10s (5.62 per cent) provided for grammar-school foundations, £3601 6s (2.89 per cent) for scholarship and fellowship endowments, and £1218 4s (0·98 per cent) for the strengthening of public libraries in London and elsewhere.

The most distinctive and pronounced characteristic of the aspirations of the professional classes was their invincible secularity. Through the whole of our long period, their gifts for the several uses of the church amounted to only slightly more than 8 per cent of all their benefactions. The scale of their intense secularism may be suggested when we note that these men gave somewhat less than half as much for the needs of the church as they gave in almshouse endowments alone. Even during the decades prior to the Reformation their benefactions for religious purposes amounted to only 52·75 per cent of all their charities. In the two decades of the Reformation the proportion of benefactions devoted to religious uses fell abruptly to 6·74 per cent of the whole. The professional classes gave in total the very considerable sum of £30,272 10s to the various charitable causes during the Elizabethan era, but of this amount only 2·76 per cent was designated for the uses of the church. The largest single sum devoted to religious purposes during this starkly secular period was £601 15s, this representing 1·99 per cent of the total charities of the class, given for church building. All the remaining church needs were treated with what can only be described as contemptuous neglect during the whole of this age. Nor was there any marked revival of religious concern during the early Stuart period, when only 5·95 per cent of the huge total of £62,618 8s given by members of the class for charities was devoted to the pressing needs of organized religion. By far the largest amount vested in this period for a religious purpose was the £1578, or 2·52 per cent, provided as endowments to enhance clerical stipends. The critical requirements of church building commanded funds totalling £901 3s (1·44 per cent) and church repairs £609 (0·97 per cent), while all other religious uses received no more than nominal support from this prosperous and, with respect to secular needs, extraordinarily generous class of enlightened men.

The charitable giving of the professional classes remained relatively substantial during the revolutionary era, their benefactions amounting to £13,416 8s in these distracted years. At the same time, however, the gifts made by the class for religious purposes were so small in number and amount as to indicate a secularism on the part of these powerful and aggressive men which was now complete. In all, their religious benefactions accounted for no more than 0·36 per cent of their charities. More specifically, they gave totals of £28 12s for church repairs, £20 for general church uses, and £1 for church building in a generation when they were pouring thousands of pounds into the care of men's bodies and the training of their minds. Thus far had the course of a great social and cultural revolution moved in the generations comprehended by this study.

N. THE UNIDENTIFIED

It remains to speak briefly of the contributions made by 867 donors of unknown social status. These men and women, and a considerable proportion of them were women, comprised 11·73 per cent of all the donors of the county and were to give to the social needs of London the substantial total of £166,409 1s, or 8·81 per cent of all the charitable wealth we have recorded. The size, the nature, and the quality of these gifts would suggest that most of these contributors were of middling urban status, including, one would deduce, a large proportion of tradesmen, a fair number of lesser merchants, and at least a few widows of great merchants. The structure of giving by these donors of uncertain social class is remarkably similar to that for the 'generality of London giving', with, for example, 33·70 per cent of their benefactions having been dedicated to the needs of the poor, as compared with 35·18 per cent for the city as a whole, and 26·14 per cent for educational uses, as compared with 27·04 per cent for the city at large. In one respect,

however, there was an important difference; a somewhat larger proportion of the gifts of these unknown men and women were disposed for
religious uses than we have observed for London at large. This fact is
accounted for by the circumstance that a considerable proportion of all
their gifts were for church building, outright benefactions for this
purpose having been gleaned from various lists where it has not been
possible certainly to identify the social class of the donor. But, broadly
speaking, this large and relatively generous group of men and women
were members of the urban middle class of London which had lent such
a full measure of devotion to the needs of the city whose economy it had
enhanced and whose institutions it had formed.

The Achievements of the Age

A. THE RELIEF OF THE POOR

1. *Household relief*

London grew steadily in population during the first half of our period;
with almost frightening speed during the second half. The great
prosperity, the excitement, the opportunities, and perhaps even the
anonymity which the metropolis provided drew men of all classes and
abilities from every part of the realm; a few of whom were destined to
become great merchants and even lord mayors; some of whom were to
become solid members of the city's middle class; more of whom were
to become at least self-supporting workmen in the myriad of trades and
occupations spawned by the surging industrial and commercial growth
of the city; and a considerable number who were to become social and
economic derelicts whom the city found itself obliged to support,
quite as much from a concern for public order as from the prompting
of an increasingly sensitive social conscience. We shall observe that the
men of London were aggressive and intelligent in assuming the responsibilities imposed by a new age and a more complex economy, founding
and endowing great social institutions for the care and rehabilitation of
the poor which were at once the model for and the envy of the realm at
large.[1] Thus the very forwardness of London, and the immense
generosity of its citizenry, created a social environment and institutions
for the relief of poverty which undoubtedly served to draw to the city
not only the unemployed but the unemployable.[2]

During the whole course of our period London suffered from no
protracted interval of economic depression or crisis such as afflicted all
the provincial cities from time to time, even including Bristol. Its
economy was at once intricately diversified and steadily expanding with
an almost irresistible momentum. Yet the problem of poverty was
chronic in London during our whole age, in the main because the city
was at all times growing rather more rapidly than its economy. There
was, then, a constant labour surplus on which expansion fed but which
in turn created social problems of very serious proportions, with which
the merchant aristocracy, controlling as it did every aspect of the

government and policy of the community, was to deal with vigour, intelligence, and a disciplined humanity.

In our period the citizens of London poured the generous total of £664,608 14s into the various forms of poor relief. The scale of their charity is suggested when we reflect that this sum exceeded the whole of the charitable wealth vested for all purposes during our period in Buckinghamshire, Bristol, Hampshire, Kent, and Lancashire. This great sum represented 35·18 per cent of the amount given by London donors for all charitable uses. The enormous aggregate of £426,972 3s was vested to secure the direct relief of the poor in their own households, specifically for the care of the aged, or for elaborate schemes of general charity which normally had the care of the poor as their central objective.[3] In all, then, 22·60 per cent of the whole of London's charity was dedicated to the outright relief of the poor. It is particularly important to observe that of the vast fortune given for outright poor relief, £371,639 13s was left in the form of endowments designed to afford in perpetuity succour for the poor and helpless, to create institutions which might come to grips with the now admitted fact that occasional unemployment and social wastage were inevitable concomitants of the new economic order. There was in addition the enormous outlay of £237,636 11s made by the most enlightened of London's donors for the foundation and endowment of almshouses in the city and elsewhere. This great sum represented 12·58 per cent of the whole of the city's charitable wealth, and nearly the whole (99·42 per cent) of these gifts were in capital form, since these donors were intent on the creation of institutions in which sanctuary might be permanently gained for those who for a variety of reasons could not compete successfully in the world in which they found themselves.

The social sensitivity of the burgher aristocracy of London was manifest even in the years before the Reformation when a total of £37,378 7s, this being 14·95 per cent of all benefactions made prior to 1540, was given for one or another form of poor relief. Approximately half the whole sum is represented in the £18,702 given for outright relief and for general charitable uses. In the years before 1510 these considerable outlays tended to take the form of funeral doles, though London donors were the first in the realm to sense that this typically medieval form of almsgiving had none save evil consequences, however much it might salve the conscience of the donor. But from 1510 onwards most of the substantial gifts and bequests for the care of the poor began to be established as capital sums under some form of trusteeship which would ensure the effectiveness as well as the permanent administration of income for the worthy purposes envisaged by the donors. During this same early interval an almost equally great sum, £18,576 7s, was provided by particularly prescient donors for the founding of new almshouses or to secure the strengthening and reorganization of older and often derelict foundations which were an inheritance from the medieval past.

A marked and an immediate quickening of concern for the needs of the poor occurred in London, as in the whole of England, with the advent of the Reformation. The substantial total of £31,481 13s given during the two decades of religious revolution represented 20·60 per cent of all charitable benefactions for this interval and was, it will be noted, but little short of the whole amount provided for the succour of the poor during the preceding sixty years. Of this impressive sum, £21,217 17s was vested for direct relief or for general charitable uses, while £10,263 16s was given for still further foundation of almshouses.

Almost exactly a third (33·38 per cent) of all Elizabethan benefactions were dedicated to one or another form of poor relief. The total of £86,891 3s so provided represents a considerable *per annum* increase over the preceding period, and it likewise possessed greater qualitative strength, since it was on balance more carefully and skilfully devised by men now practised in the art of constituting charitable trusts. Of this total, the substantial sum of £23,754 1s was given for almshouse endowments, adding most significantly to this important social resource both in London and in the provinces. But by far the larger amount, £63,137 2s, was designated by donors of this generation for household relief or for general charitable purposes in named parishes. This represented a heavy commitment of wealth for a specific and an important social need and was to bear effectively, indeed, quite dramatically, on the whole grim problem of poverty before the Elizabethan age was finished. The dedication of the London burghers to the attack on poverty was now persistent, the total given for outright relief and general charity never falling below £11,778 11s in any decade of the reign and rising during the decade of the Armada to the impressive sum of £20,004 3s.

The frontal attack on poverty was, however, made by Londoners in the course of the early Stuart period when the vast total of £388,272 9s was disposed for the several forms of poor relief, this being 40·49 per cent of all the great wealth contributed during these almost prodigally generous years. This represents, of course, an outlay of nearly £10,000 a year, in average terms, during four decades, the amount disposed for the relief of poverty alone far exceeding the whole of the charitable wealth accumulated during our entire period in any other county in the realm. By far the largest total, £244,798 12s, was given for household relief or for general charitable uses in London and elsewhere, this having been the era when massive endowments for the care of the poor were rapidly accumulated in parish after parish across the city. The amounts designated for these uses never fell during this interval below the £35,133 4s given in the first decade of this generation and rose to the enormous total of £103,445 18s in the years 1621–1630. As impressively, London donors also vested £143,473 17s in almshouse endowments, a truly immense sum when one reflects that £1000 was sufficient to build and endow a large and well-supplied institution. The incredibly generous men of the early Stuart interval supplied far more than half the total to be given for almshouse endowments in London during our whole period. Indeed, the capital given for this purpose in the one decade 1611–1620 considerably exceeded the whole amount provided for this use in all the decades from 1480 to 1610.

There was, of course, a slackening in the immense flow of funds to the institutions being framed for the succour and control of poverty during the two unsettled decades with which our period closes. But the great achievements of this short generation pale only by comparison with the interval just preceding it. The great sum of £120,585 2s disposed by London's donors for one or another form of poor relief during the revolutionary era represented giving for this purpose at an annual rate about three times that of the Elizabethan age. Further, there was a concentration of benefactions on poor relief quite unmatched in any earlier interval, 45·18 per cent of all charitable gifts having been designated for this use. Of the great sum provided by men and women during these troubled years, £79,016 12s was dedicated to outright relief or general charitable purposes, while another notable addition to the almshouse resources of the city and nation is represented in the £41,568 10s given for this end.

We should now note, at least briefly, the principal of the many gifts and bequests made during our period for the succour of the poor, including those which were vested so broadly as to be more accurately classified as gifts for general charitable uses.[4] The long interval prior to the advent of the Reformation may best be divided into two periods, since in the years before 1510 a heavy proportion (78·10 per cent) of the £7487 8s given for the care of the poor was in the form of outright alms or funeral doles, whereas in the remaining three decades of this early period a most significant change in sentiment and in the theory of charity is indicated by the fact that considerably less than half (47·64 per cent) of such benefactions were so disbursed by now more sophisticated donors. Men were, then, coming at a very early date in London to understand that ostentatious funeral outlays or large sums broadcast over a parish bred rather than relieved poverty. They began quite reluctantly but inevitably to realize that poverty was endemic and that it could be relieved only by disciplined wealth, by institutions designed to deal with it systematically and intelligently. Medieval alms had on the whole been at once eccentric and very possibly injurious to the society. They could in any case make no significant contribution to the problem of poverty as the sixteenth century came quickly to understand it. This profoundly important metamorphosis in the attitude of the society towards its responsibility for the blighting curse of poverty was to be first effected in London. But during the first generation of our period, as we shall see, men held as stubbornly as they could to the old ways.

Even the great merchants of London were addicted to lavish funeral alms and distributions during these earlier years. Thus Sir John Yong, a former lord mayor and a grocer, ordered the distribution of £60 to one hundred poor householders on his death in 1481,[5] while Sir Thomas Hill, also a grocer, who was serving as lord mayor at the time of his death in 1485, by his will distributed £10 in doles to the poor at his burial, £40 in clothing for the poor, £26 in outright alms for London's poor and £5 p.a. for four years in fuel, while ordering, as well, the outright distribution of £33 7s to the poor of Spaldwick in Huntingdonshire.[6] An earlier lord mayor, Robert Drope, who died in 1487, left in all £126 for the benefit of the poor, including outlays to be made for shirts and smocks for three hundred needy persons, gowns for one hundred, £10 to be distributed at once to the poor of Cornhill Ward, and £16 to be given in alms at his month's mind.[7] Some years later, the rich mercer, Hugh Clopton, among other great charitable bequests totalling £1314 8s, left outright £100 to be distributed to the poor of London and an equal sum to be given in doles at Stratford-upon-Avon, his birthplace and principal place of residence in his later years.[8] Viscountess Lisle, the widow of Robert Drope, on her death in 1500 left benefactions to the poor amounting in all to £175 7s and including £1 to the needy in each of the twenty-four wards of the city, to be disbursed 'by the most worshipful woman dwelling in each of them', £20 to be distributed in doles of 1d each, £10 for the poor householders of Cornhill, £4 to householders in the parish of St Thomas Acon, £4 for the poor of her birthplace, Nutley in Hampshire, and £100 'or there abouts' from the residue of her estate to be employed for the refreshment of poor householders or the redemption of poor prisoners as the 'need shall be'.[9]

But even during this first generation of our period, 1480-1510, more perceptive burghers were beginning to experiment with endowments designed to bring relief in perpetuity to the poor of London under more carefully considered arrangements. Thus in 1492 a tradesman, Thomas Reede, left real property with a capital worth of £400, the income of which was to be disbursed equally for the care of the poor and for the maintenance of roads.[10] Sir William Horne, who in 1487 had been lord mayor, by his will proved in 1496 left to his company as trustees real property charged with an annuity of £10 p.a. for poor relief, as well as providing £25 to be distributed in alms throughout the city and £7 to purchase gowns for twenty-eight poor men.[11] A rich grocer, Sir John Warde, in 1501 disposed an endowment with a capital value of £200 for the aged and infirm 'in my owne countrey' of Hertfordshire, as well as establishing a fund of £120 for general charitable purposes in London and ordering a distribution of £80 p.a. for three years for the sustenance of London's poor, this last very large amount being the estimated value which the donor placed on the residue of his estate.[12]

One of the most munificent of all the donors of this early period, Sir John Percival, a rich merchant tailor, made thoughtful provision for the poor under the terms of his will proved in 1503. Percival ordered an outright distribution of £31 to the poor of London and an estimated outlay of £80 for their clothing, with careful instructions to his executors to purchase russet cloth from Suffolk or Northamptonshire, 'for those colours are most sure', at not more than 2s 4d a yard. At the same time, he created an endowment with a capital worth of £100 to provide bread for London's poor, established a rent-charge with his company possessing a capital value of £46 to secure food and fuel for the needy of St Mary Woolnoth parish, and created a small annuity for the poor of St Dionis Backchurch.[13] In the following year, 1504, Sir William White, a great draper, by his will ordered under careful stipulations the distribution of fuel for the poor of his parish at a charge of £12 p.a. for the long term of twenty years.[14] Nicholas Alwyn, a native of Lincolnshire who had made a large fortune as a mercer and who was chosen lord mayor in 1499, on his death in 1506 charged his executors with what must have been the incredibly difficult task of distributing £25 in penny doles to 3000 of the poor of London and as many in Lincolnshire, as well as providing somwhat more than £400 for the relief of poor householders in London and £441 7s for the care of the needy in Spalding, Lincolnshire.[15]

In the next generation, 1511-1540, in the years just preceding the Reformation, there was a marked increase of concern for the plight of the poor of the city. In all, the substantial total of £11,314 12s was disposed by benefactors either for household relief or for general charitable purposes, while a much heavier proportion of this wealth was vested in the enduring and more carefully regulated form of endowments. It will have been observed that in the preceding generation all save one of the substantial benefactions for poor relief had been provided by the great merchants of the city, all but two, in fact, having been established by former lord mayors. In the generation to which we now turn, there was at least a slight enlargement of the social and economic base of these great benefactions as the tradition of social responsibility, so soundly and firmly established among the mercantile elite, began to extend to the merchant body more generally.

In 1513 Dame Thomasine Percival, the widow of the great merchant, Sir John, who proudly declared herself a 'citizen and free woman' of the city of London, by will made large charitable dispositions totalling £1373 14s. Dame Thomasine had come far indeed from the days in *ca.* 1462 when she had ventured to London from Week St Mary, Cornwall, as a servant in the household of a mercer, Thomas Barnaby, who was to become her first husband. She had later married Henry Galle, a rich merchant tailor, and finally Sir John Percival, whom she was to survive for a decade. This interesting woman's principal foundation was a well-endowed grammar school for her native Cornish village,[16] but she like-wise conveyed to her late husband's company as trustees property with a then capital worth of at least £463 to secure the distribution of food and coal to poor householders in London as well as to lend further support to certain of her husband's charities. She left, in addition, an annuity of £1 14s for the support of the services in St Mary Woolnoth, funds with a capital value of £43 7s for prayers, £20 for church repairs, and £13 7s, given earlier (1498), towards the construction of the Holborn conduit.[17]

A few years later, in 1516, a great draper, Sir William Capel, who had twice been mayor of London, died leaving generous arrangements for the poor of his city. He provided by will and by earlier gift benefactions totalling £152 for the relief of the poor, including £28 to be distributed in doles and clothing at his funeral, £10 for linen, clothing, and fuel for the needy of Walbrook Ward, capital of about £54 vested in the Drapers' Company, the income of which should be employed for alms, and a dwelling house valued at £60, the rental of which should be used for poor relief and for church repairs.[18] Henry Kebyll, also a lord mayor and a great merchant, shortly afterwards made even more generous provisions for the poor from his large estate. These distributions, totalling about £550, included iron ploughshares and coulters for 120 poor husbandmen in various parishes in Oxfordshire, Warwickshire, and Gloucestershire, five London tenements, then valued in excess of £182, to the Grocers' Company to care for the poor of that company as well as to support prayers, a total of about £300 to be paid to the poor of St Mary Aldermary parish from the profits of his considerable land-holdings in Essex over a period of fifteen years, and, finally, doles in the amount of £5 to be disbursed to one hundred of London's poor.[19]

A lesser merchant, Matthew Boughton, a draper of relatively modest estate, who died in 1523, left, in addition to 3s for church general, £23 for making an altar in his brotherhood chapel, and £80 for prayers, lands with a worth of approximately £200 which were to be sold on the death of his wife and the income employed to pay annually to every poor householder of the heavily populated parish of Allhallows Lombard Street 6d if married and 3d if single.[20] In the same year, Thomas Mirfyn, a skinner who had been lord mayor in 1518, left £182 to be paid by his company over a period of ten years to its poor, they to hear mass in the chapel where he was buried.[21] A burgher's widow, Angela Johns, in ca. 1527 established an interesting fund for the benefit of the poor when she conveyed to the churchwardens of St Leonard Shore-ditch rentals with a then value of £5 19s 8d p.a. to secure the 'dyscharge

[of] the pore people of the . . . parishe of all maner of dewties and charges for and consernyng the charges at Easter, ther iiij offeryng dayes, ther howselyng, for the pascall light to the rode lofte', suggesting the weight of customary religious dues which Londoners of the period believed bore far too heavily on the poor and those of modest means.[22]

The final decade (1531–1540) of this early period was marked at once by an increase in the amount vested for the care of the poor and by a notable spread of concern for the plight of the poor among all the burgher groups. In 1532, Elizabeth Rede, a goldsmith's widow, left a total of £166 13s 4d in coals for the poor, £66 13s 4d to be distributed at her funeral for the poor of the parish of St John Zachary, £13 6s 8d for a dinner of bread and ale for the poor, £1 for the beggars of the parish, as well as vesting more usefully property then worth £118, the income of which was to be distributed by the Goldsmiths' Company to the poor of St Leonard's Foster Lane and St Peter Westcheap.[23] At about the same date, Sir John Peche, then residing in Kent, conveyed to the Grocers' Company the substantial sum of £500 for the main-tenance of obits in Lullingstone, Kent, with a portion of the income, while the larger part was to be employed for general charitable pur-poses, including the relief of the poor.[24] A Norfolk-born mercer, William Botery (Buttry) in 1535 left to his company an endowment of £300 for general charitable uses in London, as well as £200 to be employed in assisting poor young women about to be married in his native parish of Thorpe Market.[25] In the same year, Robert Robinson, a clothworker, left £200 as capital to his company, the income to be disposed for charitable uses, as well as an endowment valued at £209 10s for the maintenance of its poor, and £21 10s for outright alms for the needy.[26]

The somewhat old-fashioned will of Sir Thomas Seymour, a mercer who had been lord mayor, in 1536 provided generous if wholly un-regulated amounts for poor relief. Seymour ordered the distribution of £10 to the poor of St Stephen Walbrook parish, £40 to the poor of Walden in Essex, from whence his family had sprung, and the large outlay of £250 to be made in outright alms to 500 poor of Weddington in Essex.[27] A very small, but significant, charitable bequest was made in 1537 by Thomas Barley, a grocer of St Thomas the Apostle, who gave £1 10s to the poor and £2 10s for the relief of prisoners in what is the earliest clearly Protestant will we have noted.[28] And we may close our rapid review of the principal benefactions for the poor in the pre-Reformation period with the bequest of Sir Christopher Askew, a draper and former lord mayor, who stood stalwartly by the old faith.[29] Askew left £10 for the poor and for prisoners in London, about £20 to the Drapers for new hangings in their hall, £20 for highways, and £100 of endowment, the income of which was to be employed during

Lent to provide fish for the poor of Edmonton, Middlesex, his birth-place.[30]

There was an immediate and most pronounced quickening of giving for the care of the poor with the advent of the Reformation. In the course of the two decades which we have somewhat arbitrarily defined as the era of the Reformation, a total of £21,217 17s was provided for the care of poor families in their own households or for general chari-table uses which included the relief of the needy as one of the central objectives of the donor. This substantial sum considerably exceeded the whole of such charitable funds given during the course of the pre-ceding sixty years and, perhaps as importantly, a heavy proportion of this wealth was now vested in enduring and on the whole skilfully framed endowments.

In 1545 Sir Michael Dormer, a rich mercer, died leaving £901 13s for various charitable uses and enjoining his heirs against any unneces-sary or vain funeral outlays.[31] Dormer left in all £159 13s for poor relief, including £16 for the needy of his own parish of St Lawrence Jewry and £2 in alms for those of Vintry Ward. He also vested funds with an estimated capital worth of £80 to ensure the delivery of coal to the poor of his parish and £40 to secure the distribution of £2 p.a. to the unfortunate of his own company. He left, moreover, £6 13s 4d out-right to the poor of his native village of Thame, Oxfordshire, and £10 to the needy of two Buckinghamshire parishes in which he had large landholdings, as well as £5 to his own poor tenants, who should also be relieved of all rentals for six months and be protected against any increase of rents by his heirs and successors.[32] In the same year Joan Milbourne, who had outlived a succession of draper husbands, by her will established a capital sum of £250, the income of which was to be disbursed in alms for poor and worthy women of the city, as well as leaving £1 5s in doles for London's poor.[33] The benefactions of Sir John Allen, a rich mercer who was well regarded by Henry VIII and who had twice served his city as lord mayor, were even more generous than those of his close friend Dormer, though they were distributed in a curiously diffuse fashion. In all, Allen left £914 6s 8d for poor relief, with an estimated £200 to be laid out in 10s alms for the needy of four London parishes and 4d each to be given to every poor and bedridden person within the walls of the city. Allen likewise set aside £100 to be used to pay the subsidy requirements of the London poor on the occasion of the next tax and about £100 to be used over the next two years in continuing his custom of feeding fifty poor on all 'fish days' a diet of 'bread and pottage and red herrings'. The will also ordered the distribution of 128 woollen gowns, costing approximately £68, to deserving poor, enjoined the distribution of £33 to the poor of four named parishes over a term of years, and established an endowment of £333 6s 8d with which fuel was to be provided to needy households. Lesser amounts were to be distributed to the poor and sick of Allen's birthplace, Thaxted, Essex, while an annual gift of £1 was ordered to the poor of Whittington College and to the thirteen poor of St Anthony's.[34] Just a year later, a lesser merchant, William Mery, a grocer, by his will disposed £268 for the benefit of London's poor, not to mention substantial amounts for other significant and needed uses.[35]

Requirements of space suggest that it might be well to accord no special comment to a number of considerable benefactions provided for the poor during the reign of Edward VI but to pass on to a few selected instances in the reign of Mary Tudor. One is struck, first of all, by the fact that the thirteen donors of this reign who left as much as £100 to the poor, it being pertinent to note that the whole of the charities of this group of rich burghers exceeded £12,000, provided no more than £1 for prayers. It seems reasonably certain, in fact, that ten of these men and women were Protestants and that the stern repression as well as the fervent evangelical efforts of Mary Tudor had little if any effect upon the beliefs or the religious habits of the dominant burgher aristocracy of the city. Their pattern of interests and their aspirations for the future of their society became, indeed, increasingly and more rigorously secular as this tragic reign wore on.

The earliest of these donors was Henry Amcottes, a fishmonger who had been lord mayor in 1548 and who died in 1554. This benefactor provided in all £151 to be distributed to the poor, including gowns for twenty poor men and as many needy women who carried torches at his funeral, £6 to the poor of Billingsgate Ward, of which he was alderman, £4 to the poor of each of the other twenty-three wards of the city, and £20 for the poor of Lincoln, his native town.[36] An even more generous distribution of £8 p.a. was ordered for the poor of St Margaret's parish, Westminster, from a large and valuable block of properties vested in the churchwardens under the will of a cordwainer, Richard Castel.[37] But by far the greatest of the benefactors of the Reformation period was Sir John Gresham, whose gifts and bequests for charitable uses may conservatively be estimated at £7873 17s. As we shall later note, during his lifetime Gresham provided an endowment of £2000 to be invested in land for the succour of poor clothiers in Bristol.[38] His will, proved in 1556, disposed £120 for clothing for the poor of London, £240 for the poor of the entire city, and an estimated £30 for coals for the benefit of the needy of his own parish of St Michael Bassishaw. More importantly, the residue of his estate, which must have yielded upwards of £2500, was to be applied for general charitable uses, the needs of the poor being central, after the foundation of his great grammar school in Norfolk had been carried forward and his large personal and family bequests paid. These notable philanthropies, so carefully and expertly arranged, were over the next generation to have most effective consequences not only in the benefits which they brought to the society but in the pattern they established for other great merchants who had known and admired this famous man.[39]

Just a year later, in 1557, Sir George Barne, a haberdasher who had been lord mayor in the dangerous days at the close of Edward VI's reign, left £20 outright to the poor of the city, his windmill at Finsbury, which seems to have been valued at about £50, to the Haberdashers as an endowment for their poor, and capital with a then value of £78 to provide bread for thirteen poor of the parish of St Bartholomew Exchange.[40] His widow, Dame Alice Barne, on her death two years later, left a generous sum of £612 for various forms of poor relief, including £10 for the poor of her ward, an estimated £60 for clothing, £400 to provide fuel for London's poor over a term of ten years, £2 outright to the needy of the Haberdashers' Company, £130 to be distributed to the destitute in all the wards of London, and £10 to aid the poor refugees just then returning from Calais.[41]

It is interesting to observe that the Elizabethan age constitutes a distinct period with respect to its treatment of the needs of the poor. In all, donors of this generation gave the very large total of £63,137 2s for the relief of the poor and for general charitable causes, a much larger sum than had been afforded during the preceding eight decades. It may be noted, too, that the flow of such benefactions during this long interval was remarkably steady, having in each decade been well over £11,000 and in only one having risen to as much as £20,000. This is a generation, also, marked by so many substantial individual benefactions for poor relief that there is space here to mention, with rare exceptions, only gifts of more than £300, an amount, it must be emphasized, which would have been regarded as a fair competence in this age in all save the highest ranges of the society.

We should also observe that though the great merchants continued to bear the principal responsibility in creating endowments for the care of the poor, other classes too were now making substantial contributions. Thus in 1562 Sir Humphrey Browne, a Justice of the Common Pleas, left real property in St Sepulchre, then possessing a capital worth of £224, for the benefit of the needy in St Martin Orgar.[42] In the next year Dame Anne Packington, a merchant's daughter but a judge's widow, left carefully devised endowments to the Clothworkers' Company, with a total capital value of upwards of £516 on condition that £3 13s 4d should each year be distributed to the poor of St Dunstan in the West, two payments totalling £7 13s 4d p.a. for the care of the poor of St Botolph without Aldgate, as well as £3 p.a. for the education of poor children, and an annual sermon in the two favoured parishes with a total stipend of £4 6s 8d p.a.[43] Two years later, Lady Isabella Gresham, the widow of Sir Richard, by bequests to the Mercers' Company added to gifts already made which in all provided a capital of £190 to secure annual payments of £3 in perpetuity to each of three London parishes in which she was personally most interested, as well as arranging by will for outright distribution of £108 to the worthy poor of London.[44]

By successive investments Sir Martin Bowes, a goldsmith and for two decades one of the most influential merchants of London, created a large charitable estate to which still more funds were added by his will upon his death in 1566. In all, Bowes left for charity £2574, of which about half, £1361, was for poor relief or general charitable purposes. The whole of the amounts provided for the poor was vested as capital, in part with the Goldsmiths and part with private trustees, for the benefit of the poor in several London parishes, for the poor of the Goldsmiths' Company, for needy persons in Woolwich and in North Cray, Kent. Included also in this large and formidably complex group of trusts was one *corpus* of property comprising a great messuage, twenty-two gardens, and a small tenement, then rented at £13 6s 8d p.a., which was conveyed in trust to the Goldsmiths with the intent that the poor of the ward of Langbourne should be wholly relieved of the weight of parliamentary subsidies. Bowes, whose almshouse foundation and substantial endowment for hospitals will be subsequently noted, likewise provided capital of approximately £193 for his company, left £60 for municipal uses, and £20 to the clergy.[45] A prosperous London cutler, Thomas Bucke, in the next year (1567) left properties in London and Surrey with a then capital value of £504 on trust with his company to secure numerous charitable undertakings, which included an annual payment of £2 to the poor of Fleet Lane, an equal amount to the deserving poor of his birthplace, Wilburton, in the Isle of Ely, and a residue then amounting to £12 17s p.a. to the poor of the Cutlers' Company.[46] Robert Harding, a rich salter, by gift and bequest devised in all £319 17s for the uses of the poor, together with numerous benefactions for other charitable purposes. Harding left £33 7s for fifty gowns for poor men and an estimated £25 for the purchase of fuel for the needy of London. In addition, he created endowments with a capital worth of £44 for the care of the poor of the Salters' Company; £67 was vested in the Fishmongers' Company, the income to be employed to relieve the needs of poor artificers and others in the neighbourhood who were obliged to purchase fish cuttings and refuse for their food; and £68 was left to the Butchers' Company, the income to be used by them for the relief of poor men who came to their shambles to buy refuse meat. In addition, Harding had in 1564 given the Fishmongers an annuity of £2 for the care of their poor and by his will, proved in 1568, left outright £22 10s for the poor of several Bedfordshire villages and £20 for the destitute of numerous Buckinghamshire parishes.[47]

Sir Thomas Rowe, a rich merchant tailor who died in 1570, left the substantial total of £1572 for various charitable uses, of which by far the largest portion was for the care of the poor. Rowe gave or bequeathed £231 outright in alms for the poor of ten London wards and the needy of the Clothworkers' Company, gowns for forty poor men, and similar helpful distributions, but his principal charity was constituted by vesting extensive London properties, then valued at upwards of £800, in the Merchant Taylors' Company, with instructions to employ the income for the needs of poor freemen of the Clothworkers, Carpenters, Tilers, Plasterers, and Armourers who because of age or infirmity were no longer able to earn their own living. It will be observed that Rowe's distributions were carefully designated for artisans in skilled trades mostly unrelated to his own commercial interests, and it may also be remarked that each householder benefiting was to receive the relatively large stipend of £4 p.a. towards his support.[48] In the same year, 1570, another prosperous merchant tailor, Thomas Walker, left numerous London tenements with a then capital worth of about £480 on trust with the stipulation that the annual income should be disbursed for the assistance of poor but worthy householders,[49] while just a year later still another merchant tailor settled an even larger capital as an endowment for poor relief. Robert Donkin, after providing an estimated £42 as a fund to secure the distribution of bread in St Michael Cornhill, by will conveyed to his company London properties then worth £520, the income on which was to be employed to clothe poor men 'of honest fame and most in need' in an annual distribution at Christmas time.[50]

William Bond, a haberdasher and a merchant adventurer, accounted one of the 'most famous in his age for his great adventures both by sea and land', on his death in 1576 left the substantial sum of £500 with which to buy and maintain a stock of grain for the poor of London, as well as £55 for various outright distributions for poor relief.[51] At about the same date, a much humbler citizen, Thomas Busby, a cooper, left two houses which two generations later possessed a capital worth of about £300, the rents from which were to be employed for the distribution of food and fuel in St Giles Cripplegate.[52] Barbara Champion, a draper's widow, in this same year, 1576, left properties with a then capital worth of £390 to her late husband's company with provision that the income be employed for the poor of the company, while also leaving £30 outright to poor prisoners and creating loan funds of £100 each for the Drapers and Skinners, for the benefit of young freemen.[53]

One of the greatest of the Elizabethan benefactors was William

Lambe, a merchant and clothworker who had settled most of his large estate in carefully ordered charities well before his death at an advanced age in 1580. A native of Sutton Valence, Kent, Lambe was known favourably to Henry VIII, who sold to him at nominal charges the hermitage chapel of St James, which Lambe was later to endow. He was an early and a strong Protestant who, according to his contemporary biographer, 'was a hearer of God's word read and preached, given to devout praier, visited by Master Nowell . . . and Master Fox in his [last] sickness'. Lambe gave in total the large fortune of £5695 for various and most thoughtfully conceived charities, almost the whole of his estate having been disposed for such uses. His benefactions for poor relief amounted to £984, including £96 to be given in doles at his funeral, a capital sum of £425 vested in the Clothworkers' Company to ensure distribution of gowns and shoes to poor men and women, £133 to provide annual gifts to the poor of the Stationers' Company, £6 to be used to purchase 120 pails for poor women who might thus carry water and the better earn a living, £24 to the needy of Sutton Valence, and £100 to aid the depressed clothiers of Long Melford, Suffolk, and £200 for the needs of poor clothiers of Bridgnorth and Ludlow, Shropshire. This great man who, it is most difficult to recall, was well into middle age with the advent of the Reformation, was one of the wisest and certainly one of the most boldly experimental of all the philanthropists of the Elizabethan age.[54]

The flow of funds into various plans for poor relief was very heavy indeed in the decade of the Armada, slightly more than £20,000 having been disposed for such uses by a great variety of donors drawn from all social classes. But the large and dominant foundations continued to be made by members of the mercantile aristocracy, by men who had reached their maturity in the age of the Reformation and whose aspirations tended to reflect the intense secularism of the new age. Thus Robert Hilson, a merchant, by earlier gifts and by bequest in 1583 disposed in all £382 3s for the care of the poor of two London parishes and a lesser annuity of £1 6s 8d for household relief in Great Stanmore, Middlesex, where he maintained a country residence in his later years.[55] In this same year large bequests for the poor of London and of Ticehurst, Sussex, were made by Barnard Randolph, Common Serjeant of London. This testator left £480, to which £20 was added by the company, to the Ironmongers' Company, which distributed £25 p.a. for the relief of the poor in twelve parishes in Queenhithe and Castle Baynard wards, in amounts ranging from 6s 8d p.a. to £3 12s p.a. for each of the favoured parishes. Some months before his death, Randolph had vested £200 in the Fishmongers, who undertook in perpetuity to distribute £1 p.a. to each of two London parishes, £2 annually to the churchwardens of Ticehurst for road repairs there, £2 p.a. to the poor of that community, and £4 p.a. to a divinity student at Cambridge. By will, Randolph likewise left £1000 to his executors, plus certain other assets whose value cannot be estimated, with the intention that the presumed income of £50 p.a. be employed for the relief of the poor in Ticehurst, which was, it scarcely wants saying, the testator's birthplace.[56] Almost equally generous and in some respects quite similar provisions were made just two years later (1585) by a rich vintner, Stephen Skidmore, for the poor of London and of Cork, Ireland. This donor left extensive properties, lately belonging to the Black Friars, in trust, after the death of his wife, to the company for uses specified in great detail. The property at that time possessed a capital worth of £900 or more, the income of which was to be annually distributed in sums of £1 to each of seventeen city parishes for the benefit of their poor, £2 12s p.a. to St Stephen Coleman Street for the weekly distribution of a dozen loaves of bread, £1 p.a. for the poor of the Vintners' Company, and £24 p.a. for the needy of the donor's native town of Cork.[57]

John Lute, a clothworker who had been master of his company, by his will proved in 1586 bequeathed to the Clothworkers extensive holdings of London shops, then leased at too low rentals, which provided a capital worth of £523. He stipulated that renewal fines should be imposed totalling £200 and employed by the company as a loan fund for its own young members and for honest householders, while the income from the properties should be disposed for the poor of the company and of St Michael Cornhill. There was also a payment of 6s 8d to be made annually for a sermon in that parish.[58] At a slightly earlier date, Sir Thomas Offley, whom Fuller described as 'the Zacchaeus of London, not for his low stature, but his high charity', left outright something like £134 for gowns for fifty poor and for fuel over a period of seven years, £103 7s for the poor of Stafford, and an estimated £867 to be used by his executors for general charitable purposes.[59] A rich mercer, John Heydon, who died in 1582, left an extraordinarily complicated structure of bequests totalling £2604 for various charitable uses. Loan funds with a capital worth of £2100 were established with the Mercers and other livery companies, as well as funds of £100 each vested in the municipalities of Bristol and Gloucester and £200 in Exeter, all of which were to be lent on reasonable surety to young men just beginning their careers as merchants or as tradesmen. Those who were thus helped in establishing themselves were to pay 3·33 per cent interest, this most favourable rate carrying its own charitable implications, the considerable income thus accruing to be employed, if we may aggregate payments in several communities and in numerous London parishes, approximately 30 per cent for the care of the poor, 30 per cent for the relief of poor prisoners, not quite 26 per cent for the support of London hospitals, 13 per cent for the maintenance of a weekly divinity lecture in St Michael Paternoster church 'by some learned man, to be elected by the persons who appoint the lecturer for the Clothworkers' in that church, and a small proportion for company uses.[60]

The trust device so carefully drawn by Heydon, under which aspiring and trustworthy young men needing capital could be helped with substantial loans at modest interest rates, the income in turn being dedicated to the assistance of the hopelessly poor, became in the later Elizabethan years a very common charitable plan. We may mention another established in 1587, a few years after Heydon's death. Sir Lionell Duckett, a former lord mayor, a mercer, and a most successful entrepreneur, vested £200 in his company as a loan fund for the assistance of four promising young men, who should pay 4 per cent interest, which was to be distributed to the 'poorest and oldest' persons in three London parishes. Duckett likewise left £30 outright for clothing, £100 to Christ's Hospital, £20 for the relief of prisoners in London, and an uncertain amount for the poor of four Nottinghamshire parishes.[61] In this same year, 1587, another great mercer, Peter Symonds, left in various funds a total of £107 for the poor of London, as well as creating trusts with a capital value of £450 for the relief of the poor of his native city of Winchester, where he likewise established a great almshouse.[62]

But by no means all the substantial endowments constituted during these years for the care of the poor were the fruit of the incredible generosity of the merchant aristocracy. In 1589 an aged lady, Blanche Parry, one of the gentlewomen of the Queen's privy chamber, left capital of £400 value for the relief of the poor of Westminster, while endowing at the same time a rather complicated trust to secure the distribution of free grain to the poor of Barton and Newton in Herefordshire, with an estimated capital worth of £280.[63] Shortly afterwards, in 1592, John Lyon, a rich yeoman of Harrow, Middlesex, and the founder of the great school there,[64] died having established an endowment with a capital value of £400 for the relief of the poor of his parish, providing £4 p.a. for the maintenance of certain highways in the county, and ordering that any residue from the school endowment be devoted to marriage subsidies and other worthy charitable uses.[65]

We should consider together the munificent and in part joint charities of Sir Thomas Ramsay, Lord Mayor of London in 1577, who died in 1590, and of his remarkable wife, Dame Mary, who survived him for about a decade. This most generous couple were over a period of almost twenty years to vest a total of £14,317 16s in carefully devised charities which took the needs of all England in view. It is evident that together they had established a pattern of charitable interests which they gradually and methodically implemented between 1583, when their first trust was created, and 1601, when Lady Ramsay's will was proved. Their benefactions for poor relief alone required a capital of £5567. Thus an endowment of £200 was conveyed to the municipal authorities to secure the payment of £10 p.a. for the relief of three particularly hard-pressed London parishes. A further endowment of £2000 was settled on the city of London as trustee, the income to be employed for divers charitable uses, including £20 p.a. for the maintenance of poor and maimed soldiers who had served in the Spanish war, £2 10s p.a. for the care of the poor of Christchurch, and a residue of approximately £36 10s p.a. for clothing and general poor relief. Ramsay by will left as well £137 outright for the relief of the poor of London, Edenbridge (Kent) and Croydon (Surrey). After her husband's death, Lady Ramsay purchased a manor in Essex which she placed in trust to support various charitable uses, including an additional £12 10s p.a. for the relief of London's poor and £10 p.a. for the succour of the poor of Acton, Middlesex, and £20 p.a. for the support of ten poor widows. She also established loan funds of £200 each in five city companies, which were to be lent on good surety at 5 per cent, with the income to be devoted to the relief of the poor of the several companies comprehended in the scheme. Lady Ramsay left as well £100 to be distributed in clothing in seven Essex parishes, £1000 to be employed in Bristol for general charitable purposes, and an estimated residue of £1200, comprising all her moneys, household effects, and all other property not specifically bequeathed, for broadly defined charitable uses in London.[66]

There could, of course, be few benefactions on the immense scale conceived and so judiciously carried forward by the Ramsays. It must be noted, indeed, that the total of their charitable giving far exceeded the worth of the whole estate of the average member of the upper gentry even in southern England during their generation and constituted a sum which would have beggared not a few of the nobility of the realm. But there were many other substantial endowments for the poor created in the closing years of Elizabeth's life, at least a few of which may be briefly noted.

Among other large charities, a draper, Thomas Russell, a native of Staffordshire, disposed in all the considerable sum of £748 4s for the relief of the poor of London and of his own native county. Rent-charges were vested, representing a capital worth of £52, for the poor of St Leonard Shoreditch, and an equal amount for the needy of Barton, Staffordshire, to which he had also given £20 outright during his lifetime; and the same capital was ensured for both Colton and Blithfield in his native county. Russell likewise conveyed to the Drapers' Company property then worth at least £453, the income of which was to be employed for the care of their poor, while by his will he ordered the distribution of substantial amounts in fuel and clothing.[67] In 1594, Sir

Cuthbert Buckle, who was then serving as lord mayor, died leaving rent-charges with a capital worth of £210 to three London parishes in which he had held property, as well as an estimated £90 for clothing the poor of his own parish (St Mary at Hill) and gowns for poor mourners attending his funeral.[68] Buckle had died of the epidemic which swept London in 1594. Throughout our period, the menace of these terrible scourges prompted men to draft their wills and may well have reminded them of their charitable responsibilities. These very human motives are exemplified in the will of William Plumbe of Fulham (Middlesex), who in 1594 left £5 to the poor at his funeral, £2 to the poor-box, and £2 to be distributed to the needy of his parish, 'knowinge that I was borne to dye and that the tyme thereof may be soe shorte a momente wthe twynckling of an eye, and fynding by daylie experience the manyfolde and intricate suytes and questions in lawe which doe arise for lacke of disposing and advisinge of such havior as yt pleaseth the allmyghtie to commytt unto us haue thought very meete and convenyent in this contagyous tyme of infecton' to make his final dispositions.[69]

Margaret Holligrave, a clothworker's widow, on her death in 1596 left valuable properties in East Smithfield, these possessing a probable worth of £680, to her late husband's company as trustees, with instructions to pay £2 p.a. to the poor of two London parishes, £1 p.a. to the relief of prisoners, and to devote the considerable remainder of the income to the care of the poor of the company.[70] A year later, William Peake, a donor of uncertain social status who possessed considerable land in Hoxton (Middlesex), devised to trustees lands with a capital value of £309 to secure payments of £5 4s annually for the poor of both St Leonard Shoreditch and Wellingborough (Northamptonshire), in addition to establishing a small endowment of £30, the income of which should be employed to provide clothing for two poor widows of Pottersbury (Northamptonshire).[71] Gregory Smith, a merchant tailor, in the same year spread over numerous and widely scattered communities bequests for the poor totalling £290, including £60 for clothing for London poor, £10 for the needy of his own company, £140 in capital and outright bequests in Wighton and Hindringham, Norfolk, £20 each to Norwich and King's Lynn for their poor, not to mention gifts for the poor in various parishes in Cambridgeshire, Suffolk, and Buckinghamshire.[72] A rich haberdasher, Thomas Aldersey, in 1593 had constituted a great endowment for the founding of a grammar school in his native town of Bunbury, Cheshire,[73] which was charged as well with the payment of £10 p.a. for the care of the poor of that community and £3 6s 8d p.a. for the needy of the Haberdashers' Company, which was named as trustee of the entire endowment. By the terms of his will Aldersey settled in addition a capital sum of £300 on the

Haberdashers, the income to be distributed to their poor, and gave £100 for the relief of prisoners in Bridewell.[74]

Thomas Owen, a respected judge of the Court of Common Pleas and himself a merchant's son, on his death in late 1598 left, in addition to outright distributions of £20 for London's poor and £5 for the poor of Westminster, property in his native city of Shrewsbury then valued at £320, the income of which was to be employed for the assistance of poor and decayed householders there. Owen likewise left a rent-charge of £2 13s p.a. which his trustees were to use for the weekly distribution of bread to twelve poor and impotent persons in the parish of Condover, Shropshire, the manor and lordship of which Owen had purchased.[75] A mercer's widow, Margaret [Mary] Sharles in 1600 bequeathed property with a then capital value of upwards of £200, the income to be used in part for the distribution of fuel to the poor of Christchurch parish and the remainder to be disposed annually at Christmas time in bread and beef for the needy of that parish. This donor likewise left £100 to the Mercers' Company as capital to be lent to poor and deserving tradesmen, apparently without interest, as well as a large capital sum for the foundation of a lectureship which will be discussed in a later connection.[76]

There had been a steady and increasing concern of the London mercantile aristocracy with the problem of the care of the poor, mounting in the Elizabethan period to a concentrated, systematic, and impressive effort to provide sufficient endowments to enable the parishes to undertake responsibility for those not hopelessly or helplessly indigent. At the same time, as we shall later note, benefactors were rapidly raising up a system of almshouse relief, in London and the provinces, for those who must be regarded as derelict, as permanent casualties in the new economy of the realm. But impressive as were these measures for outright or household relief in the course of the sixteenth century, they seem scarcely more than anticipatory when we consider them in relation to the immense outpouring of funds for this purpose in the early decades (1601–1640) of the seventeenth century. In this brief interval the enormous total of £244,798 12s was provided by London donors for household relief or for general charitable uses. The immensity of this sum, very nearly the whole of which was capital, is suggested when we reflect that it amounted to almost two and a half times as much as had been given for these uses in London itself since 1480 and that it was not much less than the amount (£284,964 5s) provided for these purposes during our entire period in all the other nine counties included in this study. The climax of this incredible generosity, which of course benefited the provinces as well as London, was reached in the years 1621–1630, when a total of £103,445 18s, of which 96·17 per cent was capital, was given to secure the care of poor men and women in their own households. We may certainly say that the social conscience of England stood mature by that date and that the burgher mind had accepted a vast responsibility which burgher wealth was implementing with effective and massively endowed resources.

The number of large benefactions made in the early Stuart period for household relief was so great that it is quite impossible to deal even briefly with more than a few of them. In the first decade (1601–1610) there were forty-seven Londoners who made capital benefactions of £100 or more for poor relief; in the next decade this number increased to ninety-seven; and in the climactic decade (1621–1630) there were 119 citizens, of whom, it may be noted, ninety-three were merchants or merchants' widows, who gave £100 or upwards for this charitable use. We must, consequently, confine our attention, save in most unusual instances, to a sampling of the great endowments of £500 or more made for poor relief by donors of this period. These are very large benefactions when it is recalled that in terms of the standards of the time the income on such a fund would have provided at least subsistence support for as many as eighteen families and would have been quite sufficient to endow the normal needs of two or three rural parishes in caring for their poor.

In 1602 a native Londoner and a tradesman, Charles Langley, bequeathed to the vicar and churchwardens of St Giles Cripplegate six messuages then possessing a capital worth of at least £960, with the provision that the income, aside from £4 p.a. reserved for the vicar, was to be employed for clothing with 'northerne cloth, or broad northern dozens' the poor of that parish and those of St Luke Finsbury, while any surplus was to be devoted to the care of the sick and lame in St Giles.[77] These same two parishes, with others, likewise benefited in 1602 from the generosity of another tradesman, Robert Rogers, a leatherseller, who by earlier gifts and his bequest gave in all £873 7s for the use of the poor. This donor provided an endowment of £90 for the distribution of coals to the needy of three parishes, gave outright £50 in doles to destitute persons, and £100 for the assistance of poor artificers, constituted an endowment of £200 for weekly bread doles, established a fund with the Merchant Adventurers' Company, of which he was also a member, with a capital of £400 for the care of their poor, and ordered the distribution of £23 6s 8d to the poor in three western towns, including Poole (Dorset), of which he was a native.[78]

Richard Beddoe, described by Strype as 'one of the ancientest' of the parish of St Clement Danes and a feoffee of the poor in that parish, under the terms of his will proved in 1603 left real property in the city with a then value of about £500, from the income of which £20 p.a. was to be employed for the relief of the poor. In addition, Beddoe bequeathed £100 which was to be lent without interest for terms of two years to fifty poor householders and 'young beginners' of the parish in order to permit as many as possible to meet their own financial problems.[79] In the same year (1603) a goldsmith, Philip Strelley, a native of Derbyshire, left the manor of U[I]lkerthorpe in that county to his company on trust with the provision that the property should be leased for £55 p.a. to sustain charitable uses, of which £10 p.a. should be paid for the relief of poor and maimed soldiers, £2 p.a. to the poor of St John Zachary, and £8 p.a. for the care of poor workmen who had served the Goldsmiths' Company.[80] Sir William Glover, an alderman and dyer, in 1604 provided in his will for the distribution of £560 15s for poor relief, including £200 left to the Dyers to be lent to young men at 5 per cent, the interest to be given to the poor of the company. This donor left an equal amount for the uses of the poor of several London parishes, £66 13s 4d for the poor of Coventry, and sixty gowns to be distributed to as many poor at a charge of £1 8s for each garment.[81] A vintner, George Clarke, by gifts and by bequests ordered under his will in 1606, provided in all £293 6s 8d for the relief of poor families in St Botolph without Aldgate, £230 for those dwelling in Whitechapel, and £106 15s 4d for the poor of St Leonard Shoreditch. Clarke likewise gave the substantial sum of £200 to secure the repair of sixteen almshouses at Town's End (Whitechapel), as well as a large endowment for Oxford University.[82]

A substantial grocer, Francis Tirrell, in 1609 left in all £781 13s for the care of the poor of London. A stock of one thousand marks was vested in the Grocers, the income on which was to be employed for the distribution of fuel to the needy of five named parishes, £50 was left for outright alms for the poor of four parishes, while smaller sums were provided for household relief in Southwark and in Croydon.[83] In the same year, 1609, a west-countryman, Robert Chilcot, who had served as clerk to the great philanthropist Peter Blundell and who had inherited a portion of his estate, ordered most generous charitable distributions totalling upwards of £2500 under his will, almost the whole of which was designated for the benefit of his native town of Tiverton, Devon. Chilcot vested rents possessing a capital worth of £1020, from which annual payments of £16 10s were to be made to fifteen of the poor of Tiverton, £15 for the relief of fifteen poor artificers of the town, and £19 10s p.a. to be disbursed in weekly sums in bread and money for the maintenance of an additional group of fifteen of the worthy poor of his native parish.[84]

By 1609 it is not too much to say that rich merchants like Tirrell and Chilcot lay under a heavy responsibility of tradition and status to make large and useful charitable dispositions either during their late years or at their death. The merchant society, in fact, viewed with extreme disfavour those of its members too penurious to assume the now well-defined burdens of the class, and it was outraged indeed when the richest merchant of his generation died making no substantial charitable provisions. Sir John Spencer, whose wealth was reckoned by his contemporaries as within the range of £500,000 to £800,000, died in 1610 selfish and obdurate to the end, with no other arrangements than for a funeral of great magnificence at which baskets of food and clothing, with a total value of perhaps £400, were to be distributed to 320 poor men who should be in attendance: a reminder to the wits of London that his only daughter had been carried away in a basket by her lover in a spectacular elopement.[85]

A London goldsmith, Richard Hanbury, by gift, probably in 1610, settled on the Grocers' Company the large endowment of one thousand marks, the income of which he ordered distributed weekly in bread to the poor of two London parishes, with the further provision that annually six prayer-books 'well buffed and bossed' should be given to as many poor children in both of the favoured parishes.[86] In the same year, George Palyn, a girdler and a native of Cheshire, among very substantial charities with a total capital worth of £3702, gave £362 for the relief of poor households in London and in his native town of Wrenbury.[87]

The flow of benefactions designed to relieve the needs of the poor rose to a flood tide of generosity in the second decade of the seventeenth century and was to be maintained for a full generation until the unsettling effects of civil disturbance began to be felt. This immense outpouring was almost wholly in the permanently salutary and institutional form of endowments, with the result that great rescources were rapidly added to those which earlier piety and generosity had created. Indeed, some responsible men were as early as 1617 in agreement with William Acton of St Katherine Coleman, who explained in his will that he was 'egiveing noe more' than £5 for poor relief 'for that I see not many take relief in this parish'.[88] But the generality of merchants were by no means persuaded that the needs of a rapidly increasing and essentially unstable working-class population enjoyed adequate security even from the massive endowments so rapidly being vested. In the decade 1611–1620 there were in all thirty-seven donors, of whom thirty-one were merchants or their widows, who by gift or bequest established endowments for the care of the poor with funds of £400 or more. We shall want to speak briefly of at least a few of these funds.

A London brewer, Edward Harvest, in 1611 left £200 as an endowment for the poor of two London parishes, while his widow, who seems to have died shortly afterwards, left city property with a then capital worth of £400, the income on which she ordered distributed amongst twenty poor widows of the parish of St Giles Cripplegate.[89] At about the same time, Florence Caldwell, a haberdasher, enfeoffed rentals with a capital value of £316, in order to provide an annuity of £2 12s for bread for the needy of St Martin Ludgate, £6 6s p.a. to secure clothing and a small cash stipend for six of the poor of his company, and £2 p.a. to the poor of his native town of Rolleston, Staffordshire, in addition to substantial charities for other purposes.[90] A large endowment of £2800 capital value was created in 1612 under the will of Robert Gale, a vintner, which, among other uses, secured the distribution of £20 p.a. to the poor of Chippenham, Wiltshire, at the discretion of the bailiff and 'six of the ancientest burgesses' of the town and an equal amount to be given each year to the poor of the city of Lincoln, the donor's birthplace, and its suburbs.[91] Sir Thomas Cambell, an ironmonger who had served as lord mayor in 1609–1610, by gift and bequest vested in his company and the municipal government of London a total capital of £800, the income of which was to be employed for the distribution of large quantities of fuel to the poor of two London parishes as well as certain parishes in Southwark.[92]

One of the most munificent of all the benefactors in the decade under review was the staunchly Puritan merchant adventurer, William Jones, who had first found employment in London as a porter when he arrived from Wales as a boy. Jones, who died in 1615, left in all the enormous sum of £19,900 for various carefully arranged charitable purposes, including £1700 of capital for the poor. The largest of these poor relief funds was an endowment of £1440 settled on the Haberdashers' Company with the provision that it was to be lent at 5 per cent interest, the income to be employed for the full care of nine of the poor of that company. In addition, Jones provided bequests of £200 for the relief of the poor of Stade, £50 for the poor of Hamburg, and an equal amount to poor Englishmen living in that German city in which he had long maintained large mercantile interests.[93]

Ann Whitmore, almost certainly a haberdasher's widow, in 1615 bequeathed to that company property valued at about £480 to secure annual payments of £19 for the clothing and general relief of the poor of the parish of St Edmund the King, as well as £2 p.a. to the church-wardens for general uses and £3 p.a. to the company for its pains.[94] An aged merchant tailor, Jeffrey Elwes [Helwys], on his death in the next year bequeathed £400 in trust to his company, the income of which was to be distributed to the poor of the city, as well as establishing an endowment of £100 for the sustenance of needy householders in Walbrook Ward, giving £7 outright to the poor of Woodford, Essex, and distributing seventy-six gowns to as many poor men following his funeral.[95] An even richer merchant tailor, Sir John Swinnerton, who died in the same year, was somewhat less generous, leaving endowments with a capital worth of approximately £350 to secure payments of £7 p.a. to the poor of a London parish, £5 4s annually to the poor of Lexden,

Essex, and an equal amount for the poor of Oswestry, Shropshire, not to mention smaller outright distributions of alms and clothing.[96] Still another merchant tailor, Randolph Wolley, a native of Staffordshire, left in all a capital sum of £940 for poor relief under quite complicated instructions. Numerous parcels of London property, with a then capital worth of about £600, were conveyed to trustees, the income to be used for the 'relief of the poorer sort of householders' in the parish of St Augustine and for other good and charitable uses; a fund of £240 value was given to the Merchant Taylors' Company to provide £12 p.a. for the care of its poor; £100 was bequeathed as an endowment to secure the payment of £5 p.a. to the needy of the donor's native chapelry, Woore, in Staffordshire; while an additional £50 was to be dispensed in alms.[97]

One of the most generous of all the benefactors of this great decade was another merchant tailor, John Vernon, who by gifts and bequests left £5950 for various charitable uses, of which £4030 was capital for the support of several schemes for poor relief. A small fund of £60 was given to his company to secure the distribution each Sunday of a dozen loaves of 'good sweet wheaten bread' at St Michael Cornhill, as well as certain lesser payments for other charitable purposes. Vernon likewise established a most substantial endowment of £800 value for the complete maintenance of ten poor and aged men, each of whom should have £4 p.a., they to be free of the Clothworkers, the Woolwinders, the Carpenters, the Tilers, the Plasterers, or the Armourers. These pensioners should likewise be provided with woollen gowns every third year. Vernon also vested in his company rents of £100 p.a., or a capital of about £2000, to be used for the maintenance of twelve aged and needy men of that fraternity, each of whom should have £6 p.a. and a gown every third year, as well as support to be lent to four of the poor of the company, who were to be named as reversioners, each of whom should have £1 6s 8d annually. This great benefactor likewise stipulated that certain residues arising from a complex series of gifts to the company should be invested at 5 per cent and the income employed for poor relief. Finally, Vernon bequeathed to the city of Chester £800, the income on which was to be used by the municipal authorities there for the care of ten poor and aged men who were members of certain of the artisan fraternities of the city, and with the further provision that each should have a gown every third year.[98]

There were many benefactions for the poor ranging in amount from £100 to £600 during the remaining years of the decade, of which at least a few examples may be given. Thus in 1618 Lady Jane Townshend left in all about £600 for poor relief, including, if we may capitalize certain rent-charges, £200 for the needy of Kensington, £100 to the poor of St Giles, where she was buried, about £74 in clothing to poor women in London, and £237 to aid the poor in four Norfolk parishes where her family held lands.[99] Henry Adams, a rich cutler, in 1618 bequeathed £1000 to his vicar and churchwardens with the stipulation that £10 p.a. should be employed for the succour of the 'ancient poore' of his parish and that an equal amount should be similarly disposed in the parish of Shorne, Kent, where he had been born; the churchwardens were also to make relatively small payments for sermons in Shorne and St Dunstan's and to lay out £4 p.a. for a dinner. Such income as remained was to be utilized for church repairs in St Dunstan's.[100] In the same year, a rich and generous salter's widow, Frances Clarke, by will provided for the distribution of sixty mourning gowns at £1 6s 8d each to poor men and £50 to supply coal to the needy of St Margaret Moses. This benefactor established as well an endowment of £200 with the Merchant Taylors' Company, the income of which was to be used for the care of the poor of Odiham, Hampshire, and capital of the same amount was vested in the Tallow Chandlers' Company to secure the annual payment of £10 for poor relief in her husband's native parish of Langham in Rutland.[101] John Sheild, a native of Yorkshire who had served the Clothworkers' Company as cook for many years, on his death in 1620 disposed charitable bequests totalling £696 11s, of which a large proportion was for poor relief in London and Yorkshire.[102] In the same year, 1620, Peter Wybo, a native of Flanders who had settled in London, left in all £310 for poor relief in widely dispersed amounts, including £20 to the poor of the French church in London, £80 in total to the poor of the Dutch congregations in Sandwich, Maidstone, Colchester, and Norwich, £10 to the destitute in his London parish, and £30 for poor relief in Newbury and £20 for the same uses in Reading. In addition, Wybo provided £100 for the care of the poor in his native town of Pittem, Flanders, £30 for the poor of the Dutch community in Calais, and £20 for those in need in Cambrai.[103] And, finally, we must mention in this representative group the substantial bequest of Walter Wilson, probably a farmer of the impost on wines, who left £500 for the care of the aged and maimed poor of London, as well as £40 for the relief of prisoners in the city and in Southwark.[104]

There remain in the later years of this decade of such incredible generosity a number of great donors who require somewhat more extended treatment. Among them was the rich and universally respected merchant tailor, Sir William Craven, whose great generosity towards his native village of Burnsall in Yorkshire will be discussed in a later volume of this study. In all, Craven's charitable dispositions totalled upwards of £8600, of which rather more than £2500 was given for various schemes of poor relief. Shortly before his death, Craven, with his wife, had conveyed to his company for charitable uses city properties possessing a capital worth of at least £2800, the major portion of which, with a capital value of £1920, was dedicated to the relief of twenty-four poor and aged men who had gained the freedom of the city by servitude or patrimony and who had lived as householders in good repute. Seven of these men should have been woollen cloth dressers who were now past labour; as many should have been tailors who could no longer support themselves because of failing eyesight; and the remainder freemen of the company, of whatever trade. Further, this endowment was charged with the payment of an annuity of £4 to the churchwardens of St Antholin's for the provision of coals to the needy of that parish and an identical amount to St Andrew Undershaft for the same purpose. Some years earlier (1595), Craven, with other donors, had subscribed the sum of £336 for the purchase of property, conveyed to the Merchant Taylors' Company as trustees, the income of which was to be employed for the support of five poor widows of the society and one other poor widow, each of whom should receive £3 9s 4d annually for maintenance. And, finally, by the terms of his will, this generous man ordered the outright distribution of £100 to London's poor, as well as £50 to be given to the poor of Tiverton, Devon.[105]

Sir James Lancaster, the famous merchant and explorer, died in the same year as Craven, and his charities were on almost as munificent a scale, though his estate was modest indeed when compared with that of his great contemporary. Lancaster was a native of Basingstoke, Hampshire, and was a principal founder of the charitable institutions of that town and of near-by Kingsclere.[106] His bequests to the poor totalled upwards of £3000, including an outright distribution of £450 to needy but respectable householders in London and £120 in alms to paupers of London and Southwark; an endowment of £400 for the support of poor widows of the Skinners' Company; and an even larger fund of £960 (£48 p.a.) to be used by his company for general charitable purposes. In addition to these large bequests for the benefit of London's poor, Lancaster vested in the Skinners as trustees an annual payment of £30 for the relief of the poor of Basingstoke who should attend the distinctly Puritan lectures he had founded there, as well as a second payment of £15 p.a. to the generality of poor in the town, and £20 p.a. to be distributed as outright alms. And, finally, he created an endowment valued at £200, the income of which should be employed to lend aid to the needy of Kingsclere.[107]

The bequests left for the poor by John Harrison, a rich merchant tailor who died in 1619, were more modest than those we have just been discussing. This benefactor settled on his company properties with a then value of upwards of £400 for the support of the poor in the parish of St Augustine, as well as devising to other trustees sixteen tenements with an estimated worth of £420, the income of which was to be employed for the relief of the poor of the city. His will likewise ordered a distribution of fifty woollen gowns to poor men at the time of his death.[108] A London draper, Robert Buck, who died in 1620, and his wife, Clare, who survived him until 1634, were likewise to make generous provisions for the poor. Buck left £300 in trust to his company to be lent at a moderate rate to three aspiring young drapers, while the £10 annual interest was to be distributed towards the needs of forty poor men and women of the society. He left as well £100 to the parish of St Andrew Undershaft, which his widow in 1623 augmented to a capital of £245 for the purchase of land, the income to be employed for gifts of bread and money for the needy of the parish, with a nominal stipend to the minister who should twice yearly preach sermons of thanksgiving for England's deliverance from the Spanish invasion. This fund the widow later further increased by a bequest of £100. Buck likewise left to his company lands in Kent then valued at £1080, the income of which was to be applied in the amount of £12 p.a. for the care of eight poor widows in the Drapers' almshouse, £19 p.a. to the company for general charitable uses, and the remaining £23 p.a. to be expended in three Essex parishes in rotation for the clothing of their poor, with an indicated preference for those bearing the name of the donor.[109]

We may conclude our discussion of the multitude of benefactions made for the relief of the poor during this remarkable decade with a brief notice of the charities of Sir William Seabright, for many years Town Clerk of London, who died in 1620. Seabright left in all £2245 for various charitable uses, of which not quite half was designated for poor relief in London and in a number of provincial parishes. His will provided that £100 was to be disbursed to eighty poor men at the time of his burial, while £400, it may be estimated, should be employed for general charitable purposes by his executors, and £30 was to be given outright to the needy of four London and Middlesex parishes. Further, this donor left £115 which was to be distributed at once to the poor of twelve parishes in Worcestershire, his native county, and in Staffordshire, while an annual payment of £3 0s 8d for the perpetual relief of their poor was to be made to each of five parishes in Worcestershire and two in Staffordshire.[110]

We have earlier noted that the climax of this remarkable generation of philanthropy occurred in the decade 1621–1630. In this brief interval a total of £103,445 18s was disposed for household relief, of which nearly the whole was in the form of capital gifts. In this decade alone, London donors bestowed more substantial amounts for the care of the poor than was to be accumulated for this use during the whole of our period in any other single county in the realm. There were, as we have noted, 119 London donors during these years who gave capital amounts for this purpose of £100 or more, so great and so general was the outpouring. Therefore, we must be highly selective indeed in commenting even briefly on representative gifts; note the very large foundations of the

period; and then discuss at greater length the enormous and most carefully devised endowment created by a London salter, Henry Smith.

A London haberdasher, Roger Jeston, by his will proved in 1622
vested rich properties in his company for charitable purposes, of which,
in capital terms, £872 was settled for the relief of the poor. Jeston's
will provided for annuities of £15 12s for the maintenance of six aged
poor of his company, of £3 to the poor of Lambeth, of £5 to the needy
of his native parish of Kinver, Staffordshire, while further distributions
of about £20 p.a. were to be made from other properties which were to
be conveyed in trust to his company.[111] At about the same time, Richard
Hale, a grocer, in addition to outright bequests totalling £130 for the
benefit of the poor of London and four Hertfordshire parishes, settled
a loan fund on his company, the income of which was to be used for the
distribution of fuel in two London parishes. Hale's will further provided a yearly rent-charge of £5 each for the benefit of the parishes of
Codicote and Kings Walden, Hertfordshire, of which £4 p.a. was in
each parish to be disbursed to the poor and £1 p.a. to two learned preachers for sermons on two occasions in each year.[112]

Edward Hewlett, possibly a stationer, by bequest in 1622 vested in
the governors of the 'Hospital of the Poor' of St Saviour lands worth
upwards of £400 and subject to a rental of £20 p.a., which they as
trustees should distribute amongst the poor of that Southwark parish.[113]
In 1624 a London lawyer, Christopher Tamworth, conveyed to trustees
£400 of endowment which he directed them to invest in land for the
support of ten poor men and women in the parish of St Botolph
Aldgate.[114] A sternly Puritan mercer, John Dunster, in the next year
left in all £570 for poor relief in numerous communities as a relatively
small fraction of the total of £3420 which he gave for various charitable
uses. Thus his will provided for the distribution of £10 to the poor of
his own parish and £20 for the needy porters of London, £100 each for
the poor of Bristol, Exeter, and Taunton, £140 for the distressed in
his native town of Donyatt, Somerset, as well as substantial amounts in
outright alms for the poor of Ilminster and Chard.[115] Robert Parker, a
merchant tailor, in 1625 bequeathed to his company a fund of £100
under agreement that £5 p.a. would be paid in perpetuity to the poor of
St Antholin parish. Parker likewise remembered his native parish of
Walsall, Staffordshire, by settling on his company £400 on condition
that £20 p.a. should be paid in varying amounts for poor relief in the
hamlets and villages of that then large rural parish. He further granted
to trustees lands in his own village of Great Bloxwich, subject to a life
interest, with the provision that £4 p.a. of the income be distributed to
the poor of the community and that the residue, then amounting to
about £3 p.a., should be treated as a stock for the repair of the local
chapel and its clock.[116]

We may now turn to the very large benefactions made during the decade 1621–1630 for the household relief of the poor. All save one of the donors providing capital of more than £800 for this purpose in these years were great merchants, members of the mercantile elite of the city. There were fourteen donors in this group, though we shall limit our attention to the seven who seem most representative and important.

The greatest of these benefactors, after Henry Smith, who stands alone,[117] was without doubt John Kendrick, a draper and a native of Reading, who died in 1624. In Fuller's eloquent words, 'His charities began at his kindred; proceeded to his friends and servants (to whom he left large legacies); concluded with the poor, on whom he bestowed above twenty thousand pounds'. Fuller does somewhat exaggerate Kendrick's immense generosity, since the full measure of his charities seems to have been £18,695, of which £1685 will be noted now as having been dedicated to direct household relief. A wise and perceptive man, Kendrick was far more interested in the rehabilitation of the poor than in their direct support,[118] though it may be said that upwards of £16,000 of his great foundation was in a true sense devoted either to the care or to the cure of poverty. Kendrick's distributions were appointed in his will, which began with his eloquent testament of faith: 'I John Kendricke ... draper ... commend and commit my soule to Almighty God, my creator, trusting most assuredly to be saved by the death, passion, and onely merits of Jesus Christ, my Sauiour and Redeemer'. Though he had lived modestly and quietly, never holding high public or company office, Kendrick's great bequests made him a famous man, and his will was printed as a public document in pamphlet form in 1625.[119] The consequence was that his generosity and his great care in the ordering of his bequests came to have added weight in the framing of the noble traditions of the rich and responsible class of which he was an exemplar.

Kendrick's benefactions for the outright relief of the poor may be briefly treated. A portion of a large endowment for various charitable uses which he lodged in the Drapers' Company was charged with the payment of £30 p.a. for the relief of the poor of London and £3 p.a. for the care of the poor of the company, these payments representing a capital worth of £660. Kendrick likewise left outright £25 to be disbursed among the 'poor religious men' of London as alms. But his largest gift for this use was a charge on £1000 of the huge gift of £7500 given in trust to the mayor and burgesses of Reading, with which lands to the value of £50 p.a. were to be purchased and the income distributed by the overseers to the poor of that town, providing always that this stipend was 'an addition and clear increase' in the rates which had normally to be assessed for their sustenance.[120]

The impact of Kendrick's great charity on the minds and consciences of his contemporaries in the livery companies must have been significantly strengthened in the next year (1625) when Richard Fishborne died leaving almost £10,000 to charitable uses, with the result that still another modest and relatively inconspicuous merchant was extolled in a funeral sermon which was printed in 1626 and which, the many subsequent citations would suggest, enjoyed a wide circulation.[121] Fishborne was a native of Huntingdonshire, being 'cut out of no mean quary, being a gentleman by extraction'. He became a mercer, entering the service of Sir Baptist Hicks,[122] and later amassed a considerable fortune in trade. Nathaniel Shute, in his funeral sermon, after an almost classically intricate wrestling with his text (*Nehem.* 13, 14), tells us that Fishborne professed 'euen on his death bed where euery man speakes, with an unmasked conscience, that to his knowledge, he had not gotten any part of his goods iniustly'. A charitable man all his life, 'he was not drie-handed to some hospitals in priuate before his death, but blessed those dead bones with his charitie . . . charitable in publicke, and that not in handfulls, but in sheaues'.[123] Warming to his task after recounting Fishborne's great charities, Shute tells us that 'as his stomacke euer kicked against Poperie, so was hee a true wouen Protestant', a lustre to his city, 'a glory to his company, a beautie to the merchants . . . a credit to the place where he liued . . . a patrone of the poore . . . the noblest, louingest, and faithfullest friend that euer poore man had . . . a second Nehemiah'.[124] Surely such preaching before the Mercers' Company, soon to be spread abroad in published form, armed the undoubted greatness of Fishborne's charity with double strength. No man could possibly have heard it or have read it without thinking of his own funeral, of his own spiritual credit, and of the true immortality which good works confer on God's children.[125]

Shute, and Fuller follows him, found a slightly more impressive total (£10,726 13s 4d) than the £9107 10s which is our reckoning of the immense sum this quiet mercer disposed for charity. Of this total, £3470 was dedicated either to the relief of the poor or to general charitable uses which comprehended the needs of the poor. Thus Fishborne charged an endowment vested with the Mercers with an annual payment of £20, representing a capital worth of £400, for the relief of the poor in the parish of St Bartholomew Exchange, this stipend to be in addition to the amounts normally collected there for the care of the poor, while settling as well £1000, the income of which should be employed for clothing the poor of his own company. In addition, Fishborne left to the Mercers, as trustees, £2000 for the benefit of his native county, Huntingdonshire, the income of which was to be employed for general charitable purposes there at the discretion of the trustees, but with the suggestion that the endowment of an almshouse or grammar school, the maintenance of a lectureship, or the care of the poor would best meet the wishes of the testator.[126] And, finally, Fishborne left £20 with which clothing was to be supplied to the desperately poor of certain London parishes and £50 for the relief of the poor in Coxwell, Essex.[127]

Still another great benefactor died in 1625. Sir Thomas Smith, the son of Customer Smith and Alice, the daughter of the famous Sir Andrew Judd, was a skinner and likewise one of the leading colonial venturers of his age. Smith left in all £4695 to various charities, including, as we shall note elsewhere, a large addition to the endowment of Judd's grammar-school foundation at Tonbridge, Kent, and the establishment of a scholarship endowment in its favour with a capital of £1420. Smith also left properties then valued at £1200 on trust with the Skinners' Company for the relief of the poor in Tonbridge and four other Kentish communities, as well as an additional sum, if we may capitalize the amount, of £600 for the same purposes from what proved to be a large residue in the estate. Moreover, Smith provided in another trust capital valued at £104 for the relief of the poor in Dover and £320 for general charitable uses there. In London, Smith left £100 outright for the clothing of the poor, £50 for the needy of the East India Company, £500 for the relief of those members of the Muscovy Company who had sustained trading losses, and £133 to the Skinners' Company for the augmentation of its charities. In all, then, it appears that this enlightened and extremely generous man had vested £2523 of capital in various trusts for the care of the poor in London and in his native county of Kent.[128]

The poor likewise benefited greatly under the terms of the will of Lancelot Andrews, who, it should be remembered, was the son of a London merchant and who had received his early education in the Merchant Taylors' School. Andrews by gift and bequest left in all £9400 for various charitable uses, including £2400 for the direct relief of poor men and women. He gave outright £100 each to the parishes of St Giles Cripplegate and St Luke Finsbury for the care of their needy, as well as £200 to be distributed to poor maidservants of good reputation. But his principal benefaction for the poor is to be found in the charitable trust created by a codicil to his will, proved in 1627, under which £4000 was vested in trustees for the purchase of lands which would produce an annual income of £200. Half this substantial stipend was, as we shall later note, dedicated to experiments in social rehabilitation, while the other half was to be paid out for the relief of poor and aged persons and for the sustenance of poor widows in numerous parishes in London and Southwark in which Andrews was particularly interested by personal association or because of his knowledge of pressing need.[129]

Sir Thomas Bennett, a renowned mercer who had served as lord mayor in 1603–1604, on his death in 1627 left a substantial and carefully disposed sum for poor relief, being 'desirous to leave some memorial of his thankfulnes to God'. The rectory and church of Kirton, Lincolnshire, with the advowson, were left to the Mercers' Company for charitable uses, the property possessing a capital value of about £3000, subject only to an annual rental to the Crown of £29. Bennett provided that £20 p.a. should be employed for the full relief of four of the poor of his company, £14 p.a. for the clothing of 'poor and naked men, women, and children, wandering in London, that have no dwelling', and that £20 p.a. should be vested in the municipal authorities of Wallingford, Berkshire, his birthplace, for the care of poor and aged persons there.[130] In the following year (1628) Samuel Middlemore, a clothworker, bequeathed £800 to his company on trust, the income to be disposed for the clothing of twenty poor men and women of his parish, St Clement Eastcheap, and for the distribution of fuel to these pensioners as well as to the oldest poor of the parish.[131]

We may fittingly conclude our notice of the great benefactions provided for the poor during this remarkable decade by a brief comment on the bequests of that very rich merchant, Baptist Hicks, Viscount Campden, who died in 1629 in his seventy-ninth year. Hicks, who gave or bequeathed more than £7000 to a variety of charitable purposes, left £200 to be invested by the churchwardens of Kensington, the income to be employed for the relief of the worthy poor of that town. In addition, his will conveyed to the corporation of the town of Tewkesbury, near which his father had been born, certain properties in Wales then worth approximately £1600, with the provision that half the income should be disbursed for the relief of the poor of the community and its outlying precincts, while the remainder should be used to augment the stipend of 'an able and sufficient preacher' in the parish, it being expressly the intention of the donor that the parishioners should not in consequence withdraw their own 'good and charitable benevolence' from the support of their minister.[132]

We have reserved for more detailed treatment our discussion of the charitable foundation created by a salter, Henry Smith, who was not only the greatest donor in this remarkable decade but who, by the great care which he exercised in the creation of his trust and in the ordering of its distribution, was profoundly to influence later merchant philanthropists in the settlement of their properties on trustees. Smith conveyed to trustees by gift and bequest the huge total of £63,800 for general charitable uses, all of which had as its central objective the relief of poor men and their social rehabilitation. This vast sum looms large even when it is considered within the scale of the benefactions of the mercantile elite of London and rears itself as a veritable charitable monadnock when we compare it with the totals accumulated during the whole of our long period for the care of the poor in such rich and generous counties even as Kent or Norfolk. Indeed, in reflecting on it even in our own century we share something of the awe of the always trenchant Thomas Fuller, who, in commenting on this immense benefaction, says that just as many simple inland people may credit the whale as a fable, 'in like manner, being now to relate the bounty of this worthy person, I am afraid that our infidel age will not give credit thereunto', regarding it 'rather a romance or fiction than a thing really performed, because of the prodigious greatness thereof'.[133]

Nor do we know much regarding the life of this great but modest man, whose personality eluded even his contemporary, Thomas Fuller, that greatest of all writers of 'characters'. Smith was born in Wandsworth, Surrey, probably in 1548, the son of humble and obscure parents. He seems to have been apprenticed to a London silversmith at an early age and to have carried on that trade for some years, though well before the close of the Elizabethan era he was at least a moderately rich man who was laying the basis for a great fortune in general trade and in almost uniformly successful real-estate speculation. When in 1608 he was chosen alderman for Farringdon Without, he was listed as a member of the Salters' Company, though, as was so often the case, this now eminently successful merchant carried on his activities as an entrepreneur and speculator quite independently of his livery.[134] Smith was married, though childless, and after the death of his wife in *ca.* 1605 evidently began to consider leaving his rapidly growing fortune to charitable uses. Boldly experimenting thenceforward, he slowly fabricated the great trust mechanism to which the bulk of his wealth was disposed on his death, at an advanced age, in 1626. Smith died in St Olave Silver Street, though there is no evidence that he ever served prominently in the affairs of this parish. This is the sum of our certain knowledge of the life of this great donor, who, it will be observed, for all his wealth was able to avoid office in his company as well as the burdens and dignities of high civic responsibility. The essence of the man is to be found in his works of charity rather than in his career.[135]

Henry Smith's charities may be divided into three units in which he was clearly seeking by somewhat different trust devices to accomplish the one purpose of relieving and assisting the poor by various schemes of social rehabilitation. The first of these was developed during his lifetime, when he gave outright £1000 of capital to each of six Surrey towns, Kingston, Croydon, Guildford, Farnham, Dorking, and Godalming, with an indication that the gift made first to Kingston was to serve as a model of administration. Each of these capital sums was conveyed to the municipal authorities of these market towns, subject only to a life income for the donor, with the stipulation that the income be employed 'for the relief, maintenance, and setting on work of the poor, and for the education of the poor . . . in some good and Christian course of life'.

The deed of gift carefully specified that the income thus gained must be regarded as an addition to sums already in hand or to be raised by taxation for poor relief. The prudent donor further prescribed that the provisions governing the administration of the trust should be suitably engrossed and conspicuously hung in the parish church of each of the towns thus favoured so 'the poor may see it' and that the Archbishop of Canterbury should enjoy full powers to intervene at his own discretion in order to secure the full performance of the trust.[136]

The second unit of charities was established by will, the donor conveying to trustees endowments for a variety of uses under conditions separating these charities from those included in his great trust. It seems probable that this decision was made because of the varied purposes contemplated and because all save £1000 of the total capital of £7450 vested in these charities was derived from debts owed to the donor. Smith clearly wished to arm his executors with particularly impressive sanctions in order to secure the full collection of these assets. This group of charities included a bequest of £100 to be distributed outright in alms for the poor, £100 as a loan fund for needy persons, £150 for the endowment of a modest fellowship in Cambridge University, £500 for general charitable uses in his native parish of Wandsworth, £1000 as a charitable endowment for Reigate, Surrey, and an addition of £1000 to the *corpus* of the gift made in 1624 to Croydon. Moreover, Smith ordered the distribution of £1000 as endowment for general charitable uses in the town of Richmond (Surrey), £500 for Hartlepool (Durham), £600 for Fetcham (Surrey); and he vested in trustees a total of £2500 for the care of the poor and other charitable uses, the income to be distributed to a considerable number of named parishes, principally in Surrey.

The substantial charitable dispositions comprehended in these first two units, as has been indicated, lie outside the great charitable trust in which Smith was to lodge the bulk of his fortune and the framing of which we can see evolving during the final years of his life. He was certainly purchasing properties in London and Sussex as early as 1615 which he intended as charitable endowments and during the next two years appears to have begun the gradual liquidation of his business holdings with a view towards simplifying the structure of his assets. In 1620 he conveyed to seven trustees all his real property in London, Middlesex, and Sussex, while by a separate deed of gift he vested all his personalty, and certain cash sums, for charitable uses to be determined by his trustees, subject only to a life income of £500 p.a. and the retention of a right of revocation. The trustees named in the instrument were the Puritan Earl of Essex, the Earl of Dorset (d. 1624), Sir Edward Francis, John Middleton, William Wingfield, Sir George Whitmore, a haberdasher who was to serve as lord mayor in 1631, and Richard Amherst, an able serjeant-at-law, who seems at this time to have been Smith's legal adviser.

Smith was not, however, content with the trust as first vested and during the months following on its institution employed agents to report on parishes all over England which stood in need of aid, while at the same time seeking to define more explicitly the purposes to which he wished his fortune to be devoted. Further, the Earl of Dorset having died in 1624 deeply in Smith's debt, the shrewd and pertinacious merchant wished for a season to regain control of the trusteed properties, particularly since he now had in mind important modifications of the original instrument. Smith accordingly filed a bill in Chancery in which he petitioned for the return of the title to the properties for his lifetime and complained that four of his trustees, Dorset aside, were in his debt to the huge total of £16,000. The Lord Keeper Coventry ordered control of the endowment returned to Smith for his lifetime, granted the donor's request that he be permitted to define by will the charitable uses intended, required the trustees indebted to Smith at once to secure their obligations, and acceded to the petitioner's request that when the number of trustees, now by revision fixed at thirteen, should fall to six, the full number should be restored by appointment by the Archbishop of Canterbury or the Lord Keeper. In 1626 Smith conveyed the properties expressly vested six years earlier, together with other assets, to his trustees, with the injunction that, when the residue of his estate should fall in by will, the moneys were, whenever possible, to be invested in units of about £1000 for the purchase of manors which would yield an income of as near £66 13s 4d as could be arranged, for the benefit of the charitable uses which he now undertook to define. The whole of the income of the trust, save as his will might otherwise direct, was to be distributed by the trustees to designated parishes in which the churchwardens were to employ the income for the general relief of the aged poor and the infirm, the assistance of married persons burdened with large families, the care of poor orphans, the apprenticing of the children of poor men, the education of poor children, and the advancement of schemes for setting the poor on useful work. It was further provided that no benefits should be paid to vagrants and unsettled persons, while men and women of poor character should likewise be excluded from any assistance. The carefully drawn instrument further provided that the churchwardens in each favoured parish were to meet monthly to consider the needs of the poor of their community, that public notice of such meetings be given, and that the pertinent portions of the deed of gift be conspicuously posted in each parish.

Shortly afterwards, Smith drew his will, in which the whole of his remaining fortune, aside from modest personal and family bequests, was left to his trustees to complete the *corpus* of this great foundation.

He asked his trustees to convey the whole of the fund to the Governors of Christ's Hospital in mortmain for them to administer in accordance with the deed of trust and, that failing, to undertake the direct administration under the instructions which he had already so carefully set forward. As Smith evidently felt they might, the Governors of Christ's Hospital declined to assume responsibility for such an immense and extra-mural burden, with the result that the trustees as named by Smith found themselves vested with control. Of the original trustees, three were drawn from the nobility, three were distinguished lawyers, six were eminent London merchants, and one, Robert Henn, was a former servant and assistant to Smith. The whole amount with which the trustees were charged may with quite close accuracy be set at £50,300, of which £15,000 comprised secured debts due to Smith. Most of the remaining assets consisted of shrewdly purchased and diversified properties, including London and suburban lands, the great manor of Knole in Kent, estates in Surrey, extensive lands in Sussex and Gloucestershire, and farms in Hampshire.

Smith's will provided that of the capital left to the trustees, £10,000 should be used for the purchase of impropriations and treated as endowment for the augmentation of the stipends and the maintenance of godly preachers and the furtherance of knowledge and religion throughout the realm. Also, £1000 was to be separately invested as an endowment the income of which was to be employed for the relief of 'poor captives being slaves under the Turkish pirates' or to secure their ransom.[137] The whole of the remainder, representing a then capital worth of £39,300, was dedicated, in accordance with the careful stipulations of the original deed of trust and the prescriptions of the will, to the care and rehabilitation of the poor on a truly national basis. The estate was large and the instructions left to the trustees at once intricate and difficult, with the result that it was not until 1641 that all the resources had been gathered and the remainder invested in seventeen parcels, mostly large manors, which at that date possessed an income of £2617 p.a., or a capital worth of £57,750, considerable increases in value already having taken place.[138] The parish distributions were spread over 219 communities in twenty-three counties in England and Wales in amounts ranging from £1 p.a. for nine thinly populated rural parishes in Surrey to stipends of £15 p.a. in twenty-nine urban parishes in various counties. Rather more than half (134) of all the parishes benefiting were in Smith's native county of Surrey, to which £835 p.a., or 48 per cent, of the original available income for parish use was assigned. This very properly sentimental interest aside, the remaining distributions were ordered in the other eighty-five parishes with an intelligent consideration for need and opportunity. Thus there were thirteen parishes favoured in Sussex, to which £138 p.a. was assigned; nine heavily populated industrial parishes in London benefited from a distribution of £122 p.a.; twelve in Hampshire received £80 p.a.; six in Durham £70 p.a.; and three in Worcestershire were allocated a total of £62 p.a. The remaining counties favoured under this remarkable trust received amounts ranging from £4 p.a. (Bedfordshire) to £57 6s 8d p.a. (Essex).[139]

Though not the largest of the charitable trusts established by private benefactors in England during our period, Henry Smith's foundation was the most important and certainly the most interesting. It is evident that the trust was the creation of a careful and thoughtful man who experimented as he proceeded. In the perfecting of his grand design, he employed the assistance of the best legal minds of his age, including the Lord Keeper (Coventry), whose revocation perhaps signified better public policy than law, and one of the ablest of the judges of his generation, Sir George Croke, who also consented to serve as one of Smith's trustees. The final structure of the great social institution created by Smith was tightly articulated, its aims were well and sensibly defined, and its purposes were set with true prescience against the most urgent of English needs at least over the next three centuries; and that is perhaps a sufficient measure for men's aspirations for their society. Prudent controls and interventions had been established, ranging from that exercised by the Archbishop of Canterbury or the Lord Keeper, whose power of appointment of feoffees ensured the quality and responsibility of administration, to the provisions so sensibly set forth for the outlay of the stipends in favoured parishes where, under pain of withdrawal of benefits, the churchwardens must perform their ultimately critical responsibilities in full view of their parishes while creating a record which was subject to the occasional audit of the agents of the trust. Smith's great trust, or more accurately the social institution which he had created, as we shall elsewhere observe in detail, lifted scores of parishes out of the 'area of blight' into the 'area of opportunity' in all those counties to which year after year, generation after generation, its funds were to flow in a fruitful and life-giving stream. Henry Smith, modest as he was, was one of the founders of modern England.[139a]

There was a slackening of the flow of funds into the various institutions which Londoners were creating for the amelioration of poverty in the next decade, 1631–1640, as the unsettlement now chronic in political life began to exercise its disturbing effect on the realm. At the same time, it must be remarked that the £54,312 12s provided during these years for the relief of poverty was a huge sum when compared with any save the almost prodigal amounts which London generosity had bestowed during the two preceding decades. It should likewise be borne in mind that this great total, and more than 96 per cent of the amount was capital, was an addition to the now massive accumulations with which English society had strengthened its institutions in a determined effort to deal courageously with a social ill which had afflicted the western society from the dawn of its history. There is also interesting evidence that in this decade there was a considerable broadening of the base of substantial giving for poor relief, the roster of the sixty-seven donors contributing £100 or more of capital funds for this purpose having included a fair number of tradesmen and not a few members of the professional classes, as well as the solid core of merchants who, as always, bore the chief burden of responsibility for the social conscience of the city. We must limit our comment first to a sampling of benefactions ranging from £300 to £800 for various schemes of household relief and then note very briefly the contribution of the really large merchant donors of this decade.

The son of a former lord mayor, Ambrose Bennett, in 1631, in addition to an outright bequest of £10 for the poor of four London parishes and an equal amount for the poor of Leicester, charged certain of his lands in Surrey with annual payments of £9 for the relief of the poor of St Bennet Fink in London, £9 p.a. to the poor of 'Redrith' [Rotherhithe], Surrey, £8 p.a. to Waterstock, Oxfordshire, and £1 p.a. to Calverton, Buckinghamshire, for the same purpose.[140] In the same year, a London salter, Barnard Hyde, among charitable bequests totalling £1440, left provisions for the poor which required an outlay of capital to the value of £490. Hyde vested in his company endowments which would secure the payment of £5 p.a. to the poor of St Dunstan in the East, £1 p.a. to the needy of Little Ilford, Essex, and £5 p.a. to ten of the poor of the Salters' Company. In addition, his will prescribed a very interesting and certainly complicated plan under which £13 10s p.a., representing the income on £270 of stock, would be paid to the churchwardens of three London parishes in sums of 5s each for fifty-four poor widows or maids, the payments to be made to eighteen such persons in each parish. A scheme of rotation was also laid down over a ten-year cycle, with the result that thirty city parishes in all were to receive at least occasional benefit from the income thus provided.[141]

Luke Jackson, a girdler and a native of Thornton, Leicestershire, by his will in 1631 bequeathed £15 outright to the poor of his company, £5 to the poor of his own parish, and £20 to needy householders of London generally. He established as well a trust with a capital worth of about £400, from the income of which £2 p.a. each was to be paid to the ministers of the churches at Nottingham (St Peter) and Thornton, Leicestershire, for two annual sermons of thanksgiving for England's deliverance from the Armada and the Gunpowder Plot, while the residue of the income was to be distributed two-thirds to Nottingham and one-third to Thornton for the relief of their poor householders.[142] More modest was the bequest of Sir Edward Barkham, a draper and former lord mayor, who by his will proved in 1634 provided in all £290 7s for the care of the poor, including an endowment to secure the annual payment of £6 13s 4d to the oldest and poorest of his company and of £6 4s for the needy of two London parishes and one in Middlesex, as well as outright gifts of £5 to the destitute of St Lawrence Jewry and £25 for the poor of five Norfolk villages.[143] One more relatively modest bequest from these years may be mentioned, this being the endowment valued at £320 which was established by Henry Loft, a yeoman of Enfield, in order to secure the payment of £12 p.a. for the support of six poor widows of his parish and of £4 p.a. to provide clothing for the poor.[144]

A very rich clothworker, Sir Ralph Freeman, in 1634 made careful provision for an elaborate schedule of charitable uses, to which he left £5810, including a total of £450 for poor relief. Freeman gave £50 outright to the poor of his parish of St Michael Cornhill, as well as an annual income of £20, derived from a loan fund established with the Merchant Adventurers, which was to be distributed £10 p.a. to the poor of the Clothworkers' Company, £5 p.a. to the needy of his own parish, and £5 p.a. to a Hertfordshire parish in which he had extensive landholdings.[145] An humbler member of the same company, Samuel Lese, in the same year bequeathed to the Clothworkers houses and lands, with certain other assets, possessing a total capital worth of approximately £520, the income of which, save for a small payment for an annual sermon, was to be employed for the relief of the poor and aged men and women of his fraternity.[146]

We are told by Fuller that the bequests and gifts made to the poor by Thomas Curzon, an armourer who died in 1636, were inspired by a strange accident. Curzon had lent a rusty musket to an actor. The gun, which was thought not to be loaded, was discharged upon the stage, killing a spectator, to the great grief of Curzon, who resolved to settle his whole estate for the relief of the poor and unfortunate. Fuller tells us further that the endowment was built up slowly, Curzon delivering sums that came to hand to the Court of Aldermen for safe keeping and investment in the later years of his life. The whole amount left, and it was all for poor relief, possessed a capital value of £569, with the annual income payable to the poor of the Armourers' Company and for the maintenance and clothing of the poor of the donor's parish of St Botolph Bishopsgate.[147]

Numerous benefactions for the poor established in 1637 by donors of various social strata may be briefly noted. Thomas Evans, a haberdasher, in that year bequeathed £25 outright to the poor of London as well as establishing an endowment of £600, the income of which was to be disposed for the care of the poor of his native parish of Charlbury, Oxfordshire.[148] Ellen Gulston, the widow of a well-known physician, vested the substantial sum of £600 in the Merchant Taylors' Company under an agreement by which the company undertook to pay £30 p.a. in perpetuity for the relief of poor widows in all parts of London.[149] In the same year, William Platt, a member of a most gifted family, charged the great benefaction which he had just made to St John's College, Cambridge, with a payment of £14 p.a. for the relief of the poor of St Pancras and £6 p.a. for the care of the needy in the parish of Hornsey.[150]

The bequests of three women donors, also of quite differing social status, made during the closing years of the decade for the care of the poor may also be mentioned. In 1638 a merchant's widow, Elizabeth Juxon, established an endowment of £300, of which £200 was dedicated to poor relief and the remainder to increasing the stipend of the minister in the parish of St Michael Paternoster.[151] In the same year, Joyce Featley, the wife of an irascible but brilliant clergyman, left £340 to be disposed for general charitable uses, as well as £4 p.a. to her parish for an annual sermon and the relief of its poor.[152] Just a year later, Frances Stuart, widow of the Duke of Lennox, died bequeathing a total of £480 in outright alms for the poor, including £100 to the poor of Holborn, £60 to three London parishes, £100 to Westminster, £200 to poor men and women at her funeral, and small legacies for the poor of two parishes in Hampshire.[153]

Mark Howse [Hawes], an embroiderer, died in 1639, completing by will the foundation of a substantial charity which he had instituted by deeds of gift in 1629 and 1633. A total of £646 13s was vested by Hawes in his company as trustee, of which capital valued at £560 was to be employed for the support of the poor in his parish of St Thomas the Apostle and of needy artisans connected with his company, while the remainder was dedicated to company uses and for putting forth annually as apprentices or servants two poor girls who had been cared for in Bridewell for at least two years past.[154] A haberdasher and former lord mayor, Sir Richard Fenn [Venn] on his death in the same year, 1639, left £20 outright for the needs of the poor as well as landed property in West Ham, Essex, valued at about £100, the profits of which were to be distributed each Sunday in bread for the poor of the parish, and an endowment valued at £200 for the relief of the poor of Wotton-under-Edge, Gloucestershire, his birthplace.[155] Sir John Hanbury, a merchant tailor, in the same year left in trust to his company £500 for the purchase of lands, the income to be applied for the relief of poor families in Feckenham and Hanbury, Worcestershire, he having been a native of the latter parish;[156] while in the closing year of the decade a vintner, Anthony Bailey, by will provided rent-charges of £4 p.a. each for five London parishes, representing a capital worth of perhaps £400.[157]

The decade under review differs interestingly from the two just preceding it in that there was no single donor who created a huge endowment for the benefit of the poor. None the less, there were a number of very substantial gifts and bequests made for this purpose, a few of which may be noted. Thus in 1631 Richard Crashaw, a goldsmith, among charitable contributions totalling £4576, left £1526 for a variety of relief plans. To the seven parishes in his ward he bequeathed £350 in outright alms, as well as £150 additional for his own parish of St Bartholomew Exchange in doles and in 'good cheese' for its poor. Crashaw left £400 to the poor of his company and £100 outright to the needy householders of 'Marton' [Markeaton] and Mackworth, Derbyshire. Finally, his most substantial benefaction was the settling of an endowment with a capital worth of £860 to secure the payment of £15 p.a. to the needy householders of Derby and £28 p.a. to such persons to Markeaton and Mackworth.[158] In the same year Henry Fryer, a London lawyer, vested in trustees extensive London properties and a manor in Cambridgeshire then valued at upwards of £2000, the income of which, to the extent of £100 p.a., was to be devoted to the relief of poor families in the parishes of St Botolph Aldgate, Chiswick (Middlesex) and Harlton (Cambridgeshire), while by a further provision an additional stipend of £10 p.a. was settled on twenty poor widows of St Botolph Aldgate.[159]

Sir Hugh Middleton, the famous merchant and projector, on his death in 1631 bequeathed from his straitened fortune £20 to the poor of his birthplace (Henllan) in North Wales, £10 to the poor of Denbigh, and £5 to Amwell, Hertfordshire, as well as leaving one share of the stock of the New River Company, which we have most uncertainly estimated as having a then value of £600, for the relief of the poor of the Goldsmiths' Company.[160] Shortly afterwards, in 1633, a London skinner, John Meredith, who was also a native of Wales, left in all £910 for the care of the poor, including weekly stipends of 15s each to three poor men and two poor women of his company, and annuities for the relief of poor householders in the parishes of St Sepulchre and St Bartholomew the Less.[161]

One of the most generous of the many substantial donors to the poor in the decade was Sir John Fenner, whose will was proved in early 1634. Fenner vested in the churchwardens of the parish of Isleworth for the relief of the poor property with an estimated worth of £200, as well as funds totalling £310 for eight London parishes as a perpetual stock, the income to be employed to purchase fuel in slack seasons for distribution to their poor during the winter. To these bequests was added a large endowment of £2200 which should annually provide an income of £110, to be distributed for the benefit of ten parishes in London and Southwark. Of this income, £60 p.a. was to be employed for the annual distribution of Bibles 'of the canonical scripture only, of the smallest volume, well printed on good paper, and handsomely bound' to deserving young persons not themselves able to purchase Bibles,

while the remaining £50 p.a. was to be given to poor and sick persons
in the favoured parishes.[162]

Though Lady Katherine Conway was the widow of a nobleman and
a great officer of state, it seems evident that most of the large total,
£2420, which she left for various charitable causes was derived from
her merchant father and her first husband, a London grocer. Lady
Conway by will disposed £30 outright in alms for the poor of London
and gave £300 to the Dutch church of London for the care of the poor
of their congregation. She left as well annuities possessing a capital
worth of £900, the Grocers being her trustees, to secure annual payments
of £5 to the needy of Luddington, Warwickshire, and of £10 to the poor
of Acton (Kensington) parish, where she had resided. Her will further
provided that the Grocers should annually pay £10 to Acton for the
care of the aged and impotent of the parish, the same amount for poor
relief in St Dunstan in the East, and still another payment of £10 for
the care of poor widows of the Grocers' Company.[163] In the same year
(1639) a Scottish lawyer, Robert Johnstone, one of the 'swarm of
Scots' who had followed the Stuarts south, died leaving great charitable
bequests totalling about £6000. Johnstone's concern was principally
centred on his native country, though he vested capital of £100 to secure
an annual payment for the relief of the poor in one London parish. His
will provided as well for the creation of an endowment of 'ane ...
thousand pund starling ... to imploy the saide sume in ane stock or
morgadge of land' towards the perpetual relief of the poor of his native
city of Edinburgh.[164]

We may fittingly conclude our discussion of the benefactions for the
poor established in this generous decade with the thoughtful dispositions made over a period of years by Mary Paradine, the wife of a
London haberdasher and the sister of two other women donors who gave
liberally for poor relief. In 1628 she vested £100 in the Embroiderers'
Company under agreement that they should annually disburse £6
among their poor and infirm. Over the next twelve years a series of endowments were established by this persistently generous woman.
Thus £100 was enfeoffed for the poor of St Andrew Holborn, the same
amount for St Leonard Shoreditch, and so on until six London parishes
were assisted with such endowments. In 1631 she gave to the municipal
authorities of London a further £400 with which lands were to be purchased to provide an annual stipend of £6 for the relief of the poor in
the town of Bedford, the remainder to be used for the clothing of poor
widows in the almshouse founded by David Smith, her father. Finally,
Mary Paradine settled £300 on the Haberdashers to secure the relief
of the poor of that company and of a London parish, as well as to provide care for four poor preachers. This woman, like so many sprung
from the now firmly entrenched merchant aristocracy, had most evi-

dently absorbed both the traditions and the aspirations of the class of which she was truly a member.[165]

The years of civil war and political experimentation by no means brought to an end the great flow of benefactions for the relief of the poor. There is evidence in many wills that the occasional and sometimes severe unemployment created by the war impelled men to make as generous provision as they found possible for the relief of poverty even during these two decades when their own fortunes were imperilled by the risks of war or diminished by the heavy weight of taxation borne by the merchant class of London. During these years the impressive total of £78,626 12s was provided by London donors for the household relief of the poor and for general charitable uses, representing an average flow of nearly £4000 p.a. for these purposes in this interval. It is, in fact, only during the desperately unsettled years 1643–1646 that the amounts provided for these uses fell sharply below this remarkably high level of contributions for poor relief. The benefactions of these two decades, difficult and tragic as they were, were in point of fact considerably more substantial than in any similar period in London's history prior to 1611, when for a generation the flood gates of charity were opened.

In dealing with this final interval it might be well to note first at least a sampling of the relatively small gifts for poor relief, heretofore ignored save as they have been incorporated in the totals we have given. We shall first comment on some of these made in 1643, when charities of all kinds were most sharply diminished, and then in 1657, when the firm and skilful hand of Oliver Cromwell had once more given the nation a most welcome stability. It will be observed that these gifts were, with few exceptions, for outright distribution, while, as we have so frequently stressed, the larger benefactions of this and earlier periods were almost invariably capital amounts. It will be noted as well that even these, for London, very small sums of £40 or less include amazingly few benefactions from the artisans or urban poor, classes which, as we have indicated, were to bear no more than a nominal share of the immense social burdens undertaken by the mercantile aristocracy of the city.[166]

Among these smaller, yet in total impressive, contributions to the needs of the poor made in 1643 was the bequest of Robert Awnsham of £40 for the relief of needy householders in two Middlesex parishes.[167] The widow of a gentleman, Barbara Barron, gave £4 in doles for St Martin-in-the-Fields,[168] while Elizabeth Benbowe, a leatherseller's wife, left £20 outright to the poor of London, £2 in doles at her burial, and £10 to the poor of St Leonard Shoreditch, as well as bequests to the destitute of two Kentish parishes.[169] Richard Benefield, of uncertain social status, gave £10 to be added to capital funds available for poor relief in St Giles Cripplegate;[170] a clergyman, Edward Bewsy, of St

Olave Silver Street, bequeathed £4 for distribution in three Essex parishes;[171] and a draper, Thomas Britten, provided £30 in capital for two Suffolk parishes, as well as leaving £10 for his own parish of All-hallows Lombard Street.[172] A tallow chandler bequeathed £2 to the poor of St Mary at Hill,[173] and a gentleman, William Butcher, gave £1 in doles for his Westminster parish.[174] The poor of St Stephen Coleman Street were left £5 by Elizabeth Clarke, a surgeon's widow, who also left £8 to two Kentish parishes,[175] while St Mary Aldermary benefited from the modest bequest of £2 left by a grocer, Robert Edwards.[176] A widow, Anne Goldsmith, left £20 to the poor of her native parish in Hertfordshire as well as £12 to twelve poor women in St Alban Wood Street 'that I used to give alms to',[177] while still other widows were leaving £3 to the poor of Croydon, Surrey,[178] and £10 to the poor of Bow Brickhill, Buckinghamshire.[179] A saddler left £2 to the poor of St Martin-in-the-Fields;[180] an apothecary £3 to St Dionis Backchurch as well as £6 to his native parish in Suffolk;[181] a tailor gave £5 to the needy of St Bride;[182] and Richard Hunt, a confectioner turned soldier, £36 13s 4d to the relief of the poor of St Mary Wool-church.[183]

We must content ourselves with an even more limited sampling of the lesser benefactions for the relief of the poor made in 1657, since in that year, when confidence and stability had been in a measure restored, there were 290 contributions for this purpose of £40 or less. It will be ob-served that in 1657 as in 1643 an amazing proportion even of these relatively humble donors left bequests for parishes in counties other than Middlesex, suggesting that much of the population of the city, as we know to be the case with the merchant class, was not London born. London was in this era truly a devourer of men.

Elizabeth Ager, a widow, by her will left £3 to her London parish as well as a total of £5 for the relief of the poor in two parishes in her native county of Shropshire.[184] A well-to-do cordwainer, Robert Allen, left £2 to the poor of St Bartholomew the Great;[185] a haberdasher left £1 to the poor of St Mary Somerset;[186] and Isabel Arnold, a widow, bequeathed £5 for poor relief in St Martin-in-the-Fields.[187] The poor of St Michael Bassishaw benefited by a bequest of £2 10s from Thomas Atkins, a merchant tailor,[188] and of £3 from Thomas Barney, a member of the same livery.[189] A London carpenter, Thomas Atkinson, left 5s to the poor of a Middlesex parish,[190] a Stepney sea captain £10 to those of his parish;[191] and a clergyman, Samuel Bamford, £6 to the poor of various London parishes and a few of his best books to Emmanuel College, Cambridge.[192] A widow, Hester Blackborow, bequeathed £1 to the needy of her London parish and the same amount to those of Mucking, Essex;[193] a widow, Joan Bradley, gave £20 to the poor of St Leonard Shoreditch;[194] a carpenter left £3 to needy householders of

St Bartholomew Exchange;[195] and Edmund Brent, a haberdasher, left
£2 to the poor of St Bride.[196]

There were many women who provided small amounts for poor relief
in this year, most of them being quite certainly wives or widows of
lesser merchants or tradesmen. Thus Margaret Beauchamp left £18 to
three London parishes, as well as £40 to St Bartholomew's Hospital;[197]
Mary Burrell £5 to the London poor and £20 to poor widows;[198] Sarah
Daniell, of Dutch descent, £5 to the poor of the Dutch congregation
and as much to those at Norwich;[199] Ann Dodington £10 to widows in
her parish of St Paul Covent Garden and the same amount for the poor
of two Kentish parishes;[200] and Mary Cox £3 to the poor of St Mary-le-
Strand, £3 to Christ's Hospital, and as much for St Bartholomew's.[201]

The poor of Stanwell, Middlesex, were benefited by the bequest of
an innkeeper, George Buckingham, who established an annuity of £1
for their care,[202] while a bricklayer, Nicholas Burt, provided £2 to be
distributed amongst the needy of St Botolph without Aldgate.[203] A
haberdasher, John Byard, left £3 to the poor of his London parish;[204]
an ironmonger, William Chenery, £1 10s to Holy Trinity;[205] a goldsmith £1 to St Mary Woolnoth;[206] a vintner, Henry Coleman, £2 10s
to the poor of Allhallows Bread Street and as much to those of Kilby
in Leicestershire;[207] and a barber-surgeon, Thomas Collins, provided
£9 for the destitute of named London parishes and £3 to the same
purpose in Camberwell, Surrey.[208] Matthew Crutchfield, a salter, bequeathed £5 to the poor of his parish;[209] Edmund Daning, a merchant
tailor, £1 for St Bartholomew the Great;[210] Henry Dickman, an apothecary, £2 to the needy of St Lawrence Jewry;[211] and a fleet surgeon, Paul
Delano, gave £1 to the poor of the French church and the same to
those of St Anne at Blackfriars.[212] A colonel, James Drax, gave £20 to
the poor of St John Zachary;[213] a tailor left £10 to the worthy poor of
St Katherine Cree, £5 to the poor of Ashborne, Derbyshire, and £10 to
Christ's Hospital;[214] while Christopher Marsh, a servant to the Countess
of Pembroke, bequeathed £5 to the poor of his native Exeter and as
much to those of his London parish.[215]

These are but a random and insubstantial sampling of the hundreds
of small gifts and bequests for the uses of the poor. We have drawn them
from two years late in our period, but it must be emphasized that there
were a great many of the same temper and quality left in every decade
after about 1560, when such bequests for this purpose became customary for almost all burghers, even of the middling and lesser sort. It is
only when we aggregate some thousands of these small benefactions,
dedicated so devotedly to poor relief, that we sense the breadth of social
concern in the London of our era with the plight of the poor. These
lesser men, quite as truly as the great donors, on whom we now con-
centrate once more, shared the view that hopeless poverty was a social

blight which must somehow be eradicated by means of private generosity.

We shall limit our attention to no more than a representative number even of the great donors for poor relief during the last two decades of our period. John Heath, a clothworker, on his death in 1641 left £100 in trust for the poor of St Giles Cripplegate, the income of which was to be distributed in bread. Heath had at an earlier date, probably in 1635, left in trust to his company the sum of £1000, from the income of which £45 p.a. was to be employed for the clothing of thirty poor men and women of the company and of his parish.[216] In this same year, Thomas Gawen of Westminster, who described himself as a 'gentleman', left outright £20 to be distributed amongst the poor of St Margaret's parish and lands then worth upwards of £800 upon trust for the relief of the twenty poorest of St Albans, Hertfordshire.[217] Another large bequest left in 1641 was that of Edmund Tuberville [Turville], a grocer, who, in addition to a loan fund of £100 for the use of his company and an annuity of £10 for a sermon at St Stephen Walbrook, provided carefully regulated annual stipends representing a capital worth of £800 for the care of poor householders in four city parishes, for the poor of his company, and the relief of poor families in his native parish in Worcestershire.[218]

Passing to 1646, the year in which the civil convulsion was perhaps at its worst, we may mention the bequest of £870 left for the poor by an East India merchant, William Fremlyn, who died shortly after his return home from a long sojourn abroad.[219] At about the same date, Henry Hazelfoot, a haberdasher, vested in his company an endowment with a capital worth of £1400, of which £720 was dedicated to the care of the poor of his company, the purchase of corn for distribution in time of need, and the relief of the poor of St Nicholas Cold Abbey.[220] In the same year another haberdasher, the venerable Sir Nicholas Rainton, by will conveyed to his company £2000 to secure several charitable uses, including charges for the relief of the poor which represent a capital value of nearly £1000. The sum of £32 10s was annually to be disbursed towards the support of twenty-five of the poor men and widows of the company, £10 8s was each year to be given to two Lincolnshire villages in order to provide bread for all their poor, while £2 p.a. was to be made available to the churchwardens of both St Edmund the King and St Mary Woolchurch for the relief of their worthy poor.[221]

We should now pass on for almost a decade in order to mention at least a few of the larger donors for the relief of the poor towards the very close of our period, when substantial political stability had been restored and men once more felt secure in their aspirations. The benefactions of a lesser merchant, John Lamotte, cannot be exactly determined, but his generosity was to be celebrated in a particularly moving funeral sermon preached in July, 1655, and published in the next year under the title, *Abrahams Interment*. Lamotte was a widower at the time of his death, his second wife, Elizabeth, having died in 1644 and leaving by the terms of her own will £5 to the poor of her parish of St Bartholomew Exchange, £100 to the poor of the Dutch community in London, £100 to the poor and destitute of the Palatinate, £15 to needy householders in Sandwich, Kent, and £10 each to parishes in Surrey and Cambridgeshire.[222] John Lamotte, a cloth merchant and alderman, was for thirty years an elder of the Dutch church, his grandfather having emigrated from Ypres to Essex in the Elizabethan period. All his life, we are told, 'streams of true Christian charity . . . issued from him', most particularly when 'any publick calamity befell the people and Church of God'. Hence since 1620 he had given continuously and generously to those persecuted in France, in Bohemia, in Germany, and above all in the Palatinate, while not neglecting the needs of those nearer home. Lamotte, his funeral preacher continued, enjoined his children to eschew strife in the settlement of the estate 'which the Lord of his mercy hath lent me'. He reminded them that, 'I having been by trade a merchant, and what by Gods blessing I have advanced, I have endeavoured and laboured to gain it honestly, and to keep faith & a good conscience always, ever acknowledging that these following parties had a share in my estate, as in all other mens, the common-wealth, the service of God, the ministers, and the poor members of Christ'.[223] These sober and moving sentiments expressed vividly the inner convictions of the merchant class to which Lamotte, one of its inconspicuous members, belonged and explain the aspirations which had resulted in the creation, in the century just preceding, of what can perhaps most accurately be described as the structure of Protestant good works.

In 1656 several London parishes benefited under the terms of the will of an innkeeper, James Glasbrooke, who left property valued at approximately £700 for the relief of poor householders.[224] A merchant's widow, Parthenia Lowman, in the same year vested endowments of £100 each in five London parishes in which poverty had long been acute, with the provision that the income, aside from a nominal honorarium for an annual sermon, should be distributed to the poor in money, food, and bread.[225] A merchant and alderman, Michael Herring, in the following year (1657) left £30 to be distributed to sixty poor men, as well as £400 for the support of ten poor widows of the London clergy.[226] Francis Van Acker, a merchant, presumably of Dutch origin, by his will proved in 1657 left, in addition to £30 for London hospitals, £40 to gain the release of prisoners, and £160 to be distributed to named clergymen, a total of £895 for the relief of the poor. Van Acker's bequests to the poor were widely dispersed, including £200 for the 'generality of the poor', £25 to the poor of two London parishes, £500 for poor members of the Dutch congregation in London, £60 for those of the Dutch church in Sandwich, £40 for the Dutch church in Colchester, and £40 in all for lesser Dutch congregations in Norfolk.[227] In concluding our discussion of the larger benefactions left in 1657 for the relief of the poor, we must mention the bequest of a notable goldsmith, John Perryn, whose charities reached the very substantial sum of £4100, of which £900 of capital was dedicated to the care of the poor. These distributions for poor relief included £5 p.a. to the poor of Bromyard, Herefordshire, his native parish, £20 to be given annually to two almsmen who had been working goldsmiths, to decayed workmen, or to their widows, £5 p.a. each to the churchwardens of St Vedast and St Sepulchre parishes in London for their poor, and £10 p.a. to the poorest and most deserving householders in East Acton, Middlesex, where the testator resided in his later years.[228]

We may conclude with examples of substantial bequests left in 1658 for the relief of poverty. A London saddler, John Cox, left to his company lands in Essex with a then capital worth of upwards of £1000, from the income of which £40 p.a. was to be dedicated to the relief of twenty poor men who had been working saddlers and the remainder to the uses of the company.[229] Gilbert Keate, a grocer and a native of Wiltshire, in the same year provided, among charitable bequests totalling £1960, funds to the value of £720 to ensure annual payments to the poor of his London parish, £16 p.a. to the needy householders of Bishopstone, Wiltshire, and £8 p.a. to the poor of St Keverne's parish near Truro, Cornwall.[230] All these late bequests for the relief of poor men were disciplined by a sense of practicality and social economy well expressed in the will of William Thurston, a merchant. He, in leaving £100 to the poor of London and lands in Easton, Huntingdonshire, possessing a capital worth of about £80, for the poor of that community, and 10s each to a hundred old men and women, said he was making the latter gift 'instead of an old custome in giving to many poore such summe of monie to furnish themselves with blacke gowne for to attend their corps on the day of their interrment wherein I have seene much abuse . . . And besides for their performance thereof they must be forced to hire an gowne and sometimes to hire one to serve in their roome'.[231] The age of eccentric and of sentimental alms had long since passed in England. Society had taken upon its conscience the full measure of responsibility for the care of poverty.

During the long course of our period the great total of £426,972 3s had been provided by private donors in London for the general uses of the poor. It is important to recall that the curve of these great benefactions had been steadily upwards during almost the whole of this age and that a heavy proportion of the total amount had been given during the last two generations of our period.[232] Moreover, this huge aggregate of funds, including as it did outright poor relief, charity general, and gifts strictly limited to the care of the aged, was very heavily concentrated on capital sums, the £371,639 13s thus given constituting slightly more than 87 per cent of the whole. This means that so massive had been these accumulations for the care of the poor that by the close of our period something like £18,582 was annually available to trustees, churchwardens, and overseers for the great assault on poverty which private charity had launched in England during the era with which we are concerned. This was, in seventeenth-century terms, an immense income, undergirding and giving effective structure to the many and the strong institutions which responsible men had created for the relief of a kind of hopeless poverty which an increasingly humane society could no longer countenance.

Limiting ourselves to a consideration of the endowments which had been vested during our period for the household relief of the poor, it is most interesting to observe that of the massive total £217,151 15s had been provided in capital sums for poor relief in London (Middlesex) and that the huge total of £154,487 18s had been given by London donors for the care of the poor in other parts of the realm. This is amazing confirmation of the breadth of view of the London mercantile aristocracy as well as offering abundant proof of the geographical fluidity of a class which through the whole of our period was drawn from every quarter of the nation. This means, in the ultimately important terms of income, that something like £7724 p.a. was available to trustees over the whole of England for the mitigation of poverty as a consequence of the generosity of London's benefactors. Since London donors believed, in average terms, that £2 p.a. was sufficient to maintain a subsistence level of life for an unemployed or unemployable family in the provinces, then something like 3862 families, or possibly 16,000 human beings, were being steadily preserved across the length and breadth of the land by London's alms alone. These same donors had provided an annual income of about £10,858 for the care of the poor in London's own teeming parishes, far exceeding even Willet's proud boast that 'in some parishes an hundred, two hundred, three hundred pounds, in some more, some lesse are giuen yeerely to the poore, in money, bread, fewell: so that one parish with another may be thought to giue fifty pound yeerely in almes, which in an 120 parishes (for so many are counted in the City and Suburbs) may arise to fiue or six thousand pound'.[233] London donors, again in average terms, reckoned that £2 15s p.a. was sufficient to provide what must have been a scant living for a completely impoverished city family, which may well mean that very nearly 4000 poor households in the city, or perhaps as many as 17,000 persons, were wholly supported by the complex and rich institutions for the care of the hopelessly poor which men of this age had created. In all, it is not too much to suggest, something like 33,000 human beings were in 1660 being lifted and maintained above the slough of utter social disaster, if not death, by the incredible generosity of a relatively small but a faultlessly responsible burgher society. These men and women had raised up institutions which were then and which remain among the noblest of those the spirit of man has ever brought into being.

2. *The founding of almshouses*

Great as was this contribution to the relief of the poor, it by no means represents the full measure of London's waxing generosity. In the course of our period London donors likewise gave the enormous total of £237,636 11s for the building and endowment of almshouses in their own city and in all parts of the realm. This great capital aggregate, for 99·42 per cent of the whole was in endowments, exceeds substantially the total (£179,778 10s) provided for this purpose in the other counties comprehended in this study, while in those counties, as we have noted, a considerable proportion of the benefactions for this use were in fact London capital. A reasonably informed estimate, which we cannot fully document, would suggest that something like half the total provided in the whole realm for almshouses from 1480 to 1660 was the gift of a relatively small group of London donors.

London's interest in almshouse foundations to be devoted to the intensely secular purpose of offering permanent haven—and withdrawal—from a now complex society to the invincibly poor and incompetent arose very early in our period. In the two generations prior to the Reformation, the impressive total of £18,576 7s was provided for this worthy use, of which, however, a considerable proportion was by royal gift. During the short interval of the Reformation, an even more intense interest was exhibited by a large number of benefactors who in these few years gave in all £10,263 16s towards foundations in London and elsewhere. In every successive decade of the Elizabethan age the total provided for almshouses rose sharply, the substantial sum of £9421 12s having been afforded for this use in the closing decade of the reign. But the great outpouring came in the early Stuart period, when the incredible total of £143,473 17s was given by Londoners for foundations in every part of the realm. The climax clearly occurred in the second decade of the seventeenth century, when the huge total of £81,512 7s, or well over a third of the sum for our entire period, was given by a great number of merchant donors who seem to have been competing with each other in their vast generosity. There was, of course, a slackening of the flow of funds into these institutions during the revolutionary era, though the impressive total of £41,568 10s was given for this humane use during the brief interval and, it must be noted, the £31,259 provided in the closing decade of our period ranks only after the prodigal outpouring we have mentioned in the second decade of the century.

Considerations of space make it undesirable to comment in detail, as we shall in other counties, on London's medieval almshouses, with particular attention to those which survived in 1480 as institutions functioning for the care of the hopelessly poor and unfit. We have counted in all twenty-two foundations made at various times in the long course of the Middle Ages which were, in terms of their social function, lepers' hospitals, general hospitals, hostelries, or almshouses within our meaning of the term. During the medieval centuries, certainly as many as ten and possibly as many as fourteen of these institutions had at least for a season offered shelter, food, and care to almspeople. But the decay of the fifteenth century, in London as elsewhere, had taken a heavy toll, with the consequence that in 1480 London, or more accurately Middlesex, would seem to have possessed not more than eight foundations which offered the social services by which the seventeenth century defined an almshouse. Further, as we shall later note, certain even of these institutions were gravely decayed, others possessed little or no endowment, and still others were in serious need of the reorganization which the Reformation was to supply. We may, consequently, conclude that London emerged from the Middle Ages with surprisingly scant resources for the institutional care of the helplessly poor when compared with several rural counties or, for that matter, with the second and third cities of the realm. Upon this most limited inheritance men of the early modern period began rapidly to build.

We know very little regarding what seems to have been the earliest foundation in our period. Robert Warren, a gentleman, by deed in 1485 and an indenture in 1489 established an almshouse in Finchley for six poor persons, to which he gave a small endowment, the whole of his foundation being roughly reckoned as of the order of £250.[234] Anthony Woodville, executed in 1483 at the command of Richard III in one of the most unjust of all that sovereign's actions, by his will, which was not proved until 1491, left the profits of three manors, representing a capital value of about £650, for the founding in Rochester of an almshouse for thirteen poor, as well as constituting a chantry richly endowed with a bequest of £666 13s 4d.[235]

The charitable intentions of monarchs seem to lie at greater hazard from time—and descendants—than do those of their subjects. Henry VII was deeply persuaded of the grave need which London and his realm had for more almshouses, there being 'fewe or noon such commune hospitalls . . . and that for lack of them, infinite nombre of pouer nedie people miserably dailly die, no man putting hande of helpe or remedie'. Towards the alleviation of this want, he began before his life was out the rebuilding of Savoy Palace as an almshouse where one hundred of the desperately poor might be succoured, 'to the laude of God, the weale of our soule, and the refresshing of the said pourer people'. The always prudent Henry had not begun his work before making a careful survey of similar institutions abroad, being particularly interested in the administration of the great hospital in Florence. The King gave the huge sum of ten thousand marks to secure the completion of his foundation and its endowment, the institution being opened in 1517 with a master and four chaplains in attendance. Though the foundation and the buildings persisted until 1702, the high designs of the benefactor were frustrated as paralysis of maladministration overtook it, most of the apartments actually having been let out to fashionable people before the sixteenth century was over.[236] A better fortune was enjoyed, however, by an almshouse for thirteen poor men which Henry VII founded and endowed, at a total charge of £3104, in the parish of St Margaret, Westminster. This foundation was incorporated by his grand-daughter into the collegiate church of Westminster and was carefully administered, the income providing full sustenance for those chosen as almsmen.[237]

In the year of Henry VII's death another substantial almshouse endowment was completed under the will of James Finch, who had served as master of the Sheremen's Company. During his lifetime, Finch had conveyed to his company on trust certain houses and a wharf, valued in all at about £250 for the benefit of Richard Whittington's famous college and almshouse, as well as conveying by will properties to the Clothworkers' Company and the Skinners, with a total value of at least £400, the income of which should be employed for the support of a divinity lecturer in the college.[238] A few years later, in 1513, a rich fishmonger and former Mayor of London, Thomas Kneseworth, left in trust to his company London properties then valued at approximately £1600 for the full support of thirteen men and women 'in poverty'. Each of his almspeople was to have 8d weekly for support as well as an annual gift of Welsh cloth for raiment. The endowment was subject also to a charge of £2 p.a. to provide prisoners in Newgate and Ludgate with 'such things as ... [they] should have most need of' and to small administrative charges, while the residue of the income was to be employed for the maintenance of the premises included in the endowment.[239]

Another pious lord mayor of the period, Sir John Tate, a mercer and a native of Warwickshire, some time before his death in 1515 demolished his brewery in Threadneedle Street in order to make room for the rebuilding of St Antholin's church, to which he was the principal contributor,[240] and also to restore a fifteenth-century hospital for thirteen poor men on which he laid out an estimated £400 of his funds.[241] Some years later, in 1523, Henry, Lord Marny, at a charge of perhaps £200 built an almshouse for five poor men at Layer Marney (Essex), which was probably connected with a chapel and a chantry, served by two stipendiary priests, for which his will also made provision.[242] Thomas Mirfyn, a skinner and a former mayor, whose benefactions for the poor have already been noted,[243] shortly before his death in 1523 conveyed to his company funds of at least £190 value, with which lands and tenements were to be purchased for the care of sixteen almsmen, while at about the same time Hugh Dennis, of uncertain social status, and his wife founded a chantry at Islesworth (Middlesex), to which they joined an almshouse, endowed with approximately £140 of capital, to secure the sustenance of seven poor men.[244]

One of the greatest and certainly the most carefully vested of all the almshouse foundations made prior to the Reformation was that of Sir John Milbourne, a draper who had in 1521–1522 served as Mayor of London. Milbourne and his wife in 1534 purchased a vacant tract of land in London from the Convent of the Holy Cross, on which they built thirteen almshouses (Stow says fourteen) at an estimated charge of £400. Milbourne then vested in his company a trust with a capital value of about £600, from the income of which payments were to be made to the thirteen almsmen, being decayed men and women who had served the company, of 7d each weekly, as well as certain administrative charges and the cost of maintenance of the property.[245] Shortly afterwards, in 1537, a courtier and favourite of the King, George Henningham, founded an almshouse for three poor widows in Tottenham High Cross.[246] In the next year Margaret, Countess of Kent, with merchant wealth which she had inherited from her father and her first husband and which she had somehow preserved from the life-long wasting of her late and noble spouse, conveyed on trust to the Clothworkers' Company an almshouse which she had erected in Whitefriars for seven poor women. Simultaneously, she settled on the company £350 as endowment with the provision that each almswoman was to enjoy $7\frac{1}{2}$d weekly for her sustenance and that in the selection of beneficiaries preference was to be given to the widows of clothworkers. This endowment the donor increased by the provisions of her will, proved in 1540, by which lands and houses in London with a capital value of about £360 were bequeathed to the feoffees for the better execution of the trust.[247] And, finally, we should mention the founding in 1536 of an almshouse and school at Ratcliffe (Middlesex) by Nicholas Gibson, a London grocer. Gibson expended something like £250 for the building of pleasant quarters for fourteen poor men and women who were fully maintained by him until his death in 1540.[248] He charged his wife, Avice, to continue this support during her own lifetime, which she faithfully did. She had married Sir Anthony Knyvett some years before her death in 1554. In 1552 this woman surrendered to trustees capital valued at about £333 for the support of the school and £373 for the endowment of the alms-houses founded by her husband. The Coopers' Company was made trustee under agreement to pay each of the fourteen poor £1 6s 8d p.a. for maintenance and to serve as overseers of this interesting and well-devised charitable institution.[249]

We have noted the principal of the almshouse foundations made during the two generations of our period prior to the advent of the Reformation. There were in all fifteen of these foundations, of which thirteen may be regarded as new; one represented a considerable aug-mentation of an older and still thriving establishment; and the one remaining was a reorganization of a late medieval institution which was nearly derelict in 1480. In all, then, foundations were projected to secure the lodging and sustenance of 242 hopelessly poor persons, of which number eighteen were in counties outside Middlesex. This represented a most substantial addition to the social resources of London, since there is doubt whether provision for the care of as many as 300 of its desperately poor existed at the beginning of our period. It will also be observed that, in the closing decade of the interval just reviewed, these foundations were much more carefully and elaborately framed by donors in order to secure secular administration and to vest the institutions with resources regarded at once by donors and trustees as adequate for carrying forward in perpetuity the aspirations which in-creasingly sensitive and responsible men held for their age and the future.

Despite the unsettlement that characterized the next two decades of religious change, the movement for the founding of almshouses by the London community of merchants began to gather very considerable momentum. During this brief interval (1541–1560), the substantial total of £10,263 16s was given by various donors either for the founding of new establishments or for the strengthening of existing institutions. Among the first of these was the creation in 1542 of a trust under the will of.William Dauntsey, a mercer, for the founding of an almshouse and school in his native village of West Lavington, just to the south of Devizes in Wiltshire. This donor settled on his company as trustee properties then possessing a capital worth of £928, the income of which was to be employed in approximately even portions for the support of the two institutions. Suitable quarters were built for the lodging of five poor and aged men and 'two honest aged poor women', each of whom was to be accorded an annual stipend of £2 3s 4d for maintenance.[250] Shortly afterward, John Hasilwood, very probably a leatherseller, built an almshouse for four men and three women of the poor of the Leather-sellers' Company at a probable cost of £200, which he endowed with annuities representing a capital worth of £242,[251] while in 1544 Elizabeth Holles, a mercer's widow, built and endowed an almshouse for six poor at a total charge of about £400 for the benefit of St Helen Bishopsgate.[252]

In the same year, George Monox, a rich draper and a former mayor of London, died leaving only modest charitable bequests, but with an indication that he had arranged shortly before his death for the founding of a carefully ordered school and almshouse in Walthamstow, Essex. Monox had built, at a cost of approximately £260, apartments for thirteen almspeople, with rooms for the school and the lodging of the schoolmaster in a storey just above. The pensioners were likewise to have the use of an adjoining close of about two acres, in which they might have their gardens, dry their clothing, and take their recreation. The thirteen almspeople, eight respectable poor men and five honest widows, were to be sustained by rent-charges on London property with a capital value of £468, which should ensure to the bedesmen £18 7s 4d annually for their keep, or £1 2s 2d each, and £5 for their coals.[253]

Among the numerous foundations of this period may be mentioned certain bequests made under covenant to the Dyers' Company on condition that an almshouse be established for their poor. In 1545 Sir Robert Tyrwhit conveyed property valued at upwards of £241 for the support of eight almspeople on such a foundation, to which in 1550 Henry West, a London dyer, added an endowment valued at £100 or more. It appears, however, that there were successive and inexplicable delays, the income being employed for the care of the company's poor in their own households until the almshouse was erected sometime after the Restoration.[254] Another small hospital was established in 1547 in St Botolph without Aldgate by a brewer's widow, Anne Wethers, who left five tenements for as many poor almswomen and a stipend of 6d each weekly, her whole foundation representing a capital worth of about £230.[255] A London leatherseller, Thomas Kendall, shortly before, 1552 built almshouses for two poor persons in St Mary Magdalen, Bermondsey, for which he also established a small endowment,[256] while in 1552(?) Emma Askew, the widow of Christopher,[257] a former Mayor of London, built at a cost of about £140 almshouses for seven poor widows which by her will, proved in 1554, she endowed with properties having a capital value of £420, in order to ensure the annual payment of £3 for the full support of each almswoman.[258] Finally, among these rather oddly assorted foundations of his subjects, we should mention the establishment by Henry VIII in 1544 of an almshouse, the Woolstaple, in Westminster, for seven decayed men, which the sovereign endowed with resources to the value of at least £742 in order to secure the payment of a very generous annuity of £5 6s each for the support of these pensioners.[259] He also, it should be noted, richly endowed the precariously existing royal College of Windsor, conveying to the Dean and Chapter by will ecclesiastical properties in eleven counties with a then value of £666 6s 8d p.a., for the support of thirteen poor knights 'decayed in warres and suche like service of the realme'. Though we have not regarded this large endowment as a charitable contribution, it may be remarked that a most useful purpose was served and that the institution, particularly as reorganized by Queen Elizabeth, was well and prudently administered.[260]

In 1556, and quite literally on his death bed, Sir William Laxton, a rich grocer and a former lord mayor, arranged by will for the founding of a notable grammar school and a generously endowed almshouse at his birthplace, Oundle, Northamptonshire. Laxton conveyed on trust to his company properties then possessing a capital worth of £1760, with the intention that the jointly administered institutions should share equally in the income. The almshouse was to shelter and afford complete maintenance for seven poor and respectable men to be chosen by the vicar, the churchwardens, and four substantial parishioners, who were to pay each almsman £1 14s 8d p.a. in weekly sums.[261] At about the same time, 1555, Thomas Lewin, an ironmonger, provided for the building of an almshouse for the care of four poor men of his company, endowing it sufficiently to ensure an annual stipend of £1 6s 8d. for each of his almsmen, the whole of the endowment amounting to approximately £208.[262] We shall deal elsewhere with the almshouse founded in 1557–1558 at Stoke Poges, Buckinghamshire, by Edward, Lord Hastings, which that peer so richly endowed with capital of £1070 for the support of his five almsmen, and we may mention also the endowment of £208 which the great Sir Andrew Judd added to secure the support of six poor in the almshouse founded in 1544 by Elizabeth Holles in St Helen Bishopsgate parish.[263] And, finally, in tracing out the almshouse endowments created during the Reformation decades, we should notice the foundation in 1559 of an almshouse for ten pensioners by John Richmond, an armourer, which on the death of his wife was to be funded with an endowment of £180 to ensure at least modest support for the poor lodged therein.[264]

The movement for the founding of almshouses suffered a surprising diminution in the first decade of the Elizabethan era when not more than £1657 14s was contributed by Londoners for this worthy purpose. But the giving for this use was fully to revive in the next decade, and thereafter to increase rapidly and steadily until in the closing decade of the century the substantial total of £9421 12s was provided by bene-factors for the founding of almshouses in London and elsewhere. In the whole course of the Elizabethan period £23,754 1s was given by Londoners for these foundations, rather more than half of which, it is interesting to note, were established in counties outside Middlesex. Most of these foundations we must treat very briefly, reserving extended comment for those that were generously endowed or notable for other reasons.

An almshouse was founded for Finchley in ca. 1561 by Thomas

Haynes, a tradesman. This establishment was supported with assets possessing a value of something like £300 and offered shelter to six of the poor of the parish.[265] A London grocer, Edmond Stile [Style] in 1564 built an almshouse in Ipswich, Suffolk, at a cost of about £200, while by his will he charged his estate with its repair but not, apparently, with any endowment.[266] As we shall elsewhere note, Sir Martin Bowes, a great goldsmith and a former Lord Mayor of London, by his bequest in 1566 completed the founding of an almshouse in Woolwich, Kent, for five almsmen on which he settled capital with a total worth of £620.[267] Laurence Sheriff, the founder of Rugby School, directed in his will that £50 should be employed by his executors for building a suitable almshouse for four poor men near the school, which he endowed with a capital of £111 in order to ensure for each pensioner 7d weekly for his maintenance.[268] In the same year, Sir Richard Champion, a draper who had served as lord mayor in 1565-1566, by his will instructed his widow to 'buy as much lands as would countervail the yearly alms of Mr. Milbourne', thereby making a capital augmentation of about £432 to the London almshouse which a fellow draper had founded just a generation earlier.[269]

Still another civic dignitary, Sir Roger Martin, a rich mercer who was lord mayor in 1567, shortly before his death in 1573 built cottages for four almspeople in his native parish of Long Melford, Suffolk, though there is no clear indication that he endowed the institution.[270] We shall elsewhere deal fully with William Lambarde's great foundation of his *Collegium Pauperum Reinae Elizabeth* in East Greenwich, Kent. The son of a London draper, this famous legal scholar was to lay out a total of £2337 8s 6d on this institution, which lent generous sustenance to twenty poor, in the years intervening between 1575, when he obtained the charter, and his death in 1601.[271] We shall also discuss elsewhere the notable almshouse established at Sutton Valence, Kent, in 1574 by William Lambe, a London clothworker, who expended in buildings and endowment about £600 in order to lend full support for twelve poor aged persons in this, his native parish.[272] Even more generous, as we shall see, was the great foundation of Peter Symonds, a mercer, at Winchester in 1587 of an almshouse, most soundly endowed with £75 p.a. for the complete support of six poor men, one poor woman, and four homeless boys.[273]

In 1587 David Smith, who described himself as 'ymbroderer to her Majesty', by a particularly complicated bequest devised to the governors of three London hospitals, as trustees, his own capital messuage and six tenements which he had recently built as almshouses for as many poor widows of his parish. The endowment of the almshouse was to consist of the rent of the messuage and the income from a capital stock of £80 bequeathed by the founder. In 1631 Smith's daughter, Mary

Paradine, left £400 to Christ's Hospital for the purchase of lands which she charged, with other charitable uses, with £6 p.a. as an augmentation of the endowment vested by her father.[274]

A London clothworker, Alexander Every, by his will proved in 1589 left £100 for the building of suitable quarters for seven almspeople in his native parish of Broadway, Somerset, as well as endowing the institution with rents then having a capital value of about £420.[275] In 1592 Sir Christopher Wray, Chief Justice of the Queen's Bench, made further provision for an almshouse which he had founded on his estate at Glentworth, Lincolnshire, where he had built a great seat. Wray expended something like £100 on the quarters, then endowing the institution with rent-charges possessing a capital value of £320 to ensure each of his six almsmen 10d and a penny loaf weekly, a gown yearly, and an ample supply of fuel.[276] Just a year later, Dame Elizabeth Powlett died, having recently settled on trustees an endowment for the establishment of an almshouse and school in her native town of Burton-upon-Trent, Staffordshire. This donor conveyed properties with a capital value of approximately £250 for the maintenance of five aged almswomen, each of whom was to have £1 6s 8d annually, while the surplus income was to be disposed for fuel and the upkeep of the premises.[277] Another woman donor, Alice Smith, the daughter of Sir Andrew Judd, by her will proved in 1598 settled on the Skinners' Company an endowment valued at £300 for the augmentation of the revenues of the almshouse in St Helen Bishopsgate so generously assisted by her father in 1558,[278] this payment being subject only to small annuities to be paid for the relief of three poor women of Allhallows Lombard Street and St Gabriel Fenchurch.[279]

In considering the larger or more interesting of the numerous Elizabethan foundations, we may well begin with the Salters' Almshouse in St Olave Cripplegate, which was the gift of Sir Ambrose Nicholas, an eminent member of the company who had served as lord mayor three years prior to his death in 1578. Nicholas conveyed on trust to the Salters twelve small tenements which he had recently built at an approximate charge of £400 for perpetual use as an almshouse for poor men and women, salters always being preferred. He vested as well London properties then having a capital worth of at least £480, the income of which should be used to ensure each almsperson an allowance of 7d weekly, the remainder being employed for the maintenance of the premises. Nicholas likewise bequeathed to his company £100 to be lent to worthy young men of the fraternity who should pay such interest as might be required to provide annually a cartload of fuel for the foundation.[280] Very probably in the same year, Cornelius Vandon, an aged yeoman of the guard and usher to four successive sovereigns, died having founded an almshouse for eight poor widows of Westminster and another near 'St Ermin's Hill, by Tuttle side' for eight additional poor but respectable women. It may be roughly estimated that Vandon's outlay on these premises, which were to serve their stipulated purpose for three centuries, was of the order of £600, though it does not seem probable that any endowment was provided beyond a payment of £13 6s 8d to the Dean and Chapter of Westminster in connection with the repair of the premises.[281] Just a year later, the renowned Sir Thomas Gresham conveyed to the municipal authorities of London by will eight almshouses which he had built and maintained in the parish of St Peter the Poor. This foundation Gresham most munificently endowed with an income of £53 6s 8d, representing a capital worth of £1067, for the complete sustenance of his almspeople as well as the maintenance of the properties.[282]

A splendidly endowed almshouse was founded at Woodbridge, in his native Suffolk, in 1587 by Thomas Seckford, a lawyer and Master of the Court of Requests. Quarters were built for thirteen poor men by the donor, while certain London properties then valued at £1888 were conveyed to trustees as endowment. From the abundant income, £5 15s annually, plus a gown, was to be paid for support to each of twelve inmates, while the thirteenth, who should be named principal, was to have £7 13s 4d p.a. and a gown. Further, three poor widows of the parish should each be paid £2 13s 4d p.a. with the obligation of attending the almsmen in the event of sickness. After these payments, there remained at the time of the foundation an income of £18 5s which the donor ordered employed for the relief of the poor of a London parish, for the salary of the paymaster of the almshouse, for the payment of a stipend of £1 p.a. to the minister of Woodbridge church for visiting and instructing the almsmen, and the residue to be devoted to the relief of poor householders in that parish.[283]

In 1587 Richard Hills, a merchant tailor too little remembered not only for his benevolence but for his great wisdom, conveyed to his company on trust thirteen tenements near the Tower, then valued at about £300, to be used as almshouses for the widows of deceased almsmen of the company. The company subscribed £400 16s 1d a few years later in order to renovate and enlarge the premises, while in 1595 additional subscriptions totalling £330 were received for the purchase of lands to serve as endowments for fourteen almswomen. This almshouse was further enlarged in 1637, when quarters for twelve more widows were built, partly by subscription and partly at corporate charge. Hills likewise left by will properties then worth £219, the income of which after certain life interests was to be paid to the poor of the company, and more particularly to impotent and poor members of the fraternity 'using or having occupied shearing with the broad shears, or rowing at the perch'.[284]

Some years later, in 1592, even more generous provisions were made under the terms of the will of John Fuller, a London lawyer and Treasurer of the Inner Temple. Fuller directed his heirs to build two almshouses, the one at Stepney for twelve poor and single men aged fifty or more and the other in St Leonard Shoreditch for twelve women of good repute, with an indication that the Mercers' Company had undertaken to act as governors. His will further provided lands with a capital worth of £2000 as endowment, in order to secure an annual income of £50 for each institution. The almshouses were built by his widow, but it seems that the endowment was not formally devised until 1623 when she, having long survived the donor, with Sir Thomas Mansell, her then husband, settled sufficient lands to accomplish the intentions which Fuller had so carefully set forward.[285]

Anne, Lady Dacre, a sister of Thomas Sackville, who had attended the Queen as a maid of honour, by her will proved in 1595 bequeathed the sum of £300 to be employed for the building of a hospital in Westminster (Emanuel Hospital) for the relief of twenty poor and aged persons and likewise for the reception and training of twenty poor children who might there be sustained until they could support themselves. She conveyed as well on trust nearly 3000 acres of land in Yorkshire, then valued at about £2000, with the instruction that it should be rented for a full century at £100 p.a., this income to be employed for carrying forward the purposes of the foundation. The trustees found it impossible, because of the limitations imposed by the long lease, to do more than administer the almshouse portion of the founder's will, though in 1736 the contemplated school for homeless children was established from the huge rental which had by that time become available.[286]

In the year following (1596), to quote Fuller, 'Mr. Balthazar Zanches [Sanchez], a Spaniard, born in Xeres in Estremadura, founded an almshouse at Tottenham High-Cross ... for eight single people, allowing them competent maintenance. Now, seeing protestant founders are rare, Spanish protestants rarer, Spanish protestant founders in England rarest, I could not pass this over with silence'. Sanchez seems to have purchased land for his foundation in 1596 and to have laid out £140 on the building of quarters for eight aged poor widows and widowers of Tottenham. His will placed on trust an endowment of £400 to secure the full support of his almspeople, as well as providing a stock of £100, the income to be used for the distribution of bread to the poor of his parish, and £300 as an endowment for the support of the French church in London.[287] And, finally, we must mention the foundation in 1599–1600 by Richard Platt, an ale-brewer, of a school and almshouse at Aldenham, Hertfordshire. Platt had completed the building somewhat earlier, then conveying to trustees properties in London and Aldenham, the income of which was principally devoted to the endowment of the school, but the residue, then possessing a capital worth of £300, was to be employed for the care of six poor pensioners, each to enjoy two rooms and a garden and have yearly £2 for sustenance, a gown worth 10s or 12s, and a load of fuel for his comfort.[288]

We have at least noted briefly the foundation of thirty-seven new and endowed almshouses in London and elsewhere by London donors in the course of the two generations extending from 1541 to the close of the century. There had been advanced by London benefactors for these creations almost £25,000 of capital, to which must be added somewhat more than £9000 given for the augmentation of these endowments, for strengthening almshouses founded prior to the Reformation, and for a number of unendowed and transitory, though none the less useful, houses where succour was afforded to men and women who were overwhelmed by the society in which they lived. In all, the foundations of the later Tudor period afforded complete sustenance to something over 300 almspeople in the city and in the provinces, as well as free lodging without support to more than 100 additional persons. It is also notable that of the thirty-seven foundations we have mentioned, a total of sixteen had been established in counties other than Middlesex, as the powerful and disciplined flow of London funds began to move out to every quarter of the realm. This is a record of notable and beneficent achievement of which any age might well be proud.

But the fact is that the age of almshouse foundations was only just at hand in London, and this, so great was merchant generosity, meant for England as well. In the relatively brief interval of the early Stuart period, the enormous total of £143,473 17s was disposed by London philanthropists for these foundations or for the strengthening of the endowments of older institutions. This means, of course, in average terms that something more than £3500 a year was provided during these four decades towards the building of bulwarks against the evil tide of abject and hopeless poverty. This great work was carried forward with an energy and an enthusiasm which suggest that the whole of the merchant class was committed to it with a singular tenacity of purpose and of aspiration. We cannot note all the endowments, particularly those that were relatively small, but we can at least sketch the broad outlines of an amazing charitable movement.

We may first notice at least a sampling of the considerable number of smaller foundations, as well as mentioning certain of the foundations made in other counties which will be more fully discussed elsewhere. Among the latter group was the substantial almshouse for eight founded at Basingstoke, Hampshire, in 1607 by Sir James Deane at a cost of about £200 for the building and endowed with funds possessing a capital worth of £1100.[288a] In the same year, Roger Owfield, a London fishmonger, left £100 for the building of an almshouse at Ashborne, Derbyshire, for the shelter of eight poor people of that town, to which his widow, Thomasine, added £76 to secure the proper completion of the structure. The widow also maintained these almspeople with an annual stipend of £1 each until 1630, when by indenture she conveyed £100 on trust to the governors in order permanently to endow the institution.[289] In 1612 Thomas Evans, who for thirty years had faithfully served as messenger to the Lord Keeper of the Great Seal, bequeathed £100 for the building of an almshouse in St Martin-in-the-Fields, as well as £100 for poor relief in Westminster and Chelsea and £100 for church repairs in Chelsea and in Lawford, Warwickshire.[290] We shall discuss elsewhere the Earl of Northampton's great endowment of Trinity Hospital in Greenwich, an almshouse for poor men at Clun (Shropshire), and another for poor women at Rising (Norfolk), on which he expended in all upwards of £9000 for buildings and endowments and which gave shelter and most generous maintenance to forty-four almspeople.

Sir Roger Wilbraham, Master of Requests under James I, in 1616 built and endowed an almshouse for six poor householders in Monken Hadley (Middlesex) at a total capital charge of about £260.[291] Just a year later, Robert Flood, who was probably a lesser merchant, left £120 for the building and endowing of an almshouse in Llangristolus, Anglesey, while at the same time bequeathing the residue of his estate, in the amount of approximately £300, for the care of the poor of that community.[292] A London grocer and a former lord mayor, Sir Stephen Soame, probably in 1617 built an almshouse at Little Thurlow, Suffolk, for nine pensioners at a cost of about £200, which he endowed in the year following with rents representing a capital value of £600 to ensure the full maintenance of his almspeople.[293] In 1621 Richard Edmonds left lands and rents, with a capital value of at least £250, to the Fishmongers' Company to finance the building and endowment of added quarters for two almsmen in their almshouse,[294] while in the same year Leonard Poure, a resident of St Sepulchre, left £200 for the building of a schoolhouse and almshouse in Bletchington, Oxfordshire, as well as lands of the certainly inadequate value of £120 to secure the support of four almspeople.[295] An even more ambitious foundation was made, shortly before his death in 1624, at Corsham, Wiltshire, by William Halliday, a rich and generous London mercer. This establishment, apparently originally designed for six almspeople, was endowed with resources representing a capital value of something like £400.[296] At about the same time (1624), Sir Nicholas Kempe, who had previously contributed £100 towards the building of the chapel in Archbishop Abbot's great almshouse foundation at Guildford, left £500 towards the endowment of that institution in which he had always shown a warm interest.[297] A draper, Thomas Weedon, as we shall see elsewhere, in 1624 founded an almshouse for four inmates at Burnham (Chesham parish), Buckinghamshire, which he endowed with a mortgage debt of £500,[298] while a year later John Dunster, a clothworker, established a similar institution for six poor at Donyatt, Somerset, with a soundly built stone house and an endowment of £700.[299]

In 1627 two relatively small almshouse foundations were made, these being Roger Pemberton's house at St Albans for six poor and worthy widows on which this merchant laid out approximately £180,[300] and Robert Pennington's bequest of £100 to the Fishmongers' Company for the strengthening of their almshouse at Newington, Surrey.[301] A merchant's widow, Mirabell Bennett, in 1628 bequeathed £250 to the stock of the Children's Hospital in Norwich,[302] while a few years later (1631) a London lawyer, Henry Hawkins, by his will gave £300 for the endowment of almshouses at Wisbech, Cambridgeshire.[303] A London stationer, William Barringer, in 1632 bequeathed the residue of his estate, with a value of about £200, for the building of an almshouse at Stevington, Bedfordshire,[304] while in the same year a merchant tailor, John Slany, who had earlier built an almshouse for six poor at Barrow, Shropshire, endowed it with properties valued at £536 at least, in order to secure a weekly stipend of 1s 4d for each inmate, as well as clothing to the value of £1 each in every second year and an adequate allowance for fuel.[305] It was also in 1632 that Elizabeth Fiennes, Lady Saye and Sele, provided shelter and support for three poor widows of the parish of St Bartholomew the Great where she purchased land and built three cottages at an estimated charge of £150, endowing the institution with rents of £7 p.a. for the maintenance of her almswomen.[306]

We may now conclude our review of a representative group of the lesser almshouses founded by London benefactors in the course of the early Stuart period. Hugh Perry, a mercer who was master of his company in 1633, the year before his death, bequeathed £300 for the purchase of a site and the building of a suitable almshouse at Wotton-under-Edge, Gloucestershire, for six poor men and as many needy women. He gave in addition £250 as an endowment for the institution, placing its management in the care of the municipal authorities and the parson and churchwardens. Perry also charged a trust fund which he had vested in the municipal authorities of Gloucester for general charitable uses with the payment of £8 p.a. to his almshouse for the clothing and support of the inmates.[307] At about the same date (1635) Thomas Isles, a clergyman, built four cottages on a spacious tract in Hammersmith (Middlesex) as an almshouse for four poor widows, endowing it with London properties then valued at upwards of £240.[308] A Lord Chancellor's widow, Alice Egerton, in 1637 founded and endowed an almshouse for six poor women at Harefield (Middlesex) at a total charge of £540.[309] In the same year, the endowment of an almshouse at Marshfield, Gloucestershire, was completed by a London skinner, Nicholas Crispe. This donor and his elder brother, Ellis, a salter, had as early as 1625 purchased suitable land in this, their native town, on which at a cost of at least £400 they built a commodious stone structure affording apartments of two rooms each for 'the perpetual harbouring and relief of eight poor householders of the town and parish'. The elder brother, by his will proved in 1625, endowed the institution with London properties, then possessing a capital value of £267, in order to ensure the maintenance of the buildings and an annual stipend of £1 10s for the support of each of the almsmen. Nicholas Crispe, on his death in 1637, bequeathed properties in Marshfield as well as an outright legacy, with a total worth of £200 or thereabouts, for the further strengthening of the endowment, as well as £6 13s in alms for the poor of Marshfield and a distribution of £8 in clothing to his almspeople.[310]

Now, to comment more extensively on the larger almshouse foundations made during the early Stuart period: there were as many as twenty-five on which their donors lavished £800 or more in securing their strong endowment in perpetuity. The earliest of this group was that established in Ruthin, Denbighshire, by Gabriel Goodman, the famous Dean of Westminster, with wealth left to him by his merchant father. Goodman had instituted this foundation in his native town in 1590, when he secured letters patent for founding an almshouse for twelve poor people, ten being men and two women, and a preacher. The statutes provided that the Bishop of Bangor was to be president of the hospital and that the poor were to be nominated from the shires of Denbigh and Flint. Goodman built the almshouse and gradually settled properties on it as endowment which by the time of his death possessed a total capital worth of £1157. The chaplain, or warden, was assured an annual stipend of £26 13s 4d, while the residue was to be employed for the sustenance of the poor in the house, each of whom was to have at least £2 12s annually.[311]

In the year following (1602) Robert Rogers, a leatherseller and merchant adventurer whose generous provision for the poor has already been noted,[312] bequeathed £600 to the Corporation of London for the building and endowment of an almshouse which would lend full support to six aged, poor, and respectable couples. The cost of the construction was £230, the donor's executors adding £30 to the remaining £370 in hand in order to provide the £400 of endowment which Rogers had evidently contemplated. Rogers likewise bequeathed the sum of £333 6s 8d to his native town of Poole, Dorset, for the erection of an almshouse there for six poor couples of that town, preference to be given to those 'decayed by sea', his executors being instructed to provide as much additional capital as might be required to build and endow the institution. The executors paid in a further sum of £33 6s 8d, the capital being employed by the municipal authorities for the purchase of the site (£10), for the erection of the building (£148 16s 4d), and the remainder (£207 17s) being invested in land for the full maintenance of twelve almspeople. Finally, Rogers bequeathed £200 as an augmentation to the endowment of the Leathersellers' almshouse, the capital to be lent to young artificers of the fraternity at a moderate interest rate, this income to be used for fuel and other needs of the almsmen of the company.[313]

A large foundation was ordered under the terms of the will of William Goddard, a wealthy fishmonger, who died in December, 1609. Goddard directed his wife, Joyce, to convey to trustees funds sufficient for the building in brick of a hospital for forty poor at Bray, Berkshire, containing an apartment for each, a chapel, and 'one kitchen and bakehouse common to all the poor people', and to entitle the foundation 'Jesus Hospital in Bray'. The Fishmongers were named governors and were to nominate the almspeople, of whom six should be aged poor of the company and the remainder 'the most aged, poorest parishioners' of Bray. Goddard likewise devised properties in London and Berkshire, which some years later may be accurately valued at £1784,[314] to secure the full maintenance of the poor members of the hospital. There were persistent legal difficulties raised by Goddard's sister, which delayed the full execution of the donor's intention, but the widow paid annually from 1610 until 1623, £66 13s 4d towards the building of the almshouse, on which about £900 was expended before it was at last completed in 1628. In that year the legal issues were finally resolved and this notable foundation began its useful and healing work.[315]

In 1609 Alice Owen, the widow of Thomas Owen, a Justice of Common Pleas and himself a considerable philanthropist,[316] purchased eleven acres of land at Islington (Middlesex), where she erected a hospital for the care of ten poor widows at a total charge of about £600. In the same year she vested rents with a capital worth of £500 in the Brewers' Company, of which her first husband had been a member, for the support of her foundation, this endowment being augmented in 1613 by a second gift of £40 when Dame Alice undertook the foundation of a free school on a site adjacent to her almshouse.[317] In 1610, George Palyn, a girdler whose large benefactions for the poor have already been noted, left £900 on trust to his company, of which £260 was to be used for the building of an almshouse for the comfort of six poor freemen of London, while the remaining £640 was to be treated as a stock which would, he hoped, supply an annual stipend of £6 13s 4d for the full and generous support of each of his almsmen.[318] The London poor were likewise benefited in 1611 by the provisions of the will of Tobias Wood, counsel to the Coopers' Company, who left on trust £600 to be employed towards the enlargement of the company's almshouse in Ratcliffe, which, as we have seen, had been founded in 1536.[319] Quarters were accordingly arranged by the company for the reception of six poor coopers, each of whom was admitted to the foundation with an annual pension of £6 as a consequence of Wood's generosity.[320]

All the benefactions of the early Stuart period were quite dwarfed by the immense charitable bequest of that somewhat enigmatic Elizabethan entrepreneur, Thomas Sutton. Sutton (1532–1611) was born in Knaith, Lincolnshire, where his father was serving as steward of the courts at Lincoln. He may have attended Cambridge for a short time and certainly was enrolled for a season at Lincoln's Inn. On his father's death in 1558, Sutton inherited a modest estate. In this year he was a captain in the garrison at Berwick-on-Tweed, where he probably remained until 1560. He was much in Lincolnshire during the next several years in what appears to have been a mixed military and civil capacity, evidently enjoying the favour of the Earl of Warwick, who in 1569 settled a life annuity of £3 1s 8d on him and who doubtless gained for him in 1570 appointment as master and surveyor of ordnance in the northern parts of the realm. While serving in the north, Sutton became interested in the mineral resources as yet quite undeveloped in Durham, gaining by purchase from the bishopric and later from the Crown most valuable coal-mining rights which he had so far exploited by 1580 as to have won a fortune then estimated at £50,000. In that year he returned south, settling his residence first in Hackney. Two years later he married Elizabeth, the widow of Sir John Dudley, who brought him another fortune as well as a pleasant estate at Stoke Newington. Sutton was during these years engaged in speculative purchases of agricultural property and certainly in money lending, but the root of his rapidly growing fortune remained his mineral properties in the north, where he permitted the Newcastle merchants to pool their interests and to operate the mines as if they were a single enterprise.[321] In 1583 he seems to have negotiated the transfer of a sub-lease on a portion of his holdings for the considerable sum of £12,000, and so competently and profitably did he manage the properties, which were principal suppliers to London, that he with some justice was blamed for having lifted the price of coal in Newcastle from 4s to 6s a chaldron.[322]

It was in 1594, when he was in his sixty-second year, that Sutton, with no legitimate children, began to consider the outlines of the great charity on which he finally settled. In that year he conveyed his Essex properties in trust for the foundation of an almshouse and school at Hallingbury, in that county, outlining the proposed foundation by a first draft of his will. Upon the death of his wife, to whom he was devoted, Sutton returned to Hackney. Though he secured an act of Parliament in 1609 to permit the foundation of the projected institution in Essex, Sutton determined, for reasons that remain quite obscure, on a radical change in his plans. Perhaps, indeed, the opportunity for a bargain proved irresistible to this shrewd old trader. The Earl of Suffolk (Thomas Howard) was straitened because of the immense outlays he was making on the rebuilding of Audley End, and from him Sutton purchased the great property of Charterhouse for £13,000, as the seat for his great charity.[323] The purchase having been made, Sutton moved with swiftness and vigour. In June, 1611, he obtained letters patent authorizing him to found his almshouse and school there rather than in Essex. A few months later he executed the deed of gift and drew his will in favour of the great institution which he had now created.

Sutton died late in this year, leaving his great project in the hands of the governors of the foundation, who were named in the letters patent, among whom were numbered such powerful and incorruptible men as Archbishop Abbot, the Lord Chancellor (Ellesmere), Robert Cecil, John King, Bishop of London, Lancelot Andrews, then Bishop of Ely and the King's Almoner, John Overall, Dean of St Paul's, Sir Henry Hobart, Chief Justice of the Common Pleas, and the redoubtable Sir Edward Coke, then Lord Chief Justice. The whole of Sutton's fortune, aside from small personal legacies and £13,829 7s designated by the donor or his executors for other charitable uses, was vested in the foundation, which would seem to have been endowed with properties then possessing the immense capital worth of £116,000, the original outlay for purchase not being included.[324] We have credited this great total in equal amounts as an almshouse foundation and as a school endowment, this evidently having been the donor's intention and one scrupulously observed by his governors. The institution was prepared to receive, with respect to its almshouse obligation, eighty old men, they being 'suche poore persons as can bringe good testimonye and certificat of their good behaviour', with a preference indicated for old 'captaynes either at sea or land, maimed soldiers, decayed merchants', or those who had been 'Turkish' captives, each of the brethren being allowed an annual stipend of £5 for his personal needs. The master and brothers dined in the great hall, while apartments for their lodging were prepared in that area of this immense group of buildings which at an earlier day had been the monastery barns, the school and scholars being separately lodged and fed.[325]

Sutton's nephew, Simon Baxter, 'suborned by others', as he was later to allege, brought a legal action to set aside the will, in which he had been left a legacy of only £300. It is evident that in this step Baxter enjoyed the powerful support of Sir Francis Bacon, then the Solicitor General, who was ever ready to bend a great mind to ignoble deeds. In another place we have dealt fully with the remarkable and really infamous brief in which Bacon urged his sovereign to set the will aside.[326] Suffice it here to say that the case was argued before the Judges in June, 1613, who determined by a majority of ten to one, one justice being ill, to uphold the trust. Some days later, the governors, indicating that they were possessed of £20,000 the use of which had not been fully determined, gave to the Crown £10,000 for the rebuilding of the ruined bridge at Berwick-upon-Tweed, a worthy action which may not have been unconnected with the resolution of the doubts Bacon had raised in the King's mind regarding the wisdom of this immense concentration of wealth upon narrowly defined charitable uses. History, it is pleasant to relate, has proved Sutton, not Bacon, abundantly right.[327]

The total contribution made by Thomas Sutton to English charitable needs was but little short of £130,000, a truly immense sum which would probably have impoverished any other private person of his generation, be he merchant or great noble. The benefaction also constituted a challenge to all men of his age, being a kind of model against which humbler but still capacious designs of good works could be measured, for, as a contemporary accurately put it, this was 'the greatest gift that ever was given in England, no abbey at the first foundation thereof excepted'.[328] And the good works of Englishmen were continued and extended at an ever-accelerating pace, as if Sutton's wedge of generosity had opened even more widely the great and fruitful stratum of philanthropic wealth.

Thus Lawrence Campe, a draper, in 1610 prepared an almshouse in the parish of Allhallows-on-the-Wall at an estimated charge of £150, which he endowed shortly afterward with an annuity representing a capital worth of £208, for the full support of six poor persons to be lodged there. Two years later, Campe vested an annuity of £7 16s for the support of twelve almsmen at Friern Barnet (Middlesex) in suitable houses which he had built there. This draper was even more generous in his dispositions for the poor of London, and most particularly for decayed silk weavers, having settled funds of £460 for household relief, not to mention £2 p.a. which he disposed for the relief of prisoners and £40 for the assistance of needy scholars.[329]

William Jones, the haberdasher whose great outlay for poor relief has been noted,[330] by the terms of his will, proved in 1615, established two richly endowed and carefully ordered almshouses. The larger institution was built at Monmouth, where a total of £10,580 was expended by the donor's executors on the founding of a school, the almshouse, and a lectureship, the whole complex charity being administered by a single board of governors. It is impossible from the available records to estimate accurately the proportion of the building costs and administration to be allocated to the almshouse, which was to offer free lodging and complete care for twenty of the poor of the town and county of Monmouth. But the endowment provided was most generous, each of the almsmen having an annual allowance of £6 10s for his support, as well as a woollen gown of the value of £1 6s. The capital required, therefore, may be most modestly reckoned at £3200 for this great foundation. This donor's other foundation, at Newland, Gloucestershire, was even more generously conceived. In this instance, £5000 was vested to secure the maintenance of a preacher, whose annual stipend was settled at £66 13s 4d., while the remainder of the endowment, with a capital worth of £3667, was dedicated to the support on a comfortable scale of the sixteen almspeople for whom the buildings were designed and for the general maintenance of the institution.[331]

A substantial mercer, John Wynne, in 1617 bequeathed £1000 for the erection and endowment of an almshouse for six worthy poor in his native town of Baldock, Hertfordshire, with the provision that each almsman should enjoy £2 p.a. for his sustenance.[332] At about the same date, Thomas Thompson, a lawyer of Barnard's Inn, built a commodious almshouse at Petworth, Sussex, at an estimated charge of £600, which he endowed by will, proved in 1619, with properties then possessing a capital worth of upwards of £1200. The trustees were enjoined to admit twelve of the native and aged poor of the parish, each of whom was to have the comfortable stipend of £5 p.a. for maintenance.[333] An even more generously conceived foundation was made at Godalming, Surrey, in 1619 by the bequest of Richard Wyatt, a master carpenter of St Bennet Paul's Wharf. This donor required his executors to spend £500 on the construction of an almshouse for ten poor, enjoining them to 'looke on the orders of Mr. Lamberd's [Lambard's] Hospital at Greenewch and follow them yf you shall thinke it good'. Each tenement was to have two rooms, access was arranged to an ample garden, and instructions were given to admit five almsmen from Godalming and the others from nearby parishes. The institution was endowed with lands then having a capital worth of £1400, each of the almspeople receiving £6 13s 4d p.a. for his full support.[334]

Sir John Jolles, a draper and a former Lord Mayor of London, by his will proved in 1622 bequeathed to the Drapers on trust properties then worth upwards of £480, the income of which should be employed for the care of eight aged almspeople in quarters which had he provided somewhat earlier in Stratford Bow, Middlesex. Jolles likewise left on trust a fund of £200 to be lent to young freemen of his company at an interest rate of 3 per cent, the income to be used for the relief of poor persons in Allhallows Barking, Stratford Bow, and a parish in the Isle of Ely.[335] We shall in another place speak at length of Thomas White's great almshouse foundation in Bristol, begun in 1613 and completed by generous bequests under the founder's will in 1624, for the endowment of which capital to the value of at least £3640 was settled on the trustees to lend complete support to twelve almspeople in his native city.[336]

White was the son of a Bristol clothier and had gained fame as the vicar of St Dunstan in the West. His will also provided ample funds for the building near Sion College, of which he was the principal founder, of an almshouse for twenty almspeople, ten being women, the government of which was to be modelled on that of the Bristol institution. Something like £1500 was laid out on this large establishment, which White endowed with lands having a then capital worth of £2400. The almspeople were to be chosen from two London parishes, from Bristol, and from the poor of the Merchant Taylor's Company, while the ordinary affairs of the house were to be administered by a matron, she being a widow and 'one of the discreetest' of the almswomen on the foundation.[337] In 1625 a merchant adventurer, Christopher Eyre, by bequest provided £240 for the erection of six substantial brick almshouses for six poor and respectable couples of his parish (St Stephen Coleman Street), as well as settling on trustees a fund of £400 to provide full maintenance for these almspeople. His will also furnished £200 for the building of identical quarters in his native city of Salisbury, while vesting £400 for the support there of six couples, they being such 'as were past labour and children, and were known to be of honest disposition, such as feared God, that they might live orderly'.[338]

One of the most remarkable of the almshouse foundations made in the early Stuart period was that of Edward Alleyn, the famous actor and theatrical entrepreneur, who according to Fuller 'was the Roscius of our age, so acting to the life that he made any part (especially a majestic one) to become him'.[339] Alleyn became almost fanatically interested in the plight of the poor in the metropolitan region during his later years, building and endowing an almshouse in St Giles Cripplegate for ten of the poor of that parish at a probable outlay of £600 in 1620. Already, however, he had begun to acquire property in Dulwich for the great foundation which was to become Dulwich College. In all, this donor provided funds to the value of £9372 for the institution which he wished to be known as 'The College of God's Gift', which was planned to afford lodging and full support for six poor men, six women, and twelve needy children. This great philanthropy, on which Alleyn was actively engaged from 1606 until his death in 1626, was likewise designed by the founder to function as a school, the full roster of those on the foundation to include, aside from the almspeople, a master, a warden, four fellows, six junior fellows who should be musicians, and up to eighty paying scholars. Alleyn's will also provided for the foundation of almshouses for ten persons in each of two London parishes, but his already great magnanimity had so far exhausted his estate that it appears his executors found themselves unable to follow this prescription.[340]

In the same period the East India Company was taking slow steps towards dealing with the problem of its poor, particularly after the establishment of its dockyard in which some hundreds of men were often employed. In 1617 Sir William Russell first proposed that an almshouse be founded by the company for the care of injured men and for the relief of widows and orphans. This plan, involving as it did contributory payments, met with little favour. In the next year the question had to be faced again when one Hugh Greet, a former factor who had been brought home a prisoner under accusations of fraud, died bequeathing to the company property valued at £700 with the stipulation that it be used for charitable purposes. The company, which had earlier denounced Greet as one who had 'carried himselfe mutinouslie, rioutously, debaushtly, and unfaithfullie', now found itself embarrassed by the bequest of property roughly to the value of the alleged fraud. Greet had named as executors Sir Thomas Smyth and Sir William Russell, men of great influence in the affairs of the society, who carried a motion in the Court held in 1619 that the legacy be used to found the desired almshouse for company servants. Sir Thomas Roe offered a further contribution of £400 if the design were carried forward promptly, but this donation was forfeited since the Court delayed until 1627, when the almshouse for twenty poor men was established in Blackwall (Poplar). The original endowment remaining from Greet's estate after construction costs was £446 10s 1d, an amount quite insufficient to carry forward the now ambitious plans of the company, but by the close of our period additional contributions and legacies totalling £1903 10s had been added to the stock of this institution.[341]

We should perhaps treat in order the almshouse foundations made, or attempted, by the Bayning family over three generations, the family fortunes having stemmed principally from the estate of Paul Bayning, a very rich London grocer who died in 1616. Bayning established, at an uncertainly estimated charge of £400, an almshouse for seven poor of the parish of St Olave Hart Street, as well as leaving £20 in outright alms for London's poor, £100 for Christ's Hospital, £104 for the uses of his company, £30 for the delivery of prisoners, and £40 for charitable purposes in Little Bentley, Essex, his birthplace.[342] The grocer's son, also Paul Bayning, greatly increased the value of his patrimony by shrewd investments and by an equally shrewd marriage, being raised to the dignity of Baron Bayning in 1628 and of Viscount Bayning shortly before his death in 1629. He bequeathed to his executors £1220 for the purchase of a site and the building and maintenance of an almshouse to lodge ten of the poor householders of his native parish of St Olave Hart Street; his will further provided the large endowment of £2280 with which his executors were charged to purchase lands for the endowment of the hospital, to assure 'releefe of tenne poore people to the worlds end'.[343] The third Paul Bayning, the only son and heir of his father, died in 1638 at the age of twenty-two. But young as he was, Lord

Bayning in his will stipulated that still another almshouse for ten poor persons of St Olave's should be founded by his executors, setting aside £3500 to provide most handsomely for the generous support of the projected institution. Bayning's estate was ample to meet his bequest, but, for reasons which still remain obscure, the foundation contemplated by this young donor was evidently never made.[344]

In 1629 Baptist Hicks, Viscount Campden, by his will endowed a large and excellently designed almshouse for twelve of the poor of Chipping Campden, Gloucestershire, which he had built some years previously at an estimated charge of £600. Hicks settled on trustees properties then possessing a capital worth of upwards of £2800, the income to be used to provide each of his almspeople with the generous stipend of £8 13s 4d p.a. for maintenance, as well as the clothing and fuel requisite for the needs of the institution.[345] A few years later, Jeffrey Kirby, a grocer, bequeathed £1000 to his company for the building of an almshouse and a rent-charge with a capital worth of £200 for its maintenance, though it seems probable that the intentions of the donor were never fully carried forward.[346] A rich merchant tailor, Robert Gray, by his will proved in 1638 provided a generous bequest of £1500 and the reversionary interest in £1000 for the augmentation of the endowment of the almshouse recently founded by his company. But this great gift by no means exhausted his generosity. Some years before his death he built an almshouse at a cost of £600 for the care of ten poor women in his native town Taunton. As we shall note elsewhere, Gray by his will settled on this foundation an endowment of £2000 for the full care of his pensioners, as well as providing instruction to ten poor children of the town in the elements of reading and writing.[347] Somewhat earlier, George Strode, a London merchant, with other members of his family, founded and endowed an almshouse for five and a school at his native town of Shepton Mallet, also in Somerset.[348] Finally, we may conclude our comment on the larger of the almshouse endowments of the early Stuart period with mention of the establishment at Putney, Surrey, of an institution designed to afford lodging for twelve almspeople. Sir Abraham Dawes built this almshouse some years before his death in 1640, by will providing an endowment of £800 to secure the full support of the poor there sheltered.[349]

We have been able to deal in this summary account with no more than the principal of the many almshouse foundations created by London generosity in the years 1601–1640. There were also in these decades many augmentations of the endowments of older foundations in capital gifts ranging from 10s to £666 13s 4d in amount, of which we can give only a sample. Thus in 1601 Edward Berkeley, a mercer, bequeathed to his company a thousand marks to be lent at reasonable interest to young men of the company, not yet of the livery, with the stipulation that the income should be paid to the almsmen of Whittington College for the 'augmentation of their diet'.[350] Some years later (1609), a London saddler, John Hall, added to the endowment of his company's almshouse by the bequest of a rent-charge possessing a capital value of £150,[351] while in 1612 a leatherseller's widow, Anne Elliott, augmented the stock of the foundation of that company with a capital bequest of £200, not to mention a legacy of £100 the income of which was to be used for university scholarships.[352] A successful London merchant, John Jossye, in 1621 provided a legacy of £666 13s 4d for the further endowment of Trinity Hospital, Edinburgh, which, founded in 1462, had enjoyed the steady support of Scottish donors since the Reformation, with the result that in a period of two generations its resources had been increased almost six times over.[353] In the next year, Edward Hewlett, possibly a stationer, left in trust to the governors of the 'Hospital of the Poor' in St Saviour's parish, Southwark, lands then worth £800 or thereabouts, with the provision that of the income £20 p.a. should be expended for the general relief of the poor of the parish, while the remainder, which was shortly to be of much greater value, was to be employed to augment the resources of the almshouse.[354] William Penifather, a grocer, by the terms of his will proved in 1638 left £233 6s 8d as a stock for the better care of the almspeople of his company, as well as providing a bequest of £100 for Bridewell Hospital and £66 15s as an endowment for household relief in the parish of St Margaret Fish Street.[355]

It will have been observed that many of the augmentations made during this period were disposed by merchants for the strengthening of the capital funds of the almshouse foundations of their own livery, a number of which had been founded in the Tudor period. The most notable of these augmentations was carried forward in the Merchant Taylor's Company, in which during the interval 1601 to 1660 we have counted twenty-six separate benefactions of members who in the course of these two generations greatly enhanced the stock of the institution with funds totalling £4394 14s.[356]

We have spoken at least briefly of fifty-five new foundations made by London donors during the early decades of the seventeenth century. Of this number, only eighteen were designed to provide additional facilities for the already extensive group of almshouse foundations in and about London. It is notable, then, that in this interval of only forty years London benefactors founded and endowed thirty-seven new institutions for the care of the hopelessly poor in other counties, as the great arc of London's generosity was extended farther and farther to the west and north as the needs of the metropolis and of the home counties came, in the judgment of sensitive men of the period, to be very nearly fulfilled. Other substantial resources were vested for the support of older endowments, in large part occasioned by the greater income which men of the seventeenth century thought necessary for the decent maintenance of pensioners on the earlier foundations. In all, we have dealt with foundations and augmentations for which the enormous sum of £140,894 was disposed in the course of this remarkable and certainly responsible generation. This capital was given by a great many donors for the care, according to their prescription, of 660 almspeople in London and elsewhere. There remains the relatively modest total of £2579 17s given in this period either for augmentations which we have not noted or for the founding of unendowed institutions, most being outside London, which were not to survive for more than a generation or two. We have at least recounted, though we have failed adequately to appraise, the noble achievements of a generation in which there occurred the greatest advance ever made in man's sense of responsibility for the welfare of his whole society.

There was a marked falling away in almshouse foundations in our final period, particularly during the war years. None the less, the total of £41,568 10s supplied by London donors for this worthy cause from 1641 to 1660 represents an amazingly high level of contribution when we take into account the political and economic unsettlement of the period and the further fact that many men now believed that London and most of the southern counties possessed quite sufficient almshouse resources for the needs of the age. In the first decade, when the scourge of civil war lay on the land, the total given for these uses was £10,309 10s, the smallest amount to be noted in any single decade since the last years of Queen Elizabeth's reign. But in the final decade, when internal peace and order had been restored by a capable and certainly vigorous revolutionary government, the astonishing total of £31,259 was provided for almshouse foundations, this having been, in point of fact, the largest sum given for this purpose in any save one preceding decade in our whole period. We shall now note very briefly certain of the smaller foundations of the revolutionary era and then turn to a somewhat more extended treatment of the larger gifts.

Mary Lake, the daughter of a London merchant and the widow of a fallen minister of state, by the terms of her will proved in 1646 established an almshouse at Little Stanmore (Middlesex), which she vested with an endowment of about £1000. The income from the stock was to be employed for the full support of seven poor men and women on her foundation, the annual sum of £32 4s being allocated for this use, while the remainder was to be distributed for the relief of poor householders of the parish.[357] At about the same time, Humphrey Hall, a London girdler, built an almshouse for seven poor widows at Brandon, Suffolk, which he endowed by will in 1648 with properties in the neighbourhood with a then capital value of £400 for the support of his almspeople.[358] Robert Jenner, who seems to have been a retired goldsmith, in 1643 built almshouses for eight of the poor of Malmesbury, Wiltshire, at an estimated charge of £400, which he endowed with an annuity of £40 for the full maintenance of the foundation.[359] In the last year of this decade, Sir John Gayer, a fishmonger and a former lord mayor, among charities totalling £1653 6s, provided a bequest of £500 for the augmentation of the stock of an almshouse which he, with two friends in Plymouth, had founded in that city in 1630.[360]

Passing to our final decade, we may note the charity of John Hawkins, who built an almshouse for five poor women at South Mimms (Middlesex) and settled a modest endowment on it in 1652, the whole outlay being approximately £300.[361] William Adams, a rich haberdasher, in 1656 built quarters for four aged and deserving almspeople in his native town of Newport, Shropshire, endowing the foundation with lands then possessing a capital value of £416.[362] In the year following (1657) Thomas Bell, an apothecary, conveyed to trustees £150 for the building of an almshouse for six persons in Kingerby, Lincolnshire, the structure to be made of brick and to provide a chimney and a garden for each inmate. His will gave an endowment valued at £360 for the full support of his pensioners, as well as an annuity of £1 10s for sermons at Kingerby and £1 10s p.a. for household relief in that parish.[363] The Earl of Southampton at about the same date gave lands valued at £200 towards the erection of an almshouse for five needy persons in St Giles Cripplegate, though the building in 1656 appears to have been carried forward at parish expense.[364] In 1657 Moses Goodyear, a London merchant, bequeathed £50 as endowment for the Plymouth almshouse and as much for the orphanage there,[365] while Thomas Nicholl built an almshouse for six at Hendon, Middlesex, at an estimated charge of £300.[366]

Sir John Wollaston, a goldsmith and a former lord mayor, built an almshouse for six of the needy of Hornsey (Middlesex), at a cost of about £300, which he endowed by will in 1658 with London properties then valued at upwards of £320, as well as vesting in his company capital to secure the payment of £10 p.a., plus a residue of uncertain value, for the support of two of their almsmen.[367] And, finally, we may mention the foundation by a merchant, Richard Higginson, at the very close of our period, of an almshouse at Bispham, Lancashire, for ten poor women, which he endowed with rents representing a capital value of £400,[368] and the modest endowment of £160 vested by John Juxon on an almshouse at East Sheen, Surrey, in which four poor widows were to be maintained.[369]

The earliest of the more substantial foundations made in these years was that provided for the Clothworkers' Company by one of its members, John Heath, who died in 1641. Heath, who also left a large endowment for poor relief in London,[370] bequeathed £1500 to his company with instructions to build an almshouse at a cost of £300 and to invest the remainder as stock for the full support of ten poor old men of the company, such as had been clothworkers or dressers, or 'other mechanics and handicraft men'. The almshouse was built by the company in St Mary Islington, but the funds provided were found to be sufficient to care for twenty of the almsmen of the company.[371]

In 1639 the famous judge, Sir George Croke, who had served as a trustee of Henry Smith's endowment and who had lent legal advice to numerous other charitable donors, built at a cost of perhaps £350 a commodious almshouse for eight persons at Studley (parish of Beckley), Oxfordshire, where he had purchased large properties some years earlier. In successive conveyances, Croke vested the institution with rents of a capital value of £1200 to ensure the full maintenance of his almspeople, four of whom were to be men aged sixty or more and four women aged fifty or more, unless deserving persons should be appointed of younger years who must in that event be lame, blind, or helpless. Croke also provided a stipend of £20 p.a. to a preacher at Studley mansion house or at the chapel of Horton, among whose duties was the reading of prayers in the almshouse twice daily.[372] At a slightly later date (1643) Mark Quested, a prominent fishmonger, left to his company on trust a manor in Kent, whose rental would suggest a then value of £3640, for the endowment of several noteworthy charities. Among these, Quested enjoined his trustees to use one year's rental (£182) and an additional £100 from his personal estate to build at his birthplace at Harrietsham, Kent, an almshouse for twelve poor, of which number half should be needy almsmen of his company and the remaining persons poor natives of Harrietsham who should be nominated by the most substantial persons of the parish. The almshouse was endowed generously with £72 p.a. to secure the comfortable maintenance of those on his foundation.[373] In the same year, Sir Edmund Wright, a grocer and a former lord mayor, died having made generous provision for an almshouse foundation at his native town of Nantwich, Cheshire, as well as leaving benefactions for various charitable uses in London, where his fortune had been made. Some years earlier, and probably in 1638, Wright had built a commodious house, with two rooms for each almsman, to provide lodging for six poor of the parish. The property was conveyed to twelve local trustees, including the clergyman, together with an endowment of £640, for the succour of six needy men of fifty years or more who should be conformable to the 'religion of the Church of England'. Applicants for admission to the foundation must be nominated by the minister, churchwardens, and overseers, and then chosen by lot, the admitting slip to bear the words, 'Praise God for thy founder'.[374]

The Haberdashers' Almshouse was founded in 1642 under the terms of the will of Edmund Hammond, a wealthy member of that livery.

Hammond left £400 for the purchase of a site and the building of an almshouse suitable for the reception of six 'poor old decayed men', who must be free of the company and who were to be designated by its master and wardens. Hammond's will also established an endowment of £60 p.a. for the complete care of his almsmen, as well as a further annuity of £20 to be distributed among the poor of the company.[375]

It is interesting to observe that no large almshouse foundation was made by any Londoner during the particularly unsettled years extending from 1643 to 1650. In 1651, however, the flow of substantial gifts and bequests for this purpose set in again, with the legacy of Susan Amyas [Amos], a widow of uncertain social status, who left on trust funds for the erection of an almshouse at a probable cost of £200 for eight of the poor of the parish of St Luke Finsbury. Her will further provided an endowment of £800, the income of which should be used to distribute £4 p.a. to each almsperson for his sustenance, £6 p.a. to provide fuel for the institution, £1 p.a. to employ someone to read prayers daily before the inmates, and £1 p.a. to bring river water into the premises for the convenience of the pensioners.[376] In the next year (1652) Alexander Stafford of the parish of St Andrew Holborn by will endowed an almshouse for fourteen poor women of Frome, Somerset, with rents representing a capital sum of £600, which we shall describe more fully elsewhere. Somewhat earlier, this same donor had built at a charge of at least £500 an almshouse on a half-acre tract near Gray's Inn Lane for the benefit of ten poor men and women of his own London parish. By his will Stafford vested in his trustees, who were to administer both foundations, rents then yielding £47 p.a. for the full support of his London almshouse, each almsman to receive £4 p.a. for his keep, and the remainder of the revenues to be devoted to maintenance and administration, including a rent of £1 10s p.a. for 'the New River water then taken in'.[377] At about the same date (1653), provision was made for the hopelessly poor of Kensington (Middlesex) by William Methold, a skinner, who had for many years been a prominent and active member of the East India Company. Some little time before his death, Methold had built an almshouse for six poor women, at a roughly estimated charge of £200, in which he had maintained the inmates with annual stipends of £4 each for their full support. By the terms of his will, Methold settled in perpetuity a rent of £24 p.a. on the institution to ensure its work.[378]

We must now attempt to separate the charitable affairs of two London merchants named John Smith who died at about the same time and both of whom raised up almshouse foundations among other and considerable philanthropic dispositions. The first, who died in 1655, was a draper of St Stephen Walbrook, who had served as master of his livery in 1644. In 1653 Smith built an almshouse at Leyton, Essex, for eight of the indigent of that parish, which his will settled on feoffees together with lands then valued at somewhat more than £400 as endowment. At an earlier date, 1645, Smith had settled £1250 on the Drapers' Company, subject only to a life estate, with the provision that upon his death half the capital should be employed by the company for its own uses and the remainder as an endowment for the care of the poor of the company.[379] Finally, by his will, Smith settled on the city of Lincoln lands then valued at upwards of £600 as an endowment for the relief of the deserving poor in two parishes of that, his native community.[380] The second John Smith, who died in the next year, by his will conveyed to trustees £200 for the erection of an almshouse at Longport (Canterbury), Kent, for the lodging of eight old men and women, as well as bequeathing capital to the value of £640 for the full maintenance of the inmates.[381] The will also provided a stipend of £20 p.a. for an 'able and orthodox' clergyman to preach each Sunday afternoon in St Paul's church, Canterbury, and £20 p.a. to the churchwardens and overseers of Hornsey, Middlesex, for the apprenticing of poor children in that parish, in which Smith apparently resided.[382]

We must distinguish, as well, between two vintners named Rowland Wilson, they being father and son. The son, who had the more interesting career, died in 1650,[383] while the father, who left the larger estate to charity, survived until 1654. The senior Wilson by his will established an almshouse at Merton, Surrey, which was built at a cost of about £200 and which he endowed with agricultural land then valued at £480 for the full maintenance of six pensioners.[384] It was probably in the same year (1654) that James Palmer, who had for many years been Vicar of St Bride Fleet Street, built at an approximate charge of £400 an almshouse and chapel in Tothill Fields, Westminster, for the comfort and care of twelve poor people, men and women being accepted in equal numbers. The grounds set aside for the institution comprised six pleasant acres, on which Palmer also built a school, to which we shall recur in later pages.[385] The almshouse was endowed, by successive gifts in 1656 and 1657, with capital funds, principally lands in Berkshire, valued at about £1000, if we may assume that half the *corpus* of the trust was devoted to the care of the poor and the remainder to education.[386]

At about the same date an equally modest and even more generous benefactor died having made most substantial dispositions for the founding of three almshouses. This donor, John Walter, a draper, had begun laying his plans as early as 1642, being moved by the fact that many poor 'had lately perished by lying abroad in the cold to the great dishonour of God'. Yet he proceeded so modestly that Fuller, writing shortly after Walter's death, says that he 'could learn little from the minister who preached his funeral, less from his acquaintance, least from his children. Such his hatred of vain-glory, that (as if charity were guiltiness) he cleared himself from all suspicion thereof'. The first almshouse, founded in 1646 in Southwark (St George's parish), was a substantial and commodious building for sixteen poor men and women, being built at a charge of about £700 by the donor. In 1650 a second was constructed at Newington, on waste lands there, for the same number of poor and doubtless at something like the same cost. The two institutions were richly endowed with rents on city properties, then valued in capital terms at upwards of £4880, the generous stipend of £128 p.a. being directly devoted to the sustenance of the thirty-two almspeople, and the remainder of the income being assigned for fuel and administration. Walter had also determined on the building of an almshouse for eight poor in London, but died before his final plan could be settled, though he left £400, or thereabouts, for the building, which was constructed in St Leonard Shoreditch. In April, 1658, his widow, Alice, conveyed to the Drapers' Company, as trustees, £500 as endowment, thus completing the remarkable charitable design.[387]

We may conclude what has been an extended discussion with some comment on the great almshouse foundation made in 1657 by Elizabeth, Viscountess Lumley. In another connection we shall speak at some length of her joint establishment of an almshouse and school at Thornton Dale, Yorkshire. This almshouse was fitted for twelve of the poor of the neighbourhood, representing an outlay of approximately £1400 for buildings and endowment. By the same deed poll, this donor established an almshouse with twelve rooms in the parish of St Botolph Aldgate for the reception of six almspeople to be chosen from that and the adjoining parish of St Botolph Bishopsgate. Each of the inmates on the foundation was to have an annual stipend of £6 13s 4d for his sustenance. The London almshouse was built at an estimated charge of £600, income from the central trust, with a capital value of £800, being charged for the support of the institution. The Yorkshire school was endowed with an income representing a capital worth of £1250, while the trustees were instructed as well to pay £10 p.a. for the relief of prisoners in York Castle, £10 p.a. to poor scholars in the universities, and £40 p.a. for the clothing and apprenticing in London of poor children from the five Yorkshire parishes in which this great donor was particularly interested. The whole of the trust, which was most skilfully ordered, enjoyed a capital of £5750.[388]

We have sketched in some detail one of the great movements in social history. The men and women of London had with their own fortunes gone far indeed towards gaining for their society relief from the most hideous aspects of poverty by providing havens of refuge for those who were for whatever reasons incurably and invincibly poor. They were evidently resolved that they would end those tragic circumstances under which helpless and derelict men and women could lie 'abroad in the cold to the great dishonour of God'. In the course of our period these donors, only the greatest of whom can we mention, had poured the vast total of £237,636 11s into the founding of almshouses in London and throughout the realm. We have counted 139 new foundations established by these donors, while there were as well another twenty-one unendowed or scantily provided institutions created by a charity which often overreached the resources of the donors. In all, these institutions offered free and permanent lodging as well as sustenance to probably as many as 2848 men and women who could not survive outside the precincts of social sanctuary. Most of these foundations were made by the great merchants of London, men who were through our whole period generously and stubbornly dedicated to the betterment of their society; men whose sense of responsibility encompassed the whole of the land.

Of the substantially endowed foundations, a total of sixty-seven were established within the limits of Middlesex or in northern Surrey for the reception of the poor of the great city which spawned poverty quite as truly as it did that wealth with which poverty was being mastered. Into these institutions there had gone the enormous total of £128,986 4s, an amount quite sufficient to provide the average stipend of £4 4s p.a. which London donors of the period believed to be required for the sustenance and diet of an almsperson. We may believe that these institutions offered complete support and succour for something like 1500 pensioners, if the average stipend be laid against the income known to have been available.[389] In addition, the sum of £26,402 7s had been provided either for the augmentation of existing London foundations or, as we have noted, for unendowed or insufficiently supported houses. The donors who had given this latter sum at least reckoned that an additional 201 almsmen might be supported by their benefactions, with the consequence that probably just over 1700 almspeople were by the close of our period maintained by the whole accumulation of capital which London had poured into these noble monuments to the social conscience of the age.

Even more remarkable, however, is the fact that London donors had at the same time vested the huge total of £82,248 in seventy-two almshouse foundations in other parts of the realm. These endowments were designed by their donors to lend full support to perhaps 1100 almsmen, which represents a most substantial addition to the social resources of the thirty-one counties in which these institutions had been founded.[390] These almshouses were studded over the whole realm, though their heaviest incidence is to be found in those counties from which London for generations drew its merchant class or with which it maintained close trade relations. Not only did these almshouses, founded usually by merchants in their native parishes, vastly improve social conditions over an immense region, but they exerted as well a direct and salutary influence on potential donors in the surrounding countryside. These institutions were carefully endowed, well administered, and were immediately and evidently beneficent in their effect on the communities in which they were sited. They thus supplied enormous social leverage, since they were models which other men consciously or unconsciously held in mind as they drew their wills for more modest foundations throughout the realm. London capital was bold, ingenious, and vastly generous. Above all else, it bore effectively on the framing of the aspirations of a whole people.

The weight of the resources mustered against poverty by the enlightened benefactions of London was indeed immense. The sum of these benefactions, as we have seen, reached the huge total of £664,608 14s, distributed in the several ways with which men of the age sought to grapple with poverty. Of this amount, whether vested in almshouse endowments or in stocks for the household relief of poor families, the great sum of £427,872 16s had been given for the mitigation of poverty and want in London proper. It has been our estimate that in all some 18,700 Londoners were by the close of our period each year relieved from the fear of abject want and starvation itself by the vast endowments which had been reared by the age against the social evils of poverty.[391] These were great resources indeed, offering by 1660 at least subsistence relief and protection to perhaps 7 per cent of the whole population of the city. But the charity of London knew no parochial bounds, for the large total of £236,735 18s had been bestowed by its benefactors in the various forms of poor relief over the whole face of England and Wales. If the steady assumption of men who must have known is correct that the control of poverty could be far less expensively established in the provinces, it would seem that another 17,000 human beings owed their support, and often their very lives, year after year and generation after generation, to the militant benevolence of these men and women of London who were determined that their nation should be a fitter and a finer habitation for free men.

B. EXPERIMENTS IN SOCIAL REHABILITATION

1. Apprenticeship foundations

The steady attention of London donors throughout our long period was fastened on the problem of poverty and its direct relief. An immense capital sum had been dedicated by private men for the control and amelioration of poverty ; a complex system of institutions had been established in London and elsewhere which by the close of our period gave reasonable assurance that no worthy family of stable abode would perish for want of food and shelter.

There was at the same time, however, a considerable group of rich and enlightened benefactors who were undertaking much bolder and ultimately even more hopeful experiments in the cure and prevention of poverty through institutions designed to afford opportunities for the social rehabilitation of poor and ignorant men. We may now turn to a consideration of a number of these institutional developments, all having their origin and their testing during our period, with which the burgher aristocracy of London was especially concerned. London donors during our whole period were to vest the very large total of £251,728 13s on these experimental undertakings, which represented the surprisingly high proportion of 13·32 per cent of the whole of the charitable accumulations of the city. The quality and the boldness of London leadership is once again suggested when we note that in no other county, save of course Bristol, where the mercantile elite were also dominant, was there a comparable degree of interest in these forward-looking ventures.*

Taking in view the whole group of charitable uses which we have regarded as dedicated to the ends of social rehabilitation, it is notable that in the years prior to the Reformation only £8429 15s was given for this general purpose, or 3·37 per cent of the benefactions for the period. But in the two decades of reformation the huge total of £66,183 14s, representing 43·30 per cent of the whole, was given for purposes of social rehabilitation, this great outpouring being principally directed to the hospitals being founded or reorganized in these fruitful years when men's aspirations were undergoing a very rapid and certainly revolutionary re-orientation. In the Elizabethan period the total given for these uses fell to £53,077 4s, which none the less represented slightly more than a fifth (20·39 per cent) of all benefactions for the period. In proportionate terms, the endowments for social rehabilitation were halved during the early Stuart period, the great sum of £87,822 8s given for this purpose amounting to slightly less than a tenth (9·16 per cent) of the whole vast capital given to charity during these four decades. There was relatively a rather sharp increase during the revolutionary decades, when the £36,215 12s vested for this use represents 13·57 per cent of all the charitable resources provided in this short interval.

We shall now turn to a necessarily brief discussion of the several uses

* The proportion of total charitable funds devoted to social rehabilitation in the several counties was as follows:

	Per cent		Per cent
Bristol	10·42	London (Middlesex)	13·32
Buckinghamshire	4·45	Norfolk	9·63
Hampshire	4·42	Somerset	2·66
Kent	4·78	Worcestershire	5·94
Lancashire	3·04	Yorkshire	4·85

It should also be said that a substantial fraction of the funds credited to this use in the other counties was in point of fact of London origin.

which we have loosely grouped under the general heading of schemes of social rehabilitation. We must confine ourselves to no more than a small sampling of an almost unlimited variety of plans and experiments with which the London merchants of the period sought to create new and very often ill-advised institutions to attack the very sources of poverty. Many of these plans were naive and short lived; but they were bold, they were enormously stimulating, and they lent social hope and dignity to the age that contrived them.

It seems most surprising that the London merchants of our period displayed so modest an interest in the founding of apprenticeship endowments. The great majority of these men had themselves come up to London from distant places as apprentices, and as a group their social origins would make it certain that their fees and expenses had been difficult for their own families to provide. Yet during our whole period endowments established to furnish precisely this kind of help totalled no more than £19,587 18s, or 1·04 per cent of the vast aggregate of London's charitable wealth. This proportion was markedly less than that to be found even in most of the rural counties we have studied and stands in quite marked contrast to the 2·04 per cent of Bristol's total charitable funds devoted to this particular use. It is especially significant that of all the donors of apprenticeship schemes only three were lord mayors and only seven were great merchants. Though the testimony is by no means as full as we should like, it seems clear that most of the great merchants viewed the whole apprenticeship system with some mis-givings, and there is abundant evidence that many of them believed that the really critical point in the career of a fledgling merchant came when his training had been completed and he stood in need of trading capital.

We have noted no apprenticeship endowment of any sort in London prior to Elizabeth's accession, and the growth of these funds was very slow indeed through the remainder of the sixteenth century. In all, the modest total of £1815 8s was given for this purpose in the Elizabethan era, far less than for any other use which may be regarded as social rehabilitation, save for the £1065 4s supplied for marriage subsidies. There was a marked increase in these gifts during the early Stuart period, though the total of £6305 10s seems unimpressive when we compare it with the huge sums given for almost all other charitable endeavours during this most generous age. The really heavy concentration of apprenticeship endowments occurred in the two revolutionary decades, when the substantial sum of £11,467 was given by a considerable number of donors to encourage the flow of talent into the livery com-panies as well as into the myriad of lesser companies making up the industrial and commercial life of the great city. At least a few of the principal of these endowments may be mentioned, with particular attention to those vested for the benefit of provincial boys.

In 1587 Peter Symonds, the great mercer, certain of whose charities have already been noted, established an apprenticeship endowment of £100 for the benefit of aspiring youths in his native city of Winchester.[1] Hugh Offley, twice master of the Leathersellers' Company, by his will proved in 1594 left £600 as endowment for apprenticeships in London, as well as £200 for the aid of worthy boys in his native city of Chester.[2]

To pass to the early Stuart period, we may mention the bequest of Philip Strelley, a goldsmith, who left in trust annuities with a capital value of £400 'towards yearly placing of poor men's sons' to be chosen from his own county of Derbyshire, from Nottinghamshire, or from the city of Worcester.[3] Moving forward almost twenty years, we may mention the endowment of £500 left in 1624 by William Halliday, a wealthy mercer, to the municipal officers of Gloucester, the income of which was to be disposed to four poor boys of that town 'who had had honest education to be apprentices, and whose parents wanted means for the same'.[4] A few years later Lancelot Andrews established an apprenticeship fund with an income of £25 p.a. for the binding of poor and fatherless children of London who might otherwise be driven to beggary or worse.[5] A London cordwainer, James Shaw, in 1630 vested properties then valued at upwards of £280 to provide apprenticeship fees for three boys and two girls who should be natives of Brampton, Derbyshire, presumably the donor's birthplace.[6] Poor boys of other Derbyshire communities were assisted by an endowment of £100 left by Richard Crashaw, whose substantial charities for the poor have already been noted, under the terms of his will proved in 1631.[7] In 1633 John Locke, a rich 'tailor on Ludgate Hill', left on trust £1000, the income of which should be employed for binding out as apprentices children who had been certified by the Governors of Bridewell Hospital, each boy to have from £5 to £10 for his fee.[8]

A selection of substantial apprenticeship foundations made in the closing years of the early Stuart period will suggest that not all these benefactions were the gift of merchants. Hugh Perry, who was a mercer, among other very generous provisions for his native town of Wotton-under-Edge, Gloucestershire, gave capital of £100 value to assist boys from that place 'that should go up to London to be bound apprentices'.[9] Lady Katherine Conway in 1639 by will provided a fund of £400 on trust to secure the binding of poor and fatherless children of the parish of Acton (Middlesex) under the trusteeship of the Grocers' Company,[10] while somewhat earlier Thomas, Lord Coventry, had vested in the Merchant Taylors' Company fee-farm rents to furnish the payment of £20 p.a. for the apprenticing of poor children from two London parishes, £10 p.a. for poor relief, and £1 16s 8d p.a. for company uses.[11] Still another fund established in 1639 may be noted, though it was hardly designed to endow apprenticeships in the ordinary meaning of the term.

John Parker, a London haberdasher, left £300 to be employed for taking up orphan boys and girls from the streets or from Bridewell and for paying their passage to New England, where they should be 'bound apprentices to some such as will be carefull to bringe them upp in the feare of God and to maintain themselves another daie'.[12] Bequests of this kind were by no means uncommon in this period, as witness the dispositions of Roger Abdy, a clothworker, in 1642 who left £100 for apprenticing ten poor boys who must be sons of freemen of London, as well as £120 to be 'bestowed upon twenty more poore boyes and girles to be taken upp out of the streetes of London as vagrants' and transported to the New World, where they might find greater opportunities.[13]

During the unsettled decade of civil war, 1641–1650, there was a steady interest in the founding of apprenticeship endowments, a total of £2352 having been given for this purpose by a considerable number of donors. Thus William Stanley in 1643 left £100 to the Drapers' Company of Coventry to be used for apprenticeships·until such time as they might be able to institute a workhouse and gave in addition £100 to the city of Coventry for setting forth freemen's sons as apprentices there and in London.[14] Shortly afterwards, Elizabeth, Viscountess Campden, left on trust to feoffees in Kensington (Middlesex) capital of £200 with instructions that half the income was to be applied for the apprenticing of a poor boy from the parish and the remainder for poor relief, while also establishing a fund of the same value and with identical provisions for the parish of Hampstead (Middlesex).[15] At about the same time, Sir Nicholas Rainton, a former lord mayor and a haberdasher, left capital with a worth of £200 for apprenticing three poor children from the parish of Enfield, Middlesex, and the same amount for three children of London, to be chosen by the mayor and aldermen.[16] We may conclude our examples of substantial apprenticeship endowments created in this decade by mentioning the gift made by Sir John Gayer, a fishmonger who served as lord mayor in 1646–1647, of £500 to Christ's Hospital as trustee, the income on which was to be used for the settling in apprenticeships of three boys annually upon the nomination of the governors.[17]

We have already noted that in the final decade of our period there was a sudden welling up of interest in apprenticeship foundations on the part of London donors. The substantial total of £9115 was provided for this use in this single decade, well over three times as much as had been so vested in any earlier decade and, almost incredibly, 46 per cent of the whole amount given for this use during the full course of our period. There were in all twenty-seven separate benefactions given for apprenticeships between 1651 and 1660, ranging in amount from £45 to £2000 in capital value, all save two of the donors having been substantial merchants. The language of the wills and the deeds of gift establishing these endowments suggest no reason for the sudden burgeoning out of interest in apprenticeships, though we may well believe that both the desire to re-create the apprenticeship system so seriously disrupted by the recent civil conflict and the restoration of political and economic stability under the Commonwealth and Protectorate may significantly have influenced the action of donors during this interval.

In 1654 a wealthy Levant merchant, Sir John Langham, vested in Christ's Hospital an endowment of £500 to secure the apprenticing each year of three boys and three girls in useful trades.[18] William Adams, a rich haberdasher, by an indenture dated 1656 settled on his company as trustees rents with a capital worth of £480, the income to be employed each year for the binding of three poor boys from Newport or Chetwin End, Shropshire, as apprentices either in London or in Shrewsbury.[19] In the same year, Godfrey Goodman, the Bishop of Gloucester, who was properly suspected of Romanist proclivities, established an apprenticeship fund with a capital worth of £300 for boys to be chosen from his native Wales.[20] Theophilus Royley, a draper, also in 1656 by will created an apprenticeship endowment with a then capital value of about £600, the income of which was to be employed for apprenticing the children of the poor of his company, an allowance of not more than £5 to be made for each boy and of not more than £3 for each girl selected.[21] In the next year, 1657, a grocer, Thomas Whitley, by will gave £200 to secure the apprenticing of named persons, as well as ordering other charitable benefactions.[22]

Towards the close of our period, Gilbert Keate, also a grocer, bequeathed £600 as an apprenticeship fund, the income of which should annually be employed for the apprenticing of six boys and girls to be chosen from Christ's Hospital, as well as providing £400 of endowment for St John's Hospital in Exeter, to be used for the maintenance and apprenticing of four children from that city.[23] It was probably in the same year (1658) that Thomas Austin, a clothworker, established an annuity of £60 which was to run for seven years and to be wholly employed for the apprenticing of London children, as well as giving £100 as endowment for the relief of the poor of the parish of St Leonard Shoreditch.[24] In the same year, another merchant, Thomas Bowyer, made generous arrangements to ensure the apprenticing of ten poor boys, while also providing for the care of ten seamen maimed in merchant service.[25] Sir John Wollaston, a goldsmith, whose generously endowed almshouse foundation has already been discussed, by the terms of his will proved in 1658 vested in Christ's Hospital as trustee a huge rent-charge of £200 p.a., representing a capital worth of £4000, to secure the apprenticing of boys at £5 p.a. each and girls at £3 6s 8d p.a. each, with the provision that if sufficient worthy candidates were not available, any residue of income should be employed for the general care of children in the hospital.[26] In concluding, we may mention a more modest provision made by Francis Ash, a goldsmith, who settled property then valued at £200 to secure annually the apprenticing of two boys, sons of poor men of his company, as well as £140 for setting forth each year one or two apprentices from his native town of Derby.[27]

Relatively modest as was the support lent by London merchants to the accumulation of apprenticeship endowments, it may none the less be said that the total of £19,587 18s provided for this purpose was to have considerable effectiveness in spreading the arc of opportunity for poor but ambitious youths in London and elsewhere in the realm. Almost the whole of these gifts had been vested in capital sums, and we may believe that by the close of our period something like £979 was each year available to feoffees for the binding of young people who might otherwise have been condemned for life to the poverty with which their own families were afflicted. Since in average terms £4 15s was regarded as sufficient for the arranging of an apprenticeship, this means that perhaps 206 youths were each year rescued and provided with the opportunity to become responsible and useful citizens. This, certainly, was no mean social gain.

2. *Loan funds*

Though London merchant donors displayed a rather limited interest in creating large endowments for apprenticeship schemes, they were zealously concerned with the problem of supplying the necessary capital for the likely and ambitious youths who had successfully completed their years of service. This problem of finding the considerable capital required for entering upon a trading career was, as we have earlier noted, a serious one if the young man could gain a starting competence neither by marriage nor by family aid. There is abundant evidence that many merchants of charitable disposition supplied the required capital by gift or, more often, loans on easy terms, to favourite apprentices. But such private charity by no means met what remained a critical social problem. It is also most vividly clear from the nostalgic evidence of many merchants' wills that even successful men remembered in their old age with some bitterness their own great difficulties in establishing themselves as young men with a sufficient trading competence. These facts doubtless serve to explain the steady accumulation of loan funds, almost from the beginning of our period, designed to relieve the dilemma of the aspiring young merchant or tradesman and to open for him the doors of economic opportunity.

During the whole course of our period the impressive sum of £43,942 1s of loan capital was provided by London donors. It should be noted that we have regarded such gifts and bequests as loan funds only if the amounts were to be lent either with no interest charge or at nominal rates up to 3 per cent, these charges being designed to secure the preservation of the principal rather than to serve other charitable ends. There was given in addition upwards of £24,000 to be lent to young merchants and tradesmen on well-secured terms and at economic interest rates, the income of which was to be disposed for prescribed charitable uses; these we have incorporated under the use to which the income was to be applied.

From 1503 onwards the accumulation of London's loan funds proceeded steadily. In the years prior to the Reformation, £1352 2s was provided by six donors for this most fruitful social purpose, while in the short interval of the Reformation the substantial total of £2320 was added. The great burst of benefactions for this charitable use came in the Elizabethan era, when the very large total of £18,795 13s was given, with a particularly heavy concentration in the first decade of the period (1561-1570), when the total was £8165. But there was no slackening of enthusiasm for this useful form of investment in social rehabilitation during the last two generations of our period, the additions being made from decade to decade within the remarkably narrow limits of from £2510 (1651-1660) to £4296 (1611-1620).

The loan funds created with such steady generosity by London donors were of two quite different types. The first were capital gifts to be lent to needy persons generally in an effort to relieve their emergency wants without subjecting them to the social stigma of pauperism. Such funds were in capital form, though the donors evidently expected that they would in time be exhausted or lost, since no interest was exacted and no, or at best inadequate, security demanded. In all, £5710 was given by a considerable number of benefactors for this salutary use. Perhaps two examples will serve to illustrate the loan funds of this sort. Thus Mildred, Lady Burghley, in 1583 vested in the Haberdasher's Company as trustees the capital sum of £210 to be lent to needy householders of several named parishes outside Middlesex. Of this amount, £120 was designated for loans in the town of Romford (Essex), her birthplace, to men of such occupations as husbandman, smith, carpenter, baker, tailor, and shoemaker, and in amounts not to exeed £20 and for a term of two years without interest. The second sum of £90 was to be lent on the same terms to needy persons of the same lowly callings who were residents of three Hertfordshire parishes near her then home at Theobalds.[28] A somewhat more restricted kind of expendable loan fund may be illustrated in the bequest of a stationer, Christopher Meredith, who in 1653 left capital valued at £200 to his company to be lent to needy and deserving stationers requiring aid, without security, and without the assessment of any interest charge.[29]

But by far the largest sum, £38,232 1s in amount, was carefully disposed by donors with the intention of creating a revolving loan fund, to be lent with great discrimination while providing the fledgling merchant or tradesman with the initial competence required for his calling. A few of the larger of these benefactions may be briefly noted. The earliest substantial loan fund of this type was endowed by a rich goldsmith, Thomas Wood, who in 1503 left to his company ten houses and fourteen shops making up 'Goldsmiths' Row', and then probably nominally valued at £800, with an additional £112 to constitute a loan fund for young men entering on their calling in these shops.[30]

The greatest of the loan funds of our period was created between 1542 and 1554 by that extraordinarily ingenious and prodigally charitable merchant tailor, Sir Thomas White, who is of course best known for his foundation of St John's College, Oxford. The son of a Reading clothier, White was apprenticed to Hugh Acton, a rich merchant tailor, who established him in business on his death in 1520 with a bequest of £100. White very quickly became a prosperous merchant, being assessed at £1000 in 1535. During this period in his life, he rose to a position of dominance in the cloth trade, establishing close business connections in many parts of England and with cities which were later to benefit from his generosity. After some resistance, he accepted election as an alderman in 1544 and was chosen sheriff in 1547. White was elected lord mayor in 1553, when his firm but temperate control of the city contributed much to Queen Mary's accession to the throne.

White's first great loan fund was established by a gift of £1400 to the city of Coventry. An estate was purchased yielding £70 p.a., the income to be lent to deserving young men of the town who were able to furnish reasonable security and who wished to become tradesmen. The indenture provided that, upon the donor's death (1567), the income was to be paid in rotation for the purposes indicated to the cities of Coventry, Northampton, Leicester, Nottingham, and Warwick. This fund, so so conservatively ordered that only the income might be used, was judiciously invested and managed, with the result that as early as 1710 the annual loan capital available was £838. White's next experimental venture was to establish a fund of £2000 for the use of the Corporation of Leicester, with the stipulation that the capital should be lent without interest to tradesmen requiring funds, in sums of from £40 to £50, and with careful provisions for security and repayment. The third great loan fund was created in 1545 by a gift of £2000 to the city of Bristol, subject to a regulation and revision of the trust made by the donor shortly before his death. The revised deed of trust provided that for a period of ten years £800 should be lent on surety to sixteen poor but deserving clothiers of the city from the income on the endowment, while £200 was to be used to supply corn for the poor of the city. Beginning with the year 1577, the then income of £104 p.a. was to be distributed in rotation to twenty-four named cities and towns in all parts of the realm, there to be lent free of interest to young men 'of honest fame, freemen and clothiers being preferred', the loans to run for the long term of ten years.[31]

To move ahead about a generation after White's huge benefactions, we may mention two loan funds most carefully devised by Robert Offley, a haberdasher, in 1596. Offley left £200 on trust with the Haberdashers with instructions that the capital be lent without interest to four deserving young men of the company for terms of not more than five years.[32] In addition, he left £600 to the city of Chester to be lent in sums of £25 to each of twenty-four worthy young men there for terms of five years. The deed of gift further prescribed that half of those eligible should have gained their freedom by apprenticeships served within the city and that loan apportionments should be made by lot among the eligible applicants.[33] A few years later, in 1601, the famous Peter Blundell, a London merchant whose benefactions total nearly £11,000, left £900 as a loan fund for the city of Exeter and the town of Tiverton, under carefully regulated and quite unusual conditions. Of the capital, £500 was to be made available in loans of £20 each to twenty-five poor but worthy artisans and handicraftsmen of Exeter at a nominal interest rate of 2 per cent to encourage repayment, while the remaining £400 was to be lent on the same terms to artificers, weavers, and tuckers of Tiverton.[34]

John Kendrick, a draper whose generous bequest to poor relief has already been discussed, by his will proved in 1624 established loan funds with a total capital value of £1900. The sum of £900 was left to the Merchant Adventurers, to be lent in the very substantial amounts of £300 to each of three 'honest, industrious, and frugal young men', just free of the company, for a period of three years without interest, five of his own servants to be first preferred by the feoffees. Kendrick's will also established a loan fund with £500 of capital, to be lent free of interest for three years to ten honest and industrious clothiers of Reading, or to other tradesmen if the funds could not be well or securely placed, while a fund in the same amount and with identical regulations was created for the town of Newbury.[35] In the next year, Richard Fishborne, a most generous mercer of London, bequeathed to the wardens of his company the substantial capital of £1000 to be lent in amounts not to exceed £200 each to young men just free of the company for terms of five years and without charges for interest.[36] We may conclude our almost random sampling of certain of the larger loan fund creations with another, having a capital of £1000, also left to the Mercers by Elizabeth, Viscountess Campden, in 1648, which was to be lent free of interest in sums of £125 each to eight young men free of the company. The fund was carefully regulated to benefit young men not yet of the livery, shopkeepers being first preferred, and then silkmen, all of whom must be of good name and able to provide good security for their credit.[37]

In all, the substantial total of £38,332 1s was provided by London donors as capital specifically designed to enable promising young men to establish themselves in business upon the completion of their apprenticeship. The whole of this capital was available to deserving young tradesmen or merchants either at no interest or at the most at nominal interest rates. It is also important to note that £9650 of this capital sum had been given by London donors for the assistance of deserving young men in various provincial towns, almost invariably towns in which these benefactors had been born or with which they had held close trading connections. There were in all 440 individual donors of loan funds during the whole course of our period. Of this number, it is interesting to observe, 346 were merchants or their widows, who as a group gave very nearly 90 per cent of the whole *corpus* of these funds. There were in addition eighty-eight donors who were tradesmen, while only six were either members of other social groups or of uncertain status. The whole conception, then, of this extraordinarily fruitful charitable instrumentality was still another bold contribution of the mercantile genius and sprang from the tender sense of responsibility which animated this group during the age under discussion. In average terms, it was considered that slightly more than £70 was required by a young merchant or retailer about to start on a trading career, and, again in average terms, donors seem to have believed that 3·6 years was a sufficient period for such an enabling loan to run. This, then, means that towards the close of our period something over 150 men in London and the provinces were each year launched on business careers—were translated into the middle class—as the consequence of this massive generosity of the merchant donors of London. It must be remembered, too, that there was in addition a large sum of about £24,000 available at economic interest rates, the donors being primarily interested in another charitable use, for young men who found it difficult to secure working capital elsewhere.[38] These great resources for social rehabilitation and advancement were extraordinarily fruitful in their consequences, and they were immensely to increase the fluidity which characterizes any healthy and aspiring society. Another very great social gain had been made.

We have been describing institutions which were being quite rapidly formed by private donors for socially hopeful purposes. The apprenticeship foundations and the loan funds were made available for youths who had already demonstrated reliability, intelligence, and probably as well clear evidence of the aggressiveness so characteristic of the mercantile fraternity in this age. But there remained the large and inert mass of the incompetent, the lazy, and the marginal elements of the society, which stood as a challenge to the Calvinistic ethic of the typical London tradesman or merchant. Remarkably generous and it was thought reasonably adequate provision had been made for the derelict, for the true casualties of the economy, in the immense endowments which had been vested for household relief and for almshouse foundations. But there were other lines of assault on poverty which were clearly inspired by hopes of social rehabilitation, of human salvaging, which we must now examine.

3. To set the poor on work

One of the most interesting of the instruments created for this purpose during our period was the vesting of capital wherewith the poor might be set upon useful and gainful work, either under rather informal controls or in the institutionalized confines of a workhouse. There was considerable enthusiasm for schemes of social rehabilitation of this sort in several of the counties we have studied, though London donors on the whole remained prudently sceptical regarding this charitable mechanism, there being a substantial body of evidence suggesting that they thought it too expensive and unreliable in relation to benefits to be gained.[39] The whole amount provided by London donors for such experiments in social rehabilitation was no more than £13,253 6s, or only 0·7 per cent of the total of the great charitable wealth accumulated by the city during our period.[40] Gifts for this use did not begin until the period of the Reformation, when the meagre total of £120 was provided, with rather more than £3000 having been given in the Elizabethan decades. During the early Stuart age, a total of £5906 6s was given for stocks for the poor, with a particularly heavy concentration of these endowments in the decade just prior to the Civil War, when £4550 was given. This interest was well maintained during the years of the Civil War, when the impressive sum of £3230 was given for this use. In point of fact, very nearly 59 per cent of the whole of the capital provided for workhouses and stocks was vested during the relatively short interval 1631–1650. We shall now mention a few of the larger and more interesting of these foundations.

The earliest of the substantial endowments of this sort was that created under the will of Thomas Hunt, a skinner, who in 1559 left £100 to provide materials upon which the poor in London hospitals might be set at work.[41] Two decades later, William Lambe, the great clothworker and philanthropist, left £200 on trust with his company to be used to set the poor on work at cloth making.[42] By far the largest of the sixteenth-century endowments for work schemes was that founded in 1588 under the will of Laurence Atwell, a skinner. This donor left the residue of his estate, an amount not far from £1800, on trust to his company under instructions to treat it 'as a stock to be employed in some good sort whereby poor people', and especially those of his own company, might be put on useful work. It was also the donor's wish that the capital should be maintained by the addition of all income received, save for certain payments for the benefit of the company and for St Bartholomew's Hospital. Atwell at the same time settled on private trustees properties valued at £600 for the founding of a similar work scheme in Exeter, which was in turn frustrated since 'the poor . . . entitled to the benefit . . . had from time to time secretly sold and disposed of the materials of the manufactures . . . and had . . . wasted the money'.[43]

Passing to the seventeenth century when, as we have said, there was much greater interest in these work schemes, we may first mention several of the smaller and more representative endowments and then conclude with a fuller discussion of the few that were really substantial. In 1616 William Parker, a merchant tailor, gave £200 to be used for the provision of tools and materials with which the poor of his native parish of Walsall, Staffordshire, might be gainfully employed.[44] Sir Thomas Hayes, a draper who had served as lord mayor in 1614–1615, on his death in 1617 provided £100 as a stock for the poor of Westminster.[45] The rich and generous merchant tailor, John Vernon, several of whose benefactions have already been described, in 1617 left £200 to his native Chester 'to remain forever' as a stock to set the poor on work. This fund, it is instructive to note, was consumed within a period of seven years.[46] Baptist Hicks (Viscount Campden), among his many generous provisions for Chipping Campden, Gloucestershire, vested the considerable sum of £500 with which the poor of that town were to be set on productive work, the feoffees to appoint two able and responsible men to manage the enterprise for half the profit. In this case, too, despite careful safeguards, the substance of the trust was soon lost, suggesting only too pointedly why the always prudent London donors viewed these experimental undertakings with so little real enthusiasm.[47] Some years later, in 1642, William Randall, of Lincoln's Inn, left funds valued at £108 each, with which the poor of Banbury (Oxfordshire) and Henley-in-Arden (Warwickshire) were to be given useful and gainful employment.[48] And, finally, in discussing certain of the relatively modest benefactions for this purpose, we may mention James Fletcher's gift in 1653 of £400 to six carefully designated trustees of Ormskirk, Lancashire, to be employed as a perpetual stock for setting on work the poor of that parish.[49]

By far the most ambitious of all the workhouse schemes undertaken by London donors in this period was that arranged under the will of John Kendrick, the draper whose great benefactions for the poor have already been noted. Kendrick died in 1624, though some time was to elapse before his great foundations were settled in Reading and New-bury.[50] Under the terms of the will, £8350 was received by the municipal authorities of Reading, with which, after various bequests for poor relief had been funded, a total of £1968 was expended on the purchase of land, the erection of buildings, and the equipping of working rooms for the poor of the town 'in trades of clothing and also in working of stuffs for dyeing or otherwise'. A remainder of £3600 of capital, with certain later additions, seems from the beginning to have been regarded as principally an endowment for poor relief, and has been so reckoned by us, though the donor evidently wished it also to support the great workhouse he had founded. The clothing trade of Reading was for many years principally carried forward in these premises, rent-free quarters being provided there for those who would employ the poor, until towards the close of the eighteenth century, when the endowments, then yielding about £590 p.a., were directly applied for poor relief. Kendrick likewise left £4000 to the municipal authorities of Newbury under similar instructions. The sum of £350 was laid out there on a workhouse, though the remaining endowment seems to have been used rather more for direct household relief than for a work scheme. In 1706 this charity plan was substantially revised, a school for the clothing and education of poor boys being established with the remaining resources of the trust.[51]

Sir Ralph Freeman, a clothworker, who died during his mayoralty in 1634, bequeathed £1000 to the town of Northampton under quite ingenious conditions. This capital was to be lent to trustworthy merchants and tradesmen at 3 per cent on condition that they set the poor of the community at work, while the income thus gained was to be distributed in clothing to the inmates of a local almshouse, to the poor of the town generally, and towards the support of the free grammar school of Northampton.[52] Later in this decade (1639), Robert Johnstone, a lawyer whose generous provision for the relief of the poor of his native Edinburgh has already been mentioned, left £1000 to the civic authorities there to be employed as a stock to set the indigent on work, with the sanguine provision that 'the incres of the said stock ... be destribut amongst the poore of the said citie'.[53]

We may conclude with the bequest made in 1642 by Sir James Cambell, an ironmonger, who left the large sum of £2000 to the Governors of Bridewell, stipulating that they establish a work scheme for the poor, and particularly for prisoners who had been released from Newgate and would find their way back there unless ready and gainful work under discipline were made available. Cambell's executors enjoyed discretionary power to invest the capital instead in those London parishes with the greatest number of poor, such as St Sepulchre's, for work programmes there to be arranged in the event the Bridewell authorities did not promptly provide a competent plan. The executors remained for some time undecided, the Governors of Bridewell as as late as 1656 having held a special court to arrange more facilities and materials, but it seems quite certain that the parochial alternative was adopted and that this goodly substance was consumed, we can only hope fruitfully, in needy London parishes.[54]

4. The care and rehabilitation of prisoners

If there was considerable doubt among London merchants regarding the utility and benefits to be found in workhouse schemes, there was none with respect to the social and human gains to be derived from lending some aid to those who were in prison. The modern mind simply declines to believe the abundant evidence on the conditions under which prisoners were kept during the whole of our period. A large proportion were prisoners for debt who had no hope of release unless they gained the help of family or friends, save in the infrequent gaol deliveries that were ordered. Unimaginable suffering came from ghastly over-crowding, complete discomfort, and utter neglect. Only most reluctantly did the state begin to assume any responsibility for the maintenance of prisoners. Successive Elizabethan statutes afforded some slight measure of maintenance,[55] but a penny a day was regarded as sufficient in many counties. Prisoners were wholly dependent upon outside assistance for their food and, if they had been lodged in gaol for debt, upon others for their redemption. Prison conditions were particularly bad in the several London prisons where so many rootless men, part of the flotsam of emigration to the city, found themselves caught up as vagrants or worse with no hope of succour.

From the beginning of our period the fate of prisoners, particularly for debt, bore heavily upon the burgher conscience. In all, the really enormous sum of £34,795 10s was provided for one or another form of prison relief during the course of our age, or 1·84 per cent of the whole of the charitable funds of the city. In no other county in the realm was there more than a token concern with this grave social problem, even Bristol having dedicated only 0·89 per cent of its charitable resources to this worthy and humane use. It is also significant to note that a large proportion (69·27 per cent) of the generous total given for this purpose was in the form of endowments, these donors being resolved to raise up formidable resources for the aid of those who could be rehabilitated, most particularly, of course, those who were imprisoned for debt.

There was some contribution towards this form of social rehabilitation in every decade of our period, the amounts given during the two generations prior to the Reformation ranging from £77 9s (1480–1490) to £795 12s (1531–1540). In the short span of the Reformation period, a total of £874 13s was given for the care of prisoners. But it was with the

Elizabethan age that the flow of these benefactions began to quicken, the substantial sum of £8259 19s having been provided for this use during this long generation. From the first decade of the seventeenth century forward for five successive decades, the total of contributions never fell below £4000, while it rose to more than £5000 in two decade intervals. In all, the large sum of £18,082 13s was given for the rehabilitation of prisoners during the early Stuart period, while in the unsettled years of political upheaval the amount was £5914 10s.

As we shall later observe, there was a considerable number of substantial endowments vested for prison relief during the course of our period. But the most significant fact in the accumulation of these resources was the general participation of all classes of the society. Thus in the decade 1501–1510 there were forty-two donors who left something for prisoners, thirty-five having given sums less than £5. Just a century later there were ninety-eight donors in all, of whom seventy-six provided amounts of less than £10. This was, in fact, one of the few charitable causes in which men of all classes were interested. From about 1580 onwards, at least a small benefaction for one or more of the London prisons came to be, with some gift to the poor and to the hospitals, almost a routine item in every merchant's will. Is it not probable that among all classes of men fear of imprisonment for debt was never quite absent from the conscious mind? Even great fortunes in this turbulent economic age, fortunes which had been won so quickly, could evaporate before the breath of fire, the hazards of storm, or a turn of fate. Men of this age, glorious though it was, were afflicted with haunting fears only recently, and one hopes permanently, dispelled.[56]

Though the massive accumulation of funds for the relief of prisoners came from the thousands of small legacies left for this use, we must content ourselves with the recital of only a few of the relatively large benefactions made for this purpose. All these gifts fall into three main types: funds left to provide food and other necessaries for those confined to prison for whatever reason, endowments or outright gifts to secure the release of prisoners held for debt, and funds established to secure the succour or redemption of prisoners held for ransom abroad.

The earliest of the really large endowments was that provided by Sir Thomas Ramsay and his widow, Lady Mary. By an indenture dated 1583, this great grocer vested in the civic authorities rents with a then value of £10 p.a. to be distributed among London prisoners for their sustenance, while his will, proved in 1590, left £24 3s 4d outright for the same broad uses. Lady Ramsay, probably in 1601, gave as well the substantial sum of £500 for the relief of prisoners in London and Southwark, it being her expressed intention to redeem as many as possible who were held for failure to pay judgments of £2 or less.[57] In the same general period, Ralph Rokeby, the Master of Requests, among other substantial charities, left a total of £720 for the care and redemption of prisoners in the London area.[58] In the next year (1597) William Peake, of St Leonard Shoreditch, left lands charged with an annual payment of £15 for the relief of those in certain London prisons,[59] while Gregory Smith, a merchant tailor, bequeathed £100 as a fund, the income to be employed for the redemption of prisoners for debt.[60]

The lot of London prisoners must have been considerably bettered when in 1601 Peter Blundell by will provided nine separate endowments of £150 each, vested in as many of the livery companies, with the stipulation that the income be employed for the relief of those held in the principal London prisons.[61] One is somewhat less certain regarding the good effects of the gift of £250 made about 1605 by Elizabeth Elliot, the income of which was to be used to pay a man for ringing a bell under the walls of Newgate between eleven and twelve on the night preceding an execution, while at the same time delivering an exhortation for the edification of the condemned man. The trust further provided that the bellman should on the day of the execution deliver still another pious address to the doomed man at St Sepulchre's churchyard, the hangman's cart being stopped for this purpose.[62] Among other substantial charities, William Walthall, a mercer, in 1608 left £30 for the relief of prisoners and £100 to secure the release of debtors,[63] while some years later (1615) Ann Whitmore, a haberdasher's widow, bequeathed £150 for the maintenance of prisoners.[64] Frances Clarke, a salter's widow, died in 1618 having some years earlier given £200 on trust to the Drapers on condition that they pay £10 p.a. to relieve and redeem poor prisoners in the Compter in Wood Street and having created an identical endowment with the Mercers as trustees for the redemption of debtors in the Poultry Compter.[65] Richard Wiseman, a goldsmith, in 1618 left £100 for the assistance of men just released from prison,[66] while in the next year John Harrison, a most generous merchant tailor, bequeathed the considerable sum of £320 to secure the release and rehabilitation of debtors.[67]

Passing to the next decade, when a total of £4376 14s was provided for the relief of prisoners, we can recount only a few of the many benefactions of these years. We have already dealt with Henry Smith's endowment of £1000 vested to secure the relief or ransom of Englishmen held by the Barbary pirates.[68] Bishop Andrews in the following year (1627) left annuities representing a capital worth of £1000 to be distributed annually in Holy Week for the relief of poor prisoners,[69] while in the same year Sir Thomas Bennett, a rich mercer, provided an annuity of £24 to secure the release of prisoners for debt in the two Compters and in Ludgate, who might be redeemed for £2 or less.[70] Lady Mary Carey, the widow of the third Lord Hunsdon, on her death in 1627 left a capital sum then valued at £120 to provide for the care of prisoners, as well as establishing annuities representing a capital worth of £200 for the poor of London and Northamptonshire, £120 for St Bartholomew's Hospital, and endowing a lectureship with an annual stipend of £6.[71]

In the decade just preceding the outbreak of civil war, the large total of £5060 13s was given by a great many donors for the relief of prisoners. We may mention a few of the more modest, though still substantial, gifts for this use made during these years as being more representative than the quite large funds we have been describing. In 1631 Richard Crashaw, the goldsmith whose generous arrangements for the poor of London and Derbyshire have already been mentioned, by the terms of his will provided an estimated £250 for the maintenance and rehabilitation of prisoners.[72] Rowland Heylyn, an ironmonger and a notable benefactor of Shrewsbury, by the terms of his will proved in 1632 left £100 to secure the redemption of debtors imprisoned for judgments of less than £4,[73] while in the same year a fellow Welshman, William Middleton, left £250 for the relief of prisoners in the two Compters and in three other London prisons.[74] At the very end of the decade, in 1639, Robert Johnstone, the lawyer whose generous provisions for the poor and for a work programme in his native Edinburgh have already been discussed, left by will £1200 (Scots) for the relief and redemption of prisoners there whose debts should in no case exceed £100 (Scots).[75]

During the two revolutionary decades, the surprisingly large total of £5914 10s was provided for the relief of prisoners by London donors. By far the largest of these benefactions was that of Sir James Cambell, an ironmonger and former lord mayor who died in 1642. In addition to an outright bequest of £200 for prison relief, Cambell vested £1000 in his company on trust with the stipulation that this capital be lent to young freemen of the livery at 4 per cent interest, the whole of the income to be employed 'with the advice of the high sheriffs of London' for redeeming debtors whose obligations did not exceed £5 each. In addition, Cambell by will settled another trust of £1000, the income of which was to be employed for the ransom of poor captives who had been taken by Turkish or other Mediterranean pirates.[76] A few years later, in 1646, Henry Hazelfoot, a haberdasher, charged his company with the distribution of £10 p.a. to secure the release of prisoners for debt,[77] while in the next year Ann Middleton, the widow of the famous Sir Thomas, settled an annuity in the same amount to gain the release of prisoners against whom stood judgments of not more than £2, save for exceptional cases when, upon the recommendation of the wardens, as much as £3 might be paid.[78] And, finally, we may note the bequest of £100 to poor prisoners in London left in 1657 by Robert Vallence, an innkeeper in Clerkenwell.[79]

5. Marriage subsidies

The least substantial of all the accumulations made during our period for the various forms of social rehabilitation were those provided by London donors for marriage subsidies. Though at least small sums were given for this purpose in all save one decade (1631–1640), the total amounted to no more than £9277 1s, or only 0·49 per cent of the whole of the charitable funds of the city. This rather old-fashioned form of charitable assistance enjoyed its greatest popularity during the first half of our period, more than half the total being accounted for by the £4821 2s provided for this use during the years prior to the Reformation. In the years of reformation (1541–1560), the sum of £1264 2s was given for marriage portions, as compared with the considerably smaller total of £1065 4s given during the much longer Elizabethan age. One would have thought this an interesting and beneficial form of social experimentation, but it simply never gained favour with the mercantile elite as it did in many counties among the perhaps more sentimentally disposed squirearchy. In point of fact, something over 80 per cent (81·12 per cent) of the whole of the capital disposed for this purpose was the gift either of women of the age or of unmarried men. Possibly the sociologist or psychologist might draw conclusions from this fact which quite elude the historian. But, in any event, we shall want to notice at least a sampling of these gifts.

In 1506 Nicholas Alwyn, a mercer who had been mayor in 1499–1500, by will bequeathed £10 to provide one hundred pewter pots for young women about to be married, as well as vesting in trust a remainder of about £100 for marriage portions.[80] A generation later, Sir Thomas Seymour, also of the Mercers' Company, bequeathed on trust £133 7s to provide portions for the marriage of two hundred poor maidens in his native county of Essex.[81] But by far the largest of all the endowments for such purposes was that left in *ca.* 1537 by Thomas Howell, a London draper of Welsh birth. Howell, who traded principally in Spain in oils, alum, iron, raisins, and fine cloths, died in Seville, leaving on trust to his company 12,000 ducats in gold to be employed to provide generous marriage portions for deserving Welsh maidens, and with an indicated preference for orphan girls of his own lineage. The company, in replying to a complaint lodged against it for delays about twenty years later, made it clear indeed that the bequest had raised many difficulties. Their historian has with justice said that these problems constituted a warning to intended benefactors 'never to leave portions to marriageable maidens, especially if they be Welsh'. Their first approach in their endeavour to secure the property had been to the Spanish ambassador, to whom they had offered £100 for his help in gaining the legacy, all of which was in Spanish goods. A year later a delegation from their own livery, aided by two Florentine merchants, had made firm representations in Madrid. In 1541 the sum of £570 was received in cash, together with a consignment of oil, in partial settlement, but despite their best efforts no more than £1962 seems to have been recovered in all. This none the less considerable endowment was at once invested in London real property, including £1200 paid to the Crown for a portion of Thomas Cromwell's estate, then yielding £105 p.a. It seems quite clear that the company built its own hall on a portion of the property, paying the trust no rental, but this minor diminution aside, every effort was made to pay out the stipends, despite the great distance and many other problems of administration. The property purchased for the endowment was vastly to increase in value, the annual rental in 1921 being £10,600, with the result that successive broadenings of the permissible uses as ordered by Chancery were to make it a notable and a most valuable charity for 'maidens, especially if they be Welsh'.[82]

There was considerable though sporadic interest in these endowments during the Elizabethan period. Thus in 1556 Elizabeth Gravener, probably a leatherseller's widow, left lands in Devon worth approximately £600, a fourth of the income of which was to be used for marriage subsidies.[83] A grocer's widow, Katherine Hall, in the next year left £5 p.a. for a term of forty years for marriage portions.[84] In 1579 Margaret Dane [Dean], the widow of William Dane, an ironmonger, among other considerable charitable endowments, vested in the Ironmongers property valued at £200 to provide in each year £10 to be distributed to twenty poor and needy maidens upon their marriages.[85] Towards the close of the Elizabethan era, another woman donor, Lady Mary Ramsay, whose generous benefactions for so many useful purposes have been noted, left property upon trust to the City of London to ensure the annual payment of £20 for marriage subsidies, as well as leaving an outright bequest of £40 for the same purpose.[86]

To conclude, we may mention a few additional funds vested to secure competences for poor girls about to be married which were established in the early Stuart period. In 1618 Isaac Duckett, a goldsmith, bequeathed £400 on trust with the ambiguous stipulation that the income was to be employed either for the rewarding of faithful maidservants in the parishes af St Andrew Holborn and St Clement Danes, or to provide stipends at the time of their marriage. A decree in Chancery in 1620 established this as a valid trust and also ruled that the income was to be employed for marriage portions for deserving maidservants from the favoured parishes.[87] The great merchant philanthropist, John Kendrick, in 1624 by will left capital of £200 for marriage portions in London, £100 in Reading, and £50 in Newbury;[88] and, finally, we may note the £200 which Lancelot Andrews left to be distributed outright in portions to poor maidservants about to be married.[89]

6. *The founding of hospitals and the care of the sick*

We turn now to a consideration of the great charitable movement with which by continuous and very large accumulations of capital London's hospitals were established, maintained, and endowed. It is a subject badly in need of full treatment and for which rich stores of sources are available, but the proportions of this study impose unhappily rigorous limitations of space. It is a record of a proud and humane accomplishment in which the burghers of London were pioneering, not only for England but for the western world, as they founded and financed a number of great institutions under secular control that were devoted to the care of the sick and helpless. A seventeenth-century writer, in speaking of St Bartholomew's, expressed the pride and devotion of Londoners in these, their creations, when he said that this 'charitable foundation so well devised by that famous and renowned King Henry the 8, hath since the times of the Gospel been much augmented: and is by the wise gouernours of the house as faithfully imployed to the comfort of many poore members of Christ, which by the charitie of that house, haue been healed of diuers diseases otherwise incurable. We reade that an angel stirred the poole of Bethesda and made it apt to cure all manner of diseases: but here not onely the angel of God goeth in and out among them, but Christ himselfe is present, assisting them in such charitable workes, and giuing a blessing thereunto.'[90]

These foundations are as interesting as they were worthy, because they represent the first really significant advance towards the assumption of civic responsibility for the cure of illness and the care of completely helpless persons. They were also experimental, the functions and purposes of at least two of the institutions having been radically altered in the course of our relatively short period. Thus we have on balance determined to regard Christ Church as a hospital during this age, though by the close of the period it was well on the way towards becoming one of England's great schools. So, too, we have classed Bridewell as a hospital, though it began principally as a workhouse and by the close of our era was usually, and rather accurately, regarded by most donors as a prison with specialized functions. Mixed and confused as the tasks of the hospitals were during a period of about a century, the testimony of many hundreds of testators is that they appealed with such an impressive tenacity to the charitable aspirations of London donors because they offered an organized, humane, and hopeful solution to the age-old problem of illness and incapacity when linked with poverty.

During the whole course of our period the amazing total of £130,872 17s was provided by London benefactors for the care of the sick and the support of the five institutions which we have regarded as hospitals.[91] This large sum accounted for well over half the total given for all those uses which we have reckoned as making due contribution to the social rehabilitation of the poor, and to almost 7 per cent of the whole of the charitable wealth of the city. Interest in the problem of treating illness institutionally was continuous, if modest, from the outset of our period, there having been contributions for this purpose ranging from £20 7s to £325 8s in every decade from 1480 to 1550. But it is with the great Edwardian foundations that the imagination and aspirations of Londoners were really stirred. For the decade 1551–1560 we have credited the huge total of £61,279 11s awarded by the Crown or given by burghers for the hospital endowments of the period. From this time forward it may be said that almost every London merchant, every lord mayor save two, and most tradesmen, as a matter of course made some testamentary provision for the hospitals of the city, while there were many who gave very large sums indeed to one or another of these institutions. During the course of the Elizabethan period, the amount contributed rose steadily from one decade to another, the substantial total of £20,024 having been provided in this generation for the five hospitals which were lending such immensely valuable support to the needs of a sprawling and essentially rootless urban complex. Almost exactly twice as much was poured into these now mature institutions during the early Stuart period, when the total of gifts in no decade fell below £8532 13s and when for the whole generation the munificent sum of £40,137 was provided. The Civil War, however, dealt a severe blow to the further growth and maturity of London's hospitals, the total of gifts for their support in this brief interval falling away to £8514 2s, with, it may be noted, few substantial endowments having been given after 1642.

St Bartholomew's Hospital, the oldest of these foundations, was of medieval origin. It was established early in the twelfth century (ca. 1122) as part of the Priory of St Bartholomew, from a very early date providing care for the poor and sick as well as for orphan children whose mothers had died there. The priory and hospital at the time of the Dissolution possessed net revenues of £304 16s 5d p.a. With the expropriation of the monasteries, the municipal authorities of London petitioned that the city might thenceforward enjoy the government of the hospital together with the revenues which it had held. After an unsuccessful attempt to reconstitute the hospital along semi-religious lines, the King in late 1546 transferred the title to the City of London for the reception of one hundred sick poor persons and vested in the foundation endowments slightly greater than it had held prior to the Dissolution. At the same time, the city undertook to raise a matching contribution of five hundred marks p.a. to provide for the operation of the institution, which was at first gathered by weekly collections in the several wards. These collections were, however, shortly abandoned, and there was by law substituted a scheme for raising operating income by levying certain duties and by assessing the city companies. The hospital was placed under the control of governors appointed by the Corporation, and in 1552 extensive and costly repairs were undertaken on the fabric. In this period the annual outlay, including payments of yearly stipends to ministers of two parishes as well as the care of one hundred patients, amounted to the impressive and certainly burdensome total of £795 2s.[92]

Even prior to the Reformation there had been at least slight evidence of community support for St Bartholomew's, seven small benefactions totalling £10 having been noted in the interval 1480–1540 for the relatively few sick being cared for in the priory during these years. But immediately the institution had been reorganized under secular control and began its great and needed works of mercy, the flow of funds for its support and endowment may be seen beginning. In the brief interval 1547–1550 a total of fifteen benefactions have been noted, amounting to £289 10s and ranging in amount from 10s to £100. In the next decade there were scores of gifts to the stock of the hospital, with the total of contributions reaching the considerable sum of £1897 12s, as the burghers of London set about the great task of funding the heavy responsibility which they had assumed. The generosity of the Reformation period was in fact not matched by Elizabethan charity, the sum of £1777 12s, most of which was endowment, having been added during these four decades. The augmentations made during the early Stuart period were at a consistently high level, ranging from £635 13s to £947 3s for the several decades and with a total addition of £3165 1s to the resources of a now great and universally honoured charitable foundation. Even during the revolutionary era there was no falling away of support, the sum of £1579 having been provided in this short interval. In the whole course of our period, London donors contributed the impressive total of £8718 15s, of which 88·17 per cent was in capital sums, towards the endowment and maintenance of what was by 1660 commonly regarded as one of the most important of all the social institutions of the city.[93] Though no hospital, whether of the seventeenth or of the twentieth century, can ever be wholly endowed, the generosity of London merchants and tradesmen had armed this notable foundation with impressive strength.

Bethlehem Hospital was likewise of medieval origin, having been founded as a convent in 1247 by Simon Fitz Mary, a London citizen. By 1330 the foundation was commonly referred to as a hospital, though less than a generation later it had apparently so far decayed that the almspeople had been dispersed. Sometime before the early fifteenth century the institution had begun to receive insane patients, an inquisition of 1403–1404 revealing that there were then residing in the house six insane persons and three other sick patients. There was only a slight endowment in hand for the support of its work, and Bethlehem was far gone in decay at the opening of our period. There were occasional benefactions made in its favour, totalling, however, no more than £1 7s for the decade 1491–1500, and £1 17s and £16 5s respectively for the two decades immediately following. In 1523 Sir Stephen Jenyns [Jennings], a merchant tailor who had served as mayor, by the terms of his will left £140 to be used by the city 'toward the recovery of the patronage or gifte' of the hospital by the mayor and commonalty of London if that could be accomplished within three years, and, if not, the bequest was to be used for other charitable purposes.[94] It seems certain that the secularization of the hospital was not then achieved, but the effort was continued until in 1546 the purchase was effected at a cost of £113 6s 8d. The hospital was opened for the care of an uncertain number of lunatics, being in 1557 placed under the management of the Governors of Bridewell. At about that time, its capital resources were of the order of £860 (£43 8s 4d p.a.). Slow but steady accumulation of endowments were made in the years that followed, though Bethlehem failed to attract any really substantial single gift, being normally remembered with relatively small bequests from a great number of burghers. In the years intervening between its secularization and 1632, when a report on the condition of the hospital was made to the Privy Council, we have reckoned capital gifts of £1070 4s in all.

The inquisition of 1632 indicated that the settled income of the foundation was then £277 3s 4d, which suggests a considerable increase in the rentals of certain urban properties long held by the governors as endowments. The hospital then housed twenty-seven demented persons, who were also assisted by outright gifts from city officials and other charitably disposed persons. Dr. Crooke, the master, had since 1629 received an allowance of 2s a week for each patient, but had, it was alleged, none the less been guilty of medical neglect of his charges. A second report, made to the Council in April, 1633, revealed that Crooke had indeed been guilty of gross misconduct. His accounts were inaccurate, he had extorted improper fees, had sold gifts in kind to the patients, and had been wholly negligent in discharging his medical obligations. A substantial reorganization was effected in the affairs of the hospital following on this investigation, which may well account for a marked and immediate increase in gifts for its support. In the first decade of the revolutionary era, another £160 of endowment was added by a number of gifts, while in the closing years of our period (1651–1660) the substantial total of £405 was provided by several interested donors. In 1642 it appears that the number of patients housed and cared for had risen to forty-four, though even with additions to the funds of the hospital not more than two-thirds of the yearly outlays could be met from the resources in hand. None the less, a fair beginning had been made in the attack on a social and medical problem which has haunted mankind from the beginning of history to our own age.[95]

St Thomas's Hospital in Southwark was also a medieval foundation. Stow tells us that it was founded in 1213 by the then Prior of Bermondsey as an almshouse. The hospital continued to be held by the monastic foundation until the Dissolution, when its extensive properties were valued by the commissioners at £266 17s 6d. Late in Henry VIII's reign, the premises were purchased from the Crown and rebuilt as a hospital for the reception of poor, lame, and diseased persons by the municipal authorities at a cost, with Christ's Hospital, of £2476. The new institution was opened for patients in 1552 under a charter from Edward VI, dated August 12, 1551, prescribing its purposes as the 'curing and sustentation of the . . . poor, sick, and weak people'. At the same time, the Crown conveyed as endowment properties with a then annual value of £154 17s 1d, or a capital worth of about £3097, for its support. In 1553 a report prepared by the civic authorities for the consideration of the King disclosed that St Thomas's had been opened and was then providing care for 260 'aged, sore, and sick' patients and that the outlays for this institution and Christ's Hospital, they being then under joint administration, was set at the very large total of £3290 5s 4d p.a. These great charges were, of course, most inadequately supported by endowments, particularly in the case of St Thomas's. The Crown lent further assistance in 1553 when by indenture Edward VI conveyed the endowments of the Savoy Hospital, then valued at approximately £12,000 for the support of the four royal hospitals. In 1557, however, the general court for the four hospitals determined, in effect, that the whole of the endowment should be employed for the heavy charges being borne by St Thomas's, while Christ's Hospital should be supported by monthly collections from the citizens and from the profits of Blackwell Hall, subject only to an annual payment of £333 6s 7d for the needs of St Bartholomew's. This arrangement, presumably meant to be temporary, became permanent when it was confirmed in 1631 subject to a capital transfer of £500 made from the funds of St Thomas's to the Governors of Christ's Hospital.

It would seem, then, that the original value of the endowments supplied for St Thomas's by the Crown may be reckoned at about £15,000. Generous though this endowment was, the income was wholly inadequate to support the outlays of this foundation, which during the remainder of our period bore the heaviest responsibility of all of London's hospitals for the care of the impoverished sick of the city. There was a steady and ever-increasing flow of private gifts and bequests to the hospital, with the result that by 1630 the total of the endowments stood at £30,890. The governors made a detailed report on the affairs of the foundation to the Privy Council in 1632, disclosing an annual income from endowments of £1839 16s 3d, and suggesting a moderate increase in rentals on earlier investments in London and Southwark properties. The total outlays were stated as £2716 7s 10d for the preceding year, the still considerable deficit being met principally by gifts to income and casual receipts. There were then somewhat more than 300 patients being cared for, the medical services being supplied by one surgeon at £51 p.a., who was expert in 'cutting the poor of the stone', two surgeons who had £36 p.a. each as stipends, a doctor of physic who received £30 p.a., an apothecary whose stipend was £60 p.a., 'an herb woman for physical herbs' at £4 p.a., and thirteen nursing sisters, each of whom received £2 p.a. The support lent by London benefactors to St Thomas's was well maintained from this time forward to the close of our period, £1443 19s being added to its endowments during this interval. In all, in the course of our period, the large total of £32,234 5s was settled as endowment on this great institution, whether by the Crown or by private benefactors.[96]

We have seen that Christ's Hospital was closely connected in administration and in original endowment with St Thomas's. Though it was built in part on the site of the Friars Minor, Christ's Hospital was a wholly new foundation, made by Edward VI shortly before his death in 1553. Inspired by Bishop Ridley's eloquent humanitarianism and the steady representations of the civic authorities regarding the miserable state of the poor, the young king was persuaded that a foundation planned to provide shelter, medical care, and education for the orphan poor of London was needed to supplement the grand design of the royal hospitals now emerging with the reconstitution and endowment of St Bartholomew's and St Thomas's. At the urging of the then mayor, Sir Richard Dobbes, subscriptions were opened in all the wards of the city, and the buildings were put in order in late 1552 for the reception of 380 homeless and helpless children. It will be recalled that £2476 was subscribed for the rebuilding of Christ's Hospital and St Thomas's, while in the next year (1553) the Crown conveyed the properties of the Savoy Hospital with the intent of thus endowing all the royal hospitals. In 1557, however, as we have noted, these endowments were in effect transferred to St Thomas's, Christ's Hospital being assigned instead the proceeds from a monthly free collection in the wards and the profits of Blackwell Hall.

Christ's Hospital during the whole of our period served principally its original function of a home and hospital for orphan and foundling children, though the first outlines of a great grammar school may be seen emerging within a generation.[97] The institution, ministering as it did to the needs of children from infancy to full maturity, rapidly undertook a great variety of services which made it an extremely complex social organism that developed in relation to the immensely important humane purposes which it endeavoured to satisfy. The good works undertaken by Christ's Hospital appealed to the generosity and the aspirations of the entire community, with the result that from the date of its foundation forward it enjoyed an ever-increasing support from the burghers of London. By 1610 the gifts and bequests made for its endowment had reached the huge total of £45,999 6s, and the hospital was then sheltering and rearing 630 cilldren, as well as sustaining fifty-four who had been put forth in apprenticeships. The children on the foundation might with some justice sing their psalm of thanksgiving:

> Wee orphants poore like mercy found, when meanes and friends were scant,
> Our gracious God a prince did move, to slake and ease our want . . .
> The ground-worke of our good thus laid, God rais'd us patrons deere
> Whose liberall hands did still prouide, to rid our hearts from feare
> You cittizens those patrons are, by you we orphants liue,
> Foode, rayment, learning, all we want, to us you largely giue
> Blesse their endeauours Lord we pray, encrease likewise their store,
> That those in plenty may abound, which helpe to feed the poore. . . .[98]

During the next two decades, 1611–1630, London benefactors poured £12,318 9s more into the already great endowments of the hospital, whose needs were proving to be insatiable as it endeavoured to keep pace with the social requirements imposed by a city growing at an incredibly rapid rate. Of the hundreds of benefactions made to the institution during these years, it is interesting to observe that there were 207 ranging in amount from 6d to £10, approximately three-fourths of these donors being tradesmen and shopkeepers, while there were thirty-nine very substantial bequests ranging from £100 to £2200, of which thirty-five were vested by merchants or their widows. The total of endowments provided by London benefactors in the not quite eighty years that intervened between the foundation and 1630 had reached the massive sum of £58,317 15s. A report of the governors to the Privy Council in the next year (1631) reviewed in some detail the operations of the great institution, which at that date offered care to 707 children. The total of receipts for the year was stated as £4625 3s, of which, it may be noted about half was from the endowment. The outlay for the year slightly exceeded the income, with a great variety of charges listed, of which the principal were £1366 5s 7d for the boarding of nursing children in London and in the country, £1296 17s for food and related necessaries, £1,017 15s 9d for clothing, £502 19s 7d for wages and administrative salaries, £101 11s 11d for education, and £718 6s 4d for miscellaneous outlays and quit-rents.[99]

The devotion of Londoners to this unique and now famous institution increased steadily and rapidly during the last generation of our period, despite political unsettlement and civil war. In the decade 1631-1640 the substantial sum of £8899 5s was left to Christ's Hospital, while in the decade of the Civil War this total was actually surpassed when £9806 was given for the hospital's uses and better endowment. But the crowning record of achievement was witnessed in the Cromwellian decade, when the enormous total of £11,900 13s was vested by London merchants for the further strengthening of the noble work of this great hospital. Thus the whole sum given to Christ's Hospital in slightly more than a century was £88,923 13s, or rather more than 57 per cent of the immense total provided by London donors for all the hospitals of their city. This is a record of achievement of which any city in any age might well be proud.[100]

Bridewell was the fifth and last of the great sixteenth-century foundations. Hardly a hospital in our sense of the term, the institution was in the course of a century to serve as a workhouse, an apprenticeship foundation on a large scale, and, towards the close of our period, as a house of correction and prison for vagrants. Bishop Ridley and a committee of the merchant elite of London in 1552 submitted to the King the thanks of the city for having 'all readie so lovingly & tenderly looked vppon that they have not only provided healpe for all malladies & disseases & the vertuous educacon & bringing upp of or myserable & poore chilldren' in the hospitals already established with royal aid.[101] At the same time, they called attention to the remaining problem of vagrancy and idleness, petitioning the King that the disused palace of Bridewell might be appropriated to the city for use in curing this 'or olde sore'. The King having expressed his approval, these civic leaders then addressed a lengthy memorandum to the Privy Council, setting out in some detail their plans for the new institution. They expressed the conviction that the only cure of idleness and beggary was to be found in labour. But many men were so far fallen because of disease or fortune that they could find no work. This situation could be aided only 'by making some general provision of work, wherewith the *willing* poor may be exercised' and the unwilling beggars compelled to labour. They proposed a most ambitious list of work schemes to be carried forward under civic supervision, and said, viewing with pride the support lent to the hospital so recently founded, 'we dout nothing of the matter wherewith' this 'the most needful and necessary' institution shall be furnished.[102] This most persuasive petition was warmly endorsed by Ridley, who, in an eloquent letter to Cecil, said, 'I must be a suitor unto you in our good Master Christ's cause; I beseech you be good to him . . . he hath lain too long abroad . . . without lodging, in the streets of London, both hungry, naked and cold. Now, thanks be to Almighty God! the citizens are willing to refresh him, and to give him both meat, drink, cloathing and firing' if lodging can only be provided. Great, empty Bridewell would be eminently suitable to this noble purpose. 'Sir, I have promised my brethren the citizens to move you, because I do take you for one that feareth God, and would that Christ should lie no more abroad in the streets.'[103]

Bridewell was conveyed to the city for the purposes so movingly described, being in 1557 incorporated as one of the royal hospitals and conjoined with Bethlehem for purposes of governance. We have seen that the Savoy endowments, meant to buttress all the foundations, were in fact almost wholly absorbed by the pressing needs of St Thomas's Hospital, with the result that Bridewell from its beginning lay as a charge upon the generosity and the tax rolls of the city. All the companies of the city subscribed amounts ranging from £100 each for the great liveries to £2 for the Long Bowstring Makers, the total of contributions being £1540, to furnish and equip the house; collection books were spread out across the city; and rates were imposed to meet the charges, which by 1579 were estimated at £2000 p.a., in order to keep the 200 inmates usefully employed.[104] From the beginning, the aspect of social rehabilitation so evidently contemplated by the founders was quite overwhelmed by the role which Bridewell played in serving as a place of detention for vagrants, rogues generally, and the destitute and root-less flotsam of the city. Necessary as these functions were, they meant that Bridewell had well before the century was out taken on essentially punitive responsibilities for the handling of the incorrigibly idle and those who could not be returned to their own parishes.[105] These mixed functions are well described in a *Report for Bridewell* in 1610 which stated that in the preceding year 1697 persons, mostly vagrants and wandering soldiers, had been housed there before being sent on to their home parishes for settled relief. Many of these men and women were wholy destitute and had to be assisted with food, clothing, and money, before they could be released. In addition, 130 persons, of whom 88 were vagrant boys picked up from London's streets, were steadily maintained by the hospital 'and kept in arts and occupations, and other . . . . workes and labours' designed to effect their social rehabilitation.[106]

In addition to the generous and enthusiastic support lent by the citizens and their companies in outright contributions to the needs of this impressive social experiment, Londoners came gradually to regard Bridewell as sufficiently important and permanent to warrant gifts and bequests for its endowment. Such gifts increased in each successive decade of the Elizabethan period, with the result that in 1600 the endowed funds of the hospital stood at £1864 13s. During the early Stuart period there was a noticeable quickening of interest in the ever-increasing needs of Bridewell, a total of £4892 13s being added to its permanent stock in the course of that generation. The largest support was, however, gained in the first decade of the revolutionary era, when the substantial total of £2933 6s was provided for its capital needs. During the whole course of our period the citizens of London contributed the impressive sum of £10,015 12s towards the endowment of an institution which they had likewise supported by steady income gifts and rates.[107] Harsh and inadequate as Bridewell and its governors may seem to us, it was none the less a most notable landmark along the road of man's humanity to man.

These five great institutions had been endowed by the close of our period with £141,131 6s of resources by the great generosity of London's benefactors, of which, as we have earlier noted, a very large proportion was specifically designated to relieve the sick and the infirm. They stood unrivalled not only in England but in the whole of the western world as a well-articulated and munificently supported system of hospitals designed to protect helpless men and women against the most grievous blows of fortune. In all, these foundations offered lodging and succour to something like 1400 of the sick and helpless of the great city by the time of the Restoration.[108] Crude and primitive as they may seem to us, a century after Bishop Ridley had spoken, Christ no longer 'lay abroad . . . without lodging in the streets of London, both hungry, naked and cold'. This achievement is the more memorable when it is recalled that almshouse foundations had been raised in London (Middlesex) by private charity during this same period which provided care and lodging for approximately the same number of persons, men and women adjudged to be permanently derelict through no fault of their own.[109] These were truly immense social gains, and they had been made by private men, the pattern of whose aspirations was altering the structure and shape of a whole culture.

But we have not yet quite concluded the remarkable story of the foundation and endowment of hospitals, or, more accurately, the provisions made for the sick and utterly helpless. There remains the substantial sum of £13,864 12s which cannot be assigned to the endowment of any one of the five London hospitals just discussed and which we have listed under the head of other provisions for the care of the sick. Of this total, the sum of £2634 12s was in gifts and bequests made for the care of the sick in other parts of the realm, the larger proportion of this considerable sum having been designated simply for outright distribution to sick persons. An even greater sum, £6305, was left by some

scores of donors to the five London hospitals, but without a clear indication to their executors, or to us, of the precise distribution to be
followed in making these gifts. Over and above this was the substantial
sum of £4925 given by London donors for the care of the sick of the
city in a bewildering variety of ways unconnected with the royal hospitals.
Something over £1500 of this amount was left for the relief of those in
the several 'pest-houses' of the city; many donors ordered distributions
made to bedridden persons in named parishes, some made provision for
the free medical care of the poor in indicated parishes by named physicians for a term of years; others for the care of sailors on ships leaving
for long and perilous voyages; and a great many for the care of poor
women in the pains and dangers of childbirth. All these donors, whether
to the great hospitals or to private schemes, we must treat as an anony-
mous aggregate. These good works were supported by an amazingly
large cross section of the men and women of London, even if, as was
always the case, the leadership and a huge proportion of the great resources supplied were contributed by the merchant aristocracy of the
city. Though considerations of space prevent us from naming even the
most generous of these benefactors, we may record that all mankind
still lies in their debt.

C. MUNICIPAL BETTERMENTS

1. *General uses*

It seems surprising that relatively little of the immense generosity of
London was directed towards purposes which were tangibly and visibly
to better the great municipality regarded with such fierce pride by its
citizens. In total, benefactions were made in the amount of £93,593 16s
for the several uses which we have grouped under the head of municipal
betterments. This sum accounts for only 4·95 per cent of the whole of the
charitable accumulations of the city and is relatively very low when
compared with the 9·10 per cent of such funds designated for this use
in Bristol, or, for that matter, with the proportion so vested in several
of the rural counties we have examined. The explanation quite certainly
is that London's interest was tightly concentrated on the creation and
endowment of a great range of social institutions and that the more
conspicious monuments and improvements to the fabric of the city
simply seemed far less important to these shrewd and far-sighted donors.
As importantly, the city had for some generations come to depend upon
the effective instrument of taxation to secure needed improvements,
whereas in rural counties and in most towns across the realm such improvements, if they were made at all, still depended upon private generosity.

The curve of London's interest in municipal betterments is remarkably level through the whole course of our period. Thus, in the decades prior to the Reformation, a total of £15,690 14s was provided for municipal purposes, this constituting 6·27 per cent of all benefactions for the age. In the Reformation years proper, the proportion of gifts made for such uses declined somewhat to 4·59 per cent of the whole, while in the Elizabethan era the £19,725 18s given for this purpose constituted 7·58 per cent of the total of benefactions. The considerably larger sum of £41,680 14s was disposed for these needs by donors of the early Stuart period, but it will be observed that this represented only 4·35 per cent of all benefactions, while the proportion declined even further in the revolutionary era to 3·55 per cent of the whole.

Though, as we have so frequently observed, London donors often constituted the municipal authorities as trustees for their charitable undertakings, the amount left directly to the city for its own use, or to secure tax relief for its citizens, was relatively very small indeed. In the course of our period we have counted no more than £9424 7s left to the municipality for its general uses, or only 0·50 per cent of the whole of London's charitable resources. At least small sums were, however, left for such purposes in every decade, with the heaviest concentration in the Elizabethan period, when a total of £3420 10s was given. Gifts of this kind were made for a bewildering variety of uses, though the larger ones tended to be for unspecified purposes. It may be well to notice at least a sampling of them.

Hugh Clopton, a mercer and a lord mayor, in 1496 left £10 each to the Chamber of London and to his company, 'for disobedience of myne othe', as well as providing an estimated £200 for building a bridge at Stratford-upon-Avon and £68 for the erection of a suitable market cross in that, his native town.[1] Still another mercer, John Cooke, just a generation later (1525) gave to the city of London for its use a 'great barge . . . upon the . . . River Thames' on which he had set two corn mills, subject only to a life annuity, as well as conveying to the city on his death in 1544 his capital messuage 'called the Duke of Norfolk's place' and other messuages situated at Broken Wharf for its 'proper use and behoof'. These properties cannot be accurately valued at the time of the gift, though their worth may be conservately estimated some years later as at least £800.[2] In the same general period, Sir Thomas Lovell, Chancellor of the Exchequer for a season under Henry VIII, gave £76 6s 8d to Lincoln's Inn in connection with the erection of its new buildings, as well as giving to the city in 1522 a magnificent set of plate for official uses with a then value of £185.[3]

Passing deep into the Elizabethan period, we may note the bequest made in 1585 by Thomas Randall, a mercer, for the comfort of the lord mayor and the chamber of the city. Randall left an annuity of £1 to the Chamber of London to the end that 'the tent that is pitched . . .

for the Lord Mayor to heare, the Whitsonday sermon may stand the other two dayes whereby they [the Chamber] maie sitt drye and out of the sonne'.[4] Some years later, Robert Offley, a haberdasher whose loan foundation has already been discussed, left to the Corporation of London property in the parish of St Mary Aldermanbury, then valued at something like £500, for such uses as they might find bene-ficial, as well as creating, in another charitable fund, an annual payment of £1 towards a yearly banquet for the mayor, aldermen, and council of the city of Chester.[5] At the close of the Elizabethan age, a grocer, John Newman, left to the city a plot of land enclosed with a brick wall and valued at about £300, to be used as a burying ground for the parish of St Michael Bassishaw, while devising by will in 1605 land and build-ings within the precincts of the Royal Exchange in equal proportions to the City of London and to the Mercers' Company for such uses as they might wish to make of the property, then valued at at least £600.[6]

Moving forward another generation, we may mention the bequest made by Rowland Heylyn, an ironmonger, of £300 for municipal uses in his native town of Shrewsbury. This bequest, made in 1632, was only one of several substantial and well-considered benefactions which this remarkable donor disposed for the improvement of life and opportunity in this western community.[7] The western reaches of the realm also benefited through the will of William Middleton, one of that great merchant family, who left £250 to the municipal authorities of Haverford for their use and £200 for the betterment of the town of Denbigh.[8] We may well conclude with the bequest made in 1644 by Daniel Oxenbridge, a Parliamentary stalwart and a merchant, of £1000 to 'the Right Hon'ble the Lords and Comons now assembled in Parlmt ... to their use for the prosecution of their designes', as well as disposing £150 to his executors for the purchase of a burial plot for the English residing in Leghorn, where Oxenbridge was carrying on his prospering trade at the time of his death.[9]

2. Merchant company uses

We have included under the general head of municipal betterments considerable amounts left to the London companies through the long course of our period for the uses of these fraternities and ultimately for the public benefit. It should be emphasized that these sums are in no sense trusteed funds for specified charitable uses. They are rather amounts left expressly to the companies for their own uses and are hence charitable funds only in a somewhat indirect sense. A great deal of this wealth was left for the strengthening of the financial resources of a donor's own livery, other sums were designated for the enjoyment of the members or the carrying forward of the internal affairs of the company, and still larger totals were accumulated from residues left over to the company for its pains in administering charitable endowments of which it was trustee. It will have been noted that the great livery companies especially were throughout our period favourite charitable trustees, not only for members but for other burghers and for many persons residing outside Middlesex who seemed to have had no personal connection of any kind with the company named as trustee of their charitable dispositions. This general confidence in the great livery companies was well reposed, and they had come by the close of our period to be vested with enormous capital sums which they administered for charitable uses as well as to hold for their own account considerable endowments which were in part at least the reward for their own good stewardship.[10]

The total of the wealth left expressly to London companies for their own uses reached the very large accumulation of £56,511 1s during the course of our period, or nearly 3 per cent (2·99 per cent) of the whole of the charitable funds of the city. These gifts increased steadily in number and size as our period wore on, but it is notable that in no decade were they ever less in sum than £545 (1480–1490), while in thirteen of the decades they aggregated more than £2000. The early merchants were extremely generous to their own companies, having given the impressive total of £8623 3s to company uses in the interval preceding the advent of the Reformation. During the next two decades (1541–1560), the total of £3425 6s was given, while in the Elizabethan era not less than £2000 was provided for company uses in any single decade, the total for the whole period being £11,535 11s. As we should expect, the great outpouring of these endowments occurred during the early Stuart age, when these benefactions rose from decade to decade until in the closing years (1631–1640) £9006 14s was given by ninety-seven individual merchants to strengthen the already impressive resources of their companies. There was, of course, a marked falling away of such benefactions during the short and unsettled era of revolution, but even so the total provided for company uses reached the not insubstantial sum of £7602 6s during these years.

As we have indicated, the benefactions made for the uses of the London companies were of a great variety. After the mid-Elizabethan period, almost every member of the great livery companies left at least a token bequest of a few pounds to his fraternity for any one of several uses, while the number of really substantial bequests likewise began to increase most markedly. We need not deal in detail with this whole group of benefactions, but it might be well to class them roughly under a few heads and notice at least a small sampling of these gifts, drawn principally from the earlier years of our period and from the early Stuart era when the climax of giving for these purposes may be observed.

During our period, most of the London companies either built or rebuilt their halls, some of which were most elaborate and expensive structures exhibiting the pride of the companies and perhaps the unconscious desire of merchants and tradesmen for the visible evidence of a status as yet not quite fully defined. Most of these considerable outlays were made from company funds and assessments, but there were as well numerous gifts for the purchase of sites, construction, finishing, and repairs by members who were evidently seeking to urge on their brethren to appropriate action. We have counted gifts of this sort to all the great livery companies and to seventeen of the lesser companies, the total worth of which may be fairly accurately estimated at £8104. Among these was the bequest made by Henry Eburton in 1494 of his mansion house to serve as a hall for the Drapers, together with certain London tenements to be used as his company saw fit.[11] In 1510 Edmund Rede, a mercer, gave to his company the substantial sum of £500 towards the building of its hall and chapel, though his irate wife some years later persuaded Wolsey, as Chancellor, to secure the refund of a portion of the gift.[12] Most gifts of this sort were of course much more modest, such as that made in 1556 by Sir John Champneys, when he bequeathed £10 to the Skinners for the ceiling of their hall.[13] Some years later, in 1559, a wealthy cordwainer, Thomas Nicholson, left the residue of his estate, with an approximate worth of £300, to his company for the building of a suitable hall, as well as establishing a loan fund of £40 for the benefit of young men of the fraternity and bequeathing a rent-charge of £1 p.a. for the general uses of the company.[14] The Ironmongers were given the site for their hall by Sir Christopher Draper,[15] while a generation later Sir Stephen Soame wainscoted and otherwise renovated the Grocers' Hall at a personal outlay of £500.[16] Finally, we may mention the bequest of James Wood, a bowyer, who in 1629 left the residue of his estate, with a then value of about £360, to his company for the purchase of a suitable hall.[17]

The pride these men took in their fraternities is also confirmed by the many bequests left for the purchase of plate for ceremonial uses. In all, we have reckoned these gifts at the considerable total of £1741 3s, with the heaviest concentration being observed in the years 1581–1620. Three examples will perhaps suffice, drawn from the later years of our period and in two instances chosen from societies other than the great and rich livery companies. Thus in 1625 Edward Ayleworth gave £10 for a gilt cup for the Middle Temple, with a most eloquent testimony of his affection for his 'nursing mother'. Sir George Bolles in 1621 provided £30 for plate for his company, the Grocers, as well as £33 for a dinner, and £50 for its general uses.[19] A generation later Martyn Dallison bequeathed £6 13s to the Scriveners' Company for appropriate plate in a will notable principally for the classically Calvinistic testament of faith with which it was prefaced.[20]

Nor were the London merchants of our period wanting in generosity in providing funds for the elaborate and extremely expensive dinners and feasts which were an important part of the life and ceremonial of all city companies. Most of these bequests were in relatively small sums of from £5 to £50 to be used outright for a single and, frequently, a commemorative dinner. In all the substantial total of £2907 has been recorded of gifts for such immediate and sumptuary use. But there were as well endowments established totalling £4731 6s in capital value towards the funding of these increasingly elaborate occasions. Thus Sir Thomas Gresham in 1579 left the enormous total of £2000 to the Mercers, the income of £100 p.a. to be used for four stated dinners of the society in each year.[21] A generation later, another mercer, Richard Fishborne, added an endowment of £420, from the income of which £20 was to be expended for a yearly dinner for the livery and £1 for an appropriate service in the company chapel just preceding the occasion.[22]

There remains the large capital sum of £39,027 12s which was in effect vested in the companies for their own uses by members either in the form of direct benefactions or as residues of known value. We may mention a few of the many benefactions of this kind, drawing our examples from two quite casually selected intervals of about a generation each. Thus there was an ever-increasing number of substantial sums provided for these quasi-charitable purposes in the generation just prior to the Reformation. William Browne, a mercer and one of the few London-born mayors of the city in our whole period, on his death in 1514 settled on his company a residue with a capital worth of £460, after vesting in the fraternity an endowment valued at £340 to secure prayers for the repose of his soul. Among other considerable dispositions, this merchant left to his company a silver goblet for its use, appraised at £18 value.[23] A few years later, in 1523, another mayor, Sir Stephen Jenyns, who during his lifetime had hung the Merchant Taylors' Hall with tapestries costing £100, left to his company silver of an uncertain value, as well as three London houses with a then capital worth of £153 for their general uses.[24] Another merchant tailor, Richard Smythe, in 1527 left to his company 'for their proper use and behoof forever' two houses and land then valued at £213 as well as a residue, with a then capital worth of about £200, from an endowment for prayers.[25] We may conclude our review of these early benefactions with a mention of still another merchant tailor, Thomas Speight, who in 1533 left his company for its general uses thirty-six houses, sixty-eight cellars, two gardens, and a wharf and crane, all possessing a then capital value of £907.[26]

Very nearly half of the company endowments were given by members during a period of about two decades (1612–1634), of which we may mention at least a few of the larger. In 1612 Robert Gale, a vintner, dedicated to the uses of his company capital to the value of £400 as part of a substantial charitable trust serving several useful purposes.[27] In the same year a haberdasher, Florence Caldwell, who had earlier given to the Armourers a cup and cover valued at £10, gave £100 each to the Haberdashers, the Vintners, the Armourers, and the Barber-Surgeons for the general needs of these fraternities.[28] Another haberdasher, the great Welsh philanthropist, William Jones, in 1614 bequeathed the large sum of £1000 to his company for their 'pains' in administering the huge charitable estate of nearly £20,000 which he had settled on them as trustees.[29] A grocer and a former lord mayor, Sir Thomas Middleton, just before his death in 1631 conveyed to his company lands and buildings in London possessing a then value not far short of £300 for the general uses of the fraternity,[30] while in 1634 Sir Ralph Freeman, a clothworker and also a former lord mayor, left to the Merchant Adventurers an estimated residue of £400 from a loan fund with which they were vested as trustees, as well as bequeathing to his own livery £50 for a dinner and £150 for the purchase of plate.[31] Finally, a large endowment was provided for the Salters' Company in 1633 when William Robson gave the company £2500 to 'remain freely and wholly to' its uses, subject only to a life interest for himself and certain of his named kinsmen, while stipulating as well that his company should have £20 p.a. from a further fund of £2500 vested in them as trustees for a number of charitable causes.[32]

3. *Public works*

Well over half the sum disposed by London merchants for the uses which we have included under the head of municipal betterments were vested in some form of support for the city companies. Their next most considerable interest was in the financing of a great variety of public works in London and in many outlying counties. In all, £27,604 8s was expended for such uses, this representing 1·46 per cent of all the charitable wealth accumulated by the city. The interest in this form of outlay was, then, relatively most modest, though it remained remarkably stable from the outset of our period until about 1640. In the years prior to the Reformation, £5073 10s was expended on such public improvements, with a proportionately larger outlay during the short interval of the Reformation, when £2363 1s was given for these uses. During the Elizabethan age the amounts designated for public works ranged from £690 19s to £1787 during the four decades, with £4769 17s being provided in the whole interval. Considerably heightened interest in such undertakings may be noted during the early Stuart age, when the substantial total of £14,848 was given, while the benefactions for such needs fell away markedly during the unsettled years of revolutionary experimentation to the modest sum of £550 for the two decades.

Many of these gifts were very small, particularly those for road and street repairs, but a fair number were substantial in amount and ingenious in conception. Our best course will perhaps be to mention a number of the larger benefactions for this purpose with the intention of suggesting the amazing variety of interests and the wide geographical spread of these charities.

Sir William Taylour, a grocer and a former mayor, in 1483 left a maximum amount of £50 to finish a road which he had begun at Edenbridge (Kent), where he had been born and where he held land.[33] Another mayor, Sir Edmund Shaa, a few years later bequeathed the considerable sum of £266 13s 4d for the erection of a new gate at Cripplegate, provided the city donated the materials from the old gate and sand and mortar; he also left £27 for the repair of certain highways in Essex.[34] At about the same time, a mercer, John Fisher, gave £333 6s 8d for the building of the new cross in the Cheap.[35] Another mayor, Richard Gardener, in 1490 provided £100, plus an additional £133 6s 8d if required, for the raising and repair of London Bridge, as well as £20 for the repair of highways in Cambridgeshire.[36]

Moving forward a full generation in our sampling, we still find the great merchants and former mayors the principal supporters of needed public works. In 1523 Sir John Rest, a grocer who had served as mayor in 1516, provided £40 for the repair of the London-Peterborough highway, as well as £66 13s 4d for the rehabilitation of the market-place in the latter town, of which he was a native.[37] In the same year, Roger Acheley, a draper, and mayor in 1511, died, having some little time earlier expended upwards of £100 on throwing up dikes and levelling the ground at Moorgate in order to provide easy access at all seasons to Moorfield.[38] A water conduit had been laid in London Wall at this gate at about this time by Sir Thomas Exmewe, a goldsmith who served as mayor in 1517, while his will ordered that any necessary repairs to this important public work should be undertaken from the residue of his estate.[39] A rich mercer, Richard Collier, in 1532 left the residue of his charitable estate, with an approximate capital value of £200 for the maintenance of highways in the vicinity of his native town of Horsham, Sussex,[40] while a few years later Sir Thomas Seymour, also a mercer and a former lord mayor, by will provided £100 for the repair of roads in and near London and £20 for the mending of roads in Essex.[41]

During the interval of the Reformation a great many gifts were made for public betterments, but the larger of these benefactions continued to be those of the lord mayors and great merchants of London. His native neighbourhood was remembered in 1542 by Sir William Holles, who left £200 to the Mayor of Coventry for the erection of a new cross in that town.[42] Another rich mercer, Sir Michael Dormer, in 1545 bequeathed £100 for the repair of London's streets,[43] while in 1557 Katherine Hall, a grocer's widow, by will provided £5 p.a. for a term of forty years for the same laudable purpose.[44] A few years later, and probably in 1560, Sir William Chester, a draper, vaulted over with brick the noisome town ditch from Aldgate to Newgate at an estimated charge of £150 and at about the same date built walls around St Bartholomew's Hospital and Christ's Hospital at an outlay of something like £100.[45]

Elizabethan merchant donors exhibited a quite varied interest in public improvements, though the total of their gifts for this purpose amounted to no more than the relatively modest outlay of £4769 17s. In 1561 Sir Rowland Hill, a mercer and a former lord mayor, died leaving extensive charitable endowments, particularly for the benefit of his native county of Shropshire. Some years before his death, he had built several London causeways at his own charge, as well as four bridges at Hodnet, Stoke, Atcham, and Tern, all in Shropshire, at an uncertain cost.[46] A few years later, in 1564, another former lord mayor, Sir John Lyon, bequeathed £100 to be used for building a needed market-house at Queenhithe Wharf, all the rents and profits to be payable to the municipality.[47] William Lambe, the great clothworker and philanthropist, 'a person wholly composed of goodness and bounty, and . . . as general and discreet a benefactor as any that age produced', rebuilt and completed the Holborn Conduit at about this same date at a personal charge of at least £1500.[48] Barnard Randolph, whose substantial provisions for the poor of London and his native Suffolk have already been noted,[49] in 1583 expended about £900 for conduits which brought water from the Thames to cisterns in the parishes of St Mary Magdalen and St Nicholas Cold Abbey, near Fish Street, for the convenience of the fishmongers and others inhabiting this part of the city, as well as establishing a small annuity of £2 for the repair of a road in the parish of Ticehurst, Sussex.[50] A few years later, in 1587, Richard Maye, a merchant tailor, gave £300 towards the building of the new and enlarged Blackwell Hall, the market-place for woollen cloths, as well as leaving £90 for the uses of Christ's Hospital.[51] Shortly afterwards Sir Cuthbert Buckle, a vintner, built a bridge at a cost of about £200 at his native village of Brough in Westmorland, as well as providing uncertain amounts for the mending of roads in that northern region.[52] To conclude the Elizabethan benefactions for municipal improvements, we may mention the gift of the famous lawyer and statesman, Sir Julius Caesar, who in 1595–1596 erected additional and badly needed buildings for the Inner Temple at a personal charge of £300.[53]

Passing to the early Stuart period, we should note at least the principal of the gifts for public uses made in the course of a generation
(1605–1630) when approximately half of the whole outlay for betterments of this kind was made by London donors. In 1605 a merchant
tailor, John Conyers, by will left £100 for bringing water into Aldgate
by conduits, as well as £100 for the repair of roads in his native Bedfordshire.[54] The bringing of adequate water supplies into the city, which,
as we have seen, had engaged the charitable interest of several donors,
was of course satisfactorily concluded by the persistent ingenuity and
skill of Sir Hugh Middleton early in the reign of James I. This was a
private business venture, but one in which London took justifiable
pride. In the words of a contemporary, it 'is now after many rubs and
lets brought to good effect, the water being now arriued at, or deriued
rather to the citie: which said water-workes, although they haue beene
taken in hand vpon hope of priuate gaine, yet because the benefit therof
is publike, and will redound both to rich and poore, they may be ranged
if not among the direct charitable, yet the magificent [sic] and commen-
dable workes of the citie'.[55]

A new market-house was provided for Croydon, Surrey, in 1609 at a
cost of £200 under the will of Francis Tirrell, a grocer, who also left
£40 for the purchase of a new bell for the church in that town.[56] We
have in earlier pages discussed the circumstances under which Thomas
Sutton, the most munificent of the philanthropists of our entire period,
became the unintended posthumous donor of the immense sum of
£10,000 for the building of a great bridge at Berwick-upon-Tweed.[57]
Sutton had also bequeathed £353 for the mending of appointed roads in
Middlesex, Essex, and Cambridgeshire, and had during his lifetime
built a conduit in London at an uncertain charge. Baptist Hicks, later
Viscount Campden, in 1612 built at his own cost the Middlesex Sessions
House at an outlay estimated at £600 on land provided by his sovereign.[58]
A rich and public-spirited merchant tailor, William Parker, in 1616 left
the large sum of £1000 for the rebuilding of Aldgate and Aldgate Wall,
the work being carried forward in the next year by the civic authorities.[59]
We shall elsewhere discuss in detail the munificent endowment of
£2000 vested by Thomas White in 1624, the income of which was to
be perpetually employed for the mending of roads in and near the city
of Bristol.[60] We may well conclude this brief survey with notice of the
gift of a water system for the town of Wotton-under-Edge, Gloucestershire, made at a cost of about £400 by Hugh Perry, a London mercer,
shortly before his death in 1634.[61]

These London merchants had made many benefactions of great
utility, both in their own city and across the whole face of England, for
municipal betterments of one sort or another. They left England a quite
different and certainly a better place in which to live, by the enduring

monuments which they had raised. Yet the whole of their outlays for municipal betterments was relatively very small and was marked by a kind of prudence unmixed with pride of ostentatious building. These men put their trust in less conspicious but more useful and enduring monuments. Their immense endowments for the care of the poor, their almshouses, and their many and generous outlays for the rehabilitation of the unfortunate and the under-privileged more adequately marked the slope and the dynamic of their social aspirations. These men viewed their society at once compassionately and objectively; they displayed a remarkable prescience as they sought to divine its needs not only for the present but for the generations to come. In no respect was their wisdom and their sense of the needs of their nation more brilliantly demonstrated than in the fanatical devotion which these great donors displayed for the broadening, we can almost say the founding, of educational opportunities in England.

D. EDUCATION

1. Grammar-school foundations

The aspirations of the London burghers and their incredible generosity are perhaps best exemplified in the steady and massive support which they lent to education during the whole course of our period. Moreover, their determined effort to found and endow an educational system held in view the whole realm and its needs, for only a relatively small proportion of the immense endowments vested was for the necessarily limited needs of London itself. These merchants believed in the virtues of education with an almost fanatical intensity, for a variety of reasons to which they gave eloquent testimony in the phrasing of their great bequests. In many cases they had themselves been handicapped by the imperfect education of their own youth. They believed that an increasingly elevated standard of education was required for the ever more complex necessities of trade and finance in the modern world. They held to a man the view that affording a competent education to aspiring youth was the surest and most fruitful way open to their society for the prevention of poverty by the destruction of the ignorance in which it was spawned. And they believed, and said so, that only a literate citizenry could create a truly godly community able to understand and defend God's truth against the enemies with which it was beset.

During the whole span of our period London donors were to contribute the vast total of £510,890 17s towards the strengthening—one can perhaps more accurately say, the foundation—of the educational resources of the realm. This great capital aggregate amounted to 27·04 per cent of all the charitable wealth accumulated by London in these years. The vastness of this wealth can perhaps be suggested when we say that it somewhat exceeded the total provided for all charitable uses during our whole period in the two great counties of Kent and Yorkshire.

The devotion of London to the cause of education, never particularly strong during the Middle Ages, was impressive even in the decades prior to the Reformation when the influence of Christian humanism began to be felt under the leadership of men who were in several instances themselves sons of London merchants. During these years, the large total of £76,581 9s was given for various educational uses, slightly more than twice as much as was provided for the poor and, remarkably enough, not incomparably less than the £111,997 1s given for religious needs in this same long generation. In the brief interval of the Reformation, the relatively large total of £32,586 5s was bestowed on educational foundations, this being rather more than twice as much as was given in these years for the whole range of religious needs. The £83,319 12s provided for educational uses during the Elizabethan era represented almost a third (32·00 per cent) of all charitable wealth given during the interval and, it will be noted, was something like five times as much as was bestowed for religious uses in this intensely secular era. The great outpouring came during the early Stuart years when the huge total of £246,492 3s was given to secure an almost revolutionary extension of the educational facilities of the realm, though it should be said that these outlays amounted to little more than a quarter (25·70 per cent) of the whole of the charitable wealth vested in this incredibly generous age. The needs of education were by no means neglected during the two decades of political disturbance with which our period ends, the large total of £71,911 8s given for these uses amounting to 26·94 per cent of all the charitable contributions of these unsettled years.

The predominant interest of London benefactors during most of our period was in the founding or the strengthening of schools across the length and breadth of England. From 1480 to 1660, there was poured into these foundations the immense sum of £259,263 2s, this representing 13·72 per cent of all charitable wealth and somewhat execeding in amount any other single charitable head save for the £331,502 4s provided for the household relief of the poor. This great sum, moreover, was almost wholly (99·67 per cent) in the form of endowments designed to build and perpetually to maintain the institutions with which this age sought forever to destroy ignorance and illiteracy. Firmly supporting these foundations, and frequently vested in them, was also a huge accumulation of scholarship and fellowship endowments, which were by the close of our period to total £92,465 8s and which were to link tightly the fabric of secondary education with that of the universities.[1]

The accumulation of grammar-school endowments began modestly enough in the years prior to the Reformation, no more than £320 of these funds having been given during the first two decades of the period. But from 1500 onward the flow of gifts for this use never really faltered. Thus during the two generations before the Reformation the impressive total of £14,559 was given by a considerable number of donors for school foundations, though this was far less than the £57,814 19s settled on the universities by London donors. What one can perhaps describe as the velocity of these contributions was approximately trebled during the Reformation period proper, the large total of £15,274 17s being provided for the further enlargement of the school resources of the city and of the realm. There were many and there were notable school foundations in the Elizabethan age, when the total vested for these institutions was £32,530, supplemented, it may well be noted, by additions totalling £18,269 5s to the scholarship and fellowship resources of the nation. But the great period stretches from 1591 to 1630, when not less than £11,093 7s was contributed in any single decade, and with the climax of generosity being attained in the second decade of the seventeenth century when the generous total of £78,386 was provided. During the early Stuart period proper, the huge sum of £148,263 17s was given for schools, this constituting slightly more than 57 per cent of the great sum given for these foundations during the whole of our long period. This incredible achievement was made despite the fact that gifts for school foundations fell away most drastically during the decade just prior to the outbreak of the Civil War, an era of profound unsettlement and un-certainty in which men could not clearly discern the outlines of the future. But there was an immediate revival of interest in bringing to com-pletion this age of foundation of the grammar-school system of England during the period of Puritan warfare and victory, for the great sum of £48,635 8s was given by men and women who, having witnessed, as they believed, the triumph of the elect, were now determined to rout finally the forces of ignorance.

We shall first treat the school foundations made in London and its outlying suburbs in the course of our period and then turn to the far larger number of institutions founded in other parts of the realm by London's donors. The amazing fact is that London possessed most limited and undistinguished grammar-school resources on which to build when our period opened. Throughout the Middle Ages the approval of the Bishop of London and the Chancellor of St Paul's was required for the establishment of a school. The ecclesiastical author-ities, despite mounting civic, parliamentary, and on occasion royal protest that became very strong in the fifteenth century, were able to maintain the monopoly of a few old but visibly declining church schools.

Three of these institutions had had their origin in the twelfth century and had once been vigorous and flourishing. St Paul's School was certainly in existence in the early twelfth century and was well established by its close. The school was unendowed and, though subjected to numerous reformations by the cathedral chapter, was at once undistinguished and weak when our period opens. The school's deserved fame rests, of course, upon its reorganization, one must in truth say re-foundation, by Colet early in the sixteenth century. The second of the older foundations was the school conjoined with the church of St Martin-le-Grand, whose origin may also be dated from the early twelfth century. It gained a modest endowment in lands and tithes in the late twelfth century, and we know that a century later its master received an annual stipend of £8. Both church and school were in decay in 1368 when the premises were badly damaged by a tempest, but the school was re-endowed in the late fourteenth century and was flourishing at least in the first generation of the fifteenth century. But it was in rapid decline after about 1440 and was wholly inconsequential, if not moribund, by the opening of our period. Finally, there was the school kept in a house in the churchyard of St Mary-le-Bow, which was also of twelfth-century foundation. Very little is known regarding its history save that it never gained endowment or any considerable public support. This school too had decayed well before 1480, having been supplanted by a newer foundation, St Anthony's, and was closed and the premises rented out for secular uses early in the sixteenth century.

These three schools were able to maintain their monopoly of London's secondary education until the middle of the fifteenth century, when civic demand for the enlargement and betterment of the educational facilities of the city became very insistent indeed. Numerous private attempts were made to found schools without ecclesiastical approbation but were invariably quashed by the threat of legal action combined with the fear of excommunication. Among those forced to close, in ca. 1440, was one taught by John Seward, a notable early humanist. But the rigid ecclesiastical controls were to a degree relaxed when in 1441 John Carpenter, the master of St Anthony's Hospital, obtained from the Bishop of London the appropriation of the annual income of sixteen marks from the Hospital of St Bennet Fink for the announced purpose of establishing a school under a competent master. The school was apparently founded in 1446, a stipend of £16 p.a. by that time being assured to the master. This school flourished and probably overtook St Paul's in popularity and prestige by the close of the fifteenth century. It was in existence at the time of the Reformation, the Chantry Commissioners reporting that the salary of £16 p.a. was still being paid, though they were uncertain from what sources. The school was unmolested and in 1560 enrolled as many as two hundred students. But it did not enjoy the favour of the seventeenth-century world and gradually declined, to be finally closed shortly after the Restoration. The second school to be opened in the mid-fifteenth century was one connected with the church of St Dunstan in the East, about which very little is known. At the time of the Chantry Commissioners' report, the institution enjoyed an income of £17 10s p.a., but it appears that it was then no more than a singing school. There is no evidence that it was closed by the chantry expropriations, but it shortly languished and disappeared, since it, like all the older foundations save St Paul's, could not compete with the richly endowed secular foundations that were by this time being made.

These most limited additions to the educational resources open to the citizenry quite failed to meet either the need or the public expectations. In 1446 the Archbishop of Canterbury and the Bishop of London sought formally to fix the number of permitted schools at the five then enjoying ecclesiastical approval. This was countered by a most eloquent petition to Parliament from four rectors of as many city churches, who stated that the approved schools were too small to meet the needs of the city and the many young boys from a distance whose families sought facilities for their education in the capital. 'Wherefore it were expedient, that in London were a sufficeant nombre of scoles, and good enfourmers in gramer, and not for the singuler availl of ii or iii persones grevously to hurte the multitude of yonge peple of all this lond . . .'.[2] Though Parliament and the King lent warm support to the petition, the ecclesiastical authorities remained adamant, expansion, not to say reformation, being delayed for two full generations, save for the probable opening of a school in conjunction with a chantry in the parish of St Mary at Hill, where the schoolmaster seems to have enjoyed an annual stipend of £8 10s. In 1458 a draper, Simon Eyre, is said to have left a huge bequest of £2000 for the endowment of a grammar school in the chapel of Leadenhall Market, but this intention, for reasons which remain obscure, was never honoured.[3]

These, then, were the school resources possessed by London at the outset of our period, and they were very inadequate indeed. They were too hopelessly unimpressive to elicit any considerable help from merchant donors, whose bequests and gifts for these schools amounted to no more than £85 from 1480 to 1500, though these men were already beginning to plant more hopeful schools, usually under secular control, in other parts of the realm. The great reformation came of course with Colet's reorganization and rich endowment of St Paul's School. This transformation began shortly after Colet was appointed Dean of St Paul's in 1505, his plans being well advanced when in 1509 he and the Mercers' Company assigned to the school a rent-charge of £8 p.a. as its first endowment. The great foundation may be said, however, to date from 1510 when Colet petitioned for permission to vest lands in mortmain for the endowment, since he 'to the pleasure of God and for and in augmentation and encrease, as well of connyng as of vertuose lyving w'in this your realme, hathe now of late edifyed within the . . . cathedrall churche a scholehouse (wherein he purposith that children as well borne as to be borne w'yn youre saide citie as elsewhere) to the same repayring shall not oonly in contynuance be substancially taughte and lernyd in Laten tung, but also instructed and informed in vertuose condicions'.

This great foundation, which literally revolutionized grammar-school education, has been too well and too often described for us to attempt to add anything of moment within the context of this treatment. But we should at least recount the particulars regarding the financing of the foundation, which was vested in a form of trust to be imitated by many later donors. Colet's father, Sir Henry Colet, had been a mercer and a master of his company, and it was from the great inheritance from his estate that the endowment was to be made. Colet began his outlays on the building of his school in 1508. When the work was completed in 1512, facilities were available for 153 students on the foundation in splendid new quarters, on which something over £3000 had been expended by the donor. Colet from 1510 forward conveyed to the Mercers' Company as trustees successive gifts of land in Buckinghamshire, Hertfordshire, Essex, Cambridgeshire, and London, to which still further holdings were added under the terms of his will, proved in 1519. When the whole of these endowments were assessed in 1524, the income was £112 0s 11d p.a., representing a then enormous capital worth of £2441. Possibly the greatest and certainly the most influential educational foundation of the century had been made by one of its choicest spirits.[4]

A second foundation was made in 1536 just to the east of London in the then village of Ratcliffe (Stepney) by a native of that place, Nicholas Gibson, a warden of the Grocers' Company. Gibson built a free school in the village, with a house for the master, maintaining the institution from his own purse until his death in 1540. By will be bequeathed substantial properties to his wife on trust, with the provision that she should maintain the school, then giving instruction to sixty boys, and with the further stipulation that she should on her death settle a sufficient endowment on the school and an associated almshouse. The widow, Avice, in 1552 settled on the Coopers' Company as trustee endowments valued at £333, the income to be used for the support of a master and an usher competent to teach young children reading and spelling and to lend instruction in 'grammatical science' to the older boys. The government of the school and its visitation the donor left in the hands of the Coopers' Company.[5] Numerous small bequests were left to this school in later years, typical examples being the legacy of 13s 4d given for school uses in 1564 by Thomas Franke, a cooper,[6] and the more substantial bequest of a half-interest in a house left in 1599 by Peter Thellow, a draper, for the joint uses of the school and almshouse.[7]

A few years later, the rich and powerful Mercers' Company opened their school in the expropriated premises of the Hospital of St Thomas Acon, where they had long worshipped. It seems probable that a school had been begun in the hospital in the mid-fifteenth century, as the parish of St Mary Colechurch, in which the hospital was situated, was one of those mentioned in the petition to Parliament as being disposed to open a school. Be that as it may, the hospital was confiscated in 1538, and the company moved at once towards negotiations for purchase under agreement to found a school on the premises. In 1541 the purchase, including substantial properties once the principal endowment of the hospital, was completed at a cost of £969 17s under a covenant to found and maintain a free grammar school for twenty-five students and to employ a learned man to preach weekly in the Mercers' church. The school was opened in the church in 1542, the company sometime later erecting a more suitable school building. The salary of the master was initially £10 p.a., but on the second appointment was increased to £12 p.a., to which was added £8 p.a. for the stipulated sermons. In 1574, when a new master was appointed, the number of scholars was increased to forty and careful statutes were drafted for the conduct of the institution. In the next year, Lady Margaret North gave £500 to the Mercers' Company, which, after specified life interests, was to be employed as an endowment to provide scholarships for four male children in the grammar school and then in either of the universities, 'if they should be found apt to learning'.[8] Aside from this substantial gift, which greatly strengthened the scholarship resources of the school, the institution was supported directly from the already large charitable funds with which this ancient company was endowed.

We have indicated in an earlier discussion that throughout our period Christ's Hospital, founded in 1552 by the energetic efforts of leading London merchants and the generosity of Edward VI, served principally as a hospital for foundling children, many of whom were infants.[9] No institution in the city was more generously or more steadily favoured by London donors. Within a generation the foundation had become exceedingly complex, serving many useful social purposes, among which, of course, was the education of its charges. Thus the outlines of the future grammar school were beginning to emerge, and an ever-increasing number of gifts and bequests were being received which were either restricted to educational uses or defined education as the central aspiration of the donor. We have, consequently, regarded this group of benefactions as part of the *corpus* of educational funds and should mention at least the principal among them.

In 1559 Richard Castel, the famous Westminster shoemaker, left the residue of his estate, with a then capital value of about £580, on trust to the governors of the recently opened hospital for its general uses, but with an indicated interest in the education of the children there.[10] At about the same date, Thomas Cutt, a merchant adventurer, who may well have been the father of one of the two first 'schoole-maisters for the petties A. B. C.' in the hospital, indicated in his will that the bequest therein contained, when taken with earlier contributions, made the total of his capital gift to the hospital the substantial sum of £550.[11] In 1589, Alice Middleton, who may have been a printer's widow, left £500 to the institution for its uses,[12] while in 1609 William Bennett left an estimated £180 to ensure the education of six poor boys, to be chosen from Abingdon, Berkshire.[13]

Very substantial augmentations were made to the endowment of Christ's Hospital during the early Stuart period, a fair proportion of which were evidently designed to strengthen the educational activities of the institution. Thus in 1612 William Stoddard, a prominent skinner, left on trust, after certain life interests, lands to the value of £66 13s 4d p.a. to be distributed £4 p.a. for two dinners for all the children of the hospital, £1 p.a. to the resident officials, £5 p.a. to the poor of the Skinners' Company, and £10 p.a. to the company for its own uses, while the balance, which represented a capital of about £933, was to be employed by Christ's Hospital for the care and education of ten poor children of men who had been associated with the Skinners' Company.[14] Robert Buck, a draper whose substantial endowment for poor relief has already been noted,[15] in 1620 left lands in Kent with an approximate capital worth of £500 for the uses of the hospital. A future president of the hospital, Christopher Clitherow, an ironmonger, in 1625 by indenture firmly established the educational functions of the institution when he conveyed to the governors rents possessing a capital worth of £200 for the founding of two exhibitions at Oxford, with a preference for St John's College, for as many graduates of the school.[16] John Locke, a tailor residing in St Martin Ludgate, in 1633 left the hospital the generous sum of £1000 as endowment, the income to be used to provide care and education for eight poor children of London freemen, two to be nominated by the President of Christ's Hospital and two each by the churchwardens and common councillors of three named London parishes.[17] Sir Hugh Hamersley, a haberdasher and lord mayor who had served as president of the hospital, left it £100 in 1636,[18] while a vintner, Anthony Bailey, bequeathed the institution a rent-charge representing a capital sum of £200 on his death in 1640.[19]

By far the largest of the numerous benefactions for the support of the educational activities of Christ's Hospital was that left in 1654 by Richard Aldworth, a rich skinner who also founded schools in Berkshire and Hampshire. Aldworth bequeathed specifically lands valued at £470 and the residue of his estate, which was secured by a lien of £7000 on crown lands. This great endowment was by the terms of the donor's will to be employed for the full support and education of forty additional children on the foundation, who should be served by a nurse and a schoolmaster. With the Restoration, these lands reverted to the Crown, and the whole great endowment stood in jeopardy. Most powerful representations were made, however, to the Lord Treasurer and to Parliament by the governors, who in turn spoke for the merchant elite of London, and the House of Commons in 1660 directed the repayment of the sum from the arrears of the old excise. These efforts did not, however, immediately prevail, and it was not until 1673 that the Crown undertook to refund the capital over a term of seven years for the founding of the famous mathematical school, which in its constitution was made to appear a royal benefaction. But a great benefactor's purposes, after the lapse of a generation, had been well, indeed brilliantly, served.[20]

At about the same time, George Dunn, a barber surgeon and a graduate of Christ's Hospital, left annuities representing a capital value of £160 for the specific purpose of teaching girls on the foundation to read the English language 'that they may the better attain unto the knowledge of God and understanding of His Word'.[21] In 1654 another skinner, Thomas Singleton, left £40 and the residue of his estate, the whole gift not being valued at more than £430, for the support of the now very important educational work of the hospital,[22] while Richard Rochdale, a brewer, in 1658 by gift and bequest left an estimated £420 to be employed in part for educational purposes and in part for loans and apprenticeships for its graduates.[23] These, then, are the chief of the many bequests left to this notable institution with a clear indication that the funds were to be employed for educational uses.[24] Though the reckoning cannot be precise, we may estimate that in all something like £13,970 had by 1660 been provided by London donors to advance the educational contributions of what may by this date be regarded as one of the great schools of London.

The next great school foundation was that made in 1560 when the Merchant Taylors' Company founded the school that has for almost four centuries so notably borne their name. The court of the company in July of that year determined on the foundation and arranged for the purchase of the 'Manor of the Rose' for the school premises, this being in the parish of St Lawrence Poultney and originally the residence of Sir John Pultney, a merchant and a mayor of the period of Edward III. The purchase price of this property was £566 13s 4d, of which nearly the whole (£500) was paid by Richard Hills, a modest but most generous member of the livery, who was later to found the almshouse that bears his company name. Not only was he the true founder of the school, but from the date of Richard Mulcaster's appointment as headmaster in 1561 until at least 1568, and more probably until 1586, this eminent merchant paid his salary of £10 p.a. as a further contribution.[25] The statutes of the school, adopted in 1561, provided for the admission of one hundred scholars who should pay no fees of any kind, fifty sons of poor parents who could pay a tuition of 2s by the quarter, and one hundred who could afford a quarterly tuition charge of 5s. The master should be competent in 'good and cleane' Latin and Greek literature and should have free lodging on the premises, while he was to be assisted by a well-educated and reliable usher.

The school was supported principally from the corporate funds of the company, though small legacies soon began to be received, such as one in 1566 from Richard Botyll for £5 and another in the same year for £2 from John Mansbridge. It was, however, immensely assisted when Sir Thomas White, a merchant tailor and a member of the court when the school had been founded, established an organic connection between it and St John's College, Oxford, which this amazing benefactor was founding and endowing in this same decade. He arranged that forty-three of the scholars on his Oxford foundation should preferably be drawn from the Merchant Taylors' School, or at least from London; that such scholars should be sons of poor men; and that each should have £4 10s annually as his stipend.[26] The school had by 1570 achieved a well-deserved reputation for the excellence of its tuition and was enrolling boys from counties as distant as Somerset and Yorkshire, though the company had in 1567 emphasized the primary responsibility of the foundation for the education of burgher youths. Mulcaster, one of the great schoolmasters of the age, had raised the instruction to great academic eminence well before his retirement in 1586. The company continued throughout our period to lend full support to the school's needs, most of the substantial bequests provided by its members being for the endowment of additional exhibitions at St John's College, Oxford, under which head they may be more appropriately considered in later pages.

Very shortly after the establishment of the Merchant Taylors' School, a free parochial grammar school was founded in St Saviour's parish, Southwark, by interested citizens there. A former monastic site was purchased and a suitable schoolhouse built in 1562 by public subscriptions amounting to upwards of £200. In the same year, the Queen chartered the school for the free instruction of one hundred youths of the parish, whether rich or poor. The governors named in the charter at once appointed a master, with a stipend of £20 p.a., and an usher, who was to have £10 p.a. The school was wholly unendowed at the outset, the liberal salary commitments being met by the modest tuition fees levied, the contributions of the governors, and very probably from local rates. But the endowment began slowly to accumulate, among the earliest benefactions to capital being the bequests of John Sayer, of Southwark, of an annuity with a capital value of £20 in 1563,[27] and of £5 from Martin Darcie, a shipwright, in 1567.[28] In all, we have recorded gifts and bequests with a total capital worth of £550 for the support of the school and its scholars given in the interval 1563–1660, including the one substantial legacy of John Bingham, a saddler and a governor of the institution, who in 1617 gave property then valued at £240 as an endowment for two scholarships for boys from the school in either of the universities.[29]

The modern foundation of Westminster School, and suitable provision for its financial needs, may be said to date from 1560 when the young and learned Queen resolved to make it the equal of Eton College. The school had, of course, medieval roots, there having been a monastic school at Westminster as early as the thirteenth century and a flourishing grammar school there in the late fourteenth century. Henry VIII's reorganization of the monastery as the 'King's New College' carefully preserved and sought to strengthen the grammar school, which was designed for forty scholars on the foundation and which placed instruction successively under two distinguished headmasters, Alexander Nowell and Nicholas Udal. Elizabeth further defined the constitution, providing new statutes resembling those of Eton, linking the foundation closely with both universities, and appointing Dr William Bill as the first dean. The Queen likewise assigned revenues from the collegiate foundation in the amount of £95 11s p.a. in order to ensure stipends of £20 p.a. and of £7 p.a. respectively for the master and the second master, with generous allowances for commons, £1 6s 8d p.a. for each of the forty scholars on the foundation, as well as commons, and provision for the election each year of six scholars who were to proceed either to Christ Church, Oxford, or to Trinity College, Cambridge. The enrolment of the school was to be limited to 120 boys.[30]

The school attracted the patronage of the great of the realm because of its undoubted excellence and, very possibly, because of the steady interest which the Queen displayed in its affairs and in its students. Thus in 1570 Gabriel Goodman, the Dean of Westminster and the founder of a grammar school in his native Wales, granted to the school the lease of the manor of Chiswick, Middlesex, and stipulated that accommodations should be built there, at a total charge of about £350, for the master and forty students, to which they could retire in times of the plague in London.[31] Lord Burghley in 1594, impressed by the 'good virtuous bringing up and education of scholars' in the school, gave a yearly rent of £13 6s 8d towards the purchase of needed books for scholars going on to the university.[32] But the greatest of the private benefactors to the school was John Williams, who undertook at his own charge a complete rehabilitation of its decayed premises and a strengthening of its resources shortly after he was appointed Dean of Westminster in 1620. Williams expended something like £2000 on the building of the school library, including £500 for books, while he may well have laid out as much as an additional £2500 on the repair of the school and abbey. Finally, Williams vested in the school rents with a then capital worth of £548 to fund the creation of four additional scholarships in St John's College, Cambridge, for boys educated in the school, two of whom should be natives of Wales and the other two natives of Lincolnshire.[33]

The next foundation of a grammar school was made just outside London in the then hamlet of Highgate, in the parish of Hornsey (Finsbury) in 1565. A royal charter was gained for this foundation by Sir Roger Cholmeley for the 'education . . . of boys and youths in grammar', the administration of the trust to be vested in six governors. The founder by successive conveyances established an endowment whose capital value reached the generous total of £1413, a most adequate stock for a relatively small grammar school in this period.[34] These resources were increased during our period by a number of gifts, totalling £291 10s, among which three may be cited as typical. A London fletcher, John Martyn, in 1574 gave £1 p.a. towards the needs of the school, and more specifically for the augmentation of the master's salary.[35] There arising some legal doubt regarding this benefaction, Jasper Cholmeley, a relative of the founder, in 1587 bequeathed an identical rent-charge in lieu of Martyn's benefaction and added as his own bequest an annuity of £1 6s 8d for the increase of the school's endowment.[36] Finally, we may mention the bequest of John Dudley, who in 1581 left £2 outright to the school, as well as a rent-charge of £40 capital worth for the augmentation of its stock.[37]

A second grammar school was provided for Southwark in 1571 when the parishioners of St Olave's built at their own charge a suitable building in which 'children and younglings, as well of the rich as the poor' of the parish might be taught. The Queen by letters patent authorized the school to offer instruction not only in grammar but also in the lower branches of knowledge for younger children, while vesting its affairs in sixteen governors chosen from the parish.[38] Its original endowment comprised sixteen acres in Horsley Down, purchased with subscriptions of unknown donors at a probable charge of £250. A sustained effort was made by the governors to increase the available endowment, John Lamb, one of their number, making the first considerable contribution in 1572 when he conveyed for the use of the school two houses in Fleet Lane, London, which a generation later possessed a capital worth of about £200.[39] There were likewise a number of small bequests made to the school in these years, betokening widespread parochial interest in this educational venture, of which John Smith's legacy of £5 in 1573[40] and Charles Pratt's gift of £2 p.a. for a term of twenty years may be regarded as typical.[41] In 1600 Dame Margaret Osborne, the widow of a former lord mayor, vested a rent-charge with a capital worth of £40 in the school,[42] while at about the same date Richard Dowsett gave another rent-charge of equal capital value for the same purpose.[43] In 1610 the stock of the school was considerably augmented by the bequest of rents possessing a total capital value of £90,[44] and a number of modest gifts continued to be made in the course of the next generation. In all, we have counted capital gifts made to the school in the course of our period totalling slightly more than £700 in original value. A fair beginning had been made by a parochial community towards the permanent endowment of a substantial and important educational institution.

We have discussed at length in earlier pages Thomas Sutton's foundation of Charterhouse in 1611, indicating that half the immense endowment of £116,000 has been credited to the almshouse and an equal amount to the great grammar school which the donor likewise wished to establish within the same premises. The instructions of Sutton placed the institution under the government of the trustees and three principal administrative officers: the master, who had general charge of the whole establishment, the preacher, who served the needs of both almsmen and students, and the schoolmaster, who should be 'careful and discreet to observe the nature and [genius] of their scholars, and accordingly instruct and correct them'. The trust provided for the appointment of a master with a salary of £20 p.a., which in 1658 was increased to £100 p.a., and of an usher at an initial salary of £10 p.a. Forty students were to be admitted on the foundation, these being boys 'whose parents have [no] estate of lands to leave unto them', who were not only to have full support and tuition but who, if qualified for admission to the university, should each enjoy a stipend of £20 p.a. for support there. In addition, both boarding and day students might be admitted, two assistant masters being appointed to help with the instruction, upon the payment of tuition fees which could hardly have covered more than a fraction of the extra expense incurred. Thus briefly must we review the founding of one of the most eminent of English schools by one of the greatest of all English philanthropists.[45]

Charles I in 1633, on the petition of numerous citizens of Westminster, founded the Green Coat School (St Margaret's Hospital) there. The petitioners presented a house for the reception of poor boys and girls of tender age where they might be lodged and instructed in the manual arts and at least the rudiments of learning. The school was endowed initially with £50 p.a. allowed by the Crown as a royal gift.[46] Shortly after its foundation, in 1636, Thomas Gawen, one of the governors, gave certain properties in Newgate and in Barking, Essex, with a then value of about £400 capital, as a further endowment of this institution, which is probably more properly to be regarded as a school than as an almshouse.[47] Certainly it may be said that historically the Green Coat School was to render services of inestimable value to the youth of Westminster.

During the revolutionary decades, two additional schools were founded to serve the ever-increasing requirements of metropolitan London. In 1647 the chaplain of the East India Company's almshouse, the foundation of which has already been described, was required to keep a school on the premises in which children might be taught and seamen instructed in the mariner's art. In 1649 a more competent master was employed whose principal function seems to have been teaching, since he was only required to 'exercise such offices of piety to the almesmen as is requisite'. Something like twenty-five children were admitted during these unsettled years, the master having £20 p.a. as his stipend from the charitable funds of the hospital.[48] And, finally, we must note the founding in 1656 of a school in Tothill Fields, Westminster, by the Reverend James Palmer in conjunction with his notable almshouse.[49] Palmer erected a pleasant school building at a cost of about £200 on a spacious site, which he also provided, and settled on the foundation an endowment of about £1000 for its educational needs. Twenty boys, drawn from St Margaret's parish, were to receive free instruction by the master, who was likewise charged with catechizing and watching after the almspeople in the adjoining institution.[50]

We have recounted all too briefly the record of an amazing cultural achievement. There were few large European cities more miserably served with educational resources than was London at the outset of our period. But by persistent effort and continuous generosity, private citizens of the metropolis had in the course of not quite two centuries provided their city with what were probably the best schools available in the western world. We have described the foundation, or re-endowment, of fifteen schools in greater London, all of which were either competently endowed, or supported by livery companies as a direct charge on their now very large charitable funds. Of these, twelve offered to ambitious boys a grammar-school education of high quality, and there were places for poor but able youths in all of them without tuition cost to the parents. By the most conservative estimate, these schools enrolled 1500 youths by the close of our period, which of course suggests that something like 5 per cent to 7 per cent of the male population of school age was at that date receiving education of a relatively high level of advancement. It seems very probable that no deserving boy with requisite ability could have failed to find a place in some London school and, given the huge scholarship resources accumulated in the universities for the benefit of London, he could have looked forward to generous assistance at the universities if he were really able.

But this was by no means the full measure of the contribution of London donors to the educational needs of the age. While the huge total of £92,940 17s had been vested in school foundations in greater London, this represents only somewhat more than a third (35·85 per cent) of the whole sum which these rich and generous men dedicated to the extension of school facilities. In all, the immense total of £166,322 5s was given by London merchants, with the help of a few additional citizens, for founding grammar schools in other parts of the realm. In the main, these foundations were made in the native parish of the donor, reflecting his memories of the inadequate schooling of his own youth and his desire to widen the ambit of opportunity in a community to which he was bound by those ties of nostalgia which age evokes in all men. In not a few cases, too, these foundations were made by wise and perceptive men in regions which they simply thought were backward and which they wished to help draw level with the remainder of the nation, this having been particularly true in those regions which Puritan London regarded as papistically inclined. There was also the feeling, not infrequently expressed after 1630, that London's own educational resources were now sufficient and that the desperate needs—the educational bargains—were to be found in the rural reaches of the realm. The foundations which we shall now briefly describe were, then, quite as much a product of the stern evangelism of London as they were a labour of love by those dedicated and generous men whose abiding monuments they remain.

These foundations in the provinces had in point of fact been well begun by London merchants before 1480, especially by men who were anxious to permit education to escape the iron grip in which the ecclesiastical authorities held it in London itself.[51] But Sir Edmund Shaa [Shaw], the earliest of these donors in our period, did not exhibit this suspicion of the church in his provision for a school and a chantry in his native parish of Stockport, Cheshire, though his will placed the endowment firmly in the hands of the Goldsmiths' Company as trustees. The London properties comprising the endowment then possessed a capital worth of £726, from the income of which £4 7s was to be devoted to prayers by a stipendiary priest, while a second priest, 'a discrete man, cunning in grammar and able to teach grammar' should enjoy a stipend of £10 p.a. and should continually keep a school in the town, open to 'all manner of persons, children, and others' who might desire to learn this 'science'.[52]

The decade which saw Colet's great foundation at St Paul's likewise witnessed the establishment of four schools in widely separated parts of England as a consequence of London generosity. In 1503, Sir John

Percival, a merchant tailor and former mayor, by will founded a school
in his native town of Macclesfield, Cheshire, also in conjunction with a
chantry, but with a careful separation of the incomes and functions of
the two. Percival declared that in and about Macclesfield 'God, of his
abundant grace, had sent, and daily did send to the inhabitants copious
plenty of children, to whose learning, bringing forth in cunning and
virtue, right few teachers and schoolmasters were in that country,
whereby many children, for lack of such teaching, fell to idleness, and
lived dissolutely all their days'. The foundation was supported by lands
which a generation later possessed a capital worth of £425 and was
declared to be open free of tuition to all good men's children of the town
and the neighbouring countryside. The school was reorganized in 6
Edward VI, after the Chantry Commissioners' report, being placed
under the trusteeship of local and secular governors and under the
direction of a master and an usher.[53]

A London grocer, Robert Beckingham, shortly before 1507 seems to
have founded the grammar school at Guildford, Surrey, when he
established the institution in a house and gardens with a then annual
value of £4 13s 4d. On his death two years later this merchant provided
for the endowment of the school with lands possessing a capital worth
of about £400. The schoolhouse was rebuilt in 1520 and again, and
much more ambitiously, in 1557, when the principal inhabitants of the
town contributed about four hundred marks for what must have been
a much more commodious structure. The foundation by letters patent
in the reign of Edward VI was apparently no more than a legal for-
mality, part of the endowment having been in chantry lands.[54] In 1563
Thomas Blank, a tradesman, of St Leonard Eastcheap, added £40 to the
endowment of the institution, while his widow, Joan, in 1569 bequeathed
£10 more to the augmentation of the stock of what was ultimately to
become a well-endowed and notable school.[55]

And we must mention the foundation, sometime before her death,
of a school at Wimborne Minster, Dorset, by that enlightened woman,
Margaret Beaufort. This institution, which was connected with a
chantry, was endowed with capital to the value of £320, the priest being
instructed 'to teche gramer frely to all theym that will come'. The assets
were expropriated under Edward VI, but were restored as a secular
foundation by the founder's great-granddaughter in 1563 on the inter-
cession of Lord Mountjoy for the local inhabitants.[56] At about the same
date, Sir Bartholomew Rede, a goldsmith and Master of the Mint,
founded a grammar school at Cromer, Norfolk, 'for gentlemen's sons
and good men's children and especially poor men's children', with an
initial endowment of £200 and the prudent provision that the cleric
serving as schoolmaster should be chosen by his company with the
advice of the Provost of King's College, Cambridge, or of Eton College.

The master should be a good grammarian, of the degree of Master of Arts, and preferably one bred either at Eton or at Winchester. Rede, if we interpret his will correctly, added as well an endowment of £200 on his death for the support of his foundation, leaving to the Prior of Charterhouse on trust certain London properties for this charitable purpose.[57]

We have also assigned quite tentatively to this decade the foundation of the free grammar school at Enfield in Middlesex County. There may possibly have been a chantry school in the town in the time of Edward IV, but the grammar school seems to have been founded about 1506 under the terms of the will of John Carew, probably a former merchant and certainly a former resident of St Sepulchre, London. Carew left a considerable charitable estate to Enfield, dedicating £6 13s 4d p.a. for the wage of a schoolmaster for the parish, and a remainder, valued at perhaps £200, as an endowment for the care of the poor.[58] Two local residents, William May and Thomas Merryweather, in 1517 by indenture added property to the endowment with a capital worth totalling £167.[59] These endowments were confirmed in 1558, the schoolmaster being required to teach the children of poor men of the parish 'to read and understand grammar, and to write Latin'. A generation later a native of Enfield, William Garrett, a merchant tailor, gave the town £50 towards the building of a new school-house, as well as providing £100 to maintain a lectureship in London and the same amount for the poor of St Antholin's parish.[60] The endowment of the school was further augmented in about 1615 when Roger Grave left an annuity representing a capital worth of £40 to aid in the teaching of poor children from the parish. By 1621 the income of the school had so much increased, either because of unrecorded gifts or, more probably, the rise in rents, that the salary of the schoolmaster was increased to £20 p.a., a substantial residue being still available for poor relief.[61]

That remarkable woman, Lady Thomasine Percival, shortly before her death in 1513 founded a chantry and a free school in her native parish of Week St Mary, Cornwall. The establishment was extensive, including a house for the master and a library, the whole outlay being probably conservatively stated at £250 for the site and buildings. The institution was endowed with rents representing a capital value of £400, the income being sufficient to defray the salary of the master and an usher, as well as the wage of a laundress to wash the clothing of the teacher. We are told by Fuller that in the reign of Henry VIII the sons of the gentry of the western region were well educated in this school, which was, however, transferred to Launceston in the time of Edward VI.[62]

In the same year, 1513, Sir Stephen Jenyns, a merchant tailor who had served as mayor in 1508, secured letters patent for the foundation of a richly endowed school in his native town of Wolverhampton, Stafford-shire. Jenyns built at an uncertain cost commodious quarters for his school and settled on it, the Merchant Taylors being his trustees, the manor of Rushocke in Worcestershire, the available rents of which were then £20 p.a. It appears, however, that a generation later the true capital worth of the manor was approximately £1600 and that by 1624, when the whole of the revenues became available to the foundation, the capital value of the estate had risen to £5000. The institution was established by Jenyns as a free grammar school to be taught by a master and an usher and to serve the needs of a large area then without educa-tional resources of any consequence.[63]

The last of the endowed schools founded in the years before the Reformation was instituted under the will of Richard Collier, a mercer who died in 1532. Collier named his company as trustee for the founda-tion and government of a free grammar school in his native Horsham, Sussex. Property with a then capital value of about £640 was to be settled as the endowment for a school for sixty students, poor boys from Horsham and its neighbouring parishes to be preferred before the sons of gentlemen. At the same time, none was to be refused admission who was apt in learning. The school was to be served by a master with a stipend of £10 p.a. and an usher with a salary of £6 13s 4d p.a., the considerable residue of income being assigned for the maintenance of the school premises.[64]

Very evidently, there was a strong and well-sustained interest on the part of London burghers in the extension, one can almost say the creation, of grammar-school facilities not only in London but in the realm at large well before the Reformation. In this relatively brief period, thirteen schools had been founded by London generosity, if St Paul's may be included, in Middlesex and in seven other counties in all parts of the nation. These institutions, it will have been observed, were for the most part anchored securely in the city companies as trustees, even when they were associated with chantry foundations. In these two generations, London donors, of whom most were great merchants, established as endowments the relatively large total of £14,559 as an earnest of their resolution to weaken and then to destroy the age-old enemy, ignorance.

This resolution was greatly strengthened by the whole movement which we call the Reformation, or perhaps one should more accurately say was itself one of the important causes of the Reformation. We have observed in county after county that even the Chantry Commissioners were painfully conscientious in their protection of educational trusts and that they were deeply sensitive to the now general conviction that Eng-land must conserve and as rapidly as possible strengthen the educational resources which were just beginning to emerge as important social assets. Consequently, in London as elsewhere even the deeply unsettled years from 1541 to 1560 witnessed, on balance, a substantial addition to these resources.

William Dauntsey, a mercer, in 1543 founded an almshouse and a school in his native parish of West Lavington, Wiltshire, a capital sum of £464 being assigned to the school by the donor. Free lodging was to be provided for the master, who should have a stipend of £10 p.a. for his labours and who should freely teach all likely children presenting themselves.[65] At about the same date, a great mercer and a former lord mayor of London, George Monox, vested in a single foundation an almshouse and school at Walthamstow, Essex, the school endowment being something like £300 in capital terms. A priest was to be appointed master at a stipend of £6 13s 4d p.a., who should provide free tuition for the children of the community as well as offering prayers for the repose of the donor's soul. A second payment of £1 6s 8d p.a., with lodging, was to be made to a parish clerk who should help with the teaching. The will offered no precise definition of the nature or quality of the curriculum, though it seems probable that it remained an English school, offering the more elementary disciplines, at least as late as 1636, when an inquisition revealed that the then schoolmaster was 'not able to teach the Latin tongue'.[66]

A school was founded in Coventry, probably in 1547, by John Hales, the reformer, under unusual circumstances. We are told that Hales on a visit to the town was impressed by the need for a grammar school and also by the evident suitability for this use of the premises of the recently dissolved priory of the white friars. Upon Hales' undertaking to found the school, the King in 1546 sold the property to his Clerk of the Hamper at an unknown price, subject to the promise to establish a free grammar school. Hales opened the school in the choir of the priory church, assigning to the master the then munificent salary of £30 p.a., to the usher £10 p.a., and to the music master £4 13s 4d p.a., which would suggest that properties with a capital worth of about £900 were being devoted by the founder to the support of the institution. The school was shortly removed to the church of St John's Hospital, but there were steady complaints that Hales was withholding certain of the monastic property for his own uses, though Sir William Cecil and the Lord Chancellor in 1565 held this not to be the case. The bickering between the founder and the citizenry continued until Hales' death in 1571, causing him to set aside a design to found in Coventry a college to rival Eton and Westminster, though the school was continuously maintained in the Hospital until 1885, when new buildings were erected.[67]

In 1551 an English merchant, Robert Tempest, founded a free school for the poor children of Calais, with a bequest of £300 (*Flemish*), though it seems certain that this institution did not survive the political catastrophe which overtook the city in the next reign.[68] We shall deal fully in another place with the great grammar-school foundation made by Sir John Gresham in 1554 at Holt, Norfolk, on which we have reckoned a total of £2620 was vested by this illustrious donor.[69] Not only was Gresham a lord mayor, but it is significant that of the four remaining founders of schools in the Reformation era, three were great merchants and former holders of that eminent civic office.

The first of these, Sir William Laxton, a grocer who was lord mayor in 1544, by the terms of his will proved in 1556 founded a notable grammar school at his birthplace, Oundle, Northamptonshire, in conjunction with an almshouse. The school was initially endowed with half the capital, which gave it something like £880 of resources, from the income of which a graduate of the degree of Master of Arts was to be employed as schoolmaster at a salary of £18 p.a. and an assistant master with a yearly stipend of £6 13s 4d. The Grocers' Company was named trustee of the institution, which was well administered and which Fuller tells us a century later 'hath been, to my knowledge, the nursery of many scholars most eminent in the university'.[70] In the year following, 1557, Robert Hammond, a rich London tradesman, founded a modest school at Hampton (Middlesex), to which he left real property then valued at about £90, with the additional provision of rents over a period of twenty-one years in the yearly amount of £9 13s for its support. This school was, it appears, suspended for uncertain reasons in 1568, or thereabouts, though in 1612 the parish under the leadership of the vicar undertook legal measures to ensure its resumption.[71]

In another volume we shall deal fully with the great grammar-school foundation made at Tonbridge, Kent, by Sir Andrew Judd, a skinner and former lord mayor. Judd vested an endowment of £1786 on this institution between 1553 and 1558, while fellow London merchants shortly afterwards established exhibitions for the school possessing a capital value of £140. Then, almost two generations later (1619–1625), his grandson, Sir Thomas Smith, another London merchant, augmented the endowment and scholarship funds of the school with gifts and bequests totalling upwards of £1900. In fact, nearly the whole of the rich endowments of Tonbridge School were derived from London generosity.[72] And, finally, in recounting briefly the grammar-school foundations of the Reformation decades, we should mention the one made by a mercer, Sir Rowland Hill, in his native town of Drayton, Shropshire, in 1556. Hill erected the building, possibly a year or two earlier, at an estimated charge of £300 and by indenture conveyed to trustees lands with a then capital value of £440 for the support of the school. He constituted the churchwardens of the parish his trustees, binding them with only general statutes for his free school and setting the initial salary of the master at £13 6s 8d p.a. and that of the usher at £6 13s 4d p.a.[73]

Both the number and the distinction of grammar-school foundations greatly increased during the Elizabethan period. There were in all thirty-eight endowed foundations made during the course of the reign, of which thirty-two were instituted in the years 1561–1600, the interval which we have, for purposes of statistical convenience, regarded as the Elizabethan era. On these foundations London donors poured out over a term of forty years the large total of £32,530 in endowments across the length and breadth of England. We can, of course, deal only briefly with this vigorous and culturally significant educational movement.

In 1561 John Deane, rector of the church of St Bartholomew the Great, founded a school in the chapelry of Witton (Great Budworth) in his native county of Cheshire. As early as 1558 Deane had been granted letters patent for the foundation of a free grammar school there 'for the good instruction of boys', and before his death in 1563 had vested in his trustees property which a generation later (1596) possessed a capital worth of £429, as its endowment. The schoolmaster was to have a salary of £12 p.a., while the surplus of income, if sufficient, was to be employed for the wages of an usher and the enlargement of the school.[74]

One of the most illustrious of all English schools was founded in 1567 by Laurence Sheriff, a moderately rich grocer, who established the institution on what at first seemed a most inadequate endowment. This was of course Rugby School. Sheriff, a native of the town, was principally intent on founding a modestly endowed almshouse there for poor men, on which he settled an income representing a capital sum of no more than £111. He had, however, some years before his death built for his own use a mansion house just opposite the church in Rugby, and this, shortly before his will was drawn, he determined to convert into a school. His will originally provided a bequest of £50 for the preparation of the schoolhouse and £100 for endowment, but this latter provision was revoked by a codicil which granted instead for the support of the master a third interest in eight acres of the Conduit Close in Middlesex, then possessing an annual value of £8. The great wealth of Rugby School was in large part derived from this providentially situated property, which a century later was let to yield £50 p.a. for the school's uses and which three centuries later had an annual rental of £5000 p.a. [75]

We can mention only in passing the foundation at Dronfield, Derbyshire, of a grammar school with an endowment of approximately £300 vested by Henry Fanshawe, the Queen's Remembrancer,[76] while in another place we shall describe at some length the grammar school founded in 1569 in his native town of Blackrod, Lancashire, by John

Holmes, a weaver, who provided it with property and endowments valued at £190 as well as vesting in Pembroke College, Cambridge, a scholarship to the value of £5 p.a. for its graduates. Richard Clough, for many years a factor in the employ of Sir Thomas Gresham, was unfortunate in the bequest of £200 which he left to his native town of Denbigh for the foundation of a grammar school there. This bequest, made in 1570, was apparently lost, as was an impropriation of the tithes of Kilken (Flintshire), which Fuller tells us was worth £100 p.a., which Clough is supposed to have intended as endowment. Certain it is that no school was functioning in Denbigh in 1591 when Thomas Middleton in a petition to Lord Burghley, expressing his intention to found a free school there and to maintain a learned preacher, indicated that for the great statesman's favour in obtaining a charter he was prepared to bestow '1000 angels' on anyone Lord Burghley might care to name.[77] But this evidently ambitious plan also came to naught. Welshmen could be dreamers.

The great age of grammar-school foundations may be said to extend from 1571 to the closing decade of our period. During this interval of three generations in only two decades—that of the Armada and that just prior to the outbreak of the Civil War—did the total of new endowments given by London's donors fall below £11,000, while the average contribution for each decade reached the incredibly high figure of £25,075. The earliest of the many foundations of this long period was that made in 1571 at Abingdon, Berkshire, under the terms of the will of John Roise [Royse], a London mercer. Some years earlier (1562), Roise had given £50 to the civic authorities of Abingdon for the preparation of quarters for the reception of sixty-three scholars in a grammar school. Roise further agreed to endow the institution with sufficient funds to make it possible to admit children from the town and the adjoining countryside, with a preference for the sons of widows and poor men, and with provision for ten additional students who might be 'any honest man's, gentleman's, or rich man's son'. The founder during his lifetime and by the terms of his will endowed the institution with rents then possessing a capital worth of about £270.[78]

The grammar school at Bedford was founded by Sir William Harper, a rich merchant tailor who served as lord mayor in 1561. Harper, a native of Bedford, had as early as 1548 begun to support a school in this town, an older institution being derelict. In 1565, or thereabouts, he built a commodious schoolhouse at an estimated charge of £300 on the site of a former chantry, the lands of which Harper also purchased, apparently for about £560, and conveyed to the school's endowment. But even more importantly, he endowed the school in 1566 with thirteen acres of what was then meadow land in St Andrew Holborn, which he then valued at £12 p.a. but which was in time to increase vastly in worth. The school and its endowment, thus fabricated over the years in piecemeal fashion, Harper conveyed to the mayor and civic authorities of Bedford some little time before his death in 1574.[79]

In 1576 a rich draper, William Parker, whose charitable benefactions for many uses totalled £2157 10s, by will provided for the foundation of a free grammar school at his birthplace, Daventry, in Northamptonshire. Parker settled on trustees rent-charges with a then capital worth of £400 to provide a stipend of £15 p.a. for the master and £5 p.a. for the usher, who should offer free and full tuition to fifty poor children in 'that liberall science of gramer and the understanding of the Latin tongue'.[80] In this same year, 1576, William Lambe, a clothworker and a great philanthropist, founded and endowed a grammar school at Sutton Valence, Kent, which we shall deal with more fully elsewhere, with a total outlay of £1000 for its support.[81] A modestly but carefully endowed school was established in 1585 in his native Woodstock (Oxfordshire) by Richard Cornwell, a London skinner. Cornwell by the terms of his will left to trustees £100 for the provision of a suitable schoolhouse and £200 for the endowment.[82]

That most interesting couple, Sir Thomas Ramsay and his equally generous wife, in 1583 by indenture conveyed property to Christ's Hospital as trustees, charged with the payment of £20 p.a. for the founding of a free grammar school at Halstead, Essex, to which Lady Ramsay in her will, proved in 1601, added an endowment of equal value. They likewise founded in Christ's Hospital a writing school where there should be taught 'as well poor men's children of the city of London as children of the said hospital to write and cast accounts', which was also endowed with £400 of capital. As we shall note in our discussion of Bristol charities, Lady Ramsay by will greatly augmented the endowment of Queen Elizabeth's Hospital there with a bequest of £1000. To complete at least a cursory review of the great educational charities of the Ramsays, we should mention their joint foundation of a scholarship fund, with a capital worth of £800, for the appointment to the university of four scholars of 'the most towardness in virtue and learning, the sons of poor men . . . born within this realm', of whom two might proceed to fellowships upon undertaking to 'enter into the ministry of God's holy word, and become a publisher and preacher of the same'. Lady Ramsay by bequest created an additional scholarship fund of £800, the income to be employed towards the maintenance of twelve poor scholars in the universities. In all, then, it would seem that these donors devoted £3800 of their great charitable estate to the enlargement of educational opportunities for the youth of London, Bristol, Essex, and, for that matter, of the whole realm.[83]

At about this time a woman donor quite as remarkable as Lady Ramsay founded a grammar school at Newport, Essex. Joyce Frankland was the daughter of Robert Trappes, a London goldsmith, and of Joan his wife, who was herself a notable benefactor to education in Kent.[84] Born in London, she first married Henry Saxey, a merchant adventurer, by whom she had an only child, William Saxey, who died in 1583. Her second husband, William Frankland, remains a completely shadowy figure, save for the known fact that he was a clothworker and that his wife outlived him. Her great benefactions to the universities will be considered later, but her wisdom and generosity are well displayed also in her school foundation. Her will, proved in 1587, makes it clear that she had never been in Newport, but was credibly informed that it was 'a great and poor town' without educational facilities, though the townspeople stood ready to employ a town house that was suitable for a grammar school if funds could be found. She accordingly settled properties then valued at £470 on trustees for 'finding a grammar school' at Newport, the appointment of the master and the ordering of the foundation to be in the hands of the Master of Gonville and Caius College, of which she was also a principal benefactor. She requested only that her own name, 'daughter of Robert Trappes, of London, goldsmith, deceased and William Saxie, her son' be suitably inscribed over the door.[85]

In 1587 a dour Puritan girdler, Richard Walter, left £500 for the founding and maintenance of a grammar school in his native parish of Finedon [Thingdon], Northamptonshire.[86] In the year following, Henry Prannell, a vintner, of St Michael Queenhithe, by his will provided an endowment with a capital worth of £133 for the teaching of poor children in Martyr Worthy, Hampshire, from a suitable age for entrance upon their studies until the age of sixteen when they were ready to be apprenticed.[87] And we may conclude our review of the schools founded in this decade with the modest beginnings of Harrow, whose original benefactor was a prosperous yeoman of the hamlet of Preston, Middlesex. John Lyon obtained a licence from the Crown to found a school as early as 1571 and for some years prior to his endowment of the institution had been giving from his own purse £13 6s 8d p.a. to secure the instruction of about thirty poor children in the parish. In 1590 Lyon drafted the statutes for the school, which was by that date well established. On his death in 1592, suburban properties then by the founder's estimate worth £100 p.a. were vested for various charitable purposes, including his educational benefactions. The income was to be accumulated for three years and the school buildings erected with these moneys, though in fact the revenues did not become available until the death of the founder's widow in 1608, and the buildings could not be completed until 1615, since the costs ran to about £700. The trusteed properties, if we may convert to capital amounts, were dedicated £400 for the care of the poor; £80 to road repairs in the neighbourhood; £200 for sermons in the parish church; £400 for four scholarships from the school to both universities; and £820 for the endowment of the school. The master was initially to have a salary of £27 p.a. and the usher £14 p.a., the remainder of the income to be applied for fuel and other maintenance charges. The lands conveyed by Lyon began to increase very rapidly in value shortly after the Restoration, as the London urban complex over-ran them, but it was not until that time that the foundation was more than an excellent and a local grammar school. One parcel of the endowment lands was sold in 1932 for upwards of £180,000, while the income of the Lyon Trust reached the enormous total of £17,477 p.a. a few years later. With Harrow, as with Rugby, fortune blessed an institution which in the modesty of its foundation is scarcely to be distinguished from scores made in this period of high hopes and earnest aspirations.[88]

Though a school seems to have been intermittently kept at Market Bosworth, Leicestershire, its true foundation dates from the gifts of Sir Wolstan Dixie, a great merchant and a former lord mayor, for its erection and endowment. It was probably in 1591 that Dixie built the school at an estimated cost of £400, and he had laid the foundation for the master's house just prior to his death in late 1593. At a later date, Dixie's nephew and heir certified that he had completed the master's lodgings at his own expense of £220, as well as devoting £700 to the purchase of lands for the proper endowment of the school, in accordance with his late uncle's wishes. The school was designed to provide a rigorous classical education for not more than sixty youths, the master to have an annual stipend of £26 and the usher £20. The master was to be learned in Latin, Greek, and Hebrew and should offer instruction in these languages in the upper school, while the usher was to teach Latin and the 'ABC primer' in the lower. To complete his foundation, Dixie, who was also one of the great benefactors of Emmanuel College, Cambridge, vested in that college a scholarship and fellowship fund with capital of £500, with the provision that of the four holding the stipends one scholar and one fellow must, if possible, be graduates of his grammar school.[89]

There were four grammar-school foundations made by Londoners in various parts of the realm in the one year, 1593. Three of these were relatively modest in amount and conception. Thus William Elkin, a mercer, bequeathed to the governors of Christ's Hospital on trust an annuity representing a capital worth of £200 for the instruction of children in the chapelry of Woore (Mucklestone) in Shropshire.[90] A stationer, William Norton, also remembered his native county with an endowment of £133 to found a school in the rural parish of Onibury, Shropshire, as well as establishing a scholarship fund with a capital of about £120 to provide books for scholars from Christ's Hospital proceeding to the universities.[91] The redoubtable Dame Elizabeth Powlett endowed the school at Burton-upon-Trent, where she had also established an almshouse, with £10 p.a. in order to secure an augmentation of £3 in the salary of the master and to make possible the employment of an usher for this Staffordshire institution.[92] And, finally, in this year of remarkable educational generosity, still another and more substantial Staffordshire foundation was made at Barton (Tatenhill) by Thomas Russell, a prominent London draper. Russell vested in his company as trustee property in London then valued at £50 10s p.a., which after a payment of £2 12s p.a. for the relief of the poor of Barton, and certain other charges, was to be devoted to the endowment of his school. The capital value of the foundation may be reckoned at about £430, to which Russell's executors added an outlay of approximately £350 for the erection of a commodious brick building in accordance with the wishes of the testator and following the plan of the school recently built at Highgate, Middlesex. The foundation was designed for seventy students, 'at the least', and was served by a master and usher who were to be nominated by the Drapers' Company. Russell, it may be noted here, also made the Drapers trustees of a scholarship fund with a then capital value of £267 in order to provide two exhibitions of £6 13s 4d each, the one at Oxford and the other at Cambridge, to advance learning throughout the realm.[93]

The lord mayors of London, and for that matter great merchants generally, were drawn in surprising numbers from tiny rural hamlets in the provinces. This fact inevitably led to an interesting pattern of dispersion for almshouse and school foundations across the face of the realm. As an example, Sir Cuthbert Buckle, a rich vintner, made most generous provision for the poor of Brough-under-Stainmore (Westmorland), where, as we have seen, he also built a much-needed bridge during his lifetime. On his death in 1594, Buckle also endowed his trust with rent-charges representing a capital worth of £160 for the free instruction of children in the elementary disciplines. The schoolhouse was subsequently built by local subscriptions and in 1608 was dedicated to joint use as a school building and as a chapel.[94] In the same year, 1594, Sir Rowland Hayward, a clothworker who had twice served as lord mayor, endowed a struggling school in his native Bridgnorth, Shropshire, with £400, which his son, Sir John Hayward, a landed gentleman of Kent, augmented with a gift of £100 in 1635. It is also likely that Sir Rowland some years before his death had paid for the erection of the school building, but the particulars remain obscure.[95]

During this decade the great needs of the northern counties evidently engaged the charitable attention of London merchants, particularly, of course, those who were natives of the region. At about this time, we are told by Fuller, 'divers well-disposed citizens of London, desirous (as yet) not to be named, being born in or near to Ashburne in the Peak, in the county of Derby, combining their loving benevolence together, have built there a fair school house, with convenient lodgings for a master, and liberal maintenance allowed thereto'.[96] The school was formally founded by letters patent in 1585, but we have found no London benefactions to it until 1597 when a stream of relatively small legacies has been noted, totalling £92, of which the bequest of £1 7s by Thomas Wood, a pewterer, is typical.[97] In 1608, however, Roger Owfield, a fishmonger, who had founded an almshouse in Ashbourne, by will added £70 to the endowment of the school, which had by this date also gained firm local support. Owfield in addition established a scholarship fund with a capital of £100 for exhibitions at Cambridge, with a strongly expressed preference for students drawn from Ashbourne, if worthy applicants could be found there.[98]

Thomas Aldersey, a haberdasher, created a large and a carefully devised charitable trust for the benefit of his native parish of Bunbury in Cheshire. Aldersey built a large schoolhouse there, well set in spacious grounds. In 1594-1595 he conveyed to trustees the rectory of Bunbury, the tithes of eleven other Cheshire parishes, and certain other properties, all with a then value of about £137 p.a. for various charitable uses within the community. As we have already noted, £10 p.a. was to be used for the relief of the poor of the parish,[99] the minister was endowed with the generous stipend of £66 13s 4d p.a., and his vicar or curate was to have £20 p.a. and a room in the preacher's house, while the residue of the income, then amounting to about £37 p.a., was to constitute the endowment of the grammar school. The school was to be served by a competent master, with a salary of £20 p.a. and the free use of a house, garden, and orchard, and by an usher, with an annual salary of £10 and free lodging in a tenement which was incorporated into the school's stock. The Haberdashers were to serve as governors, indeed for the whole trust, and were to make sure that all children born in Bunbury and in Cheshire generally should receive free instruction to a maximum number to be determined by the teachers. Girls were to be admitted to the lower forms, but might not continue past the age of nine or such earlier time as they had learned to read the English language. This generous and well-considered foundation quickly attained an excellent regional reputation and was greatly to broaden the sphere of opportunity in what was then a backward and remote area.[100]

A modestly endowed but much-needed grammar school was provided for his native parish of Dean, Cumberland, in 1597 under the terms of the will of John Fox, a successful London goldsmith. Fox left on trust £150 with the Goldsmiths' Company, with the expressed hope that lands might be purchased to the value of £10 p.a. in order to pay a 'learned and godly schoolmaster' to offer instruction to the poor children of the community. It seems probable that the school was kept in a private house until 1615 when John Fox, a prebendary of Westminster and a son of the founder, with some help from local donors, built a schoolhouse at a cost of about £100. The annuity of £10 remained the only endowment income of the school, which consequently had to impose a light tuition charge on its students, who were drawn during its first century from a considerable area around Dean.[101]

We may well conclude our review of the sixteenth-century foundations with at least a brief comment on that made by Richard Platt, whose endowment of an almshouse at Aldenham, Hertfordshire, has already been described. Platt, like his more famous son, was a projector and experimenter, evidently deeply interested in education. In 1599 he nominated his own company, the Brewers, as governors of the almshouse and the conjoined grammar school which he proposed to found at Aldenham. He indicated that he had some years previously (1596) built the school at a probable cost of £400, to which he gave by gift and bequest properties then worth £1080 as a perpetual stock for its support. The school was to admit sixty students, the poor of Aldenham and of the Brewers' Company being preferred, who should be taught in the lower forms by an usher competent in the normal disciplines and who should have £10 p.a. and lodging as his stipend. The master was to have £20 p.a., as well as a house and garden, and must be prepared to teach Latin grammar as well as 'purity of life, manners, and religion' to the older students. Platt at about the same time gave a messuage then valued at £90 for the augmentation of the endowment of the free grammar school at St Albans and sought by a bequest of £20 to secure the foundation of a school in the London parish of St James Garlickhithe, where he had at his own cost built a room in the west end of the church for this use. Platt had in view a school for the poorer children of the parish, in which reading, writing, and arithmetic, and an 'entrance into grammar rules' might be competently taught, but his aspirations remained unrewarded until 1710 when such a school was founded with Platt's bequest as part of the *corpus* of its endowment.[102]

We have already observed that in the early Stuart period there was an immense outpouring of London wealth for the founding of still more schools for the benefit of both the children of the city and those in many counties across the realm. In all, the great total of £148,263 17s was given during this fruitful interval, or substantially more than half the amount provided for grammar-school foundations during our whole period. It is true that a very considerable proportion of the whole, £58,000, is to be credited to Thomas Sutton's one great foundation,[103] but there none the less remains an immense sum devoted to a great variety of foundations, whose history we should now trace briefly. It is not too much to say that the whole structure of English grammar-school education took shape during this generation on a scale and with an excellence of conception never matched again until deep in the nineteenth century.

Dean Alexander Nowell's grammar-school foundation at Middleton, Lancashire, which he had contemplated as early as 1572, was made in succesive stages between that date and his death in 1601, probably as much as £1392 being given for its endowment.[104] In the same year, Peter Blundell, the rich and generous clothworker, by the terms of his will arranged for the endowment of the school at Tiverton, Devon, with the very large sum of £2400 and authorized his executors to expend the further sum of £1000 for the preparation of the schoolhouse and its offices. The foundation was placed in the care of twenty-seven trustees, it being provided that free instruction should be afforded for 150 local boys aged six to eighteen and that the master was to have the munificent stipend of £50 p.a. and the usher £13 6s 8d as well as his lodging. In addition, Blundell by will provided an endowment of £2000 for six exhibitions in the universities, these scholars to be chosen whenever possible from among the graduates of the great grammar school which he had just founded.[105] A few years later, Blundell's nephew and business associate, Robert Chilcot, left £400 for the building and endowment of an English school for not more than one hundred students who were to receive free instruction in preparation for entrance into Blundell's grammar school.[106] In 1600 Gabriel Goodman, the famous Dean of Westminster, completed the endowment of the hospital and free grammar school which he had begun a decade earlier for the benefit of the sparsely populated countryside around Ruthin in Denbighshire. Goodman settled on the educational foundation endowments of about £1100, with the provision that 120 students might be enrolled and with the careful stipulation that all those drawn from Ruthin and Llanelidan should receive free instruction. By his will, proved in 1601, he also established an endowment for two scholars at St John's, Cambridge, with a capital worth of £160, as well as leaving a modest residue from his estate for the general uses of the two universities.[107]

We shall speak elsewhere in some detail of the foundation in 1604 of a grammar school at Coxwold, Yorkshire, with an endowment of £733 left by Sir John Harte, a London grocer who had served as lord mayor in 1589–1590. It seems probable that Harte, who was a native of the parish, had also provided a modest house and surrounding grounds for the school then valued at about £100.[108] We shall also note elsewhere that Sir James Deane, a famous merchant of his generation, had in 1608 founded a grammar school at Basingstoke, Hampshire, which he substantially endowed with £1100.[109] The Steward of the Inner Temple, George Ledsham, by the terms of his will, proved in 1606, left £300 for the erection and maintenance of a free grammar school in his native parish of Hawarden, Flintshire. On his instructions, the trustees delayed until interest accumulations of £50 enabled them to build a small but suitable structure, devoting the income on the undepleted capital to the tasks of education in this rural parish.[110] A moderately wealthy merchant tailor, John Hide, in 1609 vested an endowment with a capital worth of £200 to provide for the maintenance of a small grammar school in the chapel at Hayfield, Derbyshire, while establishing annuities of £6 18s for the relief of the poor of London and of £5 for the sustenance of almsmen of his own company, and leaving a residue of about £15 p.a. for the redemption of prisoners for debt whose obligations did not exceed £5.[111]

Lady Alice Owen's school at Islington was founded in conjunction with the almshouse which she reared and endowed for this parish beginning in 1609.[112] In 1613 this able woman laid down the statutes for the school, which was to admit twenty-four poor students from Islington and six from Clerkenwell. The school was built at an estimated charge of £150, and it was provided under the terms of her will with an endowment of £440 for the support of the master and the repair of the building.[113] This intelligent and clear-minded woman likewise founded a scholarship at Emmanuel College, Cambridge, with an endowment of approximately £200, left £200 to the library at Oxford, and gave outright £20 for the support of the school at Edmonton, Middlesex.

The following decade was of course dominated by the great foundation of Charterhouse, but there were as well a large number of lesser schools established in every part of England by the merchant elite of London. Thus in 1611 Sir William Ryder, a haberdasher and manufacturer who had been lord mayor of London in 1600, endowed the school at Drayton, Shropshire, with London property then valued at £220, for the augmentation of the salaries of the master and usher 'so they shall the more willinglie teache and instruct poore mens' children . . . [that] they maie become good members in the comonwealthe'.[114] A somewhat less renowned haberdasher, Florence Caldwell, in the next year (1612) also augmented the endowment of an existing school when he left £5 p.a. to increase the salary of the schoolmaster at Rolleston, Staffordshire, in the hope that he might the better bring up children in 'good literature, doctrine and behaviour'.[115] We have mentioned these augmentations of existing foundations at the outset of our discussion of schools established in this decade, because they are typical of scores of similar gifts and bequests which we have simply been unable to treat more fully because of our concern with original foundations.

A school was founded in the rural parish of Standon, Hertfordshire, in 1613 under the will of Thomas Fisher, a London skinner. This donor left rents with a capital worth of about £500 for the support of instruction and for providing books, paper, and ink for poor scholars, as well as £10 p.a. to be distributed to the poor of the parish and an annuity of the same amount towards the support of the work of Christ's Hospital.[116] We shall discuss at some length in another place the foundation of a grammar school in his native Eccleston, Lancashire, in 1597 by Sir James Pemberton, a goldsmith and lord mayor, which by subsequent gifts and a generous bequest in 1613 he endowed with a total of £1600.[117] In the year following, 1614, Humphrey Walwyn, a London grocer, directed his executors to build a free school at Colwall, Herefordshire, which he endowed with £500 settled on his company as trustees, they being bound to send a learned man every third year, a stipend of £5 p.a. being provided, to examine the students on the foundation. Those children of Colwall and Little Malvern who could afford no fees were to be taught without charge, while those who could do so were to pay 10s p.a. as their tuition. The Grocers' Company was entrusted with the selection of the master, who should also be a clergyman obligated to deliver four sermons annually in Colwall and one in Little Malvern.[118] Robert Smith, a merchant tailor and attorney, began in 1606 to create a substantial charitable trust for his native town of Market Harborough, Leicestershire, which he completed well before his death in 1620. In 1609 Smith had established a lectureship in the parish with an endowment of £400, to which for some years afterwards he added £6 13s 4d p.a., to secure two lectures each week by a preaching minister. In 1614 he built a school with an apartment for the master at an approximate charge of £250, which he endowed with rents representing a total capital worth of £280 to ensure the promised stipend of £10 p.a. for the master, necessary repairs, and periodic visits of inspection and examination by the Dean and Chapter of Christ Church, Oxford.[119]

One of the largest of the foundations of this decade was that made at Monmouth by William Jones, the London haberdasher whose great generosity provided this, his native town, with a full range of social institutions. A eulogist tells us that 'because ignorance and barbarisme are chiefe enemies that hinder religion', Jones provided 'seminaries of learning and religion for the instruction of their children and took order for erecting of a free schoole in the same place and a faire house for the schoole-master'. The Haberdashers, as his trustees, were in 1615 vested with the huge sum of £9000 for the support of the almshouse, the lectureship, and the educational foundation which Jones wished to raise in Monmouth; something like £1000 was expended on the schoolhouse, while the endowments specifically dedicated to the support of the school may be reckoned at about £3500. The founder declared that he was establishing a 'free grammar school for the instruction and education of boys and youths in the Latin tongue and other ... erudition'. The school was designed for not more than one hundred students and was to be taught by a master and an usher who were to have, respectively, the generous salaries of £60 and £30 for their

pains. The preacher, also on the foundation, was to be of the degree of
Master of Arts and was entrusted with the duty of visiting the school
twice yearly and examining the scholars.[120]

A skinner's widow, Margaret Audley, in 1616 by bequest settled an
endowment with a capital worth of £400 for the maintenance of a school
in Hackney (Middlesex) as part of a trust which also provided for a
distribution of £5 4s p.a. to the poor of the parish, £4 p.a. for the repair
of a bridge which she had built 'at her own cost' to furnish a more
convenient passage from Hackney to Shoreditch, and any residue for the
maintenance of the parish church.[121] In the same year, a merchant tailor,
Randolph Wolley, by gift and will added £100 to the endowment of the
grammar school of his native town of Wolverhampton (Staffordshire)
and a second gift of the same amount with the specific instruction that
the income be used to increase the stipends of the master and usher.
At about the same date, this donor also constituted an endowment of
£100, the income to be employed for the reader at Woore chapelry
(Mucklestone), Shropshire, he henceforward to teach without charge
the needy children of that community.[122]

It has been observed that not infrequently these great merchant donors
vested a school foundation and an almshouse as a single trust under a
single corporate administration. Another such example was that created
in 1617 at Stratford Bow, Middlesex, by Sir John Jolles, a draper who
had served as lord mayor in 1615–1616. Jolles had built the schoolhouse in this, his native village, some years earlier at a probable cost of
£300. After supporting the institution during a trial period, he arranged
for its endowment by vesting in his company as trustees London
properties then valued at somewhat more than £700. The school was
designed for thirty-five poor boys who should be taught without fees
the 'secrets of grammar and the Latin tongue' by a master and usher
to be nominated by the master and wardens of the Drapers' Company.[123]
Still another school was provided for the county when in this same year,
1618, Simon Bolton, a yeoman, left a house and lands with a then capital
worth of about £200 for the maintenance of a free school for the poor
children of Tottenham, then of course a suburban village.[124]

We may mention as a group four large grammar-school foundations
made in this decade by great London merchants which will be fully
discussed in our treatment of other counties. Thus Sir James Lancaster
settled on the grammar school of Basingstoke, Hampshire, and the lesser
foundation at Kingsclere, Hampshire, generous endowments valued
at £1387, as well as scholarship trusts with a capital worth of £1200.[124a]
Sir William Craven, who with his wife, Dame Elizabeth, was a great
benefactor to Yorkshire as well as to London, in 1605 built the grammar
school at Burnsall, Yorkshire, at a cost of £400 and by his will, proved
in 1618, endowed it with an annuity of £20 for the stipend of the

master.[125] In the next year, as we have noted, John Harrison, a merchant tailor, vested in his company as trustees £500 for the building and £1100 for the endowment of a free grammar school at Great Crosby, his birthplace in Lancashire, as well as establishing a university scholarship fund with an endowment of £200.[126] And, finally, we should mention William Seabright's foundation of a grammar school at Wolverley, Worcestershire, which he built in 1618 at a charge of about £400 and endowed, on his death in 1620, with capital of the same value for the 'free teaching of the children'.[127]

A merchant tailor, Richard Osmotherlawe, in 1612 made his company feoffees for a small school in his native parish of Bromfield, Cumberland, which he endowed with rents to a capital value of £200.[128] Some years earlier, Sir Stephen Soame, a grocer who had been lord mayor in the late Elizabethan years, had erected at an estimated cost of £200 a school at Little Thurlow, Suffolk, where he had also built and endowed an almshouse. By the terms of his will, proved in 1620, Soame settled a trust with properties worth then in excess of £600 to secure the support of a grammar school for children from all parts of Suffolk who might attend without the payment of any tuition. The lower forms were to be taught reading, writing, and arithmetic by the usher, whose salary was set at £10 p.a., while the older and apter students should be grounded in the English and Latin tongues by the master, whose stipend was fixed at £20 p.a., until such time as they were prepared to proceed to the university or to be bound out as apprentices.[129]

There seems to have been an unendowed grammar school in Hertford as early as 1557, but it was kept only intermittently until its foundation in 1621 under the terms of the will of Richard Hale, a London grocer whose forbears had long been settled in the parish of Kings Walden, Hertfordshire. Hale built a large school, for one hundred or more students, in 1616 or 1617 at a probable cost of about £400 and defrayed the charges for instruction by income gifts until his death. His will provided an endowment of £800 for the support of a master and usher who should freely teach 'children and youth in the Latin tongue and other literature' under the supervision of the governors, to be composed of the mayor and nine principal burgesses of the town. For reasons not wholly clear, Hale's son and grandson did not vest the endowment until 1664, but provided from their own estates an annual rental of £40 p.a. for the full support of the institution during this interval of more than forty years.[130] In 1621 Dame Margaret Hawkins, the widow of the redoubtable Elizabethan seaman, by the terms of her will founded a grammar school in her native town of Kington, Herefordshire. Dame Margaret left in her executors' hands £140 subject to a life annuity and £800 to be wholly employed for the building and endowment of the school, which should be free to boys from three Herefordshire parishes as well as those drawn from Michaelchurch-on-Arrow in Radnorshire. Since she wished the institution to be sufficiently endowed for the full support of sixty students, she enjoined her executors to accumulate income for four years for the building of the school premises, in order to leave the endowment intact. This was done, the school being built of stone in 1625 at a cost of £240 and providing in addition to the school-rooms appropriate quarters for both the master and usher. The master was to be a learned and able divine, who should likewise preach weekly in the parish, while the usher was to be a learned and discreet man competent to instruct the children in his charge in 'literature and good education'.[131]

Another of the rare grammar-school foundations made by donors not members of the mercantile aristocracy was established at Stanwell, Middlesex, in 1622 by Thomas, Lord Knivett. Knivett, whose other claim to historical fame is having headed the search party that found the explosives in the Gunpowder Plot, set aside funds in the residue of his estate with which his wife, at a probable charge of £250, built a 'neat and convenient' schoolhouse with an adjoining master's house shortly after her husband's death. Again following his instructions, Lady Knivett vested in feoffees lands with a capital worth of upwards of £460 for the full maintenance of a master who should provide free instruction to all poor scholars of the parish.[132]

By far the largest of the foundations made in this decade was that made in Edinburgh under the terms of the will of George Heriot, a goldsmith formerly of that city who had followed the king to London, where he was to make a great fortune as the principal purveyor of jewels to the improvident king and his recklessly extravagant consort. Heriot, who died in 1624, left the residue of his estate to the Town Council Ordinary and the ministers of his native city for the founding of a hospital in direct imitation of Christ's Hospital, which by this date was already rather more famous as a grammar school than as a hospital for foundlings.[133] Heriot's fortune may be quite exactly appraised as £47,507 16s 11½d, against which were levied large legacies to relatives, including two natural daughters, and friends. The residue of £23,625 10s 3½d was not immediately available, being principally in debts owed to the donor by the King and by the Earl of Roxburgh. As funds came to hand, the governors began raising the fabric of the great institution in 1628, most prudently expending only the income received from the mounting capital of the endowment. Because of the civil disturbances first in Scotland and then in England, the work was subject to numerous interruptions but was completed in 1650 at a total charge of about £30,000. Scarcely had the premises been finished than Cromwell took possession of them for use as a military hospital, a use to which they were put until 1659 when Monck withdrew his forces.

In that year, a full generation after Heriot's great bequest had been made, the hospital was at last opened for the admission of thirty orphan boys who were to receive their whole education on the endowment, the number being increased to fifty-two just two years later.[134]

We shall deal elsewhere with the foundation in 1626 at Shepton Mallet, Somerset, of a school and an almshouse by Sir George Strode, a London merchant connected with the able and prolific family of that western county. Strode and his family built the schoolhouse and a dwelling for the master at a charge of about £100 and by successive gifts in 1627 and 1639 endowed the school with an income representing a capital worth of £260. We may conclude our discussion of the school foundations of this decade by a brief notice of two institutions built and endowed in 1627 under the will of Edward Latimer, probably a London feltmonger before his retirement to rural Middlesex with a fortune and lands that raised him at once into the lower gentry. Latimer settled on trustees lands with a very uncertainly estimated capital worth of £500 to provide a school and orphanage in Hammersmith for eight boys between the ages of seven and twelve, the income of which was to be used for their sustenance and education in English until they had attained the age of thirteen. The deed of gift further instructed that six poor and aged men should be clothed by the trustees and given partial support by an annual payment of 10s to each pensioner. Latimer likewise provided an endowment of something like £300 for a similar institution at Edmonton, Middlesex, where some years earlier a rent-charge of £2 p.a. had been left towards the establishment of a free school by another London donor. Latimer enjoined his trustees to choose eight boys aged from seven to twelve and to furnish them with clothing, care, and education 'in some petty school' until they were prepared for their apprenticeships. No funds were provided for a school building, though instruction was afforded in various inconvenient quarters until 1739 when the mounting surpluses from the valuable lands left by Latimer enabled the trustees to build a proper schoolhouse at a cost of £500.[135]

In the decade immediately before the outbreak of the Civil War, there was a pronounced decline in the total given for grammar-school foundations. In all, £6166 was provided by London donors for this use in the years 1631 to 1640, the smallest sum, it may be noted, since the eighth decade of the sixteenth century. None the less, foundations were continued by Londoners in every part of the realm at the still amazing rate of almost one a year. But these establishments were on the whole on a relatively modest scale, there having been no single massive endowment made during these years. None the less, all these institutions were useful and several of them were in succeeding generations to become schools of considerable renown.

The first of these foundations was that made in 1632 at Beccles, Suffolk, by Sir John Leman, a rich and generous fishmonger who had served as lord mayor in 1616–1617. Leman conveyed to the town authorities a large messuage then valued at about £200 to be used as a free school for the education of forty-eight scholars to be drawn from Beccles and two adjoining parishes. No student might be admitted who could not read English perfectly and instruction was not to continue for more than four years for any student. The foundation was not a grammar school, being by the founder's prescription limited to writing, reading, arithmetic, and catechizing in 'the religion established in this realm'. None the less, the institution was well endowed with properties then having a value of at least £800 for the support of a master and usher who must live on the premises.[136]

A school and almshouse were founded in his native parish of Barrow, Shropshire, by John Slany, a merchant tailor, some years before his death in 1632. The schoolhouse seems to have cost the donor not quite £200, and he in his will indicated that a six-acre tract lying about the school and almshouse was to be principally employed for the maintenance of the school. The schoolmaster was preferably to be an ordained minister, and was to have an annuity of £10 for the instruction of twenty poor scholars drawn from the countryside, they to be taught without the payment of any fee. In addition to these students on the foundation, the master was permitted to accept other scholars to a reasonable number who could afford to pay a modest tuition charge, the better to support him.[137] Just two years later, in 1634, a London mercer, Hugh Perry, who had founded a well-endowed almshouse in his native town of Wotton-under-Edge, Gloucestershire, by the terms of his will made modest provision as well for the educational needs of that community. Perry enlarged the facilities of the free school there by establishing an endowment of £160 capital value in order to defray the stipend of an usher, who should undertake without charge to offer instruction in the lower branches of knowledge.[138]

We shall comment elsewhere on the founding in 1635 of a small grammar school in his birthplace, Topcliffe (Yorkshire), by William Robinson, a London merchant. Robinson vested in the Grocers' Company an endowment of £320, the income of which was to be employed towards the maintenance of a schoolmaster who should provide tuition in the Latin and English tongues.[139] In the same year, Charles Parrett, a draper, in addition to an outright legacy of £10 for the uses of the school at Hampstead (Middlesex), left an annuity with a capital worth of £100 towards the stipend of a master competent to provide elementary English instruction for the children of poor and decayed householders in the town of Bow Brickhill (Buckinghamshire).[140]

Edward Pothan, a London skinner, in 1637 left rent-charges with a capital value of £333 for the support of a schoolmaster at Alberbury, Shropshire, while also bequeathing an identical sum for the support of a master at Hayes, Middlesex, who should have free use of the testator's 'aboade and residence' in that parish.[141] In the year following, Sir Thomas Mowlson, a grocer who had served as lord mayor in 1634, completed by will the endowment of the grammar school which he had founded some years earlier in his native community of Hargrave, Cheshire. Mowlson had spent about £400 on the construction of the school, to which he had also conveyed endowments of £320 during the later years of his life. To this he now added properties with a capital value of £400 to complete the endowment, establishing the trusteeship and providing that 'one learned, diligent, and discreet man' be appointed to instruct the youth of the village 'in grammar and virtue'. The master was to have an annual salary of £20, the residue of the income to be applied for the maintenance and improvement of the premises and towards the relief of the poor.[142]

We may conclude our review of the school foundations of this decade with a consideration of the notable educational legacies left to his native Scotland by Robert Johnstone in 1639. Johnstone, a lawyer and one of Heriot's executors, had, as we have already seen, arranged substantial bequests for a number of needed charitable uses in Edinburgh, though the largest of his benefactions were dedicated to education. He disposed something like £600 for the erection and endowment of a grammar school at Moffat (Dumfrieshire), with the careful provision that the provost, bailiffs, and ministers of Edinburgh were to serve as its governors. He left as well £1000 to establish a scholarship fund for eight poor scholars in the University of Edinburgh, of whom four were to be chosen from Moffat Grammar School and the remainder from the Edinburgh Grammar School or from Heriot's Hospital. He also bequeathed to the 'Colledge at Edinburgh' certain of his law books and historical works, as well as all his books in French, Spanish, and Italian. Johnstone likewise provided a legacy of £1000 towards the augmentation of the endowment of Heriot's Hospital, the income to be used quite specifically for the clothing of the children cared for and educated there. This great charitable trust, particularly when Heriot's even larger dispositions are borne in mind, would suggest that however much injury the Scottish followers may have wrought on the House of Stuart, they richly remembered and significantly advanced the culture and society of their native land with the wealth which they had so quickly gained in England.[143]

It appeared in the decade prior to the outbreak of the Civil War as if the enthusiasm of London merchants for the founding of schools might be waning. But this was by no means the case, since in the two decades of political and economic unsettlement with which our period closes the amounts designated by London donors for school foundations rose again to very high totals and the steady progress of this amazing cultural movement was renewed. During this brief interval of two decades, the huge sum of £48,635 8s was provided by Londoners for school endowments, thereby substantially completing the great design of widely diffused educational opportunities begun a full century earlier by the merchant aristocracy of the city.

On his death in 1641 Nathan Walworth of St Bennet Paul's Wharf finished the endowment of the school which he had founded at Ringley in the parish of Prestwich, Lancashire, some years earlier. As we shall note elsewhere, Walworth had in 1625 established a chapel at Ringley, had endowed the living in 1635, and at about this same date built a schoolhouse at an estimated cost of £100. This foundation he endowed by will with properties valued at upwards of £300, to the end that a competent schoolmaster might be employed to teach all children of the community without charge and those from other places at 'moderate and indifferent rates'.[144] In the next year, Sir James Cambell, the great ironmonger who had served as lord mayor in 1629–1630, founded a free grammar school in the town of Barking, Essex, which he generously endowed with a stock of £666 13s 4d. This institution was to afford free tuition to all children of the parish, who were to be taught to read English, to master the rudiments of grammar, and to attain some proficiency in writing and ciphering. Cambell, like so many of his contemporaries, seems to have believed that England was now sufficiently endowed with grammar schools and that the next great task was properly to endow and strengthen the elementary schools of the nation.[145] In the same year, 1642, William Randall, Esq., of Lincoln's Inn, bequeathed a third part of a rent-charge, which, being sold, yielded a capital sum of £108, for the founding of a school at Preston, Northamptonshire. This stock proving inadequate, Randall's son, of the same name, added £100 to the endowment by gift in 1653, while shortly after the Restoration a local landowner, Richard Knightley, further strengthened the resources of the institution with a bequest of £200. This is but typical of the manner in which the leaven of London funds worked in innumerable instances across the length and breadth of the land.[146]

A rich London grocer, Thomas Gamull, a native of Audlem, Cheshire, by the stipulations of his will, proved in 1643, settled on trustees the sum of £500 for the founding and endowment of a grammar school in that parish. Gamull also instructed his three executors to meet with the community 'assembled in the parish church for that purpose', to determine on the plan for the building and the investment of the endowment in freehold land. Instruction was to be offered in the school to all youths of the parish in the Latin and Greek tongues, the governance being vested in six substantial local residents. In the same year, Ralph Bolton, a merchant tailor and also a native of this parish, vested in the governors an additional sum of £466 13s 4d for the augmentation of the endowment, subject however to a life annuity. Unhappily for this interesting and well-supported institution, the surviving executor of Thomas Gamull, 'being in actual war against the Parliament' before the founding legacy could be paid over, the amount was confiscated in 1644 and dedicated to the public service until a 'fit opportunity' was found to restore it to its intended use. In 1651, with the return of political stability, restoration was ordered in the amount of £802 0s 6d, representing principal and interest on the original legacy. Meanwhile, however, Bolton had shortly before his death in 1650 advanced a loan of £40 to secure the building of the schoolhouse. Moreover, Bolton's widow, Tryphena, on her own part was to found an elementary school at Audlem for both boys and girls, with a slight endowment, then valued at perhaps £50.[147]

The rage of civil war likewise delayed and somewhat altered the bequest which Robert Lever, a London clothier, left in 1644 to secure the solid endowment of the grammar school at his birthplace, Bolton-le-Moor, Lancashire. It was not until 1655, in fact, that his executors were able to lay out a total of £785 17s 8d from this staunch Puritan's estate for the erection of the building and the endowment of the stipends of the master and usher of this school, which will be more fully described in another place.

The paralyzing effect of the Civil War on school foundations is most dramatically suggested when we note that save for the East India Company's small school at Stepney,[148] no school was established with London wealth for the four-year period 1645–1649. There had, indeed, been no interval of this length barren of foundations since the accession of Queen Elizabeth.

But the steady progress of foundations was well resumed in 1650 when the Royalist lord mayor, Sir Thomas Adams, a draper, established a school in Wem, his native parish in Shropshire. Adams, who had earlier founded the Arabic lectureship at Cambridge,[149] conveyed to fifteen substantial inhabitants of Wem as trustees funds for the construction of a school which should offer free instruction to 'all men's children' within the favoured parish. This initial endowment Adams increased by successive gifts from 1651 to 1659 of lands with a somewhat uncertainly estimated capital worth of £1400, for the support of three masters on the foundation. The junior masters were to teach the lower forms and instruct in English, while the senior was to offer instruction in the Latin and Greek languages to the older students.[150] In 1651 Robert Jenner, probably a retired goldsmith, by the terms of a nuncupative codicil to his will, founded and endowed a grammar school at Cricklade, Wiltshire. His executors, following his wishes, built a large and substantial schoolhouse at a charge upwards of £200, while the founder provided a rent-charge of £20 p.a. as the stipend of the master, who should strictly limit his instruction to a classical curriculum. The master was required to admit all qualified applicants from the two parishes in the town, but, if we read the will correctly, a tuition of 4s annually was to be collected from all students, whether paid by their parents or by the parish.[151]

A school was provided for the Isle of Man in 1654 by one of its native sons, Philip Christian, who had made a considerable fortune in London as a clothworker. His company, as trustee, apparently built the school at a charge of about £100 and then applied as endowment an annuity of £20 which Christian had designated for the support of a competent schoolmaster who would provide instruction for all the poor but aspiring children of Peel, his birthplace. The original building had become derelict by 1686 when the company rebuilt it and placed the whole foundation on a firmer basis of administration.[152] In 1654, too, Rowland Wilson, a leading London vintner, supplied a modest endowment with a capital value of £240 for the support of a school which he had founded sometime earlier at Hugill, Westmorland, for the teaching and better advancement of the poor children of that community.[153]

We have already spoken of Richard Aldworth's great legacy of £7000 to Christ's Hospital in 1654, with which some years later the notable mathematical school of that institution was established.[154] But this by no means represented the full measure of the generosity of this enlightened merchant, who dedicated most of a great fortune to educational foundations. Thus by the terms of his will Aldworth bequeathed £4,000 to the municipal government of his native Reading (Berkshire) in trust for the foundation there of the Blue Coat School on the model of Christ's Hospital. Save for an annuity of £20 to a lecturer for the parish, who was also to instruct the students in religion, all the resources of the trust were vested for the advancement of the institution. There were to be admitted twenty poor and destitute boys, each of whom should be fully clothed, fed, and maintained, with a generous provision of £6 13s 4d for each child, while an additional thirty poor boys were to receive free instruction in the school without maintenance. A fully competent schoolmaster was to be appointed, with a stipend of £30 p.a., to ensure the education of his charges, while they on the completion of the curriculum were to be apprenticed with a premium of £6 13s 4d to be supplied by the trust. Aldworth further bequeathed £2000 to the municipal authorities of Basingstoke, Hampshire, as trustees, for the establishment there of a similar school on a more modest scale. Ten boys were to be admitted to the foundation, with the same provisions for their upbringing and education, while additional children might be admitted for instruction but without maintenance or apprenticeship. These great bequests established important and extraordinarily valuable social institutions which sought quite successfully to conjoin education with a central intention of relieving the worst evils of poverty for defenceless youth. Aldworth was one of that select and generous company of donors who were bold enough to experiment with new forms of social institutions and dedicated great fortunes to the attainment of the aspirations held so tenaciously in mind.[155]

The six closing years of our period rivalled the late Elizabethan and the Jacobean eras in the number of school foundations made in various parts of the land by London donors. There were in all twelve considerable institutions endowed during these years, several of which we shall deal with fully elsewhere. Thus Henry Colborne, a rich and most generous scrivener, endowed two schools in his native Lancashire, as well as another in Hertfordshire, where he was a substantial landowner. Colborne vested in feoffees valuable properties on which annuities were charged sufficient to endow a grammar school at Kirkham, Lancashire, with an income representing a capital value of £1400, and another in Goosnargh, just to the north, with an income of £25 p.a., or a capital worth of perhaps £500. In addition, Colborne conveyed to the Merchant Taylors' Company as trustees an endowment yielding £637 10s for the founding of a grammar school at Ashwell, Hertfordshire, the company laying out £290 on the building and investing the remainder in lands for its support.[156] As we shall see, too, James Fletcher, a haberdasher, in 1654 built and endowed a grammar school at Bretherton, Lancashire, at a total charge of £436 in memory of his wife, Jane, a native of the place, she having some years earlier sought to establish a free school there with a gift of £100. By the terms of his will, proved in 1656, Fletcher likewise increased the endowment of the school at Ormskirk, Lancashire, with a bequest of £100.[157] Still another Lancashire foundation was made in 1658 by Richard Higginson, also a London merchant, for the parish of Bispham. Higginson erected the building at a probable charge of £200 and endowed the school with London properties, formerly the lands of the Dean and Chapter of St Paul's, then possessing a capital worth of £600. When these properties were restored to their rightful owners at the Restoration, Higginson's widow at once settled a new endowment of £200 on the institution, thus averting its collapse, while, happily, the lands for this new endowment were so well chosen that they possessed a capital worth of £9865 5s 10d at the close of the nineteenth century.[158]

In 1656 Sir Lancelot Lake built a school at Little Stanmore (Middlesex) at a charge of about £150, endowing it with lands with a capital worth of £300.[159] In the same year, William Adams, an immensely generous benefactor to his native town of Newport, Shropshire, founded and handsomely endowed the grammar school of that place. A school had been kept at Newport prior to the Reformation by one of the fellows of the College of Newport, the stipend of £5 p.a. for the master having been preserved by the Edwardian commissioners and protected in 23 *Elizabeth* when the former properties of the college were conveyed to trustees by the Crown. In 1633 a London salter, William Robson, settled an additional £5 p.a. on the institution, which remained an English school lending instruction in the lower branches of knowledge.[160] This school was further endowed by Adams under the terms of his will, proved in 1661, when properties with a capital worth of £180 were settled on feoffees for its support, to the end 'that the children of the poorest people of Newport, of civil and honest demeanour, might be there freely taught to read English'. But Adams' greater interest was in the foundation of a free grammar school for his native town. Sometime before 1656, he had constructed the buildings—a large and well-designed schoolhouse and residences for the master and usher—at an approximate cost of £400. Over the schoolhouse Adams provided a spacious library, which he likewise stocked with books, while around the institution he set aside a large tract as a playground and with gardens for the two teachers. The founder settled a large estate on the Haberdashers as trustees for his numerous charities in Newport, designating an income of £77 4s p.a., or a capital worth of £1544, for the support of the masters, the visitation of the school, the maintenance of the premises, and sundry smaller connected outlays. In addition, the donor disposed capital of £400 for the founding of four scholarships for graduates of the school in either university, each student to have £5 p.a. towards his support during his tenure. Such scholars should have been eminently well prepared upon leaving Newport, for the school, which was designed for eighty students, was by the provisions of the statutes, carefully and minutely drawn by the founder, to offer instruction in Greek, Latin, and Hebrew.[161]

John Perryn, a goldsmith, who was a native of Bromyard, Herefordshire, in effect refounded the grammar school there by the terms of his will, proved in 1657, when he vested an endowment of £400 on the governors, the income to be solely used for the stipend of the master 'for his better encouragement to be laborious and careful for the education and bringing up of youth'. Perryn's keen concern with the enlargement of educational opportunities in the nation was further displayed by a bequest of £5 p.a. for the work of Christ's Hospital and a scholarship endowment yielding £5 p.a. to found an exhibition in either university for the use of a scholar 'bred up a Bluecoat in Christ's Hospital'.[162] In the year following (1658), a haberdasher, William Crowder, by will provided £100 for the building of a grammar school at Weobley (Herefordshire) and an annuity representing a capital value of £400 for its endowment. Crowder indicated that an able schoolmaster, well versed in both Latin and Greek, should be employed to offer free instruction to able students drawn from Weobley and neighbouring parishes.[163]

And, finally, at the close of our period, we must mention the founding in 1659 of a trust by Walter Bigg, a merchant tailor, which he desired ultimately to be employed for the erection of a school at Wallingford, Berkshire. Bigg left an annuity of £10 which was to be accumulated until a proper building could be erected, which did not apparently occur until *ca.* 1672, the income thereafter to be employed towards the payment of a schoolmaster who should offer free instruction to poor boys in the elementary disciplines.[164] Just a little earlier, and probably in 1658, a grocer, Henry Box, had built a large and 'very fair house' standing in two acres of grounds at Witney, Oxfordshire, at a cost of upwards of £400, for the foundation of a grammar school for thirty scholars. Box conveyed to the Grocers' Company an annuity with a capital worth of £1000 for the maintenance of a master and an usher competent to offer instruction in Latin, Greek, and Hebrew, entrusting the government of the institution to his widow during her lifetime. The widow, Mary Box, in her turn in 1670 by indenture augmented the already considerable endowment with £286 of capital, the income of which was designated for the addition of a writing master to the faculty of the school.[165]

We have dealt all too hurriedly with a momentous social and cultural achievement made by a relatively small group of truly dedicated men. In the course of our period, London merchants, with the aid of a few men and women drawn from other social classes, poured the tremendous sum of £216,939 into the founding of endowed schools in greater London and in the provinces. In all, there were 153 of these foundations, of which fifteen were in the city, fifteen in the county of Middlesex, and the amazing total of 123 in other and more distant parts of the realm.* These foundations included both grammar schools and elementary schools, at least eighteen and possibly as many as twenty-three being endowed institutions of the latter sort. We have reckoned, we believe fairly accurately, that by the close of our period there were places in the schools of greater London for at least 1500 of the youth of the city, while in Middlesex and the more distant counties these foundations made by Londoners provided certain places for 5100 boys; and, if a very rough estimate may be accepted, in thirty-one instances where the size of the foundation is unknown, very probably accommodations existed for another 1400 aspiring youths. In all, then, it seems probable that London generosity had in our period provided for the nation a system of education offering, with few exceptions, free tuition and frequently scholarship assistance for as many as 8000 young people.

* Not all these foundations have been specifically mentioned, though some notice has been given to 125 of them.

This great achievement constituted a veritable cultural revolution in England. Not only had a small, though very rich, class of men translated their own aspirations into an impressive system of national education, but their example had been followed in every county by foundations, usually much more modest, made by local donors who were stirred by the same firm conviction that the opportunity for education provided the most certain weapon of attack on poverty and the curse of ignorance which had for so long robbed men of their godly estate.

These foundations were scattered over the whole of Britain in an interesting and revealing pattern, normally, as we have seen in instance after instance, determined by the genetic accident that a youth from a provincial parish had gained his fortune in London and then when the time of disposition came remembered his native village with a generously endowed grammar school, not infrequently conjoined with an almshouse foundation.* Yet in the course of our period it did so fall out that a London foundation had been made in all save six English counties; and there were as well four London foundations in Wales, two in Scotland, and one in Calais. But the most amazing concentration of these foundations was to be observed along the western borders of the realm in a block of five counties extending southward from Lancashire to Herefordshire, in which there were forty-four grammar schools established by London donors. As we shall later see,[166] a very high proportion of London merchants and tradesmen were drawn from this region, but not in sufficient numbers to explain why more than 36 per cent of all foundations made outside London and Middlesex should have been clustered in these particular counties. The deeds of gift in case after case make it clear that these were regarded as counties of marginal opportunity, as areas still inclined towards Rome, and as communities which must be brought level in terms of opportunity with the whole of the nation. We shall examine this intensely evangelical interest on the part of London donors in some detail in our study of Lancashire, but the same strong forces were evidently working as London merchants, well aware of the great need, settled their charitable estates in favour of Cheshire, Shropshire, Staffordshire, or Herefordshire. These enlightened and responsible London merchants, perhaps even more truly than the great Queen, were responsible for winning the west for Protestantism and for giving to the region the social and cultural institutions required for life in the modern world.

But we have by no means assessed the full measure of London's immense efforts to secure larger and better educational opportunities for the youth of the nation. In addition to the huge sum of £216,939 provided by them for the foundation of endowed schools in all parts of

* *Vide* Map I for distribution of these foundations.

the realm, these donors gave the impressive total of £42,324 2s for the further strengthening of the nation's secondary educational resources. This large sum was given by London benefactors for a variety of purposes: £21,674 9s was for the augmentation of existing school foundations, beyond those we have noticed in our detailed analysis, whether in London or elsewhere; £14,171 was for the erection of schoolhouses, their repair, or for founding schools which were either unendowed or supported by stocks of less than £100; £5627 16s was for a variety of worthy educational uses too diverse to classify; and the surprisingly small total of £850 17s was provided in the form of income gifts to be expended for immediate school needs.

It would require extended treatment indeed to deal adequately with these smaller augmentations and foundations, but at least a brief general comment would seem to be warranted. Thus the £21,674 9s of augmentations was spread over a total of 141 existing foundations, more than half being schools in the provinces that had been founded by local generosity. There were, as well, fifty-seven unendowed, or very scantily endowed schools founded by Londoners in all parts of the realm, of which thirty at least were intended by the donors to become grammar schools supported either by tuition fees or by endowments to be provided by future benefactors. Only two of such foundations were in London; seven were in Middlesex, forty-five in other English counties, and one each in Ireland, New Hampshire, and Massachusetts. It is interesting to observe, too, that these unendowed foundations were quite as heavily concentrated in the western reaches of the realm as were the larger and more adequately settled schools whose founding we have dealt with in some detail. Fully half, twenty-four, of all these foundations made outside London and Middlesex were located in a tier of seven western counties, in this case beginning with Cumberland to the north and stretching down county by county to Herefordshire in the south.

It need scarcely be repeated that almost the whole of the immense contribution made by Londoners to the foundation of an adequate school system for the nation was concentrated in the period of slightly more than a century extending from the accession of Elizabeth to the restoration of the monarchy. In this interval of 103 years, a total of 109 endowed schools and forty-nine unendowed institutions were founded by London donors in every part of the realm. This means that year after year for more than a century the merchant elite of London were in average terms establishing one and a half schools in England in a great movement which scarcely slackened in its momentum over this long period of time. The aspirations of these men were clearly articulated, firmly held; and they possessed the means and the generosity required to bring a new and certainly a better society into being.

2. Scholarships and fellowships

The immense contribution of London in fashioning the grammar-school system of the realm by no means represents the full measure of the devotion of these merchant donors to the enlargement of educational opportunities. These men also vested the enormous total of £92,465 8s in scholarship and fellowship endowments, occasionally, as we have seen, for the support of needy boys while in school; more often to send able graduates on to the universities; and still more frequently for the direct support of scholarships in the universities.[167] Space does not permit detailed treatment of the many benefactions comprehended in this great sum, though we have sought to notice at least the principal amongst them in our discussion of school foundations and in our remarks on benefactions to the universities. But a few quite general comments may be made.

The total of £92,465 8s provided by London donors for scholarships and fellowships constituted 4·89 per cent of all the charitable gifts of the city, the relative interest of donors in this worthy purpose being suggested by the fact that the sum considerably exceeds the amount given during our period for any specific church use save for the much larger total provided for church building. And an estimate of the greatness of London's contribution to this educational need is suggested when we reflect that the city alone gave for this purpose almost twice as much as the amount (£52,589 19s) contributed in all the other nine counties included in our study. There is reason to believe, in fact, that the great capital wealth given by Londoners for this purpose amounted to almost as much as that contributed by the whole of the remainder of the realm.

The concern of London with the building of these resources, perhaps the most effective of all the mechanisms for accomplishing social mobility, was evident even in the early decades of our period. In the years prior to the Reformation the not inconsiderable total of £4038 2s was given for scholarship and fellowship foundations, while during the brief period of the Reformation the rate of such giving was greatly accelerated, £3348 1s being so disposed in the two decades. The curve of giving to scholarship and fellowship endowments rose steeply during the Elizabethan years, the large capital of £18,269 5s having been accumulated for these uses in the course of the four decades which we have somewhat arbitrarily called the Elizabethan era. The great outpouring of funds for this purpose was, however, to occur during the early Stuart interval, when the enormous total of £51,885 was given by a great many donors. This means, of course, that well over half (56 per cent) of the entire accumulation of scholarship and fellowship endowments was concentrated in this one brief interval of four decades. There was inevitably a sharp falling away of interest in such foundations during the Puritan Revolution, when the universities were suspect and the political future uncertain. But none the less the substantial total of £14,925 was added to the now large resources with which Londoners had determined to make both secondary and higher education more generally and easily available to able and ambitious youths from all parts of the nation.

Of the great *corpus* of these endowments, the surprisingly large total of £26,235 8s was vested in schools in London and throughout England as scholarship endowments either for the support of boys on the foundation or for scholarship awards to support them in the universities upon the completion of their school curriculum. These stipends averaged £6 1s p.a., and one may estimate with fair certainty that by the close of our period something like 215 youths were being wholly or principally supported by such awards. All these grants, of course, were parish centred and were hence calculated to discover and to provide abundant opportunity for able boys in scores of communities all over England and to bring distinction to the schools which educated them and in many instances sent them on to the universities.[168]

The larger sum of £66,230 of fellowship and scholarship capital was vested in the universities under a great variety of purposes and conditions. Very frequently selection was limited to a school or an area; sometimes the donor was content with the expression of a preference in selection; while usually the choice of candidates was left wholly within the discretion of the university or college. These London endowments created at Oxford and Cambridge upwards of 181 scholarships—in some scores of cases the number of scholars to be appointed on the foundation was not prescribed by the donor—and, most remarkably, about sixty-two fellowships. In all, it would appear, then, that by the close of our period the almost prodigal generosity of London was in any given year lending full support to at least 396 scholars in the grammar schools or in the universities, as well as to the sixty-two men who might well be described as London fellows.[169] This alone would have been a massive cultural achievement, but when we reflect that these great endowments were so carefully employed to enmesh the grammar-school system, which London alone had so nearly founded, with the university system, which it revivified and immensely strengthened, the epical accomplishment of these men of trade becomes very clear indeed.

3. *Support of the universities*

London benefactors were even more generous in the continuous and effective support which they lent to university education, the great fellowship and scholarship endowments quite aside. In all, the immense total of £154,591 5s was bestowed by Londoners on new foundations, augmentations of endowments, the fabric of the colleges, and other necessities for the enlargement and betterment of the universities. This great sum represents 8·18 per cent of all London charities during our period. A remarkably large proportion of the whole was given, principally by the princes of the realm or of the church, during the years before the Reformation, when the great sum of £57,814 19s was provided for the needs of higher education. In the brief period of the Reformation the considerable total of £13,943 7s was vested for university uses, while in the Elizabethan era the total of these gifts rose to £32,503 13s, this being almost exactly the amount provided by Londoners for grammar-school foundations in this same interval. A heavy concentration of these contributions was to occur during the early Stuart period, when £43,537 6s was given by London donors, with a sharp decline during the unsettled decades of revolutionary experimentation and protest, when the sum of benefactions to the universities declined to £6792. It should be remarked that by no means the whole of the great total which we have recorded under the heading *Colleges and Universities* was left by London donors to the two ancient universities. In all, we have credited the substantial total of £19,120 given for the foundation of new and most interesting institutions of higher learning within greater London. These we may well briefly consider before turning to the universities as more conventionally defined.

The design for the foundation of Gresham College seems to have been in the mind of Sir Thomas Gresham, the great Elizabethan merchant and statesman, for many years before his death in 1579. We have not regarded as a charitable undertaking the building of the Royal Exchange which Gresham carried forward at his own charge in 1566–1568, the livery companies having contributed heavily towards the purchase of the site, on which the total outlay was upwards of £3500. The property was treated by Gresham as a commercial asset until in late 1574 he began actively to consider the founding of a college in London, to which his own university, Cambridge, raised most strenuous objections. By the terms of his will, proved in 1579, the Exchange and other properties came jointly into the hands of the City of London and the Mercers' Company for the performance of certain charitable trusts, including the establishment of Gresham College. The foundation was not to be fully effective until the death of Lady Gresham, who was left with a huge annual income of £2388 10s 6½d, which until her death in 1596 she worked assiduously to divert to her own heirs. The revenues assigned by Gresham for the support of his college represent a capital worth of approximately £8500, while the constitution provided for lecturers with an annual stipend of £50 each in divinity, astronomy, geometry, music, law, medicine, and rhetoric. The teachers were to be unmarried men who should maintain their rooms in the college buildings. Though never expanding into a true university, as Gresham hoped it might, the institution enjoyed great prestige throughout our period and has continued to carry forward useful and important educational services.[170]

An even more ambitious design was in the mind of Matthew Sutcliffe, Dean of Exeter and a notable pluralist, for a great and stalwartly Protestant divinity college to be founded at Chelsea. Sutcliffe interested James I in his dream, the King granting the charter for the institution in 1610 and conveying to the foundation lands, principally in Chelsea, with a then capital value of £600. Chelsea College was empowered to incorporate twenty fellows on the foundation, of whom seventeen must be in holy orders. Sutcliffe was named as the first provost, while such eminent divines as Abbot, Overall, Morton, Field, and Howson were made fellows by the King, with Camden and Hayward as the lay fellows 'to record and publish to posterity all memorable passages in church and commonwealth'. Fuller tells us that the college was intended as a 'spiritual garrison, with a magazine of all books for that purpose', from which an aggressive warfare of controversy and polemics could be carried forth against the Papists. Sutcliffe laid out from his own considerable fortune £3000 on an over ambitious range of buildings, but the hopes of the founder were dashed when in 1616 an appeal from the Archbishop of Canterbury for funds to be raised by collections throughout the realm brought in scarcely enough to pay the cost of collection. Sutcliffe on his death in 1629 bequeathed property to the college with a certain capital value of £6000, in addition to large but uncollectable debts owed to him; however, his will was successfully contested and it seems improbable that more than £1400 was ever received by the now collapsing institution. Thus the whole ambitious scheme withered, in Fuller's view because of the King's failure really to support it zealously, the indifference of the great prelates, the suspicion of the Puritan party in Parliament, and the bitter jealousy of the universities. Fuller, writing not long after the final collapse, regretfully composed the epitaph: 'Almost rotten before ripe, and ruinous before finished, it stands bleak and in decay.'[171]

The foundation of Sion College in 1624 under the terms of the will of Thomas White was more modest in conception but far more carefully and securely ordered. This generous clergyman, who had already settled a great almshouse foundation on his native Bristol, left the sum of £3000 to secure the founding of an almshouse in London as well as to establish near-by a college for all the clergy of greater London. His executors in 1627 purchased for £2450 the capital messuage formerly comprising the priory of Elsing Spital for the use of the college, which was dedicated to the maintenance of truth in doctrine, the advancement of mutual love among the clergy, and the repression of 'suche sinnes as followe us as men'. All the clergy of London were 'to be annexed' to the corporation and were freely each year to elect a president and two deans who should arrange and direct the affairs of the society. The first president chosen was the then Bishop of London, while John Donne, then gaining fame as White's successor at St Dunstan's, was elected vice-president. The executors settled two rent charges representing a capital value of £3200 on the institution, which speedily proved its worth as a meeting place and a centre of spiritual inspiration for the clergy of the metropolis.[172] White, to complete his educational charities, had likewise some years earlier (1621) founded a chair of moral philosophy at Oxford with a stipend of £2000 capital value and gave as well to Magdalen College five exhibitions in divinity with a yearly stipend of £8 each, plus an annuity of £4 to the principal of the college.

Generous as had been White's provisions for Sion College, no arrangement had been made for a library, which it was at once apparent would lend much greater utility to the institution and its learned members. Accordingly, in 1629, the Reverend John Simpson, Rector of St Olave Hart Street and an executor as well as a relative of White's, provided suitable quarters over one of the almshouses at a total cost of £200 and later endowed the library with a rent-charge possessing a capital worth of £320.[173] In 1629, Rebecca Romney, the widow of a lord mayor, gave £100 for the purchase of books for the library,[174] while Viscount Bayning provided an equal amount for this purpose, thereby exciting his funeral preacher to an eloquence which can only be described as extraordinary.[175] Sion College attracted a steady stream of support from the London clergy and merchants, as witness the bequest of £50 left by the Puritan clergyman Walter Travers, Hooker's great opponent at the Temple, for four sermons each year in Latin, and his own library of more than two hundred volumes,[176] and the gift of Sir Robert Parkhurst, a clothworker who served as lord mayor in 1634, of £50 for the better endowment of the library, which was proving far more useful to the clergy than the one heretofore available in St Paul's.[177]

There remains the very large capital sum of £135,471 5s which London donors lavished on the endowment and fabric of the two ancient universities, quite beyond, it will be recalled, the capital totalling £66,230 which had been vested by Londoners in scholarship and fellowship funds at Oxford or Cambridge. Somewhat surprisingly, though roughly three times as many individual benefactions were made by London donors to Cambridge as to Oxford, the total of capital given to Oxford for fabric and endowments may be reckoned at £85,954, while Cambridge received the considerably smaller total of £49,517 5s.[178] We may now deal briefly with at least the principal of the many gifts and bequests made to the universities by Londoners during our period, including as well a few of the scholarship and fellowship foundations not previously treated; these latter, however, we have not counted within the *corpus* of what we have reckoned as gifts to the universities.

The greater generosity displayed by London towards Oxford was most conspicuously evident in the first half of our period and was princi-pally the consequence of the special favour lent by great churchmen to the older university. Thus at the very outset of our period, Thomas Kempe, for more than a generation Bishop of London, gave the large sum of £666 13s 4d towards the completion of the Divinity School at Oxford, to which he likewise gave, in 1487, a library of uncertain value.[179] Somewhat later, Richard Fitz James, who was also to serve as Bishop of London from 1506 until his death in 1522, was a generous benefactor to Merton College, whose warden he was for more than two decades. Fitz James has been described as the 'second founder' of Merton, though his recorded benefactions seem to have been limited to the rebuilding of the warden's lodge and other work on the fabric, on which the outlay probably did not exceed £400.[180]

During the years prior to the Reformation, there were numerous bequests to the universities made by Londoners with at least the nominal condition that prayers should be said for the souls of the donors. To mention only two of these, Thomas Kneseworth, a fishmonger who had been Mayor of London in 1505-1506, settled on his company an an-nuity to secure £4 p.a. to each of four priests at Oxford or Cambridge, who among their other duties would pray for him.[181] A few years later, Sir Robert Rede, Chief Justice of Common Pleas, bequeathed £66 13s 4d to King's College, Cambridge, and £125 to each university for general uses, with the request that prayers should be recited, while also estab-lishing a fellowship in Jesus College, Cambridge, with an original capi-tal worth of £280.[182]

In 1511 Brasenose College was founded by William Smyth, Bishop of Lincoln, and Sir Richard Sutton, a barrister of the Inner Temple who had gained a considerable fortune at the bar and as steward of the great nunnery of Sion. The two men were truly co-founders of the college, which was licensed by the Crown to hold property to the value of £300 p.a. and to consist of a principal and sixty scholars. The founders leased Brasenose Hall from University College at £3 p.a. and laid out £40 or more for its renovation as their first act of generous piety. Sutton likewise purchased additional property from Oriel College to provide needed space for the new foundation and in gradual increments between 1519 and 1524 conveyed lands in Oxfordshire, Leicestershire, Essex, and London, with a then capital worth of something like £2000, towards the endowment of the institution, probably not far short of the funds with which Smyth had lent strength to the new college.[183] Brasenose continued to enjoy the support of London donors after the

Reformation, Alexander Nowell vesting in the foundation thirteen scholarships with a stipend of £3 6s 8d each,[184] Joyce Frankland, the daughter of a London goldsmith, endowing it with £800 for an additional fellowship and three scholarships,[185] and other donors contributing capital sums totalling £813 for lectureships, fellowships, and towards the building of the college chapel.

We may deal more briefly with Wolsey's great foundation of Cardinal College in 1524–1528, on which he is believed to have laid out as much as £20,000 of capital. Though we have after some hesitation included this great sum as a charitable benefaction, it will be remembered that most of this wealth was derived from the early confiscation of the smaller monastic foundations. The college was suppressed and expropriated on the occasion of the Cardinal's fall, but was refounded in 1532 by Henry VIII as Christ Church, this monarch expending something like £3000 on the completion of its fabric.[186]

The next foundation at Oxford, Trinity College, was likewise indirectly derived from the enormous monastic wealth which had come into the possession of Sir Thomas Pope, who in 1537 had been made treasurer of the Court of Augmentations. Pope in 1555 secured the site and the derelict buildings of Durham College, the Oxford house of Durham Abbey, which in the year following he constituted as Trinity College, to consist of a president, twelve fellows, and eight scholars. In successive conveyances from 1556 to 1558 he endowed the institution with lands with a capital worth of £4532, while by his will he left £433 7s for the fabric, with a house at Garsington to be used in time of epidemics, as well as providing college plate of an estimated value of £150.[187] The residue of his estate was left to his widow, Elizabeth, who shortly married Sir Hugh Powlett, and who, as we have seen, became a substantial philanthropist in her own right.[188] In addition to providing furnishings for the college and for the house at Garsington, Lady Elizabeth gave properties with a capital value of upwards of £400 for the further augmentation of the endowment of the college and left each scholar a gratuity of 10s by the terms of her will.[189] To this Richard Blount, a London merchant, by will added £100, with which the parsonage of Ridge in Hertfordshire was purchased in 1580 and settled on the college.[190]

But the most typically and thoroughly London of all the Oxford foundations was that made by Sir Thomas White, the great merchant tailor who served as lord mayor in 1553. It is known that White was an intimate friend of Sir Thomas Pope, and it is probable that Pope's example may have moved him to undertake the foundation of St John's College to which he devoted the remainder of his life and most of his large fortune. In 1554 he purchased from Christ Church the site of St Bernard, a dissolved Cistercian house, on whose repair and enlargement he seems to have expended something like £820 during the next two years. In the year following, he secured a royal licence, amplified in 1557, for the foundation which was to comprise a president and thirty scholars who should devote themselves to learning in divinity, philosophy, and the 'good arts'. At about the same time he purchased Gloucester Hall, which he fitted out for the use of one hundred students. The initial endowment of St John's was established with lands purchased at a cost of £1908 16s which White conveyed to the foundation in 1557, together with £36 p.a., or a capital worth of £720, due to him from the great loan fund which he had established in Coventry.[191] In the same year, the founder purchased land in Oxfordshire for £270 which he added to the endowment, followed in 1560 and 1565 by capital increments totalling £1373. During these early years, White was likewise steadily engaged on the repair, the enlargement, and the equipping of the fabric, on which he had by 1566 expended at least £1000. Meanwhile, he had revised his will, formerly drawn in favour of the twelve livery companies, to secure the augmentation of St John's endowment and the support of fifty scholarships on the foundation, with the provision that forty-three should be drawn from London and with an expressed preference for graduates of the Merchant Taylors' School, whose foundation White had encouraged. This endowment consisted of valuable London properties, which were shortly afterwards sold by the college for £3634, and a trust fund of £3000 to fall in to the college upon the death of his wife. In all, then, White's whole outlay on his foundation may with fair accuracy be reckoned as the very large total of £13,285.[192]

White's foundation commanded the continuing support of the merchant aristocracy of London throughout our period, particularly since the founder's great scholarship plan for the city's benefit was most inadequately endowed. Thus in 1610 George Palyn, a girdler whose great benefactions for the poor of London and for an almshouse foundation have already been noted,[193] left £600 for the support of scholars at St John's and Brasenose, as well as, it may be mentioned here, an identical amount for scholars in Trinity College and St John's, Cambridge.[194] The Merchant Taylors' Company undertook the responsibility for building and equipping the library of the college, Sir William Craven having subscribed £50 towards this venture and in 1613 substantially augmenting the endowment by conveying to the college a Northamptonshire living with a capital worth of upwards of £800.[195] Jeffrey Elwes [Helwys], also a merchant tailor, bequeathed £100 to the endowment of St John's in 1616, as well as £300 for other university needs,[196] while Mary Robinson, a grocer's widow, left £500 to the scholarship foundations of the college, an equal sum for 'some college or colleges' at Cambridge, and £100 to the ill-fated college at Chelsea.[197]

John Vernon, another merchant tailor, in 1617 settled on his company sufficient capital to provide £16 p.a. for scholarships at St John's, those favoured to be students of divinity.[198] Sir William Paddy, the noted physician who had been educated at the Merchant Taylors' School and at St John's, was a great benefactor of the college, in 1618 providing an expensive organ and gathering a famous collection of medical books for its library. A devoted lover of music, Paddy also gave and bequeathed a total of £3200 to his college for the improvement of its choir, the support of the choristers, and the salary of an organist.[199] George Benson, a rich merchant tailor, in 1636 gave £1000 to St John's quite specifically for the aid of the fellows and scholars on White's original foundation, as well as establishing an endowment of £120 for the relief of the poor of Thame, Oxfordshire, and £105 for the support of indigent persons at Harlow, Essex.[200]

Space permits the mention of only a few more of the individual donors to the capital needs of the universities. Typical of a great many relatively modest benefactors were Alice Smith, the wife of the famous Customer Smith, who in 1598 left £100 each to Oxford and Cambridge for their unrestricted capital needs,[201] and George Clarke, a vintner, who a few years later, in 1606, bequeathed £200 towards the endowment of a public school in the University of Oxford.[202]

It would seem to be almost a profanation to attempt to lay a monetary assessment against the benefaction of Sir Thomas Bodley to his university. His distinguished diplomatic career all but at an end on his return to England in 1598, Bodley informed the university of his intention to restore the old Public Library, to which Duke Humphrey had been a famous donor, and set about methodically to bring together the great collection that bears his name. The library was opened in 1603 and an enlargement was undertaken in 1610, while the founder began in the following year to enhance the collection and to provide for its endowment. Bodley seems to have laid out upwards of £8000 on the renovation and enlargement of the fabric of the library during his lifetime and it appears that at least £11,000 was expended by him and his friends in the acquisition of the collection and in the vesting of endowments for the benefit of the fabric and the collection.[203] Nor was this magnificently disciplined gift, creating the greatest public library then known in Christendom, quite the full measure of Bodley's generosity. He left to his own college (Merton) £100 for a dinner and £133 for a new chest and a stock for needy students, and gave £666 13s 4d to Oxford and Cambridge for gowns for their students. Bodley left, in addition, £400, or rather £20 p.a., to the poor of Totnes, Devon, capital valued at £410 for the relief of the poor of Oxford city, and a total of £520 to be distributed by his executors to the worthy poor of London.

The great English historian, William Camden, remembered his

university in 1622 by endowing a lectureship in history with the manor of Bexley (Kent), which then possessed a capital worth of £8000. The endowment was, however, restricted in the sense that for a term of ninety-nine years the income of £400 p.a. was to be settled on his friend, the noted composer, William Heather, and his heirs, subject to a payment of £140 p.a. to the lecturer until the whole of the endowment should fall in.[204] On Camden's representations, Digory Whear was appointed the first holder of the lectureship. Heather, on whom Oxford conferred the degree of Doctor of Music in 1622, died shortly afterwards, in 1627, in his turn founding a lectureship of music with a stipend of £17 6s 8d p.a. for an incumbent who should offer a music lesson weekly, keep the musical instruments of the university in proper order, and arrange for a lecture in English on musical theory.[205]

In 1624 Sir Nicholas Kempe, of Islington, Middlesex, bequeathed the considerable sum of two thousand marks to Oxford for its general uses. The bequest was promptly and somewhat inexplicably appropriated to build locks on the Thames in order to open the stream for better navigation 'for the benefit of the University and City', and with the further provision that the endowment was to be restored from wharfage and other fees to be laid against the river traffic.[206] All Souls College greatly benefited under the terms of the will of Sir John Francklyn, of Willesden, Middlesex, who left an endowment with a then capital value of £400 for the needs of its library in 1648,[207] while in 1654 John Goodridge, for some time a fellow of Wadham College and in the last years of his life the Professor of Rhetoric in Gresham College, bequeathed to Wadham lands and the residue of his estate, with a total value of about £1200, for its general uses.[208]

We have sought to do no more than set out a sampling of the rich and continuous stream of gifts which flowed to Oxford from London donors during our period. We have incidentally mentioned at least a few of the numerous fellowship and scholarship foundations, which it will be recalled were segregated for discussion in earlier pages. There remain, too, as many as sixty-one benefactions to Oxford made by relatively modest London donors which can only be gathered in the aggregate of our totals. These gifts and bequests, ranging in amount from £5 to £100, were in thirty-seven instances made by merchants to the university or its colleges, though it would seem that not more than five of their number had ever been matriculated in the university. These men, as we have seen, believed in education at all levels with a consuming passion. They helped not a little in establishing the greatness and strength of university education in England, just as they had contributed so decisively to the founding of secondary education in every part of the realm.

We have noted that London donors were, if our whole period be taken in view, much more generous towards Oxford than Cambridge. But this generosity towards the older university was mostly concentrated in the years prior to the Reformation and most of the very large sums were the gift of princely or prelatical benefactors. Cambridge gained steadily in the favour of merchants of substantial wealth, men likely to leave a university bequests of perhaps £50 almost casually among other larger dispositions for charitable purposes. Included in the £49,517 5s given by Londoners for the fabric and endowment of Cambridge and its colleges are sixty-nine individual benefactions ranging rather modestly from £5 to £100 in amount, upon which we cannot comment in detail but which evidently reflect the mercantile elite's stalwart approval of the undoubted and increasing Puritan bias of the university and certain of its colleges.

This is not to suggest, of course, that all or even most of the great foundations were made by London merchants. One of the most important of all the benefactions to Cambridge in our period was the foundation by Henry VIII in 1540 of the five Regius Professorships which possessed an original capital value of £4000 and which did much to instil new life into the university and its curriculum.[209] But an even greater princely benefactor to Cambridge had been the King's own grandmother, the incomparable Margaret Beaufort. This remarkable woman had decided as early as 1502 to devote her private fortune to the advancement of education.[210] In that year and the next she established the divinity professorships in the two universities and a preachership in Cambridge, the capital value of which cannot be accurately estimated.[211] Under Bishop Fisher's gentle guidance, she turned next to the completion of Henry VI's foundation at Cambridge, opened in 1505 as Christ's College, on which it seems probable she expended in building and endowment capital of the order of £5000, and to which she added £100 of endowment by the terms of her will. But her devotion and wealth were more fully concentrated on the founding of St John's College, which she began in 1508 and which was well advanced by the time of her death in the next year. Henry VIII, it must be remembered, sought with considerable ingenuity, though happily unsuccessfully, to divert the ordered arrangements of his grandmother's will. The work on St John's was carried forward with the funds provided, the fabric being completed in 1516 at the then immense outlay of £5000. Margaret Beaufort richly endowed her foundation with lands then possessing a capital worth of something like £8000. Fisher might well say: 'all England for her death had cause of weeping'.[212]

Lady Margaret's great foundation at St John's received the steady support of London donors throughout our period. At least a few of the principal benefactions may be noted, almost all being augmentations of the scholarship and fellowship resources of the college, which, we should perhaps repeat, have been separately reckoned for statistical purposes. John Dowman, a prebend of St Paul's, in 1515 gave lands to support five scholars at St John's, to be drawn from the grammar school at Pocklington, Yorkshire,[213] founding as well nine sizarships in the college on his death in 1526, the whole capital outlay being about £640.[214] A half century later, John Gwynne, a London lawyer of Welsh birth, vested lands with a capital worth of £800 to provide for the maintenance of three fellows and six scholars in St John's, the fellows to be natives of Wales and the scholars to be chosen from the graduates of Bangor School.[215] We shall speak elsewhere of the bequest in 1587 of Henry Hebblethwaite, a London draper, of £500 for the founding of a fellowship and two scholarships at St John's for the benefit of Yorkshire youths and also of the benefaction of a London barrister, Robert Hungate, who in 1619 established four scholarships in the college with a capital value of £523 for the benefit of the same county.[216] In 1637 William Platt of Highgate Hill (Middlesex) left property, including his wife's jointure, subject to a life income, with a then capital value of upwards of £2800, for the founding of additional fellowships and scholarships in St John's.[217] A London widow, Susannah Hill, in 1638 left in trust property then having a capital worth of £200 for the support of two poor scholars at St John's, both to be sons of clergymen, as well as £400, the income of which should be bestowed on the widows of impecunious clergymen.[218] In the same year Francis Dee, Bishop of Peterborough, and a graduate of the Merchant Taylors' School and of St John's, gave to his college his own library, in five languages, all his chapel plate, and an endowment for the support of two fellows on the foundation, the whole representing a benefaction of somewhat more than £1100.[219] A few years later (1641), John Highlord, a rich skinner of St Olave Hart Street, bequeathed £500 for additional exhibitions at St John's and the same generous sum for scholarships in Trinity College, Cambridge.[220] Finally, we should record the generosity of John Williams, statesman and Archbishop of York, who between 1623 and 1626 built and furnished the library of St John's College at a cost of more than £2000, as well as establishing, as we have earlier noted, four scholarships with a capital value of £547 for graduates of Westminster School in St John's.[221]

We shall elsewhere deal fully with the support lent in the early years of our period by Norfolk donors to Gonville Hall. The county took an almost proprietary interest in the college, which so many of its sons attended, and its refoundation as Gonville and Caius in 1557 was the great contribution of a native of Norwich, Dr John Caius, who, however, may more accurately be regarded as a London donor. Caius was himself a member of Gonville while at Cambridge, but his education was completed at Padua, which he entered in 1539 and where he pursued the medical curriculum. On his return to England in 1544, he began a series of medical lectures in London for the surgeons of the city, which he was to continue for at least two decades. He rapidly acquired great wealth in his London practice, which he early resolved to employ for the advancement of learning. In 1557 he procured letters patent permitting the reorganization and endowment of Gonville Hall, being appointed master in 1559 as he began his great task. Caius undertook at once a substantial plan of rebuilding and enlargement, on which it is reckoned he spent at least £3000, while he conveyed Norfolk lands with a then capital worth of £2000 as endowment, which he correctly estimated would possess an additional worth of £1500 when existing leases fell in. Dr Caius, who seems to have been a moderate Catholic, finding himself embroiled not only with his own fellows but with the university authorities, sought refuge in his later years in the medical and humanistic writings which have lent so much lustre to his name. By the terms of his will, proved in 1573, he ordered most of his books to be sold, the proceeds, amounting to about £400, to be invested in land for the further augmentation of the endowment of his foundation. Caius devoted his whole fortune to this great undertaking, almost the whole of the modest residue of his estate to be used to pay for his tomb and 'for cleaning and mending Mr Linacre's tomb in St Paul's'.[222]

London donors lent strong support to Gonville and Caius, disposing their benefactions almost entirely for additional fellowships and scholarships for the still inadequately endowed institution. We have counted seven fellowships and eighteen relatively modest scholarships thus settled on Gonville and Caius during the interval 1581 to 1642. Among these numerous benefactions, the most considerable one was that with a total capital value of £2080 left by Joyce Frankland, the daughter of Robert Trappes, a goldsmith, and of Joan Trappes, herself a most generous donor. Mrs Frankland's school, founded at Newport (Essex), was placed under the care of Gonville and Caius. This endowment was vested to found a chaplaincy in the college and to endow as well twelve scholarships, with a stipend of £3 6s 8d each, and six fellowships, each of which should yield £7 p.a. to the holder. The residue of the income she wished applied to increase the stipends of four scholarships founded earlier by her mother, from four marks each to the five marks to be paid on her own foundations. In addition, this benefactor, being almost a co-founder of the college, had sometime earlier (1585 ?) established a Hebrew lectureship at Caius, with an endowment of uncertain worth.[223]

But the most persistent devotion of the London mercantile aristocracy was of course attracted by Sir Walter Mildmay's foundation, Emmanuel College. Mildmay, the eminent Elizabethan statesman, was a Puritan in sympathy, though he had assured his royal mistress that his foundation was not 'contrary to your established laws'. But the college speedily assumed a Puritan tone, and, richly supported with London capital, it was within a generation to be not only one of the most distinguished academic societies in either university but in terms of historical influence certainly the most important. Its founder had from an early date exhibited a warm interest in education, being one of the original governors of the free grammar school founded in his native Chelmsford in 1550, establishing an endowment of £2 12s p.a. for Christ's Hospital in 1556, and having given to his own Cambridge college, Christ's, an endowment of £400 value in 1568 for the establishment of a Greek lectureship and the support of six scholars. His foundation at Emmanuel was begun in 1583 when he purchased the site of the dissolved Dominican house in Cambridge and about ten acres of land for £550. Mildmay gained his licence from the Queen in 1584 and four years later had completed his building at a quite uncertain but evidently rather modest cost. By successive conveyances he endowed the college with lands then possessing a capital value of £3153, a relatively scant capital stock even for the small foundation, comprising then a master, three fellows, and four scholars, with which Emmanuel was initiated.[224]

But even before Mildmay's death the augmentations had begun to pour in, with the result that within two generations there were on the foundation fourteen fellows and upwards of fifty scholars. We may sketch at least briefly the principal of these benefactions, most of which were from London donors. That remarkable woman, Joyce Frankland, who not only founded a school but was a substantial benefactor to four colleges, in 1587 added £400 to Emmanuel's endowments for fellowships and scholarships.[225] Just a year later, in 1588, another London widow, Elizabeth Walter, a staunch and certainly outspoken Puritan, left £400 to the new foundation for the endowment of two fellowships.[226] Sir Wolstan Dixie, a skinner who had served as lord mayor in 1585, contributed in the last years of his life £650 towards the completion of the fabric of the college and on his death in 1593 left £600 to endow two fellowships and two scholarships there, as well as founding at Emmanuel a lectureship in Greek and Hebrew with an endowment of uncertain value.[227] Another Elizabethan lord mayor, Thomas Skinner, a clothworker, by a gift made in 1596 added to Emmanuel's general endowment by conveying to the foundation a rent charge of £8 p.a.,[228] while in 1602 Edmund English of Westminster by will provided the large sum of £1000 for the full support of two additional fellows and six scholars.[229] Skinner's successor as lord mayor, Sir Henry Billingsley, a haberdasher, left Emmanuel £66 13s 4d as an endowment for an additional scholar, having somewhat earlier (1591) vested capital valued at £176 for the support of three scholars in St John's College, Cambridge.[230]

It will have been noted that Emmanuel enjoyed steady support from great merchant donors in London a full generation after its foundation, particularly when the Puritan temper of the college became more fully apparent. We need not sketch these contributions in detail, since most of them were for fellowships and scholarships, but we should at least record two very large benefactions made to the college at the close of our period. In 1654 Francis Ash, a goldsmith and a native of Derbyshire, settled lands on Emmanuel then possessing a capital value of £3400, the income of which was to be employed for founding ten additional scholarships with an annual stipend of £10 each, the nominees to be chosen whenever possible from the graduates of the free grammar school at Ashby-de-la-Zouch, Leicestershire.[231] A few years later, Sir John Wollaston, also a goldsmith and an intimate friend to Ash, by the terms of his will settled properties valued at £2000 on the college, to provide £50 p.a. for scholars to be chosen from Staffordshire, £30 p.a. for the endowment of a lectureship, and the remainder to be used for the general needs of the institution.[232] By such repeated acts of generosity, and these almost wholly from the ranks of the great merchants, Emmanuel College had within two generations from the day of its founding been lifted to the front of Cambridge colleges.

The last of the great London foundations at Cambridge in our period was that made in 1589 under the provisions of the will of Frances Radcliffe, Countess of Sussex. This donor left £5000, which she had gathered into a capital sum, for the erection of a new college at Cambridge under the title of 'The Lady Frances Sidney Sussex College', with a master, ten fellows, and twenty scholars on the foundation. She had drawn plans for the college during her lifetime, but it was not until 1596 that her executors purchased the estate of the Grey Friars from Trinity College and erected the necessary buildings. Two of her executors, the Earl of Kent and Lord Harington, waived legacies of £100 each left to them by the Countess in order to augment the endowment, which quickly proved to be inadequate to carry forward her purposes.[233] This college, too, whose statutes and constitution were based upon those of Emmanuel, enjoyed the firm support of London benefactors, of whom two of the earliest may be mentioned. In 1601 Leonard Smith, a fishmonger of Puritan persuasion, bequeathed £120 for the establishment of an additional fellowship with the nomination vested in his company, while from the residue of his estate £60 was employed for the endowment of a modest scholarship.[234] Just a few years later, Sir John Harte, a grocer who had served as lord mayor in 1589–1590, made generous provisions for the new institution under the terms of his will proved in 1604. Harte left £30 outright for the purchase of books for the college library, as well as an endowment of £600, the income of which was to be used to augment the stipend of the master and fellows and to found four scholarships for the free school which he had established at Coxwold, Yorkshire.[235]

It is interesting to observe that the older Cambridge foundations did not fare so well from London's merchant donors, though their funds were considerably augmented by the benefactions of other social groups in the metropolis. Thus in 1512 Jesus College was left £160 towards work then under way on its fabric by Sir John Ripley of Tottenham High Cross, as well as an annuity of twelve marks for the support of a scholar.[236] Rather more than a generation later, in 1551, John Reston, Canon of St Paul's, left the college £5 for a silver salter, as well as cash and lands with a total capital worth of £2600 for the endowment of fellowships and the creation of seven scholarships.[237] Similarly, Magdalen College was reorganized in 1542 from the ruins of the earlier Benedictine foundation, by Thomas Audley, the great Henrician Lord Chancellor, though Audley's personal contribution to the foundation probably did not exceed £700.[238] Another lawyer, Sir Christopher Wray, seems to have given something like £400 towards the fabric of Magdalen, while in 1587 he greatly augmented its endowments by a gift of land valued at £800 for the founding of two fellowships and six scholarships, to which by will he added another fellowship with a then capital worth of £133 6s 8d.[239] Sir Nicholas Bacon, Lord Keeper of the Privy Seal, gave £200 towards the building of the chapel at Corpus Christi College, as well as founding in 1577 six scholarships in the college with a somewhat uncertainly estimated endowment of £600.[240] As a final example of these non-merchant benefactions to Cambridge, we may mention the bequest of Henry Burrell, a London gentleman, who in 1627 bequeathed to Christ's College silver valued at £4 13s and an endowment with a then capital worth of £400, from the income of which £1 p.a. was to be used for the repair of the fabric, £4 p.a. for the purchase of new books and mathematical instruments, and the remainder to found a lectureship in rhetoric.[241]

We may conclude by noting a few of the remaining substantial benefactions made to Cambridge by Londoners during our period. Bishop Lancelot Andrews in 1626 left Pembroke College, which he had served as master, £1000 for the endowment of two fellowships and for other corporate uses, as well as three hundred volumes to be added to its library.[242] That ennobled mercer, Viscount Campden, in 1629 left tithes and other properties with a then capital value of £673 to Trinity College for the foundation of additional scholarships, with an expressed preference for graduates of St Paul's School.[243] At about the same date, and probably in 1631, Sir Thomas Adams, a mercer who was to serve as lord mayor during the period of the Civil War, founded the Arabic professorship at Cambridge with an annual stipend of £40, to which Abraham Wheelock was first appointed,[244] Sir Henry Spelman in 1635 adding a stipend of £20 p.a. for lectures by Wheelock in Anglo-Saxon.[245] Mark Quested, a fishmonger whose great almshouse foundation in Kent has already been discussed, in 1643 left on trust to his company a substantial endowment then valued at £960, the income to be employed for the maintenance of four Masters of Arts with a stipend of £8 p.a. each and four scholars with annual grants of £4 each 'so long as they should abide at their study' in either Cambridge or Oxford.[246] At the close of our period a girdler, Richard Andrewes, charged a manor in Kent with annual payments to Cambridge of £40, or a capital worth of £800, for the augmentation of the scholarship resources of the university.[247]

These were great and good works that we have been examining. Not only had the universities been strengthened and revitalized, but they had been organically linked through London generosity with the great system of schools which the benefactors of the capital had established in all parts of the realm. These donors, great and small, had poured the huge total of £510,890 17s into institutions with which education could be diffused through the whole structure of the society. These founders, most being great merchants, possessed for a full century very clearly defined aspirations for their community and, indeed, for the whole of the English society. They wished to banish ignorance and its handmaiden, poverty; they wished the Scriptures to be more truly read and understood; they wished to arm the secular society with the weapons of learning which heretofore had been almost wholly vested in a clerical and aristocratic social stratum; and they wished, above all perhaps, to endow men with that dignity and self-sufficiency which the modern world seemed to require of its competent citizens. Rarely have men held a nobler vision of their world; perhaps never have they moved more swiftly and surely towards the attainment of their vision.

E. RELIGION

1. *The secular trend*

The parochial organization of London was nearly complete almost three centuries before our period began. We have already dealt at some length with the contributions made to charity by the various parishes of the city and county,[1] and have noted that we reckon the number of parishes in greater London, including Westminster, at 123 in about 1600 and the number in the remainder of the county at seventy. The city was the seat of a rich and powerful diocese, with a great church which was quite as much a national as a civic monument. The life and culture of the city were also greatly influenced during the first two generations of our period by the many monastic establishments with which it was embellished, these possessing wealth and revenues greater than those of any other single county of the realm. London was a capital renowned throughout Christendom for the number and beauty of its churches, the learning of its ubiquitous clergy, both regular and secular, and the enthusiastic piety of its citizenry. The devotion and wealth which had in the course of the Middle Ages built and endowed the innumerable religious foundations of London were still strong and vigorous at the beginning of our period.

In the whole course of the period of almost two centuries with which we are concerned, benefactors of the city were to give the large total of £368,389 12s to the several religious uses, this amounting to not quite a fifth (19·50 per cent) of the immense whole of London's charitable funds. Quite surprisingly, London was on balance by no means the most severely secular of the counties we have examined, Bristol for example having bestowed not more than 13·18 per cent of all its benefactions on religious needs, and even three of the rural counties having given smaller proportions of their charitable funds for religious purposes.*

But, as we shall observe, the curve of London's giving for religious uses makes it abundantly clear that a large proportion of this generous total was heavily concentrated in two periods and that the dominant temper of the city and, more particularly, of the mercantile aristocracy who controlled it, became exceedingly and severely secular. It should also be noted that the large total of £55,723 8s, amounting to 15·13 per cent of the whole given for religious purposes, was vested by London donors in other counties of the realm and that very nearly three-fourths of this impressive sum was disposed by London merchants animated by a most pronounced Puritan bias.

During the decades prior to the Reformation, London benefactions for all religious purposes reached the huge total of £111,997 1s, this having amounted to almost 45 per cent of all charitable funds for these two generations and, most significantly, to more than 30 per cent of the total given for religious purposes in the whole course of our long period. This pious outpouring has a singularly interesting structure when more closely analyzed, the large sum of £65,898 8s, or almost 59 per cent of the whole given for religious purposes, having been vested for chantries and other arrangements for prayers for the dead. This great total is principally accounted for by the huge bequests for such uses by royal and noble personages, being by no means typical of this burgher community, though, as we shall see, there were a fair number of substantial endowments for prayers left by great merchants as well.

The flow of funds to the several religious uses was abruptly and most dramatically checked by the events of the Reformation and by the profoundly significant change in temper which accompanied that momentous historical event. During the two unsettled decades 1541–1560, the

---

* The range is from 13·18 per cent for Bristol to 31·94 per cent for Lancashire.

total given by Londoners for religious uses sank to £15,580 15s, while of this amount it should be observed that almost 61 per cent was for the semi-secular purpose of church building. This withering of concern for the needs of the church and its services is the more boldly evident because it occurred in an era when the great flow of charities for a broad spectrum of secular purposes was getting strongly under way. The amounts given for religious needs during these years accounted for only slightly more than a tenth (10·19 per cent) of all charitable benefactions, constituting, for example, only half as much as was provided for poor relief and education and less than a fourth of the great sum given for the founding of institutions for the social rehabilitation of the poor.

But the full power of this great wave of secularism did not sweep over English life and its institutions until the Elizabethan age. This immensely important historical phenomenon has been observed in every county of the realm; it is simply more pronounced in London, which was always most sensitively, almost precociously attuned to the shifts and drifts in that temper of mind from which historical change proceeds. During this long interval of forty years (1561–1600), London benefactions for all religious uses totalled no more than £17,330 13s, this amounting to the incredibly scant proportion of 6·66 per cent of all charitable funds disposed during the period and no more than 4·70 per cent of the total provided for religious needs in the whole course of our period. This amount, was, of course, only a tiny fraction of the sum provided for the great secular charitable purposes, being actually considerably less than that disposed by London donors for the various uses we have grouped under the head of municipal betterments.

It may be said of the early Stuarts, though the fact is one of the roots of their tragic historical failure, that they at least tried to reverse the vast and deep tide of secularism which had in two generations so profoundly and permanently altered not only the institutions but the temper of English life. James I lent sympathy, if no great support, to the now grievous needs of the church; his son and the archbishop who dominated his policy sought actively and dangerously to regain an age that was already long since lost. The efforts of Archbishop Laud were concentrated in London, his formidable presence was ever there, and his almost hysterically persistent chiding and exhorting bore more demonstrable results there than in the remoter reaches of the realm. But it was a shallow and essentially meaningless gain which flowed from such prodigious effort. In the interval 1601–1640 London donors gave the substantial total of £194,765 5s for religious uses, which, it should be observed, amounted to somewhat more than half (52·87 per cent) of the whole sum provided for the needs of the church during our entire period. But of this great total, somewhat more than 57 per cent was designated for church building and, most particularly, for the expensive repairs to St Paul's, which Elizabeth had neglected with an almost shocking disinterest but which Laud carried forward after he had all but bludgeoned the city into its heavy contributions.[2] Even more significantly, the large sums provided for religious purposes during this era become relatively much less impressive when viewed in the context of the truly immense out-pouring of all charities during these generous years. The amount given for religious uses comprises only a scant fifth (20·31 per cent) of that great total, being, for example, substantially less than that provided for education and only half as much as that disposed for the relief of poverty. Laud had failed, as any man must, to reverse the process of an historical change which was irrevocable.

During the revolutionary decades (1641–1660), the benefactors of London gave in all £28,715 18s for religious needs, this constituting slightly more than a tenth (10·76 per cent) of the substantial funds vested in these two decades. Of this sum rather more than £20,000 was de-voted to the desperately needed purpose of endowing some scores of parishes, in and out of London, in order to augment scandalously low clerical stipends or to found lectureships to secure the better and more fervent preaching of the Word.

2. *The general uses of the church*

Very possibly the most sensitive barometer of sentiment towards the church, its ministry, and its needs is to be found in the degree of support which men lend to its general uses. Under this head we have gathered a great variety of gifts and bequests for the support of the service, gifts for lights and church music, for special services, and for the unrestricted support of the church and its sacramental usages. We have observed in every rural county that these gifts and bequests, usually in very small amounts, were customary and are to be found in almost every will down to about 1540; in more conservative rural counties, down to the middle of the Elizabethan age. Their disappearance, and it almost invariably came so abruptly that it may be dated quite precisely, is perhaps the most reliable signal that secularism has triumphed in a parish or a county, or, even more significantly, in a social class. London differs from all of England in this most important respect, since these benefactions were never in our period universally customary among its citizenry, who in many instances were stalwartly secular in their aspirations even as our period opened. This is not to say that such gifts were rarely made, but rather that they were never particularly important in the financing of the services of London's churches and that the curve of their decline pro-ceeds from a very low relative starting level as compared with any other county in the realm.

In the whole course of our period London benefactors provided only

£16,863 11s for the general uses of the church, this being somewhat less than 1 per cent (0·89 per cent) of the charitable wealth of the city and roughly comparable to the sums provided for such secular uses as apprenticeships and workhouses. A rather high proportion (71·22 per cent) of this sum was in the form of endowments, capital vestings being particularly common for the considerable amount given by London benefactors for general church uses for parishes in other counties. Almost a third of the whole amount given for general church needs was left in the years prior to the Reformation, when £4945 18s was so designated, with sums ranging from £423 to £1449 3s having been provided in the several decades included in this interval.

There was a marked, though by no means a catastrophic, falling off of these gifts during the short interval of the Reformation, a total of £749 11s having been given for these general uses. But during the Elizabethan age such benefactions all but disappeared, no more than £631 19s having been provided through the whole of this long interval, and the total actually falling to only £55 11s in the first decade (1561–1570) of the period. There was a most pronounced revival of interest in parochial needs during the early Stuart period, when the total of such gifts rose to £9806 13s, or nearly sixteen times as much as was designated for such purposes during the preceding period of equal length. These gifts, including several substantial endowments, were heavily concentrated in the decade 1621–1630, when approximately a third of the whole amount disposed for the general uses of the church during our entire period was given. The curve of giving for these purposes fell away steeply once more with the summoning of the Long Parliament, no more than £729 10s having been provided during the last two decades of our period.

It will perhaps suffice to mention in some detail two of the larger bequests for the general uses of the church prior to the Reformation, then to note briefly a sampling of similar gifts of a more modest order chosen from the one year 1504. In 1501 Sir Robert Tate, a great merchant who had served as lord mayor in 1488, left substantial bequests for both religious and secular uses. He disposed for the general uses of his parish church of Allhallows Barking and a church in Coventry, his birthplace, funds valued in all at £120 13s, as well as £26 for the general uses of divers monastic churches. Tate's will likewise provided for the building of a chantry chapel, at a cost of about £200, in his parish church in London, which he endowed with lands yielding approximately £8 p.a., while he left a total of £36 for church repairs in London and in Coventry.[3] A fellow mercer, who was also a burgher of Calais, Sir Thomas Thwaytes, on his death in 1503 left in all £182 for the general uses of two London churches, two in Calais, and certain monastic foundations, as well as something like £240 to endow prayers in St Helen

Bishopsgate, London, in a church in Calais, and in his native parish of Ashby, Lincolnshire.[4]

We have spoken of the two largest benefactions made for the general uses of the church in the decade 1501–1510, when in all the substantial total of £1449 3s was provided. The bulk of this amount was, however, given by many scores of donors of the city who left for this use sums of £10 or less, more than half of whom, in fact, left £1 or less for the needs of their parish churches. Among these humbler donors, chosen from the year 1504, were John Andernes, a skinner, who left 1s to St Mildred Bread Street;[5] John Archer, who left quite substantial lay and religious bequests, including £7 for the general uses of St Mary Woolchurch;[6] William Ball [Bulle], who left 1s for the needs of St Magnus;[7] and William Barker, a fishmonger, who bequeathed 3s to the general uses and £2 3s for the repair of the same church.[8] The services of the church of St Augustine on the Wall were assisted by a bequest of 3s made by William Bateson, a merchant tailor,[9] those of St Edmund Lombard Street by a legacy of £1 from Thomas Bower, a baker, who also left £2 for church repairs and £2 to his company,[10] while St Dionis Backchurch received a modest £1 for its general uses from John Bownde, a draper, who, however, also left £40 towards the building of its north aisle.[11] Thomas Brown, a yeoman of Enfield, left 10s to the general uses of his parish church and 3s for its repair,[12] John Burt, an artisan, left 2s to his parish church of St Michael Wood Street,[13] Thomas Catte, a cheesemonger, left £1 14s to the general uses of his parish church and £1 to the services of a monastery,[14] while Thomas Collins, a fishmonger, bequeathed 11s to the services of St Mary at Hill and £2 for its repairs.[15] This is to mention but a few of the humbler benefactions in this year late in the reign of Henry VII.

It is interesting to observe that in no later decade did the total left by London benefactors for the general uses of the church exceed the sum of £700 until the early Stuart period, when the amounts designated for this purpose rose steeply to £3112 for the interval 1611–1620 and to £5513 2s in the decade next following. We have already discussed the circumstances which brought about this marked revival of interest in the general needs of the church and should now mention at least some of the larger gifts so designated.

In 1615 Sir John Weld, a gentleman residing at Enfield, but the son of Humphrey Weld, a great grocer, endowed a chapel which he had built at Southgate (Enfield parish) at a charge of £200, with lands valued at £550 for its full support.[16] We have with some hesitation regarded a large capital gift of £2000 made by will in 1619 as vested for the general support of the church rather than more specifically for the augmentation of clerical stipends, because of the somewhat complicated intentions of the donor. Dame Margaret Slaney, the widow of Sir

Stephen, a skinner, who had served as lord mayor in 1595–1596, left this substantial sum in trust to the Grocers' Company as a perpetual stock for the purchasing, restoring, and uniting again to the church impropriated benefices in all parts of England. Such benefices, having been purchased, were to be held in hand until the stock was restored and then were to secure the stipends of learned clergymen who were no pluralists.[17]

There were more numerous large benefactions for the support of the church in the next decade. In 1624, John Kendrick, the great merchant philanthropist, left annuities with a capital worth of £350 for the maintenance of the services in his parish church in London and in Newbury, Berkshire.[18] An even larger legacy for the support of the church was given in 1629 by Baptist Hicks, Viscount Campden, whose provision for the church at Hampstead (Middlesex) and that at Tewkesbury (Gloucestershire) may conservatively be estimated to have possessed a capital value of £673.[19] These two bequests together account for not more than a fifth of the large total provided in this decade for the general uses of the church, there having been fourteen other individual gifts or bequests totalling £100 or more given for this purpose, as well as a considerably larger number ranging in amount from £10 to £100. But, as we have observed, the belated and certainly grudging generosity of this decade did but little to restore the tradition of lending customary and substantial support to the services of the church and may well be regarded as no more than an eccentric peak in a curve of giving which documents all too convincingly the triumph of secularism in English life and thought.

3. Prayers for the dead

We have expressed surprise that London benefactors, including even merchant donors, contributed as heavily and persistently to the endowment of chantries and prayers as they did in view of the pervasive secularism which characterized the temper of London even in the decades prior to the Reformation. In all, £69,353 18s was given as endowments or as outright sums to secure such prayers, so typical of medieval piety and so suspect because of the flagrant and widespread diversion of capital sums left for this purpose. This large amount represents 3·67 per cent of the whole of the charities of the city during our entire era; more relevantly, it amounts to 17·21 per cent of all the charitable benefactions during the first eight decades of our period; and, quite amazingly, accounts for 54·36 per cent of all gifts made for religious purposes during the same eighty-year interval. It is quite true that a third (33·73 per cent) of the capital supplied for these foundations was provided by the Crown, great churchmen, and nobles, and hence is in no sense typically burgher, but, even so, London merchants and tradesmen were in each decade from 1480 forward to 1540 supplying from £3910 to £6010 7s of these pious funds on their account and for the repose of their own souls.

The great age for the foundation of chantries in London was the fourteenth century, when one authority has reckoned that about 280 of these endowments were made.[20] In the fifteenth century, we are told, another 120 such foundations were constituted, though by the close of this century probably upwards of half the endowments so carefully and piously created for perpetual prayers had already been lost or the funds diverted to other uses by the ecclesiastical authorities. Those that had survived tended to be vested in secular hands, the livery companies being favourite trustees for particularly prudent donors, with the result that the companies by the date of the Expropriation held large capital for prayers in perpetuity, the Merchant Taylors alone, as an example, reporting hereditaments with a value of £440 13s 10d p.a. for the endowment of obits and chantries when these properties were confiscated under Edward VI.[21]

We should deal at least briefly with a sampling of these bequests, including both formally endowed chantries and simpler arrangements for prayers, with perhaps a special emphasis on those which were left by the merchant aristocracy of the city. In 1485 Sir Thomas Hill, a grocer who died of the sweating sickness while mayor, though in his will 'utterly' forbidding 'any moneth mynde to be kept solemnely for me after the guyse of the world', none the less left £100 for prayers in the Mercers' Chapel and as much for its repair.[22] In this year, too, Sir William Haryot, a draper who had been Mayor of London in 1482, left something like £500 of endowment to his company as trustees to secure the maintenance of a chantry chapel and to pay in perpetuity the stipend of an honest chantry priest.[23] An older merchant, Sir Bartholomew James, who had served as mayor in 1479 and who probably died in 1481, left upwards of £80 for an elaborate month's mind and for prayers for a term of five years in St Dunstan in the East, as well as a perpetual obit to be observed there.[24] In 1489, Thomas Kempe, who had been Bishop of London since the mid-fifteenth century, finished by bequest the endowment of a chantry he had founded in St Paul's some years earlier, vesting it with lands in Essex of a somewhat uncertainly estimated value of £550.[25]

In the last decade of the fifteenth century, London donors left in all £6446 7s for prayers, though only a few of the many benefactions for this purpose can be noted. Thus in 1492 a mercer, John Reynold, left £273 10s for the endowment of a chantry in London, as well as £133 10s for the repair of the choir of St Pancras and £10 for the enrichment of its vestments.[26] A merchant and alderman, John Swan, in the same year provided the substantial sum of £400 for prayers in several churches, in addition to £20 for church repairs in London, £1 for general church uses, and £55 for the uses of monasteries in London and in his native Yorkshire.[27] In 1494 Sir Ralph Astrye, a fishmonger who served as mayor in the year before his death, bequeathed in all £267 for prayers in London and in Hitchin, Hertfordshire, for a term of from ten to twenty years, having earlier roofed and glazed his church of St Martin in the Vintry at a total charge of £175.[28] Another former mayor, Hugh Clopton, in 1496 by will provided £11 p.a. for a term of twenty years to secure prayers in his parish church, as well as £145 disposed to monasteries for prayers by the friars.[29] Still another mayor of the city, John Mathewe, a mercer, who died in 1499, left approximately £83 in outright payments for prayers in numerous churches—in his parish, in London, Westminster, and Rome—and in twelve religious houses, while also instructing his executors to maintain a priest in his parish church (St Martin Orgar) for twenty years at an unstated stipend, he to offer prayers for the repose of the donor's soul.[30]

Well over 40 per cent (42·07 per cent) of the amount given for prayers in our whole period was disposed in the single decade 1501–1510. This total of £29,177 13s owed much to the endowments with a capital value of £18,683 15s which Henry VII bestowed on Westminster Abbey for the maintenance of a staff of stipendiary priests in his not yet fully completed chapel there, as well as for prayers to be offered in the universities, in three cathedral churches, in the collegiate church at Windsor, and in thirteen religious houses in various parts of the realm.[31] But even these vast dispositions by a monarch, quite as prudent in death as in life, leave a considerable sum given by Londoners of humbler rank to secure the repose of their souls. Thus in this single decade eleven former mayors, all being great merchants, created endowments for chantries or, more commonly, gave substantial outright sums for prayers over a period of years. We shall want to comment on a fair number of the larger gifts and bequests of this kind.

In 1501 Sir John Warde, a very rich grocer who had been mayor in 1485 and who had on six occasions served as master of his company, left the large capital total of £1030 to endow prayers in London and in his native town of Hinxworth, Hertfordshire.[32] Another former mayor, Sir John Percival, in 1503 left an even larger capital (£1100) to secure the foundation of a chantry in which two stipendiary priests were to be maintained, as well as endowing an obit.[33] In the next year, Sir William White, a draper who had been mayor in 1489–1490, made more modest arrangements, providing a stipend of £6 13s 4d p.a. for prayers over a term of ten years and establishing a life interest for his wife in London tenements with an approximate capital value of £240, with the stipulation that these properties were to constitute the endowment of a perpetual chantry on her death.[34] Still another mayor, Sir John Shaa [Shaw], a goldsmith and a member of an eminent family of late medieval merchants, in his will proved in 1504 left £100 for prayers in the Mercers' Chapel and lesser amounts for five hundred masses and prayers by the five orders of friars.[35] In the next year, 1505, three former mayors died, all leaving substantial amounts for prayers. Thus Sir Henry Colet, the father of the great humanist, John Colet, and a mercer who had twice served as mayor, left a sum of £220 to ensure prayers by two 'honest chaplains' for a term of fifteen years, each priest to have a stipend of £7 6s 8d p.a.[36] Sir Bartholomew Rede, a goldsmith who had been mayor in 1502–1503, established an almost identical arrangement, having assigned £280 for prayers to be said by two honest monks over a period of fifteen years, as well as providing £20 for less rigorously prescribed observances.[37] And, finally, in this same year, John Wyngar, a grocer who had been Mayor of London in 1504–1505, left approximately £175 to ensure prayers in his parish church (St Mary Woolchurch) for a period of twenty years at eleven marks annually, an obit for the same term at £1 p.a., not to mention observances in divers religious houses and in the parish church of St Mary in Leicester, his birthplace.[38] Nicholas Alwyn, a mercer who had been mayor in 1499–1500, provided by gift and bequest a total of £370 3s for prayers, a portion of which, however, was probably property he had held in trust to secure the performance of the prayers endowed in St Thomas Acon by Sir Edmund Shaa.[39] In 1507 a rich skinner, Oliver Danyell, by will provided £410 for prayers for the repose of his soul,[40] while in 1508 Katherine Pemberton, the widow of Hugh, a merchant tailor, vested in her late husband's company the substantial sum of £400, the income of which was to be employed for the hire of a priest to sing prayers.[41] In 1508 also, William Browne, a mercer who died while serving his term as mayor, left funds to pay a priest ten marks yearly for a term of ten years for prayers in his parish church, St Mary Aldermary,[42] while, in the year following, Richard Chawry, a salter who had been mayor many years earlier, left a partly estimated total of £150 to secure prayers for the repose of his soul.[43]

This remarkable outpouring of substantial sums to secure the endowment of prayers may be regarded as a kind of watershed of traditional piety for the city of London. But for the next three decades (1511–1540) such contributions continued to be at once numerous and generous, amassing themselves in decade totals which were surprisingly stable, the range being from £7473 15s to £8429 7s during this generation. We shall content ourselves with no more than a brief recital of the principal of these endowments.

The earliest substantial endowment for prayers provided in the decade in which Lutheranism first appeared in England was that bequeathed in 1512 by Thomas Morris, a grocer, who left £153 17s for prayers as well as £267 of capital for scholarships for divinity students at Oxford.[44] William Cawley [Calley], a prosperous draper, in 1515 left to his company on trust London properties which a generation later possessed a capital worth of £527 for the maintenance of prayers in designated chantries,[45] while at about the same time Matthew Pemberton, a merchant tailor, vested in the parish church of St Martin Oteswich funds sufficient for the generous support of a stipendiary priest to say prayers in that church.[46] By gift and bequest Sir Richard Haddon, a mercer who had twice served as lord mayor, constituted complex endowments of about £573 7s capital value, his company being trustees, for the maintenance of a stipendiary priest and for the support of an obit.[47] And, to conclude our notes on the principal chantry endowments of this decade, we may mention the founding of a chantry in Charterhouse in 1517 by Sir Robert Rede, Chief Justice of the Common Pleas, at a charge of £256, which this donor endowed on his death in 1518 with a capital of £265 to secure the services of two priests for a term of twenty years, each of whom was to have £6 p.a. for his stipend.[48]

In the next decade (1521–1530), two substantial chantries were founded in St Paul's by ecclesiastical dignitaries. Richard Fitz James, Bishop of London, erected a chantry chapel, destroyed when the cathedral was struck by lightning in 1561, which he endowed with a stipend possessing a capital value of £287,[49] while John Dowman, Archdeacon of Suffolk and a prebend of St Paul's, a few years later (1526) endowed a chantry there with a capital of £440.[50] But the foundations of the great merchants of London were also continued, as witness the bequest of £200 made by Sir John Rest, a grocer and a former lord mayor, in 1522 to the Crossed Friars, to establish daily prayers for the repose of his soul,[51] and legacies totalling £261 left in the next year by Thomas Mirfyn, a skinner and also a former lord mayor, for prayers in various churches.[52] Thomas Michell, an ironmonger, in or before 1527 settled on his company properties and cash to the value of perhaps £200 for the observance of prayers in perpetuity,[53] while in the same year Sir James Yarford, a mercer and a former lord mayor, endowed a chantry with funds totalling at least £332 to secure the services of two stipendiary priests who together were to receive £16 11s 8d p.a.[54] Even more generous dispositions were made by Sir Thomas Lovell, the grocer turned statesman, who sometime before his death in 1528 endowed two chantry priests with property having a probable worth of £400, while establishing an additional fund of £300 for repairs and maintenance.[55] The flow of these benefactions was, then, still running strong in London shortly before the Reformation Parliament was convened, though even in their acts of traditional piety these London merchants displayed great caution as they arranged for secular trusteeships and guarded their endowments with reversionary clauses. This caution could on occasion suggest a disillusionment that was almost bitter, as is indicated in the bequest in 1527 of an endowment of £3 8s p.a. for prayers in his native parish of Wilmslow, Cheshire, by Thomas Etell, a tailor, provided the priest be 'no viciouse persone of lyevyng, diser, carder, bowler, cokkefyghter, noder commyne ale goer', no bull or dispensation by Pope or legate notwithstanding.[56]

It is, however, important to observe that in the decade in which the Reformation Parliament carried forward its great and revolutionary work there was no substantial falling away of gifts and bequests for prayers for the dead. Such endowments were, of course, not prohibited by law in the Henrician period, though the whole weight of a gathering Protestant temper in England, and most particularly in London, was frontally opposed both to the theory and practice of prayers for the dead. In the course of this decade (1531–1540) a total of £8345 9s was provided by London donors for these traditional observances, and we shall want to note at least the principal of these foundations.

A rich chantry was founded in Whittington College under a codicil to the will of Sir William Baily in 1532. Baily, a wealthy draper, who had served as lord mayor in 1524–1525, endowed this foundation with properties of about £650 value, of which £450 was vested in his company as trustees, while leaving in addition £22 for prayers and obits in various religious houses in London and elsewhere.[57] More modest provisions for prayers were made in the same year by another lord mayor, Sir Thomas Pargitar, a salter, who established prayers in perpetuity in his own parish church (Allhallows Bread Street), with an annual stipend of £6 13s p.a.,[58] and by Sir John Browne, Serjeant-Painter to the King, who gave in all £118 13s for prayers, including the sum of £100 owed to him by the convent of the Crossed Friars in London.[59]

The last chantry to be founded in St Paul's was endowed in 1533 by the terms of the will of Robert Brockett, a baker of St Martin Pomary, in Ironmongers' Lane. The donor vested the chantry with property of an apparent capital worth of £430, the income to be employed for the payment of two stipendiary priests to pray for the soul of John Withers, clerk, and a canon of the cathedral church, 'with whose advice and consent' Brockett had drawn up his will.[60] In the next year, Sir William Fitzwilliam, a rich merchant tailor and more recently a public servant, in addition to small sums for prayers in designated churches, left to his company £800, of which half was to be settled as an endowment for a chantry in the church at Marholm, Northamptonshire, the testator's birthplace.[61] In 1535 Robert Robinson, a clothworker, vested in his company a substantial endowment of £419, half the income of which was to be employed for the support of the poor of the company and the remainder for prayers.[62] A haberdasher and a former mayor, Sir Stephen Pecocke, in 1536 bequeathed £24 for prayers in specified churches and monasteries, having at an earlier but uncertain date settled on his church funds with a capital value of £447 for the support of prayers for the repose of his soul.[63] In the next year (1537), another lord mayor, Sir John Mundy, a goldsmith, left £71 13s in trust to his company for the founding of a perpetual obit,[64] while in 1538 still another former lord mayor, Sir Christopher Askew, left about £10 outright for immediate prayers, as well as providing a stipend of £7 p.a. for a term of twenty years to secure prayers in his parish church, St John the Evangelist.[65]

Gifts and bequests for prayers began to fall away rapidly both in number and in amount quite precisely in 1537, though they did continue in sharply diminished numbers during the two decades of the Reformation. In the decade 1541–1550, the total provided for these traditional observances was £2110 2s, this being about a fourth as much as was given for this purpose in the preceding ten years. Of this sum, a total of £675 was given for immediate use by forty-four donors in income gifts ranging in amount from 3s to £186 13s. A substantially larger sum was disposed in the form of capital, by which eighteen donors, giving within the range of 2s to £240, sought to create arrangements for prayers in perpetuity. The tragic failure of Mary Tudor is suggested by the fact that in the decade in which she undertook by such rigorous courses to restore the ancient faith, bequests for prayers fell away very steeply to a total of no more than £1331 8s, this amount having been provided, whether in capital or income designations, by twenty-five Londoners who left from 1s to £400 for this pious purpose. Needless to say, with the accession of Mary's sister, such benefactions came to an abrupt end, only £14 having been left for prayers in the first decade of the Elizabethan period.

4. The withering of the support of monasticism

A considerable proportion of the large total which London donors designated for prayers during the first eight decades of our period was vested in monastic hands, where, it was felt, a more certain observance of the prescriptions could be expected. We have not in any county treated gifts to monasteries as a separate head, but have rather distributed these gifts under the several religious uses of prayers, church building and maintenance of fabric, the support of the clergy, and the general uses of the church. At the same time, however, we have in each county treated this giving specifically in order not only to assess it in terms of amount but to determine the social structure of monastic support and to plot the curve of the decline and the final disappearance of such benefactions.

The monasteries of London, or, more exactly, of Middlesex, were the foremost in the realm, both in wealth and in prestige. In all, it has been reliably estimated, the endowments of these notable foundations produced just prior to the Dissolution a net annual income of £11,533 18s 6d, suggesting a capital worth for these great establishments of something like £230,678. Towards the support of monasticism, and 79·14 per cent of all London benefactions were to foundations within the county of Middlesex, London donors gave in the course of our period the surprisingly large total of £41,883 12s. Almost the whole of these benefactions were made prior to 1541, the sum representing 16·75 per cent of all charitable benefactions made during the interval and constituting the considerable proportion of 37·39 per cent of all gifts for religious uses made in the years prior to the Reformation. At the same time, however, it should be emphasized that this substantial sum, spread over a term of sixty years, represented an addition of no more than one-fifth to the presumed capital of the monastic foundations in the county in 1480, an increment barely sufficient to keep pace with the steady erosion of fire, time, and waste to which these establishments were proverbially liable. In part this withdrawal of support was evidently due to the fact that the monasteries of the county on the eve of the Dissolution were expending no more than £195 8s p.a. on the distribution of alms, this amounting to 1·69 per cent of their then total income and representing an almost complete abnegation of the social and moral responsibilities with which these foundations had once regarded themselves as charged. Monasticism in England was foredoomed long before the Reformation Parliament was assembled or the Crown's commissioners had begun their visitation.

The considerable total of £41,883 12s of monastic benefactions was given by 341 individual London donors. A brief analysis of the structure of these gifts suggests most decidedly that the claims of monasticism on the conscience and loyalty of men had as early as 1480 become confined to very narrow social limits and, most importantly, that they had been almost wholly repudiated by the burgher class which was to exercise such a powerful influence on the shaping of the aspirations of modern England. Well over half (58·06 per cent) of the total of gifts for monastic uses in London was represented in two benefactions from the Crown for a massive sum of £24,317 10s. Twenty of the clergy, with particularly large gifts from several of the upper clergy, gave in all £8863 7s for monastic uses, this amounting to rather more than a fifth (21·16 per cent) of the whole. In all, then the Crown and clergy together account for very nearly 80 per cent of the whole of London's benefactions for the support of monastic institutions. The merchants of the city during these two generations gave a total of only £3638 18s for monastic purposes, this constituting no more than 8·69 per cent of the whole. It is particularly significant that of the 139 merchant donors only eleven gave £100 or more, the largest single benefaction for this purpose by a member of this class being £448 4s. In fact, we may perhaps best analyze the amazing structure of these benefactions by suggesting that of the sum provided for monasteries in London, no more than 13·34 per cent was given by the typically urban classes. Monasticism had been in effect repudiated by those very classes in which so much of the wealth and power of England was to be concentrated in the years to come.

The considerable sum of £23,884 12s, this being 57·03 per cent of the whole amount, was given by London donors for the endowment of monastic chantries, or, more commonly, for prayers under more modest arrangements. Much of this great total was of course accounted for by Henry VII's huge endowment for Westminster Abbey, but we have also observed how frequently merchants, and burghers more generally, gave at least a portion of their bequests for prayers to religious houses of London and its vicinity. Well over a third (36·83 per cent) of the whole sum was given for further monastic building, for the erection of chapels, or for the care of the fabric of existing houses. Here again the total of £15,420 8s given for this purpose is swollen by the £5333 15s provided by Henry VII in connection with his magnificent building at the Abbey, though there were numerous and often substantial burgher gifts for this purpose as well. The relatively small sum of £2384 3s, this amounting to 5·69 per cent of the whole, was given for the support of monastic services generally, while the insignificant total of £194 9s was provided for the uses of designated members of the regular clergy.

Once again the tragic weakness of the Marian Counter-Reformation is demonstrated in the complete failure of the Queen to persuade her realm to lend support to those institutions upon which the ancient faith depended. In the decade of her reign (1551–1560) the really trifling total of £361 7s was given by eleven London donors, of which number, it is important to note, only two were members of the typically urban classes. The almost frantic efforts of the Queen to restore an age that was gone enjoyed but slight, almost eccentric support from the citizens of the capital. The processes of history are never reversible.

5. *Maintenance of the clergy*

One is tempted to wish that much of the large sums provided by London's donors for prayers and for the monasteries, soon to be secularized by the processes of reformation, might have been disposed for the support of the parochial clergy of London and the realm at large. In all, London benefactors were to give in the whole course of our period £34,822 for the augmentation of clerical stipends, this comprising only 1·84 per cent of the whole of the great charitable funds of the city and amounting to about the same total as the intensely secular donors of London were to provide for the relief of prisoners. Of this total, £29,292 6s was in the form of endowments to secure the permanent augmentation of livings, a sum sufficient fully to endow something like fifty parishes with stipends then regarded as adequate for the support of a godly and learned clergyman. Significantly, almost half (46·10 per cent) of the whole amount given for the maintenance of the clergy was disposed by merchant donors for other counties, not only because the need of the rural clergy was far greater than that of the moderately well-endowed benefices of London, but because the donors were, in such stubbornly conservative counties as Lancashire, consciously seeking to further the course of the Reformation by appointing staunch and undoubted Calvinists to key parishes which would serve as centres for the propagation of the true faith.[66]

The interest of London benefactors in this great need was very slight indeed until the second decade of the seventeenth century. During the years prior to the Reformation only £3174 10s was given for the augmentation of clerical stipends, more than half of this amount being in the form of outright bequests to named regular or secular clergy. But in the course of the next two generations (1541–1600), these benefactions fell away to a small total, no more than £2416 15s having been given for this worthy and now desperately needed purpose, the secularism of the age having, of course, been particularly marked during the reign of the wholly uninterested Queen. The great surge of such giving, now almost entirely in the enduring form of endowments, came in the early Stuart period when the really considerable and eminently useful total of £22,841 3s was disposed for the lifting of clerical incomes, this representing almost two-thirds (65·59 per cent) of the whole amount given for this use during the years under study. The generous total of £6389 12s was also given for this purpose during the revolutionary decades, with the result that 83·94 per cent of all clerical augmentations were constituted in the last two generations of our period.[67]

The larger of the sixteenth-century augmentations may be quickly dealt with. Dame Elizabeth Rede, a rich goldsmith's widow, in 1532 bequeathed property with a capital value of £251 for the support of a priest at St John Zachary, in addition to leaving £44 13s 4d for prayers, vestments and altar cloths valued at £20 for use in her parish church, and substantial secular charities which we have elsewhere discussed.[68] In 1557 Thomas Lewin, an ironmonger, left £10 p.a. for a 'good, sad, and honest' priest to serve at St Nicholas Olave, we think not as a stipendiary priest.[69] The strong evangelical temper of London's religious sentiment after the Reformation and the earnest desire for a learned and preaching clergy may perhaps be exemplified in the quite modest bequest of Nicholas Culme, a merchant tailor, who in 1586 left £2 13s to 'Dr. Reynolds of Corpus Christ's Colledge in Oxford... not tying him to come to London, but if he doe come my request is that he also will sometime visit our Church of Saint Augustine and there preach unto the people'.[70]

From 1611 onwards the benefactions made for the maintenance of the clergy are both numerous and generous. We must needs content ourselves with a brief mention of no more than the principal of these endowments. One of the largest, and certainly one of the most carefully devised, of the endowments for the benefit of the clergy was that ordered by the will of William Parker, a rich merchant tailor, who in 1616 left in trust to his company £2000 for charitable uses, of which £735 was to be devoted to the improvement of clerical stipends. The minister of St Antholin's, London, was to have an additional £10 p.a., while the clerk and the sexton of the parish were each to have an annuity of £2 10s. Moreover, a stipend of £20 p.a. was henceforward to be paid to a clergyman to serve the needs of the chapel of Great Bloxwich, in Walsall, Staffordshire, Parker's birthplace, the nominee preferably to be a graduate of the Merchant Taylors' School and of St John's College, Oxford.[71] Another great philanthropist of this period, John Kendrick, in 1624 left annuities and an endowment, with a total capital worth of £1000, to secure the reading of morning prayers in the parish church of St Christopher by the Stocks, the minister to have £20 p.a. and the clerk and sexton, who must attend, £2 10s each, as well as £10 p.a. each to the churches at Reading and Newbury, for the same use.[72] In this year, too, a London lawyer, Christopher Tamworth, vested £400 in order to endow a daily service at St Botolph by Aldgate and at the church of St Martin's in Leicester, as well as leaving £20 for church repairs and a large legacy for the benefit of the poor of London.[73] Henry Smith, perhaps the wisest of all London donors, as we have previously noted,[74] in 1626 established under careful trust provisions the massive endowment of £10,000 for the purchase of impropriations, the augmentation of clerical stipends, and the maintenance of learned and godly ministers in every part of the kingdom. Still another great benefactor of this amazing decade, Baptist Hicks, in 1629 settled on Tewkesbury, Gloucestershire, tithes and rents with a capital worth of about £800 for the better maintenance of an able and sufficient clergyman in that community,[75] while in 1630 John Bancks, a mercer who had served Hicks as an apprentice, left annuities and rents with a capital worth of £178 in order to endow sermons in the Mercers' Chapel and at Islington, Middlesex.[76]

A total of £2183 13s was provided by London donors as endowments to secure augmentations of livings in the decade just prior to the Civil War and, as we have earlier noted, such foundations were continued at an accelerated rate during the two decades of political disturbance, when £6,389 12s was so vested. But most of these endowments from 1631 onwards have a definitely Puritan bias, even when they are not quite specifically for lectureships, and it might be better to treat at least the larger of them under that head.

6. The endowment of lectureships

An even greater total was in fact provided for lectureships by London donors than for the augmentation of clerical stipends, the impressive sum of £49,744 10s having been given for this purpose from 1571 onwards to the close of our period. Almost the whole (99·37 per cent) of this great sum was left as capital, with the result that something like £2490 p.a. was by the close of our period available to support the sixty-four lectureships founded by London donors in their own city and in other parts of the realm. Most, but by no means all, of these foundations were made by Puritan merchants who sought by a variety of devices to secure in perpetuity the appointment of learned, godly, and preaching ministers who would spread the Gospel according to Geneva.[77] It is important to observe that of this great endowment more than half (51·67 per cent) was disposed for the benefit of parishes and congregations outside Middlesex.*

These benefactions were looked upon with distinct disfavour by the Elizabethan government, this doubtless accounting for the fact that their accumulation proceeded slowly during the period 1561-1600, when a total of no more than £3803 3s was furnished. But the flow of such benefactions increased steadily during the early Stuart years, considerably more than £10,000 having been given during the first two decades of the century and really great totals of £11,008 7s and £10,123 in the third and fourth decades respectively. As would be expected, interest in these endowments was well and steadily maintained during the Puritan interval, when the substantial sum of £14,104 was provided.

We should now turn to a discussion of at least the most important of these foundations, including also, if we may, certain other benefactions with a definitely Puritan bias which are not technically lectureships and which are not so regarded in our statistical summaries. One such was the early bequest of about £20 by Humphrey Monmouth, a rich draper and a friend of Tyndal, who as early as 1528 had been imprisoned by Sir Thomas More because of his avowed Protestantism. Monmouth left his legacy to provide for thirty sermons to be preached by Latimer, Barnes, and other reformers, while further stipulating that a sermon in English be preached at his funeral instead of masses for the repose of his soul.[78] This interesting bequest may be said to have established the tone and temper of many that were to follow, as the increasingly Protestant and then increasingly Puritan merchant aristocracy sought to bend the church to its will by the immense leverage supplied by wealth and determination.

* It should be noted that such endowments for the augmentation of livings are separately treated for statistical purposes.

Sir John Rivers, a grocer who had served as lord mayor in 1573, by his will proved in 1584 endowed four sermons annually in the church of St Bartholomew Exchange and as many at Hadlow, Kent, providing stipends of £6 13s 4d annually for the minister in each parish. Rivers, after consigning his soul to God and confessing his sins, in his testament of faith expressed the expectation that 'after this mutable worlde and transitorie lief' he might 'rise with the Electe and have eternall lief' in the world to come.[79] A devout Puritan widow, Elizabeth Walter, who, as we have seen, was also a substantial benefactor to Emmanuel College, Cambridge, by the terms of her will in 1588 left £300 for the relief of virtuous preachers and £50 for the maintenance of a godly minister in Ipswich, Suffolk.[80] Another Puritan lady, Frances Radcliffe, Countess of Sussex, in the next year ordered the distribution of £100 among poor and godly ministers in greater London and at the same time endowed with £20 p.a. two weekly lectures in Westminster Abbey, to be delivered by a 'godly and learned preacher'.[81] In 1593, to continue with the recital of a few of the Elizabethan foundations, Thomas Russell, a rich and generous draper, left annuities with a capital value of £200 for the payment of stipends of 10s each to twenty non-beneficed clergymen to preach each year at Paul's Cross.[82] Thomas Aldersey, a prominent haberdasher, in 1598 settled a very large trust with a capital worth of at least £1733 on his company as feoffees, they to appoint a godly and learned preacher at Bunbury, Cheshire, where this donor had already endowed a grammar school, the incumbent to have an annual stipend of £66 13s 4d p.a., and his curate, who must be unmarried, a salary of £20 p.a. with a room in the minister's house.[83] Concluding our notes on Elizabethan lectureships, we may mention the benefaction made in 1600 by Margaret Sharles, a mercer's widow, of rents with a capital value of £100 for the augmentation of the stipends of the vicar, curate, clerk, and sexton in Christchurch, London, and the endowment of a weekly lectureship in that church with a capital of £400.[84]

Further endowments were established at Paul's Cross for preachers having no benefices by George Palyn, a rich girdler, who left £200 for that use,[85] as well as £100 for a weekly sermon at St Mary-le-Bow, and by George Bishop who in 1611 provided £10 p.a. for the same purpose.[86] Jeffrey Elwes, an alderman and a merchant tailor, bequeathed £200 of endowment for these sermons in 1616,[87] while in 1622 Roger Jeston, a haberdasher, left £5 p.a. for preaching at Paul's Cross, as well as £6 p.a. for a divinity lecture in Lambeth parish church.[88]

Very large dispositions for the advancement of soundly Protestant preaching were made by William Jones, the staunch Puritan haberdasher and merchant adventurer, whose great charities totalling nearly £20,000 have been frequently mentioned in these pages. Jones settled on his own company as trustees £1600 as the endowment of a lectureship at St Bartholomew Exchange, the nomination to be in the hands of the company, they in 1615 appointing the eminent John Downam, who in 1616 preached a commemorative sermon for Jones under the title, *The Plea of the Poore*. Jones likewise bequeathed £1000 to be faithfully distributed by his executors amongst poor and zealous clergymen in any part of the realm. He had also, Downam tells us, for some years past maintained a preacher at Monmouth, his birthplace, with a stipend of £50 p.a., which was increased to £66 13s 4d p.a., with a free house, in connection with the great endowment for a school and almshouse at that place. And, finally, Jones included in a similarly complex foundation at Newland, Gloucestershire, a stipend of £66 13s 4d p.a. for a lecturer there, who should also have a free house. The nominee, Jones stipulated, must be of the 'quality of a Bachelor of Arts' and must preach at least weekly sermons.[89]

There were numerous lesser endowments constituted for lectureships and sermons during this decade which includes Jones's generous and carefully devised foundation. In 1617 Thomas Whetenhall established three lectures in St Anne Blackfriars, St Swithin's, and Whitechapel, as well as vesting a reversion of £12 p.a. for a lecture in St Antholin's, the total capital supplied being of the order of £1040.[90] One of the most enlightened of all donors of the period, Sir William Craven, a merchant tailor and a former lord mayor, among many other bequests endowed lectures at St Antholin's,[91] while, as we shall note elsewhere, Sir James Lancaster, a skinner and one of the pioneers of the India trade, not only left £400 to worthy clergy to be selected by his company but endowed a lectureship at Basingstoke, Hampshire, with a generous stipend of £40 p.a. [92]

The great outpouring of funds for the endowment of lectureships came in the decade 1621–1630, when the substantial total of £11,008 7s was provided for this godly purpose by men who could not be overawed by Laud and who were desperately seeking to preserve and strengthen the fervent preaching of the Word of God according to their own staunchly Protestant lights. We shall want to notice at least a sampling of the numerous foundations made in this interval, mentioning some of the smaller as well as the larger of these outlays. Thus in 1621 Nicholas Firmage, a lesser merchant, left £600 for various charitable uses in his native parish of Ashfield, Sussex, of which capital with approximately £400 value was for the support of 'a preaching minister of God's word for a Sunday sermon in the forenoon'.[93] A large endowment was left in 1623 by Dame Mary [or Margaret] Weld, the widow of Sir Humphrey Weld, a grocer and a former lord mayor. She provided £300 to the churchwardens of St Olave Upwell (Jewry) to maintain a divinity lecture in that church, as well as £150 for a lecturer at St Antholin's, already well endowed with such funds. This formidable lady likewise bequeathed £1000 to her executors to be distributed amongst poor, godly, and needy clergy under the trusteeship of the Haberdashers.[94] Moreover, Dame Mary provided the great sum of £2000 to be expended on the purchase of impropriate rectories and parsonages to which godly, learned, and preaching ministers of the Church of England should be appointed by the trustees, the rents and profits to be accumulated until the full capital sum had been recovered and then vested on the incumbents. The capital should thereupon be reinvested in livings and the same procedure repeated and so on 'until the world's end'.[95] Generous provision was made for lectureships and sermons in the next year by Thomas White, Vicar of St Dunstan's and the founder of Sion College. This donor left rents representing a capital of £1000 for a lectureship at St Paul's, three sermons to be preached weekly there in term time and the lecturer never to mention the donor's name, as well as capital of £800 value for a reader who should be named by the Lord Mayor of London. He provided as well £18 p.a. for the appointment of an 'honest and able man' to read a lecture in St Dunstan's each Sunday and Thursday afternoon. At an earlier date this great Puritan divine, who was one of the principal benefactors of his native Bristol, had endowed with rents of £26 p.a. sermons in three of the parishes of that city.[96]

In 1625 Christopher Eyre, a merchant adventurer who also founded an almshouse in his native Salisbury, established an endowment with a stipend of £20 p.a. for a lecturer to preach once weekly in St Thomas's church there, provided his executors, the mayor, and other civic officials be permitted to nominate the incumbent.[97] In the same year a most generous sum was left, under carefully devised stipulations, by Richard Fishborne, a mercer, for the support of lectureships and the Puritan clergy generally. He gave £500 to his company for maintaining sermons in their own chapel and an equal capital sum for the support of a lecturer, who should preach one day a week in the parish church of St Bartholomew Exchange. He also constituted a discretionary fund of £2000 for the general charitable needs of Huntingdon, a portion of the income of which was to be employed for the support of a lecturer in this, the donor's birthplace. Fishborne's will also ordered the distribution outright of £330 to six named clergymen, £400 to beneficed London clergy whose livings were of small value, and as much to the unbeneficed clergy of the city. In addition to these already munificent provisions, Fishborne settled on the Mercers the great capital sum of £2800 for the purchase of livings in the northern counties of England, where his trustees should 'find most want of preaching of the Word of God to be' and on which they should settle learned and godly ministers.[98]

Towards the close of this remarkable decade, Daniel Elliott, a merchant tailor, left rentals representing a capital worth of £800, half the income of which was to be employed for the support of a lecturer at Allhallows Bread Street and the remainder for a lecturer in his native parish of Beaulieu, Hampshire.[99] James Bunce, a leatherseller, provided by the terms of his will, drafted in 1630, £8 p.a. for three sermons annually in his native parish of Otterden, Kent,[100] while William Gonnell, a merchant, in the same year left £6 p.a. to the lecturer at St Antholin's and £5 p.a. for lectures in Christchurch, London.[101]

Very nearly as much was given in the next decade (1631–1640), when even the aggressive and confident merchants of London must have felt quite uncertain of the course they were taking against the stubborn and dedicated opposition of the Court and the Archbishop. None the less, in this interval they provided the huge sum of £10,123 for lectureships or for the settling, under trusted lay control, of clergy who would continue to preach in accordance with the views so stoutly held by the overwhelming majority of London donors. These endowments, almost all of which were eventually employed for the augmentation of parochial stipends, were given in the firm conviction of resolutely godly men that truth as they saw it and knew it must soon triumph. In this one firm conviction alone these remarkably prescient men and women of London failed to sense the future development of the culture whose leaders they had so recently become.

Richard Crashaw, whose great lay charities have previously been noted,[102] in 1631 made most generous provisions for godly preaching under the terms of his will. This London goldsmith left an annuity with a capital value of £400 for the founding of a weekly lecture in his parish church of St Bartholomew Exchange and founded as well a lectureship for the town of Derby with the large capital of £1250.[103] In the next year, Rowland Heylyn, an ironmonger whose nephew was the eminent divine, Peter Heylyn, left a considerable sum to the clergy, having at an earlier date financed the publication of a Welsh Bible and a Welsh translation of *The Practice of Piety*. Heylyn founded a lectureship with an annual stipend of £20 in the parish of St Alkmund in Shrewsbury, while his will ordered the distribution of £300 in outright gifts to poor clergy.[104] Barnard Hyde, a rich salter, in 1631 vested in his company £30 p.a. to secure a weekly lecture in his parish of St Dunstan in the East,[105] and in the next year Sir John Leman, a fishmonger who had been lord mayor in 1616–1617, left capital of £1000 to secure an annual payment of £10 to the preachers at Paul's Cross and £40 p.a. as a yearly stipend for a 'learned preacher of honest and good life and conversation' to preach a divinity lecture each Thursday from nine to twelve o'clock in the parish church of St Mary at Hill.[106] A rich draper, John Rainey, in 1633 settled a capital sum then valued at £1800 on his company in order to endow a chapelry at Worsborough, Yorkshire, and to found a lectureship, with a stipend of £40 p.a., in the parish church of St Michael Cornhill in London.[107] A generous mercer, Hugh Perry, who the year before his death in 1634 had served his company as master, by his will arranged for lectureships requiring capital to the value of upwards of £700. He left £200 to his company to secure the continued support of the morning lecture at St Antholin's and £270 for the maintenance of the lecturer at St Bartholomew Exchange, as well as providing £12 p.a. for establishing morning lectures at Wotton-under-Edge, Gloucestershire, where he had founded an almshouse and school.[108]

A former lord mayor, Sir Martin Lumley, a draper, by the terms of his will, proved in 1634, settled on his heirs capital of £400 value to secure the appointment by them of a lecturer in St Helen Bishopsgate, the lecturer to preach each Tuesday evening from Michaelmas to Lady Day.[109] The moderately Puritan Sir Thomas Mowlson, a grocer who had been lord mayor in 1633, by the terms of his will in 1638 vested income representing a capital worth of £800 for founding a living for the chapelry of Hargrave, Cheshire, to which a 'learned and godly preacher ... out of one of the universities' should be appointed to preach and teach the 'knowledge of God and His Word'.[110] Towards the close of the decade, Samuel Petty, a stationer, settled on trustees £600 for the purchase of lands with an income of £30 p.a., of which £26 p.a. should be devoted to lectures on divinity at St Magnus and £4 p.a. towards the relief of the poor of that London parish.[111] In the same year (1639), Margaret Astell, probably the widow of an innkeeper, by deed established an endowment with a then capital worth of £1142 for a variety of charitable uses. The largest portion of the income was to be devoted to the payment of £40 p.a. to a 'pious and learned' lecturer at St Lawrence Jewry, who should deliver a divinity lecture on each Friday throughout the year. This donor, it would appear, was no Puritan, since she required the lecturer to be comfortable to the Church of England as by law established.[112]

Endowments for sermons and lectureships continued unabated in the next decade, when despite the political and religious disturbances the large sum of £10,804 was given for the advancement of a cause which must have seemed to Puritan merchants to have been won and assured on the field of battle. We may mention a few of the larger of these numerous gifts and bequests, most of which exhibit the spiritual certainty expressed by Nathan Walworth, who in his will proved in 1641 expressed the firm hope that he would 'enjoy eternal rest amongst the chosen and elect people of God'. Walworth had earlier (1635) established a free grammar school in his native parish of Prestwich, Lancashire. He likewise built a chapel there which he endowed with lands possessing a probable value of £400, in order to secure a living for 'a godly and learned preacher'.[113] Edmund Hammond, a haberdasher, in 1642, in addition to important secular charitable bequests, left £1000 on trust to his company for the purchase of impropriations and the settlement of learned and godly ministers in such parishes, the nominees to be men who would preach at least once each Sabbath day, hold no other benefices, and reside in the parish to which they were appointed.[114]

A very large endowment for similar uses was provided under the will of Elizabeth Hicks (Lady Campden) in 1643. This donor, among other substantial charities, left £600 each to the parishes of St Lawrence Jewry and St Mary Magdalen, Milk Street, for the purchase of lands of £30 p.a. clear value, of which £4 p.a. was to be paid to the incumbent and £26 p.a. for the maintenance of a 'learned and able minister, of good life and conversation', to present a lecture on divinity on the afternoon of some convenient weekday. Lady Campden left as well £3100 on trust with the Mercers' Company for the purchase of two livings in some northern county, the ill-served regions of Yorkshire, Lincolnshire, and the Bishopric of Durham being preferred, where two young, worthy, and learned ministers, who must be at least of the degree of Master of Arts, might be settled on the nomination of the company.[115] In the same year (1646), Henry Hazelfoot, presumably a haberdasher, vested in that company by deed of gift lands valued at £18 p.a., the income to be used in such wise that the stipend of the lecturer at St Nicholas Cold Abbey be increased by £8 p.a. and the remainder distributed in bread to the poor of the parish.[116] Sir John Francklyn, of Willesden, Middlesex, who represented Middlesex in the early years of the Long Parliament, on his death in 1647 left £600 for the endowment of a weekly sermon,[117] while Thomas Boylston, a clothworker, by a conveyance made shortly before his death gave to his company the substantial sum of £800 for the founding of a lectureship in the parish church of Burton-on-Trent, Staffordshire, to be held by a 'learned and orthodox preacher of the Protestant religion'.[118]

As we have previously indicated, it is scarcely possible to separate augmentations of livings and gifts to the clergy from endowments for lectureships in the decade of Puritan supremacy in England. We shall accordingly mention a few of the larger benefactions made under both heads. In total, the considerable sum of £8430 12s was provided for these two laudable purposes in the course of these years. One of the earliest and most interesting of such endowments was that provided in 1650–1651 by Richard Coysh, a skinner, who had served as an officer in the Parliamentary Army. In the debates in Parliament on the disposition of the episcopal lands, Coysh had strongly argued that these properties should not be sold in order to gain revenues for the state, but should be dedicated to the uses of piety and charity. His view not prevailing, Coysh bought for £817 13s 4d the derelict premises of the

Bishop of London's city palace (London House), while also purchasing the land at a charge of £1201 1s 6d, 'at 13 years' purchase'. He razed the buildings and erected fifteen new structures. He then let or sold the whole of this valuable property, subject, however, to an annual charge of £84 p.a., which should be distributed £42 p.a. for a lectureship in St Gregory's church, £24 p.a. for the poor of London, £10 p.a. for exhibitions to both universities, and £8 p.a. for the propagation of the Gospel among the Indians of New England.[119]

A weekly lecture with a stipend of £20 p.a. was founded for the parish of St Olave Hart Street by Walter Hulls, a merchant tailor, in 1653, the donor also making liberal provisions for the poor of that parish.[120] Sarah Bridges, the widow of a prosperous salter, on her death in 1650 left an annuity of £15 for the further augmentation of the several lectures already endowed in St Antholin's parish, as well as vesting properties to meet certain annual charitable payments ordered under her late husband's will (1642), providing for £2 p.a. for the poor of Clapham, Surrey, and as much for the schooling of labouring men there, with a residue of rentals of uncertain value to be paid to the uses of Christ's Hospital.[121] In 1657, Michael Herring, an alderman and a haberdasher, by his will ordered outright payments of £400 to the clergy of indicated London and Surrey parishes and £400 to the widows of poor ministers, as well as £250 to be distributed towards the maintenance of ten poor scholars in the universities.[122] A London gold-smith, John Perryn, likewise in 1657, among other large benefactions, provided an endowment with a capital worth of £520 for the support of a lectureship in his native parish of Bromyard, Herefordshire. A lecture was to be given each Monday morning, this being market day, through-out the year by the six to eight learned and godly divines beneficed in the town and near-by parishes, each preacher to receive 10s for his lecture. Perryn further provided capital of £2000 value to secure the payment of £100 p.a. for the relief of aged and orthodox clergymen and their widows who stood in need.[123] The widow of Sir James Cambell, a lord mayor and ironmonger,[124] on her death in 1658 disposed £200 for the support of sermons in the Dutch church in London, as well as £10 each to the clergy of the Dutch communion.[125] In the year following (1659), Richard Higginson not only provided under the terms of his will £20 p.a. for the clergyman at Bispham, Lancashire, during the remainder of his lifetime, but created an endowment of £400 capital value to secure a like sum in perpetuity for the maintenance of a zealous and godly minister in that community.[126] Finally, we may mention the endowment of a stipend of £10 p.a. for the minister of the parish church of St Werburgh, Derby, this being his native town, made by Francis Ash, a rich and most charitable goldsmith who died at the very close of our period, as well as the foundation of a weekly lectureship in the parish church of Ashby-de-la-Zouch, Leicestershire, made by this same donor.[127]

It will have been observed that a large proportion of the benefactions left for the clergy, whether for augmentations, the founding of lectureships, or outright assistance, was the gift of merchants of Puritan persuasion, who were seeking by such means as were available to them not only to create a preaching ministry in England but also to ensure the appointment of clergy who were 'zealous and godly'. These were essentially speculative efforts, for the weight of policy and law ran steadily against such undertakings. Archbishop Laud in particular frowned upon them, being prepared to intervene when he detected any systematic effort to win the church for Geneva by the purchasing of the livings in which its clergy were seated. It is difficult to be certain, but it may be at least roughly estimated that from 1561 forward close to two-thirds of all London benefactions for the clergy possessed a Puritan bias. But here was a great area of aspiration largely barred to the merchant elite of the city who were during these years remaking all the other fundamental institutions of their society.[128]

7. *The care of the fabric*

London donors, taking our whole period in view, were relatively ungenerous in the care they lent to the maintenance of the fabric of the 117 parish churches in the city and its suburbs and to the seventy churches gracing the remainder of the county. Under the heading of church repairs and decoration, we have included not only the benefactions made for the normal repair and maintenance of the fabric but a great variety of gifts for the ornamentation of churches and their services. During the whole of our period the sum of £33,601 12s was provided, constituting 1·78 per cent of all charitable funds of the city, and this may be compared with such a relatively minor outlay as the £34,795 10s given for the relief of prisoners. A large proportion of this total (87·60 per cent) was in the form of gifts for immediate use and, it is interesting to note, only a modest proportion of these benefactions were made for the care of fabric of churches outside the county.

This so evidently insufficient total was by no means spread evenly over the whole course of our era. During the decades prior to the Reformation the substantial and just possibly adequate sum of £8734 10s was provided by pious London donors for the care of the churches of the city, the wills of hundreds of donors attesting the pride and concern of Londoners for the rich architectural and spiritual heritage which they had gained from the Middle Ages. But with the advent of the Reformation, the chilling pall of indifference to the fate of the fabric descends, deepening during the Elizabethan age and in no sense lifting until the mid-Jacobean period, which in so many historical senses marks the end of the great Elizabethan era. In this long interval of seventy years (1541–1610), the total given for church repairs amounted to no more than £3663 15s, or a scant tenth of the wholly inadequate total settled for this use during our entire period. There was a marked revival of concern for church fabric setting in about 1614 and rising to a true climax in the repairing of the now sadly derelict parochial churches in the Laudian decade (1631–1640), when almost a third of the total given during our whole period was provided by donors whose conscience, or prudence, was stirred by the Archbishop's unending activity. During the early Stuart period as a whole (1601–1640), the total of £18,708 16s was given for this use, standing in the most marked contrast to the insignificant sum of £1575 4s provided during the Elizabethan age of identical length. The gifts for this purpose fell away sharply during the years of political and religious unsettlement, though by no means to the plane of almost complete neglect that marked the second half of the sixteenth century. In all, the not inconsiderable sum of £3347 16s was given, principally by Puritan donors for the maintenance of a fabric which they are too often credited with despoiling.

The incessant needs of the fabric commanded the customary loyalty of London donors in the year prior to the Reformation, just as we have seen that men making wills usually included at least nominal amounts for the general uses of their churches in this period. These benefactions constituted a very important source of predictable parish income and were evidently in most parishes sufficient to care for the day-to-day repair of the church structures and to provide the means for the gradual improvement of ornamentation and of the sacramental objects. We have seen that for the period 1480–1540 a probably scantily sufficient total of £8734 10s was provided by pious men and women for these uses, of which, it should be emphasized, a very large proportion was given in quite modest sums by all classes of a degree above that of artisan. Thus, to take one decade for more detailed analysis, in the interval 1501–1510 the sum of £2434 18s was given for church repairs and decoration by 163 donors in amounts ranging from 1s to £202. Considerably more than half these benefactions were in sums of £1 or less, and of the total number 159 were gifts for immediate use. We shall content ourselves with the recital of only a few of these pre-Reformation gifts; most of those to be mentioned are relatively so large as to be quite untypical of the flow of many more modest contributions.

In 1491 William Caxton, the great printer, left fifteen copies of the *Golden Legend* to St Margaret's, Westminster, which unfortunately were later sold at prices ranging from 5s 4d to 6s 8d a volume.[129] Joan, Viscountess Lisle, a few years later (1500) left £90 for the repair and decoration of her parish church of St Michael Cornhill, as well as a rent charge of 13s p.a. for the care of its fabric.[130] In 1510 Thomas Bradbury, a mercer who died during his mayoralty, bequeathed £90 in all for church repair and decoration, including £10 for the repair of his own church (St Stephen Coleman Street), vestments worth £40 for the parish in Hertfordshire where he had been born, and £40 for vestments to two churches in Essex.[131] Moving forward as we must rather rapidly, we may note the bequest in 1527 of £50 for copes and vestments in St Mary Aldermary and £3 for church repairs in his native Staffordshire made by Roger Bedyll, a skinner, who also provided £1 for church general, £107 15s for prayers, £40 for the poor, and £2 for the relief of prisoners.[132] In the same year, a mercer, James Maston, left 3s to the general uses of St Magnus and £6 13s to St Peter's altar in that church, provided measures were taken to prevent its continued desecration by dogs.[133] Finally, we may mention the substantial provision made by Sir John Brugge [Bridges, Briggs], a draper, who had served as mayor in 1520–1521, for vestments to the value of about £20 for his church of St Nicholas Acon and the same amount for his native parish of Dymock, Gloucestershire. This donor also instructed his executors to repair his parish church with stone, to remake the door, to ceil it against the rain, and to provide a new gallery for the convent of Holy Trinity Minories.[134]

We have spoken at length of the withering of concern for the care of the church fabric of the city by Londoners during the next two generations. Customary gifts for this purpose all but ceased, and substantial benefactions from rich and otherwise generous merchant donors became very rare indeed. Thus in the first decade of the Elizabethan era the total given for church repairs amounted to only £279 9s, or not much more than an average of £2 for each parish church in the city. That the broad popular base of support was gone is suggested by the fact that only twenty-five donors gave or bequeathed sums for this use in amounts ranging from 3s to £120. An age of almost complete secularism was evidently at hand, and our examples of benefactions for church repair during these sixty years may be briefly presented.

The parish church of St Martin Oteswich was repaired and somewhat improved in 1555–1559 and again in 1597 at a total, and very roughly estimated, charge of £300.[135] William Heron, perhaps a woodmonger, in 1580 left a rental of £4 p.a. for a period of twelve years to be devoted to the repair of St James Clerkenwell, as well as a capital sum of £400, the income of which was to be used for the perpetual care of the fabric of that church and of St Sepulchre.[136] A few years later, Edmund Chapman, Master Joiner to the Queen, provided pews and the choir for the parish church of St James Garlickhithe at a charge of upwards of £80, as well as making other charitable provisions which were celebrated in particularly atrocious doggerel in his epitaph.[137]

As we have noted, a marked and certainly a desperately needed revival of interest in the state of the church fabric of the city set in about 1610, which was directed and intensified by the valiant efforts of Laud and his episcopal supporters. A fair number of substantial gifts and bequests were accordingly made in the interval 1611–1640, some of which seem suspiciously close to benefactions made under an almost intolerable pressure. One most useful contemporary authority, writing in about 1613, boasted that in the past twenty or thirty years 'generally all' the parish churches of the city had been 'beautified and adorned' at a cost of from £100 to £200 for each parish, [138] in some cases by voluntary gifts and subscriptions, with which we have been concerned, and in others by parish rates. This writer also estimated that the total outlay for building as well as repairs during this interval was of the order of £10,000, which is certainly a gross underestimate of the large amount we know to have been provided for these combined uses.[139] We should now comment on at least a sampling of the more substantial of these benefactions for the repair and adornment of the fabric.

A London merchant, Robert Chilcot, in 1609 provided an annuity representing a capital worth of £200 for the perpetual care and repair of the parish church of Tiverton, Devon, as part of the great trust which he created for the founding and support of the social institutions of that community.[140] Two years later, Thomas Savage, a goldsmith, by will left property with an estimated worth of £200 to secure in perpetuity the care of the fabric of St Alban Wood Street.[141] St Giles Cripplegate, not yet a century old, was repaired and somewhat enlarged by the addition of a gallery in 1612–1618 at a total charge of £77 13s.[142] Numerous donors, most of whom were merchants, expended about £137 for repairs and pews for the parish church of St Stephen Walbrook at about the same time.[143] In 1616, William Parker, a rich merchant tailor, several of whose large secular charities have previously been mentioned, left £100 as a stock for the care of the fabric of Allhallows Bread Street, having as well, we may note here, contributed £143 10s towards the rebuilding of St Antholin's, and having given £500 towards the major renovations being undertaken on St Paul's.[144] Another principal subscriber to the great work being carried forward at St Paul's was Sir William Craven, a merchant tailor, who likewise left, in 1618, £100 for the repair of St John the Evangelist and who some years before his death extensively repaired and decorated the church in his native parish of Appletreewick (Burnsall), Yorkshire, at a cost of perhaps £200.[145]

Some nine of London's parish churches received extensive repairs during the next decade (1621–1630), when we have recorded £4536 5s given for church renovations in London and elsewhere. Among these, there were repaired principally by voluntary contributions St Bartholomew Exchange, on which £235 was spent in 1621 and £240 in 1635,[146] and Allhallows Lombard Street, which was repaired in 1622–1623 at a total outlay of £171 9s,[147] while £220 was expended on badly needed repairs for Allhallows London Wall in 1627.[148] Much more extensive repairs and alterations were undertaken on St Botolph by Aldgate at about the same time, upwards of £400 having been spent there between 1616 and 1633.[149]

We may conclude with brief mention of at least the principal outlays made for church repairs and decorations in the decade 1631–1640, when, as we have noted, the really considerable total of £10,231 19s was given or bequeathed for this use. Thus in 1631 outlays of not quite £250 were made on the fabric of St Edmund Lombard Street,[150] while shortly afterwards ambitious repairs costing £437 were effected at parish charges at St Olave Hart Street.[151] The steeple of St Peter Cornhill was repaired in 1629 and great repairs and renovations were undertaken there four years later, all costing somewhat more than £1000.[152] There are numerous contributions recorded for work being carried on for some years in St Clement Danes, these repairs amounting to almost a rebuilding and being completed in 1633 at a total cost of £1586.[153] General repairs were also carried forward in the rich church of St Helen Bishopsgate in 1632–1633, the whole cost of which was £1322 3s 2d,[154] while at the same time badly needed repairs were completed at St Bennet Fink at a charge of about £400.[155] Numerous subscriptions totalling £450 were made, principally by merchants, for the repair of St Christopher by the Stocks in 1635–1636,[156] while £300 was collected for renovations and repairs at St Dunstan in the East in 1638.[157] Sir John Wolstenholme, a founder of the East India Company and a Customer, in 1634 gave £100 towards the repair of Allhallows Barking and bequeathed £200 of endowment for the perpetual care of a church which he had built in 1632 at a cost of something over £900 for the parish of Great Stanmore, Middlesex.[158] In concluding, we should record two substantial outlays made during the revolutionary era, upwards of £1100 having been laid out on the extensive and badly needed repair of St Swithin's church in 1647–1648,[159] and £1000 having been given in 1658 by George Holman, son of a London grocer, for the ornamentation of the church of St Bennet Fink.[160]

8. *The decline of church building*

The distinction we have drawn between outlays for church repairs and church building is often most arbitrary and occasionally perhaps indefensible. By the latter term, however, we have understood benefactions made for the building of a new church, the rebuilding of one that had to be razed or that had been destroyed, and the extensive enlargement or structural re-edification of an existing church. In all, the very large total of £164,004 1s was given by London donors during the whole course of our period for these uses, this having been well over 40 per cent (44·52 per cent) of the total provided for all religious purposes and constituting

8·68 per cent of the whole amount given for all charitable purposes.*
It should be said at once that almost a third (30·73 per cent) of this massive sum was expended on two structures, Westminster Abbey and St
Paul's, in the one case in the early decades of our period, in the other
principally during the Laudian era.

There was extensive church building in London from the beginning of
our period until well into the era of the Reformation, the impressive
total of £38,085 15s having been provided between 1480 and 1550 for
this purpose. But, save for the grudging support which the Queen gave
for the really feeble effort to restore the badly damaged St. Paul's
Cathedral, the whole outlay for this purpose from 1551 to the close of
the century was no more than about £4000. The outlay for building, or
more accurately for rebuilding, mounted steadily after the accession of
James I, to reach the very large sum of £80,960 8s in the decade of
Laud's great power and all but fanatical efforts. During the early Stuart
period as a whole, the massive total of £111,571 6s was provided for
church building, an amount at least roughly comparable to that laid out
for the building and endowment of almshouses in the same interval.
These outlays fell away immediately and very sharply during the two
closing decades of unsettlement and religious turmoil, when the modest
sum of £4145 was given for church building.

We have suggested that the population of greater London increased
by a factor of 7 or 8 during the course of our period and that almost the
whole of this tremendous growth occurred during the short interval of
about a century and a quarter extending from the advent of the Reformation to the restoration of the monarchy. There was relatively little
church building in the city to accommodate this immense expansion of
population. In the course of our period, four new churches were built,
wholly or in part by voluntary contributions, within the boundaries of
greater London, while seven were built in newly formed county parishes
which may well have been experiencing an even more rapid proportionate
growth. In addition, we should note that ten of the expropriated monastic
churches were converted to parochial needs, the remainder being put to
such uses as private residences, storehouses, hospitals, and manufac-
tories. The facilities for worship were also to some extent bettered by
the rebuilding of twenty-five London churches and one county church
during our period, for with few exceptions these structures were considerably enlarged when they were reconstituted. We shall see, too, that
church building was almost wholly confined to two periods: the medieval
building being completed in the interval prior to the Reformation, and

* Most amounts mentioned in our discussion of church building are estimated. The basis for such estimates and the difficulties of the problems are
discussed in the first volume of this study (Jordan, W. K., *Philanthropy in
England*, 33–34, 52).

approximately the same number of churches being built, rebuilt, or enlarged in the generation 1608–1637, when persistent effort was made to repair the immense dilapidations of the preceding half-century, if not to meet the crisis created by the growth in the population of the city. London, like most of the rural counties of the realm, may very well have been over-churched in 1540; but it was as certainly under-churched in 1640. It would seem probable that in rough average terms there were something like 500 inhabitants for each parish in 1540, while in 1640 there may very well have been as many as 3000.

We have observed that in the two generations prior to the Reformation the substantial total of £29,243 15s was provided for church building, as pious men and women completed the fabric of the medieval ecclesiastical establishments of London. More accurately, much of this great and certainly expensive effort was dedicated to the replacement of decayed or inconvenient medieval structures, ten churches having been rebuilt in this rather brief period, while only three new edifices were being provided in London and the county. We should now turn to what must needs be a most cursory review of the church building of this early period.

In 1480 a chapel was provided for the church of St Dionis Backchurch by John Derby at an estimated charge of £200,[161] while at about the same date a stone tower was added and bells hung in the parish church of Brentford, Middlesex, at a cost of about £300.[162] Robert Hewelett [Hulett] built a small chapel in Charterhouse at about the same time (1481), while Robert Byfield, an ironmonger, left £200 for the erection of a chapel in St Dunstan in the East in 1482,[163] and Sir William Haryot, a draper and mayor, in 1485 built and decorated a chapel on the opposite side of that church at a partly estimated charge of £225.[164] Sir Edmund Shaa had built a chapel in the Mercers' Church (St Thomas Acon) sometime before endowing it as a chantry on his death in 1488.[165] The building of St Margaret's, Westminster, was begun in 1491, the edifice being dedicated in 1523, to the erection of which Lady Mary Billing was a principal contributor, having provided something like £500 towards the cost.[166]

The substantial total of £7950 was provided for church building by London donors in the last decade of the fifteenth century. Numerous gifts have been noted for the rebuilding of Allhallows London Wall (*ca.* 1494), which was carried forward at an estimated charge of £800.[167] In the same year, a much-needed church was built at Hadley, Middlesex, at a roughly estimated cost of £600 by unknown donors.[168] Sir Hugh Brice, a goldsmith who had served as mayor in 1485, some while before his death in 1496 contributed upwards of £350 for the building of a chapel in St Mary Woolnoth and for work on the steeple and the body of that church.[169] The small church of St Mary at Hill was rebuilt in *ca.* 1497 at a charge of perhaps £800,[170] while a tower and clerestory were added to the church at Littleton, Middlesex, towards the close of the decade.[171] Important and expensive work was likewise carried forward in this decade at Westminster Abbey, John Esteney, who served as Abbot from 1474 to 1498, having laid out something like £4400 on what amounted to a rebuilding of the whole of the outer fabric of the great pile. Esteney pursued this work with an almost fanatical preoccupation, leaving £600 to meet an accumulated debit at the time of his death.[172] Henry VII began his great work on his immortal chapel in the same decade, it being completed in 1519, towards the finishing of which and for work on the west end of the Abbey proper he left the large sum of £5333 15s.[173]

The next decade (1501–1510) was notable for the amount of rebuilding undertaken by donors of the period. In the first year, Sir Robert Tate added a chapel to the church of Allhallows Barking at a charge of something like £200,[174] while at about the same date extensive renovations and enlargements were carried out on the church at Ruislip, Middlesex, at a total outlay of perhaps £310.[175] The church at Hornsey (Finsbury), Middlesex, was completed at an estimated charge of £700, in large part from materials salvaged from a decayed hunting lodge in the vicinity.[176] A former mayor and a draper, Sir William White, who died in 1504, had some years earlier carried forward extensive repairs on and had added a fourth aisle to St Katherine Coleman at a total outlay of something over £280.[177] John Wyngar, a grocer and a former mayor, is said to have been a generous contributor towards the completion of St Mary Woolchurch, though we have no particulars, and his will makes no considerable provision for this, his parish church, beyond a substantial legacy for prayers.[178] St Bride's was in effect rebuilt in *ca.* 1507,[179] while Blackfriars at about the same time gained a chapel as a consequence of the piety of Richard Spencer.[180] The rebuilding of the important parish church of St Mary Aldermary was begun in 1510 and was completed in 1518, apparently almost wholly at the charge of Henry Kebyll, a rich grocer, who in 1511 gave the large sum of £1000 for this purpose and who in 1517 bequeathed an additional £1000 for the completion of the work.[181]

Though at a markedly lessened tempo, the flow of funds for the building and renovation of churches was continued during the first decade of Henry VIII's reign. Thus in 1511 John Kyrkeby, a merchant tailor, bequeathed £100 for the building being done at Lichfield by the Grey Friars and a second £100 if as much should be required.[182] Rather more than £300 was expended from 1512 to 1516 on building a lofty steeple, and some other work, on St Mary-le-Bow, to which a considerable number of merchants made generous contributions.[183] Sir William Capel, a draper, in 1509 or thereabouts built a chapel at a cost of perhaps

£260 in his parish church of St Bartholomew the Less, in which he wished to be buried.[184] A famous mayor, John Tate, was occupied in this decade with the rebuilding of St Antholin's, the cost of which he bore almost alone. Tate razed a brewery which he had inherited from his father and which occupied a site adjoining the Hospital of St Anthony, in order to make room for the building, bearing as well a large part of the cost of the work, which seems to have been completed during the years 1499–1513.[185] Still another London merchant, Henry Coote, a goldsmith, shortly before his death in 1513 added a chantry chapel at St Vedast's at an estimated charge of £200, which he endowed with properties of a slightly lesser worth.[186] Finally, we may note that All-hallows Lombard Street was in effect rebuilt in the years 1494–1516 at a cost of approximately £1250, much aid being given by the Pew-terers' Company, and the south aisle being completed by John Warner, a grocer (d. 1510) and his son (d. 1555).[187]

Church building was carried forward at an impressive but none the less a markedly lowered rate during the next generation (1521–1550), when somewhat more than £15,000 was given by London donors for this pious purpose. Thus the important city church of St Andrew Undershaft was rebuilt, probably in the years 1520–1532, at a total out-lay of something like £2100. Sir Stephen Jenyns, a merchant tailor who had served as mayor in 1508, was the prime mover in the work, though not a resident of the parish, building at his own charge the north side of the middle aisle, roofing and repairing the north aisle, and contributing the pews. The work was finished principally by a merchant tailor, Sir William Fitzwilliam, who also built the chancel of the church at Marholm, Northamptonshire, shortly before his death in 1534.[188] John Chambers, who was somewhat incongruously at once physician to Henry VIII and the last Dean of St Stephen's, was engaged from 1526 until perhaps 1530 in building at the heavy cost of upwards of £7000 the beautiful cloisters of that collegiate chapel after the style of Henry VII's Chapel in the Abbey and very probably with the aid of the same workmen.[189] A humbler contribution was made at about the same time when Henry Froune [Frowyke], a London merchant, built the north aisle of the church at South Mimms, Middlesex, adorning it as well with a chantry chapel.[190] Sir James Yarford, a mercer, in or about 1527 built a chapel in the parish church of St Michael Bassishaw at a charge of perhaps £250,[191] while at about the same date Sir Thomas Lovell, a grocer, completed building under way at Holywell Nunnery in London, on which he laid out as much as £300.[192] Still another great merchant, Sir John Rudstone, who died in 1531, gave £20 towards the building of monastic premises in Rome, as well as about £300 for the building of a cloister and lodgings for the choristers in St Michael Cornhill.[193] The church of St Peter ad Vincula was rebuilt at a probable cost of about £1000 in *ca.* 1532 after a serious fire which occurred in 1512,[194] while the greatly decayed parish church of St Alphage was at least substantially repaired in *ca.* 1535, the parishioners failing to secure a licence for its rebuilding.[195] St Margaret Pattens was all but rebuilt in 1538 at a probable outlay of £900,[196] while St Peter the Poor was completed two or three years later at a charge of perhaps £1200.[197] The parish church of St Martin's, Westminster, was rebuilt in 1544 principally at the King's charge,[198] and St Giles Cripplegate was restored shortly after 1545, when the medieval structure was seriously damaged by fire.[199]

As we have already emphasized, church building was almost wholly neglected in and by London for a full half-century (1551–1600) during the era of cool Elizabethan secularism. Half-hearted and most limited repairs were carried out when St Paul's was badly damaged in 1561 by a great tempest, something over £6000 being expended on the roof of the great medieval structure, of which the Queen presumably gave one thousand marks and one thousand loads of timber. But the great outlays were to be delayed for two generations until Laud took in hand the work of repair and renovation.[200] All the rest of the building of this generation and more may be briefly dealt with. One of the several great London benefactors to Shropshire, Sir Rowland Hill, some little time before his death in 1561 built a church to serve Hodnet and Stoke in that county at a cost of about £600.[201] In the year following (1562), William Patten, an Exchequer official and a justice of the peace for Middlesex, greatly improved the parish church of Stoke Newington, Middlesex, where he was lord of the manor, by adding the south aisle, a tower, and the vestry, at an estimated outlay of £450.[202] Similarly, an extensive improvement of the fifteenth-century parish church at Chiswick, Middlesex, was made in 1570 when the chancel was rebuilt.[203] The Roman Catholic Lord Hastings, a privy councillor in the Marian government, left funds in his will, proved in 1571, for the building of a chapel in the church of Stoke Poges, Buckinghamshire, where he was to be buried.[204] A chapel was built on Highgate Hill (Hornsey, Middlesex) in 1576 at a quite uncertain charge.[205] Almost two decades were to elapse before any further substantial outlays were made by Londoners for church building, when the chancel of Allhallows the Less was in effect rebuilt in 1594 at a probable charge of not more than £400. A few years later (1597), the slow rebuilding of St Anne Blackfriars was completed, the edifice having been damaged by fire in 1548 and then pulled down by Sir Thomas Carwarden, who provided chambers over a stair for worship. But this modest building was from the outset far too small for the parish, particularly because of the 'great thronging from all parts' to hear the learned and vigorous sermons of the great Puritan divine, William Gouge, after 1621. Gouge greatly enlarged the church, procuring £1500 'by collections at his lectures, and by letters written to his friends, whereby it was enlarged to this stately and beautifull structure without any briefs at all'. In total, something more than £2600 was expended on the enlargement of this famous church, most of which was raised by the admirers of the redoubtable Gouge well after the close of the Elizabethan age.[206]

We have previously remarked that a considerable renewal of interest in church building and enlargement got under way with the accession of the new sovereign. The substantial total of £15,523 9s was expended for this purpose during the first two decades of the seventeenth century. Thus the church of St Martin's, Westminster, rebuilt only two generations before, was considerably enlarged in 1607 at a probable cost of £600.[207] The rebuilding of Holy Trinity Minories was started in 1608, contributions being noted for the work at scattered dates until 1633 and the whole outlay being perhaps conservatively estimated at £1100.[208] Very extensive improvements and enlargements were likewise begun in 1608 on the Temple, the total charge reaching the substantial sum of £2300.[209] The rebuilding of St Olave Silver Street was begun in 1609,[210] while the renovation and enlargement of St Mary Mounthaunt, on which £900 or more was expended, was undertaken in the same year.[211] In the early seventeenth century, extensive renovations were also made on the parish church of St Michael Crooked Lane,[212] and the small but ancient church of St Ethelburga was all but rebuilt in 1612–1615 at a charge of about £1000.[213] The far too small church of St Andrew in the Wardrobe was greatly enlarged and repaired in 1613, upwards of £1500 being spent,[214] while shortly afterwards St Antholin's, rebuilt in 1513 by one London merchant,[215] was extensively repaired and renovated by seven of the mercantile fraternity, who together subscribed £1000 for this purpose.[216] Sir John Weld, as we have already noted, built and endowed a chapel at Southgate (Enfield), Middlesex, in 1615,[217] while shortly afterwards (1617) a church was built at Wapping, first possessing the status of a chapel to Whitechapel, at a charge of about £600, principally by the subscriptions of London merchants concerned about the needs of this already crowded community.[218] In the same decade, the rebuilding of St Vedast's was undertaken, a most uncertainly estimated total of £1100 having been expended on its renovation.[219] The parish church of Allhallows Bread Street was rebuilt somewhat later, the largest single contributor being a clothworker, John Dunster, who in 1625 bequeathed £200 towards the finishing of the work.[220] And, finally, we should mention the building during this period of the beautiful chapel for Lincoln's Inn, John Donne having preached the dedicatory sermon on its completion in 1623. The project was first begun in 1609, though building was delayed until 1620. The cost of the structure was only a little short of £3000, towards which individual benefactions totalling not quite half the whole outlay have been noted.[221]

Considerable progress towards repairing at least the worst of the dilapidations and a modest beginning in meeting the spiritual requirements of a greatly increased population had been made in the course of the first two decades of the seventeenth century. But a really great outpouring was to come in the two decades 1621–1640, when Laud kept an almost steady pressure on the Bishop of London, the parishes, the government, and the city companies. In this brief interval, the huge total of £96,047 17s was provided by donors, most of whom evidently gave somewhat grudgingly, for the building or rebuilding of London churches, or for quite extensive repairs and enlargement. This impressive total, it should be noted, represents rather more than 58 per cent of the sum given for this purpose in the whole course of our long period, though we should remark at once that the great outlays made on St Paul's comprise a heavy proportion of the whole.

Of this very large total, something like £20,000 was expended for the construction of new churches, or, more commonly, for the rebuilding and re-edification of older structures. Thus the parish church of St John the Baptist seems to have been rebuilt in 1621, though we have few particulars and have found no subscriptions at all towards the outlay.[222] St Giles in the Fields had to be completely rebuilt in 1623–1631 after the twelfth-century church had collapsed. The Dowager Duchess of Northumberland, Alice Dudley, was the principal contributor to the outlay of £2068 incurred for a new fabric, as well as providing the largest of the new bells and the furnishings and fittings at a charge of £589.[223] A few years later, St Augustine's was rebuilt at a cost of £1200,[224] while at about the same time (1628–1631) St Katherine Christchurch underwent repairs and renovations so extensive as to amount almost to a rebuilding.[225] Sir Robert Pye, an Exchequer official, and George Darell, a prebendary of Westminster, were the principal contributors to the building of the New Chapel in Tothill Fields, which was to serve as a much-needed chapel of ease to St Margaret's Church, Westminster. The building was carried forward from ca. 1631 until its completion in 1636, something over £1100 having been spent.[226] During these same years, a large church (St Paul's) was erected at Hammersmith, Middlesex, at a cost of about £2000, the rich merchant and entrepreneur, Sir Nicholas Crispe, being the principal subscriber with a gift of about £700.[227] As we have earlier observed, Sir John Wolstenholme, another great merchant who had established a seat in the suburbs, had in 1632 built the parish church of Great Stanmore, Middlesex, at his own charge.[228] The old church of St Martin in the Vintry was reconstituted in 1632 with an outlay of something like £1000,[229] while the important church of St Dunstan in the East was all but rebuilt in the next year at a total charge of over £2400.[230] Inigo Jones was the architect in charge of the rebuilding of St Albans (*ca.* 1633),[231] as well as the building of a new and large church for St Paul's Covent Garden in 1632–1638, the heavy cost of £4500 being defrayed by Francis, Earl of Bedford.[232] To conclude this account of a short but remarkable period of church building, we should note that the important city church of Allhallows Barking was very nearly rebuilt in 1634 at a cost of £1250, most of this sum being contributed by a relatively small group of great merchants.[233]

This considerable yet wholly inadequate mending and enlarging of the church fabric of London and its suburbs was accomplished only because of the hammering insistence and perseverance of Archbishop Laud.[234] So too was the work now undertaken for the restoration of the fabric of St Paul's, which, as we have seen, had stood damaged and all but untended for two full generations. In 1631 careful and elaborate plans were laid for carrying forward the work under Inigo Jones's supervision, with funds which were to be raised by at least technically voluntary gifts from the nation at large.[235] The repairs were begun in 1633 and were continued during the next nine years, the steeple being rebuilt, the fabric renovated, and the whole church enlarged. Though a much larger sum was raised, it appears that the total outlay on this great work, when it was suspended with the fall of the Archbishop, was £35,551, or well over five times the amount so grudgingly laid out in the Elizabethan period for emergency repairs. The King pledged £500 p.a. as his contribution, later undertaking to complete the repair of the whole of the west end of the church as his special responsibility.[236] Pressure was brought to bear on the parish churches of London, the Inns of Court, and the great livery companies to pledge substantial assistance to the great undertaking.[237] A careful and continuing record of bequests left for this charitable use was kept, it being reported in 1637 that by that date a total of £2749 13s 4d had been so devised by pious testators.[238] Earnest and persistent pressure was laid on all parts of the realm to make substantial and continuing gifts, though relatively little save further ill will for the Archbishop was gained from this grand design. Thus the Mayor of Poole, Dorset, dourly reported in 1634 that he could collect no more than £10 10s 10d and that further collections would not be feasible.[239] The total reported for Merioneth was £6 8s 10d, while the whole amount raised in the county of Cardigan was £39 18s 4d, it being most firmly stated in the report that no annual solicitation could be undertaken.[240] The heaviest burden of contribution lay, as usual, on the great city merchants who were all but required to come forward with conspicuously substantial benefactions for the work then under way. At least a few of these should perhaps be mentioned. The notable philanthropist, John Kendrick, had as early as 1624 left a legacy of

£1000 towards the projected repairs.[241] The rich clothworker, Sir Ralph Freeman, who had served as lord mayor in 1633–1634, by the provisions of his will proved in 1634 left £1000 towards the work then in progress on the west end of the cathedral church.[242] Sir Paul Pindar, a famous Customer, in 1631 gave £10,000 towards the renovation about to be begun and pledged himself to further contributions, though it seems doubtful that these commitments were ever fulfilled because of the rapidly declining fortunes of this once rich man.[243] Sir James Cambell, an ironmonger who had served as mayor in 1629–1630, gave £1000 towards the need, though his will, proved in 1642, seems a decidedly Puritan document.[244] These are but the largest of many contributions made by the great merchants towards the rehabilitation of St Paul's, there being nineteen such donors of amounts exceeding £100. This was a work which all men knew must be done, the neglect of which stood as a kind of symbol of the all but complete secularism of Elizabethan England.[245]

Well-sustained and certainly desperately needed efforts were also made during the two decades under consideration (1621–1640) to effect major repairs and in several instances enlargements of the parish churches of the city and its environs. At least the principal of these undertakings may be mentioned. St Leonard Eastcheap was repaired and thoroughly renovated in 1618–1621 at a charge of £850,[246] while extensive repairs were completed on St Margaret Lothbury[247] and St Mary Bothaw in 1621.[248] Something like £700 was spent on the repair and enlargement of St James Garlickhithe in 1624,[249] and very heavy outlays totalling £1400 were made on St James Clerkenwell from 1623 to 1627 to repair the great damage occasioned by the collapse of its steeple.[250] The parish churches of St Magnus and St Alphage were repaired at about the same time at a charge of something like £500 for each.[251] Extensive repairs were begun in 1626 on the church of St Mary Aldermary, to which parishioners subscribed £634,[252] while £183 was expended at the same date on St Mildred Poultry.[253] In 1628 St Mildred Bread Street was repaired and a large new window installed,[254] while in the same year great repairs and alterations costing nearly £1000 were completed in the important church of St Bartholomew the Great.[255] An impressive square tower was provided for the church at Hillingdon, Middlesex, in 1629.[256] Sir William Garway, a rich draper, had in 1615 given £400 for the enlargement of St Peter the Poor, imploring his fellow parishioners to carry forward a complete renovation, to provide a turret and a gallery, and to hang new bells. The whole work was completed in 1630 at an outlay of £1587.[257] A more modest enlargement of the church of St Katherine's by the Tower was carried forward in 1629, perhaps wholly at the charge of Sir Julius Caesar, who gave £250 for the work.[258]

Despite the great continuing need, this pace of repair and rehabilitation could not be maintained in the next decade, particularly because of the heavy drain the repairs on St Paul's were making on the so evidently reluctant interest of the city. But none the less something was done. In 1631 a lofty and beautiful tower was added to the church at Staines,[259] while work begun somewhat earlier was completed at St Andrew Undershaft at a charge of more than £600.[260] Extensive repairs, costing in all £275 5s 6d, were completed on St Margaret Pattens in 1632,[261] and a new turret and better framing for the bells at St Dionis Backchurch were provided in the same year.[262] The great merchant church, St Helen Bishopsgate, was extensively repaired and restored in 1632–1633 at a cost of upwards of £1300, the city companies and numerous great merchants defraying the costs. At about the same date, St Gabriel Fenchurch was lengthened nine feet and thoroughly renovated at a cost of £537 7s 10d,[263] while in 1637 St Martin Oteswich was thoroughly repaired and redecorated at a somewhat greater cost.[264]

As we have previously indicated, the outlays for church building, or more exactly building and major renovation, were very sharply reduced during the two decades of political and religious upheaval. But the church fabric of the city was by no means neglected, the considerable sum of £4145 being expended on major undertakings and, as we have earlier noted, £3347 10s being laid out for ordinary repairs and maintenance. We may mention at least the larger of the outlays during these years for church building. The north gallery of St Margaret's, Wesminster, was built in 1641, just as the church was all but pre-empted by the House of Commons for its innumerable sermons and days of thanksgiving and prayer. The Commons voted £200 for the repair of the church in 1647, and further repairs were carried out in 1651, though neither of these renovations has been regarded as a charitable benefaction. Robert Gayer, a fishmonger, in 1649 left £100 towards the building of a new church in Plymouth, Devon,[265] while a few years later a large chapel and a suitable vicarage were provided at Poplar, Middlesex, by members of the East India Company, the total outlay being £2250.[266] The thirteenth-century church at Chiswick, Middlesex, partly rebuilt in the sixteenth century, was enlarged and greatly improved from 1649 to 1658, the total charge, borne by leading parishioners, amounting to upwards of £600.[267] The Puritans, then, were neither despoilers of churches nor insensitive to the needs of their fabric; in point of fact, the Lord Protector's daughter worshipped at Chiswick and was one of the supporters of the renovation program carried forward on this church. But they were not unaffected by the deep-seated, the now prevailing secularism which had overwhelmed England in the half-century following on the Reformation. They, and this includes most of the mercantile elite of London, were simply more interested in other causes, more devoted to other and, as they thought, more pressing and more godly needs. These men and their predecessors had permitted the church fabric of London and of England to fall into a state uncomfortably close to ruin, but their prodigal generosity had at the same time built great and effective institutions which may well have provided an even nobler habitation for mankind.

London and the Nation

The great gifts flowing out from London to every part of the realm had immensely important consequences. In three-fourths of all the English counties these great benefactions were of a size and quality which were to make them dominant in the shaping of the institutional life and the culture of the areas thus favoured. We have observed that these benefactions were with few exceptions large in amount, were concentrated on useful purposes, and were made relatively early in the social development of each county. They tended to mould the institutions of a favoured county into a pattern of aspirations in keeping with the vision these enlightened men had of a new age and a new society. We have dealt with at least the larger and more significant of these great and decisive charities, but we should now attempt a somewhat more general comment on them and their distribution, as well as seeking some explanation for the extraordinary want of parochialism on the part of these great London donors.

We have noted in the course of our period gifts in the enormous total of £584,741 8s (gifts to the universities and for university fellowships being excluded) made by Londoners to areas lying outside the confines of Middlesex.[1] The tremendous weight and significance of this massive sum is suggested when we reflect that very nearly a fourth (23·55 per cent) of all the charitable funds of the nine counties, London aside, we have examined were derived from London sources. And we may safely assume that for the whole of the realm something like this formidable percentage prevails. But the social and historical effectiveness of these great benefactions far exceeded their quantitative weight, for a very large proportion of them were in capital form, they were skilfully devised and administered, and they were on balance dedicated to purposes which reflected the needs not only of the present but of the future. These benefactions made for the needs of other parts of the realm represented very nearly a third (30·95 per cent) of the enormous total of the charitable wealth disposed by Londoners during the whole course of our period. We shall later observe that an overwhelming proportion of the whole sum was given by merchant donors and that almost 40 per cent (37·80 per cent) of all merchant benefactors left some charitable bequest outside the county of Middlesex. Very evidently, then, these donors saw the needs of their age from the point of view of the realm as a whole, and they were moved by an evangelical fervour as they sought to secure the translation of their cultural and historical aspirations into institutional form.

It should be noted, too, that London benefactors displayed a quite different structure of aspirations as they contemplated the needs of the nation at large than when they took in view the institutional requirements of their own city. Thus, they gave in all £228,270 18s to the needs of the poor outside the capital, this representing 39·04 per cent of the extra-London total as compared with the 35·18 per cent of their charitable wealth given for the needs of the London poor. Moreover, a considerably larger proportion of their gifts for poor relief in other counties was in the institutional form of almshouse endowments than was the case in London proper. Roughly speaking, London donors gave about as much proportionately to schemes of social rehabilitation and to municipal betterments beyond the county borders as within London itself. It is most instructive to observe, however, that they gave the enormous sum of £199,049 4s (university gifts not being included) to the educational needs of all parts of the realm, this representing rather more than a third (34·04 per cent) of all their extra-mural benefactions and standing in sharp and important contrast to the 27·04 per cent of London benefactions generally dedicated to educational requirements. But an even more striking contrast is presented when one considers that somewhat less than a tenth (9·78 per cent) of their gifts for the needs of other counties was designated for religious purposes, while proportionately almost twice as much (19·50 per cent) of the whole of London's charitable wealth was disposed for religious uses.*

The special strength of these London benefactions is to be discovered in the fact that they were in most cases very large and that they were almost invariably disposed in carefully disciplined capital sums. Thus of the generous total of £228,270 18s vested for various forms of poor relief, the significantly high proportion of 89·76 per cent was in capital, thereby creating effective social institutions in all parts of the realm for dealing with the appallingly difficult problems of indigence. The largest of these endowments was of course that created by Henry Smith,

* The various proportions are as follows:

	Extra-Middlesex gifts by Londoners Per cent	London totals Per cent
Poor relief	39·04	35·18
Social rehabilitation	12·30	13·32
Municipal betterments	4·85	4·95
Education	34·04	27·04
Religion	9·78	19·50

which vested capital of £39,300 for carefully defined and skilfully administered poor relief in 219 parishes spread over more than half the counties of England and Wales.[2] The all-pervading effect of London's concern for the problem of poverty is suggested when we observe that its benefactors were in the course of our period to establish endowments of £100 or more in 367 additional parishes in various parts of the realm, with the consequence that, Smith's trust being included, substantial capital sums were disposed by London generosity in 577 communities in all parts of England and Wales.[3] Some of these individual benefactions were really huge, there having been twenty-eight which established for as many communities endowments for the care of the poor ranging upwards from £1000. In twenty-seven of the English counties, London donors had established capital sums for the relief of poverty totalling more than £1000, and no county in the realm failed to participate in some measure in the boundless generosity of these merchant donors.

As we have noted in detail in earlier pages,[4] a very considerable proportion of the sums disposed by London donors for poor relief in other parts of the realm were in the socially useful and effective form of almshouse endowments. In all, the massive total of £82,248 was vested by these benefactors in the founding of seventy-two almshouses in all parts of the kingdom. Some measure of the extent and vitality of this concern is suggested by the fact that for a generation and more, from 1601 forward to 1634, London benefactors were in average terms founding one almshouse a year in counties other than Middlesex. Though these foundations were heavily concentrated in the southern third of England, there were few counties indeed which did not benefit at least to the extent of one such foundation. Nor was this all. These were on balance large, well-endowed, most carefully administered, and socially useful institutions which served in most counties of the realm as conspicuously successful models which in their turn were to excite local donors to undertake smaller but none the less important foundations. London benefactions tended, then, to possess a considerable qualitative strength, since these merchant donors were animated by prescient aspirations for their age and culture.

Quite as notable was the immensely important role played by the merchant benefactors of London in establishing a remarkable system of endowed education in all parts of the realm. In all, London donors gave the huge total of £199,049 4s for the educational needs of England outside Middlesex, not taking into account the large sums which they gave as well to the universities and for university scholarships and fellowships. A large proportion of this great capital sum was vested in the foundation of 123 endowed schools in all parts of the realm, not to mention the institution of a fair number of unendowed schools and the substantial augmentation of the funds of a considerable number of scantily endowed foundations. This was perhaps the most significant single achievement of the merchant aristocracy of London as it sought to create a new society in the terms of its enlightened and intensely evangelical aspirations. Though at least one of these foundations was vested in all save six English counties, there was, as we have earlier noted, a very heavy concentration of these schools established along the western borders of England. In the tier of eleven counties extending southwards from Cumberland to Somerset, fifty-eight such foundations were made by London generosity in regions which were on the whole backward in their cultural resources and in considerable stretches of which a stubbornly surviving Catholicism was equated with ignorance by these sternly Puritan donors.* Very nearly half of all these great endowments were sited in this area of greatest need, with another considerable concentration in Yorkshire and in the counties lying in a great arc around London itself. Eastern England generally, and East Anglia more particularly, received relatively few of these foundations because these were comparatively prosperous and advanced regions, because they were firmly and staunchly Protestant, and because they supplied relatively few of the store of men from which the mercantile aristocracy recruited itself.

The spread of London's benefactions over the several counties of the realm suggests a most interesting and certainly a complex pattern of concern on the part of these donors. We have endeavoured on the appended map to portray the flow of these charitable funds by dividing the favoured counties into five roughly defined categories of amount.†
More precise detail is afforded in the likewise appended table which provides not only the total given by London donors for each of the great charitable heads in all the counties, but which indicates as well the relation of the place of birth to the benefaction and suggests the social status of the principal benefactors.‡

In very general terms, it may be observed that the great weight of London benefactions was concentrated in three fairly well-defined areas. There were first the seven counties lying close about Middlesex which were intimately connected culturally and economically with the capital and constituted a favourite region for investment in landed properties and often for retirement by the great merchants of London.[5] The enor-

---

* These counties are:

Cumberland	2	Staffordshire	5
Westmorland	2	Herefordshire	4
Lancashire	15	Worcestershire	4
Cheshire	7	Gloucestershire	
Derby	3	(including Bristol)	2
Shropshire	9	Somerset	5
			58

† *Vide* Map II.
‡ *Vide* Table II (Appendix).

mous total of £233,456 1s was vested by London donors for the charitable institutions of these most favoured counties, this being almost 40
per cent of the whole of the great sums provided by the capital for the
regions outside Middlesex proper. In each of these counties, upwards of
£10,000 was given, while in four of them more than £20,000 of endowments were concentrated for the building of those institutions upon
which the liberal society was to be founded. In all these counties we may
say with certainty that the influence of London and of its aspirations was
to be decisive. We have already mentioned and to a degree analyzed the
nature of the ties which bound London so closely with these counties,
lying as they did in a great arc around the city. But probably most important of all was the fact that of the 403 great merchants noted in the
whole course of our period almost exactly a fifth (20·60 per cent) were
natives of these counties, being men who had come up to London as
apprentices and who had gained great fortunes in the bitter, but occasionally fabulously rewarding commercial competition of the age.
These were men who, when the time came to order their affairs, almost
invariably remembered their native parish with rich endowments which
would give youth in these rural areas fair opportunity and make available
to them the competences required by a new and a much more highly
complicated society. Much, then, depended in this spread of London's
generosity on genetic accident and the traditions by which the inflow of
apprentices was regulated. Hampshire and Kent supplied a large number of apprentices who became merchants and a fair number, twenty-six
in all, who became great merchants. Sussex, lying not much more distant, was to give London only three great merchants in our entire period,
and the total of London's benefactions to that populous county was to
be no more than relatively modest £5541 15s.

But these were old, populous, relatively settled, and near-by counties
which would inevitably have been subject to a considerable degree of
influence and leadership from the teeming and immensely prosperous
London of our period. More interesting, therefore, is the tier of seven
counties on the western borders of the realm all very distant, all lying
well to the west of the economic watershed of London's commercial
dominance, and in five instances relatively poor and backward.[6] Yet it
was precisely in this area that London's evangelical fervour was to be so
heavily concentrated. It was here that a large proportion of the grammar
schools were founded by London benefactors, and it was here as well
that great endowments for poor relief and for almshouses were disposed.
In each of these seven counties, well over £10,000 was vested, an amount,
particularly when the nature of the trusts is taken into account, which
was to exercise an immediate and certainly a dominant effect in the
shaping of the institutions and the culture of this entire area. In all, the
huge total of £116,417 2s was poured into these western reaches, this

constituting about a fifth (19·91 per cent) of the whole of the extra-mural endowments made by Londoners.

The explanation for this extraordinary concentration of charitable funds is clearly two fold. The first and perhaps more important is that this great region, mostly marginal in sixteenth-century economic terms and on balance quite thinly populated, was through the whole course of our period a continuous supplier of men, of leadership, to London. Of the tightly defined mercantile elite, these distant counties supplied fifty-nine of the 403 great merchants of the period, or almost 15 per cent (14·64 per cent) of the whole number. Thus Shropshire alone was to give to London ten lord mayors during our era and was in all to provide sixteen of the great merchants of the age. London, by which we really mean these men, rewarded this remote county with charitable endow-ments totalling £15,304 16s, including three well-endowed almshouses, nine endowed schools, and substantial agumentations of the funds of other existing schools. Secondly, the needs of this remote and institu-tionally backward area appealed to the evangelical aspirations of London merchants more generally. In will after will, eloquent reference is made to the needs, the shortcomings, and the poverty of these 'rude', 'popish', or 'ignorant' reaches of the realm. Hence, though the proportion of charitable endowments concentrated in these seven counties by native sons was very large indeed, it is important to note that of the total of 310 London donors who made benefactions in this region, fifty-eight were not western-born. These men of London were moved by a vision of a new and a better England. They were men emancipated from all parochialism, who took the whole of the realm in view as they framed institutions of a society which broke sharply and irrevocably with the medieval past.

The evangelical compulsions which animated these great donors is quite as clearly seen in the extraordinary and continuous interest taken by London benefactors in Wales, lying as it did just to the west of the region we have been discussing. In all, the large total of £20,281 was given by Londoners for the development of Welsh institutions, with a particularly heavy outlay of £13,102 for the educational needs of this truly remote and certainly retarded area. Wales, too, was a supplier of men to London, nine of the great merchants, of whom three became lord mayors, having been natives of the region. In total, however, the great charitable sum just mentioned was provided by forty-one individual London donors, of which number only twenty-three were certainly Welsh-born and of whom twelve were certainly English-born. Most of these great extra-mural benefactions were rooted in sentiment, as per-haps all human actions should be, but they were quite evidently dis-ciplined as well by a cool and hard sense of the importance of vesting funds in relation to need and opportunity.

There was, as well, an interesting grouping of four highly favoured counties in the far reaches of the north.[7] The very large total of £107,091 9s was disposed by London benefactors for the building of the charitable institutions of these remote regions, in two of these counties a conscious and a most successful effort having been deliberately undertaken to win stubbornly and conservatively Catholic areas to the ranks of the godly. The extraordinarily high proportion of 18·31 per cent of all the extra-mural charities of London were concentrated in this region, an amazingly large fraction of the whole having been given by men who were not native sons but who had been persuaded that the interests of the kingdom required the lifting up of these distant areas by the extension of opportunity and a concerted assault upon ignorance and poverty. Several of the greatest of these benefactions were disposed with almost scientific dispassion as donors, whether native or not, sought carefully and systematically to create a wholly new structure of opportunity in the north.

We have dealt in some detail with widely separated groupings of counties in which London's almost prodigal generosity was largely concentrated. More precisely, rather more than four-fifths (81·62 per cent) of all the massive total provided for counties outside Middlesex was disposed for the benefit of these highly favoured regions. It is likewise important to comment on certain other groupings which were either only modestly or most scantily provided for from the immense flow of London's charitable benefactions. A glance at the accompanying map or the preceding table will suggest that the Midland counties generally received modest, or average, support for their charitable needs.* But, more significantly, there is a group of six Midland and East Anglian counties, all being contiguous, which received very little indeed from London donors.[8] In total, these counties as a group received only £12,812 2s of London funds. Some suggestion of the relative meagreness of this amount is gained when we say that there were thirteen counties in England each of which received more than this aggregate sum, and four more each of which benefited by nearly this amount. These counties as a group gained no more than 2·19 per cent of the whole of London's extra-mural charities. There are evidently at least two explanations. All these counties were old, well led by a strong local gentry, solidly Protestant, and on balance among the most properous of all the reaches of the realm. There was not, then, clear evidence of need; this was not an area inviting prudent and needed investment in social institutions. As important, and perhaps because they were in themselves areas of opportunity, these counties were not in any real sense suppliers of men, of leadership, to London. This great region was to supply only twenty-four of all the great merchants of our

* *Vide* Map II and Table II.

period, there being an evident and interesting correlation between the fact that it was to produce 5·95 per cent of the great liveried merchants and was to gain no more than 2·19 per cent of London's immense charitable wealth disposed for the aid of the realm at large.

This important correlation can be even more dramatically demonstrated by a somewhat artificial selection of the four counties least favoured in all the realm, though they represent no regional grouping. These counties, Cumberland, Dorset, Nottinghamshire, and Rutland, were the only four in the entire kingdom to receive less than £1000 each of London's charitable benefactions. Only one, Cumberland, was truly remote and backward, Dorset being probably marginal in terms of its prosperity, population, and connections with the metropolis. But, in all, these four counties gained only £1489 of the charitable wealth being disposed by London donors, amounting to the insignificant proportion of 0·25 per cent of the whole of London's extra-mural charities. The reason is in this case very evident indeed, since these four counties supplied only six of the great merchants of our period, three of whom, it so happened, were substantial donors to the charitable needs of London but scarcely more than nominal benefactors to their native counties.

Dorset is a particularly interesting example of a neglected area, since it stands in such dramatic contrast to the well-favoured counties which ringed it about. These neighbouring counties—Devon, Somerset, Wiltshire, and Hampshire—together benefited enormously from London's great generosity, having received the massive sum of £71,653 6s for their charitable and institutional needs. This amounts to the sizeable proportion of 12·25 per cent of the whole of London's extra-mural charitable dispositions and is surely to be explained by the fact that thirty-two of the great merchants of our period (7·94 per cent of the whole number) were natives of these counties and that of this number the extraordinary total of nineteen reached the eminence of the mayoralty. Dorset, in the most gloomy contrast, received no more than £437 17s in charitable funds from London during the whole of our period. This insignificant total is composed of eleven separate gifts, ranging in time from 1557 to 1657, of which only one, given by a tradesman, was much more than nominal in amount. Only four of the merchant donors of London in our period were drawn from Dorset, and of these only one was of the dignity and wealth with which we have defined the great merchants. Of the remaining London donors to Dorset, one was a widow of uncertain social status, three were tradesmen, two were artisans, and one a decidedly impecunious lawyer. Of the eleven London donors, ten were certainly natives of Dorset, but these men and women were in terms of quality as well as number among the least important of all the county groups from which London recruited its workers and its leaders. Intensely parochial in this period, bound to the sea, proud and self-sufficient, Dorset was simply neglected and isolated as the immense flood of London's generosity poured out over the kingdom.

We have seen that there is a clear and important relationship between the place of birth of these great London donors and the disposition of their charitable estates. It has been noted that of the 2677 merchant donors, including lesser as well as greater merchants, who left charitable bequests in the whole course of our period, the amazing proportion of 37·80 per cent gave charitable sums outside London, while almost a third (30·95 per cent) of the immense total of London's charitable wealth was vested for the uses of counties other than Middlesex. This amazing fact is fully explained because a really incredible proportion of the leaders of this great urban complex were born outside London and by the closely related fact that only rarely indeed was a great merchant house continued through the second generation in the same family. The mercantile aristocracy of London was an all but completely fluid society, recruited almost wholly from outside the metropolis. The commercial life of London was cruelly competitive, fortunes were quickly made and as quickly lost, and it was only the agile, the fit, and the prudent who ended their term of years as lord mayors, as great civic dignitaries, and as great benefactors. This nervous, this kaleidoscopic, and this immensely vital society deserves close and analytic study, but a few observations immediately pertinent to our present concern may well be made.

There were in all 438 great merchants who were charitable donors in London in the course of our period, thirty-five of this number being wives or widows who were often rich and extremely generous in their own right. In all, then, there were 403 great merchants, more strictly defined, with whom we are concerned as a social and economic group of extraordinary interest and significance. Included in this relatively very small group of the commercial elite, are 172 lord mayors who died in the interval 1480–1660, of which number, it may be noted, 166 left substantial charitable benefactions. Quite incredibly, only fourteen of all the London mayors of our period were London-born, this representing no more than 8·14 per cent of the whole number.[9] But the lord mayors were only part of a larger group of great merchants which, as we have said, numbered 403 in all, and it is this body of civic leaders with which we have been and are now principally concerned. Of this class, only thirty-four (8·44 per cent) were London-born, the place of birth of fifty-eight (14·39 per cent)[10] is unknown, while all the remainder were born elsewhere in the realm. This very thin proportion of merchant leaders recruited from London held practically level through our whole period, the proportion of London-born merchant leaders who died in the interval 1480–1560, for example, being 7·83 per cent, sinking slightly in the Elizabethan era, and then rising to slightly more than 13 per cent during the last two generations of our period. The great reservoir of ability on which London drew lay in the west, almost a quarter (23·57 per cent) of all the great merchants of the capital having been drawn from a bank of eight counties, Wales being counted as one, extending southwards from Lancashire to Devon.[11] Staffordshire and Shropshire alone supplied more of the great merchants of our period (37) than did London itself, while this grouping of western counties taken as a whole was to provide nearly three times as many. And, as we have previously emphasized, it was quite precisely in this great western region that so large a proportion of London's charitable wealth was to be vested. Another block of four counties along the eastern coast of the realm, extending southward from Yorkshire to Suffolk, was to give to London 47 of its great merchants during our period,[12] while four peripheral counties, these being Essex, Hertfordshire, Kent, and Surrey, were to supply 62 merchant leaders. In all, these three regions were together to produce more than half of all the great merchants of our period. At the same time, however, as a glance at the appended map* and our table† will suggest, the remarkable fact is that the great merchants were drawn from every part of the realm during our era, at least one being produced by every county save Durham, and that London itself was to contribute so few of these extremely able and very powerful men.

Though our data regarding the place of birth of all merchant donors, greater and lesser, leaves much to be desired in terms of completeness, the findings do seem strikingly and convincingly similar. We have in all recorded charitable contributions from 2677 merchant donors in London in the course of our period. Of this very substantial number, 185 were the wives or widows of merchants, while the birthplace of another large

* *Vide* Map III.

† Birthplaces of London great merchants whose dates of death fall in the period 1480–1660:

London	34	Hampshire	7	Staffordshire	21
Middlesex	9	Herefordshire	4	Suffolk	11
		Hertfordshire	15	Surrey	13
Bedfordshire	5	Huntingdonshire	5	Sussex	3
Berkshire	7	Kent	19	Warwickshire	8
Buckinghamshire	7	Lancashire	9	Westmorland	1
Cambridgeshire	5	Leicestershire	5	Wiltshire	5
Cheshire	14	Lincolnshire	11	Worcestershire	3
Cornwall	1	Norfolk	11	Yorkshire	14
Cumberland	1	Northamptonshire	4		
Derbyshire	6	Northumberland	1	Ireland	3
Devon	9	Nottinghamshire	2	Wales	9
Dorset	1	Oxfordshire	5	Scotland	2
Durham	0	Rutland	2	Abroad	4
Essex	15	Shropshire	16	Isle of Man	1
Gloucestershire	6	Somerset		Uncertain	58
		(including Bristol)	11	*Total:*	403

group of 1679 has not been definitely determined.[13] There remain 813 liveried merchants whose birthplace is known, and of this number only seventy-five, or 9·22 per cent, were natives of London, while another twelve were drawn from rural or suburban Middlesex. The distribution of birthplaces of this large group of important and responsible commercial leaders is somewhat more evenly spread over the whole realm than is the case with the great merchants, though the large total of 307, amounting to almost 38 per cent (37·76 per cent) of the whole number, was drawn from nine quite scattered counties.[14] There were only five counties in the whole of the kingdom supplying fewer than five merchants to London, while a considerably larger proportion of foreigners were able to attain the status of merchant than great merchant.[15]

Most surprisingly, an even smaller proportion of the tradesmen of London seem to have been city-born. We have been able to determine the place of birth of a substantial group of 389 of these shopkeepers and retailers, of whom only fifteen (3·86 per cent) were natives of London. There were, in fact, seven counties, these being Buckinghamshire, Essex, Hertfordshire, Kent, Lancashire, Surrey, and Yorkshire, in which more of these lesser but still substantial burghers were born than in the city in which they carried on their business and to which they contributed so substantially in terms of leadership and philanthropic responsibility. Moreover, the evident fact that the rich and responsible citizenry of London were with few exceptions drawn from the kingdom at large is further substantiated by our record that of the 130 members of the several professional classes whose birthplace can be ascertained, only nine, or 6·92 per cent, were natives of London or Middlesex.

The city of London, growing rapidly throughout our period, was a mecca for restless and ambitious youths. It drew very heavily indeed on the whole of the realm for its ability and its leadership just as it did for its skilled and unskilled labour. It was a vigorous and a versatile urban complex in which opportunities, and risks, were greater than in any other single community in the western world during our whole era. But just as it drew great talent from the whole of England, so, as we have observed, it repaid its debt and more in the swelling flow of charitable funds which reached out into every nook and cranny of the kingdom. It was a society led and completely dominated by rich, highly articulate, and very powerful men who shared an uncommonly tight and disciplined body of aspirations for themselves, for their city, and for their whole society. There was much of prescience, and much of wisdom, in their view of their own age and the age that was to follow. They possessed the wealth, the courage, and the solidity of purpose required to make their vision of the future of their society become an historical reality. These were the men who were the architects of modern England and, it is not too much to say, of the western world.

Notes

CHAPTER I. THE CITY AND ITS PEOPLE

1. Besant, Walter, *London in the time of the Stuarts* (L., 1903), 172–173.
2. Creighton, whose careful work on population estimates for the city remains impressive, arrived at a population of about 46,000 for 1377 by an analysis of the poll-tax rolls for that year. [Creighton, Charles, 'The population of old London', *Blackwood's Edinburgh Magazine*, CXLIX (1891), 477–496].
3. Creighton estimated the population as 339,824 in 1634.
4. Latimer, John, *The history of the . . . merchant venturers of Bristol* (Bristol, 1903), 144.
5. Steele, Robert, ed., *A bibliography of royal proclamations . . . 1485–1714* (Oxford, 1910, 2 vols.), No. 749.
6. *35 Eliz., c. 6* (1593).
7. Maitland, William, *et al.*, *The history . . . of London* (L., 1756, 2 vols.), I, 279.
8. Steele, *Proclamations*, No. 927.

CHAPTER II. GENERAL COMMENTS ON THE DATA

1. We should say again that here and throughout the study the terms London and Middlesex will be used interchangeably. The total of benefactions given is that for the county of Middlesex, a very large proportion of which was, of course, from London proper. More precisely, 79·41 per cent of the whole was given by London residents, 7·34 per cent by inhabitants of Westminster, and 13·25 per cent by the rest of the county, there being a very heavy proportion of gifts by London merchants technically resident in rural parishes in this latter total.
2. The average benefactions for the several counties are as follows:

	£	s	d		£	s	d
Bristol	173	6	9	London	255	12	2
Buckinghamshire	51	3	10	Norfolk	65	10	10
Hampshire	44	10	2	Somerset	32	2	3
Kent	37	15	10	Worcestershire	66	17	10
Lancashire	110	9	10	Yorkshire	28	4	6

3. Only Bristol, where 10·42 per cent of all charitable funds were devoted to this purpose, is at all comparable.

4. The statement remains true even though we are not wholly content with the decision to regard the early gifts for the endowment of Christ's Hospital as founding a hospital rather than an almshouse or a school. *Vide post*, 191–192, 212–214, for a more detailed discussion of the problem.

5. It should, however, be remarked that this prudence was general. The proportion of capital gifts ranges from 76·83 per cent for Lancashire to 91 per cent for Bristol.

6. The proportion left by will ranges eccentrically and widely in the counties studied from 27·60 per cent in Buckinghamshire to 77·75 per cent in Bristol.

CHAPTER III. THE ASPIRATIONS OF WOMEN DONORS

1. *Vide* Jordan, W. K., *Philanthropy in England, 1480–1660* (L., 1959) 327, 328, 353–355, 382–383 for a general discussion of the role of women in the social history of the period and for particulars regarding the extent of their contributions to the charitable needs of the several counties included in this study.

2. It should be added that seven of this group are not absolutely identified as of the merchant class, though the size and nature of their fortunes, as well as the structure of their benefactions, seem so nearly to establish identification as to permit inclusion in this particular analysis.

CHAPTER IV. THE WEB OF PARISHES

1. *Vide ante*, 15–16.

2. Stow lists 119 churches, the Westminster parishes being excluded. Camden's count was 121 for the city and its suburbs, 73 in the remainder of Middlesex (*Britain*, Philemon Holland, trans., L., 1637, 437). An undated, but evidently late Tudor, count of uncertain authorship of the 'number and names of parishes within the city, liberties and suburbs' lists the number as 115 (*BM Royal MSS.*, 18 D iii, f. 3b). *Vide* Firth, C. H., and R. S. Rait, eds., *Acts and ordinances of the Interregnum* (L., 1911, 3 vols.), I, 750–753, for the count at the close of our period.

3. *Vide post*, 151–153, 205, 218.

4. *Vide post*, 117–122, 182.

5. The amounts given by residents of this parish in the various intervals tell us a great deal about its rise as a merchant centre:

	£	s
1480–1540	1,553	7
1541–1560	1,399	14
1561–1600	431	15
1601–1640	19,697	7
1641–1660	22,116	19
	45,199	2

CHAPTER V. THE STRUCTURE OF CLASS ASPIRATIONS

1. The proportion of donors identified in Bristol (88·32 per cent) was very nearly the same.

2. Thrupp, S. L., *The merchant class of medieval London* (Chicago, 1948), 6.

3. *Ibid.*, 200–204, 208–210. Miss Thrupp reckons that from 1436 to 1527 between 28 per cent and 38·7 per cent of London merchants died leaving no male heirs.

4. Breton, Nicholas, *A poste with a packet of mad letters* (L., 1602, 1637), 77–79.

5. We must necessarily treat the subject of merchant fortunes and, more particularly, the landholdings of the class with brevity in the present context. We hope at a later date and in a more relevant connection to present the data in hand more fully and adequately.

6. We shall be content with stating that the worth of the lesser merchants, there being 212 estates of such donors which can be accurately valued, was simply of a different order of magnitude. The average estate, for the whole period, of members of this group was £2806 7s 4d, or only a fraction of the worth of their great contemporaries. None the less, it must be remarked that their wealth compares very favourably indeed with that of the lower gentry in the same period. These donors likewise gave substantially smaller proportions of their whole wealth for charitable purposes, the proportion for our whole period being 11·08 per cent. The difference in social responsibility was, then, quite as marked as in wealth.

7. It appears that 172 lord mayors died in the course of our period. Of this number 166 left charitable bequests, though in some cases relatively small ones, and are accordingly included within the group under discussion.

8. The median gift made by the mercantile elite was that of Robert Hilson, a mercer who died in 1583, it being in the amount of £897 3s. The average was, of course, swollen by a considerable number of immense bequests left by members of the class.

9. Interestingly, 37·07 per cent of all the charitable contributions of Bristol's merchants were made in this interval. Bristol was beginning to decline in the next period, whereas London was just entering on an era of immense growth in wealth and in population. For London as a whole, only 13·78 per cent of all charities were vested in the Elizabethan age.

10. The totals given to charitable uses by the great merchants by decade intervals during the early Stuart period were as follows:

	£	s
1601–1610	57,400	9
1611–1620	212,274	2
1621–1630	161,972	11
1631–1640	104,255	5
	535,902	7

11. It will be recalled that this last sum is to be compared with the total of £9 14s given by members of this group for general church uses during the whole of the Elizabethan age.

12. The proportion of total benefactions designated by the great merchants for educational uses was as follows for the several intervals:

	per cent
1480–1540	12·82
1541–1560	28·97
1561–1600	35·89
1601–1640	29·32
1641–1660	20·35

For London as a whole, the proportion of total charities dedicated to educational uses actually increased from 25·70 per cent in the early Stuart interval to 26·94 per cent in our last period.

13. *Vide ante*, 55, for a working definition of the term 'tradesman'.

14. The proportions given by tradesmen for the various forms of poor relief in the successive time intervals may be usefully compared with those for London as a whole:

	Tradesmen per cent	London per cent
1480–1540	33·71	14·95
1541–1560	47·89	20·60
1561–1600	47·27	33·37
1601–1640	47·55	40·48
1641–1660	60·96	45·18

15. Very nearly a fourth (24·17 per cent) of this whole group were widows.

16. Thrupp, *Merchant class*, 41–51, provides a particularly careful and detailed study of the structure of London's commercial population in the early years of our period.

CHAPTER VI. THE ACHIEVEMENTS OF THE AGE

A. The relief of the poor

1. The history of the enlightened concern of London's municipal authorities with the problem of poverty and vagrancy has been well and fully treated for our period (Leonard, E. M., *The early history of English poor relief*, Cambridge, 1900, 23–40, 95–101). Our interest is, of course, directed more to the role of private charity in dealing with these grave social problems.

2. The Recorder of London (Fleetwood), in reporting to Lord Burghley on measures recently taken to repress vagabondage in and around the city, indicated that 250 such persons had been arrested and punished. Only twelve of the number were residents of Middlesex and Surrey, and few, if any, of the remainder had been in London for more than three or four months. The remainder had been drawn to the city from all parts of the realm, but with the largest number from Wales, Shropshire, Cheshire, Somerset, Berkshire, Oxfordshire, and Essex. (Tawney, R. H., and

Eileen Power, eds., *Tudor economic documents*, N.Y., 1924, 3 vols., II, 335–336).

3. Here and in later statistical summaries we are assuming inexactly that the whole of London's charitable dispositions were made specifically for London's benefit. To do otherwise would be greatly to complicate an already intricate discussion. The great flow of London's charitable wealth to other parts of the realm will, however, be fully discussed in a separate treatment (*vide post*, 308–318).

4. We can, of course, lend special treatment only to the very large or the very unusual bequests in London; the wealth of material is simply too great. In other counties it has been our roughly defined rule to give some notice to donors providing as much as £100 for charities. But in London so vast was the giving that in general we can comment only on those benefactors who gave a total of at least £400 for charitable uses and as much as £100 for a specific charitable purpose. This imposes a rigorous limitation, for £400 was in our period a most comfortable competence.

5. PCC 4 Logge 1481; Beaven, *Aldermen*, II, 12, 165. Yong likewise left £30 for prayers and £50 for various monastic uses. He was the son of Thomas Yong, Mayor of Bristol, and was distantly related to the famous Thomas Canyng, Mayor of Bristol in 1456. Yong, who was a merchant of the staple, as well as a leading grocer, having been master of his company on three occasions, was a Member of Parliament for London in 1455 and for Guildford in 1467. He was chosen sheriff in 1455, was mayor in 1466, and was knighted in 1471.

6. PCC 17 Logge 1485; Russan, L., *Old London city* (L., 1924), 170; Beaven, *Aldermen*, II, xxviii, 15, 166; Stow, *Survey*, I, 211; Thrupp, *Merchant class*, 176–177. Hill's charities reached the substantial total of £560 13s out of an estate valued at about £2400. In addition to large gifts for prayers (*vide post*, 274) and church repairs, he left £11 for general church uses, £30 to three prisons for bread for five years, £33 6s 8d for a conduit to carry water to Paddington, and £66 13s 4d for a conduit to carry water to Gracechurch, if the work could be carried forward within five years, and £13 6s 8d for street and road repairs. Hill wished to be buried in St Thomas Acon, but utterly prohibited 'any moneth mynde to be kept solemnely for me after the guyse of the world' or any funeral dinner save for bread, cheese, and ale for the priests. He was thrice master of his company, had been auditor in 1473 and 1480, and was chosen mayor in 1484. He died of sweating sickness while in office, as did his successor and four other aldermen then serving.

7. PCC 4 Milles 1487; Sharpe, R. R., ed., *Calendar of wills proved . . . in the Court of Husting, London* (L., 1889–1890, 2 vols.), II, 592–593; Thrupp, *Merchant class*, 337; Cook, G. H. *Mediaeval chantries* (L., 1947), 40; Beaven, *Aldermen*, II, 13, 165. Drope, a native of Huntingdonshire, was a draper, serving his company as master on at least two occasions. He was mayor in 1474. His widow, Joan, married Edward Grey, Viscount Lisle, and was herself a generous benefactor to the needs of the city. Drope, while mayor, greatly enlarged the reservoir feeding the Cornhill conduit. By his will he also left £20 in marriage subsidies for sixty poor

maids, £61 for prayers, £2 for general church uses, £86 for vestments and church repairs, £10 to his company for general purposes, and £21 for the relief of prisoners.

8. PCC 2 Horne 1496; Beaven, *Aldermen*, II, 18, 167; *Husting*, II, 595; Herbert, William, *The history of the twelve great livery companies of London* (L., 1834–1836, 2 vols.), I, 252; DNB. Clopton was the younger son of John de Clopton, lord of the manor of Clopton, near Stratford-upon-Avon. He made a great fortune as a mercer and was chosen successively master of his company, sheriff, and mayor (1492), in which latter year he was knighted. He built a house in Stratford which was somewhat more than a century later to be purchased by Shakespeare. He died in 1496 at his town house in St Margaret Lothbury, where he was buried. Clopton never married. In addition to his large bequests for municipal uses and prayers (*vide post*, 197, 275), he left £68 for marriage portions in Stratford, £20 for prisoners, £8 to hospitals, an estimated £40 to Whittington College, and £45 for scholarships at Oxford and Cambridge.

9. PCC 10 Moone 1500; Stow, *Survey*, I, 197; Nicolas, N. H., *Testamenta vetusta* (L., 1826, 2 vols.), II, 466–467; Kent Archaeological Society, *Kent Records III* (Canterbury, 1914), 127–145; Cokayne, G. E., ed., *The complete peerage* (L., 1887–1898, 8 vols.), V, 166; Albertson, Mary, *London merchants* (Philadelphia, 1932), 29. Her outlays for religious uses will be treated in later pages (*vide post*, 293).

10. PCC 9 Dogett 1492; Reede, a native of Essex, was a dyer by trade.

11. PCC 1 Horne 1496; Stow, *Survey*, I, 246; *The citizen's pocket chronicle . . . of London* (L., 1828), 313; Fuller, Thomas, *The history of the worthies of England* (L., 1840, 3 vols.), I, 241; Beaven, *Aldermen*, II, 16. Horne also left £1 for church general, £20 for the redeeming of prisoners, £42 to monasteries for prayers, and £20 towards new bells in St Thomas Apostle. He likewise bequeathed £333 6s 8d for the mending of the road from London to Cambridge, but this bequest failed, presumably because the charitable bequests (£674 13s) considerably exceeded the sum available after family and personal bequests had been met. Horne was a native of Snailwell, Cambridgeshire, to whose church he left £20 for the repairing of an image and the making of a tabernacle, as well as placing glass in the east window to portray his parents and their twenty-four children, with himself and his wife and their twelve children. This salter's original name was Littleberry, but he had been renamed Horne by Edward IV, who knighted him on the field, because of his mastery of that instrument. He served as mayor in 1487.

12. PCC 11 Moone 1501; Thrupp, *Merchant class*, 267, 372; *London and Middlesex Archaeological Society Transactions*, n.s., VI (1931), 66; Beaven, *Aldermen*, II, 15. Warde, in addition to a large capital bequest left for prayers (*vide post*, 275), also provided £40 for marriage portions, £4 for an almshouse, £50 for the relief of prisoners, £10 for bedridden persons, £20 for the repair of London streets, £30 for roads in his native county of Hertfordshire, and £73 for church repairs there. In all, his charities reached the imposing total of £1889. Warde was six times master of the Grocers' Company, on three occasions represented London

in Parliament, served as alderman from 1478 to 1501, and was chosen mayor in 1485.

13. PCC 23 Blamyr 1503; *PP* 1816, XVI, i, 794, 798; *PP* 1820, V, 121; *PP* 1826–7, X, 429; *PP* 1837–8, XXIV, 518; Fry, G. S., ed., *Abstracts of inquisitiones post mortem . . . London . . . 1485–1561* (L., 1896), 20; Thrupp, *Merchant class*, 360; *Husting*, II, 605; Beaven, *Aldermen*, I, 168, 207, II, 17, 167; Clode, C. M., *Memorials of the . . . Merchant Taylors* (L., 1875), 90; Clode, C. M., *The early history of the . . . Merchant Taylors* (L., 1888, 2 vols.), I, 139–140, 411, II, 8–20. Percival left in all £2781 10s for charitable uses, the great outlays having been made for prayers and for a grammar-school foundation in his native parish of Macclesfield in Cheshire (*vide post*, 221, 275). He left as well £50 over a period of five years for prisoners, £1 10s to London hospitals, £80 for road repairs in London, and £20 for the same use in Cheshire, £100 owed to him to be employed for marriage subsidies and roads, an estimated £162 for church repairs in London and Cheshire, and 251 oz. of plate for the use of his company. Percival, who served as alderman from 1485 to 1503, was chosen mayor in 1498, being the first member of his company to gain that dignity.

14. PCC 4 Holgrave 1504; Thrupp, *Merchant class*, 374; Beaven, *Aldermen*, II, 17; Johnson, A. H., *The history of the . . . Drapers of London* (Oxford, 1914–1922, 5 vols.), I, 158, II, 201, III, 140; *Husting*, II, 631–632. White also left large sums for church building and for prayers (*vide post*, 275, 299). He was for five terms master of his company, served as auditor from 1479 to 1482 and again from 1488 to 1490, represented London in Parliament in 1489, and was mayor in 1489. He was a native of Tickhill, Yorkshire.

15. PCC 2 Adeane 1505; Beaven, *Aldermen*, I, 17, 109, 256, 273, II, 19; *Husting*, II, 611–612, 625–626; Thrupp, *Merchant class*, 321; Butcher, Richard, *The survey . . . of Stamford* (L., 1717), 91; Brayley, E. W., *et al.*, *A topographical and historical description of London* (L., 1810–1816, 5 vols.), II, 447. Alwyn also left relatively small sums for the poor of the Mercers and the Cutlers, £4 19s to almshouses, £3 7s for roads and streets, £73 7s for the repair of the London Guildhall, £109 13s for church repairs, and £4 for general church uses, £20 13s to monasteries, and an estimated £100 for university scholarships. A man of wide concerns, he also left £4 for harbour repairs at Dover, £6 13s each to Somerset and Surrey for road repairs, while at his birthplace in Lincolnshire, in addition to his large bequest for the poor, he provided £117 13s for roads, £40 for church repairs, and £3 for the clergy. His provisions for social rehabilitation and prayers will be discussed in later pages (*vide post*, 184, 276). Alwyn was a merchant of the staple as well as a prominent mercer. He was auditor from 1482 to 1484 and sat in Parliament for London in 1491. Though a mayor, he seems never to have been knighted. The bulk of Alwyn's considerable estate was in staple. He left, in addition to his charities, money bequests totalling £1100 6s 8d, including £25 13s 4d to scriveners for drafting his wills. He was served by four apprentices and six servants.

16. *Vide post*, 222.

17. PCC 28 Fetiplace 1513; *Husting*, II, 618–619; Clode, *Merchant Taylors*, I, 412, II, 11, 20–21; Freshfield, Edwin, ed., *Minutes of the vestry . . . of St Christopher le Stocks* (L., 1886), 67; Brooke, J. M. S., and A. W. C. Hallen, eds., *The transcript of the registers of . . . S. Mary Woolnoth* (L., 1886), xvi; *L. & M. Arch. Soc.*, n.s., VI (1931), 62; *PP* 1816, XVI, i, 794; *PP* 1826–7, X, 429; *PP* 1837–8, XXV, 404; Fuller, Thomas, *The church history of Britain* (L., 1837, 3 vols.), II, 272.

18. PCC 13 Holder 1516; *Husting*, II, 626; Freshfield, Edwin, ed., *The vestry minute books . . . of St Bartholomew Exchange* (L., 1890), viii; White, J. G., *History of the ward of Walbrook* (L., 1904), 180; Strype, *Stow's Survey*, II, v, 127–128; Beaven, *Aldermen*, II, 18, 167. Capel, in addition to large sums left for prayers (£210) and church building (*vide post*, 299–300), also gave £5 for church general, £60 for church repairs, £1 for hospitals, £17 7s for the relief of prisoners, and £93 (£4 13s p.a.) for company uses. A native of Suffolk, he was the second son of Sir John Capel. He made a large fortune in trade as a draper, being seven times master of his company. He represented London in Parliament and served as mayor in 1503 and again in 1510. Capel was very rich, leaving, in addition to £738 7s for charities, personal bequests of about £2500 and plate to the value of £733. His landed property was vast, including fourteen manors in Hertfordshire, Essex, Middlesex, Norfolk, Kent, and Suffolk, as well as smaller tracts in several other counties. Capel was one of the victims of Empson and Dudley, being imprisoned for a short season and heavily fined. His elder daughter married the first Marquess of Winchester, while his son, Sir Giles, was ancestor of the Earls of Essex.

19. PCC 30 Holder 1517; *PP* 1822, IX, 267; Herbert, *Livery companies*, I, 356; Beaven, *Aldermen*, I, 115, 146, 256, II, 20, 168; Heath, J. B., *Some account of the . . . Grocers* (L., 1869), 237; Hasted, Edward (H. H. Drake, ed.), *Kent . . . Blackheath* (L., 1886), 169; Besant, Walter, *London city* (L., 1910), 49; *L. & M. Arch. Soc.*, I (1860), 262. Kebyll's charities totalled £2841 8s by gift and bequest. In addition to his bequest to the poor and a large gift for the rebuilding of his parish church (*vide post*, 299), he set aside £90 for prayers, £66 13 4d for marriage portions in Warwickshire, £10 for the work being done on Rochester Bridge, and £6 13s 4d for harbour work at Dover, £245 for church repairs and decoration in Warwickshire and London, not to mention smaller sums for monasteries and hospitals. He left as well the substantial sum of £200 for the mending and making of roads between London and Coventry. The son of a London grocer who had been master of his company on several occasions, Kebyll early gained a very large fortune in trade as a grocer. He was four times master of his company and was mayor in 1510. He left six manors and other lands in Northamptonshire, two manors in Kent, lands in Leicestershire and Essex, and valuable real property in Coventry and London.

20. PCC 14 Bodfelde 1523. Boughton's testament of faith might be cited as typical of pious merchants in these years just prior to the Reformation: 'I . . . praysing to Almighty God and to his blessed moder the Virgin Mary and to all the holy company of hevyn . . . bequeath and

recommende my soule unto almighty God my maker redeemer and saviour and to the blessed lady Saint Mary the Virgin his glorious moder and to all the holy family in hevyn.'

21. PCC 13 Bodfelde 1523; Beaven, *Aldermen*, II, 22, 168; Wadmore, J. F., *Some account of the . . . Skinners* (L., 1876), 157. Mirfyn also left large bequests for an almshouse and for prayers (*vide post*, 138, 277). In addition, he bequeathed £1 for general church needs, £1 for prisoners, £20 to his company, £170 15s for church repairs, £33 6s 8d for marriage portions, and £66 13s 4d for poor Cambridge scholars. A native of Ely, Mirfyn was apprenticed as a skinner. He married well, his wife's stepfather, Sir Robert Dynson, providing a dower of £1,074 4s 8d on condition that a jointure of £40 p.a. be established in her favour. Mirfyn rose rapidly, becoming master of his company on five occasions between 1509 and 1516, and having been named mayor in 1518. One of his daughters married the great merchant, Sir Andrew Judd, and another Sir Robert Cromwell, she being the great-grandmother of both Oliver Cromwell and John Hampden.

22. *Exchequer Augmentations*, Certificates of chantries and colleges, XXXIV, 126.

23. PCC 22 Thower 1532; *PP* 1816, XVI, i, 790, 800; *PP* 1820, V, 110; Herbert, *Livery companies*, II, 209–210; McMurray, William, *The records of two city parishes* (L., 1925),229. This donor, the widow of Sir Bartholomew Rede, also left £44 13s for prayers and £20 for church repairs, as well as a substantial bequest to the clergy which will be noted in later pages (*vide post*, 282).

24. *PP* 1822, IX, 267–268. This endowment was compounded after the Reformation, the company undertaking to pay £9 4s p.a. for the care of the poor. Peche also left an endowment with a value of about £20 to provide 5s annually for the relief of prisoners in London.

25. PCC 30 Hogen 1535. Sir John Gresham, the executor of this estate, stated that £200 was the amount intended for marriage portions, rather than the £100 which the will seems to contemplate.

26. PCC 27 Hogen 1535. Robinson also left 4s for general church uses, £3 12s for marriage portions, £20 to secure the discharge of those longest in prison, but no more than £1 10s for any one person, and a large endowment for prayers (*vide post*, 278).

27. PCC 31 Hogen 1536; Strype, *Stow's Survey*, II, v, 130; Beaven, *Aldermen*, II, 24. Seymour likewise left large amounts for marriage subsidies and road repairs (*vide post*, 184, 203), with nominal amounts for church repairs, almshouses, and prayers. His charities totalled £656 7s. Seymour was knighted in 1520, was lord mayor in 1526, and sat in the Reformation Parliament as a member for London. He was twice master of the Mercers' Company.

28. PCC 8 Dyngeley 1537. Barley's testament of faith follows: 'I bequeth my soule to God Almightie trusting to be saved by the Blode of Cryste onely and that the father loveth mee for his sonnes sake and that I shall partake of his passion'.

29. Askew testified, 'I bequeth my soule to almighty God my creator

and redemer to his glorious moder our blissed Lady Saint Mary the Virgyn and to all the holy company of heaven'. He also left a substantial sum to Oxford and Cambridge for scholars who were to be men of sound learning and 'of sure doctrine of oure mother holy churche'.

30. PCC 30 Dyngeley 1539; Beaven, *Aldermen*, II, 25. We shall later note his bequest for prayers (*vide post*, 279). Askew served as mayor in 1533 and was thrice master of the Drapers.

31. But Dormer was by no means dour, for he left his great house and lands in Buckinghamshire to his wife for her lifetime for 'her own use and to take hir passetyme therin, to make mery with my friends and hers. And that the poor may be the better relevd'.

32. PCC 38 Pynnyng 1545; Beaven, *Aldermen*, II, 27; Fry, *Inq. p. m., London*, I, 58–59. Dormer also left £40 to marriage subsidies, £40 for church repairs, £133 for prayers, £33 to clergy, £133 to his company, the income (£6 13s 4d) to provide a dinner, £6 to prisoners, £63 to Oxford, where he had been educated, £200 to his livery for loans, and an endowment for roads which will be noted later (*vide post*, 204). Dormer served as an alderman from 1531 to 1545, as lord mayor in 1541. He was knighted in 1542 and was twice master of his company. He was a very rich man, with extensive landholdings in Berkshire, Buckinghamshire, Oxfordshire, Essex, Middlesex, Hertfordshire, Kent, Worcestershire, Sussex, and Surrey. He also held considerable property in Calais and real property in London which in the year of his death was worth £59 6s 5d p.a.

33. PCC 36 Pynnyng 1545; *L. & M. Arch. Soc.*, III (1870), 151–152; Johnson, *Drapers*, II, 82n. This donor was the wife of Sir John Milbourne, her earlier husbands having been named Chester and Wells. Some years prior to her death, she had vested an endowment of £124 in St Catharine's College, Cambridge, to secure an annual sermon in the Mercers' Chapel in memory of her second husband. Her will also provided £20 in marriage subsidies, £8 10s for prayers, £6 13s 4d to the Drapers' Company, and lesser amounts for prisoners and for the general uses of the church.

34. PCC 1 Alen 1546; Lyell, Laetitia, and F. D. Watney, eds., *Acts of court of the Mercers* (Cambridge, 1936), 531; Watney, John, *Some account of the hospital of St Thomas of Acon* (L., 1906), 105; Beaven, Aldermen, II, 23, 169; *PP* 1822, IX, 285. This benefactor left additional and substantial charities. He gave £5 for church general, £40 to church repairs in Thaxted, £153 for prayers, £33 for prisoners, £1 7s for hospitals, £73 13s to his company's uses, £30 to marriage subsidies in London and Essex, and a 'silver collar' for the use of the lord mayor. Allen was an alderman 1515–1545, lord mayor in 1525 and again in 1535, a privy councillor, and thrice master of the Mercers' Company. Stow and other authorities say that he was a bachelor, but his will distributed large landholdings to three children. It is only human to wish to know more regarding Elizabeth Jay, who was left his London house and lands in Kent and Middlesex, and who should have 'the keping of John my foole'.

35. PCC 40 Alen 1547; Moore, Norman, *St Bartholomew's Hospital* (L., 1918, 2 vols.), II, 199. Mery left £20 to prisoners, £100 for repairs on a grammar school, and £10 for the renovation of an almshouse, £100 for

public works, £10 for church general, £13 7s to the Grocers, and £100 of endowment to St Bartholomew's Hospital.

36. PCC 9 More 1554; Beaven, *Aldermen*, II, 30, 170. Amcottes also left 10s. to church general, £1 for prayers, £30 for marriages in London and Lincoln, £40 for the repair of streets in London and the road from London to Rye, £10 to almshouses, £23 to hospitals, £35 for prisoners, and £40 to his company. He was forced into the acceptance of civic responsibility: in 1536 he was chosen alderman, but declined to serve until after he had been fined £40, and his shop and goods sequestrated, and had spent a week in Newgate. He was made sheriff in 1542 and mayor in 1548, having been knighted in the latter year.

37. PCC 37 Chaynay 1559; *PP* 1816, XVI, i, 816; *PP* 1840, XIX, i, 90; Blunden, Edmund, *Christ's Hospital* (L., 1923), 16; Wilson, J. I., *Christ's Hospital*, (L., 1821), 35. Castel was known as the 'cock of Westminster', since he was for years at his shoemaker's bench at three or four o'clock every morning. The residue of his estate, which was large, was left to Christ's Hospital (*vide post*, 212–213).

38. In our discussion of Bristol's charities, and *vide post*, 225.

39. PCC 28 Ketchyn 1556; *PP* 1825, X, 103; *PP* 1884, XXXIX, iv, 229; Beaven, *Aldermen*, II, 30; Leveson Gower, W. G. G., *Family of Gresham* (L., 1883), 30–35; Fox Bourne, H. R., *English merchants* (L., 1866, 2 vols.), I, 172; DNB. Gresham also left £100 in marriage portions, £30 17s to church general, £48 to prisons, £5 to lazar houses, £116 13s to hospitals, £50 to roads, and £13 7s to the Mercers. He was very rich, his landed estates in Kent, for example, being worth £109 19s 4d p.a., and those in Surrey £177 4s p.a. His executors were Sir Rowland Hill, Sir Andrew Judd, and his nephew, Thomas Gresham, all of whom in their turn were to be great benefactors.

40. PCC 13 Noodes 1557; *Virginia Magazine*, XXIX (1921), 112–114; *PP* 1823, VIII, 252; Beaven, *Aldermen*, II, 31, 170; Russan, T. S., *The Muscovy merchants of 1555* (Manchester, 1953), 29, 73. Barne also left £20 to his company and £100 to St Bartholomew's and St Thomas's hospitals. He was principally concerned in trade with Spain and left £40 to a servant 'so that he shall do his diligence in gathering up of my goodes' in that country. His testament of faith suggests that he was a staunch Protestant. Barne was one of several leading burghers whom Northumberland was at first able to persuade to attest to Edward's will naming Lady Jane Grey as his successor, but took no part in proclaiming her at London. He served as alderman from 1542 to 1556 and as mayor in 1552, being knighted in the next year. Barne was a 'principall doer' in promoting the first Russia voyage in 1553 and was also an important supporter of the Guinea voyages in 1553 and 1554. He was probably a native of Somerset. His son, George, was lord mayor in 1586; one daughter married Sir Francis Walsingham; and another was the wife of Sir John Rivers, who was lord mayor in 1573.

41. PCC 32 Chaynay 1559; *Va. Mag.*, XXIX (1921), 114–117. Dame Alice also left £10 for prisoners, £10 for church repairs in Shropshire and as much for bridge maintenance there, £20 to the universities, £6 13s 4d

for marriage subsidies, £10 to her late husband's company, and £101 for hospitals. A native of Shropshire, she married first Richard Relfe, a vintner, who died in 1528.

42. PCC 2 Chayre 1562; *PP* 1816, XVI, i, 792; *PP* 1904, LXXI, 800; Madge, S. J. ed., *Abstracts of inquisitiones post mortem . . . London . . . 1561–1577* (L., 1901), 8. This property in 1904 possessed a capital value of £19,391 13s 3d.

43. PCC 10 Stevenson 1563; *PP* 1819, X-B, 59–60; *PP* 1823, VIII, 293; *PP* 1829, VII, 260; *PP* 1884, XXXIX, iv, 604. This lady was the daughter of Henry Dacres, a merchant and sheriff of London. Her husband, Sir John Packington, a native of Worcestershire, had been educated at the Inner Temple. He early enjoyed special marks of favour from Henry VIII. In 1532 he was made serjeant-at-law and in 1535 a justice in North Wales. He trafficked extensively and profitably in monastic lands. He died in 1560.

44. PCC 16 Morrison 1565; *PP* 1816, XVI, i, 790, 794, 802; *PP* 1820, V, 115–117; *PP* 1884, XXXIX, ii, 10; Leveson Gower, *Gresham*, 76 ff. This was but the largest of the charitable outlays of this donor. Lady Gresham also left £130 to London hospitals, £100 to the universities, £66 13s 4d for marriage subsidies, £40 to scholarships, £45 for the succour of prisoners, and £20 for the uses of the Mercers and the Goldsmiths. Lady Gresham, *née* Worsopp, was a widow when she became Gresham's second wife.

45. PCC 3 Stonard 1566; Beaven, *Aldermen*, I, 11, 91, 147, 169, 251, II, 29; *PP* 1823, VIII, 326; *PP* 1840, XIX, i, 92; Prideaux, W. S., ed., *Memorials of the Goldsmiths' Company* (L., 1896–1897, 2 vols.), I, 43, 63; Herbert, *Livery companies*, II, 257. Bowes was the grandson and great-grandson of former mayors of York, where he was born in 1500. He was apprenticed to a London goldsmith and by 1530 was Deputy Keeper of the Exchange at the Tower of London. He was lord mayor in 1545. Bowes was knighted in 1541 and sat for London in Parliament on five different occasions. He was appointed Treasurer of St Bartholomew's Hospital in 1547, served as Comptroller-General of the Hospitals from 1557 to 1566 and as Master of the Mint from 1533 to 1544. He was prime warden of the Goldsmiths from 1559 to 1562. *Vide post*, 142.

46. PCC 9 Stonard 1567; *PP* 1823, VIII, 315; Baker, Thomas, *History of the College of St John* (Cambridge, 1869, 2 vols.), I, 547; Welch, Charles, *History of the Cutlers' Company* (L., 1916, 1923, 2 vols.), I, 215, II, 156. Bucke also charged the trust with an annual payment of £3 6s 8d to provide for a scholar in St John's College, Cambridge, from the Isle of Ely or from the Cutlers' Company, annuities of £2 each to Christ's Hospital and St Thomas's, and £1 p.a. for the repair of his parish church, St Sepulchre.

47. PCC 26 Babington 1568; Pearce, Arthur, *History of the Butchers' Company* (L., 1929), 93; Madge, *Inq. p. m., London*, 117; Beaven, *Aldermen*, II, 38; *PP* 1822, IX, 333; *PP* 1824, XIII, 191; *PP* 1825, X, 109. Harding left as well £66 15s for apprenticeships for children to be drawn from Christ's Hospital, £70 to various London hospitals, £12 to prisoners,

and £30 to scholars at Oxford and Cambridge. A native of Bedfordshire, Harding served as auditor from 1558 to 1560 and as sheriff in 1568. His estate, with lands in Southwark, Bedfordshire, and Buckinghamshire, was valued at upwards of £4000.

48. PCC 29 Lyon 1570; Stow, *Survey*, I, 114; Jupp, E. B., *An historical account of the . . . Carpenters* (L., 1887), 21n., 643; Besant, Walter, *London in the time of the Tudors* (L., 1904), 377; Clode, *Merchant Taylors*, I, 228; *Husting*, II, 686–687; Wilson, H. B., *The history of the Merchant-Taylors' School* (L., 1813–1814, 2 vols.), I, 31n.; Beaven, *Aldermen*, II, 35, 172; *PP* 1826–7, X, 431; *PP* 1884, XXXIX, iv, 384. A tailor's son, Rowe married a daughter of Sir John Gresham and rose rapidly in his company. He served as lord mayor in 1568. He was President of St Thomas's Hospital in 1567 and master of his company in 1557. He was cousin to Sir William Rowe, lord mayor in 1592, father to Sir Henry, lord mayor in 1607, and grandfather to Sir Thomas Roe, the famous author, traveller, and diplomatist. Rowe resided at Hackney, where he was buried. In addition to loan funds of £100 each for the Merchant Taylors and the Clothworkers, he left £70 for prisoners, £100 for municipal uses, £20 for scholarships, £20 for marriage subsidies, and lesser amounts for numerous other charitable causes.

49. *Husting*, II, 686; *PP* 1816, XVI, i, 798; *PP* 1837–8, XXVI, 333–334; *PP* 1904, LXXI, 930.

50. PCC 25 Holney 1571; *Husting*, II, 688; Clode, *Merchant Taylors*, I, 155–156; *PP* 1826–7, X, 432; *PP* 1830, XII, 15. Donkin was a freeman prior to 1530 and was admitted to the livery in 1557. He served his parish (St Michael Cornhill) for some time as churchwarden. The properties conveyed to his company increased enormously in value, a convalescent rest home having been built at Bognor from surplus income in 1872.

51. PCC 26 Carew 1576; Beaven, *Aldermen*, II, 38, 173; *PP* 1824, XIII, 230; Blackburn, E. L., *An architectural . . . account of . . . Crosby Place* (L., 1834), App. III, 81–92; Russan, *Muscovy merchants*, 81. Bond was a merchant engaged in many great enterprises. He was a shipowner, exported cloth to Flanders, imported wine from France, and traded both to Spain and to the Baltic. His personal estate was valued at upwards of £4200. He also left £40 for prisoners, £58 for marriage subsidies in two London parishes, £40 to maintain scholars at Oxford, £53 7s to hospitals, as much to his company for 'any good use', and a loan fund of £100 to be lent gratis to young freemen of his company. He was an alderman for some years and was sheriff in 1567. A brother, Sir George, was lord mayor in 1587.

52. PCC 29 Pyckering 1576; *PP* 1816, XVI, i, 748; *PP* 1829, VII, 304; Baddeley, J. J., *St Giles without Cripplegate* (L., 1888), 76; Harper, C. G., *More queer things about London* (L., 1924), 31–32. The benefaction was immortalized by one of the longest and crudest examples of the art of epitaph composition that we have observed:

This Busbie willing to releeve the poore, with fire and with breade,
Did give that howse whearin he dyed, then called ye Queenes heade:
Four full loades of ye best charcoales, he would have bought each year

And fortie dozen of wheaten bread for poore howsholders heare:
To see these things distributed, this Busby put in trust
The vicar and church wardenes, thinking them to be just:
God grant that poore howsholders here, may thankful be for such
So God will move the mindes of moe, to doe for them as much
And let this good example move, such men as God hath blest
To doe the like before they goe with Busby to there rest . . .

Still, crude and blatant as it may be, generations of men and women reading and probably memorizing these lines during dull sermons at St Giles may well have been moved decisively by these sentiments and this exhortation. The catalysts of human action are rarely known certainly, even by those who are themselves moved.

53. PCC 28 Carew 1576; Herbert, William, *History of the . . . Skinners* (L., 1837), 373; *PP* 1837–8, XXVI, 434; *PP* 1884, XXXIX, iii, 131–133. This woman was the widow of Sir Richard Champion, merchant and alderman of London, who served as lord mayor in 1565 (*vide post*, 142). The properties left in trust to the Drapers were taken in the nineteenth century to clear the approaches to London Bridge, £11,000 in compensation being paid.

54. PCC 19 Arundell 1580; Fuller, *Worthies*, II, 157; Fleming, Abraham, *A memoriall of the . . . almes-deedes of William Lambe* (L., 1580), *Epitaph on William Lambe* (L., 1580); Besant, *London . . . Tudors*, 377–378; Bruce, A. K., *Memories and monuments . . . of . . . London* (L., 1931), 138; Ashton, John, *The Fleet* (L., 1888), 179–180; Allen, Thomas, *The history . . . of London* (L., 1839, 5 vols.), I, 293. We shall treat Lambe's great benefactions for almshouses, social rehabilitation, municipal uses, and schools in later pages (*vide post*, 142, 177, 204, 228).

55. PCC 20 Butts 1583; *PP* 1816, XVI, i, 754, 788, 796; *PP* 1822, IX, 224, 296; Davenport, Percy, *Old Stanmore* (Stanmore, Middlesex, 1933), 73. Hilson was a mercer and a brother-in-law of Barbara Burnell, also a considerable donor. He built a gallery for Great Stanmore church during his lifetime and left an endowment to secure lectures there and in his London parish church. He also left an annuity of £10 14s 8d for the purchase of clothing for the children in Christ's Hospital.

56. PCC 27 Butts 1583; Stow, *Survey*, I, 19; Besant, Walter, *London city* (L., 1910), 212; *PP* 1820, V, 144; *PP* 1825, X, 110; *PP* 1837, XXIII, 677; Besant, G. B., 'The city churches before . . . 1666', *Parthenon*, X (1936), 291; Pendrill, Charles, *Wanderings in medieval London* (L., 1928), 165. Randolph likewise left a large sum for municipal betterments in London (*vide post*, 204). As a result of a suit in Chancery, half the Ticehurst annuity was ordered paid to a grandson for whom no provision had been made.

57. PCC 56 Brudenell 1585; *PP* 1820, V, 147; Ware, John, *An account of the . . . charities of St. Leonard, Shoreditch* (L., 1836), 1; *Husting*, II, 709.

58. PCC 9 Spencer 1586; *Husting*, II, 710–712; *PP* 1822, IX, 224–225.

59. PCC 39 Tirwhite 1582; Beaven, *Aldermen*, I, 11, 182, II, 33, 171; Stow, *Survey*, I, 114; Wilson, *Merchant-Taylors' School*, I, 4; *L & M.*

Arch. Soc., n.s. VIII (1938), 40; Clode, *Merchant Taylors*, I, 228; Daniell, A. E., *London city churches* (N.Y., 1896), 33; Fuller, *Worthies*, I, 295–296; Machyn, Henry, *Diary* (L., 1848), 353. The will bequeathed £267 plus half the residue for this purpose. Wilson (*Merchant-Taylors' School*) and Fuller estimate Offley's total estate at about £5000, which would establish a much larger residue, but the will and other sources suggest a worth which may be more modestly set at £2600, and hence, other bequests being taken into account, the charitable residue would be much as we have reckoned. Offley, a native of Stafford, was sent to London to attend William Lilly's school in about 1517, afterwards being apprenticed to a merchant tailor. He became master of his company in 1547 and lord mayor in 1556. He was knighted in 1557. He was well known for the frugality of his tastes; Machyn cites a popular rhyme, 'Offley three dishes had of daily rost: An egge, an apple, and (the third) a toast'. But his munificence was great, his charities totalling £1366 4s and including, in addition to his benefactions for the poor, £100 for Christ's Hospital, which he had served as president, £100 for prisoners in Chester and £12 for London prisoners, £20 for university scholarships, and numerous lesser distributions.

60. PCC 14 Butts 1583; *PP* 1820, V, 141–142; *PP* 1822, IX, 294; *PP* 1823, VIII, 68, 597; *PP* 1826, XII, 31; *PP* 1884, XXXIX, ii, 28; Seymour, Robert, *A survey of . . . London* (L., 1734, 2 vols.), I, 244. Heydon was a native of Woodbury, Devon, to which he left £6 13s 4d outright as well as an annuity of £3 6s 8d for its poor, to be paid from the income on one of the loan funds held by the Mercers' Company. Heydon was chosen sheriff in 1580 and was serving as master of his company in 1582, the year of his death. This donor also left £500 as an endowment for Christ's Hospital.

61. PCC 9 Rutland 1587; *PP* 1822, IX, 297; Seymour, *Survey*, I, 249; O'Donoghue, E. G., *Bridewell Hospital* (L., 1923, 1929, 2 vols.), I, 255; Beaven, *Aldermen*, II, 37; Russan, *Muscovy merchants*, 92–93. Duckett was long regarded as one of the richest men in London, but his will suggests that his estate had been considerably diminished by the time of his death. He was particularly interested in mining ventures in Cumberland, where he used German labour, and in smelting operations in Germany. Duckett was one of the adventurers supporting Frobisher's search for a northwest passage. He traded in cloth and wine, was a promoter of the Guinea voyage of 1558 and of later slaving voyages. He was also an active member of the Mines Royal and a member and onetime governor of the Russia Company. All new enterprises seem to have attracted him. A native of Nottinghamshire, he had been apprenticed as a mercer. He served as an alderman from 1564 to 1587, as lord mayor in 1572; he was four times master of the Mercers and at various times president of St Thomas's Hospital, Bethlehem, and Bridewell. His testament of faith was strongly Calvinistic in temper.

62. Symonds, a wise and most generous benefactor, left in all £4416 7s for charitable uses. His great charitable dispositions in Winchester will be fully treated in another place. *Vide post*, 142, 169.

63. PCC 16 Drury 1589; Home, Beatrice, *Westminster Abbey* (L., 1925), 172; Strype, *Stow's Survey*, II, vii, 45; *Lansdowne MSS.*, LXII, 51.

64. *Vide post*, 229–230.

65. *PP* 1823, IX, 261; *PP* 1894, LXIII, 'Paddington', 27–33; Bryant, P. H. M., *Harrow* (L., 1936), 1–23; Venn, John, *Biographical history of Gonville and Caius College* (Cambridge, 1897–1912, 4 vols.), III, 230; Laborde, E. D., *Harrow School* (L., 1948), 22; Druett, W. W., *Harrow* (Uxbridge, 1935), 121, 152–153, *Pinner* (L., 1937), 89; Staunton, Howard, *The great schools of England* (L., 1865), 307–308; Norden, John, *Speculum Britanniae* (L., [1593] 1723), 23. We have not seen Lyon's will, though Venn indicates that there is a copy in Cambridge.

66. PCC 39 Drury 1590; PCC 64 Woodhall 1601; Beaven, *Aldermen*, I, 101, 123, II, 37, 173; *PP* 1816, XVI, i, 782, 786, 794, 800; *PP* 1820, V, 82; *PP* 1823, VIII, 332; *PP* 1840, XIX, i, 101–106; *PP* 1867–8, LII, i, 23; Blunden, *Christ's Hospital*, 18. *Vide post*, 181, 185, 228. A native of Kent, Ramsay was apprenticed to a grocer and maintained a steady interest in the affairs of that company. He was chosen an alderman in 1566, sheriff in 1567, and lord mayor in 1577. He served as President of Christ's Hospital in 1582–1590 and was Surveyor-General of Hospitals during the four last years of his life. Lady Ramsay was born in Bristol, the daughter of William Dale, a merchant there. She enjoyed considerable wealth in her own right and was completely trusted by her husband in business as well as charitable affairs.

67. PCC 56 Nevell 1593, sentence 88 Dixy 1594; *Husting*, II, 717–719; *PP* 1816, XVI, i, 772; *PP* 1822, X, 302; *PP* 1837–8, XXVI, 435; *PP* 1867–8, LI, ii, 16–17; *PP* 1884, XXXIX, iii, 165–167; Johnson, *Drapers*, II, App., 526; Boyd, Percival, ed., *Roll of the Drapers' Company* (Croydon, 1934), 159. *Vide post*, 231, 285, for Russell's large benefaction for educational uses and for a lectureship. His charities totalled £2033 11s. Russell was bound apprentice in the Drapers' Company in 1543; he was twice warden of his company, though never its master. He held no high civic office.

68. PCC 55 Dixy 1594; *Husting*, II, 721–722; *L. & M. Arch. Soc.*, III (1870), 459; Milbourn, Thomas, *The Vintners' Company* (L., 1888), 86–88; Beaven, *Aldermen*, II, 41; *PP* 1823, VIII, 383, IX, 665. Buckle was a native of Brough, Westmorland, where he founded a school. He was a vintner; he served as an alderman from 1582 to 1594, as sheriff in 1582, and as President of St Thomas's in the last years of his life. *Vide post*, 204, 231.

69. PCC 24 Dixy 1594; Feret, C. J., *Fulham old and new* (L., 1900, 3 vols.), I, 239–241.

70. PCC 68 Drake 1596; *PP* 1822, IX, 225–226; *PP* 1884, XXXIX, iv, 589; *PP* 1904, LXXI, 858.

71. PCC 2 Cobham 1597; Ware, *Charities of St. Leonard's*, 7; *PP* 1826, XII, 221; *PP* 1830, XII, 309; *PP* 1837–8, XXVI, 520. *Vide post*, 182.

72. PCC 89 Cobham 1597. Smith was a native of Wighton. *Vide post*, 182.

73. *Vide post,* 232.

74. PCC 10 Kidd 1598; Herbert, *Livery companies,* II, 543; Hatton, Edward, *A new view of London* (L., 1708, 2 vols.), II, 734; *PP* 1824, XIII, 193–195; *PP* 1884, XXXIX, iv, 431–435; Beaven, *Aldermen,* I, 25, 64, 275, 289. Aldersey sat in the House of Commons for London in 1572 and again in 1581. He served as an alderman from 1581 to 1588. *Vide post,* 285, for his lectureship foundation.

75. PCC 15 Kidd 1599; *PP* 1831, XI, 258, 379; DNB. Owen's father was a successful merchant in Shrewsbury. Owen was educated at Oxford and at Lincoln's Inn. He became a reader in his inn in 1583 and a serjeant in 1589. He was made Queen's Serjeant in 1593 and a judge in 1594; he was greatly trusted by Burghley, whom he advised on personal legal matters. This donor's charities were quite dwarfed by those of his widow, Alice (*vide post,* 150, 235).

76. PCC 75, 79 Wallop 1600; *PP* 1816, XVI, i, 786; *PP* 1820, V, 82; *PP* 1884, XXXIX, ii, 33. *Vide post,* 285, for her lectureship foundation.

77. PCC 45 Montague 1602; *PP* 1816, XVI, i, 748; *PP* 1829, VII, 314; Baddeley, *St Giles,* 83; Harper, *More queer things,* 30–31. Langley, who was an alebrewer, was born in London in *ca.* 1558.

78. PCC 16 Montague 1602; *S. P. Dom.,* 1638[?], CCCCVIII, 129; Fuller, *Worthies,* I, 461; Baddeley, J. J., *Cripplegate Ward* (L., 1922), 231–232; *PP* 1816, XVI, i, 748, 810, 812; *PP* 1824, XIII, 183, 242; *PP* 1837, XXIII, 29; *PP* 1840, XIX, i, 108; *PP* 1903, L, 31–32; *The Corporation of London* (L., 1950), 230–231; Seymour, *Survey,* I, 245. Rogers was a very large charitable donor, the whole of his philanthropies amounting to upwards of £3000 and including substantial benefactions for loans, almshouses, hospitals, and scholarships (*vide post,* 149–150). We have not assigned to him a fund of £100 given to the Bakers' Company for the benefit of the poor of St Michael Bassishaw (*PP* 1816, XVI, i, 796), as this was more probably the gift of another leatherseller, William Rogers, who died in 1597 (PCC 31 Cobham). Rogers, who was a bachelor, was buried in Christ's Hospital, which he had served as a governor. His memory was celebrated in a popular ballad circulated shortly after his death and praising his charitable deeds:

> . . . when good men dye, the memorie remaines,
> Of their true vertues and most Christian wayes . . .
> . . . as God blest him with aboundant wealth,
> Like to a carefull steward he imployde it:
> Squaring his guifts out in his best of health,
> As glad to leave it, as when he inioyde it.
> . . . In sundry callings and vocations,
> Where he could heare of them were rightly poore:
> As men decayed by their occupations,
> Yet held by shame from begging at the doore,
> Such succoured he . . .
> . . . to what poore wanting heart,
> Was he not liberall in the largest kinde?

Such as were hopefull, and had any parte
Of Christian zeale, felt freely his good minde.
Preachers, poore handy-crafts, and parishes:
From Rogers purse have liberall legacies.

There then followed a detailed list of Rogers' charities, which the author totalled as £2960 6s 8d, and an exhortation to other rich men to emulate this worthy donor. ['A living remembrance of . . . Robert Rogers', in *Ballads and broadsides*, H. L. Collman, ed. (Oxford, 1912)].

79. PCC 106 Bolein 1603; Strype, *Stow's Survey*, II, iv, 114; Hatton, *New view*, I, 204–205; *PP* 1837, XXIII, 809; *PP* 1901, LII, 10, 49. Beddoe was a native of Shropshire, probably a member of a gentle family long settled there. We are not certain of his social status, though the nature of his will and his London holdings would suggest that he may have been a retired merchant. His wife, Margaret, on her death in 1633, added £20 to the *corpus* of her late husband's loan fund.

80. PCC 72 Bolein 1603; Chaffers, William, *Gilda aurifabrorum* (L., 1899), 54; *PP* 1823, VIII, 332–334; Herbert, *Livery companies*, II, 249; Fry, Herbert, ed., *Royal guide to . . . charities* (L., 1939), 116–117; McMurray, *Two city parishes*, 234. Strelley also provided that the rent-charge should be employed for apprenticeships and scholarships (*vide post*, 169).

81. PCC 44 Harte 1604; Beaven, *Aldermen*, II, 48; Strype, *Stow's Survey*, I, iii, 60. A native of Coventry, Glover was first chosen an alderman in 1601, in which year he also served as sheriff. His estate was valued at about £8500, most of which, it may be noted, was invested in well-secured mortages from merchants and gentry. Glover also left £200 to the endowment of London hospitals.

82. PCC 25 Stafford 1606; Seymour, *Survey*, I, 276; Delaune, Thomas, *Angliae metropolis* (L., 1690), 62; *PP* 1837–8, XXVI, 513, 561; Ware, *Charities of St Leonard's*, 34–35. *Vide post*, 259. This donor's benefactions totalled £845 2s 2d.

83. PCC 86 Dorset 1609; Walford, Edward, *Greater London* (L., 1884, 2 vols.), II, 155; *Va. Mag.*, XXVII (1919), 150–152; *PP* 1822, IX 279; *PP* 1826, XII, 571. Tirrell left amounts ranging from £4 to £40 for such purposes as prisons, hospitals, church repairs, and the clergy, as well as a substantial bequest for municipal uses which will be noted later (*vide post*, 205). He was a younger son of a gentleman, while his mother was a daughter of Sir Edward Montague, Chief Justice of England.

84. PCC 87 Dorset 1609; Seymour, *Survey*, I, 244; Harding, William, *History of Tiverton* (Tiverton, 1845, 1847, 2 vols.), II, 167; *PP* 1820, IV, 141. Chilcot's principal benefaction was the well-endowed school which he founded at Tiverton (*vide post*, 234). He left in addition £100 for the endowment of Christ's Hospital, £100 for the redemption of poor debtors whose obligations did not exceed £5, £20 for road repairs, and a substantial sum for church repairs (*vide post*, 295). Chilcot (*alias* Comyn) was a nephew of Blundell, serving him first as clerk and then as business associate. He was one of the overseers of Blundell's will.

85. PCC 57 Fenner 1612 (sentence); DNB; Andrews, William, ed., *Bygone Middlesex* (L., 1899), 99; Ellis, W., *The campagna of London* (L., 1793), 90–91; Beaven, *Aldermen*, II, lii, 42. Spencer was a native of Suffolk. He established a large trade with Spain and the Mediterranean, having been accused in 1591 of engrossing the whole trade with Tripoli. He was a member of the Clothworkers' Company, serving as alderman from 1583 and as lord mayor in 1594. The Privy Council found him difficult, he being particularly sensitive regarding all the traditional liberties of the city. His daughter was married to Lord Compton (later Earl of Northampton), who had Spencer imprisoned for a season for the ill treatment he had meted out to her. Spencer grew more obdurate as his years grew longer, declining to contribute to a royal aid and being in arrears on a company account of £200 at the time of his death. It is impossible accurately to estimate his fortune, though it is doubtful that it exceeded £380,000 at the time of his death.

86. *PP* 1816, XVI, i, 748, 812; *PP* 1829, VII, 310. This large gift was in part bestowed by Richard Budd, evidently a friend of Hanbury's.

87. PCC 92 Wingfield 1610; Fuller, *Worthies*, I, 280; Seymour, *Survey*, I, 247; Hatton, *New view*, I, 134; *PP* 1822, IX, 260–261; *PP* 1826, XII, 550; *PP* 1830, XII, 27; *PP* 1837–8, XXVI, 513; *PP* 1902, LXXVI, 'St Mary-le-Bow', 6; *PP* 1903, L, 209. Palyn left as well £100 for church repairs, £60 to prisoners, £30 for general church uses. His large benefactions for almshouses, universities, and lectureships will be considered in later pages (*vide post*, 150, 258, 285).

88. PCC 80 Weldon 1617.

89. PCC 24 Wood 1611; *PP* 1816, XVI, i, 748, 812; *PP* 1829, VII, 316, 345; *PP* 1867–8, LII, i, 45; Daniell, *London churches*, 66; Seymour, *Survey*, I, 181, 248. Edward Harvest likewise left lands then having a capital worth of £184 for the repair of roads between Tyburn and Edgware (Middlesex) and £150 to London hospitals.

90. PCC 91 Fenner 1612; *PP* 1816, XVI, i, 792; *PP* 1824, XIII, 198; *PP* 1884, XXXIX, iv, 454; *Miscellanea Genealogica et Heraldica*, 2d. ser., III (1890), 106–107; *L. & M. Arch. Soc.*, n.s., II (1912), 318. For his bequests to London companies and for the support of a school in Rolleston, *vide post*, 202, 235.

91. PCC 77 Fenner 1612; Seymour, *Survey*, I, 247; *PP* 1835, XXI, ii, 1248; *PP* 1839, XIV, 363; *PP* 1840, XIX, i, 112. Gale's generous provision for London hospitals, his company, and university scholarships will be dealt with later (*vide post*, 202).

92. PCC 22 Lawe 1614; *PP* 1816, XVI, i, 792, 810; *PP* 1822, IX, 212; Nicholl, John, *Some account of the . . . Ironmongers* (L., 1866), 473; Seymour, *Survey*, I, 181; Beaven, *Aldermen*, I, 48, II, 47. A large portion of this charity was lost when in 1657 the trustee, one William Wall, failed. Cambell was a native of Norfolk. He was an alderman after 1599 and was twice master of his company. His son, Sir James (*vide post*, 179–180, 183, 243, 305), who was likewise an ironmonger and a lord mayor, was a very rich man and a great philanthropist.

93. PCC 117 Rudd 1615, sentence 54 Cope 1616; Seymour, *Survey*, I,

248; Fuller, *Worthies*, II, 439; *PP* 1824, XIII, 200–210; *PP* 1884, XXXIX, iv, 460. Fuller tells us that Jones left his native Monmouth because of his inability to pay a debt of ten groats. His 'brains being better than his back', he early abandoned his work as a porter to become a factor. He lived for many years in Hamburg, where he 'made such a vent for Welch cottons, that what he found *drugs* at home, he left *dainties* beyond the sea'. The learned preacher John Downam extolled Jones in a moving sermon preached before the Haberdashers in 1616. Downam praised Jones not only for his great generosity, but for the consistent modesty of his good works. 'In his lifetime he did much good unto many, and then freely parted with his riches.' He praised Jones, too, for the breadth and scope of his charity, embracing as it did many good causes in places to which the donor found himself attached. 'So let me exhort you . . . that you will show yourselves no lesse faithfull stewards unto God, and whereas he hath committed unto the most of you many talents . . . you will stirre up Gods graces of mercy and liberality in you, for the performing of like works of mercy and Christian charity.' (Downam, John, *The plea of the poore*, L., 1616.) Jones's other great foundations will be noted in later pages (*vide post*, 153–154, 202, 236, 285–286).

94. PCC 93 Rudd 1615; *PP* 1816, XVI, i, 788; *PP* 1824, XIII, 199; *PP* 1884, XXXIX, iv, 477; Hatton, *New view*, II, 734; Seymour, *Survey*, I, 181. This donor also left £150 for the uses of Bridewell and £60 as an endowment for St Bartholomew's Hospital. *Vide post*, 182.

95. PCC 36 Cope 1616; Beaven, *Aldermen*, II, 50, 176; *PP* 1826–7, X, 457. Elwes, a native of Nottinghamshire, served as alderman after 1605, sheriff in 1607, and was master of his company in 1604. He was a cousin of Sir Gervase Elwes, the Lieutenant of the Tower who was executed for his complicity in the Overbury murder. Two of his sons were to become prominent merchants. Elwes left an estate valued at £12,600. *Vide post*, 258, 285, for his benefaction to Oxford and his lectureship endowment.

96. PCC 125 Cope 1616; Orridge, B. B., *Some account of the citizens of London* (L., 1867), 233; Simon, A. L., *History of the wine trade in England* (L., 1907–1909, 3 vols.), II, 61; Beaven, *Aldermen*, II, 48; *PP* 1820, V, 81; *PP* 1831, XI, 483; *PP* 1837–8, XXV, 555. Swinnerton was a native of London. He served as an alderman after 1602, as lord mayor in 1612. He twice represented provincial constituencies in the House of Commons and was knighted in 1603. The bulk of his fortune was derived from his office as farmer of the imposts on French and Rhenish wines, for which in 1599 he paid the Exchequer for the rental of his office £15,000. His estate was valued at £16,850, with manors and lands in Essex, Shropshire, and London worth, in addition, at least £170 p.a. Besides his bequests to the poor, Swinnerton left £130 for London hospitals and £20 to the relief of prisoners.

97. PCC 130 Cope 1616; *PP* 1822, X, 185; *PP* 1825, XI, 275; *PP* 1826–7, X, 439; *PP* 1840, XIX, i, 113–114; *PP* 1884, XXXIX, iv, 389; Seymour, *Survey*, I, 181; Clode, *Merchant Taylors*, II, 36, 345. Wolley likewise left £103 to London hospitals and £100 to his company to be lent without interest to four worthy young men of the Merchant Taylors, as

well as funds for the support of a grammar school in Staffordshire (*vide post*, 237).

98. PCC 9 Weldon 1617; Seymour, *Survey*, I, 181, 248; Howard, J. J., and G. J., Armytage, eds., *The visitation of London . . . 1568* (L., 1869), 97; Freshfield, Edwin, Jr., *The communion plate of the churches in . . . London* (L., 1894), xxxvi, 39, 78; Clode, *Merchant Taylors*, II, 343; *PP* 1826–7, X, 441; *PP* 1837–8, XXIV, 373; *PP* 1884, XXXIX, iv, 387. Vernon, a native of Cheshire, was admitted to the freedom of his company in 1595 and became its first warden in 1604 and its master in 1609. He was blind. *Vide post*, 178, 259.

99. PCC 24 Meade 1618. This donor was the widow of Henry, Lord Berkeley, but her will makes it clear that her affection remained with her first husband, Sir Roger Townsend, with whom she wished to be buried.

100. PCC 71 Meade 1618; *Genealogical Quarterly Magazine* (Salem, Mass., 1900–1905, 5 vols.), IV, 44; *PP* 1816, XVI, i, 808; *PP* 1823, VIII, 285. Adams likewise left £76 for outright distribution to the poor, £35 to hospitals, and £6 for a dinner for his company.

101. PCC 73 Meade 1618; *PP* 1822, IX, 290, 341; *PP* 1826–7, X, 438; *PP* 1837–8, XXVI, 431; *PP* 1884, XXXIX, iii, 134, v, 287. This benefactor left in all £1601 for charitable uses. Her endowments for prisoners will be considered later (*vide post*, 182). She also left generous amounts for hospitals and university scholarships.

102. PCC 35 Soame 1620; *PP* 1816, XVI, i, 784; *PP* 1837–8, XXVI, 465. Sheild's benefactions for the poor and other charities had in part been established by endowments of £540 given to the Cooks' Company in 1617. Sheild also left £80 for the relief of prisoners, £40 for marriage portions, £75 11s for company uses, £40 for the clergy, £20 for church general, and £3 to Christ's Hospital.

103. PCC 79 Soame 1620; *PP* 1837–8, XXV, 52, 349; Lea, J. H., ed., *Abstracts of wills . . . Register Soame, 1620* (Boston, 1904), 309. Wybo also provided £100 (Flemish) for the support of a girls' school in Bruges, £95 for the assistance of named preachers, £30 for the aid of students maintained by the Dutch church, and £50 for hospitals, as well as £200 for the support of the Dutch church in London.

104. PCC 5 Soame 1620; Lea, *Reg. Soame*, 16–17.

105. PCC 75 Meade 1618; Beaven, *Aldermen*, I, 115, II, 47, 176; *PP* 1826–7, X, 433, 440; *PP* 1902, LXXVI, 'St Mary-le-Bow', 10; DNB; Clode, *Merchant Taylors*, II, 306, 310, 312, 322–323; Brayley, E. W., *London and Middlesex* (L., 1810, 1814, 2 vols.), II, 242; Delaune, *Angliae metropolis*, 32: Hatton, *New view*, II, 734; Daniell, *London city churches*, 236. We shall treat in later pages Craven's gifts to schools, the universities, and the church (*vide post*, 237, 258, 286, 295). He likewise left in all £155 for the relief of prisoners, £345 for church repairs, and £120 for his company.

His son, John, the founder of the Craven scholarships at Oxford, was created Baron Craven in 1623. Craven was an immensely rich man, his will disposing of bequests totalling £42,167 and the whole estate, which cannot be exactly valued, certainly amounting to well over £120,000.

106. We shall discuss these charities in our study of Hampshire.

107. PCC 65 Meade 1618; *PP* 1823, VIII, 360; Wadmore, *Skinners*, 210 ff.; DNB. *Vide post*, 237, 286, for his benefactions for schools, scholars, and the lectureship. Lancaster's charitable gifts totalled very nearly £7000 from an estate of not much more than £10,000.

108. PCC 72 Parker 1619; *PP* 1816, XVI, i, 784; *PP* 1826–7, X, 445; *PP* 1884, XXXIX, ii, 421; *PP* 1904, LXXI, 782–784; Clode, *Memorials*, 19, 492. Harrison's larger bequests for schools, scholarships, and relief of prisoners will be considered in later pages (*vide post*, 182, 238). Harrison's father was a native of Great Crosby, Lancashire, which the son so richly remembered. The father was admitted to the Merchant Taylors by redemption in 1558 and the son by patrimony in 1591. Harrison died childless.

109. PCC 112 Soame 1620, sentence 59 Dale 1621; *PP* 1837–8, XXVI, 346, 445; *PP* 1884, XXXIX, ii, 176, iii, 121–122, 128. The details for the Essex distributions were very complicated. Two of the younger master wardens of the company were each year to purchase thirteen yards 'of broad Kentish cloth of decent mingled colour' at about 10s a yard, sixteen yards of Devon kersey at 6s 8d a yard, fifteen yards of black baize cloth at 2s 6d a yard, fifteen yards of black cotton at 8d a yard, 'nine leather sheepskins dressed in oil', six yards of sackcloth, four and a half ells of brown holland, ten yards of white jean fustian, six yards of russet fustian, two and a half ells of roan canvas, three men's Monmouth caps and three felt hats for women, and then were to transport the materials to the favoured parish for distribution there by the churchwardens as directed in the will.

110. PCC 97 Soame 1620; *PP* 1821, XII, 441; *PP* 1833, XVIII, 600; Cokayne, G. E., ed., *Complete baronetage* (Exeter 1900–1906, 5 vols.), II, 4; *Index to the . . . Remembrancia of London* (L., 1878), 31; *Students admitted to the Inner Temple* (L., 1877), 57. Seabright, a native of Wolverley, Worcestershire, was admitted to the Inner Temple in 1565. He was granted the reversion of the office of Town Clerk in 1568 and the office itself in 1574. He surrendered his post in 1613. Seabright also founded a grammar school at Wolverley (*vide post*, 238). He had made shrewd investments in real property and died a rich man. His Worcestershire charities will be noted in a later volume of this study.

111. PCC 85 Savile 1622; *Husting*, II, 748; *Surrey Record Society Publications*, XLIV (1943), 221, 267; *PP* 1824, XIII, 211; *PP* 1884, XXXIX, iv, 459; Fry, *Royal guide*, 124–125. Jeston's charitable contributions totalled £2432. His other charities included £160 for the use of his company, £400 for hospitals, £400 for loans, and £400 for scholarships at Cambridge. *Vide post*, 285, for his lectureship foundation.

112. PCC 20 Dale 1621; *PP* 1822, IX, 278; *PP* 1834, XXI, 282; *PP* 1835, XXI, 370; Fuller, *Worthies*, II, 58; *VCH, Herts.*, II, 69. Hale also left £40 for hospitals, £30 to poor scholars at the universities, £6 13s 4d for marriage portions, £60 for the sustenance of prisoners, and £20 to company uses, in addition to the generous provision for a grammar-school foundation in Hertford (*vide post*, 238).

113. PCC 106 Savile 1622; *PP* 1822, IX, 563; *PP* 1840, XIX, i, 13, 117, 424; Nichols, J. G., *Historical notices of the Stationers* (L., 1861), 10. Hewlett likewise made large bequests for almshouses (*vide post*, 158), and he gave lands valued at £1000 for the endowment of three London hospitals.

114. PCC 72 Byrde 1624; *PP* 1816, XVI, i, 804; *PP* 1829, VII, 265–267; *PP* 1839, XV, 30; *PP* 1902, LXXVI, 8–10; Hatton, *New view*, I, 161–162. Tamworth also left a substantial legacy to secure services daily in St Botolph Aldersgate and to provide divine services in a church at Leicester (*vide post*, 283).

115. PCC 147 Clarke 1625; *PP* 1823, VIII, 599; *PP* 1826, XIII, 329, 338; *PP* 1902, LXXVI, 'St Mary-le-Bow', 7; *S. P. Dom.*, 1628, CXXI, 58; *London parishes* (L., 1824), 23. Dunster held property abroad which he valued at more than £10,000. His total worth was of the order of £30,000, though his affairs at the time of his death were tangled in suits at law. We shall later refer to his benefactions for the clergy, for church building, and to his almshouse foundation (*vide post*, 148, 302).

116. PCC 76 Clarke 1625; Clode, *Merchant Taylors*, II, 329; *PP* 1823, IX, 582, 605; *PP* 1826–7, X, 447. Parker also established an endowment of £100 for the support of an organist in Walsall church and left the same amount to his company for its uses. He had served Sir William Craven as an apprentice; his former master at his death remembered him with a legacy of £100.

117. *Vide post*, 117–122.

118. *Vide post*, 175, 178–179, 185, 273, 283, 304.

119. *The last will and testament of Mr. John Kendricke* (L., 1625).

120. PCC 116 Byrde 1624; Fuller, *Worthies*, I, 136; *PP* 1819, X-A, 37; *PP* 1820, V, 92; *PP* 1837–8, XXV, 30, 336, XXVI, 432; *PP* 1840, XIX, i, 120, 499; *PP* 1884, XXXIX, iii, 154–155; Hatton, *New view*, I, 199–201; Seymour, *Survey*, II, 388 ff.; Johnson, *Drapers*, III, 466.

121. Shute, Nathaniel, *Corona charitatis* (L., 1626).

122. *Vide post*, 117.

123. Shute, *Corona*, 31–32.

124. *Ibid.*, 42–45.

125. For a discussion of the impact of these funeral sermons extolling the good works of the charitable benefactors of this period, *vide* Jordan, *Philanthropy in England*, 215–228.

126. The income has been used for various purposes over the years, including a lectureship, educating and clothing poor girls, binding out poor boys as apprentices, and for poor relief more generally.

127. PCC 57 Clarke 1625; Fuller, *Worthies*, II, 106–107; Shute, *Corona, passim; PP* 1822, IX, 307; *PP* 1884, XXXIX, ii, 22–23; Hatton, *New view*, II, 735; Ware, *Charities of St Leonard's*, 86; Freshfield, Edwin, ed., *Account books of . . . St Bartholomew Exchange* (L., 1895), 61; Freshfield, *Vestry minute books, St Bartholomew*, 77; Hill, Christopher, *Economic problems of the church* (Oxford, 1956), 271. *Vide post*, 175, 201, 287, for a discussion of his other great benefactions.

128. PCC 107 Clarke 1625; Beaven, *Aldermen*, II, 47; *Archaeologia*

cantiana, XX (1893), 82 ff.; DNB; *PP* 1819, X-A, 153; *PP* 1823, VIII, 354–358; *PP* 1837, XXIII, 489; *PP* 1867–8, LII, ii, 52; *PP* 1884, XXXIX, iv, 333; Rivington, Septimus, *Tonbridge School* (L., 1869); Hasted, Edward, *History of Kent* (Canterbury, 1797–1801, 12 vols.), IX, 609; Rees, J. A., *The English tradition* (L., 1934), 183. Smith also left £100 to London hospitals, £100 each to Virginia and Bermuda for church buildings in those colonies, as well as his great educational foundation in Kent.

Smith's testament of faith may be quoted as revealing something of the nature of the man: 'I commend my soule into the handes of almightie God to whom I render all my humble thanks for his infinite mercie and blessings bestowed upon me whch are more in number than I am able to expresse, especially for the death of his deere sonne my blessed lord and only saviour Jesus Christ by whose death and passion I do assure myselfe of salvation . . . and as concerning all and singular my mannors, messuages . . . and hereditaments . . . I do dispose and devise the same in manner and forme following. That is to say first because there is a portion due unto the poore of all the wealth that God blesseth man withall in this transitory life . . .'

129. PCC 109 Hele 1626, 23, 24 Skynner 1627; Wilson, *Merchant-Taylors' School*, I, 576, 658; Maskell, Joseph, *Allhallows Barking* (L., 1864), 168; *PP* 1816, XVI, i, 748, 780, 814; *PP* 1837–8, XXVI, 836–839; *PP* 1903, L, 1–3; *PP* 1904, LXII, 2. *Vide post*, 169, 182, 185, 266.

130. PCC 21 Skynner 1627; *PP* 1822, IX, 301–305; Hatton, *New view*, II, 735; Marsh, J. B., *The story of Harecourt* (L., 1871), 5; Beaven, *Aldermen*, I, 19, 176, 208, 256, II, 45, 175. In all, Bennett left charitable bequests with a capital worth of £2720. His benefactions for other charitable uses will be noted later (*vide post*, 182). Bennett had served as alderman for several wards; he was on three occasions master of his company, was president of Bethlehem and Bridewell (1606–1613) and of St Bartholomew's (1623–1627). He married the daughter of a London mercer. His second son and heir, Simon, was created a baronet.

131. PCC 87 Barrington 1628; Phillimore, W. P. W., *Family of Middlemore* (L., 1901), 88–89; *PP* 1822, IX, 235; *PP* 1903, L, 'St Clement's', 12–13; *PP* 1904, LXXI, 799. Middlemore also left relatively small bequests to the London hospitals and to poor prisoners. He was a native of Staffordshire, the son of a merchant.

132. PCC 101 Ridley 1629; Brett-James, N. G., *Growth of Stuart London* (L., 1935), 223–224; Barratt, T. J., *Annals of Hampstead* (L., 1912, 3 vols.), I, 103–112; Howitt, William, *Northern heights of London* (L., 1869), 6; *Bristol and Gloucestershire Archaeological Society Transactions*, XXI (1898), 236; Scott, J. D. G., *St Mary Abbots* (L., 1942), 33; *Complete peerage*, II, 130; Gilbert, Richard, *Liber scholasticus* (L., 1829), 92, 115; McDonnell, M. F. J., *St Paul's School* (L., 1909), 163, 202; Picciotto, Cyril, *St Paul's School* (L., 1939), 20; *PP* 1820, IV, 237, V, 168; *PP* 1829, VIII, 140, 197; *PP* 1884, XXXIX, ii, 20, iv, 6.

Hicks was London born (1551), his father, Robert, having been a substantial mercer. His widow, Elizabeth, was also a most generous charitable donor (*vide post,* 170, 175, 290), though Hicks had settled great fortunes on his two daughters and heirs well before his death. His epitaph recites that he had given £10,000 in charitable benefactions, though the total, so far as we can determine it, was more accurately £7058. Hicks's generous gifts for an almshouse, stocks for the poor, scholarships, municipal uses, and church general are noted in later pages (*vide post,* 157, 178, 205, 266, 273, 283). There is an excellent memoir in the DNB.

133. Fuller, *Worthies,* III, 217.

134. The Salters' records were lost in the Great Fire; so there is very little information to be had regarding his connection with the company.

135. PCC 1 Barrington 1628; Bray, William, *Collections relating to H. Smith, Esq.* (L., 1800), 5–7, 27–28, *et passim*; Seymour, *Survey,* II, 285; Lysons, Daniel, *Environs of London* (L., 1792–1796, 4 vols.), I, 512 ff.; Beaven, *Aldermen,* II, 51, 177; Gwilt, C. P., *Notices relating to Thomas Smith* (L., 1836); *Misc. Gen. et Her.,* 3d. ser., V (1904), 293; *VCH, Surrey,* IV, 110; Manning, Owen, and William Bray, *History of Surrey* (L., 1804–1814, 3 vols.), I, 405, III, 344–345; Brayley, E. W., *Topographical history of Surrey* (L., 1850, 5 vols.), III, 494, *et passim*; *Surrey Archaeological Collections,* XX (1907), 170; *PP* 1837, XXIII, 891, 896.

136. There is a detailed account in *PP* 1820, V, 448–466.

137. This sum, with an additional £1000 which we have not regarded as a charity, to ensure the relief of Smith's poor relations and their immediate descendants, was invested by the trustees in suburban property (Kensington and Chelsea) and was to increase enormously in value. With the gradual decline of piracy in the Mediterranean, the income from this fund began to accumulate very rapidly, and Parliament in 1772 passed an act enabling the trustees to employ this half of the endowment as well for the relief of Smith's poor kin, who appear to have been descendants of Smith's only sister, Joan, the wife of Henry Jackson.

138. This income was in 1641 allocated by the trustees in accordance with Smith's will in the following amounts:

	£
Parish benefits	1,737 p.a.
Specified towns	256
Poor clergy	500
Captives	65
Odd amounts	15
unassigned	44
	2,617 p.a.

It may be mentioned here that the income of these trusteed funds has increased relatively modestly, since so large a proportion was invested in agricultural properties. In 1823 the yield was £5250 19s, distributions to each parish being revised upwards on the basis of the 1641 allocations; in 1873 the income was £13,663 19s 8d; and at the last reporting date (1952), about £60,000.

139. The parishes benefiting under the trust, with the totals originally distributed under the 1641 agreement:

County	Number of parishes benefiting	Amount of annual stipend		
		£	s	d
Bedfordshire	1	4	0	0
Berkshire	1	13	0	0
Buckinghamshire	1	5	0	0
Cambridgeshire	1	6	13	4
Cheshire	2	16	0	0
Durham	6	70	0	0
Essex	6	57	6	8
Gloucestershire	2	16	0	0
Hampshire	12	80	0	0
Hertfordshire	3	29	0	0
Lancashire	1	9	0	0
Middlesex (London)	9	122	0	0
Norfolk	2	14	0	0
Oxfordshire	2	50	0	0
Radnor	1	5	0	0
Somerset	4	55	0	0
Staffordshire	3	44	0	0
Suffolk	4	32	0	0
Surrey	134	835	0	0
Sussex	13	138	0	0
Warwick	2	22	0	0
Wiltshire	6	52	0	0
Worcestershire	3	62	0	0
	219	1,737	0	0

139a. The writer is grateful to the trustees of the Charity for their courtesy in supplying information regarding its present charitable concerns. The capital worth of the Charity in 1958 was approximately £4,128,000, while the gross income was very nearly £220,000. This suggests, of course, that the worth of the Trust has increased something like sixty-five times over in the course of the past three centuries, an amazing fiduciary achievement even for London trustees. Charitable distributions are made directly by the trustees under twelve charitable heads, while distributions are still made, as well, in proportions set by the donor, to 202 parishes.

140. PCC 29 St. John 1631; *PP* 1820, IV, 433; *PP* 1822, IX, 183; *PP* 1823, VIII, 559; *PP* 1834, XXI, 132; *PP* 1839, XV, 24; *Va. Mag.*, XXV (1917), 390–391; Phillimore, W. P. W., ed., *London and Middlesex notebook* (L., 1892), 56–57. This donor was the son of Sir Thomas Bennett. He died unmarried at the age of forty-two. The rent-charge was legally defective, the lands having previously been conveyed to Bennett's brother, but the defect was cured by the will of the brother's widow in 1632, which provided a sum of £666 13s 4d to purchase other lands, if need be, to meet the requirements of the legacy.

141. PCC 83 St. John 1631; Beaven, *Aldermen*, II, 53; *PP* 1820, V,

104–106. Hyde likewise left £150 for the benefit of his company, £200 for a loan fund, and a large benefaction for a lectureship (*vide post*, 288). He was first chosen an alderman in 1614 and also served as sheriff. He was master of his company in 1611 and was for some time a commissioner of customs.

142. PCC 2 St. John 1631; *PP* 1829, VII, 479; *PP* 1839, XV, 215. Jackson also left £150 to the endowment of Christ's Hospital, £15 to his company, £20 to prisoners, and £500 for a loan fund to be employed to assist young girdlers in establishing themselves.

143. PCC 1 Seager 1634; Beaven, *Aldermen*, II, 52, 177; *Complete baronetage*, I, 219; *PP* 1822, IX, 193; Cokayne, G. C., *Lord mayors and sheriffs of London* (L., 1897), 92; Coleraine, H. H., *History . . . of Tottenham* (L., 1792), 56. Barkham also left an endowment of £133 to Christ's Hospital, £40 to clergy, and £20 to his company. He died and was buried at Southacre, Norfolk, where he was lord of the manor. An aged man, he had none the less been active in mercantile and civic affairs until shortly before his death. He had begun his career as a leatherseller, but had been translated to the Drapers in 1621, the year of his mayoralty. He had been master of both his companies. His son was created a baronet in 1623. Barkham's daughter, Susanna, was the great-grandmother of Sir Robert Walpole.

144. PCC 28 Audley 1632; *PP* 1823, IX, 200. Loft also left £4 p.a. towards the support of a lectureship in his parish church.

145. PCC 29 Seager 1634; *PP* 1816, XVI, i, 794; *PP* 1840, XIX, i, 123; *S. P. Dom.*, 1643, CCCCXCVIII, 11; Beaven, *Aldermen*, I, 38, 125, II, xxviii, 57. Freeman was a native of Northampton. He was first chosen alderman in 1622. He was long a member of the East India Company and of the Levant Company, serving on several of their committees. He was master of his own livery company in 1620 and was serving as lord mayor at the time of his death. Freeman's will disposed of £46,100 in personal and charitable bequests. He held at the time of his death a manor and other lands in Surrey, a manor in Kent, one in Hertfordshire, five manors in Devon, and several in Ireland, not to mention lands and mills in Derbyshire. He also left to an heir 'all manors and lands lately bought of King Charles', which are not, however, specified. Freeman's large bequests for other charitable uses will be noted in later pages (*vide post*, 179, 202, 305).

146. PCC 72 Seager 1634; *PP* 1816, XVI, i, 754; *PP* 1822, IX, 229–230.

147. Fuller, *Worthies*, II, 384; *PP* 1822, IX, 341, X, 193; *PP* 1884, XXXIX, v, 10.

148. PCC 39 Goare 1637.

149. PCC 119 Goare 1637; *PP* 1826–7, X, 449; *PP* 1884, XXXIX, iv, 375. She was the daughter of George Sotherton, a rich and well-known merchant tailor.

150. PCC 158 Goare 1637; Fuller, *Worthies*, II, 385; *PP* 1826, XII, 201; *PP* 1828, XX, 384; London County Council, *Survey*, XIX (1938), 40–41; Lloyd, J. H., *History of Highgate* (Highgate, 1888), 119; Howard, H. F., *An account of the finances of the college of St. John* (Cambridge,

1935), 61. *Vide post*, 262, for a discussion of Platt's great scholarship foundation at Cambridge and its somewhat tangled history. Platt was a grandson of Richard Platt, a brewer and alderman of London who had founded a school and an almshouse at Aldenham, Hertfordshire (*vide post*, 145–146, 233). His father, Sir Hugh, was an author, agriculturalist, and inventor of extraordinary talent (*vide* the DNB for an excellent short treatment). William Platt was educated at St John's, Cambridge, and maintained a large residence at Highgate Hill. He married a daughter of Sir John Hungerford of Gloucestershire.

151. PCC 5 Lee 1638; *PP* 1816, XVI, i, 798; *PP* 1820, V, 140. This donor was the daughter of John Ireland, a London salter.

152. *PP* 1823, VIII, 259; Gataker, Thomas, *Saint Stevens last will* (L., 1638). This lady had married Daniel Featley in 1622, being twice a widow and much his senior. Gataker tells us that 'divers pensioners she had that in a constant course received the fruits of her bounty ... and she had skill in physick and chirurgerie ... by waters and medicines to help the poore, being not onely as physician but as apothecarie also to them'.

153. PCC 158 Harvey 1639; *Arch cant.*, XI (1877), 232–250. This donor was the daughter of Thomas Howard, first Viscount Binden, and the widow of Sir Edward Seymour, Earl of Hertford, his third wife. She was also the widow of Henry Prannell, merchant and vintner of London.

154. PCC 67 Harvey 1639; *PP* 1830, XII, 70; *PP* 1884, XXXIX, v, 70.

155. PCC 190 Harvey 1639; Beaven, *Aldermen*, II, 59, 179. Fenn also left £100 towards the repair of St Paul's, £50 to his company for loans, and £40 for a dinner, £20 to prisoners, £15 to three named preachers, and £150 to London hospitals. Fenn, who left an estate valued at about £14,000, had since 1626 been an alderman and was lord mayor in 1637. He was long a member of the East India Company and twice master of his livery.

156. PCC 97 Harvey 1639; *PP* 1826–7, X, 450; *PP* 1884, XXXIX, iv, 375.

157. PCC 163 Coventry 1640, *PP* 1826, XII, 148, 186; *PP* 1829, VII, 33; *PP* 1830, XII, 30, 106; *PP* 1840, XIX, i, 124. Bailey likewise left a substantial bequest for Christ's Hospital, which will be noted later (*vide post*, 213).

158. PCC 69 St. John 1631; *Va. Mag.*, XXX (1922), 274–277; Freshfield, *Accounts, Vestry minute books, St Bartholomew;* Seymour, *Survey*, I, 251. Crashaw, a native of Derbyshire, was godfather to the poet who bore his name, to whom he left his house in London, property in Surrey, and money for his education. *Vide post*, 169, 183, 288, for his other benefactions.

159. PCC 104 St. John 1631; *PP* 1826, XII, 177; *PP* 1840, XIX, i, 121. Fryer did not clearly indicate the division he wished to be made of the income among the three favoured parishes, this being determined by a decree of Chancery in 28 Charles II. The residue of his estate was left to Christ's Hospital. The grandson of a well-known physician, John Fryer,

who had the distinction of being accused of Lutheran heresies in his early life and of popery in later life, Henry Fryer was educated at Gray's Inn.

160. PCC 137 St. John 1631; *PP* 1823, VIII, 335; *PP* 1884, XXXIX, iv, 317; Aikin, John, *History of the environs of London* (L., 1811), 61; Nichols, J. G., ed., *Wills from Doctors' Commons* (L., 1863), 92–97; Newcome, Richard, *An account of ... Denbigh* (Denbigh, 1829), 48; Fox Bourne, *English merchants*, I, 234–235, 246–252, 256–258; DNB. Middleton was a member of a great merchant family. He was born in Denbigh, where his father was serving as governor of the castle. He was a member of the Goldsmiths' Company and of the Merchant Adventurers. His brothers Thomas and Robert were charter members of the East India Company. Middleton is best remembered for his building of the New River Company's water conduit from the River Lea into London. His outlays greatly strained his resources, and he found himself forced to sell twenty-eight of his thirty-six shares of the capital stock, in order partially to retrieve his fortune. The first dividend was paid in 1633 at the rate of £15 3s 3d a share, but not many years later the shares had become very remunerative. In 1882 the Goldsmiths derived income of £2854 19s from the Middleton bequest.

161. PCC 13 Russell 1633; *Husting*, II, 755; *PP* 1823, VIII, 367–370; Wadmore, *Skinners*, 220–221. Meredith also left £100 to be lent without interest to young freemen of his company, £88 for the sustenance of prisoners, and an endowment yielding £10 p.a. to be paid to two poor preachers to be chosen by his company.

162. PCC 9 Seager 1634; *PP* 1816, XVI, i, 750, 768, 772, 806, 810; *PP* 1822, IX, 578; Inderwick, F. A., *et al.*, eds., *Calendar of ... Inner Temple records* (L., 1896–1936, 5 vols.), II, lxxxvi; Clinch, George, *Bloomsbury and St. Giles's* (L., 1890), 13. Fenner also left £100 for plate for the Inner Temple church and gave a window to the church of St Giles in the Fields.

163. PCC 124 Harvey 1639; *Complete peerage*, II, 345; *PP* 1820, V, 101; *PP* 1822, IX, 273; *PP* 1884, XXXIX, ii, 143; Baker, W. K., *Acton* (Acton, 1912), 138. This donor was the daughter of Giles Hueriblock, a Flemish merchant who settled in London. Her first husband, who died in 1614, was Richard Fust, citizen and grocer of London. She married Conway in 1619, who in 1623 was made one of the principal secretaries of state and who in 1627 was created Viscount Conway. We shall later note Lady Conway's gift for apprenticing (*vide post,* 169). She was also a generous donor to educational needs.

164. PCC 165 Harvey 1639; Fraser, William, *The Annandale ... book of the Johnstones* (Edinburgh, 1894, 2 vols.), I, 86; Wood, Marguerite, ed., *Records of ... Edinburgh* (Edinburgh, 1927–1950, 6 vols.), III (1626–1641), 232; *Gazetteer of Scotland* (Dundee, 1803), II, 363. Johnstone was educated at the University of Edinburgh and later seems to have taken a law degree in Europe. He came to London shortly after James's accession and in 1604 gained appointment as clerk of the deliveries of the ordinance. He was a close friend of Heriot (*vide post,* 239–240), serving as executor of that rich merchant's will. Johnstone left a volu-

THE CHARITIES OF LONDON 1480–1660

minous manuscript history of English and Scottish relations from 1572 to 1628, a portion of which was in 1642 published in Amsterdam. The extent of his charitable benefactions has been greatly exaggerated, though they were very generous indeed. *Vide post*, 179, 183, 242, for his large gifts for education and for social rehabilitation, all being for Scottish uses.

165. PCC 80 Essex 1648; *PP* 1816, XVI, i, 754, 802; *PP* 1824, XIII, 215; *PP* 1826, XII, 102, 571; *PP* 1830, XII, 58, 69; *PP* 1837–8, XXVI, 515; *PP* 1840, XIX, i, 122; *PP* 1884, XXXIX, v, 70; *PP* 1904, LXXI, 895, 982.

166. *Vide ante*, 80–82.

167. PCC 15 Crane 1643.

168. PCC 17 Crane 1643.

169. PCC 7 Crane 1643.

170. *PP* 1829, VII, 381; *PP* 1900, LXI, ii, 543.

171. PCC 32 Crane 1643.

172. PCC 35 Crane 1643.

173. PCC 10 Crane 1643.

174. PCC 24 Crane 1643.

175. PCC 15 Crane 1643. This donor also left £30 to prisons, £20 to hospitals, and £5 to the Surgeons' Company for plate.

176. PCC 27 Crane 1643.

177. PCC 9 Crane 1643.

178. PCC 20 Crane 1643. This donor, Thomasine Goodakers, also left £20 to twenty London parishes.

179. PCC 43 Crane 1643.

180. PCC 39 Crane 1643.

181. PCC 22 Crane 1643.

182. PCC 6 Crane 1643.

183. Commissary Court of London, Reg. 29, f. 213; *New-England Historical and Genealogical Register*, LIV (1900), 216–217. Hunt also left £33 for the aid of eleven ministers and £20 towards the founding of a library in New England.

184. PCC 300 Ruthen 1657. She likewise left £1 to the clerk and sexton of her own parish and £5 to church building in Shrawardine, Shropshire.

185. PCC 272 Ruthen 1657; Dale, T. C., ed., *Inhabitants of London in 1638* (L., 1931), 96.

186. PCC 110 Ruthen 1657.

187. PCC 272 Ruthen 1657.

188. PCC 519 Ruthen 1657.

189. PCC 168 Ruthen 1657.

190. PCC 4 Ruthen 1657.

191. PCC 290 Ruthen 1657.

192. PCC 343 Ruthen 1657.

193. PCC 524 Ruthen 1657; McMurray, *Records of two parishes*, 214.

194. PCC 124 Ruthen 1657.

195. Freshfield, *Accounts, St. Bartholomew*, 157.

196. PCC 456 Ruthen 1657.
197. PCC 12 Ruthen 1657.
198. PCC 385 Ruthen 1657.
199. PCC 7 Ruthen 1657.
200. PCC 3 Ruthen 1657.
201. PCC 524 Ruthen 1657. This donor's testament of faith may be quoted as typical of thousands carefully composed during these later years of our period: 'In the name of God Almighty . . . I Mary Cox of Covent Garden in the countie of Middlesex being weake in bodie but in perfect memory and considering my great age and the uncertainty of the tyme of my dissolution doe therefore make this my last will and testament . . . First I commend and willinglie surrender my soule into the hands of my saviour Jesus Christ through the merritts of whose death onlie I trust to be saved, and I committ my bodie to the earth trusting through the power of the resurrection of my saviour it shall be raised to glorie att the last day.'
202. PCC 520 Ruthen 1657.
203. PCC 215 Ruthen 1657.
204. PCC 338 Ruthen 1657.
205. PCC 223 Ruthen 1657.
206. PCC 520 Ruthen 1657.
207. PCC 3 Ruthen 1657.
208. PCC 373 Ruthen 1657; *Va. Mag.*, X (1902–1903), 406.
209. PCC 212 Ruthen 1657.
210. PCC 374 Ruthen 1657.
211. PCC 372 Ruthen 1657.
212. PCC 248 Ruthen 1657.
213. McMurray, *Records of two parishes*, 389.
214. PCC 454 Ruthen 1657.
215. PCC 64 Ruthen 1657.
216. PCC 75 Evelyn 1641; Freshfield, Edwin, ed., *Accomptes of . . . St. Christofer's* (L., 1885), 99; *PP* 1816, XVI, i, 748; *PP* 1822, IX, 230; *PP* 1829, VII, 323; Brayley, E. W., *Series of views of Islington* (L., 1819), 11. Heath likewise gave a large endowment for the founding of an almshouse (*vide post*, 160–161).
217. PCC 42 Evelyn 1641; Foster, Joseph, ed., *Alumni oxonienses . . . 1500–1714* (Oxford, 1891–1892, 4 vols.), II, 553; *PP* 1833, XVIII, 184; *PP* 1901, LI, 100; *PP* 1903, XLIX, 287; *PP* 1905, C, 154. Though the King was in his debt in the amount of £1000, Gawen was evidently a staunch Puritan who hoped 'to inherit a place among the members of the elect'. For his gift (1636) to the Green Coat School, *vide post*, 218–219.
218. PCC 7 Cambell 1642; *PP* 1822, IX, 277–278; *PP* 1884, XXXIX, iii, 102.
219. PCC 30 Twisse 1646; Ware, *Charities of St. Leonard's*, 40–41; *PP* 1837–8, XXVI, 516; Foster, William, *John Company* (L., 1926), 154; Sainsbury, E. B., ed., *Court minutes of the East India Company* (Oxford, 1907–1938, 11 vols.), I–V, *passim*. Fremlyn went out to India as a company agent at the age of eighteen. He rose rapidly in the company's

service and on his retirement in 1645 was in command at Surat. After nineteen years of eastern service he died, on his return, at the age of thirty-eight. Of his bequests, £200 was for the purchase of lands for the support of the poor of his native parish of St Leonard Shoreditch. *Vide post*, 155–156.

220. *PP* 1824, XIII, 218; Fry, *Royal guide*, 122. The indenture is dated August 22, 1646. Hazelfoot stipulated that the remainder was to be devoted to the needs of London hospitals and to secure the release of prisoners (*vide post*, 183). The gift to three London hospitals provided a capital worth of £400.

221. PCC 129 Twisse 1646; Beaven, *Aldermen*, II, 55, 178; *PP* 1824, XIII, 219; *PP* 1884, XXXIX, iv, 475. In 1884 the income on this endowment, invested in London properties, was £1530 3s 5d p.a. Rainton also left substantial benefactions charged on the above trust for other charitable uses, including £12 p.a. for London hospitals and £20 2s p.a. for company uses. For his apprenticeship endowment, *vide post*, 170.

Rainton was born in 1569 in Washingborough, one of the Lincolnshire villages remembered in his will. He traded as a mercer, though he was twice master of the Haberdashers. He served as an alderman from 1621, as lord mayor in 1632. In 1634 he was elected President of St Bartholomew's Hospital. He was one of four aldermen briefly imprisoned in 1640 when they refused to provide the Privy Council with a list of citizens who might contribute to a great loan to the King. He married a sister of Sir Thomas Mowlson, lord mayor in 1633.

222. PCC 4 Rivers 1644. This donor had first married Levinius Monk, one of the Six Clerks, and by inheritance from him and her father was rich in her own right. The will disposes, charities included, upwards of £2000, with manors and lands worth more than £500 p.a.

223. PCC 86 Aylett 1655; Bellers, Fulk, *Abrahams interment* (L., 1656).

224. PCC 81 Berkeley 1656; Beaven, *Aldermen*, II, 77. Glasbrooke was one of the few men of his status to be chosen as an alderman and, in 1651, as sheriff.

225. *PP* 1816, XVI, i, 792, 808, 812, 814; *PP* 1823, VIII, 290; *PP* 1826, XII, 149; *PP* 1830, XII, 244; *PP* 1837–8, XXVI, 373, 376. This donor, who died in 1666 (PCC 79 Mico), gave additional endowments for this same general purpose after our period closed.

226. PCC 168 Ruthen 1657; Beaven, *Aldermen*, I, 95, II, 79, 184; Green, M. A. E., ed., *Calendar of . . . Committee for Compounding* (L., 1889–1892, 5 vols.), *passim*. Herring was a treasurer of the Committee for Compounding. His charities totalled £1080, and he also left substantial amounts for scholarships and for the benefit of the clergy (*vide post*, 291).

227. PCC 165 Ruthen 1657. Van Acker's estate totalled upwards of £16,000.

228. PCC 107 Ruthen 1657; Beaven, *Aldermen*, I, 29, II, 84, 185; Baker, *Acton*, 140–142; Chaffers, *Gilda aurifabrorum*, 62; Prideaux, *Goldsmiths*, II, 118, 323; *PP* 1816, XVI, i, 760, 802; *PP* 1823, VIII, 338; *PP* 1884, XXXIX, iv, 297. Perryn was chosen an alderman in 1654 and secured his

discharge in 1656 on payment of a fine of £700. He served as prime warden of the Goldsmiths in 1655. In 1637 he, with other leading goldsmiths, had been severely punished and fined for melting heavy coins into ingots and exporting them. Perryn left £20 to general charity, £60 to his company, and large bequests for a school in his native town, for the support of the clergy, and for the endowment of lectures (*vide post,* 247, 291). In 1812 his company built twenty almshouses at Acton at a cost of £12,000 from surplus income from Perryn's trust, there being sufficient capital remaining to secure an annual income of £1277.

229. PCC 713 Wootton 1658; *PP* 1837–8, XXVI, 482; *PP* 1884, XXXIX, v, 252.

230. PCC 366 Wootton 1658; Beaven, *Aldermen,* II, 73; *PP* 1816, XVI, i, 780, 788; *PP* 1820, V, 100; *PP* 1822, IX, 276; *PP* 1840, XIX, i, 131; Freshfield, *Communion plate,* 35. For Keate's large legacies for apprenticeships, *vide post,* 171. This donor also established loan funds with a total value of £240.

231. PCC 663 Wootton 1658. Thurston also left £100 to St Bartholomew's and St Thomas's hospitals, as well as £100 and unspecified amounts owed to him to Christ's Hospital.

232. See Graph, *Appendix,* p. 425.

233. Willet, Andrew, *Synopsis papismi* (L., 1634, 5th ed.), 1224. This work, a general and violent attack on Catholicism, was first printed in 1592. The 1634 edition contains an appendix entitled 'A catalogue of good workes done since the times of the Gospell', from which our quotation is taken.

234. Biggers, J. R., *Finchley* (L., 1903), 22–23; *PP* 1816, XVI, i, 746; *PP* 1824, XIII, 318; Cooke, G. A., *Topography of Great Britain* (L., n.d., 47 vols.), VII, 97. Warren also gave a rent-charge of £2 p.a. for the relief of the poor of his parish and the same amount for the repair of 'foul and feeble highways' and other charitable uses within his parish.

235. PCC 40 Milles 1491; Nicolas, *Testamenta vetusta,* I, 379–381; DNB.

236. Clay, R. M., *The mediaeval hospitals of England* (L., 1909), 12, 80, 88, 122; Godfrey, W. H., *The English almshouse* (L., 1955), 38; 'St. Mary-le-Savoy', *British Archaeological Association Journal,* n.s., III (1897), 221–231; *The will of King Henry VII* (L., 1775). The King also intended that great almshouses should be built at York and Coventry as a charge on his estate, but these wishes were never fulfilled. *Vide post,* 275, 299.

237. *PP* 1824, XIII, 272; *PP* 1901, LII, 38.

238. PCC 16 Bennett 1509; *PP* 1884, XXXIX, iv, 576; *Husting,* II, 614, 624–625. Whittington's foundation had been made in 1423. The almshouse was endowed, somewhat inadequately, for the support of thirteen poor men. Finch's bequest was evidently designed to lend support more directly to the college, it being vested with a large chantry foundation, than to the associated hospital. The college was of course expropriated in 1548, though the almshouse was continued, at Highgate, by Whittington's company, the Mercers.

239. PCC 12 Fetiplace 1513; Beaven, *Aldermen*, I, 35, 123, II, 20; *PP* 1825, X, 94; Price, J. E., *The Guildhall of . . . London* (L., 1886), 130; Pendrill, *Wanderings*, 171; Fry, E. A., ed., *Abstracts of inquisitiones post mortem . . . London . . . 1577–1603* (L., 1908), 319; Herbert, *Livery companies*, II, 102–105. The endowment, being charged as well with a stipend of £4 p.a. each to four priests at Oxford and Cambridge (*vide post*, 256) to pray for the testator's soul, was expropriated, but in *4 Edward VI* it was returned to the Fishmongers, who undertook to maintain the charities. In 1618 the income from the trust was £118 p.a., of which £60 p.a. was distributed to thirteen poor in the company's almshouses at Newington, Surrey. This donor also gave £60 towards building a conduit in London. Kneseworth, a native of Cambridgeshire, was chosen alderman in 1503, and he was mayor in 1505.

240. *Vide post*, 300.

241. PCC 4 Holder 1515; Herbert, *Livery companies*, I, 253; Stow, *Survey*, I, 184, II, 143, 242; Chester, J. L., and G. J. Armytage, eds., *Parish registers of St. Antholin* (L., 1883), 9; Beaven, *Aldermen*, I, 168, 249, 273, II, 17; Strype, *Stow's Survey*, II, v, 123. In addition to his benefactions for an almshouse and church building, Tate left £26 14s for church repairs, £20 10s for church general, £144 8s for prayers, £20 to be disbursed at the mayor's discretion, £16 5s to poor householders, £8 8s to hospitals, £20 for roads, £66 13s 4d for marriage portions, and £40 for the aid of scholars in the universities. Tate became a mercer rather late in his career, being first an alebrewer; he was chosen alderman in 1485. He was twice mayor, in 1496 and 1514; he served in two parliaments, was four times master of his company. The total of his charitable gifts was £1762 12s.

242. PCC 9 Bodfelde 1523; Nicolas, *Testamenta vetusta*, II, 609–612.

243. *Vide ante*, 92.

244. Cooke, *Topography*, VII, 63.

245. PCC 35 Hogen 1536; Beaven, *Aldermen*, I, 10, 123, 155, II, 22; Johnson, *Drapers*, II, 36; PP 1837–8, XXVI, 395; Archer, J. W., *Vestiges of old London* (L., 1851), XVIII, 1–2; Stow, *Survey*, I, 147–148. Stow accused the Drapers of not fully honouring their commitments, but it appears that it was not before the mid-seventeenth century that the income from the trusteed properties equalled the obligations.

Milbourne, a native of Suffolk, was four times master of his company. He was probably knighted in 1522. He also endowed a fellowship at Cambridge, and his will ordered distributions of about £85 for masses, £43 6s 8d for the poor and for prisoners, £12 to lazar houses, £6 for hospitals, and £20 for marriage subsidies in his native town of Long Melford, Suffolk.

246. PCC 13 Dyngeley 1537; Coleraine, *Tottenham*, 55; *PP* 1826, XII, 163.

247. PCC 20 Alenger 1540; *Complete peerage*, IV, 354; *PP* 1822, IX, 216; *PP* 1884, XXXIX, iv, 590; Fry, *Royal guide*, 66–67. This woman was the daughter of James Finch, whose own almshouse foundation has been mentioned (*vide ante*, 137). She had first married Oliver Curteys,

a gentleman who died in 1503, and then John Dawes, a grocer who died in 1514. She then took as her third husband Richard Grey, Earl of Kent, who served as a soldier and courtier but was more distinguished for the wasting of his fortune at the gaming table. Grey died in 1524.

248. PCC 12 Alenger 1540; *Husting*, II, 654; Daniell, A. E., *London riverside churches* (L., 1897), 267; Stow, *Survey*, I, 116; Beaven, *Aldermen*, II, 28; *PP* 1819, X–A, 185 ff.; *PP* 1837–8, XXVI, 468; *PP* 1905, C, 200–201. Gibson had served as an alderman for Castle Baynard and as sheriff in 1538. His epitaph records that:

> By Avise my wyff children were left me non,
> Which we both did take as God had it sent;
> And fixed our myndes that joyntly in on,
> To releve the poore by mutuall consent.
> Now, mercifull Jesu, which has assysted owre intent,
> Have mercy on owre sowles, and for the residew
> If it be Thy will, Thou mayst owre act continew.

249. Foster, William, *The Ratcliffe Charity* (L., 1936); *History of the . . . Coopers* (Cambridge, 1944), 117; Elkington, George, *The Coopers* (L., n.d.), 185. *Vide post*, 211.

250. PCC 28 Spert 1543; Beaven, *Aldermen*, I, 156, 168, 299, II, 28, 170; *PP* 1822, IX, 286–289; *PP* 1867–8, LII, ii, 38–39; *PP* 1884, XXXIX, ii, 106. Dauntsey also left £200 to the Mercers' Company to be lent to four young men, each of whom would give, as interest, two loads of coal to the poor of St Lawrence Jewry and the same to those of St Antholin's. He was a member (for Thetford) of the Reformation Parliament, had been an alderman for a long time, master of his company in 1532, and sheriff in 1530. His wife was a daughter of Sir Thomas More. *Vide post*, 224, for his school.

251. PCC 6 Pynnyng 1544; *PP* 1824, XIII, 242; *PP* 1884, XXXIX, v, 180; Black, W. H., *History . . . of the Leathersellers* (L., 1871), 89.

252. PCC F. 5 Pynnyng 1544; Cox, *St. Helen*, 237.

253. PCC F. 5 Pynnyng 1544; Fry, *Inq. p. m.*, *London*, I, 52; Cook, *Mediaeval chantries*, 8; Stow, *Survey*, I, 112; Johnson, *Drapers*, II, 15; Beaven, *Aldermen*, I, 18, 256, 274, II, xxviii, 22; *PP* 1833, XVIII, 129. *Vide post*, 224, for his school foundation. Monox was first chosen an alderman in 1507, was mayor in 1514, and in 1523 was elected mayor a second time. Refusing to serve again, he was fined £1000, which was, however, remitted on his plea of ill health. He also was a Member of Parliament and six times master of his company.

254. *PP* 1822, IX, 252; *PP* 1884, XXXIX, v, 123–124, 141; West's will is in PCC 22 Coode 1550.

255. PCC F. 51 Alen 1547; Fry, *Inq. p. m.*, *London*, I, 100.

256. PCC 18 Powell 1552; Fry, *Inq. p. m.*, *London*, III, 143–145; *PP* 1826–7, IX, 349.

257. *Vide ante*, 93.

258. PCC 8 More 1554; Baddeley, *Cripplegate*, 232; *PP* 1837–8, XXVI, 404; *PP* 1884, XXXIX, ii, 175, iii, 120–121; Stow, *Survey*, I,

19. This donor was the mother of Anne Askew, who was in 1546 burned for heresy.

259. *PP* 1824, XIII, 272; *PP* 1901, LII, 38, 218; Humpherus, Henry, *Company of Watermen* (L., 1887, 3 vols.), I, 89. This almshouse served its function until it was pulled down in 1830 and the then almsmen pensioned with life annuities of £3 each.

260. *S. P. Dom.*, 1559, V, 5–14; *S. P. Dom.*, 1574, XCIX, 24.

261. PCC 12 Ketchyn 1556; Beaven, *Aldermen*, I, 4, 175, II, xxxi, 29; Heath, *Grocers*, 241; *PP* 1822, IX, 268; *PP* 1884, XXXIX, ii, 139–140; *Husting*, II, 665–666; Fuller, *Worthies*, II, 519. *Vide post*, 225. Laxton was chosen lord mayor (possibly being the first so entitled) in 1544. His executors set over the door of the school an inscription in Latin, Greek, and Hebrew, the Latin version being:

> Oundellae natus, Londini parta labore,
> Laxtonus posuit senibus puerisque levamen.

262. PCC 30 More 1555; *Husting*, II, 662–664; *PP* 1824, XIII, 233; Beaven, *Aldermen*, II, 30; Fry, *Inq. p. m., London*, I, 169–170. Lewin likewise left an annuity of 17s for poor relief, a residue of certain properties conveyed to his company, of perhaps £262 capital value, for general charitable uses, and £2 13s p.a. for prayers, as well as bequests for scholarships, Eton College, and the clergy. *Vide post*, 282.

263. PCC 58 Noodes and 54 Welles 1558; *PP* 1823, VIII, 358; Herbert, *Livery companies*, II, 332–339. *Vide post*, 225; for Elizabeth Holles's almshouse, *vide ante*, 139.

264. PCC 38 Chaynay 1559; *L. & M. Arch. Soc.*, n.s., II (1912) 314; *B. & G. Arch. Soc.*, XXI (1898), 261; *Husting*, II, 697; *PP* 1822, X, 191–192.

265. *PP* 1816, XVI, i, 746, 750, 810; *PP* 1824, XIII, 319. Haynes likewise established two endowments of £50 each, the income of which was to be devoted to the care of the poor of a London and a county parish.

266. PCC 7 Stevenson 1564; Russan, *Muscovy merchants*, 124. Stile also left £139 6s to the poor of London, Ipswich, and Hadley (Suffolk), £20 to his company for general charitable uses, £60 to London hospitals, £15 to Ipswich for a loan fund, and £1 to St Nicholas church, Ipswich.

267. *Vide ante*, 97, for Bowes' large benefactions for the poor. He also left £419 to the endowment of London hospitals. His almshouse foundation will be fully treated in a later volume of this study.

268. PCC 27 Stonarde 1567; *PP* 1835, XXI, ii, 1186; Rouse, W. H. D., *Rugby School* (L., 1898); DNB; Rees, J. A., *The Company of Grocers* (L., 1923), 86; Heath, *Grocers*, 248; Chase, C. A., *Some great charitable trusts of Great Britain* (Worcester, Mass., 1887), 34; Staunton, *Great schools*, 353–354. In addition to his great school foundation (*vide post*, 226), Sheriff left £5 to Rugby church for new pews, £10 to the poor, £3 for the repair of Rugby market-cross, and £2 for repairing a bridge there. He likewise left £13 7s to the uses of his company and as much to London hospitals.

Sheriff's bequest for the school and almshouse was modest, the property comprising eight acres of land in the London suburbs then renting for £8 p.a., but so sited that it increased enormously in value within two generations.

269. PCC 23 Babington 1568; Johnson, *Drapers*, II, App., 484, 526; Moore, *St. Bartholomew's*, II, 221; Beaven, *Aldermen*, II, 35; Strype, *Stow's Survey*, II, v, 134; *PP* 1820, V, 98; *PP* 1837–8, XXVI, 434, 447; *PP* 1884, XXXIX, iii, 130–133. Champion also left £117 13s to the poor, £30 to prisoners, £100 to St Bartholomew's Hospital, and £20 to his company, as well as establishing a loan fund of £250 to be lent free of interest to four young men of his livery. *Vide ante*, 98, for his widow's generous benefaction for poor relief.

270. PCC 1 Martyn 1574; Orridge, *Citizens*, 228; *PP* 1822, IX, 290; *PP* 1829, VII, 569; Beaven, *Aldermen*, II, 35, 172; I'Anson, Bryan, *The Martyn family* (L., 1935), 21–22. Martin also bequeathed £66 13s 4d for clothing the poor in four London parishes and an equal amount for the relief of two hundred poor in Long Melford. He left £16 13s 4d in alms for other London poor, £6 13s 4d for twenty sermons in the Mercers' Chapel, and £33 6s 8d for cups for various companies. He also left £200 for the relief of prisoners and £100 to university scholars.

271. In our treatment of Kent. Lambarde also left £200 to the Drapers' Company, to be lent to four young men of the livery without the exaction of interest.

272. Again, in our discussion of Kent. Also, *vide ante*, 99, and *post*, 177, 204, 228.

273. *Vide ante*, 101.

274. PCC 56 Spencer 1587; *PP* 1816, XVI, i, 784, 788; *PP* 1831, XI, 118; *PP* 1840, XIX, i, 98. *Vide ante*, 127, for Mary Paradine.

275. PCC 34 Leicester 1589. Every likewise left £50 capital for church repairs in London, £50 as a loan fund for his parish, £100 to the poor of the Clothworkers' Company, and £3 8s in alms for London's poor. In a later volume, we shall treat this Somerset foundation in greater detail.

276. PCC 47 Harrington 1592; Purnell, E. K., *Magdalene College* (L., 1904), 82; *PP* 1839, XIV, 412, 453; DNB. Wray was also a most generous donor to Cambridge University (*vide post*, 266).

277. PCC 15 Dixy 1593; *PP* 1824, XIV, 553, 558; Warton, Thomas, *Life of Sir Thomas Pope* (L., 1780), 165, 193–202; Wood, Anthony, *History of the colleges . . . in . . . Oxford*, John Gutch, ed. (L., 1786), 521. This generous woman left charities totalling approximately £1000. We shall later notice her school foundation and her gift to Oxford (*vide post*, 231, 257). She married first Anthony Beresford of Derby, then Sir Thomas Pope, and finally Sir Hugh Powlett of Hinton St George, Somerset. Pope was the founder of Trinity College, Oxford, trusting his widow to complete his work of foundation; she, with her brother (William Blount), served as executor of his estate.

278. *Vide ante*, 139, 141.

279. PCC 42 Lewyn 1598; *PP* 1823, VIII, 358 ff.; Wadmore, *Skinners*, 207; Herbert, *Skinners*, 330; *Arch. cant.*, XVII (1887), 205, 208, XX

(1893), 76; Rivington, *Tonbridge School*, 17. This donor was the wife of a famous merchant, 'Customer' (Thomas) Smith, who, like her father, was a generous benefactor to Kent. In addition to her bequest to the universities (*vide post*, 259), she left £320 to hospitals, £85 to poor women in London, £10 to needy preachers, and £20 to poor scholars.

280. PCC 22 Langley 1578; *PP* 1822, IX, 328–329; Fuller, *Worthies*, II, 106; White, *Walbrook*, 208; Beaven, *Aldermen*, I, 48, 182, 218, II, 37. Nicholas also left £100 to London hospitals, £81 to the poor of London and Huntingdonshire, and £10 to his company for a dinner. A native of Huntingdonshire, Nicholas served as treasurer of St Bartholomew's Hospital from 1559 to 1561 and again from 1562 to 1566.

281. Stow, *Survey*, II, 123, 380; Daniell, *London riverside churches*, 177; *PP* 1816, XVI, i, 816; *PP* 1824, XIII, 274; *PP* 1904, LII, 40, 153–154. Vandon, who was aged ninety-four at the time of his death, was a native of Brabant who entered Henry VIII's service as a soldier during the French campaigns. He was in 1546 listed as a servant of the Queen, when he was given a passport for a journey to Germany (*L. & P. Hen. VIII*, XXI, i, 371). He was truly described as a man 'of honest and vertuous lyfe, a careful man for poore folke'.

282. PCC 47 Bakon 1579; *Husting*, II, 699–700; Nicholas, *Doctors' Commons*, 57–67; Leveson Gower, *Family of Gresham*, 141–142; *Corporation of London*, 205, 229–230; Fuller, *Worthies*, II, 517; Ward, John, *Lives of professors of Gresham College* (L., 1740), 19; *PP* 1822, IX, 291; *PP* 1884, XXXIX, ii, 108–109; *PP* 1892, LIX, App., 1–39; DNB. *Vide post*, 201, 253, for a fuller discussion of Gresham's great charities, which totalled £13,097.

283. PCC 4 Rutland 1587; Foster, Joseph, ed., *Admissions to Gray's Inn* (L., 1889), 14; *PP* 1831, XI, 489, App., 618. Seckford was the son of Thomas Seckford, Esq., of Seckford Hall, Suffolk. A student at Gray's Inn in 1540, he became in 1558 one of the Masters of Request in Ordinary and Steward of the Court of Marshalsea. He served in Parliament and on several special judicial commissions.

284. PCC 36 Drury 1590; *Husting*, II, 712–713; Wilson, *Merchant-Taylors' School*, I, 1–23; Clode, *Merchant Taylors*, II, 58, 161, 231, *Memorials*, 18, 291, 365, 437; Staunton, *Great schools*, 212; *PP* 1826–7, X, 433. Hills had in 1560 given £500 to purchase the site for the Merchant Taylors' School, to which he added £10 p.a. for endowment, being far more truly its founder than the famous Sir Thomas White (*vide post*, 214–215). This remarkable man had been born in *ca.* 1514 in Milton, Kent. He early became a leading Protestant burgher, a friend of Cranmer, and a protector of Coverdale and Hooper. He went abroad in 1539 because of his advanced religious views, returning in 1548 and becoming a link between foreign Protestants and the leaders in the Edwardian church. He was admitted to the livery of his company in 1549 and was chosen its master in 1561.

285. PCC 46 Harrington 1592; *PP* 1816, XVI, i, 770, 774; *PP* 1837–8, XXVI, 503; Stow, *Survey*, I, 115; *Students admitted to the Inner Temple*, 32. Fuller also left property valued at £200 or more, the income

to be employed for the redemption of poor debtors, not more than £1 6s 8d to be expended on the release of any one prisoner.

286. PCC 41 Scott 1595; *Lansdowne MSS.*, LXXIV, 39, 'Draught of a book for founding an hospital at Westminster'; *PP* 1816, XVI, i, 744; *PP* 1819, X–B, 69; *Complete peerage*, III, 4; DNB; Scott-Giles, C. W., *Emanuel School* (L., 1935), 31–34. This donor was the daughter of Sir Richard Sackville. Her mother was a daughter of Sir John Bridges, a London merchant. Gregory Fiennes, Lord Dacre, her husband, was restored in blood and honour in 1558, his father having been hanged at Tyburn for murder. Much abler than her reportedly 'crack-brained' husband, she none the less lived happily with him, he alone being spared from her imperious temper. The endowment of this trust at the most recent reporting date (1950) was valued at £109,134 11s (*Corporation of London*, 225–227).

287. Fuller, *Church history*, III, 153; Bedwell, William, *Description of ... Tottenham Highcrosse* (L., 1631), 114; Coleraine, *Tottenham*, 80–81; Robinson, William, *History of ... Tottenham* (L., 1840, 2 vols.), II, 238, 242; *PP* 1826, XII, 157. Sanchez was the first confectioner in England, having early in his career been comfit-maker to Philip.

288. PCC 70 Wallopp 1600; *Husting*, II, 726–727; *PP* 1819, X–A, 78, 168; *PP* 1823, VIII, 300; *PP* 1833, XVIII, 178; *LCC Survey*, XIX (1938), 24. *Vide post*, 233, for Platt's ambitious school endowments. Platt was a very rich man, as well as a most generous one. He was the father of Sir Hugh Platt, the well-known agricultural writer, and the grandfather of William Platt, whose career and benefactions have been noted in earlier pages (*vide ante*, 125).

288a. PCC 52 Windebanck 1608; *PP* 1816, XVI, i, 790, 800; *PP* 1837–8, XXVI, 447; *London Top. Rec.*, V (1908), 32; Povah, Alfred, *Annals of St. Olave* (L., 1894), 266. *Vide post*, 234.

289. PCC 111 Windebanck 1608; Seymour, *Survey*, I, 247; *N. E. Hist. & Gen.*, XLVII (1893), 289; *PP* 1828, XI, 20. Owfield also left £100 to Christ's Hospital, £30 to the poor, £50 to the clergy, and a school and scholarship endowment for Ashbourne which will be discussed later (*vide post*, 232).

290. PCC 79 Fenner 1612; Hatton, *New view*, I, 348.

291. PCC 109 Cope 1616; Firth, J. B., *Middlesex* (L., 1906), 102; *L. & M. Arch. Soc.*, IV (1875), 274–275.

292. PCC 32 Weldon 1617.

293. PCC 1 Soame 1620; Heath, *Grocers*, 254; *PP* 1830, XII, 197; *PP* 1884, XXXIX, ii, 130; Beaven, *Aldermen*, I, 102, 251, 276, II, 43. Soame was also a very generous benefactor to his company and founded a school at Little Thurlow. He was a native of Beetley, Norfolk, but had married a woman (Anne Knighton) who was born in Suffolk. First a girdler, Soame in 1598 was translated to the Grocers. He served as lord mayor in that year. He was a member of the House of Commons for London in 1601, served as President of Bethlehem and Bridewell from 1598 to 1599, as Surveyor-General of Hospitals in 1609, and as Comptroller-General of Hospitals from 1610 to 1619. *Vide post*, 200, 238.

294. PCC 51 Dale 1621; *PP* 1825, X, 100; Herbert, William, *History of the . . . Fishmongers* (L., 1837), 85; *S. P. Dom.*, 1618, CIII, 7.

295. PCC 93 Dale 1621; *PP* 1825, X, 294–295.

296. PCC 21 and 51 Byrde 1624; *PP* 1826, XII, 34; *PP* 1884, XXXIX, ii, 33; Beaven, *Aldermen*, I, 131, II, 54, 178; Watney, *Hospital of St. Thomas Acon*, 215; Baddeley, J. J., *Aldermen of Cripplegate Ward* (L., 1900), 59. Halliday left charitable bequests totalling £1376 15s and including £60 outright to the poor, £66 13s 4d for charity general, £110 for hospitals, and £40 for prison relief. His large apprenticeship endowment will be separately noted (*vide post*, 169). A native of Wiltshire, Halliday was admitted to the Mercers' Company in 1589, and became its master in 1617 and again in 1624. He served as sheriff in 1617 and was a member of the Committee of the East India Company from 1614 to 1624. He married the daughter of Sir Henry Rowe, a former lord mayor, and his own daughters married Sir Henry Mildmay and Sir Edward Hungerford. He left an estate of more than £28,000, including a bequest of £14,000 to Mildmay's wife in trust for the purchase of land within one hundred miles of London for the benefit of her children and herself.

297. PCC 74 Byrde 1624; *PP* 1837–8, XXIV, 885; Thacker, F. S., *The Thames highway* (L., 1914), 68–69; Wood, Anthony, *The history . . . of . . . Oxford*, John Gutch, ed. (Oxford, 1792–1796, 2 vols.), I, 353; Nichols, John, *The progresses of King James* (L., 1828, 4 vols.), III, 439. Kempe also left £200 to the repair of St Paul's, £20 to the poor of London, and a great endowment for Oxford University which will be noted later (*vide post*, 260).

298. This benefaction will be dealt with more fully in our treatment of Buckinghamshire.

299. *Vide ante*, 113, for Dunster's endowment for poor relief, and *post*, 302, for his other very large benefaction. The Donyatt foundation will be more fully described in a later volume.

300. PCC 117 Skynner 1627; *N. E. Hist. & Gen.*, XLIII (1889), 294. Pemberton bequeathed £10 to his godson, Roger Williams.

301. PCC 36 Skynner 1627.

302. PCC 32 Barrington 1628; *PP* 1820, V, 99–100. This donor also left the residue of her estate, which yielded £220, in trust, the income to be used for the relief of the poor of her parish, St Dunstan in the East.

303. PCC 2 St John 1631; *PP* 1837–8, XXIV, 283. Hawkins also left £300 for the relief of distressed Protestant clergy in Germany, £100 to Peterhouse, Cambridge, for the teaching of 'Bible clerks', £100 to the poor of the French congregation in London, and £300 for the purchase of impropriations.

304. PCC 42 Audley 1632.

305. PCC 42 Audley 1632; *PP* 1820, IV, 300; Clode, *Merchant Taylors*, II, 345. Slany also founded a free school at Barrow, which was vested, with the almshouse, in joint trusteeship (*vide post*, 241).

306. PCC 51 Audley 1632; *PP* 1824, XIII, 265; *PP* 1902, LXXV, 2; *PP* 1904, LXXI, 785–786, 985, 988; Webb, E. A., *Records of St. Bartholomew's Priory* (Oxford, 1921, 2 vols.), I, 554; *Complete peerage*, VII, 67.

This donor was the daughter and coheir of Henry Codingham, auditor of the Mint, and Lord Saye and Sele's second wife.

307. PCC 108 Seager 1634; Beaven, *Aldermen*, II, 62; Fuller, *Worthies*, I, 567; *PP* 1822, IX, 315; *PP* 1826–7, X, 347. A native of this community, Perry was a leading member of both the Mercers' Company and the East India Company. He was chosen sheriff in 1632. His widow married Lord Newburgh, and his three daughters married respectively a knight and two baronets. We shall later have occasion to note Perry's substantial contributions for other charitable uses in his native county (*vide post*, 169, 205, 241, 289).

308. *PP* 1816, XVI, i, 762; *PP* 1837–8, XXVI, 489–490; *PP* 1900, LXI, iii, 41.

309. PCC 70 Goare 1637; *PP* 1825, X, 127. This donor was the daughter of Sir John Spencer of Althorpe. She had married first Ferdinando, fifth Earl of Derby, who died in 1594, and then, as his third wife, Baron Ellesmere, the great Jacobean chancellor. Ellesmere's seat was in Harefield. Alice Spencer was a patron of letters, and much of the best of the great library at Bridgwater House came to Ellesmere by this marriage.

310. Beaven, *Aldermen*, I, 140, II, xxxix, 58, 179; *PP* 1822, IX, 334; *PP* 1828, XX, 370; *Misc. Gen. et Her.*, 2d ser., V (1892–1893), 92–93.

Ellis Crispe (PCC 120 Clarke 1625) also left £150 on trust to the Salters' Company to be lent at 4 per cent to young men of the company, the income to be distributed: £4 p.a. to Marshfield for sermons, £1 p.a. to the poor of St Mildred Bread Street, and £1 p.a. to the poor of the company. Crispe served as sheriff in the year of his death. His son, Nicholas, was created a baronet.

Nicholas Crispe (PCC 164 Goare 1637) also left £4 13s to London poor, £25 for the uses of his company, £21 14s to various London hospitals, and £10 for the relief of prisoners.

311. PCC 49 Woodhall 1601; Widmore, Richard, *History of . . . St. Peter, Westminster* (L., 1751), 143; Chamberlain, Henry, ed., *New and compleat history of . . . London* (L., 1769), 143; Keepe, Henry, *Monumenta westmonasteriensia* (L., 1682), 226; Newcome, Richard, *Memoir of Gabriel Goodman* (Ruthin, 1825), 1–56; Fuller, *Worthies*, II, 534; DNB; *PP* 1837–8, XXVII, 84–99. Goodman also founded a richly endowed grammar school at Ruthin and a generous scholarship endowment (*vide post*, 216, 234). His will disposed as well £66 for the poor, £45 in stock for the poor, £25 for municipal betterments in Ruthin, £20 for hospitals, £2 p.a. to the clergy, and £140 (estimated) of residue to Oxford and Cambridge for their needs.

312. *Vide ante*, 105.

313. A popular ballad memorialized the charity of this man; *vide ante*, note 78.

314. The properties in Berkshire, comprising 224 acres, had been purchased by Goddard in 1597 and 1599 at a cost of £1400.

315. PCC 109 Dale 1621 ('admon. *t. a. i.* of William Goddard . . . Dec. 13, 1609, to relict Joyce'); Kerry, Charles, *History of hundred of Bray*

(L., 1861), 30, 74–75, 89, 124, 129, 165; *Husting*, II, 733; *PP* 1825, X, 114; *PP* 1884, XXXIX, iv, 225. Goddard was a native of Bray.

316. *Vide ante*, 104.

317. PCC 84 Capell 1613, sentence 51 Rudd 1615; DNB; Beaven, *Aldermen*, II, 42, 174; *S. P. Dom.*, 1608, XXXIV, 9; Hatton, *New view*, II, 748; *PP* 1819, X–A, 190; *PP* 1823, VIII, 297; Strype, *Stow's Survey*, I, i, 279–280. Dame Alice, as she was universally known in her old age, though Owen was never knighted, in addition to her almshouse and educational foundations (*vide post*, 235), left £66 13s 4d for hospitals and £50 for church repairs. Her charities totalled £3016 13s. She was the daughter of Thomas Wilkes, a landowner in Islington. Strype relates that she narrowly escaped death as a girl when an unskilled archer pierced her hat with an arrow while she was playing on the site of her future almshouse. Her first husband, Henry Robinson, was a brewer; her second, William Elkin, was a merchant. Her brother was a brewer, and several of her numerous children married London merchants or their daughters. Dame Alice's trust for the almshouse and school, being invested in lands in Islington and Clerkenwell, was later to increase enormously in value. Thus in 1897 the properties yielded £10,357 16s 2d. p.a.

318. *Vide ante*, 107, and *post*, 258, 285. This income also increased greatly, being reported as £1198 16s 3d in 1902.

319. *Vide ante*, 138.

320. PCC 69 Wood 1611; *PP* 1830, XII, 92; *PP* 1837–8, XXVI, 469; Venn, John, ed., *Alumni cantabrigienses* (Cambridge, 1922–1954, 10 vols.), I, iv, 455. Wood also left on trust London property then possessing a capital worth of £120 for the relief of London poor, £2 p.a. for sermons in St Botolph Aldgate, and £20 towards the rebuilding of the chapel at Lincoln's Inn. He was London born, having been educated at Cambridge and at Lincoln's Inn. He was called to the bar in 1583 and was made a bencher in 1596.

321. Nef, J. U., *Rise of the British coal industry* (L., 1932, 2 vols.), I, 151.

322. No considerable research has been done by us on Sutton's career, which has been fully treated in numerous studies. Principal reliance has been placed in Trevor-Roper, H. R., 'The bishopric of Durham', *Durham University Journal*, n.s., XXXVIII (1945), 45–58; Taylor, W. F., *The Charterhouse* (L., 1912); Davies, G. S., *Charterhouse* (L., 1921); Bearcroft, Philip, *An historical account of Thomas Sutton* (L., 1737); and in the article in the DNB, which last, it may be added, cleared away much of the myth that surrounded this most interesting man.

323. Some indication of the steep rise in the value of London real property is gained when we reflect that this property had been purchased by Suffolk's father (Thomas Howard, Duke of Norfolk) for £2500 in 1565.

324. *Vide post*, 218, for a discussion of the founding of the school.

325. PCC 101 Wood 1611, sentence 46 Fenner 1612; Blanchard, W. C., *Charterhouse* (L., 1849), 69–80; Bearcroft, *Sutton*, 78–109, *et passim*; Burrell, Percival, *Suttons synagogue* (L., 1628); Sutton, Thomas, *King*

James his hospitall founded in the Charter-House (L., 1614), 8–17; Roper, W. J. D., *Chronicles of Charterhouse* (L., 1847), 62 ff.; Adlard, George, *The Sutton-Dudleys* (N. Y., 1862), 16, 159–160; Collins, Francis, ed., *Registers . . . of Charterhouse Chapel* (L., 1892), 81; Cooper, C. H., *Memorials of Cambridge* (Cambridge, 1860–1866, 3 vols.), I, 369; Fuller, *Worthies*, II, 294.

326. Jordan, *Philanthropy in England*, 285.

327. Sutton by will provided as well £690 to be disbursed to the poor in various parishes in Lincolnshire, Essex, Middlesex, Yorkshire, Northumberland, and Cambridgeshire; £353 for roads and bridges in Essex and Middlesex; £1000 in loans for young London merchants; £20 for church repairs; £200 for the relief of prisoners; £500 to Magdalen College, Cambridge; and £333 6s 8d to Jesus College, Cambridge, as well as an impropriation and an advowson of the value of £400.

328. Willet, *Synposis papismi* (1634), 1231.

329. PCC 4 Lawe 1614; Boyd, *Roll of Drapers*, 34; *PP* 1816, XVI, i, 746; *PP* 1820, V, 76, 107; Seymour, *Survey*, I, 248.

330. *Vide ante,* 108.

331. *Vide post,* 202, 236, 285–286.

332. PCC 119 Weldon 1617. Wynne also left £100 to Christ's Hospital and £40 to his company.

333. PCC 1 Parker 1619; *Students admitted to the Inner Temple,* 101; *PP* 1837, XXIII, 781. The endowment was not completed until 1624 when Nicholas Thompson, a brother, added sufficient rents from his own estate.

334. PCC 110 Parker 1619; *Surrey Arch. Coll.,* III (1865), 292 ff.; Jupp, *Carpenters,* 251–256; Jupp, E. B., *Genealogical memoranda . . . Richard Wyatt* (L. ? 1866 ?), 17–21; *PP* 1820, V, 157; *PP* 1822, IX, 368; *PP* 1824, XIV, 630. Wyatt also left stipends for the poor of Isleworth, Queenhithe Ward, and his company, with a capital value of £186; £6 13s. for his company; and £16 13s for the uses of the poor in Bridewell.

335. PCC 61 Dale 1621; Beaven, *Aldermen,* I, 201, II, 49; *PP* 1819, X–B, 136; *PP* 1823, VIII, 433; *PP* 1837–8, XXVI, 405; *PP* 1884, XXXIX, iii, 153–154; *PP* 1895, LXXIV, 'St. Mary, Stratford-le-Bow', 1; Johnson, *Drapers,* III, 30. Jolles also founded a school at Stratford Bow, which will be mentioned later (*vide post,* 237). A native of Stratford Bow, he was twice master of his company, lord mayor in 1615, and Colonel of the Trained Bands from 1618 to 1621.

336. In our discussion of Bristol charities.

337. PCC 22 Byrde 1624; Reading, William, *Sion College* (L., 1724); *PP* 1823, VIII, 286, 575; *PP* 1835, XXI, 458; *PP* 1840, XIX, i, 121; *PP* 1902, LXXII, 5, 16–17; *PP* 1904, LXXI, 809; *S. P. Dom,* 1630, CLIX, 65; Kennett, White, MS. notes in his own copy of *The case of impropriations* (L., 1704), in the Bodleian Library. *Vide post,* 205, 255, 287.

338. PCC 9 Clarke 1625; *PP* 1816, XVI, i, 800; *PP* 1820, V, 149; *PP* 1833, XIX, 367, 384; Haskins, Charles, *Ancient trade guilds of Salisbury* (Salisbury, 1912), 317. *Vide post,* 287.

339. Fuller, *Worthies*, II, 385.

340. PCC 146 Hele 1626; *PP* 1822, IX, 568; *PP* 1829, VII, 357; *PP* 1830, XII, 43; *PP* 1835, XXI, ii, 895; *S. P. Dom.*, 1619, CIX, 104; Collier, J. P., *Alleyn papers* (L., 1843); Blanch, W. H., *Dulwich College* (L., 1877); Hosking, G. L., *Life and times of Edward Alleyn* (L., 1952); DNB.

341. Foster, *John Company*, 154–160; Brett-James, *Stuart London*, 199; Sainsbury, *Court minutes, East India Company*, I–V, *passim*. Among the larger of the later benefactions to this institution were £500 bequeathed in 1646 by William Fremlyn (*vide ante*, 131) and £100 given by Captain Thomas Kerridge (PCC 39 Wootton 1658). The scheme of the foundation was later enlarged to include a school and the building of a chapel, which will be discussed in later pages (*vide post*, 219, 244, 306).

342. PCC 99 Cope 1616; *L. & M. Arch. Soc.*, n.s., V (1925), 199; Beaven, *Aldermen*, II, 44. Bayning was a member of the East India Company from its foundation, serving as its treasurer in 1600–1602. He was chosen sheriff in 1593.

343. PCC 91 Ridley 1629; *Complete peerage*, I, 272; *PP* 1829, VII, 238; *L. & M. Arch. Soc.*, VI (1890), 107; Willan, Robert, *Eliah's wish* (L., 1630), 39. Bayning also left £100 to Christ's Hospital, £150 to London hospitals, £100 for the relief of prisoners, £100 for books for Sion College (*vide post*, 255), and lesser sums for miscellaneous charitable uses. Bayning, who succeeded to his father's great estate in Essex, married Ann, Dowager Viscountess Dorchester, the daughter of Sir Henry Glenham and of Ann, the daughter of Thomas Sackville, Earl of Dorset. His personal estate reached the immense total of £153,000, there being as well great landed properties in Essex and Suffolk.

344. PCC 127 Lee 1638; Parton, John, *Some account of . . . St. Giles* (L., 1822), 198; Povah, *Annals of St. Olave*, 238; *Complete peerage*, I, 272; *PP* 1829, VII, 239. Bayning, who had paid the Crown £18,000 for his own wardship, left an estate valued at approximately £78,330. He left as his heirs two daughters who both died childless. Parish records indicate that a judgment was found against Bayning's executors in 1653 for non-performance of the bequests, but a further enquiry conducted in 1817 disclosed no record of a recovery. Bayning also left £300 to Oxford, his own university, which was apparently never paid. He likewise left £200 to St Paul's Cathedral, £270 to London hospitals, £150 for the relief of prisoners, and £60 to the poor of several parishes.

345. *Vide ante*, 117, and *post*, 178, 205, 266, 273, 283.

346. PCC 126 Audley 1632; Beaven, *Aldermen*, I, 117, II, 62; Birdwood, George, ed., *East India Company letters 1600–1619* (L., 1893), 163 ff., 279, 295; Sainsbury, *Court minutes, East India Company*, I, 102, 120; *S. P. Dom.*, 1629, CXLIX, 31, CLII, 60; *S. P. Dom.*, 1631, CLXXIV, 81. Kirby also left £133 6s 8d. to his company, £100 to London hospitals, and £100 for prisoners. He served as one of the executors under the first Viscount Bayning's will. He traded principally in the East India Company and in the Levant Company, being a charter member of the former. In 1629 he was repaid a total of £24,000 which he had lent to the govern-

ment. Assignments totalling £4300 made by his widow suggest that he was still actively engaged in the East India trade at the time of his death. The Grocers' Company records provide no clue to the failure of his alms-house bequest.

347. PCC 150 Lee 1638. The Taunton foundation will be more fully treated in a later volume. Gray left in addition £170 to London hospitals, £200 to the charities of two Yorkshire towns, £110 for prisoners, and smaller sums for church repairs, the clergy, and municipal uses. It may be noted that the PCC document is not a will, but rather memoranda regarding the examination of Mr. George Langham with respect to a 'large sheet of paper' which must have been accepted as a nuncupative will.

348. This foundation will also be discussed in a later volume.

349. PCC 137, 162 Coventry 1640; *PP* 1826, XII, 596–597; *S. P. Dom.*, 1609, L, 84; *S. P. Dom.*, 1627, DXXVI, 14; *S. P. Dom.*, 1628, XCIV, 53; *S. P. Dom.*, 1637, DXL, 120; *L. & M. Arch. Soc.*, II (1864), 141; *Dale, Inhabitants of London*, 166. Dawes also gave £100 for the repair of All-hallows Barking church. He was a parishioner of St Olave Hart Street, where he paid £50 p.a. rental. By patrimony a skinner, Dawes was appointed Surveyor of Customers' and Comptrollers' Books in all ports save London in 1609, Supervisor of Customs and Subsidies in 1627, and, with his son, Collector of Customs Inwards for London in 1628. He died a very rich man.

350. PCC 83 Woodhall 1601; Herbert, *Livery companies*, I, 289; *PP* 1837–8, XXVI, 458.

351. PCC 92 Dorset 1609; *Husting*, II, 732–733.

352. PCC 11 Fenner 1612, sentence 122 Capell 1613; *PP* 1824, XIII, 242; *PP* 1884, XXXIX, v, 180, 184.

353. PCC 68 Dale 1621; Wood, *Edinburgh records*, III (1626–1641), 52; *Edinburgh 1329–1929* (Edinburgh, 1929), 35.

354. *Vide ante*, 113, for comment on his other large charities.

355. PCC 56 Lee 1638; Hatton, *New view*, II, 735; *PP* 1822, IX, 273; *PP* 1903, L, 'St. Margaret', 5.

356. We have included a bequest of £500 made by Sir Robert Ducie in 1634, to which his widow, Elizabeth, added £100. This bequest seems to have inspired the erection of twelve additional almshouse rooms in 1638 to augment the accommodations built in about 1593 for fourteen almsmen. Ducie also contributed £500 to the London hospitals, £100 to St John's College, Oxford, £140 to church repairs, and numerous other, but lesser, benefactions. PCC 61 Seager 1634; Herbert, *Livery companies*, II, 485; *PP* 1826–7, X, 448.

357. PCC 101 Twisse 1646; *PP* 1823, IX, 271. The daughter and coheir of Sir William Ryder, a rich London merchant, this donor was the wife of Sir Thomas Lake, who held minor official posts in Queen Elizabeth's late years and who, despite limited abilities, was appointed Secretary of State by James in 1616. Lake was ruined when, in a particularly ugly family quarrel, he and his daughter, the wife of Lord Roos, defamed the admittedly dubious character of the Countess of Exeter.

After a short imprisonment, Lake retired to Little Stanmore, to the estate of Canons, which he had purchased in 1604.

358. PCC 165 Essex 1648; *N. E. Hist. & Gen.*, XLVII (1893), 249; *PP* 1830, XII, 159. The income of £20 p.a. for the almshouse was subject to a life annuity of £4 to the testator's brother, Daniel, 'whom God hath in his mercy chastized by taking from him his estate'.

359. PCC 242 Grey 1651; *PP* 1823, VIII, 336; *PP* 1835, XXI, ii, 1274, 1333. Jenner also left in trust with the Goldsmiths London property with a capital worth of £870 charged with the payment of £15 p.a. to needy goldsmiths, £15 p.a. for the support of St Bartholomew's Hospital, and £25 p.a. towards the relief of the poor in three London parishes. Jenner likewise founded a school in Cricklade, Wiltshire (*vide post*, 244–245).

360. PCC 133 Fairfax 1649; Beaven, *Aldermen*, II, lv, 63; Bell, W. G., *London tells her story* (L., 1938), 164; Cobb, Gerald, *Old churches of London* (L., 1941), 87; *PP* 1821, XII, 243, 246; *PP* 1834, XXII, 209; *PP* 1837–8, XXVI, 635; *PP* 1840, XIX, i, 125; DNB; Worth, R. N., *History of Plymouth* (L., 1871), 311; Bracken, C. W., *History of Plymouth* (Plymouth, 1931), 148, 150; Hardy, Nathaniel, *A divine prospective* (L., 1654). Gayer also left £300 to the relief of the poor of London, £100 to the Fishmongers to provide a yearly distribution to the poor of the Hospital of St Peter's in Newington, Surrey, and a gift of £500 to Plymouth for the poor of that city. He provided as well funds for glazing all the windows of a church in Plymouth and for sermons there, while giving £133 6s to the municipal authorities of Coventry, the income of which was to be used for clothing the poor of that city in woollen cloth of a 'sad heere coller'. Nathaniel Hardy preached his funeral sermon at St Katherine Cree-church, where Gayer had endowed an annual sermon with a stipend of £1, it is said to commemorate his escape from a lion when as a merchant he was travelling in Arabia. Hardy praised him as an upright magistrate who 'behaved himself faithfully, courageously and discreetly . . . in the highest office of dignity . . . . A true patriot indeed he was, losing, for a time, his liberty, hazarding his estate, shall I say his life'. Hardy likewise praised his great charity, for 'as God had blessed him with a faire estate, so he gave him a large heart . . . dividing much . . . among those that were indigent'. The preacher could not refrain from reminding his auditors that that 'which was no small incouragement to him, and may be to others, in shewing workes of mercy; he found that he gathered by scatter-ing, his store encreased by distributing'. Gayer also established a substan-tial apprenticeship foundation at Christ's Hospital which will be noted later (*vide post*, 170).

361. Brittain, F., *South Mymms* (Cambridge, 1931), 41. The institu-tion survived until 1927, when the premises were closed and the income employed for pensions to needy persons.

362. PCC 135 May 1661; *PP* 1821, XII, 409, 416; *PP* 1884, XXXIX, iv, 420–430; Beaven, *Aldermen*, II, 71, 182; Fuller, *Worthies*, III, 67. Fuller tells us that Adams had a 'heart and hand proportionable to his estate'. He was chosen an alderman in 1649 and was brother to Sir Thomas Adams, a Royalist, who served as mayor in 1645. *Vide post*, 171, 247,

for a discussion of his other charities in Newport. Adams also left £22 p.a. to the poor of his company. His charities totalled £3680.

363. PCC 124 Ruthen 1657; Barrett, C. R. B., *History of the . . . Apothecaries* (L., 1905), 53.

364. Chancellor, E. B., *London's old Latin Quarter* (L., 1930), 75–76; *PP* 1826, XII, 186; *PP* 1905, C, 140–141.

365. PCC 220 Ruthen 1657.

366. *PP* 1820, V, 167.

367. PCC 248 Wootton 1658; Beaven, *Aldermen*, I, 6, 65, 140, 159, 251, 257, II, 64, 230; *PP* 1823, VIII, 340; *PP* 1828, XX, 391; *PP* 1840, XIX, i, 132; Chaffers, *Gilda aurifabrorum*, 58; Marcham, W. M., ed., *Parish of Hornsey* (L., 1929), xxi–xxii. Wollaston left a total of £6020 for various charities. He bequeathed £520 in all for poor relief, with substantial amounts for his own parish of St John Zachary and £10 p.a. for Tettenhall, Staffordshire, near which he was born. Wollaston also left £400 (£20 p.a.) to the uses of Bethlehem Hospital, £80 to named preachers, and £10 p.a. to the preacher at Highgate (Middlesex). His great bequests for an apprenticeship scheme and for education will be considered later (*vide post*, 171, 265).

Wollaston was knighted in 1641 and was elected lord mayor in 1643. A staunch supporter of Parliament, he was appointed Colonel of Trained Bands in 1641. He served at various times as president of Bethlehem, Bridewell, and Christ's Hospital, all of which were generously remembered in his will. Towards the close of his life, he invested heavily in lands just to the north of London.

368. PCC 438 Pell 1659; *Chetham Soc.*, n.s., X (1887), 68; *PP* 1824, XIV, 222; *PP* 1843, XVIII, 45; *VCH, Lancs.*, VII, 244. Higginson also left £60 to the poor of several London parishes and £100 each to Christ's Hospital and St Bartholomew's Hospital. *Vide post*, 246, 291.

369. PCC 537 Pell 1659; *PP* 1826, XII, 587.

370. *Vide ante*, 131.

371. Heath also directed his company to provide a sermon yearly on the day of his burial, to be attended by the company, and to pay £5 p.a. to divinity students at Oxford and Cambridge.

372. PCC 58 Cambell 1642; *PP* 1825, X, 222; DNB; Ward, *Professors of Gresham College*, 312; Parton, *St. Giles*, 198; *L. & M. Arch. Soc.*, VI (1890), 107. Croke also left £10 p.a. to augment the stipend of the clergyman at Chilton, Buckinghamshire, his birthplace, and contributed £100 to the library of Sion College.

373. PCC 9 Crane 1643; *PP* 1825, X, 121; Herbert, *Livery companies*, II, 95–97; Thornley, J. C., ed., *Guilds of London* (L., n.d.), 31. The remainder of the endowment of this charitable trust was devoted to a scholarship fund and to the support of Christ's Hospital.

374. PCC 21 Crane 1643; Beaven, *Aldermen*, I, 117, II, 62, 180; *PP* 1837–8, XXIV, 646; Brett-James, N. G., *Middlesex* (L., 1951), 161–162. He also left £121 to the poor of London, including £100 to be distributed to twenty poor widows of the clergy, £16 to the poor of certain Lincolnshire parishes, £50 for the relief of prisoners, £50 to his company

for plate, £130 to London hospitals, and £100 to his company for a loan fund. Wright was chosen mayor in 1640. His personal estate was valued at £24,000. His three daughters all married baronets, his manor of Swackley (near Uxbridge) being left to one (the wife of Sir James Harrington, a member of the court that tried Charles I) on condition that she entertain her sisters for fourteen days each year.

375. PCC 44, 49 Cambell 1642; PP 1824, XIII, 217; Entick, John, New history and survey of London (L., 1766, 4 vols.), IV, 248; Godwin, George, Churches of London (L., 1839), 'Allhallows', 5; Hatton, New view, II, 735. Hammond also left £10 p.a. to the poor of Allhallows, £100 to the endowment of Bridewell, a bequest of £500 for a loan fund for poor young men of his company, and a lectureship (vide post, 289–290).

376. PCC 107 Grey 1651; PP 1829, VII, 353; Green, M. A. E., ed., Calendar of Committee for Advance of Money (L., 1888, 3 vols.), 1209. This donor also left an annuity of £5 for the relief of the poor of St Martin Vintry. She describes herself in her will as residing at Burnham, Somerset, but it is clear that her property and her family connections were in London. She was in difficulties in 1650 as an alleged delinquent, which might well have caused her to withdraw to the country.

377. PCC 183 Bowyer 1652; PP 1820, IV, 320; PP 1826, XII, 112; PP 1833, XIX, 191–192. Stafford had also probably built three small cottages at Harlow, Essex, where his wife had been buried, for poor widows of that parish. His will conveyed fee-farm rents of £12 p.a. to local trustees, of which £2 p.a. was to be used towards the support of almswomen in these quarters, £5 p.a. for the relief of poor householders of the parish, £2 p.a. for the maintenance of the church clock and bell, and the remainder for various church uses.

378. PCC 321 Brent 1653; Beaven, Aldermen, II, 68, 181; PP 1820, V, 176. Methold was a native of Norfolk, being a nephew of Sir William Methold, Chief Baron of the Exchequer in Ireland. He entered the service of the East India Company in 1615 and was the first Englishman to visit the diamond mines of Golconda. In 1633 he carried out a mission for the company in Persia. He seems to have returned to England to reside permanently in 1636, and in 1647 he was chosen as an alderman.

379. Smith's will suggested a change in the terms settled by the indenture of 1645. If the company would build and endow an almshouse in or near London with half the total capital, his executors would add £175 to the stock. The company elected to abide by the earlier covenant.

380. PCC 344 Aylett 1655; Beaven, Aldermen, II, 71; PP 1835, XXI, 159; PP 1837–8, XXVI, 44; PP 1839, XIV, 366; PP 1884, XXXIX, iii, 167; Johnson, Drapers, III, 180.

381. The Longport foundation will be treated in our discussion of Kent.

382. PCC 211 Berkeley 1656; PP 1837, XXIII, 292; PP 1828, XX, 384.

383. PCC 56 Pembroke 1650; Sedgwick, Obadiah, Christ the life (L., 1650). The younger Wilson was lieutenant-colonel of a London regiment in the early months of the Civil War, being promoted to colonel in 1646. He was a convinced Independent. A member of the Vintners' Company, he was elected alderman in 1648 and to the Council of State in 1649 and

1650. He sat in Parliament for Calne from 1646. Sedgwick, in his funeral sermon, called him 'an excellent man to the state, and a precious Christian to God'.

384. PCC 41 Alchin 1654; *L. & M. Arch. Soc.*, n.s., I (1905), 343, VI (1933), 30, 65, 67; Whitelocke, Bulstrode, *Memorials of the English affairs* (Oxford, 1853, 4 vols.), I, 223, II, 375; *PP* 1822, X, 499; *PP* 1825, X, 578. Wilson founded a grammar school in Westmorland (*vide post*, 245), where he likewise provided an annuity of £2 12s for bread distribution, making arrangements for an equal distribution for the poor of Merton, Surrey. He gave £100 to Christ's Hospital for an annual dinner of roast meat for the children, £63 12s as capital for the poor of St Martin Oteswich, and several lesser benefactions. A native of Kendal, the elder Wilson married the daughter of a London merchant and as early as 1630 paid a fine of £500 when he declined to serve as sheriff. He was the leading vintner of his generation, though his principal investments were in land possessing a capital value of at least £40,000 at the time of his death.

385. *Vide post*, 219.

386. PCC 61 Nabbs 1660; Fuller, *Worthies*, II, 427; *PP* 1819, X-A, 181; *PP* 1840, XIX, i, 824-825; DNB.

387. PCC 171 Ruthen 1657; Fuller, *Worthies*, II, 80–81; *PP* 1837–8, XXVI, 46, 49, 406, 508; *PP* 1884, XXXIX, iii, 168; Boyd, *Roll of Drapers*, 193; Johnson, *Drapers*, III, 97. Walter also left £9 13s p.a. for his company's use, £32 p.a. to the poor of London and his company, and £20 p.a. to the poor of his native city of Hereford. The total of his charitable gifts would seem to have a capital worth of £8416, though Fuller's estimate of nearly £10,000 could well be more accurate.

388. PCC 356 Pell 1659; *Complete peerage*, V, 179; *PP* 1822, X, 771; Jeffery, R. W., *Thornton-le-Dale* (Wakefield, 1931), 131–132, 212–214; *VCH, Yorks., North Riding*, II, 475–476; Drake, Francis, *Eboracum* (York, 1788, 2 vols.), I, 312. We shall deal at some length with these great Yorkshire foundations in a later volume and shall then provide biographical particulars.

389. The certain count is 914 in those foundations for which the donors or the executors clearly indicated the number of almspeople on the foundation.

390. The average stipend indicated by London donors for their foundations was £3 10s 1d p.a., this being, incidentally, a very high figure by provincial standards. The certain count is 667 when the details of the foundation are fully known.

391. *Vide ante*, 133–135. This estimate assumes that 4000 families were protected by endowments for household relief, while 1700 were cared for under almshouse foundations.

B. Experiments in social rehabilitation

1. *Vide ante*, 101, 142.

2. PCC 82 Dixy 1594; Beaven, *Aldermen*, II, 43, 174; Wilson, *Merchant-Taylors' School*, I, 4; *L. & M. Arch. Soc.*, n.s., VIII (1940), 40–41;

Black, *Leathersellers*, 65; Fry, *Inq. p. m., London*, III, 224–225. Offley left as well rents of £4 p.a. for poor relief, £97 to various hospitals, £77 for scholarships, and £20 for prisoners, as well as large loan funds totalling £540 for the benefit of young London leathersellers, young shopkeepers, and merchants of Chester.

3. *Vide ante*, 106, for his benefactions for poor relief. Strelley also left a residue worth £100 for the uses of his company.

4. *Vide ante*, 147. The fund was by will established as a loan fund, with the interest of £30 p.a. to be used to secure the apprenticeships. Halliday's widow obtained a Chancery decree setting aside the loan provisions and dedicating the use solely to apprenticeships, while increasing the number of boys assisted from four to six. Halliday also left £200 to the Mercers as a loan fund, to be lent without interest to worthy young merchants.

5. *Vide ante*, 116, and *post*, 182, 185, 266.

6. *PP* 1816, XVI, i, 808; *PP* 1822, IX, 248; *PP* 1826, XII, 126; Gilbert, *Liber scholasticus*, 434. Shaw also left £8 p.a. to his company to maintain two scholars in the universities, £270 in capital and doles for the poor of London and Derbyshire, £1 p.a. for sermons, and £7 1s 4d p.a. for company uses.

7. *Vide ante*, 126, and *post*, 183, 288.

8. PCC 5 Russell 1633; *PP* 1820, V, 133; *PP* 1840, XIX, i, 123, 426; *Husting*, II, 754; O'Donoghue, *Bridewell*, II, 70–71. Locke also left £1000 to Christ's Hospital (*vide post*, 213).

9. *Vide ante*, 148, and *post*, 205, 241, 289.

10. *Vide ante*, 127. She also left substantial legacies to hospitals and for education.

11. PCC 1 Coventry 1640; *PP* 1816, XVI, i, 746; *PP* 1826–7, X, 448; *PP* 1884, XXXIX, iv, 370; Lewis, Samuel, *St. Mary, Islington* (L., 1842), 441; Parton, *St. Giles*, 198; Scott, *St. Mary Abbots*, 33; *DNB*. Coventry also left £42 for church repairs and ornamentation and £37 for company uses. His bequests to the poor possessed a total capital value of £280.

12. PCC 142 Harvey 1639.

13. PCC 108 Cambell 1642; Beaven, *Aldermen*, II, 62. Abdy also left £120 for the poor of several London parishes and one hundred gowns for those needing clothing.

14. PCC 19 Crane 1643. Stanley also left a total of £546 for the relief of the poor in London and in various Warwickshire communities, including an annuity of £10 each to two maidservants who had served their employers faithfully for at least seven years. His charities totalled £1265; he gave £135 for various company uses, £20 for church repairs, £39 to the clergy, £120 for St Bartholomew's Hospital, and £100 each to the Drapers' Company of Coventry and to the Dyers' Company of London for loans without interest charges. This donor was a merchant tailor.

15. PCC 109 Rivers 1643; *PP* 1816, XVI, i, 762, 786; *PP* 1820, V, 168; *PP* 1822, IX, 194, 316; *PP* 1825, X, 146; Mitton, G. E., *Hampstead and Marylebone* (L., 1902), 33. Lady Campden also left £200 for poor

relief in London and suburban parishes, £100 for the relief of prisoners, £330 for the Mercers' Company, £100 to Sion College Library, and large benefactions for loans and for lectureships (*vide post,* 175, 290). This donor was the daughter of Richard May, a rich merchant tailor, a sister of Sir Humphrey May (1573–1630), a Parliamentarian and Privy Councillor of moderate political persuasion, and the wife of Baptist Hicks, Viscount Campden, whose great charities are noted in this work (*vide ante,* 117, 157, and *post,* 178, 205, 266, 273, 283). Her own benefactions reached the impressive total of £6430.

16. *Vide ante,* 131, for mention of his other charities.

17. *Vide ante,* 160.

18. *PP* 1840, XIX, i, 130. Langham (1584–1671) was of the Grocers' Company, had served as sheriff in 1642, and sat in Parliament in 1654.

19. This charity was part of an elaborate foundation made to secure an almshouse (*vide ante,* 160) and an educational trust (*vide post,* 247) for the benefit of his native town of Newport, Shropshire.

20. PCC 65 Berkeley 1656; Newcome, *Memoir of Gabriel Goodman,* 56 ff. Goodman also left £1 for church repairs, £1 10s to the poor in alms, and property with an estimated capital worth of £100 for poor relief in Wales, a residue of £116 for the relief of sequestered clergymen, and a substantial sum for a travelling fellowship.

21. PCC 125 Berkeley 1656; *PP* 1837–8, XXVI, 427; Johnson, *Drapers,* III, 473. Royley also left £20 p.a. to the poor of his company, £1 10s p.a. to the minister of St. Mary-le-Bow, and £8 10s p.a. for his company's needs.

22. PCC 339 Ruthen 1657. Whitley also left a total of £236 for poor relief, £268 for sermons and for plundered ministers, £50 to Christ's Hospital, £50 for loans, and £50 for marriage portions.

23. *Vide ante,* 133.

24. Ware, *Charities of St. Leonard's,* 87; Ellis, Henry, *History of . . . St. Leonard Shoreditch* (L., 1798), 11; *PP* 1837–8, XXVI, 522.

25. PCC 149 Pell 1659; Hardy, Nathaniel, *Carduus benedictus* (L., 1659), 31. Hardy in his funeral sermon described Bowyer as 'a garden with . . . flowers of many excellent virtues . . . the marygold of piety . . . the rose of charity . . . a virtue which ever attendeth upon the former, the love of God and of our neighbour being inseperable. The charity of this our brother, was though extended to all, yet especially directed towards the poor and needy . . .'. He must be commended, too, for bestowing so much of charity during his lifetime. 'He gave when it was in his power to have kept, he scattered his almes with both hands, and yet the one hand must not know what the other did: by all which it appeareth he was a truly charitable man.' Bowyer also gave £100 to be distributed among poor clergymen and their widows.

26. *Vide ante,* 160, and *post,* 265.

27. PCC 22 Nabbs 1660; *PP* 1823, VIII, 337; *PP* 1826–7, X, 6; *PP* 1839, XV, 346; Shuckburgh, E. S., *Emmanuel College* (L., 1904), 218; Cooper, *Memorials of Cambridge,* II, 362; Beaven, *Aldermen,* I, 59, II, 69. Ash likewise provided 10s. p.a. for each of eight working gold-

smiths who stood in need, wiredrawers being excepted, £3 p.a. for the relief of the poor of Derby, and approximately £7 p.a. from surplus income for the uses of his company. His larger educational foundation and his endowment for a lectureship in Derby will be noted later (*vide post*, 265, 291). Ash served as auditor of the city 1644–1646, as an alderman after 1648, and as prime warden of his company in 1649. He was at one time master of the Muscovy Company.

28. *PP* 1824, XIII, 192; *PP* 1884, XXXIX, iv, 454; Smith, A. M., *Roll-call of Westminster* (L., 1912), 114; *Historical description of Westminster-Abbey* (L., 1753), 31. Lady Burghley also gave £200, the income of £10 p.a. to be expended as follows: £2 13s 4d p.a. for sermons at Cheshunt, £4 6s 8d p.a. for the relief of poor householders there, and £3 p.a. for wool and flax on which the poor of that parish might be set on work. She is likewise remembered as the founder of a scholarship in St John's College, Oxford. Her loan fund was reported exhausted in 1670. The second wife of the great Elizabethan statesman, Lady Burghley was a daughter of Sir Anthony Cooke of Essex. Roger Ascham described her as one of the two most learned women in all England.

29. PCC 229 Brent 1653; *PP* 1830, XII, 80; *PP* 1884, XXXIX, v, 281. Meredith also left £6 p.a. to provide books for needy scholars in the school at his birthplace, Kempsey, Worcesterhire; £4 p.a. for Bibles to be distributed in Christ's Hospital; and he had earlier (1644) given three hundred books to Sion College Library.

30. PCC 2 Holgrave 1503; Ditchfield, P. H., ed., *Memorials of old London* (L., 1908, 2 vols.), II, 32; Beaven, *Aldermen*, II, 19, 167; Chaffers, *Gilda aurifabrorum*, 38; Stow, *Survey*, I, 295–296, 345. Stow tells us that these houses were 'vniformely builded foure stories high, bewtified towardes the streete with the Goldsmithes armes and the likenes of woodmen, in memory of his name, riding on monstrous beasts, all which cast in lead, richly painted ouer and gilt'. Wood also left £16 7s for general church uses, £10 8s to church repairs, £5 for prayers, an estimated £103 for the poor of London, £2 to almshouses, £4 for prisoners, and £20 for marriage subsidies, as well as £66 13s 4d for church uses and £6 13s for church repairs at his birthplace, Bocking in Essex.

31. PCC 36 Stonarde 1567; Clode, *Merchant Taylors*, II, 103, 146, 178, 183, 193–194, *Memorials*, 13, 432, 456–457; Stevenson, W. H., and H. E. Salter, *St. John's College, Oxford* (Oxford, 1939), 114–115, 137, 141; Coates, Charles, *History of . . . Reading* (L., 1802), 407–410; *Husting*, II, 678; *PP* 1823, VIII, 585–590; *London Topographical Record*, XV (1931), 92; DNB. White's great educational foundation will be discussed in later pages (*vide post*, 257–258). He also gave or bequeathed £1100 for municipal uses in Bristol and £65 for the same in London. The sequence of the rotation of his loan fund was as follows:

1577—York	1582—Worcester	1587—Southampton
1578—Canterbury	1583—Exeter	1588—Lincoln
1579—Reading	1584—Salisbury	1589—Winchester
1580—Merchant Taylors	1585—West Chester	1590—Oxford
1581—Gloucester	1586—Norwich	1591—Hereford

1592—Cambridge   1595—Bath   1598—Colchester
1593—Shrewsbury   1596—Derby   1599—Newcastle
1594—Lynn   1597—Ipswich   1600—Bristol

32. It is pleasant to relate that only £50 of the capital was lost in the first 250 years of this loan fund's operation.

33. PCC 30, 31 Drake 1596 (a series of four wills drawn by this prudent testator); Wilson, *Merchant-Taylors' School*, I, 4; *PP* 1824, XIII, 195–196; *PP* 1837–8, XXIV, 376; *Husting*, II, 714. Offley also left bequests for municipal uses and for scholarships. *Vide post*, 198.

34. PCC 50 Woodhall 1601; *PP* 1820, IV, 135, 140, App., 132; Seymour, *Survey*, I, 181, 244; Harding, *Tiverton*, II, 101 ff.; DNB. Blundell also left £20 p.a. to be used to apprentice four poor boys of Tiverton annually in husbandry, £100 for road repairs in the vicinity of Tiverton and £50 to the church there, as well as £200 for company uses. His great benefactions for the relief of prisoners and education will be considered later (*vide post*, 182, 234). His gifts to hospitals totalled £1260. Blundell was born in 1520 in Tiverton, where as a lad he first worked for cloth carriers. After his removal to London, he quickly became a great figure in the cloth trade, first as a merchant and later as a manufacturer.

35. *Vide ante*, 114, and *post*, 178–179, 185, 273, 283, 304, for Kendrick's other benefactions.

36. *Vide ante*, 115, and *post*, 201, 287.

37. For this donor's other benefactions, *vide ante*, 170, and *post*, 290.

38. *Vide ante*, 173.

39. The fact is that London, Somerset scantly aside, devoted the lowest proportion of its total charitable funds to this use, of all the counties of England. These proportions are:

	per cent		*per cent*
Bristol	1·68	London	0·70
Buckinghamshire	0·75	Norfolk	2·21
Hampshire	1·65	Somerset	0·69
Kent	1·67	Worcestershire	0·73
Lancashire	0·82	Yorkshire	1·14

40. We should at once say that after some hesitation we have classified Bridewell as a hospital rather than as a workhouse. As we shall later note (*vide post*, 193–195), it possessed a curiously mixed as well as a changing function during our whole period, the workhouse aspect so importantly present in the earlier decades of its existence rapidly withering away. It may be remarked here that we have counted benefactions totalling £10,015 12s made to Bridewell during our period.

41. PCC 14 Chaynay 1559; *PP* 1823, VIII, 350; Wadmore, *Skinners*, 201; Seymour, *Survey*, I, 181. Hunt also left property valued at £800 to his company to be lent to its young freemen at 5 per cent, the interest to be added to principal until the income should reach £400 p.a., at which time it should be distributed to the poor of the company. This aspiration was attained in about 1800.

42. *Vide ante*, 99, 142, and *post*, 204, 228.

43. PCC 9 Leicester 1588; *Husting,* II, 713; Wadmore, *Skinners,* 206; *PP* 1822, IX, 135; *PP* 1823, VIII, 374–376.

44. PCC 47, 130 Cope 1616; *PP* 1823, IX, 577; *PP* 1826–7, X, 444; *PP* 1840, XIX, i, 113; *PP* 1884, XXXIX, iv, 382; *PP* 1902, LXXVI, 'St. Antholin's', 14; Archer, *Vestiges of old London,* 14; Bell, W. G., *et al., London Wall* (L., 1937), 89; Delaune, *Angliae metropolis,* 32; Seymour, *Survey,* I, 247. Parker was a substantial philanthropist, whose charities totalled almost £5000. He gave £220 to the endowment of the Merchant Taylors' almshouse and £160 for the relief of prisoners, as well as large benefactions for municipal betterments, schools, his company, and religious uses (*vide post,* 205, 283, 295).

45. PCC 91 Weldon 1617; Beaven, *Aldermen,* II, 48, 176; Strype, *Stow's Survey,* II, v, 140. Hayes also left a total of £175 to the poor of London and Weybridge, Surrey, £130 to London hospitals, £26 14s to the clergy, £30 to his company, and £25 for the relief of prisoners. He was moderately rich, having left £8700 in personalty, the lease of a manor and other properties in Surrey, a manor in Essex of a capital worth of £500, 150 acres of land in Suffolk, and other scattered real property.

46. *Vide ante,* 109, and *post,* 259.

47. *Vide ante,* 117, 157, and *post,* 205, 266, 273, 283.

48. PCC 100 Cambell 1642; *PP* 1825, XI, 22; *PP* 1826, XII, 586; *New York Genealogical Record,* XLI (1910), 283; Baildon, W. P., ed., *Records of Lincoln's Inn, Admissions* (L., 1896, 2 vols.), I, 196; Walker, C. D., ed., *Records of Lincoln's Inn, The Black Books* (L., 1897–1898, 2 vols.), II, 302. The bequest was a term rental of £100 p.a. on certain lands which were sold by the executor for £324 and settled in equal amounts on these two endowments and a school foundation (*vide post,* 243). The Warwickshire fund was saved by being converted, well before 1696, into an apprenticeship endowment. The Banbury capital was soon exhausted.

49. PCC 140 Berkeley 1656; *Historic Society of Lancashire and Cheshire, Transactions,* n.s., XXIV (1908), 30, XL (1925), 91; *PP* 1826, XIII, 141; *PP* 1829, VII, 109. This endowment was apparently lost. James Fletcher, a haberdasher, left £10 to the poor of his parish and £15 to rigorously Presbyterian divines. He left £10 to the poor of Bretherton, Lancashire, and £30 to build a causeway in that, his wife's native town. We shall later notice his substantial educational foundations in Lancashire (*vide post,* 246).

50. *Vide ante,* 114, 175, and *post,* 185, 273, 283, 304.

51. We have here followed principally the detailed account of Kendrick's charities set out in *S. P. Dom.,* 1631, CXCI, 37, CXCII, 76, CCII, 24, CCIII, 39, CCIV, 36–37, CCV, 46, CCVI, 63; *S. P. Dom.,* 1632, CCX, 95–97, CCXI, 27, CCXXII, 45. A full-scale investigation of the handling of the charity by the local authorities was undertaken under a commission from the Attorney-General in 1631–1632, on the basis of a petition from certain residents of Reading, complaining that the trust stipulations were not being fully or sensibly carried out.

52. *Vide ante,* 124, and *post,* 202, 305.

53. *Vide ante,* 127, and *post,* 183, 242.

54. PCC 1 Cambell 1642; Beaven, *Aldermen,* I, 25, 176, 251, II, 54, 176; *PP* 1824, XIII, 237; *PP* 1835, XXI, 113, 115; *PP* 1840, XIX, i, 406; Strype, *Stow's Survey,* I, i, 274; Nicholl, *Ironmongers,* 536–543. Cambell's certain charities total £10,534. He provided £970 for poor relief, including an addition of £500 to an endowment for supplying free coals to the poor begun by his father, £120 in clothing, £100 to the French and Dutch poor, and £200 to the poor of two London parishes and of Barking, Essex; a total of £541 13s to his own and other companies; and £250 for the building of a bridge near Wanstead, Essex. His larger benefactions for prisoners, schools, and the clergy will be discussed in later pages (*vide post,* 183, 243, 305). Both Cambell's will and other sources make it seem at least remotely possible that an additional £10,000 may have been laid out by the executors at their discretion for other 'charitable and pious uses'. But this hardly seems likely, since there is no historical trace of what would have been a very large additional sum. Cambell's father, Sir Thomas, was an ironmonger who was chosen lord mayor in 1609 (*vide ante,* 108). The son followed the father's trade and was elected lord mayor in 1629. He was thrice master of his company, President of St Thomas's Hospital, and for many years a member of the Committee of the East India Company.

55. *14 Eliz., c. 5; 39 Eliz., c. 3; 43 Eliz., c. 2.*

56. An undated petition (STC 25969) from prisoners in the Wood Street Compter to an unstated benefactor sets out the pathos of the condition of prisoners in this period: 'In all lamentable manner, most humbly beseecheth your good worship, wee the miserable multitude of very poore distressed prisoners in the hole of Woodstreet Counter, in nomber fiftie poore men, or thereabouts, lying upon the bare boordes, still languishing in great neede, colde and miserie, who, by reason of this daungerous and troublesome time, be almost famished . . . and hunger starved to death: others very sore sicke and diseased for want of reliefe and sustenance by reason of the great number which dayly increaseth, dooth in all humblenes, most humbly beseech your good worship, even for Gods sake, to pitie our poore lamentable and distressed cases: and nowe helpe to relieve and comfort us with your Christian and godly charitie against this holie and blessed time of Easter. And wee, according to our bounden duties do, and will, dayly pray with Almighty God for your long life and happy prosperitie. We humbly pray your Christian and godly charitie to be sent unto us by some of your servants'.

57. *Vide ante,* 101–102, and *post,* 185, 228.

58. PCC 54 Drake 1596; Delaune, *Angliae metropolis,* 59; Johnson, *Drapers,* II, App., 486; Nichols, J. B., *Account of royal hospital of St. Katharine* (L., 1824), 45; Stow, *Survey,* II, 39. Rokeby also left £100 to the Drapers, the fund to be used for loans, with the interest payable to the poor of Queen Elizabeth's Hospital, Greenwich; £20 to the poor of St Katharine's Hospital and £2 each to its almspeople; £100 to Christ's Hospital; and a scholarship foundation. A Yorkshireman, Rokeby was educated at Cambridge and Lincoln's Inn. He served in Ireland for some years as a

legal adviser and judge, returning to England in 1572. He was appointed Master of Requests in 1576, Master of St Katharine's Hospital in 1580.

59. *Vide ante*, 103.

60. *Vide ante*, 103.

61. *Vide ante*, 175, *and* post, 234.

62. Apperson, G. L., *Bygone London life* (L., 1903), 130–131.

63. PCC 85 Windebanck 1608; *Va. Mag.*, XXVIII (1920), 34–37; Beaven, *Aldermen*, I, 158, II, 49, 176; *PP* 1822, IX, 299; *PP* 1826–7, X, 12. Walthall, who had served as an alderman, sheriff, and master of his company, also left £40 to the poor of London, £86 13s for various hospitals, £500 to the Mercers' Company to be lent to ten young men of the fraternity with interest of £25 p.a. to be divided: £10 p.a. to Christ's Hospital, £9 p.a. to poor Cambridge scholars, and £6 p.a. for company uses. He likewise left £246 13s 4d in trust to St Peter Cornhill parish, to be lent to shopkeepers at moderate interest rates for the benefit of the poor of the parish, as well as £100 to his native city of Derby for the same general uses.

64. *Vide ante*, 108.

65. *Vide ante*, 110.

66. PCC 119 Meade 1618. Wiseman also left £100 for the poor of various London parishes and £20 for the needy of his company, £100 to Christ's Hospital, £40 for the general uses of the Goldsmiths, and £10 for church repairs. His estate, not including a manor and other lands in Essex, may be valued at £15,308.

67. *Vide ante*, 111, and *post*, 238.

68. *Vide ante*, 121.

69. In 1904, £980 p.a. was being paid from this fund towards the rehabilitation of prisoners. *Vide ante*, 116, 169, and *post*, 185, 266, for Andrews' other benefactions.

70. *Vide ante*, 116–117, for his gifts to the poor. Bennett also left £20 p.a. for the succour of the children of Christ's Hospital.

71. PCC 34 Skynner 1627. A native of Herefordshire, this donor had been left a widow in 1617. John Carey, her husband, served as Warden of the Eastern Marches and in a number of diplomatic missions. On the death of an elder brother in 1603, Carey succeeded to the title first conferred on his father.

72. *Vide ante*, 126, 169, and *post*, 288.

73. PCC 23 Audley 1632; Beaven, *Aldermen*, I, 132, II, 57; Nicholl, *Ironmongers*, 560; [Owen, Hugh,] *History of Shrewsbury* (L., 1825, 2 vols.), II, 270; Cokayne, *Lord mayors*, 101; Baddeley, J. J., *Aldermen of Cripplegate Ward* (L., 1900), 61–62. Heylyn left £300 in trust for the benefit of the poor of Shrewsbury, bequeathed £100 to Bridewell and £50 to Christ's Hospital, left £200 capital to his company for loans to its young men, and provided an endowment of £100 for an annual sermon on England's deliverance from the Gunpowder Plot. He is, however, best remembered for having in *ca.* 1625 principally financed the translation of the Bible into Welsh and for having promoted the publication of a Welsh dictionary. A native of Shrewsbury, Heylyn was apprenticed in London

in 1576 and was admitted to the freedom of the Ironmongers in 1584. He served as an alderman after 1624, was sheriff in 1624, and was twice master of his company. Peter Heylyn, the eminent preacher, was his nephew. *Vide post*, 198, 288, for Heylyn's substantial bequests to municipal uses, the clergy, and for the founding of a lectureship.

74. PCC 13 St John 1631. *Vide post*, 198. He likewise gave substantially for the augmentation of clerical stipends.

75. *Vide ante*, 127, 179, and *post*, 242.

76. *Vide ante*, 179, and *post*, 243, 305.

77. *Vide ante*, 131.

78. PCC 21 Fines 1647; *PP* 1822, IX, 274–276; Hubbard, J. J., *Allhallows the Great* (L., 1843), 85–86. Lady Middleton had intended that this annuity should amount to £40, but by codicil indicated that since the parish of Forden, Montgomeryshire, had no settled maintenance for its minister, her executors should have power to apply £30 p.a. of the legacy for this use unless Parliament should settle a stipend in the parish. By a decree of Chancery, the disposition contemplated by the codicil was ordered carried out. This donor also left £640 of endowment (£32 p.a.) for the relief of the poor, including the widows of poor ministers, £70 for almshouses, and £60 for apprenticeships. She also gave £200 to London hospitals.

79. PCC 270 Ruthen 1657. Vallence likewise left £100 to his company for its uses, as well as £50 for its poor, £100 to the poor of St Botolph Bishopsgate, and £50 to those in his own parish, and £100 for church repairs in his parish.

80. *Vide ante*, 91, and *post*, 276.

81. *Vide ante*, 93, and *post*, 203.

82. PCC 24 Alen 1546; Johnson, *Drapers*, II, 44–45, 83 ff., III, 490 ff.; *PP* 1837–8, XXVI, 421; *PP* 1884, XXXIX, ii, 193, iv, 150; *Econ. Hist. Rev.*, 2d ser., III (1950–1951), 365. In 1860 schools for girls were built at Llandaff and Denbigh by the trustees at a cost of upwards of £41,000 and, with other Welsh educational institutions, were for many years supported in whole or in part by the great revenues of this endowment.

Howell was apprenticed to the Drapers' Company, gaining his freedom in 1507 and the livery sometime prior to 1521. In that year, he entered his name as a subscriber to Cabot's proposed voyage. In 1527 he was elected fourth warden of his company. From 1517 until his death—which we cannot date more precisely than 1536–1538, he lived mostly in Spain, where he conducted a large business in bringing in English cloth and exporting to England a variety of merchandise.

83. PCC 4 Wrastley 1556; *PP* 1824, XIII, 243–244; *PP* 1884, XXXIX, v, 181. Another fourth was vested for the maintenance of roads, another for alms, and the remaining fourth for the relief of London prisoners.

84. PCC F. 28 Wrastley 1557. *Vide post*, 204. This donor also left £100 to be lent to deserving young tradesmen, £55 to the poor of her parish, and a residue of perhaps £120 for the relief of honest but distressed householders who had suffered from fire or some such calamity.

85. PCC 42 Bakon 1579; Nicholl, *Ironmongers*, 524; *PP* 1824, XIII, 234–235; *PP* 1835, XXI, 308. This donor's charities were based on a bequest of £2000 to the Ironmongers' Company, to be lent on good surety to twenty trustworthy young men of the company, the company in turn to guarantee the principal and to administer a charitable fund of £100 p.a., which was to be employed, in addition to the marriage subsidies, £30 p.a. for the benefit of three London hospitals, £10 p.a. for the diet of prisoners in all London and Westminster gaols, £25 p.a. for fuel for the poorest householders in London, £10 p.a. for an annual dinner for the company, and £5 p.a. for the endowment of a projected school at Bishop's Stortford, Hertfordshire. Margaret Dane was the daughter of Edmund Kempe, a substantial London mercer. Her husband was a native of Bishop's Stortford.

86. *Vide ante*, 102, 181, and *post*, 228.

87. PCC 29 Meade 1618; *PP* 1816, XVI, i, 754, 802, 814; *PP* 1826, XII, 88; *PP* 1837, XXIII, 810. Duckett, who was probably a brother of Gregory Duckett, Rector of St Andrew Holborn from 1611 to 1624, also left £66 13s 4d to be used as a loan fund.

88. *Vide ante*, 114, 115, 178–179, and *post*, 273, 283, 304.

89. *Vide ante*, 116, 169, and *post*, 266.

90. Willet, *Synopsis papismi* (1634), 1223.

91. The total of contributions to the five hospitals (and for the care of the sick in other ways) was £154,995 18s, but £24,123 1s of this total has been assigned to other charitable uses as intended by the donors.

92. This brief sketch is based on Moore, Norman, *The history of St. Bartholomew's Hospital* (L., 1918, 2 vols.); *PP* 1840, XIX, i, 1–73; Fuller, *Church history* (1837), II, 251–253; Tawney and Power, *Tudor econ. doc.*, II, 305–306; and *The ordre of the hospital of S. Bartholomewes* (L., 1552). This latter work was published on the order of the lord mayor to answer 'certayne busie bodies' who had criticized the operation of the hospital. The outlays of the preceding year are set out in detail, but would seem to total £795 2s rather than the £798 2s indicated in the text itself. In the previous year 800 patients had been discharged and 172 had died. If people would but consider the 'excessyve prices of all thynges at this day', they would wonder that so much had been done with the revenues in hand.

93. The royal endowment, being in effect a transfer of medieval benefactions given in large part for other purposes, has not been included as a charitable gift.

94. PCC 8 Bodfelde 1523; Clode, *Merchant Taylors*, II, 22, 35, *Memorials*, 85; Cooke, *Top. of Great Britain*, VII, 227; Beaven, *Aldermen*, I, 91, 138, 175, II, 19; *PP* 1820, V, 349; Cobb, *Old churches*, 38; Bruce, *Memories and monuments*, 156; Bumpus, T. F., *Ancient London churches* (L., 1923), 149; *London parishes* (1824), 29; DNB. Jenyns also left £11 for church general, £50 for prayers, £4 to the poor, £20 for marriage subsidies, £10 for roads, as well as substantial benefactions for church building, his company, and education, which will be noted later (*vide post*, 201, 222–223, 300). His benefactions totalled £2693, a very large sum

for this early period. A native of Wolverhampton, Staffordshire, Jenyns married, after completing his apprenticeship, the widow of a former master of the Merchant Taylors' Company. He was chosen an alderman in 1499 and sheriff in the same year. He was master of his company in 1489 and mayor in 1508.

95. *PP* 1840, XIX, i, 471 ff.; *S. P. Dom.*, 1632, CCXXIV, 21; *S. P. Dom.*, 1633, CCXXXVII, 5; *A true report of the great costs . . . of the foure hospitals . . . in London* (L., 1644).

96. *PP* 1840, XIX, i, 614 ff.; Willet, *Synopsis papismi* (1634), 1223; *S. P. Dom.*, 1632, CCXVI, 114.

97. It should be noted that all bequests clearly intended for the support of the educational functions of the institution have been credited under school foundations rather than under hospitals.

98. *A psalme of thanksgiving to be sung by the children of Christs Hospitall* (L., 1610).

99. *S. P. Dom.*, 1631, CLXXXIX, 22. The number of children being cared for had in 1637 risen to 'near upon 1000' (*S. P. Dom.*, 1637, CCCLVI, 145).

100. *PP* 1840, XIX, i, 74–384; Lempriere, William, ed., *John Howes' MS., 1582* (L., 1904); Pearce, E. H., *Annals of Christ's Hospital* (L., 1901); Blunden, *Christ's Hospital; The Christ's Hospital book* (L., 1953); *A true report.*

101. *Howes' MS.*, 47–48.

102. Tawney and Power, *Tudor econ. doc.*, II, 306–312.

103. Ridley, Glocester, *The life of Dr. Nicholas Ridley* (L., 1763), 377.

104. *Howes' MS.*, 58–59.

105. *London. Orders for setting roges to work* (L., 1580?).

106. *Psalme of thanksgiving: A report for Bridewell* (L., 1610).

107. In 1631 the income of Bridewell from all sources was £1025 2s 2d; its outlays £1133 8s (*S. P. Dom.*, 1631, CXC, 10).

108. The number in 1658 seems to have been even larger. For a most interesting account of the hospitals and their services during the period of political dislocation, *vide Bute broadsides* (Houghton Library, Harvard University), I, 44, 53, 65, 76–77.

109. *Vide ante*, 164–166.

C. Municipal betterments

1. *Vide ante*, 90 and *post*, 275.

2. Stow, *Survey*, II, 10, 358n.; *Husting*, II, 648–649. Cooke was also a merchant adventurer and probably a merchant tailor. His capital messuage had been purchased from Sir Richard Gresham, who in turn had bought it from the Duke of Norfolk.

3. PCC 27 Jankyn 1528; *Husting*, II, 635; *LCC Survey*, VIII (1922), 154; Hodson, G. H., *History of Enfield* (Enfield, 1873), 69; Hope, W. J. St. J., ed., *Corporation plate . . . of England and Wales* (L., 1895, 2 vols.), II, 124–125; Walker, *Lincoln's Inn Black Books*, I, 148, 184, 187; Dasent, A. I., *Speakers of the House of Commons* (L., 1911), 105; DNB. In Nor-

folk, Lovell's native county, he made charitable bequests totalling £397. For an account of his religious benefactions, *vide post*, 277, 300.

4. PCC 40 Brudenell 1585. Randall also left £50 to the Mercers' Company, to be lent to young tradesmen, £10 to the poor of his company, and £50 for loans to young clothiers in his native Coventry.

5. *Vide ante*, 175, for Offley's loan funds. He also created a large scholarship endowment.

6. *Husting*, II, 725–726, 730; *PP* 1822, IX, 280; Seymour, *Survey*, I, 181, 246. Newman also left £16 to London hospitals, £100 for loans to be made by the Grocers, and £1 p.a. to the poor of St Sepulchre.

7. *Vide ante*, 183, and *post*, 288.

8. *Vide ante*, 183, for Middleton's large bequest for the relief of prisoners; he also left about £55 for the relief of the poor and a substantial amount for the support of the clergy.

9. Commissary Court of London, Reg. 29, f. 239; *N. E. Hist. & Gen.*, LIII (1899), 116–118. Oxenbridge was a member of a highly gifted family. His brother Clement was a pioneer in the establishment of the English post office, and another brother, John, was a leading spirit in the colonization of the West Indies and a close friend of both Cromwell and Milton.

10. The following table plots the ever-increasing importance of the twelve great livery companies as charitable trustees. We have accumulated by decades the amounts left to these companies for their own or other charitable uses, over a period of more than four centuries, having made an arbitrary assumption of a 5 per cent yield on trusteed funds for this very long period.

Decade	Income value		Estimated capital value	
	£	s	£	
pre–1450	117	13	2,353	
1451–1460	39	6	786	
1461–1470	4	12	92	
1471–1480	8	3	163	
1481–1490	16	0	320	
1491–1500	35	0	700	
Fifteenth-century totals	220	14	4,414	0·96% of whole
1501–1510	43	17	877	
1511–1520	55	3	1,103	
1521–1530	13	7	267	
1531–1540	210	18	4,218	
1541–1550	50	7	1,007	
1551–1560	554	12	11,092	
1561–1570	230	13	4,613	
1571–1580	1,206	18	24,138	
1581–1590	399	12	7,992	
1591–1600	591	14	11,834	
Sixteenth-century totals	3,357	1	67,141	14·53% of whole

Decade	Income value		Estimated capital value	
	£	s	£	
1601–1610	828	3	16,563	
1611–1620	3,004	7	60,087	
1621–1630	871	3	17,423	
1631–1640	1,019	9	20,389	
1641–1650	1,222	17	24,457	
1651–1660	1,155	3	23,103	
1661–1670	835	19	16,719	
1671–1680	918	3	18,363	
1681–1690	1,273	10	25,470	
1691–1700	674	12	13,492	
Seventeenth-century totals	11,803	6	236,066	51·11% of whole
1701–1710	382	5	7,645	
1711–1720	1,986	7	39,727	
*1721–1730	994	15	19,895	
1731–1740	14	10	290	
1741–1750	212	0	4,240	
1751–1760	2	10	50	
1761–1770	153	15	3,075	
1771–1780	8	0	160	
1781–1790	148	5	2,965	
1791–1800	383	18	7,678	
Eighteenth-century totals	4,286	5	85,725	18·56% of whole
1801–1810	199	13	3,993	
1811–1820	433	0	8,660	
1821–1830	228	6	4,566	
1831–1840	667	6	13,346	
1841–1850	359	11	7,191	
1851–1860	1,233	0	24,660	
1861–1870	63	2	1,262	
1871–1880	244	18	4,898	
Nineteenth-century totals to 1880	3,428	16	68,576	14·85% of whole
GRAND TOTALS	23,096	2	461,922	

The parliamentary Commission in 1884 estimated the corporate income of these London companies as between £700,000 and £800,000 in 1879. Much of this total, of course, represented capital appreciation derived principally from the increase in value of London real property.

11. PCC F.13 Vox 1494; *Husting*, II, 595, 601–602; Johnson, *Drapers*, II, 354–355, 392. Eburton also left property valued at about £40 for the general uses of his parish church, an annuity of £4 4s for poor relief,

* We have not included for this decade the large Betton charity (1723), the value of which we cannot accurately assess.

with £1 p.a. to the Drapers for administering the trust, and by gift (1485) £200 to his company for the repair of certain of its properties in Southwark.

12. Watney, John, *History of the Mercers* (L., 1914), 6.

13. PCC 22 Ketchyn 1556; Beaven, *Aldermen*, II, 26; Stow, *Survey*, I, 133. Champneys also left a small fund to provide two loads of coal yearly for seven years for the poor of his ward. He was chosen an alderman in 1527, served as mayor in 1534, and was six times master of his company. He left a very small estate, having retired from business well before his death, possibly because of blindness. Stow tells us that he was struck blind because of his pride in raising a 'high tower of bricke' on his house in Mincing Lane so that it overlooked his neighbours.

14. PCC 6 Mellershe 1559; *Husting*, II, 673–674; Thornley, *Guilds*, 168; *PP* 1884, XXXIX, v, 109; Mander, C. H., *A descriptive account of the Cordwainers* (L., 1931), 110. Nicholson also left to his company as trustees an annuity of £5 to be distributed to the poor of St Clement Eastcheap, and he gave Christ's Hospital an outright sum of £5.

15. PCC 22 Darcy 1581; Seymour, *Survey*, I, 249; Herbert, *Livery companies*, II, 607; Fry, *Inq. p. m.*, *London*, III, 37; Rogers, Mark, *Down Thames Street* (L., 1921), 91; Beaven, *Aldermen*, II, 35, 210. Draper was a native of Leicestershire. He was first chosen an alderman in 1556, one of his first actions being to appoint a bell-ringer to patrol the ward (Cordwainer) to warn the inhabitants to watch their fires, to help the poor, and pray for the dead. He was chosen lord mayor in 1566, Surveyor-General of the Hospitals in 1573, and he was six times master of his company. The tightness of the mercantile society is suggested by the fact that three of his daughters married future lord mayors. Draper gave £68 to prisoners during his lifetime, £100 to the Ironmongers to be lent at 2 per cent, £68 7s for poor relief in London, Leicestershire, Surrey, and Hertfordshire, £60 for the repair of roads, £20 to 'cleanse the river Thames', and numerous smaller bequests for a variety of useful purposes.

16. We have discussed a substantial almshouse foundation made by this donor (*vide ante*, 147) and shall later mention his endowment of a school in Suffolk (*vide post*, 238). Soame, whose charities totalled £2350, also gave £200 as capital to provide food for poor prisoners, and during his lifetime contributed £50 towards the completion of the north window in St Paul's.

17. PCC 70 Ridley 1629, sentence 103 Ridley; *PP* 1820, V, 155–156; *PP* 1840, XIX, i, 120. Wood also left £100 as a loan fund for young men of his company, annuities representing a capital sum of £125 for poor relief, £4 p.a. to Christ's Hospital, and a substantial scholarship endowment.

18. Ingpen, A. R., ed., *Master Worsley's Book* (L., 1910), 206n.

19. PCC 75 Dale 1621; White, *Walbrook Ward*, 218; Beaven, *Aldermen*, II, 51. Bolles also left £50 to Christ's Hospital, £20 to St Bartholomew's, £20 for the release of prisoners, and £19 13s for poor relief. First chosen an alderman in 1607, he was lord mayor in 1617, when his stern Puritanism was demonstrated in a prohibition laid against all carriage traffic

through the city during the hours of divine services. A native of Lincolnshire, Bolles was master of his company in 1606 and in the same period served as a member of the East India Company Committee. He married the daughter of Sir John Harte, lord mayor in 1589.

20. PCC 635 Wootton 1658.

21. We have discussed Gresham's great almshouse (*vide ante*, 144) and shall deal with his educational foundation later (*vide post*, 253–254). Also noteworthy is his endowment, vested in the City of London, of £1000, the income to be employed for the relief of prisoners in all the prisons of the city.

22. *Vide ante*, 115–116, 175, and *post*, 287.

23. PCC 13 Fetiplace 1514; *Husting*, II, 640–641; *PP* 1884, XXXIX, ii, 8; Beaven, *Aldermen*, I, 101, 115, II, 21, 166, 168; *Notes and Queries*, 7th ser., V (1888), 151. Browne left in all £1432 12s for charitable uses. Among other benefactions, he gave £70 for church repairs, £24 for the relief of prisoners, £100 for the 'common weal' of the city, £168 4s for poor relief, £20 for marriage subsidies, £40 for the repair of highways, and £90 for exhibitions in the universities. The son of Sir John Browne, this donor married first a daughter of Sir Edmund Shaa, mayor in 1482, and secondly a daughter of Henry Kebyll, mayor in 1510. One of Browne's daughters married Sir John Mundy, mayor in 1522, and a second Sir William Petre, Secretary of State to Edward VI. A cousin of Browne's, of the same name, was mayor in 1507; Browne himself was mayor in 1513.

24. We have noted in an earlier connection (*vide ante*, 189) that Jenyns advanced funds for the purchase of Bethlehem Hospital by the city. His large benefactions for education and church building will be discussed later (*vide post*, 222–223, 300). It should be remarked that the London property given to his company had in 1523 a rental value of £7 13s 4d p.a. In 1888 this property yielded an income of £1700 p.a. to the company.

25. PCC 20 Porch 1527; Clode, *Merchant Taylors*, I, 149, 412; Fry, *Inq. p. m., London*, I, 45.

26. *PP* 11 Hogen 1533; *Husting*, II, 642; Clode, *Merchant Taylors*, II, 339, 414.

27. Of this endowment, totalling £2,800, £800 was for poor relief, £400 for Christ's Hospital, £330 for general charitable uses, and £400 for university scholarships. *Vide ante*, 108.

28. *Vide ante*, 107, and *post*, 235.

29. *Vide ante*, 108, 153–154, and *post*, 236, 285–286.

30. PCC 94 St. John 1631; Hatton, *New view*, II, 735; *Home Counties Magazine*, V (1903), 16–26; Beaven, *Aldermen*, II, 48, 176. Middleton also left £120 to London hospitals and £70 for the relief of the poor in London and Essex. The brother of the more famous Sir Hugh, this donor, having served his apprenticeship, was admitted to the livery in 1593. He traded principally in Antwerp. He was elected an alderman first in 1603, when he was knighted, and served as mayor in 1613. He sat in Parliament for a Welsh constituency in 1597 and for London in 1624. He married a daughter of Sir Richard Saltonstall, lord mayor in 1597.

31. *Vide ante*, 124, 179, and *post*, 305.

32. PCC 109 Lee 1638; *PP* 1822, IX, 331; Gilbert, *Liber scholasticus*, 383. The second charitable gift of £2500 provided that capital sums should be established in the indicated amounts: for the poor of the company, £400; for the poor of Newport, Shropshire, the donor's birthplace, £200; for London hospitals, £450; to the Salters for charitable outlays, £400; for clerical stipends, £150; for university scholarships, £400; and for the schoolmaster at Newport, £100. *Vide post*, 247.

33. PCC 10 Logge 1483; Beaven, *Aldermen*, II, 11. Taylour also left £64 for prayers, £3 7s to the priest of St Mary Aldermary parish, £6 13s 4d to the church at Edenbridge, and an estimated £30 for the poor there. It may be noted that he left to a cousin 'my newe boke of engelish that I bought'. Taylour's first service as an alderman was in 1458. He was mayor in 1468 and was knighted in 1471. He was M.P. for London in 1483 and four times master of his company.

34. PCC 12 Milles 1488; Beaven, *Aldermen*, II, 14, 166; *PP* 1823, VIII, 323; *PP* 1837–8, XXIV, 551; *PP* 1884, XXXIX, iv, 299; Cook, *Mediaeval chantries*, 35; Watney, *St. Thomas Acon*, 56; DNB. Shaa also left £301 for prayers for the repose of his own soul and that of Edward IV, £140 to the poor of London and of his birthplace, Stockport, Cheshire, £100 for church repairs, and larger amounts for a school foundation and church building (*vide post*, 220, 298). He was a very rich man, with a long and distinguished public career, but in his will he did not forget that forty years earlier he had taken two oxen by distress from a man in Derby, whose heirs were to be remembered by his executors in the amount of £1.

35. PCC 18 Logge 1485; Grafton, Richard, *Chronicle* (L., 1809, 2 vols.), II, 161; Stow, *Survey*, I, 266; Lyell, *Acts of court*, 86.

36. PCC 35 Milles 1490; Beaven, *Aldermen*, II, 14. Gardener likewise left £62 for the poor of London and parishes in Suffolk and Cambridgeshire, £13 7s to his company, £26 13s in marriage portions, £53 7s for prayers, and lesser sums to other charities. A native of Suffolk, Gardener made a large fortune in trade as a mercer. He was first chosen an alderman in 1469, served as mayor in 1478 and as M.P. for London the same year.

37. PCC 3 Bodfelde 1523; Beaven, *Aldermen*, II, 22, 168. Rest left in addition £66 13s 4d for the needs of the poor of Peterborough, £20 for marriage portions there and as much for London, £19 8s for church general, including gifts of £11 to monasteries, and lesser amounts for various other charitable needs. His chantry endowment will be considered later (*vide post*, 277).

38. PCC 13 Bodfelde 1523; Strype, *Stow's Survey*, II, v, 128; Bell, *London Wall*, 81; Freshfield, *Minutes of St. Christopher*, 67. Acheley, a native of Shropshire, was twice master of his company. His other charitable bequests were not much more than nominal, and the tone and provisions of his will suggest that he died in somewhat straitened circumstances.

39. PCC 3 Jankyn 1529; Beaven, *Aldermen*, II, 22, 168; Strype, *Stow's Survey*, II, v, 129. Exmewe was a native of Flintshire. He first appears as an alderman in 1508 and was twice prime warden of the Gold-

smiths. He left £48 to the poor, £50 to church general, £40 for church building, £32 10s for prayers, £20 to poor scholars, and £10 to his company for a dinner at his burial.

40. PCC 24 Thower 1532; *PP* 1819, X-B, 167; *PP* 1884, XXXIX, ii, 104–105. *Vide post*, 223, for Collier's school foundation at Horsham.

41. *Vide ante*, 93, 184.

42. PCC 14 Spert 1542; Cox, *St. Helen*, 234–236; Beaven, *Aldermen*, II, 26. Holles also left £20 for the repair of his parish church, £13 7s for poor relief, £80 to his company, £13 7s to named clergy, and £10 (estimated) for marriage portions, as well as a substantial endowment for prayers. Holles was a rich man, his personal estate being valued at £10,380 and his lands, in seven counties, at £365 p.a. He was admitted to the Mercers' Company in 1499 and became its master in 1538. He was first chosen an alderman in 1528, served as mayor in 1539. His widow, who died in 1544, endowed six almshouses in St Helen Bishopsgate (*vide ante*, 139).

43. *Vide ante*, 94.

44. *Vide ante*, 185.

45. Waters, R. E. C., *Genealogical memoirs of the . . . family of Chester of Chicheley* (L., 1878, 2 vols.), I, 36–38; Wilson, *Christ's Hospital*, 33; *PP* 1840, XIX, i, 13, 24, 35; Beaven, *Aldermen*, II, 34; Russan, *Muscovy merchants*, 87. (The DNB article needs correction.) Chester also bequeathed valuable lands and dwellings, with an estimated capital worth of £600, for the support of six poor women patients in St Bartholomew's. A native of London, his father, John Chester, being a draper, Chester was born in 1509. He was educated at Peterhouse, Cambridge, and entered trade at once upon leaving the university. He, with associates, set up the first sugar refinery in England in 1544, from which the partners drew great gains. He was six times master of his company and from 1553, when he was first chosen an alderman, was prominent in civic affairs. He was knighted in 1557, served as lord mayor in 1560, and sat in Parliament for London from 1563 to 1567. He was a governor of the Muscovy Company, traded in Persia, and sent voyages to the African coasts. Following his wife's death in 1572, Chester retired to Cambridge, where he was admitted as a fellow-commoner and where he lived happily engrossed in his studies until his death. He had previously distributed his considerable fortune of perhaps £15,000 to his children.

46. PCC 33 Loftes 1561; *Husting*, II, 651–652; Herbert, *Livery companies*, I, 253; Fuller, *Worthies*, III, 67; Brayley, *Top. hist. of London*, III, 274–275; *PP* 1831, XI, 300; Beaven, *Aldermen*, II, 31, 170. Hill left in all £189 13s to the poor of London and Shropshire, £50 for the uses of his company, £120 to three London hospitals, as well as generous funds for education and church building (*vide post*, 225, 301). He had previously given £200 to St Bartholomew's Hospital and £600 to Christ's Hospital. Hill was born at Hodnet, Shropshire, in 1492. He served his apprenticeship with Thomas Kitson and was admitted to the freedom of the Mercers' Company in 1519. He was four times master of the company. A staunch and early Protestant, he was chosen mayor in 1549. Hill's

fortune was quite as much based on the purchase of monastic properties as upon a successful trading career.

47. PCC 3 Morrison 1564; Strype, *Stow's Survey*, II, v, 133; Beaven, *Aldermen*, II, 32, 210. Lyon also left forty gowns for poor men, £100 to London hospitals, and £200 to be lent at nominal rates to two merchants and two retailers by the Grocers' Company. Chosen an alderman in 1547, Lyon served as lord mayor in 1554, as President of St Bartholomew's in 1557-1559, and four times as master of his company. He left an estate of moderate size, with landholdings in Lincolnshire, Yorkshire, Nottinghamshire, Berkshire, Essex, Middlesex, and London.

48. *Vide ante*, 99, 142, 177, and *post*, 228. The Holborn Conduit was finished by Lambe long before his death in 1580 and very probably in the interval 1557-1560.

49. *Vide ante*, 99-100.

50. Randolph did not intend that his money should be used in lieu of the customary and statutory individual labour on the highways, but in addition to it: 'To the churchwardens . . . to bestow 40s . . . for amending the horseways, after that the parishioners should have done their days work limited by statute, from the church of Ticehurst . . . to Wetherington bridge . . . to Hook bridge . . . and to Flymwell . . . and towards Wadhurst.'

51. PCC 52 Spencer 1587; Stow, *Survey*, I, 115; Seymour, *Survey*, I, 246.

52. *Vide ante*, 103, and *post*, 231.

53. PCC 34 Pile 1635; *Reliquary*, XX (1879-1880), 46, n. 65; Cox, *St. Helen*, 295; Parton, *St. Giles*, 198; Nichols, John, ed., *Bibliotheca topographica britannica* (L., 1780-1790, 8 vols.), II, i, App., 86. Caesar left £53 to the poor of London, £15 to hospitals, and £35 to prisoners. In 1623 he made a modest contribution to the building of St Giles' church and in 1629 repaired St Katherine's at a personal charge of £250. The DNB has a full and admirable biographical notice.

54. PCC 3 Hayes 1605; Cass, F. G., *East Barnet* (Westminster, 1885), 47-48; *PP* 1816, XVI, i, 804; *PP* 1884, XXXIX, iv, 370. Conyers also left £100 in trust with his company to secure yearly payments to the poor of St Botolph Aldgate and an estimated £40 for clothing the poor. Conyers held valuable property at East Barnet, Middlesex, where he resided in later life. He had settled one son on a Yorkshire manor and owned as well a manor in Lincolnshire.

55. Willet, *Synopsis papismi* (1634), 1224. For Middleton's own charitable benefactions, *vide ante*, 126.

56. *Vide ante*, 106.

57. *Vide ante*, 151-153.

58. *Vide ante*, 117, 157, 178, and *post*, 266, 273, 283.

59. Parker was a substantial and certainly a thoughtful donor. *Vide ante*, 178, for his endowment for social rehabilitation and *post*, 295, for his other outlays.

60. *Vide ante*, 154-155, and *post*, 254-255, 287.

61. *Vide ante*, 148, 169, and *post*, 241, 289.

D. Education

1. Scholarship and fellowship endowments have been treated statistically as a separate entity, but, for purposes of the discussion following, these funds will be described in connection with our analysis of the gifts to schools and to the universities.

2. Leach, A. F., *Educational charters* (Cambridge, 1911), 419.

3. Stow, *Survey*, I, 153–154.

4. PCC 22 Ayloffe 1519; *PP* 1820, IV, 230 ff.; *PP* 1884, XXXIX, ii, 36–43; Lupton, J. H., *A life of John Colet* (L., 1887), 177, 232; *Husting*, II, 640; DNB; McDonnell, *St. Paul's School*, 14, 37, 68; Knight, Samuel, *Life of John Colet* (L., 1724); Nicolas, *Testamenta vetusta*, II, 568–573; Leach, A. F., *Schools of medieval England* (L., 1915), 277–281; Stow, *Survey*, I, 73–74.

5. *Vide ante*, 138–139.

6. PCC 2 Stevenson 1564.

7. PCC 47 Kidd 1599; *PP* 1837–8, XXVI, 470–471. This donor's father was a cooper. His was a nuncupative will.

8. PCC 49 Pyckering 1575; *L. & M. Arch. Soc.*, n.s., I (1898), 115 ff.; Carlisle, Nicholas, *Endowed grammar schools* (L., 1818, 2 vols.), II, 44–47; Leach, *Schools of medieval England*, 267, 319; Watney, John, *The Mercers' School* (L., 1896), 1–13; *PP* 1822, IX, 309. Lady North was the daughter of a London merchant, and Edward North, who was her fourth husband, was the son of a merchant. There is a biographical notice of North, who was Chancellor of the Court of Augmentations, in the DNB.

9. *Vide ante*, 192–193.

10. *Vide ante*, 95.

11. PCC 63 Windsor 1586; Pearce, *Christ's Hospital*, 24, 146.

12. PCC 16 Drury 1589; *PP* 1840, XIX, i, 99.

13. PCC 19 Dorset 1609; Feret, *Fulham*, I, 116. Bennett also left a house in Marlborough, Wiltshire, on trust, the income to be employed for the poor of that town.

14. PCC 92 Fenner 1612, 23; 55 Capell 1613; *PP* 1823, VIII, 377.

15. *Vide ante*, 112.

16. PCC 140 Evelyn 1641; *PP* 1837–8, XXV, 868; *PP* 1840, XIX, i, 120; Beaven, *Aldermen*, II, 59, 179; DNB; *Home Counties Mag.*, V (1903), 213; Nicholl, *Ironmongers*, 475; Noble, T. C., *A brief history of the Ironmongers* (L., 1889), 55. Clitherow also left a rent-charge of £3 p.a. for the poor of an Essex parish, £4 p.a. for the relief of the poor of St Andrew Undershaft, and £10 to his company for the purchase of plate. Clitherow was born in London, the son of an ironmonger who was thrice master of his company. The son was a member of his father's company but had wide-ranging mercantile interests, particularly in the East India Company, of which he was deputy governor in 1625 and governor in 1638. He also served as governor of the Eastland Merchants and was twice master of the Ironmongers. From 1625 forward he was an alderman, he served in Parliament in 1628 and he became lord mayor in 1635.

17. For Locke's large apprenticeship foundation, *vide ante*, 169.

18. PCC 103 Pile 1636; Beaven, *Aldermen*, II, 54, 196. Hamersley also left £25 to the repair of St Paul's, £26 13s 4d for the relief of prisoners, and £20 as a stock for the poor of his own parish, and a gilt salt cellar to his company. He became an alderman in 1619, served as lord mayor in 1627, as President of the Honourable Artillery Company from 1619 to 1633, and as President of Christ's Hospital from 1634 to 1636. He was at various times master of his company, on the Committee of the East India Company, and governor of both the Levant Company and the Russia Company.

19. *Vide ante*, 125. Bailey also left an annuity of £10 for the support of St Thomas's Hospital.

20. PCC 202 Alchin 1654; *PP* 1819, X-A, 48; *PP* 1826, XII, 390; *PP* 1837-8, XXV, 54; *PP* 1840, XIX, i, 86, 126; Wadmore, *Skinners*, 222; Pearce, *Christ's Hospital*, 102; Beaven, *Aldermen*, I, 116, II, 60. Aldworth also left about £725 for the relief of the poor of London, £20 p.a. for a lectureship in Reading, Berkshire, and great school foundations at Reading and at Basingstoke, Hampshire, which will be discussed later (*vide post*, 245). The total of his charitable benefactions was upwards of £15,000. A native of Reading, he gained the freedom of the Skinners' Company in 1600. He served in Parliament for Reading, was master of his company in 1630, and was a governor of Christ's Hospital. His executor, a relation of identical name, was fined for delinquency in 1646, having commanded a troop of horse in the King's army.

21. PCC 55 Bowyer 1652; Lempriere, William, *History of the Girls' School of Christ's Hospital* (Cambridge, 1924), 6. Dunn also left £2 p.a. for the care of the poor of his parish, St Katherine Cree.

22. PCC 322 Alchin 1654; *PP* 1840, XIX, i, 129. Singleton also established two fellowships in Brasenose College, Oxford, for natives of Lincolnshire.

23. PCC 92 Wootton 1658; *PP* 1840, XIX, i, 131-132; *PP* 1884, XXXIX, v, 54. Rochdale also made Christ's Hospital trustee for the payment of £6 13s 4d p.a. to the poor of St Giles and £3 p.a. to the needy of the Brewers' Company. He gave outright £20 to the poor of St Giles, £20 to the poor of St Leonard Shoreditch, £10 to St Thomas's and St Bartholomew's Hospitals, £82 for gowns for poor men, £35 to the Brewers' Company for its own uses, £40 to the poor of other parishes, and £59 'unto orthodox silenced ministers' or their widows.

24. We have not included a bequest of £200 p.a., or capital of £4000, left to Christ's Hospital by Simon Clarke, a London merchant, after the death of his wife. This, a charge on lands in Wiltshire, was never paid. (PCC 155 Alchin 1654; *PP* 1840, XIX, i, 129).

25. *Vide ante*, 144.

26. *Vide post*, 257-258, for a discussion of White's collegiate foundation.

27. PCC 4 Chayre 1563.

28. PCC 33 Stonarde 1567.

29. PCC 112 Clarke 1625; *PP* 1819, X-A, 210; Strype, *Stow's Survey*,

II, iv, 16; Willet, *Synopsis papismi* (1634), 1224; Allen, *History of London*, IV, 510.

30. Tanner, L. E., *Westminster School* (L., 1951), 11–25; Sargeaunt, John, *Annals of Westminster School* (L., 1898), 11 ff.; Forshall, F. H., *Westminster School* (L., 1884), 93 ff.; Airy, Reginald, *Westminster* (L., 1902), 3–12; Fuller, *Church history*, II, 466.

31. *Vide ante*, 149, and *post*, 234.

32. Tanner, *Westminster School*, 26.

33. Brayley, E. W., *History of . . . St. Peter, Westminster* (L., 1818, 1823, 2 vols.), I, 134–138, II, 297; Tanner, L. E., *Westminster Abbey Library* (L., 1933), 6; Barker, G. F., and A. H. Stenning, eds., *Record of Old Westminster* (L., 1928, 2 vols.), II, App., 1109; Howard, *Finances of St. John's*, 60, 289; Mullinger, J. B., *St. John's* (L., 1901), 105–106; DNB. Archbishop Williams also left an endowment of £240 for the relief of the poor of Walgrave, Northamptonshire, a rent-charge with a capital value of £27 for the care of the poor of Llandegveth, Monmouthshire, and land, then valued at about £160, to secure a bread distribution at Honington, Suffolk. For his great benefaction to St John's College, Cambridge, *vide post*, 262.

34. PCC 24 Morrison 1565; Madge, *Inq. p. m.*, London, 41–44; PP 1819, X-B, 101 ff.; Norden, *Speculum* (1593), 22; Howitt, *Northern heights*, 294; Spilsbury, W. H., *Lincoln's Inn* (L., 1850), 127. Cholmeley was the natural son of Sir Richard Cholmeley, a Yorkshire knight and soldier. He was educated at Lincoln's Inn. In 1535, being appointed Recorder of London, he began a long period of legal service, being made King's Serjeant in 1545 and in the next year Chief Baron of the Exchequer. In 1552 he was appointed Chief Justice of Common Pleas, but was dismissed and for a time imprisoned by Queen Mary.

35. PCC 8 Carew 1576; PP 1828, XX, 390.

36. PCC 17 Rutland 1587.

37. PCC 15 Darcy 1581; *Bib. top. brit.*, II, ii, 1–8; PP 1828, XX, 390.

38. Strype, *Stow's Survey*, I, i, 172; PP 1819, X-A, 207.

39. PCC 30 Daughtry 1577; PP 1819, X-A, 208.

40. PCC 19 Peter 1573. Smith was a brewer.

41. PCC 19 Martyn 1574. Pratt was a London leatherseller.

42. *PP* 1819, X-A, 208. This donor was the widow of Sir Edward Osborne, a clothworker; she later married Sir Robert Clarke, one of the Barons of the Exchequer.

43. *PP* 1819, X-A, 208; *PP* 1826, XII, 569–570.

44. PCC 97 Wingfield 1610. This donor, Wessell Webling, was a Flemish immigrant who became a prosperous brewer.

45. *Vide ante*, 151–153.

46. Entick, *London*, IV, 411; *PP* 1819, X-A, 180; *PP* 1903, XLIX, 192.

47. *Vide ante*, 131, for his generous provision for the poor of St Albans.

48. *Vide ante*, 156.

49. *Vide ante*, 163.

50. This foundation was typical of many: the 'almshouse with a chapel

388   THE CHARITIES OF LONDON 1480–1660

and schoolhouse', under the supervision of private, self-perpetuating trustees.

51. Perhaps the earliest instance was William Sevenoaks' notable foundation in Kent in 1432, which will be mentioned in some detail in our later treatment of that county.

52. The school was undisturbed by the Reformation. *Vide ante,* 203, for an account of Shaa's other secular benefactions and *post,* 298, for his church building.

53. *Vide ante,* 91, and *post,* 275.

54. PCC 21 Bennett 1509; *PP* 1824, XIII, 617 ff.; Williamson, G. C., *Royal Grammar School of Guildford* (L., 1929), 1–13; Rees, *Grocers,* 93. Beckingham lived in Southwark. He also left £60 to his company, £20 to poor relief, £22 for prayers, and lesser outright bequests for various charitable uses.

55. PCC 39 Chayre 1563 (Thomas Blank); PCC 1 Lyon 1569 (Joan Blank); *Surrey Arch. Coll.,* X (1891), 112; Fry, *Inq. p. m., London,* III, 135–137. Blank also left rent-charges with a capital value of £140 for the relief of the poor of St Mary at Hill and St Leonard Eastcheap. He was a native of Guildford.

56. PCC 31 Bennett 1510; Cook, *Mediaeval chantries,* 24; Nichols, John, ed., *Wills of the kings and queens of England* (L., 1780), 356–403; Brayley, *St. Peter, Westminster,* I, 100; Smith, *Roll-call of Westminster,* 75; Smyth, G. L., *Biographical illustrations of Westminster* (L., 1843), 4–16; Clark, J. W., ed., *The endowments of Cambridge* (Cambridge, 1904), 57–78; Cooper, *Memorials of Cambridge,* II, 9; Cooper, C. H., *Memoir of Margaret Countess of Richmond and Derby* (Cambridge, 1874); Routh, E. M. G., *Lady Margaret* (L., 1924); Halsted, C. A., *Margaret Beaufort* (L., 1839); Fisher, John, *The funeral sermon of Margaret, Countess of Richmond and Derby* (L., 1708). This donor's great benefactions were, of course, to the universities, for which *vide post,* 261. She also founded two almshouses, the one near Westminster Abbey and the other at Hatfield, about which we have no particulars. She left as well £133 7s to the poor, £206 to the clergy, and lesser benefactions for various charitable causes.

57. PCC 40, 41 Holgrave 1505; Beaven, *Aldermen,* I, 101, II, 19; *PP* 1823, VIII, 323; *PP* 1884, XXXIX, iv, 298–299; *PP* 1904, LXXI, 778–781; Thrupp, *Merchant class,* 269, 363; Herbert, *Livery companies,* II, 254. Rede left in all £1102 8s for charitable uses. In addition to a large foundation for prayers (*vide post,* 276), he provided £59 13s for church general in London, £16 7s for church repairs, £5 for the poor, £4 14s for prisoners, £44 for marriage portions, £66 13s 4d for roads in and near London, £40 for university scholarships and £7 7s to King's College, Cambridge, as well as a 'great silver gilt plate' of 380 oz. weight for the use of the Corporation of London. His grammar-school endowment, together with annuities of £1 13s 4d for prayers in his parish church and of £1 to the poor of his parish, was secured by valuable city properties vested in the Goldsmiths, with the remainder, which we are unable to estimate, to the company for its uses. He likewise left relatively small charitable sums to various parishes in Norfolk, Surrey, and Kent. Rede

was mayor in 1502; he also served as Master of the Mint from 1482 to 1497 and as prime warden of his company in 1492.

58. PCC 16 Adeane 1506; Brett-James, *Middlesex*, 275; Carlisle, *Endowed grammar schools*, II, 116; *PP* 1819, X-B, 82.

59. *PP* 1816, XVI, i, 740; *PP* 1823, IX, 187.

60. PCC 59 Windsor 1586; Hodson, *Enfield*, 37; *PP* 1822, IX, 202.

61. *PP* 1816, XVI, i, 740; *PP* 1819, X-B, 84.

62. *Vide ante*, 91–92.

63. *Vide ante*, 189, 201, and *post*, 300.

64. *Vide ante*, 203.

65. *Vide ante*, 139, for the almshouse foundation.

66. *Vide ante*, 140.

67. Hales, John (Elizabeth Lamond, ed.), *A discourse of the common weal* (Cambridge, 1893), xviii–xx; *VCH, Warwick.*, II, 322; *BM MSS.*, G, 15,594, 'An account of the loans and charities belonging to Coventry' (1733); DNB.

68. PCC 30 Bucke 1551, sentence 36 Chaynay 1559; Moore, *St. Bartholomew's*, II, 209; Waters, *Family of Chester*, I, 39–40. Tempest, who was a son-in-law of William Chester, died in Antwerp. He also left £50 to St Bartholomew's Hospital, £10 to poor householders in London, £25 to the poor of Antwerp, and £20 to the needy of Calais.

69. This great school foundation will be fully discussed in our treatment of Norfolk. *Vide ante*, 95, for a review of his other benefactions.

70. *Vide ante*, 141.

71. PCC F.18 Wrastley 1557; Garside, Bernard, *History of Hampton School* (Cambridge, 1931), 7–50; Carlisle, *Endowed grammar schools*, II, 118–119; *PP* 1816, XVI, i, 766; *PP* 1823, IX, 281. Hammond also left £106 10s for prayers, £31 10s to the poor, and £45 for bridge repairs. He was a yeoman's son, having been born in Kingston, Surrey. He became a prosperous London brewer and woodmonger and was by 1547 the largest property owner in St Andrew by the Wardrobe. He retired to Kingston some little time before his death.

72. The particulars will be fully set out in our treatment of Kent.

73. *Vide ante*, 204, and *post*, 301.

74. PCC 36 Chayre 1563; Webb, *St. Bartholomew's Priory*, I, 545, II, 299–307; *PP* 1824, XIII, 265; *PP* 1837–8, XXIV, 438; Madge, *Inq. p. m., London*, 33. Very nearly the whole of Deane's estate was devoted to this foundation. He left as well £24 7s to the poor of his London parish and those of his birthplace, and nominal amounts for hospitals, prisons, and church repairs.

75. *Vide ante*, 142, for his other charities.

76. PCC 21 Babington 1568; Oxley, J. E., *History of Barking* (n.p., 1936?), 28.

77. PCC 23, 37 Lyon 1570; Fuller, *Worthies*, III, 540–541; *PP* 1837–8, XXVII, 6, 8; *S. P. Dom.*, 1591, CCXXXVIII, 80; Williams, John, *Ancient and modern Denbigh* (Denbigh, 1856), 295. Clough was an intimate of Gresham's and, according to Fuller, persuaded him to found the Royal Exchange on the model of the Bourse at Antwerp, where Clough

had resided during much of his career. Another account of the school at Denbigh would have it that Clough had lent £100 during his lifetime to the town of Denbigh for the founding of a school. It seems probable that Clough's bequest was simply misappropriated. Fuller apparently so understood it, for he says he doubts whether 'repentance without restitution will secure such who are the causers thereof'. In 1640 a local investigation was made, and Clough's gift was declared lost. There was certainly an unendowed school in Denbigh as early as 1547, but it seems to have been closed at the time of Clough's gift. The present foundation dates from 1727.

78. PCC 34 Holney 1571; *PP* 1819, X-A, 5; *VCH, Berks.*, II, 259; Townsend, James, *History of Abingdon* (L., 1910), 95; Preston, A. E., *St. Nicholas, Abingdon* (L., 1929), 297. Roise also left £8 16s to Whittington College, £20 to municipal uses in Abingdon, £12 for marriage portions, £8 to St Bartholomew's, £20 for the relief of prisoners, and lesser sums for other charitable uses. A native of Abingdon, Roise was a mercer who late in his life seems to have become a 'money scrivener'. The will would suggest that he was almost certainly a Roman Catholic.

79. PCC 14 Martyn 1574; Fuller, *Worthies*, I, 172; *L. & M. Arch. Soc.*, IV (1875), 70–93; Clode, *Merchant Taylors*, I, 228, II, 254; Beaven, *Aldermen*, I, 63, 139, II, 34; *PP* 1822, IX, 5; Sargeaunt, John, *Bedford School* (L., 1925); Farrar, C. F., *Harper's Bedford charity* (Bedford, 1930). The income on the Holborn property in 1888 was £13,227 p.a. The purposes of the charity were greatly enlarged to include the school, marriage portions, exhibitions, hospitals, apprenticeships, almshouses, and similar uses in *33 George III*.

A native of Bedford, where he was born in 1496, Harper served his apprenticeship in the Merchant Taylors and was admitted a freeman in 1533. He was mayor (1561) during the period when the Merchant Taylors' School was being founded, but made no recorded contribution to its needs. He purchased for his own use the great mansion in Lombard Street formerly the property of Sir John Percival.

80. PCC 13 Carew 1576; *PP* 1825, XI, 9; *PP* 1837–8, XXVI, 437, 447; *PP* 1884, XXXIX, iii, 161; Seymour, *Survey*, I, 247; Johnson, *Drapers*, IV, 482; Hatton, *New view*, I, 134; *LCC Survey*, XV (1934), 21–22. During his lifetime Parker gave £500 to Christ's Hospital and £200 to Bridewell. His gifts to his company included £40 to repair the Drapers' almshouse and (in 1540) a great house in Mark Lane valued at £400 for company uses. He left £50 as a stock for the poor of St Antholin's, in addition to £29 for poor relief, £80 to the hospitals, £12 10s to prisoners, £100 to his company for a loan fund, £120 of endowment to secure a semi-weekly lecture in St Antholin's, and an annuity of £10 for the relief of the poor of Daventry.

81. *Vide ante*, 99, 142, 177, 204.

82. PCC 29 Brudenell 1585; *PP* 1825, X, 321.

83. *Vide ante*, 101–102.

84. These educational gifts will be treated fully in our discussion of Kentish charities.

85. PCC 17 Spencer 1587; *PP* 1837–8, XXV, 798; Gilbert, *Liber scholasticus*, 23; Wood, *Oxford colleges*, 240, 260, 358; Venn, *Caius College*, III, 229, 246, 286, IV, ii, 41, 57; Mallet, C. E. *A history of . . . Oxford* (L., 1924, 3 vols.), II, 10; *Brasenose College quartercentenary monographs* (Oxford, 1909, 3 vols.), I, iv, 20. *Vide post*, 257, 263, 264, for her benefactions to the universities.

86. PCC 20 Rutland 1587; Seymour, *Survey*, I, 244; *PP* 1830, XII, 326; *PP* 1843, XVIII, 196; *S. P. Dom.*, 1597, CCLXII, 20; Whalley, Peter, ed., *History of Northamptonshire* (Oxford, 1791, 2 vols.), II, 261; *VCH, Northants.*, III, 196. Walter also left £50 to his company as a loan fund, £25 to named Puritan clergymen, and £50 more to 'such godlie faithful and honest preachers as are put from their livings for matters of ceremonies', £40 to scholars in the universities, £20 to the hospitals, £34 to London and Northamptonshire poor, and lesser amounts to various other causes. That Walter was a man of stern and definite views is suggested by his testament of faith, which concludes: 'I will that there be no . . . sermon made [at his burial] not for that I doe not allow of preaching for I am fullie perswaded it is the onelie way declared in the worde whereby we must atteyne to faithe without the which we cannot be saved But for that the funerall sermons are comonlie used for custome which in tyme maye growe to supersticion rather then for any profitable edificacion . . .'.

Walter was born in Finedon in 1542. There was delay in settling the foundation, though the schoolhouse was built in 1595 and the licence was obtained to vest the endowment on trustees.

87. PCC 81 Leicester 1589; *PP* 1825, X, 523; *PP* 1840, XIX, i, 99. Prannell served as an alderman and sheriff. His widow married first the Earl of Hertford and then the Duke of Richmond and Lennox.

88. *Vide ante*, 101. Norden, who wrote before Lyon's death, says that the founder had given £300 to establish the school and had already constituted an endowment of £40 p.a. for its support.

89. PCC 1 Dixy 1593; *PP* 1823, VIII, 376; *PP* 1839, XV, 151, 183; *PP* 1840, XIX, i, 100; Beaven, *Aldermen*, I, 18, 74, 251, II, 39, 173; Brett-James, *Stuart London*, 44; *L. & M. Arch. Soc.*, V (1881), 147; Wadmore, *Skinners*, 167–168; Herbert, *Skinners*, 318; Walker, T. A., ed., *Biographical register of Peterhouse* (L., 1927, 1930, 2 vols.), II, 19; Shuckburgh, *Emmanuel*, 218; Fuller, *Worthies*, II, 106; Willet, *Synopsis papismi* (1634), 1255. Dixie left in all £4484 13s for charitable uses. In addition to the school foundation and gifts to the universities (*vide post*, 264), he vested a loan fund of £500 in the Skinners' Company, to be lent in amounts of from £30 to £50 to thrifty young men at nominal interest rates, £10 p.a. for a weekly lecture in St Michael Bassishaw, £100 for marriage subsidies, a total of £1040 to London hospitals (including £200 for building a new pesthouse), £54 for poor relief, £90 13s to prisoners, and £4 p.a. to his company.

Dixie was born in Huntingdonshire in 1525. He was apprenticed to Sir Christopher Draper (*vide ante*, 200), an ironmonger, whose daughter he married. Draper was a native of Melton Mowbray and from him Dixie inherited extensive landholdings in that community. Dixie was chosen alderman in 1573 and lord mayor in 1585.

90. PCC 78 Nevell 1592; *PP* 1837–8, XXVI, 458; *PP* 1840, XIX, i, 100; Beaven, *Aldermen*, II, 42, 174; Seymour, *Survey*, I, 249; Herbert, *Livery companies*, I, 250; Baddeley, *Aldermen of Cripplegate*, 53. Elkin also left £2 12s p.a. for the poor of St Michael Bassishaw, £65 to the universities, £200 in loan funds, with interest payments to almshouses, £60 to prisoners, £120 to his company, and £548 (£27 8s p.a.) to Christ's Hospital for its uses. Elkin had served as an alderman, was sheriff in 1586, and was master of his company. He was a native of Shropshire.

91. PCC 8 Dixy 1593; Brown, Frederick (F. A. Crisp, ed.), *Abstracts of Somersetshire wills* (n.p., 1887–1890, 6 vols.), V, 94; Plomer, H. R., *Abstracts from wills of English printers* (L., 1903), 31–32. Norton, who was thrice master of his company and in 1583 Treasurer of Christ's Hospital, also left £6 13s 4d p.a. to his company for loans, and an estimated £40 in outright gifts to the poor.

92. *Vide ante*, 143, for her almshouse foundation and *post*, 257, for her substantial benefaction to Trinity College, Oxford.

93. *Vide ante*, 102, and *post*, 285.

94. *Vide ante*, 103, 204.

95. PCC 24 Dixy 1594; *PP* 1820, V, 80, 227; *PP* 1831, XI, 403; Baddeley, *Cripplegate*, 202; *L. &. M. Arch. Soc.*, n.s., IV (1918), 184, VI (1931), 509; Beaven, *Aldermen*, II, 36. Hayward also left an annuity of £4 for a bread distribution to the poor of St Alphage. The son of a Shropshire cordwainer, he was apprenticed to a clothworker. He was in 1555 a member of the Muscovy Company, in 1559 master of the Clothworkers, most successful both in trade and in land speculation. He was one of the small committee that acquired the site for the Royal Exchange. Hayward served as lord mayor in 1570, as President of St Bartholomew's from 1572 to 1593, and sat in Parliament for London in sessions from 1572 to 1583. The Queen visited him in his newly acquired manor at Hackney. In 1591 he filled out Sir John Allott's term as lord mayor. The Bridgnorth school stems from a chantry foundation, but it seems probable that it had all but suspended its work until Hayward's refoundation occurred.

96. Fuller, *Worthies*, I, 377.

97. PCC 107 Cobham 1597.

98. *Vide ante*, 146–147.

99. *Vide ante*, 103.

100. Herbert (*Livery companies*, II, 543) places the value of the trust endowment at about £180 p.a. *Vide ante*, 103–104, for further treatment of this and other benefactions for the poor.

101. PCC 57 Cobham 1597; *PP* 1821, XII, 54; *PP* 1823, VIII, 332; Maitland, *London*, II, 1120; Chaffers, *Gilda aurifabrorum*, 55; *Cumberland and Westmorland Antiquarian Society Trans.*, n.s., IV (1904), 113.

102. *Vide ante*, 145–146.

103. For a discussion of this foundation, *vide ante*, 151–153.

104. PCC 11 Montague 1602; Strype, John, *Annals of the Reformation*

(Oxford, 1824, 4 vols.), II, i, 353–354. *Vide post*, 257. This foundation will be discussed in detail in our treatment of Lancashire.

105. *Vide ante*, 175, 182.

106. *Vide ante*, 106, and *post*, 295, for particulars of his other charities.

107. Goodman was also a benefactor to Westminster School (*vide ante*, 216). For particulars on his almshouse foundation, *vide ante*, 149.

108. PCC 1 Harte 1604; *PP* 1822, IX, 593; *PP* 1903, L, 1; *PP* 1904, LXXI, 924; Edwards, G. M., *Sidney Sussex College* (L., 1899), 52; Freshfield, *Accounts, St. Bartholomew*, 26; Seymour, *Survey*, I, 245; Cooper, *Memorials of Cambridge*, III, 20; Beaven, *Aldermen*, II, 41. Harte also gave by will £224 13s to the poor of Coxwold and Kilburn (Yorkshire) and East Ham (Essex); £112 13s to London hospitals; £100 for loans; £30 for marriages and as much to his company; £23 for the relief of prisoners; and lesser amounts for other charitable uses. He left, as well, a large fellowship foundation which is noted later (*vide post*, 265–266).

Harte served as alderman from 1580, as sheriff in 1579, and as a Member of Parliament on two occasions. He was Treasurer of St. Bartholomew's from 1573 to 1574 and its president from 1593 to 1604. He was one of the principal founders of the East India Company, serving as its governor in 1602. We shall deal at length with his foundation at Coxwold in the third volume of this study.

109. *Vide ante*, 146, for Deane's almshouse foundation. This donor also left £268 to the poor of London and £80 to the needy in various parishes in Surrey and Hampshire. He gave, also, £300 to the Drapers' Company for loans, £120 to London hospitals, £70 for prisoners, and lesser amounts for other charitable causes. His charities totalled £3494. The Hampshire benefactions will be described more fully in our treatment of that county.

110. PCC 63 Stafford 1606; *PP* 1837–8, XXVII, 200; Inderwick, *Inner Temple records*, I, 305.

111. PCC 73 Dorset 1609; Clode, *Merchant Taylors*, II, 344; *PP* 1826–7, X, 435; *PP* 1884, XXXIX, iv, 381.

112. *Vide ante*, 150.

113. PCC 84 Capell 1613; *PP* 1816, XVI, i, 750; *PP* 1819, X–A, 190; *Ambulator* (L., 1800), 123; Cromwell, Thomas, *History of Clerkenwell* (L., 1828), 386; Hatton, *New view*, II, 748.

114. PCC 94 Wood 1611; Hatton, *New view*, II, 734; Beaven, *Aldermen*, II, 44, 174; *PP* 1831, XI, 300. This school had been founded in 1556 by Sir Rowland Hill (*vide ante*, 225–226). Ryder also left £105 to the poor of his native Staffordshire and to the poor of Low Leyton, Essex, £24 to London hospitals, £20 to the relief of prisoners, and some years before his death had given £100 to Bridewell. He was a most enterprising London merchant, specializing in the manufacture of stockings from woollen yarn. He was made Collector of Customs Inward in 1603, and in 1606 Collector of Toll, Tonnage, and Poundage for London.

115. *Vide ante*, 107–108, 202, for Caldwell's charities for the poor and for the uses of his company.

116. PCC 27 Capell 1613; *PP* 1835, XXI, 287; *PP* 1840, XIX, i, 113; *N. E. Hist. & Gen.*, XLIX (1895), 378. Fisher, who was an alderman and

resident in St Margaret Lothbury, also left £120 for the release of prisoners, £66 13s 4d for his company, and lesser amounts for other charities.

117. PCC 83 Capell 1613; PP 1823, VIII, 334; PP 1826, XIII, 156; Husting, II, 737; Beaven, Aldermen, I, 37, 92, II, 48, 176. Pemberton expended about £400 on the building of his school, which will be discussed in our treatment of Lancashire. He also left £500 of endowment to Christ's Hospital, £100 to other London hospitals, £200 to the poor of the Goldsmiths' Company, and other charitable legacies.

118. PCC 20 Lawe 1614; PP 1822, IX, 272; PP 1837-8, XXVI, 130. Walwyn also provided £5 p.a. for the poor of St Martin Orgar, to be paid in coals to 'those godly poor who lived peaceably with their neighbours'.

119. PP 1824, XIII, 183; PP 1834, XLV, 342; PP 1839, XV, 276; Nichols, John, History of the county of Leicester (L., 1795-1815, 4 vols.), II, ii, 498; Fuller, Worthies, II, 242. Smith also left funds to secure the distribution of £3 18s in bread and £2 6s 8d for Bibles for the poor of his native town.

120. Vide ante, 108, 153-154, 202, and post, 285-286.

121. PCC 2 Weldon 1616; PP 1823, VIII, 362; PP 1897, LXVI, ii, 214; Seymour, Survey, I, 181. In addition, this donor left £100 to the Skinners' Company for loans to its young men and £50 to St Bartholomew's Hospital.

122. Vide ante, 109, for Wolley's generous provision for the poor of London and Staffordshire. The total of his charities was £1493.

123. Vide ante, 154.

124. PCC 18 Meade 1618; Bedwell, Tottenham, 118-119; Coleraine, Tottenham, 84-85.

124a. Vide ante, 111, and post, 286.

125. Vide ante, 110-111, and post, 258, 286, 295.

126. Vide ante, 111, 182.

127. Vide ante, 112.

128. PCC 38 Fenner 1612; PP 1826-7, X, 438; PP 1884, XXXIX, iv, 382; PP 1904, LXXI, 789. Osmotherlawe also left £7 6s 8d p.a. to the poor of London, 13s 4d p.a. to the clergy, and £2 10s p.a. to London hospitals.

129. Vide ante, 147, 200.

130. Vide ante, 113, for Hale's substantial gifts for the poor of London and Hertfordshire.

131. PCC 3 Dale 1621; PP 1837-8, XXVI, 275, 281; Hawkins, M. W. S., Plymouth Armada heroes (Plymouth, 1888), 76-78. Lady Hawkins likewise left £150 to the poor as follows: £50 to those of the parish of Kington, where she was born, £10 to those of 'Amelly', Herefordshire, where she was nursed, and the remainder to various parishes where she had lived, including £50 to St Dunstan in the East, 'where I do dwell and have lived for a long time'. Lady Hawkins, Sir John's second wife, was the daughter of Charles Vaughan.

132. PCC 78 Savile 1622; (Lady Knivett) PCC 84 Savile 1622; PP

1816, XVI, i, 766; *PP* 1823, IX, 308, 316; *Complete peerage*, IV, 424; *L. & M. Arch. Soc.*, III (1870), 130; *S. P. Dom.*, 1638 [?], CCCCVIII, 129. Knivett also left a capital sum of £20 for the relief of the poor 'under the directions of the statute of 43d. Elizabeth'. Knivett was the son of Sir Henry Knivett of Escrick, Yorkshire. He was Gentleman of the Bed-chamber to Elizabeth and to James and was a justice of the peace for Westminster. As a reward for his share in the detection of the Gunpowder Plot, he was summoned to Parliament as 'Lord Knyvet de Escrick' in 1607. His wife was a daughter of Sir Rowland Hayward (*vide ante*, 231).

133. *Vide ante*, 191–193.

134. PCC 8 Byrde 1624; DNB; Chaffers, *Gilda aurifabrorum*, 53; Maxwell, H. E., *Edinburgh* (L., 1916), 156; Arnot, Hugo, *Edinburgh* (Edinburgh, 1788), 565; Fox Bourne, *English merchants*, I, 259; Wood, *Records of Edinburgh*, II (1604–1626), 250, 257, 302, III (1626–1641), xlvi *et passim*. The institution was carefully administered and its funds well invested. The income became sufficient in the late nineteenth century to establish Heriot Free Schools in other parts of Edinburgh as well as to endow the Heriot-Watt College for technical instruction.

135. PCC 15 Skynner 1627; *PP* 1819, X–B, 86; *PP* 1823, VIII, 287, 429, IX, 174; Faulkner, Thomas, *Fulham and Hammersmith* (L., 1813), 180. Latimer also left lands with a capital value of upwards of £104 for the benefit of the indigent of the parish of St Dunstan in the West.

136. PCC 30 Audley 1632; *PP* 1816, XVI, i, 794, 796; *PP* 1825, X, 101; *PP* 1830, XII, 103, 230; *PP* 1834, XLV, 342; *PP* 1840, XIX, i, 122; *PP* 1903, L, 8; Beaven, *Aldermen*, I, 124, 169, 183, 251, II, 50, 176; Locks, W. A., ed. *East London antiquities* (L., 1902), 125; Hatton, *New view*, II, 735; Moore, *St Bartholomew's* II, 230; DNB. Leman, the son of a Dutch refugee merchant, was a notable benefactor. He provided £13 p.a. by will for the poor of various London parishes and £12 p.a. for the needy in his company's almshouses. He left lands in Whitechapel with a then capital value of £2000 for the uses of Christ's Hospital, which he had served as president from 1618 until the time of his death, as well as £150 to St Bartholomew's and Bridewell. We shall later note his large capital gift for a lectureship (*vide post*, 288).

137. *Vide ante*, 148, for a discussion of the conjoined almshouse.

138. *Vide ante*, 148, 169, 205, and *post*, 289, for Perry's other sub-stantial charities. This merchant in effect established by his generosity all the social institutions of his native parish.

139. PCC 2 Sadler 1635; Watney, *St. Thomas Acon*, 223; *PP* 1822, IX, 273.

140. PCC 17 Sadler 1635; *PP* 1834, XXI, 119; Boyd, *Roll of Drapers*, 140. Parrett left a variety of charitable benefactions, including £32 10s to the poor of his parish of St Dunstan in the East, £10 towards the building of a workhouse in London, £20 to his company, £210 (including capital and outright bequests) for poor relief in various Buckinghamshire parishes, £5 p.a. for apprenticeships in Bow Brickhill, and £1 p.a. for two sermons annually in the church there. We shall comment further on his school in our discussion of Buckinghamshire.

141. PCC 10 Goare 1637. We have been able to find little regarding these schools.

142. PCC 180 Lee 1638; *PP* 1822, IX, 280; *PP* 1837–8, XXIV, 428; Freshfield, *Accomptes of St. Christopher*, 79; Beaven, *Aldermen*, II, 57. Mowlson left in all £2795 10s for various charitable uses, including £50 for church repairs in London, £52 to the poor of divers London parishes, £180 to London hospitals, £90 to the uses of his own company, £400 to the Grocers and Merchant Adventurers as a loan fund, £54 to the clergy, £7 in alms, £40 (£2 p.a.) to the parish clerk at Hargrave, and a substantial endowment for a lectureship at Hargrave, which will be considered later (*vide post*, 289).

Mowlson served in Parliament in 1628, was governor of the Merchant Adventurers in 1632, and was elected President of Christ's Hospital shortly before his death. He married Ann, daughter of Anthony Radcliffe, a rich London merchant. His widow, who was gifted in finance, greatly increased her inheritance and was the first considerable donor to Harvard College. Radcliffe College, the women's institution connected with Harvard University, was named to honour her.

143. *Vide ante*, 127, 179, 183.

144. PCC 6 Evelyn 1641; *PP* 1826–7, IX, 240. *Vide post*, 289, for his lectureship foundation. The son of a Lancashire yeoman, Walworth served as steward to the Earl of Pembroke.

145. *Vide ante*, 179–180, 183, and *post*, 305.

146. *Vide ante*, 178.

147. (Gamull) PCC 23 Crane 1643; *PP* 1826–7, X, 454; *PP* 1837–8, XXIV, 625; (Bolton) PCC 2 Pembroke 1650; *PP* 1884, XXXIX, iv, 368. Gamull, a grocer, also left a total of £148 to the poor of London and Walthamstow, Essex, £100 for church repairs in Audlem, and £200 to his company as a loan fund. It is by no means certain that the suggested total of £1258 13s came fully into the hands of the governors. The cost of the building is unknown, but the principal investment made by the trustees seems to have been £400 laid out on lands in 1653. Bolton also left £100 of endowment for a bread charity for the benefit of the poor of Audlem and the adjoining parish of Hankelow.

148. *Vide ante*, 155–156, 219.

149. *Vide post*, 266.

150. PP 1831, XI, 328; *PP* 1837–8, XXVI, 442; Beaven, *Aldermen*, I, 26, 124, 183, 251, 277, II, lv, 64, 90, 181; Johnson, *Drapers*, III, 163; Fuller, *Worthies*, III, 67; Hardy, Nathaniel, *The royal common-wealths man* (L., 1668). Born in 1586, Adams was by 1618 a prominent and wealthy draper. He became an alderman in 1639 and lord mayor in 1645. He was twice imprisoned as a suspected royalist. Adams retired to his estates purchased some years before in Norfolk, and he is said to have remitted as much as £10,000 to Charles II in exile. At the Restoration, the King knighted him and shortly afterward made him a baronet. Adams died at a great age in 1668.

151. *Vide ante*, 159–160, for his almshouse foundation at Malmesbury.

152. PCC 174 Alchin 1654; *PP* 1822, IX, 236; *PP* 1884, XXXIX, iv,

574; Brabner, J. H. F., ed., *Comprehensive gazetteer of England* (L., n.d., 6 vols.), V, 157; Moore, A. W., *History of Isle of Man* (L., 1900, 2 vols.), I, 472. Christian also left, as part of the same trust, property with a then capital value of £140 for the care of the poor of the company, as well as a smaller annuity for his company, of which he had been warden, for its uses. His family had for some time past been prominent in the affairs of the Isle of Man as deputies of the Earl of Derby.

153. *Vide ante*, 163.

154. *Vide ante*, 213–214.

155. Unlike many other great benefactors of our period, Aldworth held no high municipal office. In 1629, he was chosen alderman for Cordwainer Ward; he was sworn and discharged the same day on payment of a fine of £600.

156. PCC 88 Aylett 1655; *PP* 1824, XIV, 239, 249; *PP* 1826–7, X, 454; *PP* 1884, XXXIX, iv, 135–136, 370; Hatton, *New view*, I, 134. Colborne also left £400 to the Drapers' Company, £10 to the poor of his parish, and £5 p.a. each to the parishes of Kirkham and Goosnargh for their needy. He also bequeathed £50 to the school at Clapham, and he intended the Merchant Taylors to have £1000 for the school at Ashwell, though they seem to have received only £637 10s of that sum. The Kirkham school will be more fully discussed in a later volume.

157. *Vide ante*, 178, for Fletcher's substantial endowment of a work scheme for the benefit of the poor of Ormskirk.

158. *Vide ante*, 160, and *post*, 291.

159. Cooke, *Top. of Great Britain*, VII, 126; *PP* 1816, XVI, i, 754; *PP* 1823, IX, 275. This donor's mother, Mary Lake, had founded an almshouse in the parish in 1646 (*vide ante*, 159).

160. *Vide ante*, 202.

161. *Vide ante*, 160, 171, for an account of his almshouse foundation and his apprenticeship fund, both being for the benefit of Newport. Adams also left £20 p.a. for a lectureship at Newport.

162. *Vide ante*, 133, and *post*, 291.

163. PCC 249 Wootton 1658; *PP* 1837–8, XXVI, 206. Crowder also left £28 to named clergymen, £40 to Christ's Hospital, and £20 to St Bartholomew's, as well as £73 to the poor of fifteen parishes in London, Surrey, Shropshire, and Herefordshire.

164. PCC 514 Pell 1659; *PP* 1819, X-A, 65; *PP* 1826–7, X, 456; Beaven, *Aldermen*, II, 82. Bigg also bequeathed £200 to the poor of his company and an equal sum for the relief of the poor of Wallingford. This donor was chosen sheriff in 1653, master of his company in 1654, and was sitting in Parliament for Wallingford at the time of his death.

165. PCC 94 Laud 1662; *PP* 1837–8, XXVI, 698; *PP* 1884, XXXIX, ii, 140; Beaven, *Aldermen*, I, 59, II, 73, 183; Moore, *St. Bartholomew's*, II, 710. Box was chosen as sheriff in 1639. In 1650 he was committed to Newgate for refusing to accept office as an alderman, but was released later that year when he consented to be sworn in; he was then discharged upon payment of £500 as a fine.

166. *Vide post*, 311 ff.

167. *Vide* Jordan, *Philanthropy in England*, 291 for a discussion of the want of precision with which the terms 'scholarship' and 'fellowship' were used in the seventeenth century.

168. We should make it clear that we have not here counted as scholarship endowments or as scholars those boys wholly supported on such foundations as Christ's Hospital, Charterhouse, or Aldworth's foundation at Reading.

169. Willet, in his valuable survey of benefactions to the two universities, estimated the total number of fellowships established in the 'period of the Gospel' as 68 at Cambridge and 27 at Oxford, and the number of scholarships as 291 and 62 in the two institutions respectively. But Willet seems to include all known benefactions from the whole of England for the period 1540–1630, though he none the less frequently refers to a period of sixty years. Assuming an interest rate of 5 per cent, his total for fellowship and scholarship endowments received by the two universities in the period would be £68,800. (Willet, *Synopsis papismi* [1634], 1233–1243).

170. *Vide ante*, 144, 201, for Gresham's other benefactions. A full memoir will be found in the DNB.

171. PCC 94 Ridley 1629; *BM Add. Charters*, 18,205 (Lord Ellesmere *et al.*, to the King, March 4, 1609); Fuller, *Church history*, III, 235; Aikin, *Environs of London*, 65; *LCC Survey*, XI (1927), 1–6; Beaver, Alfred, *Memorials of old Chelsea* (L., 1892), 262–263; Blunt, Reginald, *Handbook to Chelsea* (L., 1900), 128; DNB.

172. *Vide ante*, 154–155, 205, and *post*, 287.

173. PCC 90 Russell 1633; Pearce, *Sion College*, 8, 16–17; Baddeley, *Cripplegate*, 201–202; *PP* 1835, XXI, 461. This cost would seem much more probable than the £2000 which has been occasionally suggested.

174. PCC 3 Crane 1643; *PP* 1824, XIII, 216; Cokayne, *Lord mayors*, 18–19; Hatton, *New view*, II, 735. This donor, who was the daughter of Robert Taylor, a London merchant, also left £200 as a loan fund for young haberdashers, £70 to Bridewell, £500 as an endowment for the relief of the poor of the Haberdashers, and £500 with that company to fund four scholarships for men likely to become ministers in Cambridge University.

175. *Vide ante*, 156, for a biographical notice and an account of this donor's great almshouse foundation. His funeral sermon (1629) was preached by Robert Willan and was published in 1630 under the title *Eliah's wish*. Willan paid tribute to Bayning for having given so generously towards the furnishing of the library with books, for 'bookes are the rivers of Paradise watering the earth: the deaw of Hermon making the vallies fertile . . . the magazine of piety and arts'. He exhorted the great and wealthy city of London to raise up a library equal to those of ancient Athens and Alexandria. 'Were the meanes of your industrious preachers answerable to their mindes, this good and great worke needed no other supply, for they like Plato would give 3000. Graecian pence for three

small volumes of Pythagoras.' The clergy require a learned and free library that they may pronounce the 'true and ancient doctrine'.

176. PCC 4, 7 Sadler 1635; Pearce, *Sion College*, 96, 177–178. Travers also left £100 as a scholarship endowment for Emmanuel College, Cambridge, and as much for the uses of Trinity College, Dublin.

177. PCC 14 Goare 1637; Beaven, *Aldermen*, II, 57; Pearce, *Sion College*, 14–15. Parkhurst had been the owner of the site of Sion College and the vendor to White's executors. Parkhurst also left £140 to Christ's Hospital, £100 to Bridewell, £100 to poor clergymen and their widows, £85 to secure the release of prisoners for debt, £30 to the poor of London, and lesser sums for other charitable uses.

178. Our reckoning agrees rather closely with that made by Willet in his valuable study of seventeenth-century benefactions (*Synopsis papismi* [1634], 1233–1243). Excluding, as we have done, scholarship and fellowship endowments from this particular computation, Willet arrives at a total of £139,400 (if we may assume an interest rate of 5 per cent) given to the universities for endowment, fabric, and libraries, as compared with our total of £135,471 5s. The closeness of the two figures is, however, somewhat accidental, since Willet includes numerous and large non-London benefactions, while dealing with a much shorter period. He concludes that £83,300 had been provided for Oxford 'during the time of the Gospel', and £56,100 for Cambridge.

179. PCC 28 Milles 1489; Cook, *Mediaeval chantries*, 115; Newcourt, Richard, *Reportorium ecclesiasticum ... Londinense* (L., 1708, 2 vols.), I, 23; Fisher, Payne (G. B. Morgan, ed.), *Tombs in S. Paul's* (L., 1885), 143–145. *Vide post*, 274.

180. PCC 3 Ayloffe 1522; Cook, *Mediaeval chantries*, 115; Allen, *History of London*, II, 314; Marriott, J. A. R., *John Colet* (L., 1933), 117–118; Lupton, J. H., *Erasmus's lives of Vitrier and Colet* (L., 1883), 39n.; Newcourt, *Reportorium*, I, 25; Dugdale, William, *History of St. Paul's* (L., 1648), 382. *Vide post*, 277. As we shall elsewhere note, Fitz James, with his nephew (or brother), Sir John, was also the founder of a school in his native Somerset.

181. *Vide ante*, 137, for his other charities and for more particulars regarding the trust of which this benefaction was part.

182. PCC 13 Ayloffe 1518; Hope, W. St. J., *History of London Charterhouse* (L., 1925), 98; Cooper, *Memorials of Cambridge*, I, 268; Clark, *Endowments of Cambridge*, 261–268. Rede left large bequests for prayers (*vide post*, 277). He also left small sums for the poor of London, as well as legacies to hospitals and prisons. He held great landed estates in Kent, leaving £20 for roads, £10 to the poor, £11 13s for church repairs, and £1 to church general in Chiddingstone, in that county. Rede was educated at Cambridge and Lincoln's Inn; he was appointed King's Serjeant in 1494, Justice of the King's Bench in 1495, and Chief Justice in 1506. Rede likewise founded three public lectures in Cambridge, to be read annually.

183. (Smyth) PCC 26 Fetiplace 1513, 16 Crumwell 1539; (Sutton) PCC F.27 Bodfelde 1524; DNB; Wood, *Oxford colleges*, 354; *Brasenose monographs*, I, iv, 7, vi, 10, II, ix, 7.

184. *Vide ante,* 234.

185. *Vide ante,* 229, and *post,* 263, 264.

186. Mallet, *Oxford,* II, 35–38.

187. PCC 10 Chaynay 1559; Blakiston, H. E., *Trinity College* (L., 1898), 28–74; Warton, *Sir Thomas Pope,* 158–168. Pope was born in Oxfordshire in 1507 of yeoman parentage. He was educated at Banbury and at Eton, entering the service of the Lord Chancellor, Thomas Audley, as a youth. From 1532 onwards, he rose rapidly in the government service and grew rich after his appointment to the Court of Augmentations. He held about thirty manors, all of which had been monastic properties. None the less, he seems not to have been in sympathy with the religious changes of the period. He retained the confidence of both Mary and Elizabeth

188. *Vide ante,* 143, 231.

189. She also made generous outright bequests to the poor, prisoners, and the sick, in addition to her almshouse and school foundations.

190. PCC 47 Pyckering 1575; Wood, *Oxford colleges,* 521.

191. *Vide ante,* 174, for White's great loan fund endowment.

192. The DNB provides a memoir of this great donor, but a full-scale study would be useful. *Vide ante,* 215, for his connection with the Merchant Taylors' School.

193. *Vide ante,* 107, 150.

194. *Vide post,* 285, for his support of the clergy.

195. *Vide ante,* 110–111, 237, for a biographical notice of this great merchant tailor and a discussion of his other charities; *vide post,* 286, 295, for his lectureship foundation and gifts to religion.

196. *Vide ante,* 108, and *post,* 285, for other benefactions by this donor.

197. PCC 88 Meade 1618; *Va. Mag.,* XVI (1908), 193; *PP* 1822, IX, 271, 280, 309. Mary Robinson left substantial charities, totalling £3455, for a variety of uses: £580 for the relief of the poor of London and of Monmouth, £200 to hospitals, £400 for loans, £150 in stocks for the poor, £100 to the clergy, £200 to help the people in Virginia in building a church there, £50 for bridge repairs in Monmouth, £80 for the relief of prisoners, and numerous other smaller charitable sums. She was the daughter of William Ramsay, a rich London grocer, and a niece and namesake of Lady Mary Ramsay (*vide ante,* 101–102). Her husband, John Robinson, was chief searcher of the customs at London and a member of the Virginia Company.

198. *Vide ante,* 109, 178. for Vernon's other charities.

199. PCC 109 Seager 1634; Hutton, W. H., *S. John the Baptist College* (L., 1898), 111; Wood, *Oxford colleges,* 541; Skelton, Joseph, *Pietas oxoniensis* (Oxford, 1828), 85. Paddy was graduated from Oxford in 1573 and gained his M.D. at Leyden in 1589. He was appointed physician to James I in 1603 and was four times President of the College of Physicians.

200. PCC 192 Twisse 1646; Skelton, *Pietas,* 85; Beaven, *Aldermen,* I, 93, II, 65; *PP* 1823, VIII, 553; *PP* 1833, XIX, 187.

201. *Vide ante,* 143.

202. *Vide ante,* 106, for his substantial provision for the poor of London.

203. PCC 37 Capell 1613; DNB; Willet, *Synopsis papismi* (1634), 1236; Bodleian Library, *Registrum donationum* (1600–1660). Bodley in his will displays prescience with respect to the insatiable needs of a modern library: 'And now forasmuch as the perpetuall preservation support and maytenise of the publique library of the Universitie of Oxford ... greatlie supports all my other worthy causes and because I do foresee that in proces of tyme there must of necessitie be very greate want of conveyanice and stowage for bookes by reason of the endles multitude of those that are presentlie there and like hereafter to be continuallie bought and broughte in ...' He goes on to bequeath funds for the addition and betterment of existing library facilities, for more room for storage, for adorning and augmenting the library; he feels certain his estate can accomplish this and have left as well a substantial endowment for future needs. (Willet arrives at a considerably larger total of £28,000 as the full measure of Bodley's generosity.)

204. PCC 111 Swanne 1623; Wilson, *Christ's Hospital*, 151–153; Mander, *Cordwainers*, 84; DNB.

205. PCC 86 Skynner 1627; Chester, J. L., ed., *Registers of St. Peter, Westminster* (L., 1876), 126; *L. & M. Arch. Soc.*, III (1870), 131; *Parochial charities of Westminster*, 1890), 77; *PP* 1816, XVI, i, 766; *PP* 1823, IX, 311. Heather also left £110 for the benefit of poor children in the hospital at Tothill Fields, Westminster, £3 p.a. to Eton College, and £2 p.a. to provide books, pens, and ink for the school at Stanwell, Middlesex.

206. *Vide ante*, 147, for his almshouse foundation, made with Archbishop Abbot.

207. PCC 85 Fines 1647, 90 Essex 1648; Green, *Committee for advance of money*, I, 259, 426; *S. P. Dom.*, 1640, CCCCLXI, 103; *Alumni oxon.*, II, 530; *Alumni cantab.*, I, ii, 175; *Catalogue of archives of All Souls* (L., 1877), 138; Brunton, Douglas, and D. H. Pennington, *Members of the Long Parliament* (Cambridge, Mass., 1954), 232. Francklyn was a member of the Long Parliament, lending moderate support to the Parliamentary cause. He also left £320 to the poor of Middlesex, £200 for apprenticeships, £200 for roads, £33 to the poor of several counties, and a substantial lectureship endowment (*vide post*, 290).

208. PCC 442 Alchin 1654; Ward, *Professors of Gresham College*, 316.

209. Clark, *Endowments of Cambrige*, 153–156.

210. *Vide ante*, 221, for her school foundation.

211. The endowment was hopelessly mixed with one of £90 p.a., or £1800 capital value, vested in Westminster Abbey to support three monks who were to celebrate masses and maintain her anniversary there, as well as for the support of the three chairs. After the Dissolution, the stipends were continued by decree, with the readers having £13 6s 8d p.a. each and the preacher £10 p.a. (Clark, *Endowments of Cambridge*, 57).

212. By will, she directed that all her plate, jewels, vestments, and books should be divided between the two colleges at Cambridge; no estimate of this gift can be made.

213. This foundation will be described in the third volume of this study.

214. PCC 14 Porch 1526; Howard, *Finances of St. John's*, 8; Dugdale, *St. Paul's*, 29. *Vide post*, 277.

215. PCC 27 Martyn 1574; *Alumni cantab.*, I, ii, 277; Baker, *St. John's College*, I, 206, 421. Gwynne had been graduated from Cambridge (Queen's) in 1548 and proceeded to his LL.D in 1560. He sat in the House of Commons for Cardigan in 1563–1567 and for Carnavonshire in 1572–1574. He also left £4 p.a. for the repair of roads in Carnavon and £58 outright to the poor of fourteen named parishes in Wales.

216. This will be discussed in the third volume of this work.

217. *Vide ante*, 125. The gift to his college was subject not only to a life income for his wife but to payments of £34 p.a. to the poor of certain London parishes. Platt indicated that the property thus bequeathed had a then value of £214 p.a. and should be worth £600 p.a. when the leases fell in. There was long litigation regarding the trust, not settled until 1684, when the income available for scholarships and fellowships represented a then capital value of £2800 net. The property left by Platt increased enormously in worth and by 1881, when the rents were £3000 p.a., had become one of the most valuable of the endowments of the college.

218. PCC 103 Lee 1638; Cooper, *Memorials of Cambridge*, II, 98, 265; Howard, *Finances of St. John's*, 308; Gilbert, *Liber scholasticus*, 87.

219. PCC 134 Lee 1638; Wilson, *Merchant-Taylors' School*, I, 252–255. There is a short memoir in the DNB.

220. PCC 150 Evelyn 1641; Beaven, *Aldermen*, II, 63; Howard, *Finances of St. John's*, 292; *PP* 1816, XVI, i, 800. Highlord also gave £50 to Bridewell Hospital, £2 p.a. to the poor of his parish, and £2 13s 4d p.a. for a quarterly sermon there. The son of a skinner, he rose rapidly in the affairs of the company. He was first chosen an alderman in 1634 and was sheriff in the next year. He traded principally in the East India Company, serving on the committee of the company almost continuously from 1630 until his death.

221. *Vide ante*, 216–217, for Williams' benefactions to Westminster School. The new library cost £2991 1s 10d., towards which Williams gave £2011 13s 4d. He intended to found two fellowships as well as four scholarships, but the endowment was insufficient. He also left his library to St John's; it was, however, mostly a duplication of an already strong collection. The duplicates were sold for £382, and this amount was funded for the purchase of new books.

222. PCC 38 Peter 1573; Cooper, *Memorials of Cambridge*, I, 74–87; Venn, *Caius College*, I, 45–75. *Vide* DNB for an excellent memoir, on which we have depended heavily for these biographical particulars.

223. Mrs Frankland likewise gave £3 p.a. towards the augmentation of scholarships founded by her mother in Lincoln College, Oxford, and endowments totalling £1840 in capital worth to Brasenose for its general uses and for the strengthening of its fellowship funds. *Vide ante*, 229, 257, and *post*, 264. Her educational benefactions totalled £4840.

224. PCC 51 Leicester 1589; Cooper, C. H., ed., *Athenae cantabrigienses* (Cambridge, 1858–1913, 3 vols.), II, 55; Shuckburgh, *Emmanuel*

College; Cooper, *Memorials of Cambridge*, II, 343; *PP* 1840, XIX, i, 91; Blott, Walter, *Chronicle of Blemundsbury* (S. Norwood, 1892), 195; Webb, *St. Bartholomew's Priory*, I, 547–551, II, 262 ff. Mildmay left as well £200 outright to the master and scholars of his college and £30 in plate, £20 to Christ College, £40 to Christ's Hospital, £40 for London prisoners, £100 to the poor of Apthorpe, Northamptonshire, and £400 for tax relief in that parish, £100 for poor relief in London, Essex, and Northamptonshire, and £20 to poor preachers in Northamptonshire. He made personal bequests totalling £8680.

225. *Vide ante*, 229, 257, 263.

226. PCC 15 Leicester 1588; Cooper, *Memorials of Cambridge*, II, 361; Strype, *Stow's Survey*, I, i, 279; *N. E. Hist. & Gen.*, XLVII (1893), 286–287. This donor also left £10 to the schoolmaster at her birthplace, Ipswich, Suffolk, £50 to poor widows and orphans, £50 to poor householders of London and Ipswich, £10 to an Ipswich almshouse, £20 to prisoners, and £100 for the relief of 'poor and godly strangers ... to enjoy the freedom of their conscience'. She left, as well, a substantial lectureship foundation (*vide post*, 285).

227. Dixie was earlier interested in Peterhouse, to which he lent £100 in 1578–1579, and where he for some years seems to have maintained a fellow by annual contribution. *Vide ante*, 230, for his school foundation and other charities. Willet (*Synopsis papismi*, 1255) suggests that the lectureship was rather founded by Lady Dixie and that it was endowed at £8 p.a.

228. PCC 51 Cobham 1597; Shuckburgh, *Emmanuel College*, 216; Baddeley, *Aldermen of Cripplegate*, 56. Skinner, a native of Essex, also left £20 to the poor of his parish, £120 to hospitals, £30 to prisoners, and £20 to his company.

229. PCC 25 Bolein 1603; *PP* 1824, XIII, 285; *PP* 1831, XI, 177; *PP* 1840, XIX, i, 107; *Alumni cantab.*, I, ii, 104. English also left £100 to Christ's Hospital, £240 to the relief of Westminster's poor, and £100 to be used as an endowment for the relief of forty poor in Peterborough, Northamptonshire.

230. PCC 91 Stafford 1606; Parsons, F. G., *St. Thomas's Hospital* (L., 1932–1936, 3 vols.), I, 230; Beaven, *Aldermen*, I, 83, 201, 276, II, xlii, 42; Baker, *St. John's*, I, 434; DNB. Billingsley also left £10 to prisoners, £35 to hospitals, and £200 endowment for the relief of the poor of his parish (St Katherine Coleman), provided grants be not made to those poor persons living in newly erected houses or in great houses divided into tenements, and provided further the parson and churchwardens trouble not his heirs concerning an addition to his own house standing in the churchyard or his coach house abutting on the street. Billingsley was a native of Canterbury and studied both at Oxford and at Cambridge. He became a very rich merchant but never lost his interest in scholarly concerns, being the first translator of Euclid into English. He was chosen sheriff in 1584. The Queen disliked him, perhaps because of his pronounced Puritanism, and ordered that he be passed over, though senior alderman, in 1596, with the result that Thomas Skinner was elected lord

mayor. Skinner died within two months, and Billingsley was then chosen, with a strong protest from the court of aldermen at the royal interference with 'auncient coustoom'. Billingsley indicates in his will that he had already distributed £13,000 in portions to his children; his will disposes of £5150, two London messuages, and coal mines valued at £200 p.a.

231. *Vide ante*, 172, and *post*, 291.

232. *Vide ante*, 160, 171, for Wollaston's other great charities.

233. PCC 82 Leicester 1589; *Complete peerage*, VII, 335; Blomefield, Francis, *History of Norfolk* (L., 1805–1810, 11 vols.), I, 517 ff.; Cooper, *Memorials of Cambridge*, II, 68; Edwards, *Sidney Sussex College*; Smith, *Roll-call of Westminster*, 117. This donor also left £100 to London hospitals, £100 to poor and godly London ministers, and endowed a generous lectureship at Westminster Abbey (*vide post*, 285). She was a daughter of Sir William Sidney and an aunt of the famous Sir Philip. She married Thomas Radcliffe, third Earl of Sussex, in 1555. He was M.P. for Norfolk in 1553, was Lord Lieutenant of Norfolk and Suffolk in 1557, Lord Chamberlain of the Household in 1572–1583, dying in the latter year.

234. PCC 34 Woodhall 1601; Herbert, *Livery companies*, II, 76; Hatton, *New view*, I, 134; Edwards, *Sidney Sussex College*, 49. Smith also left £50 for a lectureship at St Antholin's and £20 to be lent at no interest charge to the poor of his company.

235. *Vide ante*, 234, for Harte's grammar-school foundation.

236. PCC 8 Fetiplace 1512; Williams, E., *Early Holborn* (L., 1927, 2 vols.), II, section 37. Ripley also left £160 for a chantry and £43 5s outright for prayers.

237. PCC F.23 Bucke 1551; Hackett, Maria, *Correspondence respecting the ancient collegiate school* (L., 1832), xlxi; *Alumni cantab.*, I, iii, 442; Cooper, *Athenae*, I, 106. Reston also left £300 (partly estimated) to maintain the choir of St Paul's and for general church uses, £10 to Christ's Hospital, and nominal sums for other charitable causes.

238. PCC F.1 Alen 1545; Reade, A. L., ed., *Audley pedigrees, II* (L., 1932), 100; Cooper, *Memorials of Cambridge*, II, 162–165; DNB.

239. *Vide ante*, 143, for his almshouse foundation.

240. PCC 1 Bakon 1578; Stokes, H. P., *Corpus Christi* (L., 1898), 73.

241. PCC 26 Skynner 1627; Peile, John, ed., *Biographical register of Christ's College* (Cambridge, 1910, 1913, 2 vols.), I, 267.

242. *Vide ante*, 116, 169, 185.

243. *Vide ante*, 117, 157, 178, 205, and *post* 273, 283.

244. *Vide ante*, 244, for notice of his school foundation. William Sclater, in his funeral sermon for Wheelock (*The crowne of righteousnesse*, L., 1654), extolled Adams' generosity in these terms: '. . . about two and twenty yeares past . . . he [Wheelock] was chosen the first publique professor, and reader of Arabick there; a lecture first founded at the sole and proper charges of an eminent and truly religious gentleman of this citie of London . . . who ever since continued it by his bounty to him, of full 40l. *per annum* . . . for which munificent act he deserves of all schollers . . . an honorable mention, and of all learned posterity an everlasting memoriall.'

245. Sclater, continuing, praised Spelman, who 'erected, about ten yeares past, a Saxon lecture in the same university, establishing it by an annuall pension of 20l. . . . since continued by [his son and] grandchild . . . and this lecture also was first publickly read by this same professor'. Sir Henry Spelman (1564–1641), the great legal historian, has an excellent memoir in the DNB.

246. *Vide ante*, 161, for his almshouse foundation. Quested also left a rent-charge of £40 p.a. for the needs of Christ's Hospital.

247. PCC 303 Wootton 1658; *PP* 1822, IX, 261, 350. Andrewes also left a total of £421 to the poor of London, Middlesex, Berkshire, and Surrey, and to the needy of his company, £360 for general company uses, and £20 p.a. for sermons in Canterbury.

E. Religion

1. *Vide ante*, 33–46.

2. *Vide post*, 304–305, for a discussion of this great work.

3. PCC 18 Mooᵫe 1501; *LCC Survey*, XII (1929), 25, 89–91; *L. & M. Arch. Soc.*, II (1864), 247–248; Thrupp, *Merchant class*, 369; Beaven, *Aldermen*, II, 16. Tate likewise gave £10 to the relief of prisoners, £4 to lazar houses, £33 for marriage subsidies in Coventry, £2 for bridge repairs there, £100 for general charitable uses there, and £10 to be 'distributed amongst the mynstrels called the waytes of London in considerayion of theire grete labore and poor lyving'. Tate was a mercer, having served his company as master in 1482, 1490, and 1498. He represented London in Parliament in 1483 and again in 1491. *Vide post*, 299.

4. PCC 24 Blamyr 1503; *Husting*, II, 621–622. (One sheet of the will is missing.) Thwaytes also left small amounts to church repairs, the clergy, and to an almshouse in Calais.

5. PCC 11 Holgrave 1504.

6. PCC 16 Holgrave 1504. Archer also left £108 6s for prayers, £20 for church repairs, £41 7s to the universities, and £4 for poor relief.

7. PCC 7 Holgrave 1504. Ball likewise left £1 7s for church repairs and an estimated £6 for distribution to the poor in clothing.

8. PCC 26 Holgrave 1504.

9. PCC 14 Holgrave 1504.

10. PCC 24 Holgrave 1504.

11. PCC 17 Holgrave 1504. Bownde left in all £288 for charitable uses. He provided, in addition to the amounts noted above, £173 10s for prayers, £18 for vestments in Essex churches, £20 for marriage portions, £20 for roads, £9 to the poor, and lesser amounts for other secular uses.

12. PCC 9 Holgrave 1504.

13. PCC 23 Holgrave 1504. Burt also left £1 for prayers, a total of £4 for church repairs, and £2 1s for poor relief.

14. PCC 13 Holgrave 1504. This donor also provided £8 for prayers and £3 for poor relief.

15. PCC 13 Holgrave 1504.

16. PCC 20 Swann 1623; Mee, Arthur, *Middlesex* (L., 1940), 170;

Cass, *East Barnet*, 32, 34–36. Weld also left £99 10s to the poor, £20 to schools, and £10 to the clergy.

17. PCC 42 Parker 1619; *PP* 1822, IX, 271, 280–282; *PP* 1830, XII, 269; *PP* 1840, XIX, i, 115; *PP* 1884, XXXIX, ii, 142–143; Wadmore, *Skinners*, 107. Dame Margaret also endowed a lectureship in St Swithin's church with a capital of £133 6s 8d., left £300 to the uses of Christ's Hospital, £200 to the Skinners' Company, and £40 for the apprenticing of poor children in West Wickham, Kent. The Grocers at once purchased the impropriation of Norhill, Bedfordshire, and in 1663 Allhallows Staining, London. Two other livings were purchased with the income in the eighteenth century, but the full terms of the bequest proved to be difficult to carry out. Two churches were built at a cost of £19,000 in the nineteenth century and were endowed with accumulations of income.

18. *Vide ante*, 114, 175, 178–179, 185, and *post*, 283, 304.

19. *Vide ante*, 117, 157, 178, 205, 266, and *post*, 283.

20. Cook, *Mediaeval chantries*, 39. This authority must err in his belief that only thirteen foundations were made from 1503 to the suppression of the chantries. Our count is twenty-seven for this interval, though it should be noted that, of these, ten were founded by Londoners in counties other than Middlesex.

21. Clode, *Merchant Taylors*, I, 144.

22. PCC 17 Logge 1485; Russan, *Old London*, 170; Stow, *Survey*, I, 211; Beaven, *Aldermen*, II, xxviii, 15, 166. *Vide ante*, 90, for biographical particulars and comment on his other benefactions.

23. PCC 21 Logge 1485; Thrupp, *Merchant class*, 349; Beaven, *Aldermen*, II, 14; *PP* 1820, V, 96; Johnson, *Drapers*, I, 151. Haryot was a native of Leicestershire and, according to Fabyan, 'a merchant of wondrous adventures into many and sundrie countries'. He was first chosen alderman in 1469 and sat in Parliament for London in 1483 and 1484. He was twice master of his company. He also left £29 to the poor, £13 to prisoners, £40 for the improvement of the Guildhall, smaller amounts for various religious purposes, and a substantial sum for church building (*vide post*, 298).

24. *Husting*, II, 587–588, 598; Beaven, *Aldermen*, II, 13; *PP* 1820, V, 95; Chandlery, P. J., *Tower to Tyburn* (L., 1924), 88; [Woodburn, S., ed.], *Ecclesiastical topography* (L., 1811), I, No. 2; White, *Walbrook*, 178; Strype, *Stow's Survey*, II, v, 124. James was the son of a London upholder. He was knighted in the field by Edward IV; he served twice as master of the Drapers.

25. *Vide ante*, 256, for his benefactions to the universities.

26. PCC 12 Doggett 1492. Reynold also left £1 for the general uses of his parish church, £40 to London conduits, £33 to marriage portions, and £12 to the poor.

27. PCC 17 Doggett 1492; Beaven, *Aldermen*, II, 17. Swan also left £13 6s 8d to the poor of Helmsley, Yorkshire, and £6 13s 4d for marriage portions there.

28. PCC 19 Vox 1494; Hatton, *New view*, II, 429; Waters, R. E. C., *Genealogical memoir of . . . Chesters of Bristol* (L., 1881), 55–58; Stow,

Survey, I, 248; Beaven, *Aldermen*, II, 17, 167. Astrye likewise left 10s to the general uses of the church, £9 to prisoners, £1 to the sick, £20 to his company, £10 (estimated) to the repair of Rochester Bridge, and a residue of perhaps £100 for general charitable uses. A native of Hitchin, he left £46 13s 4d for vestments and sacramental objects there. Astrye had served his apprenticeship under a former lord mayor, Sir William Hampton, and gained his initial competence by marrying a widow who had previously been the wife of two successive aldermen.

29. *Vide ante*, 90, 197. Clopton also built during his lifetime a chapel at his native Stratford-on-Avon, Warwickshire, at an estimated charge of £150.

30. PCC 29 Horne 1499; Stow, *Survey*, I, 18; Strype, *Stow's Survey*, II, v, 126; Beaven, *Aldermen*, II, 16. Mathewe also left £7 for church general, £29 7s for church repairs and vestments, £23 10s for designated clergy, £60 to road repairs and conduits, £6 13s 4d for marriage portions, and lesser sums to the poor and to his company. A native of Buckinghamshire, Mathewe had first been a linen-draper but was translated to the Mercers. He was an alderman from 1482, mayor in 1490, master of his company in the same year. Strype says he was a bachelor, but his will mentions a wife and son.

31. Brayley, *Westminster*, I, 99–100; Lethaby, W. R., *Westminster Abbey* (L., 1906), 167; Allen, *History of London*, IV, 11–14; Brooke-Hunt, Violet, *Westminster Abbey* (N.Y., 1902), 124 ff. *Vide ante*, 136–137, and *post*, 299, for this monarch's other charitable dispositions.

32. *Vide ante*, 90–91.

33. *Vide ante*, 91, 221.

34. *Vide ante*, 91, and *post*, 299.

35. PCC 13 Holgrave 1504; Archer, *Vestiges of old London*, xxv, 2; Beaven, *Aldermen*, II, 19, 167; Strype, *Stow's Survey*, II, v, 127. Shaa also left £48 to the poor of London, £20 for highways in his native Essex, and lesser amounts for church general, prisoners, and the sick. He was a nephew of Sir Edmund Shaa. He became an alderman in 1496, was knighted in 1497, and was chosen mayor in 1501. He represented the city in Parliament in 1495 and 1503 and was twice Master of the Mint.

36. PCC 41 Holgrave 1505; Marriott, *Colet*, 47; DNB; Beaven, *Aldermen*, II, 15. Colet also left £100 for roads, £100 for marriage portions, £100 for scholarships at Oxford and Cambridge, and lesser amounts for church repairs and church general.

37. *Vide ante*, 221–222.

38. PCC 2 Adeane 1505; Brooke and Hallen, *St. Mary Woolnoth*, xliv; Beaven, *Aldermen*, II, 19; Besant, *London city*, 121. Wyngar also left £21 13s for church general, £6 13s for church repairs, £48 7s to poor relief, £1 for alms, £4 to prisoners, £33 6s 8d for roads, and £33 6s 8d for marriage portions.

39. *Vide ante*, 91, 184.

40. PCC 21 Adeane 1507. Danyell's charities, including his bequest for prayers, totalled £480 5s.

41. PCC 2 Bennett 1508; *L. & M. Arch. Soc.*, n.s., VI (1931), 62, 77.

This donor also left £133 7s to St Catharine's College, Cambridge, and £5 for the general uses of her parish church, St Martin Oteswich.

42. PCC 1 Bennett 1508; Beaven, *Aldermen*, II, 20. Browne, a native of Rutland, was master of his company in 1497 and 1504. He had important commercial interests in Calais as well as in London. He also left £13 for the general uses of the church, £10 towards building a chapel in his parish church, £42 to the poor, £13 6s 8d for marriage portions, and lesser sums for prisoners and lazar houses.

43. PCC 22 Bennett 1509; *PP* 1884, XXXIX, iv, 509; Beaven, *Aldermen*, II, 16. Chawry left in all £193 7s for charitable uses. A native of Kent, he became an alderman in 1481, mayor in 1494, and sat in Parliament in 1497 for London. He was an aged man at the time of his death in November, 1509.

44. PCC 8 Fetiplace 1512. Morris also left £23 3s to the poor, £12 for marriage portions, and smaller sums for church general, church repairs, the clergy, prisoners, and hospitals.

45. PCC F.7 Holder 1515; *Husting*, II, 622–625; Johnson, *Drapers*, II, App., 347; *PP* 1825, X, 454; *PP* 1884, XXXIX, iii, 130. Cawley also left £53 to the poor of London and Cromer, Norfolk, £10 to Rochester Bridge, and an estimated £20 for church repairs.

46. PCC 6 Ayloffe 1517; *L. & M. Arch. Soc.*, n.s., VI (1931), 62; Clode, *Memorials*, 107.

47. PCC 29 Holder 1514; Orridge, *Citizens*, 224; *Husting*, II, 630; Lyell, *Acts of court of Mercers*, 691; Locks, *East London antiquities*, 136–137; Beaven, *Aldermen*, II, 19, 167. Haddon likewise left £62 for church repairs, £30 for the poor, £8 for prisoners, and lesser sums for other religious uses. The son of a London mercer, he was first chosen an alderman in 1499, was knighted in 1497, and served as mayor in 1506 and 1512. He was master of his company in 1500 and 1508.

48. *Vide ante*, 256, for a discussion of Rede's large secular charities.

49. *Vide ante*, 256, for his great educational charities.

50. *Vide ante*, 262, for Dowman's other charities.

51. *Vide ante*, 203. Rest also left smaller sums totalling £10 13s 4d, for masses.

52. *Vide ante*, 92, 138.

53. PCC 22 Porch 1527; *Husting*, II, 632–633; Nicholl, *Ironmongers*, 470, 514–515; Herbert, *Livery companies*, II, 612. Michell also left lands in London of a capital worth of about £500 to the uses of his company, as well as small sums for religious and secular charities.

54. PCC 20 Porch 1527; *PP* 1884, XXXIX, ii, 8; Cook, *Mediaeval chantries*, 39; Fry, *Inq. p. m., London*, I, 88–89; Beaven, *Aldermen*, II, 22, 168. Yarford left £53 7s for poor relief, £28 additionally for prayers, £13 6s 8d for marriage portions, £10 to prisoners, and other smaller benefactions, as well as having built a chapel in his parish church (*vide post*, 300). A native of Wales, Yarford was apprenticed to Stephen Gibson, to whose two children he left £10 each. He was first chosen alderman in 1509, mayor in 1519. He was thrice master of his company and sat in Parliament for London in 1509. Yarford held real property in

London worth £40 p.a., as well as extensive lands in three Kentish parishes, in Surrey, Essex, Middlesex, and Calais.

55. *Vide ante*, 197, for a discussion of Lovell's gifts for municipal uses, and *post*, 300 for an account of his generous outlays for church building.

56. *Husting*, II, 633–634.

57. PCC 21 Thower 1532; Johnson, *Drapers*, II, 51; Beaven, *Aldermen*, II, 23. Baily's charities totalled £920 14s. A native of Essex, he was first a member of the guild of Shearmen and to their great wrath arranged for his translation to the Drapers when in 1514 he attained the eminence of an alderman. He was sheriff in 1515 and was twice master of his company. He left a large estate, including lands in Kent, Surrey, and Suffolk.

58. PCC 19 Thower 1532; Malcolm, J. P., *Londinium redivivum* (L., 1803–1807, 4 vols.), II, 7; Beaven, *Aldermen*, II, 27. Pargitar left £17 13s to the poor, £6 13s 4d for marriages, and lesser sums for other charitable uses. A native of Oxfordshire, he had been chosen alderman in 1528 and lord mayor in 1530. His fortune at the time of his death was modest.

59. PCC 21 Thower 1532; *L. & M. Arch. Soc.*, n.s., II (1910), 65; Pitman, W. H., *Company of Painters* (L., 1913), 23; Englefield, W. A. D., *History of the Painter-Stainers* (L., 1923), 51; *Archaeologia*, XXXIX (1863), i, 23–25. Browne also left £40 to church repairs, property valued at £70 to his company for its uses, about £52 for poor relief, and smaller amounts for a variety of religious and secular uses.

60. PCC 5 Hogen 1533; Dugdale, *St. Paul's*, 41; Cook, *Mediaeval chantries*, 118; *Husting*, II, 637.

61. PCC 17, 33 Hogen 1534; Clode, *Merchant Taylors*, II, 39; Cobb, *Old churches*, 38; Bruce, *Memories and monuments*, 156; Bumpus, *Ancient London churches*, 149; *London parishes* (1824), 29; Beaven, *Aldermen*, II, 21; Nicolas, *Testamenta vetusta*, II, 665–669; DNB. Fitzwilliam also left £49 to religious houses, £50 for road repairs in Huntingdonshire, £100 in marriage portions, £50 for highways in Essex, £70 to scholars in the universities, and £33 to the priests attending his funeral, as well as contributing generously to church building during his lifetime (*vide post*, 300). A native of Leicestershire, he was chosen sheriff in 1506, having served as master of his company in 1499. He became chamberlain to Wolsey, and he served as Chancellor of the Duchy of Lancaster and Keeper of the Privy Seal. He was knighted in 1522.

62. *Vide ante*, 93.

63. PCC 35 Hogen 1536; *PP* 1884, XXXIX, iv, 475; Freshfield, *Communion plate*, 65; Beaven, *Aldermen*, II, 25. Pecocke left in all £626 15s to charity. He was a native of Ireland, first named an alderman in 1524, chosen sheriff in 1526, and mayor in 1532. His only surviving son was a monk.

64. PCC 9 Dyngeley 1537; Beaven, *Aldermen*, II, 23, 168; Chaffers, *Gilda aurifabrorum*, 42. Born in Buckinghamshire, Mundy was a grandson of Sir Edmund Shaa, mayor in 1482, and a son-in-law of William Browne, mayor in 1513. He was first chosen alderman in 1513 and was mayor in 1522. He was elected prime warden of his company in 1519. In 1533 he

was committed to prison for 'disobedyence to my lords the mayer and my maisters the aldermen'.

65. *Vide ante*, 93-94. Askew was a conservative in his religious views.

66. We are told, for example, that in 1633 it was the custom 'for the merchants and other tradesmen that lived in London, so many of them as were al borne in the same county, to meet at a solemn feast (upon their own charges) together in London, and then to consult what good they might to do their native county by settling some ministers (or some other good works) in that county' [*Surtees Society*, LXV (1875), 126].

67. It should be noted that an even larger proportion (92·35 per cent) of all endowments for lectureships was concentrated in this same interval. *Vide post*, 284 ff., for treatment of this closely related subject.

68. *Vide ante*, 93.

69. *Vide ante*, 141, for his almshouse bequests. Lewin also left an annuity of about £8 for the uses of Eton College and £5 p.a. for the maintenance of a poor scholar in either of the universities.

70. PCC 43 Windsor 1586. The bequest was for John Reynolds (1549-1607), then a fellow of Corpus Christi, which he served as president from 1598 until his death. Reynolds was a moderate Puritan.

71. *Vide ante*, 178, 205, and *post*, 295, for further particulars regarding this great benefactor's charities, which totalled £4943.

72. *Vide ante*, 114, 175, 178-179, 185, 273, and *post*, 304, for the full account of the massive charities of this draper.

73. *Vide ante*, 113.

74. *Vide ante*, 117-122.

75. *Vide ante*, 117, 157, 178, 205, 266, 273, for biographical particulars and full accounts of the complex charities of this great mercer turned nobleman.

76. PCC 84 Scroope 1630; *PP* 1820, V, 132; *PP* 1822, IX, 305; *PP* 1884, XXXIX, ii, 16-17; Freshfield, *Communion plate*, 77; *L. & M. Arch. Soc.*, n.s., I (1902), 341. Bancks, the son of a London barber, also left £167 for poor relief, £13 for municipal uses, £200 to be lent to young men of the Mercers' Company at 3 per cent, £20 for church repairs, and £170 for the uses of his company.

77. Christopher Hill (*Economic problems of the church*, 297) has an interesting and helpful discussion of this important matter.

78. PCC 12 Dyngeley 1537; Beaven, *Aldermen*, II, 28, 169; *VCH, London*, 267; *L. & M. Arch. Soc.*, II (1864), 252-253; Ogilvy, J. S., *Relics and memorials of London* (L., 1909), 21. Monmouth was a great cloth manufacturer and exporter who employed hundreds of workmen in Suffolk.

79. PCC 37 Butts 1584; White, *Walbrook*, 209; Beaven, *Aldermen*, II, 37, 173. Rivers also left small benefactions to the poor, prisoners, and his company. He was born in Penshurst, Kent, his father being steward to the Duke of Buckingham. He married the daughter of one lord mayor and was brother-in-law to another. He was first chosen an alderman in 1565, and he served as President of St Thomas's Hospital from 1580 to 1584.

80. *Vide ante*, 264.
81. *Vide ante*, 265, for her great foundation of Sidney Sussex College.
82. *Vide ante*, 102, 231.
83. Kennett, MS. notes in his own copy of *Impropriations*, Bodleian. *Vide ante*, 103, 232, for biographical particulars and comments on Aldersey's other great bequests. It should be noted that this capital sum of £1733 has been divided for statistical purposes equally between lecture-ships and maintenance of the clergy.
84. *Vide ante*, 104.
85. *Vide ante*, 107, 150, 258, for his other charities. Palyn also left £100 for bells for St Mary-le-Bow.
86. PCC 2 Wood 1611; *PP* 1830, XII, 77; *PP* 1840, XIX, i, 108; Aldis, H. G., ed., *Dictionary of printers . . . in England* (L., 1910), 35. Bishop was a stationer, serving five times as warden and master of his company between 1589 and 1608. He was a native of Shropshire. He left as well £10 to the poor outright, £6 p.a. for interest-free loans to young men of his company, £6 p.a. to Christ's Hospital, and, according to one source (Aldis), £60 p.a. to three scholars at Christ Church, Oxford, where his only son had died when a student. We cannot establish this last large benefaction and wonder whether it might not have been an income gift for a term of years for young men then members of the college.
87. *Vide ante*, 108, 258, for his other benefactions.
88. *Vide ante*, 113.
89. *Vide ante*, 108, 153–154, 202, 236, *Vide* also Kennett's MS. notes in his own copy of *Impropriations*, in the Bodleian.
90. PCC 8 Weldon 1617; *PP* 1897, LXVI, ii, 531; *S. P. Dom.*, 1617, XC, 73; Clarke, Charles, *Architectura ecclesiastica londini* (L., 1820), 105 ff.; Wilson, *Merchant-Taylors' School*, I, 195–199; Seymour, *Survey*, II, 698. Whetenhall also left about £8 to the French church of London and £123 to London's poor, as well as £133 7s to named Puritan clergy-men of London. He was an ardent, as well as a learned, Puritan. His will disposed of copies of the Scriptures in French, Italian, and Spanish, in Latin, Greek, and Hebrew. His library also included the works of all the leading Puritan divines of his age.
91. *Vide ante*, 110–111, 237–238, 258, and *post*, 295, for a full recital of his charities and a biographical notice.
92. This will be described in our discussion of Hampshire. *Vide ante*, 111, 237.
93. PCC 62 Dale 1621. This donor also left annuities with a capital value of about £130 for poor relief in various places and £50 for church repairs.
94. The Merchant Taylors declined to administer the trust.
95. PCC 28 Swann 1623; *PP* 1822, IX, 204–206; *PP* 1824, XIII, 212–213; *PP* 1826–7, X, 427; *PP* 1840, XIX, i, 117; Hatton, *New view*, I, 134; Cooper, *Memorials of Cambridge*, II, 264. Three rectories were purchased before 1633 and two more after the Restoration. Since 1708 the five rectories have been presented jointly by the Haberdashers and the

governors of Christ's Hospital. In 1819 an additional vicarage was purchased for £2670. Dame Mary also left £500 to Christ's Hospital, £6 p.a.
to a chapelry in Middlesex, £20 to poor persons, £100 in capital for
teaching children in West Wickham, Kent, £200 as a loan fund to the
Skinners, and £32 p.a. to Trinity College, Cambridge, for an exhibition.
Her charities totalled more than £5100.

96. *Vide ante*, 154–155, 205, 255.

97. *Vide ante*, 155, for his almshouse foundations in London and
Salisbury.

98. *Vide ante*, 115–116, 175, 201, for biographical particulars and a
discussion of his other large charities. The company laid out £3145 4s 6d,
interest apparently being accumulated, for livings in Northumberland and
Lincolnshire, settling two vicars and two lecturers with the sufficient
stipends under their control.

99. PCC 71 Ridley 1629; Clode, *Merchant Taylors*, II, 346; *VCH,
Hampshire*, IV, 655. This donor also left £10 to named London poor and
£20 to the poor of Beaulieu, £60 to university scholarships, £35 to
named Puritan clergy, and £6 to the poor of his company.

100. PCC 10 Audley 1632; *PP* 1824, XIII, 249; *PP* 1837, XXIII,
588.

101. PCC 95 Scroope 1630; Strype, *Stow's Survey*, I, i, 146. Gonnell
also left £100 to the ill-fated Chelsea College (*vide ante*, 254), £100
for books for Sion College, and £300 for general charitable uses.

102. *Vide ante*, 126, 169, 183.

103. Seymour quotes a tablet in the church of All Saints, Derby, 'A
man pious and liberal to the poor in the great plague . . . neglecting his
own safety, he abode in the city to provide for their relief . . . did many
pious and charitable acts in his life-time; and by his will left about
£4000 to the maintenance of lectures, relief of poor, and other pious
uses'.

104. *Vide ante*, 183, 198, for a discussion of his other substantial
bequests. Heylyn was a liberal contributor to the repair of St Paul's and,
undoubtedly with Laud's approval, was in 1631 named one of the
commission for the rebuilding of the cathedral. He was certainly not a
pronounced Puritan.

105. *Vide ante*, 123.

106. *Vide ante*, 241, for his grammar-school foundation.

107. PCC 30 Russell 1633; *PP* 1826–7, X, 789; *PP* 1837–8,
XXVI, 439; *PP* 1884, XXXIX, iv, 163–164; Johnson, *Drapers*, III, 472;
Freshfield, *Communion plate*, 5. Rainey also left £200 to the Drapers for
their poor, £10 p.a. to the company for its uses, and gave St Bennet
Gracechurch a silver flagon valued at about £20. In 1922 the Drapers
derived £2140 from the property vested in them as trustees. They had
redeemed the two lectureship stipends. Rainey's Yorkshire foundation
will be more fully discussed in the third volume of this work.

108. *Vide ante*, 148, 169, 205, 241.

109. PCC 65 Seager 1634; Beaven, *Aldermen*, II, 53, 177; *PP* 1823,
VIII, 257; Freshfield, *Communion plate*, 47. Lumley also left an annuity

of £7 4s to the poor of his parish and a silver flagon with an estimated value of £30 to his church. He was the grandson of a Genoese who had settled in England in the time of Henry VIII. Lumley was first elected an alderman in 1614, was lord mayor in 1623, and served twice as master of his company. He was President of Christ's Hospital from 1632 to 1634. His son, Martin, was created a baronet in 1641, served in the Long Parliament from Essex, and was a Parliamentary supporter.

110. *Vide ante*, 242, for a biographical sketch and a treatment of his large charitable dispositions.

111. PCC 179 Harvey 1639; Clarke, *Architectura*, 288; PP 1903, L, 'St. Magnus', 2.

112. PP 1822, IX, 193. This gift also included payments of £2 p.a. for the general uses of St Lawrence church, £1 p.a. to the clerk, £3 2s p.a. for distribution to the poor of the parish, £5 p.a. to the needy of St Giles Cripplegate, and £6 p.a. for Christ's Hospital, to be used for the education there of poor and deserving girls. This donor also left substantial bequests to the poor on her death in 1665, which have of course been excluded from our reckoning.

113. *Vide ante*, 243. These foundations will be more fully treated elsewhere in our discussion of Lancashire charities.

114. *Vide ante*, 161–162. Two livings were purchased by the company in Gloucestershire in 1657 at a charge of £1400, interest having been accumulated, and appointments were made in accordance with the terms of the will.

115. *Vide ante*, 170, 175, for a biographical notice and discussion of her other large benefactions. The Mercers being unable to purchase impropriations, lectureships with a stipend of £75 p.a. each were founded at Wakefield, Yorkshire, and at Grantham, Lincolnshire.

116. PP 1823, VIII, 275; PP 1824, XIII, 218; PP 1904, LXXI, 894.

117. *Vide ante*, 260.

118. PCC 128 Essex 1648; *Husting*, II, 766; PP 1822, IX, 235; PP 1884, XXXIX, iv, 573. Boylston, a native of Staffordshire, also left £50 to the poor of his parish (St Gabriel Fenchurch), gave £50 to Christ's Hospital, and assigned a loan of £100 due him from Parliament to his company for annual distributions to their poor.

119. PCC 3 Bowyer 1652; *L. & M. Arch. Soc.*, n.s., I (1898), 50; *S. P. Dom.*, 1654[?], LXXVII, 109.

120. PCC administrations, 1653–1654, Vol. I, fol. 114; PP 1816, XVI, i, 800; PP 1829, VII, 243; PP 1837, XXIII, 466; PP 1884, XXXIX, iv, 380; Clarke, *Architectura*, 446–447. Hulls also left property then valued at about £400, the income to be used for the relief of the poor of his parish, an annuity of £2 4s for the care of the poor of his company, and lands in Lewisham, Kent, then valued at an estimated capital worth of £100, for general charitable uses in that community.

121. PCC 60 Pembroke 1650; PP 1840, XIX, i, 127; *Harvard College Records* (Boston, Mass., 1925–1935, 3 vols.), I, 54; Freshfield, *Communion plate*, 70. The husband, Francis Bridges, had in 1641 donated £50 to the committee which solicited in England for funds desperately needed for

the support of Harvard College, Lady Mowlson being the principal contributor (*vide ante*, 396, n.142). Bridges by will left £4 p.a. to the relief of poor children in Christ's Hospital, £2 p.a. for the poor of Clapham, and £2 p.a. for like use in the parish of St Michael Queenhithe.

122. *Vide ante*, 132.

123. *Vide ante*, 133, 247. The total of Perryn's charities was £4100.

124. *Vide ante*, 179, 183, 243, *post*, 305, for her husband's charities.

125. PCC 622 Wootton 1658. This donor, Rachel Cambell, also left £100 for gowns for poor women, £200 to the poor of the Dutch church, £5 to the poor of Barking, Essex, and £3 to the poor of St Olave, Jewry, London.

126. *Vide ante*, 160, 246.

127. *Vide ante*, 172, 265.

128. This matter has been more fully discussed in the first volume of this work.

129. Besant, Walter, *Westminster* (L., 1902), 194; Walcott, M. E. C., *History of church of St. Margaret* (Westminster, 1847), 57.

130. *Vide ante*, 90, for her secular bequests. This donor also disposed a sum of £152 (partly estimated) for prayers.

131. PCC 26 Bennett 1510; Strype, *Stow's Survey*, II, v, 128; Beaven, *Aldermen*, II, 20.

132. PCC 24 Porch 1527.

133. PCC 28 Porch 1527.

134. PCC 21 Jankyn 1530; Strype, *Stow's Survey*, II, v, 129; Beaven, *Aldermen*, II, 22, 168. Brugge likewise provided £71 for general church uses, about £190 for prayers, £13 for the relief of prisoners, £10 in marriage portions, and upwards of £43 7s for the relief of the poor, if we interpret his confused instructions correctly. Brugge sat in Parliament for London in 1509 and was thrice master of his company. His daughter, Winifred, married Sir Richard Sackville, by whom she was the mother of Thomas, Earl of Dorset. She later married the second Marquess of Winchester.

135. *L. & M. Arch. Soc.*, n.s., VI (1929), 32; there were nine individual gifts which need not be noted in detail.

136. PCC 32 Arundell 1580; *PP* 1816, XVI, i, 746; *PP* 1822, IX, 223–224; *PP* 1884, XXXIX, iv, 579. Heron also left rents representing capital values of £320 for the relief of the poor of Clerkenwell and St Sepulchre, £160 for road repairs, and £200 for scholars in both universities.

137. PCC 6 Leicester 1588; Phillips, H. H., *Annals of the Joiners* (L., 1915), 10; Rogers, *Down Thames Street*, 69.

138. Willet, *Synopsis papismi* (1634), 1224. The dating of this catalogue of charitable works presents difficulties. It did not appear in earlier editions of the *Synopsis*, but was certainly written by Willet before his death in 1621. The catalogue itself is dedicated to Sir Thomas Middleton, Lord Mayor of London, who held that office in 1613, and the preface to the reader is signed by Willet as from Barley, Hertfordshire, in 1613. There are, none the less, references which extend somewhat beyond 1613.

It would seem, therefore, that the catalogue was composed by Willet in 1613 and that minor additions were made prior to posthumous publication in 1634 by the author's son-in-law.

139. Willet seems here to refer to the period very roughly from 1590 to 1620. Our total of benefactions for church repairs for this generation is £4108 7s and for church building £16,823 9s, or £20,931 16s in all.

140. *Vide ante*, 106, 234.

141. PCC 78 Wood 1611; Freshfield, *Communion plate*, xxxv. Savage also left relatively modest sums to his company, to the poor of his parish, the poor of his native Lancashire, and to Christ's Hospital. In 1606 he had given a silver cup of 5 oz. weight to his parish church.

142. Baddeley, *St. Giles*, 153. We shall not ordinarily recite individual gifts and legacies for London church repairs unless they amount to a substantial fraction of the whole outlay.

143. *L. & M. Arch. Soc.*, V (1881), 338.

144. *Vide ante*, 178, 205, 283.

145. *Vide ante*, 110–111, 237, 258, 286.

146. Freshfield, *Accounts, St. Bartholomew*, 62, 100. Sir Francis Jones, a haberdasher, who was serving as lord mayor at the time, gave £20 towards these repairs in 1621.

147. *Parthenon*, X (1936), viii, 291.

148. *London parishes* (1824), 26.

149. Atkinson, A. G. B., *St. Botolph Aldgate* (L., 1898), 130–131; there were eleven legacies and gifts which cannot be noted in detail.

150. Delaune, *Angliae metropolis*, 36.

151. Bruce, *Memories and monuments*, 174; Delaune, *Angliae metropolis*, 54.

152. *London parishes* (1824), 90.

153. Daniell, *London riverside churches*, 199.

154. *LCC Survey*, IX (1924), i, 20–21; Cobb, *Old churches*, 37.

155. Delaune, *Angliae metropolis*, 33.

156. Freshfield, *Accounts, St. Christopher*, 79–80.

157. Brett-James, *Stuart London*, 192–193, 209.

158. PCC 172 Harvey 1639; *PP* 1816, XVI, i, 754; *PP* 1823, IX, 268; *PP* 1826–7, IX, 236; Aikin, *Environs of London*, 103; *L. & M. Arch. Soc.*, II (1864), 141; DNB. This donor also left £100 of capital for the use of the poor of St Olave Hart Street and £200 as a stock for the poor of Great Stanmore.

159. *S. P. Dom.*, 1647–1648, DXVI, 19.

160. PCC administrations, 1659, fol. 310; Freshfield, *Communion plate*, 93.

161. *Husting*, II, 579–580. Derby, a draper and an alderman, also left London properties with an estimated value of £360 capital for perpetual prayers in his chapel.

162. Mee, *Middlesex*, 14.

163. PCC 5 Logge 1482; Stow, *Survey*, II, 177; Nicholl, *Ironmongers*, 35; Beaven, *Aldermen*, I, 154, 190, 199; Herbert, *Livery companies*, II, 600. Byfield also left £281 for prayers, £12 for church general, and cash

and plate to his company to the value of £30 6s, as well as small amounts for hospitals and poor relief.

164. *Vide ante*, 274, for his other substantial benefactions.

165. *Vide ante*, 203, 220.

166. Sinclair, M. L., *Windows of parish church of House of Commons* (L., 1906), 1; Walcott, *St. Margaret's*, 30; Daniell, *London riverside churches*, 157. She was the widow of Sir Thomas Billing, Chief Justice under Edward IV.

167. Hughes, M. V., *The city saints* (L., 1932), 83.

168. Perry, J. T., *Memorials of old Middlesex* (L., 1909), 17.

169. PCC 2 Horne 1496; *Husting*, II, 600–601; Brooke and Hallen, *St. Mary Woolnoth*, ix; Chaffers, *Gilda aurifabrorum*, 37; Strype, *Stow's Survey*, I, ii, 160; Beaven, *Aldermen*, II, 15. Brice, who wished no pomp at his funeral and no month's mind, left in all £53 6s for prayers, about £41 for church repairs and ornaments, and lesser amounts for prisoners, hospitals, lazar houses, and the poor. A native of Dublin, Brice became an alderman in 1476, served as Master of the Mint from 1480 till his death, and was on three occasions prime warden of his company. His contribution to his church was in part for the completion of its fabric, begun many years earlier.

170. Acres, W. M., *London and Westminster* (L., 1923), 13.

171. Briggs, M. S., *Middlesex* (L., 1934), 287.

172. Brayley, *Westminster*, I, 97; Westlake, H. F., *Westminster Abbey* (L., 1921), I, 152, 192–193.

173. *Vide ante*, 137, 275.

174. *Vide ante*, 271.

175. Mee, *Middlesex*, 164.

176. Briggs, *Middlesex*, 114.

177. *Vide ante*, 91, 275.

178. PCC 2 Adeane 1505; Brooke and Hallen, *St. Mary Woolnoth*, xliv; Beaven, *Aldermen*, II, 19.

179. Hughes, *City saints*, 147.

180. *Archaeologia*, LXIII (1912), 66.

181. *Vide ante*, 92.

182. PCC 4 Fetiplace 1511. This donor left in total £284 4s for prayers, £4 2s for church general, £100 to the poor of London, £100 for marriage portions, and lesser sums for other charitable uses.

183. Cooke, *Top. of Great Britain*, VII, 189; Davis, E. J., 'The transformation of London', in *Tudor studies*, R. W. Seton-Watson, ed. (L., 1924), 295.

184. *Vide ante*, 92.

185. *Vide ante*, 137. We have estimated that Tate expended at least £1100 on this pious work. The almshouse was built on the same site.

186. PCC 12 Fetiplace 1513; Beaven, *Aldermen*, II, 18, 167; Chaffers, *Gilda aurifabrorum*, 42.

187. *Parthenon*, X (1936), viii, 291; Hughes, *City saints*, 78; Stow, *Survey*, I, 202.

188. *Vide ante,* 189, 201, 222–223, for a biographical sketch of Jenyns and his other large charities; *vide ante,* 278, for Fitzwilliam.

189. PCC F.36 Populwell 1549; DNB; Salter, H. E., ed., *Registrum annalium . . . Mertoniensis* (Oxford, 1923), 476; Allen, *History of London,* IV, 165; Fell, B. H., *Palace of Westminster* (L., 1930), 68; Henderson, B. W., *Merton College* (L., 1899), 75. The DNB provides an excellent memoir of this most interesting and truly Renaissance figure.

190. Firth, *Middlesex,* 193; Pevsner, Nikolaus, *London (Middlesex),* (L., 1952), 142.

191. *Vide ante,* 277, for a biographical notice and comment on his other charities.

192. *Vide ante,* 197, 277, for further notice of this donor. Lovell enjoyed building, having contributed generously to construction at Lincoln's Inn and having made heavy outlays on the repair of properties which he had vested as chantry endowments.

193. PCC 7 Thower 1531; Brayley, *Top. of London,* III, 258; Entick, *Survey,* IV, 109; Johnson, *Drapers,* II, 55, 61; Beaven, *Aldermen,* II, 24, 169. Rudstone, a draper, was a native of Yorkshire. He became an alderman in 1521, served in 1528 as lord mayor, and was twice master of his company. He married a daughter of Sir Robert Dymoke, who after his death married Sir Edward Wotton, a privy councillor and the grandfather of Sir Henry Wotton. Rudstone also left £135 for prayers, £30 for scholars in the universities, £53 to the poor, £20 for marriage portions, and lesser amounts for other charitable uses.

194. Acres, *London,* 11.

195. *London parishes* (1824), 27.

196. Acres, *London,* 16.

197. Clarke, *Architectura,* note under plate.

198. Acres, *London,* 117.

199. Cobb, *Old churches,* 36; Clarke, *Architectura,* note under plate. *Vide ante,* 295.

200. Cooke, *Top. of Great Britain,* VII, 239; Gilbertson, Lewis, *Fabric of St. Paul's* (L., 1894), 9; *S. P. Dom.,* 1561, XVII, 34–37; *S. P. Dom.,* 1562, XXII, 69; *S. P. Dom.,* 1566, XXXIX, 89; Rowse, *England of Elizabeth,* 195.

201. *Vide ante,* 204, 225, for a full account of his other large charities.

202. Cooke, *Top. of Great Britain,* VII, 153; Pevsner, *London,* 428; Stow, *Survey,* II, 282. Patten was the son of a London clothworker.

203. Perry, *Memorials of Middlesex,* 20; Pevsner, *London,* 31.

204. Nicolas, *Testamenta vetusta,* II, 740–742. *Vide ante,* 141. Hastings' secular charities in Buckinghamshire will be fully discussed in our treatment of that county.

205. Briggs, *Middlesex,* 114, 116; Pevsner, *London,* 113.

206. Acres, *London,* 31; *London parishes* (1824), 32; Delaune, *Angliae metropolis,* 32; Jenkyn, William, *A shock of corn* (L., 1654), 35. *Vide* DNB for an admirable notice of Gouge.

207. Walford, Edward, ed., *Old and new London* (L., 1897, 6 vols.),

III, 155; Young, E. and W., *Old London churches* (L., 1956), 152. *Vide ante*, 301.

208. Hill, Thomas, *Holy Trinity Minories* (L., 1851), 12; Acres, *London*, 28; Willet, *Synopsis papismi* (1634), 1224.

209. Bellot, H. H. L., *The Temple* (L., 1922), 51–54; Acres, *London*, 93.

210. Our records of individual benefactions so suggest.

211. Jenkinson, Wilberforce, *London churches before the great fire* (L., 1917), 201; Willet, *Synopsis papismi* (1634), 1224.

212. Acres, *London*, 40.

213. Clarke, *Architectura*, note under plate; Hughes, *City saints*, 180; Cobb, *Old churches*, 36.

214. Godwin, *Churches of London*, 'St. Andrew', 2.

215. *Vide ante*, 300.

216. *London parishes* (1824), 33, and divers records of individual benefactions.

217. *Vide ante*, 272.

218. Brett-James, *Stuart London*, 195; Pevsner, *London*, 411.

219. Hughes, *City saints*, 305; Tabor, M. E., *City churches* (L., 1919), 105.

220. *Vide ante*, 113, 148, for his other charitable outlays and for biographical comment. Dunster also left £200 as an endowment, the income to be used for the repair of this church.

221. Bellot, H. H. L., *Gray's Inn and Lincoln's Inn* (L., 1925), 158; Walker, *Records of Lincoln's Inn*, II, vi–viii.

222. Acres, *London*, 26–27; Young, *Old London churches*, 91.

223. *LCC Survey*, V (1914), ii, 128–129; Freshfield, Edwin, Jr., *Communion plate of ... Middlesex* (L., 1897), xxviii, 1; Baker, *Acton*, note under 'corrections'; Grey, E. C. W., *St. Giles* (L., 1905), 51–52; Seymour, *Survey*, II, 766. This donor, a daughter of Sir Thomas Leigh, died in 1669, aged ninety. In addition to the generous dispositions noted above, she gave in the course of our period the communion plate and a carpet to the church at Acton in 1640, communion plate to Ladbrooke, Warwickshire, in 1623, and in 1646 a house to serve as the parsonage for St Giles.

224. Clarke, *Architectura*, note under plate.

225. Cobb, *Old churches*, 37; Bruce, *Memories and monuments*, 17 ff.; Young, *Old London churches*, 93–94. This church survives as the only completely Jacobean church in London.

226. Allen, *History of London*, IV, 216. Pye gave £500 towards this work. He became Remembrancer of the Exchequer in 1618, was knighted in 1621, and represented Woodstock in the Long Parliament. He was a supporter of the Parliamentary cause. Darell's will is in the PCC, 135 St John 1631.

227. *LCC Survey*, VI (1915), 16; Daniell, *London riverside churches*, 80–82; Faulkner, *Fulham and Hammersmith*, 96–97. Crispe was the son of Ellis Crispe, a salter and a highly respected merchant (*vide ante*, 149). The son made a great fortune in the Guinea trade, building a house in

Hammersmith in 1630 at a reputed cost of £23,000. He was a farmer of the customs and a most zealous Royalist. A younger brother, Tobias, was an eminent Puritan divine. Crispe died in 1665.

228. *Vide ante,* 296.

229. Acres, *London,* 27.

230. [London County Council], *Proposed demolition of nineteen city churches* (L., 1920), 15; Delaune, *Angliae metropolis,* 35.

231. Bruce, *Memories and monuments,* 73.

232. *B. & G. Arch. Soc.,* XXI (1898), 108–109; Clarke, *Architectura,* note under plate; DNB; Young, *Old London churches,* 154.

233. The west end of the church was damaged by an explosion in 1649. The damage was repaired, and a brick tower built, in the Cromwellian period.

234. Archbishop Laud's own charities were principally limited to assisting with the work being done on the fabric of his Oxford college. A memorandum (dated 1630) survives, which suggests that he had given careful thought to the ultimate disposition of his estate, his plans being frustrated, of course, by the tragedy of his end. He planned further work on St John's College and its chapel, though much of this portion of the memorandum has been crossed through, perhaps as partially completed. If he were unable to carry forward this intention, then he proposed 'to give a stock to Reading and Ockingham after Sir Thom. White waye'. He also intended to establish a large hospital at Reading, his birthplace, for poor men and women of the town, under the joint control of the local authorities and St John's College. (*S. P. Dom.,* 1630, CLXXII, 68).

235. *S. P. Dom.,* 1631, CLXXXVII, 95, CLXXXVIII, 28, 37, CXCIII, 82; *S. P. Dom.,* 1632, CCXXIII, 60; *S. P. Dom.,* 1633, CCXXXII, 14; most of Volume CCXIII (February, 1632) of the State Papers is concerned with plans for the work on St Paul's.

236. *S. P. Dom.,* 1634, CCLIX, 22, CCLXVI, 21.

237. *S. P. Dom.,* 1634, CCLXII, 53; *S. P. Dom.,* 1638, CCCXCI, 47.

238. *S. P. Dom.,* 1637, CCCLXVI, 26.

239. *S. P. Dom.,* 1634, CCLXXIII, 65.

240. *S. P. Dom.,* 1635, CCLXXXVIII, 64, CCXCVIII, 38.

241. *Vide ante,* 114, 175, 178–179, 185, 273, 283.

242. *Vide ante,* 124, 179, 202.

243. PCC 76 Grey 1651; Benham, William, *Old St. Paul's* (N.Y., 1902), 67; Pennant, Thomas, *Antiquities of London* (L., 1818), 29; *L. & M. Arch. Soc.,* II (1864), 141, n.s., VI (1930), 219; Brayley, *Top. of London,* III, 159–160; Besant, *London city,* 188. This great speculator deserves a full-scale biography. A native of Northamptonshire (b. 1566), he was at the age of sixteen apprenticed to an Italian merchant and lived in Venice for many years. Returned to England, he made a great fortune as a farmer of general customs and from his management of the soap and alum monopolies. His fortune at about the time of his gift to St Paul's was estimated at £250,000, and his will when drafted would seem to lend credence to this estimate. But his affairs were tangled, his fortune declined with the outbreak of the Civil War, and he enjoyed no favour as an ardent

Royalist during the Puritan regime. His will disposed a fortune to his native town, to Christ's Hospital, to Bridewell, and the other London hospitals, but in fact he died insolvent. His executor found the estate so involved that he was unable to settle it and committed suicide in 1655. Though his bequests have not been reckoned, Pindar did make certain other considerable charitable gifts during his lifetime. In 1611 he gave a small but valuable collection of Arabic and Persian manuscripts to the Bodleian, in 1633–1634 he gave £325 for the relief of the poor of his parish (St Botolph Bishopsgate) as well as communion plate to its church valued at £113 13s 4d; his gifts to St Bartholomew's Hospital totalled £250; in 1638 he presented Peterborough Cathedral with valuable communion plate and gave £200 to maintain the organ in his own parish church.

244. Cambell's gifts to the clergy totalled £500. *Vide ante*, 179–180, 183, 243, for biographical particulars and some discussion of his secular charities.

245. From late 1630 until 1640 amounts were, apparently quite arbitrarily, assigned to the cathedral building fund from remainders left by charitable donors for unspecified 'pious uses'. Upwards of eighty such instances have been noted, in amounts ranging from £3 10s to three of £500 each. (*S. P. Dom.*, 1640, CCCCLXXIII, 109).

246. Delaune, *Angliae metropolis*, 42.

247. Hughes, *City saints*, 216.

248. Acres, *London*, 26.

249. Niven, William, *London city churches destroyed since 1800* (L., 1887), 40.

250. Cromwell, *Clerkenwell*, 81–82; Brett-James, *Stuart London*, 217–218; Young, *Old London churches*, 191.

251. Delaune, *Angliae metropolis*, 30, 42.

252. *L. & M. Arch. Soc.*, I (1860), 262.

253. Milbourn, Thomas, *Church of St. Mildred the Virgin* (L., 1872), 11.

254. *Parthenon*, X (1936), viii, 291.

255. Bumpus, *Ancient London churches*, 61.

256. De Salis, Rachel, *Hillingdon* (Uxbridge, 1926), 64; Firth, *Middlesex*, 148; Pevsner, *London*, 111.

257. Delaune, *Angliae metropolis*, 56; Britton, John, and Augustus Pugin, *Illustrations of the public buildings of London* (L., 1838, 2 vols.), I, 110; Jenkinson, *London churches*, 134.

258. *London parishes* (1824), 128.

259. Firth, *Middlesex*, 195; Pevsner, *London*, 143–144.

260. Delaune, *Angliae metropolis*, 30.

261. *London parishes* (1824), 60; Delaune, *Angliae metropolis*, 43.

262. *Parthenon*, X (1936), viii, 291.

263. *Ibid.*; Delaune, *Angliae metropolis*, 37.

264. *L. & M. Arch. Soc.*, n.s., VI (1933), 32.

265. PCC 31 Fairfax 1649; PP 1825, X, 124; PP 1867–8, LII, ii, 22–23; PP 1903, L, 12. Gayer's brother, Sir John, was a Lord Mayor of London. Gayer also left £140 to London hospitals, £100 to the poor of

his company, and £50 to the poor of his native Plymouth. He left in addition £70 to the poor of London, £50 in plate to his company, and £50 to the clergy.

266. *Vide ante,* 155–156, 219. The East India Company, on the petition of the inhabitants of the community, gave the ground for this chapel, the tract lying just behind the company almshouses. The chapel appears to have been begun in about 1650, the East India Company contributing £250 towards the total cost. The building was completed in 1654 at the substantial cost of £2250, there having been at least four large merchant donors who assisted in the enterprise. This chapel did not become a parish church until 1858.

267. Draper, W. H., *Chiswick* (L., 1923), 92; Pevsner, *London,* 31. Divers benefactions have been noted. For the earlier rebuilding, *vide ante* 301.

CHAPTER VII.   LONDON AND THE NATION

1. We should here comment at length on what is an important under-statement and at the same time make a critical comment on our method. This study is confined to ten representative counties, London being one, though our research was substantially completed for Surrey and Northumberland as well, the former being not included in the study because it differed too little from Kent and the latter because it so closely resembled Yorkshire.

For the nine counties fully discussed, London aside, the total of London benefactions noted when the research on London was being done was £166,625 3s. But in the course of what we believe to have been equally thorough research in these counties, additional London benefactions amounting to the very large sum of £119,101 13s were discovered and noted. Hence the *true totals* of gifts from London for these nine counties as a group is the huge sum of £285,726 16s, which of course means that our research in London sources disclosed only 58·32 per cent of the true sum. It should also be said that there were considerable variations in accuracy from county to county, ranging from the 44·02 per cent of London's benefactions to Norfolk disclosed by research in London sources to the 80·73 per cent for Bristol.

Our study *of London sources* has established benefactions totalling £299,014 12s made by London donors to the remaining English counties, to Scotland, Wales, and Ireland, and, in relatively very small amounts, to other areas. If we may assume that this total also represents 58·32 per cent of the true total which would be revealed were intensive investigation carried forward in these remaining regions, it would appear that the true measure of London's generosity in these counties was of the order of £512,713 16s. When we add the £285,726 16s of the definitely established total of gifts to our nine counties, the grand total of London's extramural benefactions may probably be rather accurately estimated as £798,440 12s, instead of the £584,741 8s definitely established by our investigations.

The reasons for this substantial understatement are numerous. A fair number of trusts created during a donor's lifetime for the exclusive benefit of another county may not have been noted if no mention is made of the gift in the donor's will or if there was no will. In a larger number of cases, these London donors had retired to estates purchased in the county to be favoured, with the result that either a gift or a bequest to the county of residence is likely not to be disclosed by research in London sources, even though the wealth thus bestowed was in fact merchant capital which ought properly to be so regarded, despite the social translation which was in process of consummation. These circumstances account for most of our 'sins of omission', though there are several other relatively unimportant possibilities of error as well. Throughout our discussion of the massive and certainly dominant weight of London generosity on the institutions of the realm, it must, then, be borne in mind that the data provided do not fully represent the whole extent of the immense outpouring of charitable wealth from London.

2. *Vide ante*, 117 ff.

3. Nine of the parishes benefiting from Smith's bequests were in Middlesex and are not here included.

4. *Vide ante*, 133–134, 164–166.

5. These counties are Kent, Surrey, Hampshire, Berkshire, Buckinghamshire, Hertfordshire, and Essex.

6. These counties are Cheshire, Shropshire, Worcestershire, Gloucestershire, Bristol, Somerset, and Devon.

7. These are Lancashire, Yorkshire, Northumberland, and, if we may so regard it for convenience of discussion, Scotland.

8. These are Bedfordshire, Cambridgeshire (it is to be remembered that gifts to the universities are excluded), Huntingdonshire, Leicestershire, Nottinghamshire, and Rutland.

9. The place of birth of two of these men is uncertain, but in both cases we do know that they were not native Londoners.

10. We are least certain that thirty-six of these fifty-eight men were not Londoners. It is statistically impossible that more than one or two of the remainder could have been born in London.

11. These counties were Cheshire, Devon, Gloucestershire, Lancashire, Shropshire, Somerset, Staffordshire, and Wales.

12. These were Lincolnshire, Norfolk, Suffolk, Yorkshire.

13. The proportion of uncertain birthplaces is of course very large (62·72 per cent), but could probably be reduced to something like that (14·14 per cent) for the great merchants by further research. We are, however, reasonably sure that further investigation would not substantially change the proportion of those known to have been Londoners by birth.

14. These counties are Cheshire, Devon, Essex, Hertfordshire, Kent, Norfolk, Shropshire, Staffordshire, and Yorkshire.

15. There were twenty-nine foreign-born merchants in this group, eleven being Flemings, eight Dutch, seven French, and one each being German, Italian, and Portuguese.

	Poor £	s	Social Rehabilitation £	s	Municipal Betterments £	s	Education £	s	Religion £	s	Totals £	s
1480–1490	1,646	7	207	4	2,467	13	1,073	10	9,069	3	14,463	17
1491–1500	2,966	14	586	4	2,048	12	1,458	7	17,211	16	24,271	13
1501–1510	16,167	1	1,904	0	2,281	2	26,718	16	41,538	8	88,609	7
1511–1520	5,692	2	644	2	2,075	18	15,377	3	15,748	13	39,537	18
1521–1530	3,367	4	502	7	3,547	19	30,585	13	12,258	6	50,261	9
1531–1540	7,538	19	4,585	18	3,269	10	1,368	0	16,170	15	32,933	2
Pre-Reformation	37,378	7	8,429	15	15,690	14	76,581	9	111,997	1	250,077	6
	(14·95%)		(3·37%)		(6·27%)		(30·63%)		(44·78%)		(13·24%)	
1541–1550	13,328	7	1,750	14	2,682	7	12,558	4	11,874	9	42,204	1
1551–1560	18,153	6	64,433	0	4,326	16	20,018	1	3,706	6	110,637	9
Reformation	31,481	13	66,183	14	7,009	3	32,586	5	15,580	15	152,841	10
	(20·60%)		(43·30%)		(4·59%)		(21·32%)		(10·19%)		(8·09%)	
1561–1570	13,436	5	13,508	15	4,565	6	20,013	11	8,791	17	60,315	14
1571–1580	21,389	1	9,668	17	6,071	11	23,742	19	1,828	16	62,701	4
1581–1590	26,815	10	14,459	16	3,961	0	20,783	13	2,941	3	68,961	2
1591–1600	25,250	7	15,439	16	5,128	1	18,779	9	3,768	17	68,366	10
Elizabethan	86,891	3	53,077	4	19,725	18	83,319	12	17,330	13	260,344	10
	(33·37%)		(20·39%)		(7·58%)		(32·00%)		(6·66%)		(13·78%)	
1601–1610	52,298	1	18,728	1	4,082	17	27,289	16	10,702	8	113,101	3
1611–1620	133,419	5	21,058	6	18,789	10	99,670	7	25,771	8	298,708	16
1621–1630	131,546	3	19,660	6	8,366	13	81,291	7	54,290	6	295,154	15
1631–1640	71,009	9	28,375	15	10,441	14	38,240	13	104,001	3	252,068	5
Early Stuart	388,272	9	87,822	8	41,680	14	246,492	3	194,765	5	959,032	19
	(40·48%)		(9·16%)		(4·35%)		(25·70%)		(20·31%)		(50·76%)	
1641–1650	53,600	12	19,912	19	4,031	19	29,504	18	14,260	5	121,310	13
1651–1660	66,783	10	16,302	13	5,452	8	42,406	10	14,455	7	145,400	8
No Date	201	0			3	0			0	6	204	6
Civil War	120,585	2	36,215	12	9,487	7	71,911	8	28,715	18	266,915	7
	(45·18%)		(13·57%)		(3·55%)		(26·94%)		(10·76%)		(14·13%)	
TOTALS	664,608	14	251,728	13	93,593	16	510,800	17	368,389	12	1,889,231	12
	(35·18%)		(13·32%)		(4·95%)		(27·04%)		(19·50%)			

NOTE REGARDING THE COMPOSITION OF
TABLE I (page 423)

Difficulties of tabular representation make it inconvenient to present in full the data included in the first table. In our discussion in the text, however, full treatment is given to the data under each of the sub-heads as well as for the five great charitable heads. There are in all twenty-four categories (sub-heads) under which we have listed charities, these being in turn gathered under the five great heads which are presented in the preceding table. The full classification is as follows:

POOR
Outright relief
Almshouses
Charity General
Aged

EDUCATION
Schools
Colleges and Universities
Libraries (non-university)
Scholarships and fellowships

SOCIAL REHABILITATION
Prisons
Loans
Workhouses and stocks
Apprenticeship schemes
Sick and hospitals
Marriage subsidies

RELIGION
Church general
Prayers
Church repairs
Maintenance of the clergy
Puritan lectureships
Church building (estimated)

MUNICIPAL BETTERMENTS
General uses
Companies for public benefit
Parks and recreation
Public works (Roads, *etc.*)

For a full discussion of the categories employed and a synthesis of the statistical evidence for the whole group of ten counties, *vide,* Jordan, *Philanthropy in England,* 40–53, 369–375.

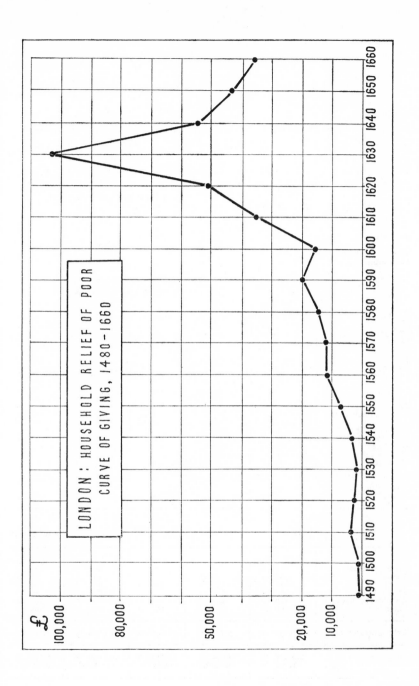

LONDON : HOUSEHOLD RELIEF OF POOR
CURVE OF GIVING, 1480-1660

TABLE

EXTRA-LONDON BENEFACTIONS

(University benefactions

County	Poor	Social Rehabilitation	Municipal Betterments	Education	Religion
	£ s	£ s	£ s	£ s	£ s
Bedfordshire	1,119 6	80 8	120 0	1,800 0	159 0
Berkshire	6,793 8	9,197 0	20 0	6,293 0	929 16
Bristol	10,473 0	2,180 0	3,120 0	1,320 0	1,067 0
Buckinghamshire	7,590 11	1,535 0	4,256 0	510 0	1,128 6
Cambridgeshire	1,642 3	231 7	89 8	167 0	275 18
Cheshire	2,418 0	1,420 0	420 0	7,320 0	3,188 18
Cornwall	247 1	—	—	800 0	— 7
Cumberland	56 0	—	10 0	662 0	—
Derby	2,245 3	781 0	5 0	701 7	1,805 0
Devonshire	2,262 10	2,975 0	116 13	5,600 0	326 10
Dorset	92 19	333 0	—	4 0	7 18
Durham	20 10	1,400 0	—	50 0	10 0
Essex	4,160 15	1,537 0	694 0	3,293 13	1,012 14
Gloucestershire	9,737 0	1,450 0	400 0	—	2,843 6
Hampshire	13,846 1	737 0	1,750 0	6,496 0	2,623 19
Herefordshire	456 0	—	15 0	1,905 0	34 7
Hertfordshire	4,364 16	665 0	187 5	5,287 10	1,710 1
Huntingdonshire	208 17	1 0	100 0	2,000 0	59 0
Kent	50,466 16	7,454 0	2,130 18	31,425 10	11,099 0
Lancashire	4,135 12	1,850 0	137 14	19,366 6	3,589 17
Leicestershire	894 7	1,000 0	16 0	1,605 0	920 5
Lincolnshire	3,063 1	310 0	168 3	200 0	1,814 0
Norfolk	10,075 18	1,249 11	979 0	10,656 0	545 14
Northamptonshire	2,451 3	1,080 0	180 0	2,708 0	1,087 6
Northumberland	79 7	—	10,000 0	—	1,563 6
Nottinghamshire	107 10	—	—	—	4 0
Oxfordshire	3,191 12	12 0	—	2,445 0	605 2
Rutland	211 13	—	—	—	—
Shropshire	8,012 3	102 0	548 0	5,280 0	1,362 13
Somerset	17,001 10	588 13	93 0	8,661 6	4,015 17
Staffordshire	2,702 4	1,230 0	50 0	3,350 0	1,778 11
Suffolk	5,357 13	690 10	—	1,860 0	904 8
Surrey (not incl. Brixton hundred)	25,308 17	16,765 0	485 1	1,090 0	612 4
Sussex	2,039 19	2,861 0	145 12	440 0	55 4
Warwickshire	979 3	3,087 6	550 0	240 0	1,051 1
Westmorland	60 0	20 0	200 0	807 12	128 0
Wiltshire	2,346 7	1,090 0	—	700 0	423 0
Worcestershire	6,585 19	1,068 14	130 0	3,449 13	879 17
Yorkshire	8,735 2	1,190 9	596 13	12,833 7	6,102 3
Grand totals for English counties	221,539 16	66,171 18	27,713 7	151,327 4	55,723 8

(Extra-English

	Poor	Social Rehabilitation	Municipal Betterments	Education	Religion
	£ s	£ s	£ s	£ s	£ s
Channel Islands	1 0	—	—	430 0	—
Ireland	486 5	8 0	—	100 0	16 0
Wales	3,251 7	3,253 0	480 0	13,102 0	194 13
Scotland	1,991 13	2,210 0	10 0	32,700 0	—
American colonies	100 0	242 0	—	960 0	640 0
Foreign	900 17	10 0	150 0	430 0	599 0
Extra-English totals	6,731 2	5,723 0	640 0	47,722 0	1,449 13
Grand totals	228,270 18 (39·04%)	71,894 18 (12·30%)	28,353 7 (4·85%)	199,049 4 (34·04%)	57,173 1 (9·78%)

II

(SUMMARY TABLE)

excluded)

Total	Number of London donors	Those born in the county	Merchant donors	Tradesman donors	Professional classes	Other or unknown
£ s						
3,278 14	42	29	19	6	3	14
23,233 4	38	27	21	4	3	10
18,160 0	19	15	12	4	2	1
15,019 17	71	53	30	19	4	18
2,405 16	38	25	16	7	5	10
14,766 18	40	36	24	8	4	4
1,047 8	11	6	6	1	0	4
728 0	9	9	3	5	0	1
5,537 10	32	30	13	9	2	8
11,280 13	50	42	33	3	3	11
437 17	11	10	4	3	1	3
1,480 10	5	3	2	1	1	1
10,698 2	161	83	98	15	8	40
14,430 6	43	31	25	4	5	9
25,453 0	118	72	50	24	10	34
2,410 7	20	16	10	3	2	5
12,214 12	104	73	56	14	5	29
2,368 17	23	19	13	2	1	7
102,576 4	290	167	75	51	17	147
29,079 9	55	44	30	10	3	12
4,435 12	40	33	17	10	1	12
5,555 4	36	24	20	1	9	6
23,506 3	42	34	20	11	3	8
7,506 9	49	41	15	12	3	19
11,642 13	5	2	4	1	0	0
111 10	5	4	2	2	1	0
6,253 14	47	26	18	2	4	23
211 13	3	2	2	0	0	1
15,304 16	61	54	31	8	4	18
30,360 6	69	51	33	17	8	11
9,110 15	60	51	43	8	1	8
8,812 11	50	40	25	6	6	13
44,261 2	83	36	42	20	10	11
5,541 15	31	21	15	2	2	12
5,907 10	40	31	22	6	6	6
1,215 12	7	6	5	1	0	1
4,559 7	24	23	9	5	3	7
12,114 3	28	23	9	8	1	10
29,457 14	171	104	83	25	16	47
522,475 13	2,031	1,396	955	338	157	581

Benefactions)

Total	Number of London donors	Those born in the county	Merchant donors	Tradesman donors	Professional classes	Other or unknown
£ s						
431 0	2	2	1	1	0	0
610 5	5	3	2	0	1	2
20,281 0	41	23	17	4	10	10
36,911 13	10	8	4	2	2	2
1,942 0	20	0	11	3	2	4
2,089 17	34	12	22	5	1	6
62,265 15	112	48	57	15	16	24
584,741 8	(2,143)	(1,444) (67·38%)	(1,012) (47·22%)	(353) (16·47%)	(173) (8·07%)	(605) (28·23%)

Reproduced from the Ordnance Survey Map with the sanction of the Controller of H. M.
Stationery Office. Crown copyright reserved.

MAP I

X *Endowed Schools founded by London donors outside London.*

I *Unendowed Schools (and substantial augmentations of existing endowments) founded by London donors outside London.*

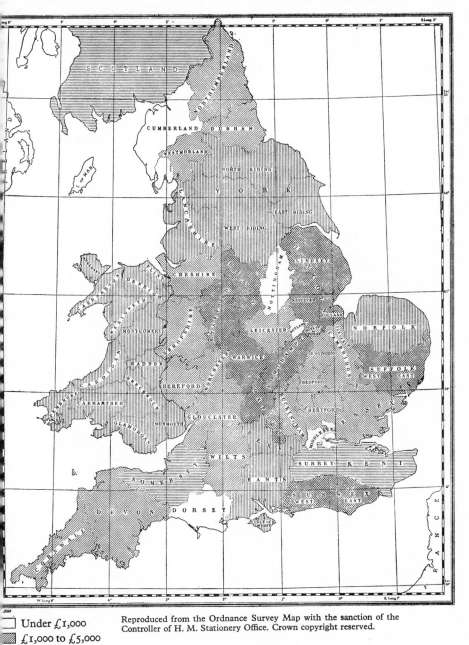

MAP II

Geographical distribution of London benefactions

Under £1,000
£1,000 to £5,000
£5,000 to £10,000
£10,000 to £20,000
£20,000 to £30,000
over £30,000

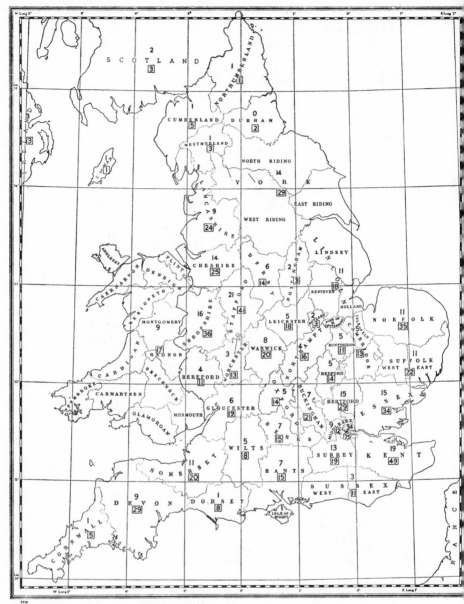

1 **Great Merchants**

3 **All Merchants**

MAP III

Geographical origins of London Merchants

General Index

(An asterisk denotes a benefiting parish or institution)

Middlesex, charities for—*cont.*
  religion, 138, 272, 273, 283,
    290, 296, 298, 299, 300,
    301, 302, 303, 305, 306,
    332, 412
  social rehabilitation, 163, 169,
    170
  merchants from, 317, 318
  parishes in, 42
  Vide also 29, 41, 53, 103, 119,
    322, 326, 328, 384
*Middlesex Sessions House, 205
*Middle Temple, 200
Middleton, John, 119
Middleton, Robert, 347
*Middleton (Lancs), 234
Midland counties, 314
*Moffat (Dumfriesshire), 242
Monasteries, decay of, 279–280
Monck, George, 239
Monk, Levinius, 350
*Monken Hadley (Middlesex), 147
*Monmouth, 153, 236–237, 286,
  400
Monmouthshire, charities for,
  153, 236–237, 286, 387, 400
Montague, Sir Edward, 336
*Montgomeryshire, 375
More, Sir Thomas, 284, 353
Morton, Bishop Thomas, 254
Mountjoy, Lord, 221
*Mucking (Essex), 129
*Mucklestone (Staffs), 230, 237
Mulcaster, Richard, 214, 215
Municipal betterments, 21, 23, 25,
  30, 43–46, 58–63, 66–72, 75,
  76, 79, 196–206, 309; *vide
  also* Public Works, Roads
*Muscovy Company, 116; *vide also*
  370, 383, 392
Musicians, 82, 155; *vide also*
  Professional classes

*Nantwich (Cheshire), 161
Newburgh, Lord, 359
*Newbury (Berks), 179, 185, 283
*Newcastle, 371; merchants of, 151

*New England, 291, 348; *vide also*
  170
*Newgate, 137, 179, 182, 204, 218,
  329
New Hampshire, 250
*Newington (Surrey), 148, 164,
  352, 364
*Newland (Glos), 154, 286
*Newport (Essex), 228, 263
*Newport (Salop), 160, 171, 246,
  269, 382, 397
*Newport, College of, 247
New River Company, 126, 347;
  vide also 162
*Newton (Herefs), 101
Nobility, 15, 31, 38, 44, 45, 48,
  57–58
Norfolk, charities for, 74, 319, 388
  education, 95, 221, 225
  poor, 93, 103, 109–110, 124,
    130, 133, 147, 344, 408
  social rehabilitation, 93, 148,
    167, 370, 371
  donors from, 262, 317
  Vide also 38, 42, 263, 326, 334,
    337
*Northampton, 174, 179
Northamptonshire, charities for:
  education, 141, 179, 225, 228,
    229, 243
  municipal betterments, 203
  poor, 103, 141, 179, 183, 382,
    387, 390, 391, 403
  religion, 278, 300, 403, 420
  social rehabilitation, 174, 179,
    382
  donors from, 317
  Vide also, 91, 326
*North Cray (Kent), 97
*Northumberland, 361; merchant
  donors from, 317
Northumberland, Earl of, 329
*North Wales, 126
Norton Folgate, 44
*Norwich, 103, 110, 130, 148,
  370
Notaries, 82
*Nottingham, 123, 174

Index of Donors

(Biographical data appear on pages indicated in bold type)